Revolutionizing Urban Development and Governance With Emerging Technologies

Ali Al Maqousi
University of Petra, Jordan

Ammar Almomani
Higher Colleges of Technology, UAE

Amjad Aldweesh
Shaqra University, Saudi Arabia

Mohammad Alauthman
University of Petra, Jordan

IGI Global
Scientific Publishing
Publishing Tomorrow's Research Today

Vice President of Editorial — Melissa Wagner
Director of Acquisitions — Mikaela Felty
Director of Book Development — Jocelynn Hessler
Production Manager — Mike Brehm
Cover Design — Phillip Shickler

Published in the United States of America by
IGI Global Scientific Publishing
701 East Chocolate Avenue
Hershey, PA, 17033, USA
Tel: 717-533-8845
Fax: 717-533-7115
Website: https://www.igi-global.com E-mail: cust@igi-global.com

Library of Congress Cataloging-in-Publication Data

Names: Al Maqousi, Ali, 1963- editor
Title: Revolutionizing urban development and governance with emerging technologies / [edited by] Ali Al Maqousi, Ammar Almomani, Amjad Aldweesh, Mohammad Alauthman.
Description: Hershey, PA : IGI Global Scientific Publishing, [2025] | Includes bibliographical references and index. | Summary: "The primary goal of this book is to bridge the gap between technology and urban planning by exploring how cutting-edge innovations can revolutionize urban development and governance"-- Provided by publisher.
Identifiers: LCCN 2025006157 (print) | LCCN 2025006158 (ebook) | ISBN 9798337313757 hardcover | ISBN 9798337313764 paperback | ISBN 9798337313771 ebook
Subjects: LCSH: City planning--Technological innovations | Smart cities
Classification: LCC HT166 .R453 2025 (print) | LCC HT166 (ebook) | DDC 307.1/416--dc23/eng/20250429
LC record available at https://lccn.loc.gov/2025006157
LC ebook record available at https://lccn.loc.gov/2025006158

British Cataloguing in Publication Data
A Cataloguing in Publication record for this book is available from the British Library.

Table of Contents

Detailed Table of Contents

Urban infrastructure drives economic growth and sustainability, yet cities like Kuwait face challenges from aging systems, urbanization, and climate change. Given Kuwait's oil-dependent economy, resilient infrastructure is key for diversification. This chapter explores asset management strategies, particularly Structural Health Monitoring (SHM), to enhance efficiency and sustainability. Kuwait's major projects, like metro systems and renewable energy, require effective management. SHM integration enables predictive maintenance, reduces costs, and extends infrastructure lifespan. IoT, AI, and remote sensing optimize monitoring and resource allocation. Despite its benefits, SHM adoption faces policy gaps, financial constraints, and institutional resistance. Addressing these requires reforms, investment, and public-private collaboration. Embracing SHM will strengthen Kuwait's infrastructure, attract investment, and drive sustainable urban development.

Cities now implement artificial intelligence to optimize public services. Policymakers face issues concerning data management, fairness, and oversight. This chapter examines how governments handle privacy and accountability when deploying new digital tools in diverse contexts. Research explores regulations, community

Mahapara Abbass, Department of Civil Engineering, Maharishi Markandeshwar Engineering College, Maharishi Markandeshwar University (Deemed), Mullana, India
Shalom Akhai, Department of Mechanical Engineering, Maharishi Markandeshwar Engineering College, Maharishi Markandeshwar University (Deemed), Mullana, India
Arti Chouksey, Department of Civil Engineering, Deenbandhu Chhotu Ram University of Science and Technology, Murthal, India
Swati Pathak, Department of Civil Engineering, Chandigarh Engineering College, Jhanjeri, India
Uzma Abbas, Department of Law, Dogra Law College, Jammu, India
Sana Abass, Department of Civil Engineering, Mahant Bachittar Singh College of Engineering and Technology, Jammu, India

Rapid urbanization in developing countries presents significant governance challenges, including socio-economic inequalities, environmental sustainability issues, and infrastructure deficiencies. Emerging technologies such as Artificial Intelligence (AI), the Internet of Things (IoT), blockchain, and Geographic Information Systems (GIS) offer transformative solutions for inclusive and sustainable urban governance. Smart city initiatives leverage these technologies to enhance service delivery, optimize infrastructure, and foster transparent decision-making, aligning with global sustainability efforts like the United Nations Sustainable Development Goals (SDGs). This chapter explores digital inclusion, partnerships, and data-driven governance to bridge the digital divide and promote equitable growth. It recommends smart infrastructure, climate resilience, and participatory governance to create inclusive, resilient cities.

Urban areas, densely populated and often located in vulnerable coastal regions, are particularly susceptible to the impacts of climate change. This chapter explores the diverse ways technology can be leveraged to enhance climate resilience in these urban environments. Focusing on mitigation and adaptation strategies, the study examines the potential of smart city technologies, including sensor networks, data analytics, and AI, to improve infrastructure management and disaster preparedness. Specific examples include real-time flood monitoring systems, predictive modelling for extreme weather events, and optimized energy grids for reduced carbon emissions. Furthermore, the chapter investigates the role of digital platforms in facilitating community engagement and fostering collaborative responses to climate-related challenges. Furthermore, the importance of equitable access to technology and the need for robust data governance frameworks to ensure that technological interventions effectively contribute to building climate-resilient and sustainable urban futures is explored

Urban settings in developing contexts face pressures arising from population growth, restricted resources, and evolving policy demands. Research insights from universities often fail to guide governance actions or inform new strategies. This chapter examines how academic leadership can connect theoretical work with practical applications in contexts that adopt emerging digital tools. The purpose is to assess ways to align faculty resources, research units, municipal agencies, and community stakeholders. Findings reveal that administrative support, collaborative programs, and targeted capacity-building foster tangible outcomes in key areas such as infrastructure, resource management, and service delivery. The chapter concludes that universities can accelerate digital adoption by shaping policy agendas and funding pathways, providing a structured route toward more effective governance outcomes.

The rapid advancement of digital technologies has transformed traditional governance models, paving the way for Smart Governance—a data-driven, technology-enabled approach that enhances transparency, efficiency, and public service delivery. The integration of Artificial Intelligence (AI), Internet of Things (IoT), Blockchain Technology, and Big Data Analytics has revolutionized urban management, ensuring real-time decision-making, optimized resource allocation, and improved citizen engagement. This paper explores the transformative potential of smart governance, focusing on its core technologies, implementation strategies, and associated challenges.

This chapter presents strategies to enhance the intelligence and energy efficiency of smart parking systems by integrating PSO and ACO. Using real-time IoT sensor data, the system optimizes driver routing to available parking spots while minimizing energy consumption. PSO is applied during the planning phase for approximate route estimation, while ACO adapts dynamically to reduce energy use and interruptions. The chapter also introduces a method to improve system reliability in challenging conditions, such as fog, by employing PSO-optimized fog-detectable sensors. This adaptive approach optimizes sensor usage and path planning based on weather conditions. Overall, the combination of global and local optimization techniques boosts parking efficiency, cuts energy use, and enhances the driver experience.

Smart transportation systems enhance urban mobility by addressing challenges like congestion and carbon emissions. With growing urbanization, their role is crucial in ensuring sustainability. This paper examines how smart transport can achieve sustainable mobility through intelligent infrastructure. IoT applications aid real-time traffic control, parking management, and data-driven policies for better urban planning. AI and machine learning optimize traffic modelling, public transport

management systems, smart electrical grids, and IoT-enabled waste management solutions. Moreover, IoT fortifies governance by promoting data-informed decision-making, fostering citizen participation, and enabling real-time surveillance. The chapter further discusses the challenges encountered, such as data privacy concerns, cybersecurity threats, and scalability issues, while accentuating IoT's capacity to contribute to the creation of resilient, sustainable, and equitable urban environments.

A necessary step in creating a sustainable, secure and resilient smart cities is the integration of renewable energy systems. The expansion of cities and the increasing energy demand make the adoption of the renewable energy technologies, solar, wind and geothermal power, vital to reduce carbon footprint and to create clean and highly efficient use of energy. Digital innovations such as the Internet of Things (IoT), artificial intelligence (AI) and blockchain bring about a framework for smart city usage for renewable energy resources management and optimization. This chapter discusses technological, economic, and policy aspects of incorporating renewable energy into urban context from a perspective of smart grids, energy storage options, decentralized power generation, and intelligent energy management systems. However, there are tremendous benefits for the integration of renewable energy, from conservation of the environment, to economic progress, as well as augmentation of a community's resilience. Further research and advancement of the infrastructure to be able to overcome the technical challenges for instance the issues of energy intermittency, storage limitations, and the complexities of grid integration. Limited funds test economic and financial constraints, especially, the high initial cost of renewable energy projects necessitate innovative funding mechanism and supportive policy frameworks. There are also social equity concerns that must be managed that provide for the utilization of clean and affordable energy for all communities, regardless of income.

By enabling the quick expansion of urban areas and efficiently managing resources through sustainable and scalable innovations, smart cities are crucial components in the continuous pursuit of improving urban living standards. Smart city applications face multiple obstacles, one of which is the risk of sensitive data being exposed without authorization, due to the proliferation of new technologies such as the Internet of Things (IoT), big data analytics, fog computing, and edge computing.

Thanks to their adaptability in natural language processing and other areas, large language models (LLMs) as Chatbots have garnered a lot of interest. Data collecting systems for LLM fine-tuning, LLM embedding of power system-specific tools, and a retrieval augmented generation (RAG)-based knowledge pool to improve LLM answers and LLMs in safety-critical use cases are important areas for future research initiatives. This chapter discusses how LLMs can lead to energy efficiency and sustainability in smart cities, by using literature review and case studies, as well as providing future directions.

6G in a rising innovation which can handle the robotized vehicular communication environment well in revolutionizing urban development and governance. It may be a promising innovation which can result in encouraging moo idleness, less communication overheads, etc. Security and protection is the major challenge confronted in 6G environment due to its energetic environment. Conventional ML procedures were sent prior but due to expanding vehicles on street and with various associated IoT gadgets, it has ended up exceptionally troublesome to recognize a genuine and solid source of information which is drifted wirelessly over the arrange. We offer an outline of different confirmation plans proposed over time which are utilized in 6G IoE-based vehicular communication environment. Within the setting of 6G vehicular communication, we examined potential security employments of the Internet-of-Everything (IoE) and open inquire about issues on security conservation in revolutionizing urban development and governance.

Cities worldwide seek new approaches to urban development that prioritize people, governance, and sustainable progress. Human-centered design focuses on social inclusion, participatory planning, and context-based methods to guide technology adoption in city environments. This chapter examines how integrating social factors into policy frameworks leads to smarter cities that strengthen equity and civic trust. It explores planning strategies that incorporate community voices, institutional shifts that facilitate inclusive governance, and the importance of shaping technology to serve public needs. The research gathered qualitative and quantitative data from global initiatives and identified best practices for participatory design in urban projects. The findings suggest that citizen empowerment and transparent processes promote balanced and ethical smart city ecosystems. This work highlights a transformative pathway toward people-first urban innovation.

Early warning and public warning systems exist to reduce harm in urban regions through timely alerts and coordinated actions. Officials often face challenges in converting high-volume data into clear messages for residents, which shows a gap in existing systems. This chapter examined how digital twin platforms and social intelligence approaches boost alert dissemination in dense metropolitan areas. The analysis included peer-reviewed research, policy documents, and selected case studies. Findings showed that merged sensor data and social input enhanced detection and

Preface

The rapid evolution of urban spaces in the face of growing populations, environmental challenges, and technological advancements presents both significant opportunities and challenges. As cities worldwide continue to develop and adapt to the complexities of modern governance, emerging technologies are transforming the ways in which urban development and governance are approached. This edited volume, *Revolutionizing Urban Development and Governance With Emerging Technologies*, aims to explore how innovations like Artificial Intelligence (AI), the Internet of Things (IoT), and renewable energy technologies are reshaping the landscape of urban infrastructure, management, and policy. By offering diverse perspectives from leading scholars and professionals across the globe, this book provides a comprehensive examination of how these technologies can be harnessed for smarter, more sustainable, and resilient cities.

Throughout this volume, we delve into various facets of urban transformation, from advanced infrastructure management to disaster risk reduction, and the crucial role of ethics, governance, and citizen engagement in shaping the future of cities. Each chapter reflects the collaborative efforts of experts from different disciplines, focusing on practical applications and strategic frameworks for adopting and scaling emerging technologies. As editors, we sought to compile insights that not only highlight the challenges of integrating these technologies but also offer innovative solutions and recommendations for overcoming barriers such as financial constraints, policy gaps, and institutional resistance.

As we stand at the threshold of a new era in urban governance, this book underscores the need for continuous research, multi-stakeholder collaboration, and a commitment to ethical practices in the use of technology. The integration of emerging technologies into urban governance requires careful consideration of privacy, accountability, and equity to ensure that all citizens benefit from the advancements that these innovations promise. Our hope is that this volume will inspire policymakers, scholars, and practitioners to embrace the transformative potential of emerging technologies while navigating the complexities of urban development in a rapidly changing world.

Chapter 1: Advancing Urban Infrastructure Through Innovative Asset Management

By Shaikha AlSanad, Kuwait Institute for Scientific Research (KISR), Kuwait

This chapter addresses the challenges faced by urban infrastructure in cities like Kuwait, including aging systems, urbanization, and climate change. The focus is on Structural Health Monitoring (SHM) as a key asset management strategy to improve efficiency, reduce costs, and ensure sustainability. SHM, integrated with IoT, AI, and remote sensing, can enable predictive maintenance and extend the lifespan of infrastructure. However, barriers like policy gaps and financial constraints hinder SHM adoption, necessitating reforms, investments, and collaboration between the public and private sectors.

Chapter 2: Building Trust in AI-Driven Urban Environments - Privacy, Accountability, and Ethical Frameworks

By Mohammad Alauthman, Saad Alateef, Ahmad Al-Qerem, Ala Hamarsheh, and Amjad Aldweesh

As cities implement AI to optimize public services, concerns about data privacy, fairness, and accountability arise. This chapter delves into how governments can address these issues by focusing on strong governance, ethical guidelines, and community involvement. It emphasizes the role of transparency, public feedback, and continuous auditing in building trust in AI-driven decisions, contributing to the broader discourse on responsible AI deployment in urban settings.

Chapter 3: Disaster Risk Reduction and Management with Emerging Technologies: Applications of IoT, AI, and Data Analytics for Resilient Urban Infrastructure

By Mahapara Abbass, Shalom Akhai, Arti Chouksey, Swati Pathak, Uzma Abbas, and Sana Abass

This chapter explores how emerging technologies such as IoT, AI, and data analytics can enhance disaster risk reduction and management (DRRM) in urban areas. IoT-enabled sensors and AI-driven analytics improve early warning systems, infrastructure monitoring, and resource allocation during disasters. The chapter discusses challenges such as data quality, scalability, and cybersecurity, while highlighting the role of public involvement and international cooperation in building resilient urban infrastructures.

Chapter 4: Leveraging Emerging Technologies for Inclusive and Sustainable Urban Governance

By R Sowmiya and M Velavan, SASTRA Deemed to Be University, India

Focusing on the governance challenges of rapidly urbanizing developing countries, this chapter explores how emerging technologies—AI, IoT, blockchain, and GIS—can be harnessed to create inclusive, transparent, and sustainable urban governance. It discusses how smart city technologies can improve service delivery, optimize infrastructure, and support decision-making in alignment with the UN Sustainable Development Goals (SDGs). The chapter advocates for digital inclusion, participatory governance, and resilience-building strategies.

Chapter 5: Leveraging Technology for Climate Resilience in Urban Areas

By Ananya Pandey and Manshu Goyal, Christ University, Bangalore, India

Urban areas, particularly those in vulnerable regions, are at the forefront of climate change impacts. This chapter discusses how smart city technologies such as AI, data analytics, and sensor networks can enhance climate resilience. It focuses on mitigation and adaptation strategies like real-time flood monitoring and predictive modelling for extreme weather events. The chapter also examines community engagement through digital platforms and stresses the importance of equitable access to technology and robust data governance.

Chapter 6: The Role of Academic Leadership in Accelerating Smart Urban Governance

By Faisal Aburub, Saad Alateef, Ala Hamarsheh, and Amjad Aldweesh

This chapter explores the role of academic institutions in bridging the gap between theoretical research and practical urban governance solutions. It examines how universities can drive smart urban governance by fostering collaborations with municipal agencies, community stakeholders, and faculty researchers. By focusing on capacity building, administrative support, and targeted programs, the chapter highlights how academic leadership can contribute to the acceleration of digital adoption in urban settings.

Chapter 7: Smart Governance and Citizen Engagement Platforms: The Role of Technology in Smart Governance

By Mohammad Ishrat, Wasim Khan, Syed Faisal, and Md. Ansari

This chapter focuses on how the advancement of digital technologies is transforming governance models through the implementation of smart governance systems. The integration of AI, IoT, blockchain, and big data enables real-time decision-making, improves citizen engagement, and optimizes urban management. The chapter outlines the core technologies behind smart governance, its implementation strategies, and the challenges that come with this transformative shift in urban management.

Chapter 8: Smart Parking in Foggy Conditions - Real-Time Efficiency with PSO, ACO, and IoT Sensors

By Tanisha Thakur, Lavanya Srivastava, Aradhana Panda, and Hitesh Mohapatra

This chapter presents innovative strategies for enhancing smart parking systems by integrating Particle Swarm Optimization (PSO) and Ant Colony Optimization (ACO) with IoT sensors. It discusses how real-time data can optimize driver routing to available parking spaces while minimizing energy consumption. Special attention is given to improving system reliability under challenging conditions like fog, with the use of PSO-optimized fog-detectable sensors to enhance efficiency and reduce energy use.

Chapter 9: Smart Transportation Systems and Sustainable Urban Mobility

By Venkata Ramana Kaneti, Yamini B, Nagarajan S, Adaikkammai A, Anto Gracious L. A., Siva Subramanian R, and Girija P

This chapter explores the role of smart transportation systems in enhancing urban mobility and achieving sustainability. By leveraging IoT, AI, and GIS technologies, cities can address challenges such as congestion, carbon emissions, and resource optimization. The chapter discusses how data-driven policies, machine learning, and renewable energy integration can improve traffic flow, optimize public transport, and promote sustainability in urban environments.

Chapter 10: AI-Driven Curriculum Transformation and Faculty Development in Developing Universities

By Wael Hadi and Mohammad AlShaikh-Hasan

Higher education institutions in developing regions face constraints related to curriculum design and faculty readiness. This chapter examines how the integration of machine learning tools and data-driven methodologies can enhance teaching processes and address learner-centered outcomes. It discusses the importance of continuous professional development for faculty and highlights how adaptive platforms can boost student engagement and performance. The chapter proposes context-based innovations that respond to local constraints and offers strategies for replicable practices that transform curriculum and institutional frameworks.

Chapter 11: Securing the Digital Backbone of Smart Cities: Threat Detection, Infrastructure Hardening, and Data Governance

By Mohammad Alauthman, Wael Hadi, and Ahmad Al-Qerem

Smart cities rely on interconnected digital systems, which face security gaps that expose them to cyber threats. This chapter investigates key vulnerabilities in urban digital infrastructures and outlines methods for analyzing malicious behavior. It presents layered security strategies for protecting sensor networks, communication protocols, and control systems. The chapter emphasizes proactive detection algorithms, infrastructure hardening, and decentralized data governance models, offering a framework for securing the digital backbone of smart cities and improving resilience against cyber threats.

Chapter 12: IoT Applications in Urban Infrastructure and Governance

By Md Shamsul Haque Ansari, Nafees Akhter Farooqui, Mohammad Ishrat, and Wasim Khan The Internet of Things (IoT) is revolutionizing urban ecosystems by enhancing governance efficiency and enabling smarter infrastructure. This chapter explores IoT applications across sectors such as transportation, energy, waste management, and public safety. It discusses the role of IoT in optimizing resources, mitigating environmental impacts, and improving service delivery. The chapter also addresses challenges like data privacy concerns, cybersecurity risks, and scalability, while emphasizing IoT's potential to create resilient, sustainable, and equitable urban environments.

Chapter 13: Integration of Renewable Energy Systems into Smart Cities

By S. Ida Evangeline

The integration of renewable energy systems is essential for building sustainable, secure, and resilient smart cities. This chapter examines the role of renewable energy technologies like solar, wind, and geothermal power in reducing carbon footprints and improving energy efficiency. It discusses the technological, economic, and policy aspects of incorporating renewable energy into urban environments, focusing on smart grids, decentralized power generation, and intelligent energy management systems. The chapter highlights the benefits of renewable energy integration, including environmental conservation, economic growth, and enhanced community resilience.

Chapter 14: Integration of LLMs in Smart Cities for Sustainable Energy Solutions

By Dina Darwish

This chapter explores the potential of large language models (LLMs) in smart cities, focusing on how they can drive energy efficiency and sustainability. It examines the role of LLMs in managing urban resources, with an emphasis on energy optimization and the management of smart grids. The chapter discusses challenges related to data privacy, the use of emerging technologies like IoT and big data analytics, and the integration of LLMs into safety-critical energy systems. It offers insights into future research directions that leverage LLMs to promote sustainable urban energy solutions.

Chapter 15: Edge Artificial Intelligence Enabled 6G Communication Security System for Connected Vehicles in Revolutionizing Urban Development and Governance

By Priya Kohli and Sachin Sharma

The rise of 6G technology promises to revolutionize urban development and governance by enabling efficient communication for connected vehicles. This chapter explores the challenges of securing communication in 6G-based vehicular environments, including the need for low latency and minimal communication overhead. It examines the role of edge artificial intelligence in enhancing security and detecting malicious behavior in IoE-based vehicular networks. The chapter also highlights research on security mechanisms, protocols, and the integration of 6G in urban development to enhance mobility and governance.

Chapter 16: Human-Centered Design for Smart Cities: Integrating Social Aspects in Planning and Policy

By Ali Maqousi, Kashinath Basu, Ammar Almomani, and Mouhammd Alkasassbeh

This chapter explores the role of human-centered design in creating smarter cities that prioritize social inclusion and governance. It examines how integrating social factors into policy frameworks strengthens equity, civic trust, and public needs. The chapter focuses on participatory planning strategies, institutional shifts for inclusive governance, and the importance of designing technology to serve people. It draws on global initiatives and best practices for participatory design in urban projects, advocating for citizen empowerment and transparent processes to build ethical smart city ecosystems.

Chapter 17: Digital Twins and Social Intelligence for Urban Early Warning Systems

By Ali Al Maqousi, Ahmad Al-Qerem, Kashinath Basu, Amjad Aldweesh, and Mouhammd Alkasassbeh

This chapter investigates how digital twins and social intelligence can enhance urban early warning systems for disaster preparedness. It explores the challenges of translating high-volume data into actionable alerts for residents. The chapter discusses how merging sensor data with social intelligence platforms improves detection and coverage, enhancing real-time response capabilities. It provides an overview of how digital twin technologies can align institutions, communities, and technologies to ensure consistent, reliable early warning systems that mitigate the impact of disruptive events in urban areas.

Chapter 18: Challenges and Opportunities in Implementing Smart City Technologies in Developing Countries

By Syed Faisal, Wasim Khan, and Mohammad Ishrat

Smart city technologies present significant opportunities for developing countries, but also come with challenges such as inadequate infrastructure, financial constraints, outdated policies, and digital divides. This chapter discusses how IoT, AI, and big data can optimize resources and enhance urban governance. It highlights successful initiatives in India, Kenya, and Brazil and outlines strategies to strengthen digital infrastructure, foster public-private partnerships, and invest in digital literacy. The chapter advocates for collaborative efforts to leverage smart city solutions for sustainable urban growth and improved quality of life.

Chapter 19: Comprehensive Framework for Smart City Assessment Indicators, Methods, and Practical Applications

By Ali Maqousi, Ahmad Al-Qerem, Kashinath Basu, and Saad Alateef

This chapter presents a comprehensive framework for assessing smart city projects. It addresses the challenge of selecting robust indicators and methodological tools to evaluate complex urban systems. The chapter proposes an adaptable assessment framework that integrates context-specific requirements with performance tracking criteria. It discusses case reviews and existing standards, emphasizing the need for cities to align evaluation processes with clearly articulated priorities. The chapter aims to guide urban practitioners in assessing and refining smart city projects across different global contexts.

Chapter 20: Digital Solutions for Urban Household Waste Management: Challenges and Opportunities for Sustainable Cities

By Utkarsh Singh and Kavita Indapurkar

This chapter explores the challenges and opportunities of using digital solutions to address urban household waste management. It examines the role of digital platforms, such as apps and web-based services, in promoting waste reduction, segregation, and recycling behaviors. The chapter also discusses issues like inadequate infrastructure and electronic waste handling, offering suggestions for improving waste collection systems and fostering collaboration between government bodies, tech businesses, and local authorities. The findings underscore the importance of coordinated efforts to promote sustainable urban waste management practices and create cleaner, healthier cities.

CONCLUSION

In conclusion, *Revolutionizing Urban Development and Governance With Emerging Technologies* serves as both a comprehensive resource and a call to action for cities striving to evolve in response to new technological landscapes. The book captures the intersection of innovation, governance, and sustainability, illustrating the diverse ways in which emerging technologies can be leveraged to create smarter, more resilient urban environments. Through the chapters presented, we aim to provide practical insights and frameworks that will assist city leaders, planners, and researchers in navigating the complexities of modern urban challenges.

While the adoption of emerging technologies brings immense potential for improving urban infrastructure and governance, it also necessitates a broader conversation about inclusivity, ethical responsibility, and long-term sustainability. The contributions in this book highlight the importance of adopting a balanced approach—one that fosters technological advancement while safeguarding the rights and welfare of citizens. We believe that through transparent governance, public-private partnerships, and investment in innovation, cities can harness these technologies to address some of the most pressing issues of our time, from climate resilience to equitable urban development.

As editors, we hope that the knowledge shared in this volume will ignite further research, discussions, and actions that can accelerate the transition towards smart, sustainable, and inclusive cities. The future of urban development and governance is undoubtedly shaped by the technological advancements discussed in these pages, but their successful implementation will depend on collective efforts to navigate the challenges ahead. We invite readers to engage with the ideas presented herein and contribute to the ongoing dialogue that will drive positive change in cities across the globe.

Acknowledgment

The completion of this book, *Revolutionizing Urban Development and Governance With Emerging Technologies*, would not have been possible without the valuable contributions and support of many individuals and organizations.

First and foremost, we extend our sincere gratitude to the contributing authors, whose expertise, dedication, and hard work have been instrumental in shaping the high-quality content of this book. Their insights, research, and forward-thinking perspectives have enriched the discussions on the transformative role of emerging technologies in urban development and governance.

We are deeply thankful to the reviewers and editors who provided thoughtful feedback, guidance, and suggestions throughout the development of this book. Their meticulous attention to detail and commitment to academic excellence have ensured that this volume meets the highest standards of scholarly rigor and relevance.

We also acknowledge the support of academic institutions, research organizations, and professional communities that fostered the exchange of ideas and provided the resources necessary for the development of this book. Their encouragement and collaboration have been invaluable in bringing this project to fruition.

A special thanks goes to the team at IGI Global for their professionalism, patience, and expertise in guiding this book from conception to publication. Their unwavering support and dedication to academic publishing have been pivotal in ensuring the success of this project.

Finally, we would like to express our appreciation to our families, friends, and colleagues for their encouragement and understanding throughout this journey. Their support and belief in the importance of this work have motivated us to push forward and complete this endeavor.

This book is the result of collaborative efforts, and we are honored to share it with readers around the world. We hope it serves as a valuable resource for scholars, practitioners, and policymakers working to create smarter, more sustainable, and inclusive urban environments.

Thank you to everyone who played a role in making this book possible.

Editors:

Ali Al Maqousi

Ammar Almomani

Amjad Aldweesh

Mohammad Alauthman

Chapter 1
Advancing Urban Infrastructure Through Innovative Asset Management

Shaikha AlSanad
https://orcid.org/0000-0001-8857-7215
Kuwait Institute for Scientific Research, Kuwait

ABSTRACT

Urban infrastructure drives economic growth and sustainability, yet cities like Kuwait face challenges from aging systems, urbanization, and climate change. Given Kuwait's oil-dependent economy, resilient infrastructure is key for diversification. This chapter explores asset management strategies, particularly Structural Health Monitoring (SHM), to enhance efficiency and sustainability. Kuwait's major projects, like metro systems and renewable energy, require effective management. SHM integration enables predictive maintenance, reduces costs, and extends infrastructure lifespan. IoT, AI, and remote sensing optimize monitoring and resource allocation. Despite its benefits, SHM adoption faces policy gaps, financial constraints, and institutional resistance. Addressing these requires reforms, investment, and public-private collaboration. Embracing SHM will strengthen Kuwait's infrastructure, attract investment, and drive sustainable urban development.

DOI: 10.4018/979-8-3373-1375-7.ch001

1. INTRODUCTION

Urban infrastructure is the cornerstone of modern cities, playing a critical role in supporting the economic, social, and environmental pillars that enable communities to thrive. Key infrastructure systems, such as roads, bridges, water supply networks, energy grids, and public transportation systems, are integral to the daily functioning of cities ((OECD). 2024; Al-Saidi & Zaidan, 2024; AlSanad & Parol, 2023). These systems not only facilitate the efficient movement of goods, services, and people but also enhance the quality of life for urban residents by providing access to essential services and ensuring a safe and comfortable environment. Well-functioning infrastructure is essential for economic growth, as it enables commerce, attracts investment, and promotes social mobility. Furthermore, in an era of environmental consciousness, the development of sustainable infrastructure has become increasingly important, as it reduces environmental impacts, conserves resources, and contributes to the mitigation of climate change(Chan et al., 2022).

However, the rapid pace of urbanization that many cities are experiencing presents significant challenges in maintaining and upgrading existing infrastructure. As populations grow and urban sprawl expands, the demand for infrastructure services outpaces (De Pryck & Hulme, 2022; Sundararajan & Suriyagoda, 2016; United Nations Environment Programme (UNEP), 2020) the capacity of traditional systems, leading to strain on services and an increase in infrastructure degradation. Many urban areas are confronting aging infrastructure, where existing systems have surpassed their intended lifespan, resulting in costly repairs and frequent system failures. Additionally, the growing frequency and severity of climate-related events—such as extreme weather, flooding, and rising sea levels—pose new threats to the stability and functionality of urban infrastructure. These factors underscore the urgent need for cities to invest in resilient and adaptive infrastructure systems that are not only capable of withstanding current demands but also equipped to meet future challenges(Pathak et al., 2022; World Bank, 2016; Yunusa-Kaltungo et al., 2024).

Kuwait, like other rapidly urbanizing nations, is facing these same challenges. As the country continues to expand and modernize its urban landscape, the need for robust and sustainable infrastructure has become a central focus of national development. Kuwait has embarked on ambitious infrastructure projects, such as the construction of the Kuwait Metro, the development of a new international airport, and investments in renewable energy sources (AlSanad, 2017, 2018, 2024a; AlSanad, 2016; EPA, 2019 ; Kuwait, 2019; Kuwait, 2023). These large-scale initiatives are part of the nation's broader strategy to diversify its economy and reduce its dependence on oil revenues. However, as these infrastructure projects progress, it is essential to ensure that they are accompanied by effective asset management strategies that can maintain their operational efficiency over the long term. Without proper asset management, even the most advanced infrastructure can deteriorate prematurely, resulting in unnecessary costs, service disruptions, and inefficiencies.

Asset management is a systematic approach to the care and maintenance of infrastructure assets throughout their lifecycle. It involves planning, operating, and maintaining infrastructure in ways that maximize value, minimize risk, and extend the useful life of assets (AlSanad & Parol, 2023). Traditional asset management strategies often rely on reactive maintenance, where issues are addressed only after they occur. This approach, while common, can lead to higher repair costs, longer downtimes, and inefficient use of resources. In contrast, modern asset management strategies incorporate proactive and predictive maintenance practices, which are supported by advancements in digital technologies such as Structural Health Monitoring (SHM), the Internet of Things (IoT), and Artificial Intelligence (AI). These technologies provide real-time monitoring, data analytics, and predictive insights, enabling cities to detect potential issues before they escalate, optimize maintenance schedules, and extend the lifespan of critical infrastructure(Al-Qazweeni et al., 2020).

The importance of integrating advanced asset management practices is particularly evident in Kuwait's infrastructure sector, where both the aging infrastructure and rapid urban development necessitate a forward-thinking approach (AlSanad, 2024a; AlSanad & Parol, 2023). With an emphasis on sustainability and resilience, innovative asset management strategies can help Kuwait address the twin challenges of modernizing its infrastructure while mitigating the impacts of climate change. By leveraging technologies like SHM, IoT, and AI, Kuwait's infrastructure systems can be better managed, ultimately contributing to the country's broader goals of economic diversification, resource conservation, and sustainable development (Al-Qazweeni et al., 2020).

This chapter aims to examine the role of modern asset management strategies in improving urban infrastructure. It explores how emerging technologies and data-driven approaches are transforming the way cities approach infrastructure management, with particular emphasis on enhancing operational efficiency, sustainability, and resilience. Moreover, it addresses the challenges faced in implementing these strategies, including policy constraints, financial limitations, and institutional barriers. The chapter will highlight the need for comprehensive reforms in infrastructure management, including enhanced policy support, strategic investments in research and innovation, and cross-sectoral collaboration, to ensure that infrastructure systems are not only efficient and cost-effective but also adaptable to the changing needs of urban populations in Kuwait and other growing cities worldwide.

In an era where urban infrastructure faces an increasing array of challenges—from rapid urbanization and climate change to economic pressures—the need for innovative asset management strategies has never been greater. It is only through the adoption of forward-looking asset management practices that cities can build and maintain infrastructure systems that are capable of meeting both current and future demands.

2. THE IMPERATIVE FOR INNOVATIVE URBAN INFRASTRUCTURE ASSET MANAGEMENT

Urban infrastructure forms the backbone of contemporary societies, underpinning economic activities, promoting social welfare, and fostering environmental sustainability. Essential components such as roads, bridges, water supply networks, transportation systems, and energy grids play a crucial role in maintaining urban functionality and ensuring residents' quality of life(AlSanad, 2024b; Chan et al., 2022; World Bank, 2020). However, the convergence of rapid urbanization, climate change, and aging infrastructure has created significant challenges for cities worldwide in effectively maintaining these vital assets. Traditional asset management practices, which primarily rely on reactive maintenance and short-term solutions, are proving increasingly inadequate in addressing these evolving challenges. Consequently, there is a pressing need for innovative asset management approaches that incorporate technology, data-driven decision-making, and long-term strategic planning to enhance the resilience and sustainability of urban infrastructure(Chan et al., 2022).

Asset management encompasses a comprehensive process involving the planning, maintenance, upgrading, and optimization of infrastructure assets to maximize their lifespan, efficiency, and reliability. Effective asset management ensures that cities can continue to provide essential services while minimizing disruptions and long-term costs(Hallegatte et al., 2019). As infrastructure systems age and urban populations expand, cities must transition from conventional maintenance strategies to proactive, predictive, and technology-driven asset management approaches. This shift is particularly crucial for cities like Kuwait, where environmental factors such as extreme heat, sandstorms, and coastal exposure accelerate infrastructure deterioration.

2.1 Limitations of Traditional Asset Management Approaches

Traditional asset management has predominantly been reactive, focusing on repairs and replacements only after infrastructure failures or visible deterioration occur. This reactive approach leads to inefficiencies, often resulting in emergency interventions that are costly, unplanned, and disruptive to urban services. Reliance on reactive maintenance creates vulnerabilities within infrastructure networks, as unexpected failures can lead to economic losses, safety hazards, and service disruptions (Balali et al., 2020; Piryonesi & El-Diraby, 2020).

One of the primary issues with reactive maintenance is the financial burden it imposes on governments and urban planners. Emergency repairs are often significantly more expensive than planned preventive maintenance due to the urgency of the situation, the need for immediate labor and materials, and potential secondary damages caused by delayed interventions. Furthermore, prolonged neglect of infrastructure components increases overall maintenance costs in the long run, as minor issues escalate into major structural failures(Balali et al., 2020; Piryonesi & El-Diraby, 2020).

In addition to financial inefficiencies, traditional asset management approaches contribute to operational instability. Infrastructure failures, such as road collapses, water pipeline leaks, or power outages, disrupt daily urban activities, affecting transportation, trade, and essential public services. In a country like Kuwait, where high temperatures place additional stress on infrastructure materials, relying on reactive maintenance can lead to premature asset degradation, requiring frequent and costly replacements(AlSanad & Parol, 2023; Chan et al., 2022).

A more effective approach is proactive asset management, which focuses on preventive maintenance, early detection of structural weaknesses, and the integration of monitoring technologies to assess infrastructure conditions in real time. Predictive maintenance, supported by artificial intelligence (AI) and the Internet of Things (IoT), allows infrastructure managers to anticipate potential failures and take corrective actions before issues become critical. This transition from reactive to proactive management enhances infrastructure longevity, optimizes resource allocation, and minimizes economic and social disruptions(Balali et al., 2020; Economic & Affairs, 2020; Piryonesi & El-Diraby, 2020).

2.2 The Impact of Aging Infrastructure, Urbanization, and Climate Change on Infrastructure Performance

Aging infrastructure presents one of the most pressing challenges for urban development. Many cities worldwide operate with infrastructure systems that were constructed decades ago and are now struggling to meet the demands of expanding populations and evolving urban needs. As materials degrade over time, the structural integrity of roads, bridges, buildings, and public utilities declines, increasing the risk of failures. Without strategic asset management, the continued reliance on aging infrastructure threatens urban resilience and economic stability ((OECD).

2024; Agreement, 2020; Allam et al., 2023; De Pryck & Hulme, 2022; Kourtis & Tsihrintzis, 2021).

In Kuwait, infrastructure aging is further exacerbated by harsh environmental conditions. Extreme heat accelerates material degradation in roads, bridges, and energy systems, leading to thermal expansion, cracking, and increased maintenance requirements. Sandstorms contribute to erosion, blocking drainage systems and affecting the performance of electronic and mechanical infrastructure components. Coastal areas face additional risks due to saltwater exposure, which causes corrosion in steel-reinforced structures and weakens overall infrastructure durability. These environmental stressors underscore the need for a modernized asset management approach that accounts for Kuwait's specific climatic challenges (EPA, 2019 ; Kuwait, 2019).

Urbanization is another key factor placing immense pressure on infrastructure systems. Rapid population growth, increasing vehicle numbers, and expanding urban footprints contribute to higher infrastructure demand, particularly in transportation networks, water supply systems, and energy distribution grids. In many cities, urban expansion has outpaced infrastructure development, resulting in congestion, overuse, and service capacity limitations. For example, road networks originally designed to accommodate lower traffic volumes are now frequently experiencing congestion, leading to increased wear and tear, higher fuel consumption, and greater maintenance costs. Similarly, water supply and sanitation systems must expand to serve growing populations, requiring continuous monitoring and resource allocation to prevent shortages or service failures (Almaaitah et al., 2021; De Pryck & Hulme, 2022; Kourtis & Tsihrintzis, 2021; Pathak et al., 2022; Sundararajan & Suriyagoda, 2016).

Climate change further complicates infrastructure management by introducing new environmental risks that cities must adapt to. Rising temperatures, extreme weather events, and shifting climate patterns increase the likelihood of infrastructure failures and disruptions. In hot climates like Kuwait's, sustained high temperatures place additional stress on asphalt roads, causing softening and deformation that can lead to premature failures. Bridges and steel structures are also vulnerable to heat-induced expansion, which affects their stability and load-bearing capacity (Al-Qazweeni et al., 2020; AlSanad, 2024a, 2024b; Kuwait, 2019; Kuwait, 2023).

Additionally, Kuwait's urban infrastructure is at risk from flooding caused by extreme weather events. While the country experiences limited annual rainfall, sudden heavy downpours can overwhelm drainage systems, resulting in localized flooding that damages road networks, weakens foundations, and disrupts essential services. Without an advanced asset management system that incorporates climate adaptation strategies, cities will continue to face escalating maintenance costs and reduced infrastructure resilience in the face of environmental uncertainties (Kuwait, 2019).

2.3 The Strategic Importance of Asset Management for Sustainable Urban Growth

Strategic asset management is essential for ensuring that urban infrastructure supports long-term economic growth, social development, and environmental sustainability. Well-maintained infrastructure facilitates economic productivity by providing reliable transportation, communication, and utility services. Efficient road networks and public transportation systems enable trade and commerce, while robust water and energy infrastructure support business operations and industrial activities. By investing in asset management, cities can improve economic competitiveness, attract investments, and enhance overall urban efficiency(Almaaitah et al., 2021; da Silva & de Souza, 2022).

From a social perspective, effective asset management ensures that essential public services remain accessible and reliable. Infrastructure failures disproportionately impact lower-income communities that may lack alternative resources or adaptive capacity. Poorly maintained roads, bridges, and public transit systems create mobility barriers, while unreliable water supply and sanitation networks pose public health risks. By adopting data-driven and technology-enhanced asset management practices, cities can improve service reliability, enhance safety, and promote equitable access to urban resources (da Silva & de Souza, 2022; De Villiers, 2018) .

In Kuwait, asset management plays a critical role in national development efforts, particularly in supporting economic diversification and sustainable urban planning. As the country invests in large-scale infrastructure projects—such as the Kuwait Metro, smart city initiatives, and renewable energy developments—ensuring their long-term sustainability will require comprehensive asset management frameworks. Incorporating real-time monitoring technologies, artificial intelligence-driven predictive maintenance, and integrated digital infrastructure management systems will help optimize infrastructure performance and resilience (AlSanad & Parol, 2023).

Moreover, strategic asset management aligns with global sustainability goals, including the United Nations Sustainable Development Goals (SDGs). Specifically, SDG 9 (Industry, Innovation, and Infrastructure) and SDG 11 (Sustainable Cities and Communities) highlight the importance of resilient infrastructure in promoting sustainable urban growth. By integrating innovative asset management solutions, Kuwait can enhance its infrastructure resilience, improve service efficiency, and create a more sustainable urban environment that meets the demands of future generations (Economic & Affairs, 2020).

3. STRUCTURAL HEALTH MONITORING (SHM) AND ITS ROLE IN ASSET MANAGEMENT

Urban infrastructure is a vital component of modern societies, supporting economic activities, social well-being, and environmental sustainability. Roads, bridges, tunnels, and buildings must function efficiently to ensure the stability and safety of urban environments. However, maintaining these assets presents significant challenges, especially as infrastructure ages and urban populations grow. Traditional approaches to infrastructure management often rely on periodic inspections and reactive maintenance strategies, which may not be sufficient to prevent sudden failures. In response, Structural Health Monitoring (SHM) has emerged as an essential tool for enhancing asset management practices. SHM leverages advanced sensing technologies and data analytics to provide real-time assessments of structural conditions, enabling proactive maintenance and long-term sustainability (Al-Qazweeni et al., 2020; Husain et al., 2023). By integrating SHM into urban infrastructure management, decision-makers can enhance resilience, improve safety, and optimize maintenance efforts.

3.1 Definition and Key Principles of SHM

Structural Health Monitoring (SHM) refers to the continuous process of assessing the condition and performance of infrastructure assets using advanced sensor systems, data acquisition technologies, and analytical models (Allam et al., 2023; Vijayan et al., 2023; Wang & Ke, 2024). Unlike conventional inspection methods, which are often labor-intensive and subject to human error, SHM provides a scientific and data-driven approach to infrastructure evaluation. SHM systems collect real-time data on various structural parameters, such as load-bearing capacity, material stress, vibration levels, and temperature variations. These data points help engineers detect early signs of deterioration and make informed maintenance decisions before problems escalate (Scuro et al., 2021; Vijayan et al., 2023; Wang & Ke, 2024).

The key principles of SHM revolve around several core aspects:

- **Continuous and Automated Monitoring:** SHM operates continuously, tracking changes in structural conditions without requiring frequent manual inspections. This allows for real-time decision-making and early detection of structural deficiencies.
- **Integration of Advanced Technologies:** SHM employs a combination of sensors, wireless communication networks, and cloud-based data processing systems to provide accurate and timely assessments of infrastructure health.

- **Predictive and Preventive Maintenance:** Unlike traditional reactive approaches, SHM enables infrastructure managers to anticipate maintenance needs and implement timely interventions, reducing the risk of costly emergency repairs.
- **Enhanced Decision-Making Through Data Analytics:** The vast amount of data collected by SHM systems is analyzed using machine learning and artificial intelligence (AI) algorithms, improving the accuracy of risk assessments and maintenance planning.
- **Adaptability to Various Infrastructure Types:** SHM can be applied to diverse infrastructure assets, from bridges and tunnels to high-rise buildings and water pipelines. The flexibility of SHM technologies makes them a valuable tool for urban asset management.

3.2 SHM as a Transformative Tool for Proactive Maintenance

Traditional infrastructure maintenance relies heavily on scheduled inspections and reactive repairs, which may not always detect early warning signs of structural weaknesses. This approach can lead to unexpected failures, posing safety risks and incurring high costs for emergency interventions. SHM transforms this process by introducing a proactive maintenance approach, where infrastructure conditions are continuously monitored, and maintenance decisions are based on real-time data rather than predetermined schedules (Al-Qazweeni et al., 2020; Al-Sanad et al., 2023; AlSanad & Parol, 2023; Husain et al., 2023).

One of the most significant advantages of SHM is its ability to detect hidden structural vulnerabilities before they become visible. Small cracks in bridges, corrosion in steel structures, or weakening of concrete due to temperature fluctuations may go unnoticed in standard inspections. However, SHM sensors can detect minute changes in structural behavior, alerting engineers to potential problems before they escalate. This capability is especially important in high-risk environments where infrastructure failure can have catastrophic consequences (Al-Sanad et al., 2023; AlSanad & Parol, 2023; Husain et al., 2023).

Furthermore, SHM enhances maintenance efficiency and cost-effectiveness by prioritizing repairs based on actual structural conditions. Infrastructure managers can allocate resources more effectively, ensuring that maintenance efforts focus on assets that require immediate attention while avoiding unnecessary repairs on well-functioning structures. This targeted approach optimizes budget allocation and extends the lifespan of infrastructure assets, ultimately contributing to long-term sustainability (Abdulkarem et al., 2020; Al-Qazweeni et al., 2020).

The role of SHM in enhancing safety is also significant. By continuously monitoring structural integrity, SHM systems provide early warnings of potential hazards, allowing for prompt interventions that prevent accidents. For example, in earthquake-prone regions, SHM can detect structural stress caused by seismic activity, enabling engineers to assess damage and implement reinforcements as needed. Similarly, in extreme weather conditions, such as those experienced in Kuwait, SHM can monitor temperature-induced material expansion and contraction, ensuring that infrastructure remains stable under fluctuating environmental conditions.

Another key benefit of SHM is its ability to support asset lifecycle management by providing comprehensive historical data on infrastructure performance. Over time, this data helps engineers and policymakers make informed decisions about infrastructure investments, retrofitting strategies, and long-term planning. Instead of relying solely on subjective assessments, infrastructure stakeholders can use SHM data to optimize the design, construction, and maintenance of future urban assets(AlSanad & Parol, 2023).

3.3 How SHM Technology Improves Infrastructure Resilience and Operational Efficiency

The resilience of urban infrastructure is crucial for ensuring that cities can withstand and adapt to external stressors, including environmental changes, increasing population demands, and aging structural components. SHM plays a central role in improving infrastructure resilience by enabling cities to identify and address vulnerabilities before they lead to failures (Allam et al., 2023; Ongkowijoyo & Doloi, 2018; Scuro et al., 2021; Vijayan et al., 2023; Wang & Ke, 2024).

One of the most pressing challenges in urban infrastructure management is the impact of climate change on structural performance. Rising temperatures, extreme weather events, and increasing humidity levels can accelerate material deterioration and reduce the lifespan of critical assets. In Kuwait, where high temperatures and sandstorms are common, SHM systems can monitor the effects of these environmental conditions and suggest maintenance adjustments to mitigate their impact. By continuously tracking temperature-induced stresses and material degradation, SHM ensures that infrastructure remains robust despite changing climatic conditions.

Moreover, SHM contributes to disaster risk management by providing real-time data on infrastructure stability during and after extreme events. In the case of earthquakes, floods, or industrial accidents, SHM can assess structural damage in real time, assisting emergency response teams in prioritizing rescue and repair efforts. This capability significantly enhances urban resilience by minimizing post-disaster recovery times and reducing economic losses associated with infrastructure failures (AlSanad & Parol, 2023; Balali et al., 2020; Carlson et al., 2012; Piryonesi & El-Diraby, 2020).

Beyond resilience, SHM improves operational efficiency by reducing the frequency of manual inspections and optimizing maintenance schedules. Traditional inspection methods often require road closures, workforce deployment, and significant time investments. In contrast, SHM enables remote monitoring of infrastructure conditions, eliminating the need for frequent on-site assessments and reducing operational disruptions (Al-Sanad et al., 2023; AlSanad & Parol, 2023).

The integration of emerging technologies further enhances SHM capabilities. The use of Internet of Things (IoT) sensors, machine learning algorithms, and cloud-based data platforms allows for more sophisticated infrastructure monitoring and predictive analysis. IoT sensors enable the collection of real-time structural data, while AI-driven analytics process this data to identify patterns and predict maintenance needs. This digital transformation of asset management results in smarter infrastructure systems that can self-diagnose issues and suggest maintenance actions with minimal human intervention (Scuro et al., 2021).

Additionally, the implementation of SHM supports sustainable urban growth by promoting long-term infrastructure planning and investment. As cities expand, the demand for reliable and efficient infrastructure increases. SHM provides policymakers with the necessary data to develop evidence-based infrastructure policies, ensuring that future urban development aligns with sustainability goals. By reducing resource wastage, minimizing unexpected failures, and optimizing asset lifespans, SHM contributes to the creation of resilient, cost-effective, and environmentally sustainable urban environments (Vijayan et al., 2023; Wang & Ke, 2024).

4. THE TRANSFORMATIVE IMPACT OF TECHNOLOGY ON ASSET MANAGEMENT

The integration of technological innovations has instigated a paradigm shift in asset management practices, moving away from conventional reactive strategies towards proactive and predictive methodologies. These advanced approaches are designed to enhance infrastructure performance, prolong its lifespan, and bolster resilience against unforeseen challenges. Contemporary technologies facilitate real-time monitoring, sophisticated data analytics, and automation, thereby significantly improving the efficiency and effectiveness of infrastructure maintenance and management protocols. These advancements directly address persistent issues such as suboptimal maintenance scheduling, elevated operational expenditures, and the inherent risks associated with infrastructure degradation and potential failures (AlSanad & Parol, 2023; De Villiers, 2018; Piryonesi & El-Diraby, 2020).

The advent of digital technologies, notably the Internet of Things (IoT), Artificial Intelligence (AI), automation and robotics, and Big Data analytics, has fostered the development of more dynamic and data-centric decision-making frameworks. Furthermore, the incorporation of satellite imaging, remote sensing technologies, and digital twins has revolutionized the assessment of infrastructure conditions, enabling comprehensive, real-time monitoring capabilities across extensive networks. These technological progressions have been instrumental in augmenting infrastructure resilience, promoting sustainability initiatives, and optimizing the operational efficiency of asset management systems (Scuro et al., 2021).

4.1 The Pivotal Role of Digital Technologies in Contemporary Asset Management

Digital technologies have become essential components of modern asset management, providing the capacity for continuous monitoring, predictive maintenance, and automated decision-making processes. The implementation of these technologies allows for the real-time tracking of infrastructure conditions, thereby reducing reliance on traditional manual inspections and ensuring that interventions are more precise and timely. Among the most impactful digital innovations are the Internet of Things (IoT), Artificial Intelligence (AI), automation and robotics, and Big Data analytics, each contributing uniquely to the enhancement of infrastructure resilience, the reduction of operational costs, and the improvement of long-term asset performance (AlSanad & Parol, 2023; De Villiers, 2018; Piryonesi & El-Diraby, 2020; Scuro et al., 2021).

4.2 Internet of Things (IoT) Applications in Asset Management

The Internet of Things (IoT) has revolutionized the field of asset management by establishing interconnected networks of sensors, which are embedded within infrastructure components to facilitate continuous data collection and analysis. These sensors are engineered to monitor a diverse array of critical parameters, including structural stress, temperature variations, vibration levels, humidity, corrosion rates, and load-bearing capacity. IoT-driven monitoring systems are designed to provide real-time alerts regarding the structural health of assets, which enables maintenance teams to implement proactive measures before critical failures occur (Du et al., 2020; Lattanzi & Miller, 2017; Schnebele et al., 2015).

A significant advantage of IoT technology is its capacity to support remote infrastructure monitoring. For extensive infrastructure networks, such as transportation corridors, power grids, and water distribution systems, traditional manual inspections can be impractical and economically prohibitive. IoT devices mitigate these challenges by transmitting real-time data to centralized monitoring systems, where AI algorithms analyze the incoming data to detect anomalies and early indications of deterioration(Du et al., 2020; Lattanzi & Miller, 2017; Schnebele et al., 2015).

Moreover, IoT technology plays a crucial role in facilitating integrated asset lifecycle management. By continuously tracking performance data throughout the lifecycle of an asset, IoT systems enable infrastructure managers to make informed decisions regarding repair schedules, resource allocation, and future upgrades. This approach not only reduces maintenance costs and minimizes downtime but also extends the useful life of infrastructure assets(Du et al., 2020; Lattanzi & Miller, 2017; Schnebele et al., 2015).

4.3 Artificial Intelligence (AI) in Predictive Maintenance and Risk Assessment

Artificial Intelligence (AI) has emerged as a transformative force in asset management by enhancing the precision of data analysis, automating decision-making processes, and optimizing predictive maintenance strategies. AI algorithms are capable of processing vast datasets derived from IoT sensors, historical maintenance records, and environmental condition reports to identify patterns indicative of structural vulnerabilities or operational inefficiencies (AlSanad, 2024a; Chan et al., 2022; Jardine et al., 2006; Yunusa-Kaltungo et al., 2024).

One of the most valuable applications of AI in asset management is predictive maintenance. By analyzing historical and real-time infrastructure performance data, AI models can forecast potential component failures, enabling maintenance teams to take preemptive actions. This predictive capability minimizes unplanned downtime, prevents catastrophic failures, and enhances cost efficiency by transitioning from reactive to proactive maintenance approaches(Jardine et al., 2006).

AI is also employed in risk assessment and asset prioritization. Infrastructure managers utilize AI-powered risk models to assess which assets require immediate intervention and which can continue to operate under current conditions. This risk-based approach ensures the efficient allocation of maintenance resources, focusing on high-risk infrastructure components.

Furthermore, computer vision and machine learning techniques are improving infrastructure inspection processes. High-resolution images, captured by drones, satellites, and surveillance cameras, are analyzed using AI to detect structural defects such as cracks, corrosion, deformations, and material degradation, thereby increasing the accuracy and speed of inspections and reducing the reliance on manual assessments(Jardine et al., 2006).

4.4 Automation and Robotics in Infrastructure Management

Automation and robotics have significantly enhanced asset management by reducing the need for manual labor, increasing inspection precision, and improving safety in hazardous environments. Autonomous drones and robotic systems are now frequently used to inspect infrastructure components, including bridges, tunnels, offshore structures, and high-rise buildings (Lattanzi & Miller, 2017; Paul et al., 2010) .

Drones equipped with high-resolution cameras and LiDAR sensors perform aerial inspections, providing detailed visual and topographical data on infrastructure conditions. These drones can detect cracks, deformations, and signs of wear without the need for physical access to the structure. Similarly, robotic systems are utilized for underwater inspections of pipelines, dams, and offshore platforms, where human intervention is challenging and costly.

In addition to inspections, robotic systems are being developed for automated repair and maintenance tasks. Robotic arms can perform welding, coating applications, and material reinforcement, reducing downtime and minimizing risks associated with manual repairs in high-risk environments. Automated road maintenance systems are also being introduced to detect potholes, apply repairs, and optimize road surface conditions with minimal human intervention (Lattanzi & Miller, 2017; Paul et al., 2010).

4.5 Big Data and Predictive Analytics for Proactive Maintenance

The emergence of Big Data analytics has equipped infrastructure managers with advanced tools for processing, analyzing, and interpreting large volumes of asset performance data. Predictive analytics, a key application of Big Data, enables the identification of trends in asset deterioration and the development of proactive maintenance strategies (Deepa et al., 2022; McMahon et al., 2020).

By combining historical data with real-time monitoring, predictive analytics helps asset managers to anticipate future infrastructure failures, schedule maintenance more effectively, and optimize resource allocation. This approach reduces the likelihood of costly emergency repairs and ensures the sustainability of infrastructure assets (Deepa et al., 2022; McMahon et al., 2020).

Another critical application of Big Data is real-time operational optimization. Smart infrastructure systems use data analytics to adjust energy usage, water distribution, and traffic flow based on demand fluctuations. These optimizations improve system efficiency, reduce waste, and enhance sustainability efforts(Deepa et al., 2022; McMahon et al., 2020).

4.6 Satellite Imaging and Remote Sensing for Large-Scale Monitoring

Satellite imaging and remote sensing technologies provide large-scale, real-time monitoring capabilities that are essential for assessing infrastructure conditions and detecting structural weaknesses. These technologies utilize high-resolution imagery, LiDAR scanning, and synthetic aperture radar (SAR) to monitor land movements, ground subsidence, and structural deformations (Du et al., 2020; McMahon et al., 2020).

A primary advantage of satellite imaging is its ability to track infrastructure performance over time, identifying gradual changes that may indicate structural instability. This is particularly useful for bridges, highways, dams, and coastal structures, where environmental factors such as erosion, subsidence, and climate-related stressors can compromise structural integrity(Du et al., 2020; McMahon et al., 2020).

Remote sensing also facilitates the development of early warning systems for disaster-prone regions. By analyzing satellite data, asset managers can assess flood risks, earthquake damage, and land subsidence trends, enabling timely interventions to mitigate risks and enhance infrastructure resilience (Du et al., 2020; McMahon et al., 2020).

4.7 Digital Twins for Enhanced Infrastructure Planning and Management

The development of digital twins represents a significant innovation in asset management. A digital twin is a virtual replica of a physical asset that integrates real-time data, predictive analytics, and AI-driven simulations to optimize infrastructure performance.

Digital twins enable infrastructure managers to test different operational scenarios, simulate environmental impacts, and evaluate maintenance strategies before implementing them in the real world. This virtual modeling capability enhances decision-making, allowing for cost-effective, data-driven asset management(Kritzinger et al., 2018; Melesse et al., 2020).

The primary benefits of digital twins include:

- Predictive maintenance through AI-driven simulations.
- Scenario modeling to assess the impact of environmental changes and traffic fluctuations.
- Real-time monitoring of infrastructure conditions, enabling rapid response to potential failures.
- Lifecycle optimization, allowing for long-term infrastructure planning and resource management.

The integration of digital twins with smart city planning is also expanding, supporting urban infrastructure development, traffic management, and sustainable energy distribution. These digital models enhance long-term asset resilience, making infrastructure systems more adaptive and responsive to future challenges(Kritzinger et al., 2018; Melesse et al., 2020) .

4.8 Cybersecurity and Data Protection in Digital Asset Management

As asset management becomes increasingly digital, cybersecurity threats pose significant risks to infrastructure operations. Unauthorized access, data breaches, and cyber-attacks can compromise sensitive information and disrupt essential services. Implementing robust cybersecurity measures, such as blockchain technology for secure data management, AI-driven threat detection, and encryption protocols, is essential to protecting infrastructure systems. Cyber resilience strategies ensure that digital asset management platforms remain secure and reliable (El Mrabet et al., 2018; Tatipatri & Arun, 2024).

4.9 Edge Computing in Infrastructure Monitoring

Edge computing is transforming infrastructure monitoring by processing data closer to its source, reducing reliance on centralized cloud servers. This enhances real-time decision-making, minimizes data transmission delays, and improves security. Edge computing is particularly valuable for remote infrastructure sites, where immediate data processing is necessary for operational safety and efficiency (Satyanarayanan, 2017).

4.10 5G Networks for Enhanced Digital Infrastructure Monitoring

The deployment of 5G networks has significantly improved data transmission speeds and network reliability, enabling seamless communication between IoT devices, AI analytics, and cloud computing systems. Faster connectivity enhances high-frequency data collection, allowing infrastructure managers to detect and respond to structural issues more efficiently. The low latency of 5G technology also facilitates the implementation of autonomous maintenance systems and smart grid management (Ongkowijoyo & Doloi, 2018).

4.11 Blockchain for Secure Data Management

Blockchain technology is gaining prominence in asset management for its ability to provide tamper-proof data records, transparent auditing, and secure asset tracking. By decentralizing infrastructure data management, blockchain enhances trust among stakeholders and ensures accurate maintenance records. This technology is particularly useful in tracking infrastructure contracts, recording maintenance histories, and enhancing digital twin applications (Alamri et al., 2019; Deepa et al., 2022).

4.12 Augmented Reality (AR) and Virtual Reality (VR) for Advanced Infrastructure Inspections

AR and VR technologies are being increasingly utilized in infrastructure inspections and maintenance training. AR overlays digital information onto physical assets, allowing engineers to visualize structural conditions in real-time without requiring physical access. VR enables immersive simulations, which are beneficial for training maintenance personnel and testing infrastructure stress scenarios. These technologies enhance accuracy in asset assessments and improve workforce preparedness (Klasa et al., 2021).

The Future of Asset Management

The integration of these technological innovations into asset management has significantly improved infrastructure resilience, operational efficiency, and sustainability. By leveraging digital tools, asset managers can adopt a proactive approach to infrastructure maintenance, optimize resource allocation, and ensure long-term urban development. The continuous evolution of smart technologies will further enhance the effectiveness of asset management strategies, contributing to the creation of resilient and sustainable cities.

5. ECONOMIC ADVANTAGES OF SOPHISTICATED ASSET MANAGEMENT METHODOLOGIES

The deployment of sophisticated asset management methodologies represents a paradigm shift in infrastructure development. It provides an encompassing framework for the administration of assets throughout their complete lifecycle. These methodologies synergize state-of-the-art technology with robust decision-making protocols to optimize the value extracted from infrastructure investments. The economic advantages of such methodologies are multifaceted, impacting critical areas such as the mitigation of maintenance expenditures, enhancement of operational efficiency, prolongation of infrastructure lifespan, fostering economic diversification, and elevating the overall quality of urban living. A thorough examination of these interconnected aspects reveals that advanced asset management not only contributes to the efficiency of infrastructural operations but also significantly bolsters the broader economic stability and developmental trajectory of a nation.

5.1 Reduction in Maintenance Costs and Enhancement of Operational Efficiency

A salient economic benefit derived from sophisticated asset management lies in the appreciable curtailment of maintenance costs. Traditional maintenance paradigms frequently depend on reactive interventions, whereby infrastructural problems are addressed only post-identification. This reactive strategy can precipitate elevated repair expenditures and augmented service disruptions. Conversely, advanced asset management emphasizes proactive, predictive maintenance, leveraging real-time data streams, sensor networks, and comprehensive monitoring systems to preemptively anticipate potential failures. By identifying and rectifying minor anomalies early in their manifestation, the imperative for extensive repairs and unscheduled maintenance interventions is substantially mitigated. This proactive strategic orientation not only averts costly emergency repairs but also curtails unforeseen service downtimes, thereby diminishing the economic ramifications of service interruptions. Furthermore, the judicious allocation of resources culminates in a more efficacious utilization of budgetary provisions, as maintenance efforts are strategically directed toward the most critical and high-risk assets, thus augmenting overarching operational efficiency (Alqasi et al., 2024).

Operational efficiency is further amplified through the strategic optimization of asset utilization. With advanced asset management systems, infrastructure managers can meticulously plan and schedule operational activities predicated on data-driven insights, thereby guaranteeing that assets are deployed in the most efficacious manner conceivable. This strategic approach not only ameliorates the functionality of individual assets but also enhances the aggregate performance of the entire infrastructural network, culminating in more cost-effective operations and heightened productivity across diverse sectors(AlMetwally et al., 2020; Sun et al., 2023).

5.2 Extension of Infrastructure Lifespan and Reduced Service Disruptions

Infrastructure systems constitute the backbone of any thriving economy, and the protracted longevity of these assets directly correlates with the value they accrue. Advanced asset management contributes substantively to the extension of an asset's lifespan through persistent monitoring protocols, preventive maintenance regimens, and thorough performance analyses. By discerning the gradual wear and tear on infrastructural components early in the degradation process, maintenance interventions can be strategically planned and implemented preemptively, thereby effectively prolonging the lifecycle of the asset. Consequently, the frequency and associated costs of asset replacements are markedly reduced, culminating in substantial long-term savings (Al-Qazweeni et al., 2020; Deraemaeker et al., 2008; Husain et al., 2023; Morgan et al., 2022).

In addition to the augmentation of asset longevity, this methodological approach also curtails service interruptions. Infrastructural failures, such as the breakdown of transportation networks, energy grids, or potable water distribution systems, can precipitate significant economic losses stemming from interrupted services and diminished productivity. Advanced asset management systems serve to ensure that maintenance activities are executed prior to the actualization of a failure, thereby diminishing the probability of unscheduled service interruptions. This operational stability engenders trust in public infrastructure and bolsters the sustained functionality of critical sectors, including transportation, utilities, and healthcare, which are foundational to sustained economic productivity(Al-Qazweeni et al., 2020; Deraemaeker et al., 2008; Husain et al., 2023; Morgan et al., 2022). .

5.3 Contribution to Economic Diversification and Investment Attractiveness

The capacity to manage infrastructure assets efficiently and sustainably represents a pivotal component of a nation's broader efforts to diversify its economic landscape. By adopting sophisticated asset management strategies, countries can ensure the continued reliability, resilience, and readiness of their infrastructure to effectively support emerging industries and attract foreign direct investment. For example, in regions endeavoring to transition from conventional industries to more diversified, technology-driven sectors, a modernized infrastructure system can serve as a compelling incentive for prospective business investments and economic partnerships. Investors are more inclined to allocate capital to regions where infrastructure is managed with optimal efficiency, as this signals a stable and predictable environment for business operations and sustained economic growth (Al-Saidi & Zaidan, 2024; Allam et al., 2023; Economic & Affairs, 2020; Forum., 2022; Zhang et al., 2023).

Furthermore, countries that prioritize advanced asset management practices convey a clear message to international investors regarding their unwavering commitment to long-term sustainable development. In the specific context of Kuwait, the adoption of advanced asset management strategies can significantly enhance the attraction of foreign direct investments in key sectors such as renewable energy generation, advanced technology industries, and the development of smart city initiatives (AlSanad & Parol, 2023). These sectors inherently demand reliable and modern infrastructure to operate efficiently, and investors are more likely to engage in markets where infrastructure reliability is rigorously ensured. Thus, advanced asset management not only safeguards existing investments but also cultivates an environment conducive to pioneering economic ventures, thereby driving the progressive diversification of the economy. In the context of developing nations or economies heavily reliant on a limited number of industries, the role of infrastructure in facilitating diversification cannot be overstated. By enhancing infrastructure reliability and sustainability, advanced asset management can support the broader economic transition, making the economy less vulnerable to external shocks and contributing to long-term economic resilience.

5.4 Smart Urban Development and Enhancement of Quality of Life

As urbanization trends accelerate on a global scale, the imperative for smart urban development becomes increasingly critical. Smart cities are fundamentally built upon a robust foundation of well-managed and interconnected infrastructure systems. These systems leverage data analytics and advanced technology to enhance city-wide operations and significantly improve the overall quality of life for urban residents. Advanced asset management is an integral component of this transformative development. By utilizing cutting-edge technologies such as Internet of Things (IoT) sensor networks, Geographic Information Systems (GIS), and smart grid technologies, cities can proactively monitor and manage infrastructure assets in real-time. This real-time capability facilitates more efficient utilization of resources, enables better strategic planning for urban growth, and reduces operational costs across various municipal departments (Al-Saidi & Zaidan, 2024; El Mrabet et al., 2018; Gunderia et al., 2024).

The economic benefits of smart urban development extend far beyond mere operational efficiency gains. A well-functioning and intelligently designed urban environment offers enhanced levels of comfort, security, and overall sustainability for its residents. For instance, advanced traffic management systems designed to optimize traffic flow can effectively reduce congestion and lower fuel consumption, leading to tangible cost savings for both individual commuters and businesses operating within the urban area. Similarly, energy-efficient buildings and infrastructure can substantially reduce operating costs for industries, commercial enterprises, and residential households, thereby contributing to overall economic savings at both the micro and macro levels. Furthermore, the strategic integration of advanced asset management principles into urban development initiatives significantly improves the accessibility and long-term sustainability of essential public services. A city that proactively maintains its infrastructure effectively can provide more reliable and efficient public transportation options, enhance waste management processes, and optimize energy distribution systems, all of which collectively enhance the overall livability and attractiveness of urban areas. This, in turn, improves the quality of life for residents, makes cities more attractive to skilled labor, and supports economic growth through increased productivity and innovation (Chan et al., 2022; De Pryck & Hulme, 2022).

5.5 Broader Economic Stability and Resilience

Advanced asset management contributes significantly to the broader economic stability and resilience of a nation by reducing the vulnerability of critical infrastructure to external shocks, such as natural disasters, economic crises, or unforeseen technological disruptions. By ensuring that infrastructure assets are meticulously maintained, continuously monitored, and operated with optimal efficiency, a country can cultivate enhanced resilience to both immediate and long-term challenges. In the face of ongoing climate change, for instance, infrastructure systems that are designed and constructed with resilience as a primary consideration will be better equipped to withstand extreme weather events, thereby minimizing potential damage and reducing the imperative for costly post-crisis repairs and reconstruction efforts(AlSanad & Parol, 2023; Piryonesi & El-Diraby, 2020).

This resilience extends comprehensively to the economic sector as well. A nation with a well-maintained and efficiently managed infrastructure network is inherently better positioned to navigate economic downturns and periods of financial instability, as the overall efficiency and reliability of its core infrastructure systems support continued economic activity, even in challenging times. The ability to effectively mitigate disruptions, minimize operational downtime, and proactively manage assets collectively strengthens the economy's overall capacity to adapt to evolving circumstances and remain competitive on a global scale(AlSanad & Parol, 2023).

6. CHALLENGES IN ADOPTING INNOVATIVE ASSET MANAGEMENT PRACTICES

While the integration of advanced asset management strategies, including Structural Health Monitoring (SHM), presents numerous benefits, several challenges must be addressed for successful implementation. These challenges range from data integration and policy gaps to financial constraints and institutional resistance. Overcoming these obstacles will require careful planning, collaboration, and commitment to creating a supportive environment for the adoption of innovative technologies. This section explores the key challenges faced by Kuwait and other regions in adopting innovative asset management practices.

6.1 Data Integration and Interoperability Issues

One of the most significant challenges in adopting innovative asset management practices is the integration of data from various systems and sources. In the case of infrastructure management, assets are often handled by multiple departments or organizations, each using different tools, software, and technologies to monitor, maintain, and track the condition of infrastructure. This fragmentation leads to difficulties in consolidating data, making it harder to assess the overall health of infrastructure assets accurately.

In addition, many existing asset management systems were not designed with interoperability in mind. For instance, newer technologies like SHM and IoT devices may not easily communicate with legacy systems, leading to inefficiencies and data silos. This lack of seamless communication prevents stakeholders from obtaining real-time insights into the condition of infrastructure, which is crucial for timely maintenance and decision-making.

To address this challenge, Kuwait and other regions must invest in technologies that promote interoperability and ensure that data from disparate sources can be integrated into a central platform. This may include developing standardized protocols for data sharing, implementing open-source technologies, or creating a universal dashboard that allows various systems to communicate effectively. Furthermore, adopting cloud-based platforms that store and process data centrally can provide the flexibility needed to manage large amounts of real-time data from various infrastructure assets. These efforts would help stakeholders make data-driven decisions and support proactive maintenance strategies, enhancing the overall efficiency and resilience of infrastructure.

6.2 Policy Gaps and Regulatory Challenges

The successful integration of innovative asset management practices also depends on the regulatory environment. Many current policies governing infrastructure management were designed based on traditional methods, which often rely on reactive maintenance practices. These policies may not account for emerging technologies such as SHM, AI, or IoT, which represent a shift from conventional approaches to more proactive, predictive management.

Furthermore, some regulations may inadvertently create barriers to the adoption of new technologies. For example, certain policies may limit the use of new materials or technologies due to outdated safety or building codes, or they may restrict the use of real-time data for monitoring purposes. As a result, these outdated regulatory frameworks can slow down the integration of advanced asset management strategies.

To overcome these policy gaps, there is a clear need for reform. This includes updating building codes, safety standards, and environmental regulations to accommodate the integration of SHM and other smart technologies. Governments must also take the initiative to create incentives for innovation, such as tax breaks or subsidies for companies investing in new infrastructure technologies. Additionally, there is a need for clear guidelines on how public-private partnerships (PPPs) can play a role in the development and deployment of these technologies, as these collaborations can provide the necessary resources and expertise to overcome regulatory hurdles.

6.3 Financial Constraints and the Cost of Implementing SHM Technologies

Financial constraints represent one of the most substantial challenges in adopting advanced asset management technologies. While the long-term benefits of SHM technologies, such as reduced maintenance costs, extended infrastructure lifespan, and improved operational efficiency, are well-documented, the initial capital required for implementation can be prohibitively high. For many municipalities, especially in emerging economies, the cost of installing sensors, developing monitoring platforms, and integrating these technologies into existing infrastructure may exceed budget constraints.

Moreover, the cost of training staff and building capacity to use and maintain new technologies adds an additional financial burden. Although these investments are expected to pay off over time through reduced maintenance costs and improved asset performance, the initial upfront costs may be difficult to justify, especially when funds are limited.

To overcome this financial challenge, alternative financing mechanisms are essential. Public-private partnerships (PPPs) can play a significant role by facilitating joint investments between the public sector, private companies, and financial institutions. This collaborative approach can help spread the financial risk associated with implementing SHM technologies while also ensuring that infrastructure projects benefit from the expertise and innovation provided by private partners. Additionally, governments can look into creating dedicated funds for the digitalization of infrastructure, offering interest-free loans or grants for municipalities and organizations seeking to invest in these technologies.

Moreover, the government could explore financing models that allow for a gradual implementation of SHM systems. Rather than installing these technologies across all infrastructure at once, a phased approach can target high-priority assets first, allowing for manageable upfront costs and more focused implementation efforts. This strategy enables authorities to prioritize investments in critical infrastructure while spreading the cost of full-scale implementation over time.

6.4 Institutional Resistance to Change and the Need for Capacity-Building

Institutional resistance to change is a well-known barrier in the adoption of new technologies, and it applies to asset management practices as well. Many organizations are accustomed to traditional, reactive approaches to maintenance, where problems are addressed only when they occur. These conventional practices have become deeply ingrained in organizational cultures, and there is often resistance to shifting towards proactive strategies driven by real-time monitoring and predictive analytics.

The resistance to adopting SHM and other smart technologies can also stem from concerns about the complexity of new systems, potential disruptions to existing workflows, or a lack of understanding regarding the long-term benefits of such innovations. Employees may feel overwhelmed by the need to learn new skills or adapt to new technologies, while management may worry about the perceived risk or return on investment.

To address these issues, building institutional capacity is critical. This requires not only training staff on the technical aspects of SHM systems but also fostering a culture of innovation and continuous improvement within organizations. This can be done by providing educational resources, offering workshops on new technologies, and encouraging leadership to actively support the digital transformation of asset management practices. Moreover, emphasizing the long-term financial and operational benefits of these technologies—such as lower maintenance costs, improved asset lifespan, and greater service reliability—can help win over skeptical stakeholders and promote the widespread adoption of SHM technologies.

Furthermore, there is a need for strong leadership within institutions to drive change. By setting clear objectives and ensuring alignment across departments, organizations can create a shared vision for the future of asset management. Leadership must also advocate for the required investments in technology and human resources, ensuring that staff members are equipped to meet the challenges of a rapidly changing infrastructure landscape.

6.5 Lack of Standardization in Technology Implementation

A significant challenge in the adoption of SHM and other smart asset management technologies is the lack of standardization. In the field of infrastructure management, various technologies, tools, and platforms are often developed by different vendors or organizations, each with their own protocols, interfaces, and systems. This lack of standardization can create difficulties when attempting to integrate different technologies or expand systems over time. It can also lead to issues with compatibility, increasing costs, and complicating the long-term maintenance of infrastructure.

In the context of SHM, different infrastructure monitoring solutions may use different sensors, measurement techniques, and data formats, making it difficult to aggregate data from various sources. For Kuwait, where large-scale infrastructure projects are being developed in diverse sectors, the adoption of non-standardized technologies can slow down the integration process and increase operational costs.

To address this challenge, there is a need for industry-wide standardization efforts. Government bodies, industry groups, and research institutions can collaborate to develop common standards for infrastructure monitoring and data collection. This could include the creation of standardized frameworks for sensor technologies, data formats, and communication protocols. By implementing such standards, Kuwait could ensure that various systems can communicate effectively, reducing long-term costs and promoting the seamless integration of future technological advancements.

6.6 Limited Awareness and Knowledge of Advanced Technologies

A further challenge to adopting innovative asset management practices is the limited awareness and knowledge of advanced technologies among key stakeholders, including government agencies, engineers, and the private sector. Many decision-makers may not fully understand the capabilities and potential benefits of technologies like SHM, AI, and IoT in infrastructure management. Without a solid understanding of these technologies, it may be difficult to gain support for their implementation, and critical opportunities for investment in new systems may be overlooked.

For Kuwait, increasing awareness and knowledge about the value of advanced asset management technologies is essential. Public officials, engineers, and other professionals must be educated about the role of SHM and other smart technologies in enhancing infrastructure performance, reducing maintenance costs, and contributing to economic diversification. A concerted effort in knowledge dissemination, including seminars, workshops, and industry collaborations, is required to bridge the knowledge gap.

Furthermore, collaboration with international organizations and academic institutions can help bring global expertise into the local context, ensuring that Kuwait is exposed to best practices and cutting-edge technological solutions. Building partnerships with global leaders in SHM technologies and asset management can help accelerate the adoption of these innovations, positioning Kuwait as a forward-thinking leader in infrastructure management.

6.7 Cybersecurity Risks and Data Privacy Concerns

As infrastructure management increasingly relies on digital technologies and real-time data collection, cybersecurity risks and data privacy concerns become paramount. SHM systems, IoT sensors, and AI-driven platforms generate vast amounts of data that must be securely transmitted, stored, and processed. These systems are also vulnerable to cyberattacks, which can compromise data integrity, disrupt operations, and cause significant financial and reputational damage.

For Kuwait, where major infrastructure projects are being developed in transportation, energy, and urban development, the protection of data and infrastructure is critical. A cyberattack targeting infrastructure monitoring systems could lead to widespread service disruptions, delays, and increased maintenance costs. Moreover, there is a growing concern about the privacy of data collected by smart technologies, particularly when it comes to personal or sensitive information.

To mitigate these risks, Kuwait must prioritize cybersecurity in the digitalization of infrastructure management. This involves implementing robust encryption, secure data storage protocols, and real-time monitoring to detect and respond to potential cyber threats. Additionally, stakeholders must adhere to best practices for data privacy, ensuring that personal and sensitive information is protected. Governments and organizations should also invest in the development of specialized cybersecurity expertise and training for staff involved in infrastructure management.

6.8 Shortage of Skilled Labor and Expertise

The integration of advanced asset management practices, including SHM systems, requires specialized skills and expertise that may be lacking in the current workforce. Engineers, data scientists, and technicians trained in emerging technologies like SHM, AI, and IoT are in high demand globally. As Kuwait seeks to adopt these technologies, it may face a shortage of qualified professionals capable of designing, implementing, and maintaining such systems.

To overcome this challenge, Kuwait must invest in human capital development. Educational programs and vocational training focused on advanced infrastructure technologies should be prioritized to develop a skilled workforce capable of supporting the digital transformation of infrastructure management. Partnerships with universities and research institutions, both locally and internationally, can also help build capacity and attract experts in the field.

Moreover, Kuwait can create incentives for professionals to specialize in these emerging fields, offering scholarships, training programs, and career development opportunities. By ensuring that the workforce is adequately trained and equipped to handle the demands of modern asset management, Kuwait can secure the long-term success of its infrastructure modernization efforts.

6.9 Integration of Sustainability and Environmental Considerations

In the context of smart infrastructure and asset management, sustainability considerations are often an afterthought or not fully integrated into the planning and design of technological systems. However, for Kuwait, where sustainability is a critical national goal, integrating environmental considerations into asset management systems is essential. The adoption of SHM and other advanced technologies must align with the broader objectives of reducing the environmental impact of infrastructure and promoting sustainability.

To ensure that technological advancements support sustainability, Kuwait must integrate environmental performance metrics into asset management systems. For instance, SHM systems should not only monitor the structural health of infrastructure but also track its environmental impact, including energy consumption, emissions, and material use. By ensuring that asset management practices contribute to environmental sustainability, Kuwait can advance its commitment to green urban development and sustainable economic growth.

7. OVERCOMING BARRIERS TO IMPLEMENTATION

The successful integration of Structural Health Monitoring (SHM) technologies into asset management systems in Kuwait faces several critical challenges. These barriers range from policy and regulatory obstacles to financial constraints, institutional resistance, and capacity-building needs. Addressing these challenges is pivotal for enabling the transformation of Kuwait's urban infrastructure, fostering economic diversification, and ensuring long-term sustainability.

7.1 Policy Reforms and Regulatory Support for SHM Integration

A major barrier to the adoption of SHM in asset management is the lack of comprehensive and updated policies that support technological integration. Traditional infrastructure management systems are often governed by outdated regulations that were not designed to accommodate modern technologies like SHM. This misalignment between existing regulatory frameworks and technological innovation can hinder the implementation of SHM systems.

To address this, Kuwait's regulatory environment must be modernized to support the integration of SHM technologies. This involves creating new policies that provide clear guidelines for the use of smart technologies in infrastructure projects, ensuring that they align with international standards. These policies must also focus on data privacy, the standardization of technology, and the use of interoperable platforms that enable seamless data sharing and integration across various stakeholders.

Moreover, regulations should incentivize the adoption of SHM by offering favorable conditions for businesses and developers to integrate these technologies into their projects. Policy changes can include tax benefits for infrastructure projects incorporating SHM systems, as well as allowances for businesses that provide SHM-related services.

7.2 Financing Mechanisms (Public-Private Partnerships, Alternative Investment Models)

The upfront cost of implementing SHM systems is a substantial challenge, particularly given that such technologies require investment in both hardware (sensors, monitoring systems) and software (data management and analysis). This financial burden may deter governments or private sector entities from investing in SHM, despite its long-term benefits.

To mitigate this, alternative financing mechanisms should be explored. Public-Private Partnerships (PPPs) are an effective model that allows the government to share the financial load with the private sector. Through these partnerships, the private sector can invest in SHM technology in exchange for a stake in the infrastructure projects, while the government provides the necessary regulatory support and infrastructure for these technologies to flourish.

Additionally, Kuwait could consider alternative investment models, such as green bonds, impact investing, or crowdfunding, to attract investments in sustainable infrastructure. Green bonds, for instance, could be issued to fund projects that focus on smart technologies, including SHM, thus allowing for targeted investments that align with national sustainability goals.

Other financing models could involve collaboration with international development banks, which may offer concessional financing to support the adoption of SHM and other technologies aimed at improving urban resilience.

7.3 The Role of Academic Research and Innovation in Advancing Asset Management

To overcome barriers to SHM integration, academic research plays a critical role in the development and improvement of asset management technologies. Research institutions are instrumental in advancing the capabilities of SHM systems, exploring new ways to integrate data analytics, artificial intelligence (AI), and Internet of Things (IoT) technologies to improve the precision and efficiency of monitoring and predictive maintenance.

In Kuwait, there is a need to strengthen the relationship between academia, industry, and government to promote innovation in asset management. Universities can conduct research on the effectiveness of SHM systems in Kuwait's unique environmental conditions, including extreme heat, humidity, and sandstorms, and develop tailored solutions that increase the accuracy and longevity of SHM systems. Research institutions can also evaluate the cost-effectiveness of SHM, helping to make the case for its long-term economic benefits.

Moreover, academia can contribute by providing training and capacity-building programs focused on SHM technology, data analytics, and infrastructure management. By equipping the next generation of engineers, technologists, and urban planners with the skills needed to implement and manage SHM systems, Kuwait can create a sustainable workforce capable of supporting infrastructure innovations.

7.4 Collaboration Between Government, Private Sector, and Research Institutions

Collaboration between government entities, the private sector, and research institutions is crucial for overcoming the barriers to SHM adoption. Each stakeholder brings essential resources, expertise, and insights into the process of integrating SHM technologies into infrastructure management.

- **Government**: The government can play an essential role by creating a supportive environment for SHM implementation. This includes developing policies, providing financial incentives, and ensuring the smooth integration of SHM into public infrastructure projects. The government can also foster collaboration by organizing forums or platforms that bring together key stakeholders to discuss challenges, opportunities, and best practices.
- **Private Sector**: The private sector, with its technical expertise and innovation capacity, is well-positioned to drive the deployment of SHM technologies. By collaborating with the government and research institutions, private companies can contribute valuable insights on how to scale SHM systems across infrastructure projects. This collaboration can also lead to cost-sharing arrangements, making SHM implementation more financially feasible.
- **Research Institutions**: Collaboration with academic and research institutions is essential for developing customized SHM solutions tailored to Kuwait's specific infrastructural needs. These institutions can drive innovation, enhance system design, and ensure that SHM technologies are effective in the long term. They also play a vital role in educating the workforce, ensuring that the necessary skills are developed to manage and operate SHM systems.

7.5 Capacity-Building and Institutional Resistance to Change

Institutional resistance to change is another challenge to the adoption of innovative asset management practices. Traditional practices in infrastructure management often prioritize reactive maintenance over proactive and predictive approaches, which may lead to reluctance in embracing modern technologies such as SHM. In many cases, decision-makers may lack the technical understanding of SHM systems or may be wary of changing established procedures.

Addressing this resistance requires significant capacity-building efforts. These efforts should include training government officials, private sector professionals, and engineers on the importance and benefits of SHM technologies. Developing awareness through workshops, seminars, and pilot projects that showcase the effectiveness of SHM can help overcome the resistance to change. Additionally, incentivizing knowledge-sharing among institutions can foster a more receptive environment for innovation.

7.6 Data Privacy and Security Concerns

As SHM systems collect vast amounts of data, data privacy and security are essential considerations. The integration of digital technologies in infrastructure management introduces the risk of cyberattacks or misuse of sensitive data. Governments and private institutions must work together to establish stringent data protection protocols to safeguard the information collected by SHM systems.

Ensuring that SHM technologies comply with international cybersecurity standards is vital for building trust among stakeholders. This includes securing the data infrastructure, using encryption technologies, and establishing clear guidelines on data access, ownership, and usage.

8. FUTURE TRENDS IN ASSET MANAGEMENT AND SMART INFRASTRUCTURE

The future of asset management in smart infrastructure is being shaped by technological advancements that promise to transform how we manage, maintain, and optimize our urban environments. As the demand for efficient, resilient, and sustainable infrastructure increases globally, several trends are emerging that will define how cities handle their assets. These trends include advancements in Artificial Intelligence (AI), blockchain, digital twins, and a growing emphasis on sustainability and resilience. These innovations not only hold the potential to improve the performance and longevity of infrastructure but also address the numerous challenges faced by cities, including climate change, population growth, and economic instability.

8.1 Advancements in AI-Driven Predictive Analytics

AI-driven predictive analytics represents one of the most transformative trends in the future of asset management. Predictive analytics uses machine learning and data-driven models to forecast potential issues in infrastructure systems before they manifest, thereby enabling more proactive management of assets. By collecting and analyzing data from various sensors embedded in infrastructure, AI systems can predict when an asset, such as a bridge or tunnel, is likely to require maintenance or when a failure could occur. These predictions allow asset managers to carry out maintenance or repairs before the problem escalates, which can save significant costs in the long run.

The key benefit of AI-driven predictive analytics is its ability to process vast amounts of data in real-time, detecting patterns and trends that might be invisible to human analysts. For example, AI systems can monitor the condition of an asset, identify anomalies, and recommend the most appropriate interventions based on a variety of factors, such as environmental conditions, wear and tear, or even usage patterns. This makes it possible to optimize the asset's lifecycle and reduce downtime, ensuring that critical infrastructure remains operational when needed most.

Furthermore, as AI continues to evolve, its ability to predict more accurately and handle increasingly complex datasets will enhance the capacity for managing large-scale infrastructure networks, such as transportation systems, utilities, and communications networks. For cities and nations looking to transition to more sustainable urban development, AI will also be instrumental in managing green infrastructure, helping to identify areas where resources can be used more efficiently or where new sustainable solutions need to be implemented.

8.2 The Potential Role of Blockchain in Infrastructure Asset Management

Blockchain technology, most commonly associated with cryptocurrencies, has potential far beyond financial applications. Its decentralized, transparent, and secure nature makes it particularly valuable for managing infrastructure assets. Blockchain could revolutionize asset management by providing a secure way to record transactions, track asset ownership, and monitor maintenance history without the need for a centralized authority.

By utilizing blockchain, asset managers can ensure the integrity and traceability of infrastructure data. For example, every action related to an infrastructure asset—whether it's inspection, maintenance, or upgrade—could be recorded on a blockchain ledger. This would create a transparent and immutable history for each asset, ensuring that all stakeholders have access to reliable data. The use of blockchain reduces the risks of fraud, enhances accountability, and facilitates collaboration among stakeholders by offering a shared, trusted platform for information exchange.

Blockchain also has the potential to improve the efficiency of public-private partnerships (PPPs) in infrastructure development. Smart contracts, powered by blockchain, could automate processes such as payments, compliance checks, and contract execution. These contracts automatically trigger payments or actions based on predefined conditions, reducing administrative overhead, enhancing trust between parties, and speeding up decision-making processes.

As the application of blockchain in infrastructure asset management expands, it is likely to play an essential role in creating a more efficient, transparent, and secure system for managing public and private infrastructure investments. This will ultimately lead to improved governance and decision-making, particularly in regions where trust and data transparency are essential to successful collaboration.

8.3 Evolution of Digital Twins and Real-Time Simulations

The concept of digital twins and real-time simulations is quickly becoming a central part of the future of asset management in smart infrastructure. A digital twin is a virtual replica of a physical asset, such as a building, bridge, or water treatment facility, that uses data to simulate the behavior of that asset in real time. These virtual models are fed with continuous data from sensors, which helps simulate and predict how the asset will perform under various conditions.

The primary advantage of digital twins lies in their ability to provide real-time insights into the performance of an asset. By simulating scenarios such as increased traffic load, extreme weather conditions, or wear and tear, asset managers can make informed decisions about necessary repairs or upgrades before a potential failure occurs. For example, a digital twin of a road network can simulate traffic patterns and wear, helping engineers understand when resurfacing or maintenance might be required.

Furthermore, digital twins allow for comprehensive risk analysis, enabling cities to anticipate the impact of various scenarios on their infrastructure. When combined with AI, digital twins become even more powerful by predicting future outcomes based on current data, enabling asset managers to prepare for possible disruptions or failures. The ability to model complex systems and scenarios with digital twins is particularly important for cities facing challenges such as aging infrastructure, population growth, and climate change.

Digital twins also enable better collaboration between different stakeholders, as the model can be shared in real-time across teams, agencies, and departments. The data-driven nature of digital twins allows for a more coordinated approach to infrastructure planning, design, and maintenance. The integration of digital twins with other technologies, such as IoT (Internet of Things) devices, will further enhance the ability to manage infrastructure efficiently and sustainably.

8.4 The Role of Sustainability and Resilience in Future Urban Development Strategies

Sustainability and resilience will be fundamental components of urban development strategies in the future. As cities continue to grow and face challenges like climate change, resource scarcity, and rapid urbanization, there is an increasing emphasis on creating infrastructure that not only meets present needs but can also adapt to future environmental, social, and economic changes.

Sustainable infrastructure management involves considering the long-term impacts of materials, energy usage, and environmental factors. For example, using renewable materials, enhancing energy efficiency, and incorporating low-carbon technologies into infrastructure designs are crucial for reducing the environmental impact of urban development. In the future, urban planning and infrastructure development will prioritize environmental sustainability, ensuring that buildings, transportation networks, and public services minimize their carbon footprints while maximizing resource efficiency.

On the other hand, resilience focuses on the ability of infrastructure to withstand and recover from disruptions, whether they are caused by natural disasters, economic shocks, or technological failures. As climate change exacerbates the frequency and intensity of extreme weather events, cities will need to ensure their infrastructure is adaptable and capable of functioning in the face of such challenges. For instance, building flood-resistant infrastructure, ensuring energy grid resilience, and designing flexible urban spaces that can withstand changing climatic conditions are key considerations in future urban development strategies.

The integration of sustainability and resilience in future infrastructure systems also aligns with the principles of circular economy, where resources are used more efficiently and waste is minimized. This shift toward sustainable and resilient infrastructure will require collaboration between governments, private companies, research institutions, and communities. Effective policies and regulations, coupled with strategic investments, will be crucial in fostering a transition toward infrastructure that is both environmentally sustainable and capable of adapting to future challenges.

9. CONCLUSION

The integration of advanced asset management strategies into urban infrastructure development represents a crucial paradigm shift with far-reaching economic and societal implications. Moving beyond traditional, reactive maintenance approaches to proactive, data-driven methodologies empowers nations to realize substantial benefits across multiple sectors. These advantages include significant reductions in maintenance costs and optimized operational efficiencies, achieved through predictive maintenance, efficient resource allocation, and strategic asset utilization. As highlighted in the context of Kuwait, embracing such strategies is particularly pertinent given the challenges posed by aging infrastructure, rapid urbanization, and the imperative to diversify the economy away from oil dependence.

Furthermore, advanced asset management demonstrably extends the lifespan of critical infrastructure assets, minimizes disruptive service interruptions, and fosters greater trust in public services. The adoption of Structural Health Monitoring (SHM) technologies, coupled with real-time data analytics, enables early detection of potential issues, thereby preventing costly failures and ensuring the sustained functionality of essential systems. Beyond these operational improvements, such strategies are pivotal in attracting foreign direct investment and supporting economic diversification, particularly in developing economies seeking to transition to technology-driven industries and enhance their global competitiveness. As evidenced by Kuwait's strategic investments in renewable energy and smart city initiatives, a commitment to advanced asset management signals a dedication to long-term sustainability and resilience.

As urbanization intensifies globally, the integration of advanced asset management principles into smart city initiatives promises enhanced quality of life for residents through improved resource management, optimized public services, and increased resilience to external shocks. The application of IoT sensors, GIS, and smart grids facilitates real-time monitoring and proactive intervention, leading to more efficient use of resources and better-informed urban planning. Ultimately, the adoption of these sophisticated approaches strengthens a nation's economic stability and competitiveness in an increasingly interconnected and volatile global landscape, positioning it for sustained growth and prosperity. By prioritizing the proactive and intelligent management of infrastructure assets, countries can build resilient economies capable of adapting to future challenges, capitalizing on emerging opportunities, and ensuring a sustainable and thriving urban environment for generations to come. Moreover, embracing innovative financing mechanisms, such as Public-Private Partnerships (PPPs), and addressing policy gaps will be critical in overcoming implementation challenges and realizing the full potential of advanced asset management in transforming urban infrastructure.

REFERENCES

Abdulkarem, M., Samsudin, K., Rokhani, F. Z., & Rasid, A. (2020). Wireless sensor network for structural health monitoring: A contemporary review of technologies, challenges, and future direction. *Structural Health Monitoring, 19*(3), 693–735. DOI: 10.1177/1475921719854528

Agreement, P. (2020). *United Nations Framework Convention on Climate Change (UNFCCC).(2015).* Climate Change Secretariat.

Al-Qazweeni, J., Parol, J., Kamal, H. A., Al-Enezi, A., Bin-Nakhi, A., Sun, H., & Büyüköztürk, O. (2020). Structural health monitoring system for Al-Hamra tower in Kuwait City. *Gulf Conference on Sustainable Built Environment*

Al-Saidi, M., & Zaidan, E. (2024). Smart cities and communities in the GCC region: From top-down city development to more local approaches [Original Research]. *Frontiers in Built Environment, 10*, 1341694. Advance online publication. DOI: 10.3389/fbuil.2024.1341694

Al-Sanad, S., Parol, J., Wang, L., & Kolios, A. (2023). Design optimisation of wind turbine towers with reliability-based calibration of partial safety factors. *Energy Reports, 9*, 2548–2556.

Alamri, M., Jhanjhi, N., & Humayun, M. (2019). Blockchain for Internet of Things (IoT) research issues challenges & future directions: A review. *Int. J. Comput. Sci. Netw. Secur, 19*(1), 244–258.

Allam, Z., Cheshmehzangi, A., & Jones, D. S. (2023). The economic landscape of cities and climate change. In *Climate and Social Justice: The Political Economy of Urban Resilience and Mercantilism* (pp. 25-41). Springer. DOI: 10.1007/978-981-99-6624-0_2

Almaaitah, T., Appleby, M., Rosenblat, H., Drake, J., & Joksimovic, D. (2021). The potential of Blue-Green infrastructure as a climate change adaptation strategy: A systematic literature review. *Blue-Green Systems, 3*(1), 223–248. DOI: 10.2166/bgs.2021.016

AlMetwally, S. A. H., Hassan, M. K., & Mourad, M. H. (2020). Real time internet of things (IoT) based water quality management system. *Procedia CIRP, 91*, 478–485. DOI: 10.1016/j.procir.2020.03.107

Alqasi, M. A. Y., Alkelanie, Y. A. M., & Alnagrat, A. (2024). Intelligent infrastructure for urban transportation: The role of artificial intelligence in predictive maintenance. *Brilliance: Research of Artificial Intelligence*, *4*(2), 625–637. DOI: 10.47709/brilliance.v4i2.4889

AlSanad, S. (2017). Megaproject and risk management: A case of Kuwait. Book of Proceedings 5th International Conference On Sustainable Development

AlSanad, S. (2018). Barriers to implementation sustainable cement manufacturing in Kuwait. *European Journal of Sustainable Development*, *7*(4), 317–317. DOI: 10.14207/ejsd.2018.v7n4p317

AlSanad, S. (2024a). Challenges in Kuwait. *Key Themes in Energy Management: A Compilation of Current Practices. Research Advances, and Future Opportunities*, *100*, 437.

AlSanad, S. (2024b). From Vision to Reality: Addressing Renewable Energy Infrastructure Challenges in Kuwait. In *Key Themes in Energy Management: A Compilation of Current Practices, Research Advances, and Future Opportunities* (pp. 437-470). Springer.

AlSanad, S., & Parol, J. (2023). Asset management–Towards adaptive resilient infrastructures. In *Life-Cycle of Structures and Infrastructure Systems* (pp. 2904–2908). CRC Press. DOI: 10.1201/9781003323020-353

AlSanad, S. A. (2016). Green practices in the Kuwait building industry: Drivers and barriers. *IABSE Congress: Challenges in Design and Construction of an Innovative and Sustainable Built Environment*, Stockholm, Sweden, 21-23 September 2016 DOI: 10.2749/stockholm.2016.1704

Balali, F., Nouri, J., Nasiri, A., & Zhao, T. (2020). *Data Intensive Industrial Asset Management*. Springer. DOI: 10.1007/978-3-030-35930-0

Carlson, J., Haffenden, R., Bassett, G., Buehring, W., Collins Iii, M., Folga, S., Petit, F., Phillips, J., Verner, D., & Whitfield, R. (2012). *Resilience: Theory and Application*.

Chan, M., Jin, H., & van Kan, D. (2022). Assessment of driving factors for sustainable infrastructure development. *Resources, Conservation and Recycling*, *185*, 106490. DOI: 10.1016/j.resconrec.2022.106490

da Silva, R. F., & de Souza, G. F. M. (2022). Modeling a maintenance management framework for asset management based on ISO 55000 series guidelines. *Journal of Quality in Maintenance Engineering*, *28*(4), 915–937. DOI: 10.1108/JQME-08-2020-0082

De Pryck, K., & Hulme, M. (2022). *A critical assessment of the Intergovernmental Panel on Climate Change*. Cambridge University Press. DOI: 10.1017/9781009082099

De Villiers, J.-M. (2018). *A framework for implementing lean practices and tools to support ISO 55000 compliance for physical asset management*. Stellenbosch University.

Deepa, N., Pham, Q.-V., Nguyen, D. C., Bhattacharya, S., Prabadevi, B., Gadekallu, T. R., Maddikunta, P. K. R., Fang, F., & Pathirana, P. N. (2022). A survey on blockchain for big data: Approaches, opportunities, and future directions. *Future Generation Computer Systems, 131*, 209–226. DOI: 10.1016/j.future.2022.01.017

Deraemaeker, A., Reynders, E., De Roeck, G., & Kullaa, J. (2008). Vibration-based structural health monitoring using output-only measurements under changing environment. *Mechanical Systems and Signal Processing, 22*(1), 34–56. DOI: 10.1016/j.ymssp.2007.07.004

Du, C., Dutta, S., Kurup, P., Yu, T., & Wang, X. (2020). A review of railway infrastructure monitoring using fiber optic sensors. *Sensors and Actuators. A, Physical, 303*, 111728. DOI: 10.1016/j.sna.2019.111728

Economic, U. N. D. o., & Affairs, S. (2020). *The Sustainable Development Goals Report 2020*. United Nations. https://doi.org/https://doi.org/10.18356/214e6642-en

El Mrabet, Z., Kaabouch, N., El Ghazi, H., & El Ghazi, H. (2018). Cyber-security in smart grid: Survey and challenges. *Computers & Electrical Engineering, 67*, 469–482. DOI: 10.1016/j.compeleceng.2018.01.015

EPA. (2019). *Kuwait National Adaptation Plan 2019-2030.* .

Forum, W. E. (2022). *The Global Risks Report 2022*. W. E. Forum.

Gunderia, A., Agarwal, P., Nikam, V., & Bambole, A. (2024). AI Approaches for Predictive Maintenance in Road Bridge Infrastructure. *2024 International Conference on Smart Applications, Communications and Networking (SmartNets)* DOI: 10.1109/SmartNets61466.2024.10577641

Hallegatte, S., Rentschler, J., & Rozenberg, J. (2019). *Lifelines: The resilient infrastructure opportunity*. World Bank Publications. DOI: 10.1596/978-1-4648-1430-3

Husain, R., Al-Sanad, S., & Parol, J. (2023). Structural Health Monitoring of Bridges: State of the Art. *IABSE Symposium: Long Span Bridges*, Istanbul, Turkey, 26-28 April 2023 DOI: 10.2749/istanbul.2023.0620

Jardine, A. K., Lin, D., & Banjevic, D. (2006). A review on machinery diagnostics and prognostics implementing condition-based maintenance. *Mechanical Systems and Signal Processing*, *20*(7), 1483–1510. DOI: 10.1016/j.ymssp.2005.09.012

Klasa, K., Galaitsi, S., Trump, B. D., & Linkov, I. (2021). Systems Applications to Aging Resilience. *Resilience and Aging: Emerging Science and Future Possibilities*, 53.

Kourtis, I. M., & Tsihrintzis, V. A. (2021). Adaptation of urban drainage networks to climate change: A review. *The Science of the Total Environment*, *771*, 145431. DOI: 10.1016/j.scitotenv.2021.145431 PMID: 33736174

Kritzinger, W., Karner, M., Traar, G., Henjes, J., & Sihn, W. (2018). Digital Twin in manufacturing: A categorical literature review and classification. *IFAC-PapersOnLine*, *51*(11), 1016–1022. DOI: 10.1016/j.ifacol.2018.08.474

Kuwait, E. (2019). *Kuwait national adaptation plan 2019–2030: enhanced climate resilience to improve community livelihood and achieve sustainability*. Environmental Protection Authority.

Kuwait, U. N. (2023). *State of Kuwait - 2nd Voluntary National Review Report 2023*. UNDP, RCO, .

Lattanzi, D., & Miller, G. (2017). Review of robotic infrastructure inspection systems. *Journal of Infrastructure Systems*, *23*(3), 04017004. DOI: 10.1061/(ASCE)IS.1943-555X.0000353

McMahon, P., Zhang, T., & Dwight, R. (2020). Requirements for big data adoption for railway asset management. *IEEE Access : Practical Innovations, Open Solutions*, *8*, 15543–15564. DOI: 10.1109/ACCESS.2020.2967436

Melesse, T. Y., Di Pasquale, V., & Riemma, S. (2020). Digital twin models in industrial operations: A systematic literature review. *Procedia Manufacturing*, *42*, 267–272. DOI: 10.1016/j.promfg.2020.02.084

Morgan, C., Sparling, B., & Wegner, L. (2022). Use of structural health monitoring to extend the service life of the Diefenbaker Bridge. *Journal of Civil Structural Health Monitoring*, *12*(4), 913–929. DOI: 10.1007/s13349-022-00585-1

Ongkowijoyo, C. S., & Doloi, H. (2018). Risk-based Resilience Assessment Model Focusing on Urban Infrastructure System Restoration. *Procedia Engineering*, *212*, 1115–1122. https://doi.org/https://doi.org/10.1016/j.proeng.2018.01.144. DOI: 10.1016/j.proeng.2018.01.144

Pathak, M., Slade, R., Pichs-Madruga, R., Ürge-Vorsatz, D., Shukla, R., & Skea, J. (2022). [Mitigation of Climate Change: Technical Summary.]. *Climatic Change*, •••, 2022.

Paul, G., Webb, S., Liu, D., & Dissanayake, G. (2010). A robotic system for steel bridge maintenance: Field testing. *Proceedings of the 2010 Australasian Conference on Robotics and Automation, ACRA 2010*

Piryonesi, S. M., & El-Diraby, T. E. (2020). Role of data analytics in infrastructure asset management: Overcoming data size and quality problems. *Journal of Transportation Engineering. Part B, Pavements*, *146*(2), 04020022. DOI: 10.1061/JPEODX.0000175

Satyanarayanan, M. (2017). The emergence of edge computing. *Computer*, *50*(1), 30–39. DOI: 10.1109/MC.2017.9

Schnebele, E., Tanyu, B. F., Cervone, G., & Waters, N. (2015). Review of remote sensing methodologies for pavement management and assessment. *European Transport Research Review*, *7*(2), 1–19. DOI: 10.1007/s12544-015-0156-6

Scuro, C., Lamonaca, F., Porzio, S., Milani, G., & Olivito, R. (2021). Internet of Things (IoT) for masonry structural health monitoring (SHM): Overview and examples of innovative systems. *Construction & Building Materials*, *290*, 123092. DOI: 10.1016/j.conbuildmat.2021.123092

Sun, J., Han, Z., & Zhang, Z. (2023). Resource allocation framework for optimizing long-term infrastructure network resilience. *Journal of Infrastructure Systems*, *29*(1), 04022048. DOI: 10.1061/JITSE4.ISENG-2083

Sundararajan, S., & Suriyagoda, N. (2016). *Climate risks and resilience in infrastructure PPPs: issues to be considered.* World Bank Group.

Tatipatri, N., & Arun, S. (2024). A comprehensive review on cyber-attacks in power systems: Impact analysis, detection, and cyber security. *IEEE Access : Practical Innovations, Open Solutions*, *12*, 18147–18167. DOI: 10.1109/ACCESS.2024.3361039

United Nations Environment Programme (UNEP). (2020). *Emissions Gap Report 2020.* https://www.unep.org/emissions-gap-report-2020

Vijayan, D. S., Sivasuriyan, A., Devarajan, P., Krejsa, M., Chalecki, M., Żółtowski, M., Kozarzewska, A., & Koda, E. (2023). Development of intelligent technologies in SHM on the innovative diagnosis in civil engineering—A comprehensive review. *Buildings (Basel, Switzerland)*, *13*(8), 1903. DOI: 10.3390/buildings13081903

Wang, G., & Ke, J. (2024). Literature Review on the Structural Health Monitoring (SHM) of Sustainable Civil Infrastructure: An Analysis of Influencing Factors in the Implementation. *Buildings (Basel, Switzerland)*, *14*(2), 402. DOI: 10.3390/buildings14020402

World Bank. (2016). *Climate Change and Development: A Framework for Action*. World Bank Publications.

World Bank. (2020). *Innovative Infrastructure Financing Mechanisms for Sustainable Development*. World Bank.

Yunusa-Kaltungo, A., Ray, S., AlSanad, S., Sokunbi, I., Manu, P., Cheung, C. M., & Mohandes, S. R. (2024). Assessment of safety climate perception of maintenance workers during major overhauls, outages, shutdowns or turnarounds (MoOSTs). *Quality and Reliability Engineering International*, *40*(5), 2936–2953. DOI: 10.1002/qre.3532

Zhang, L., Li, Y., Yu, S., & Wang, L. (2023). Risk transmission of El Niño-induced climate change to regional Green Economy Index. *Economic Analysis and Policy*, *79*, 860–872. DOI: 10.1016/j.eap.2023.07.006

Chapter 2
Building Trust in AI-Driven Urban Environments:
Privacy, Accountability, and Ethical Frameworks

Mohammad Alauthman
https://orcid.org/0000-0003-0319-1968
Department of Information Security, University of Petra, Amman, Jordan

Saad Alateef
https://orcid.org/0009-0002-3219-0833
Newcastle University, UK

Ahmad Al-Qerem
https://orcid.org/0000-0003-2187-6194
Computer Science Department, Faculty of Information Technology, Zarqa University, Jordan

Ala Hamarsheh
https://orcid.org/0000-0002-4736-7331
Department of Computer Science, Faculty of Information Technology, Arab American University, Palestine

Amjad Aldweesh
https://orcid.org/0000-0001-9358-1323
College of Computing and Information Technology, Shaqra University, Saudi Arabia

DOI: 10.4018/979-8-3373-1375-7.ch002

ABSTRACT

Cities now implement artificial intelligence to optimize public services. Policymakers face issues concerning data management, fairness, and oversight. This chapter examines how governments handle privacy and accountability when deploying new digital tools in diverse contexts. Research explores regulations, community involvement, and ethical guidelines that shape AI-driven decisions. Findings indicate that strong governance, public feedback, and continuous auditing can bolster trust. This chapter shows how transparency measures and technical controls influence equitable data use and civic trust. Insights contribute to the evolving discourse on responsible AI deployment. The analysis extends current understanding of urban governance by offering multidimensional methods for evaluating trust-building in AI-powered city landscapes.

1. INTRODUCTION

Urban administrations are adopting artificial intelligence (AI) for applications that range from optimizing traffic signals to forecasting public safety risks (Reddick, Chatfield, & Ojo, 2023). Officials view computational tools as a means to streamline resource allocation, interpret real-time sensor data, and deliver public services more efficiently (Bosco, Riccardi, Sciarrone, D'Amore, & Visvizi, 2024). Although these promises generate optimism about modernizing local governance, questions remain about whether such systems adequately protect individual privacy, safeguard public values, and fulfill accountability requirements (Barns et al., 2023).

Trust stands out as a core factor in the relationship between municipal governments and residents (Cugurullo & Xu, 2024). Without mechanisms that clarify how data is collected, processed, and applied in policy decisions, citizens may hesitate to accept AI-driven services (Castro, McLaughlin, & McQuinn, 2023). Societies hold different expectations about whether governments should collect extensive data to improve administrative tasks (Hong Kong Digital Policy Office, 2023). Public officials must address cultural, ethical, and regulatory dimensions to ensure that AI integration aligns with local norms and legal structures (OECD, 2023a).

Systems that process large volumes of personal information can raise concerns about potential misuse or unauthorized sharing (AlgorithmWatch, 2024). Municipal administrations often partner with private vendors, creating complex relationships that involve proprietary algorithms (Conti & Seele, 2023). These algorithms can automate decisions in areas like welfare distribution, policing, and housing, leading to disputed outcomes if biases surface in the models (Phillips & Jiao, 2023). Researchers emphasize that unintended discrimination may arise from historical data patterns, negatively impacting vulnerable communities (Sanchez, Brenman, & Ye, 2024).

The idea of accountability enters discussions whenever advanced technology influences public well-being (National League of Cities, 2024). City officials must balance innovation with safeguards that prevent harm, and they must remain prepared to assume responsibility if AI-related failures occur (Goldsmith & Yang, 2025). Oversight bodies, ethics committees, and impact assessments are often highlighted as critical instruments for verifying compliance with ethical standards (OECD, 2023b). While some jurisdictions have launched robust frameworks, others have struggled with a lack of technical expertise or clear legal definitions (New York City Office of Technology & Innovation, 2023).

Ethical guidelines play an important role in steering AI development (Zwitter & Helbing, 2024). These guidelines frequently include fairness, beneficence, autonomy, and transparency as foundational concepts. Policymakers interpret these principles in diverse ways, shaped by local resource constraints, political will, and cultural norms (Cugurullo, 2024). Some city governments create specialized administrative offices to draft AI policies, set privacy requirements, and define the scope of accountability (Bloomberg Philanthropies & Johns Hopkins University, 2023). Others rely on national or international standards.

This chapter explores privacy, accountability, and ethical frameworks that guide AI-driven urban environments. It provides historical context on AI in city governance, outlines privacy considerations, and discusses mechanisms that foster accountability. Ethical frameworks receive detailed coverage, with attention to stakeholder engagement and adaptive governance. Implementation challenges highlight issues that municipalities confront when seeking to enact responsible AI policies (Son et al., 2023). Strategies for building public trust are examined, and policy implications are considered in light of ongoing regulatory changes (OECD, 2023a).

The conclusion synthesizes insights from empirical experiences and theoretical debates, emphasizing the evolving nature of AI technologies. Future research avenues focus on longitudinal trust assessments, refined fairness metrics, new AI paradigms, and the global legal landscape (Tonnarelli & Mora, 2025). By presenting a conceptual framework for trust in AI-driven governance, the chapter underscores interdependencies among regulatory strategies, technical safeguards, and public engagement. This integrated perspective is essential for building and sustaining confidence in AI-enhanced public services (Barns et al., 2023).

The pages ahead intend to address multiple audiences: academic researchers, policymakers, industry collaborators, and the public. Recognizing that AI systems in cities operate across legal, cultural, and sectoral boundaries, the discussion underlines the importance of comprehensive oversight and adaptive practices (Bosco et al.,

2024). Emerging frameworks and best practices, illustrated by case insights, serve to guide further innovation that respects fundamental rights and ethical obligations.

2. BACKGROUND ON AI-DRIVEN URBAN ENVIRONMENTS

2.1. The Growth of AI in Municipal Governance

Municipalities have adopted AI to tackle challenges such as traffic congestion, waste management, public safety, and administrative efficiency (Son et al., 2023). Advanced software processes real-time data streams from sensors, closed-circuit cameras, and user-generated inputs, allowing administrators to detect patterns and optimize interventions (Cugurullo & Xu, 2024). For instance, traffic control systems that rely on AI can dynamically adjust signal timing to reduce bottlenecks. Welfare departments can analyze socioeconomic indicators to allocate limited resources effectively (Bloomberg Philanthropies & Johns Hopkins University, 2023).

Despite these capabilities, the introduction of automated decisions into public sectors raises serious questions. Historically, public officials relied on established procedures, often subject to manual checks or public scrutiny (National League of Cities, 2024). The shift toward algorithmic tools may accelerate services but sometimes reduces the role of human oversight (Phillips & Jiao, 2023). Legislators and analysts highlight the need for clarity concerning legal liability if an algorithmic recommendation leads to erroneous decisions (Sanchez et al., 2024). This issue grows more complicated when private vendors own the software, limiting external audits or disclosure of proprietary models (Cugurullo, 2024).

2.2. Data Sources and Analytical Methods

AI-driven systems in cities rely on data collected from multiple sources, including sensor grids, smartphone location data, social media feeds, utility readings, and geospatial databases (Javed et al., 2023). These varied inputs feed into machine learning algorithms that predict patterns or classify outcomes. Deep learning approaches process large datasets to uncover hidden correlations that administrators could overlook (Castro et al., 2023). Although advanced modeling provides powerful insights, it may incorporate biases if underlying data misrepresents particular segments of the population (Phillips & Jiao, 2023).

Managing these data streams requires computing infrastructure for storage and fast retrieval, which can strain municipal budgets (Bosco et al., 2024). Technical solutions like cloud-based platforms and distributed storage help address scalability. However, these arrangements also raise security and privacy questions if sensitive data traverses multiple servers (Hong Kong Digital Policy Office, 2023). Encryption and secure architectures remain essential, but re-identification techniques can still reveal personal details from "anonymized" data (Cugurullo & Xu, 2024).

2.3. The Foundations of Public Trust in AI

Trust is a cornerstone for the successful implementation of AI in governance (AlgorithmWatch, 2024). When people believe that data collection and algorithmic processing occur without adequate oversight, they may avoid participating or even attempt to circumvent the system (Barns et al., 2023). Trust emerges when city residents feel that these tools promote shared benefits without harming individuals or groups (Conti & Seele, 2023). Emerging literature suggests that public trust is influenced by perception of transparency, fairness, reliability, and the existence of recourse in the event of errors (Cugurullo, 2024).

Studies also emphasize that trust builds over time when pilot programs clearly demonstrate benefits and maintain robust checks (Reddick et al., 2023). Overreliance on AI-based decisions without explaining how these outputs were generated can backfire, as communities grow suspicious about black-box processes (Sanchez et al., 2024). Such skepticism has led some jurisdictions to require publicizing algorithmic methodologies or hosting open forums to discuss specific deployments (New York City Office of Technology & Innovation, 2023). This illustrates that technology alone cannot drive acceptance; administrators must continuously engage with stakeholders.

2.4. Shifting Regulatory Contexts

Governments at local, national, and international levels have introduced principles and guidelines related to AI governance (OECD, 2023a). These guidelines address privacy, accountability, and ethical usage. Yet there is no universal standard across cities, leading to patchwork regulations that vary widely (Castro et al., 2023). Some localities establish advanced regulatory frameworks, while others proceed with minimal or outdated rules (UK Department for Science, Innovation and Technology, 2023). International bodies, including the United Nations and the OECD, issue guidance that encourages responsible AI practices, but enforcement depends on local or national authorities (UN-Habitat, 2024).

Municipalities often adopt these global principles, adapting them to local cultural and legal norms (Bloomberg Philanthropies & Johns Hopkins University, 2023). In some cases, new laws explicitly target AI operations, such as requiring transparency reports on algorithmic decision-making (Cugurullo & Xu, 2024). Elsewhere, older data protection laws are extended to encompass AI. This diversity in approaches highlights the interplay between global aspirations for responsible AI and the complexities of local governance (Zwitter & Helbing, 2024).

3. PRIVACY CONSIDERATIONS IN AI-DRIVEN URBAN SETTINGS

3.1. Foundations of Privacy

Privacy involves limiting external access to personal information and ensuring that individuals retain control over their data (Sanchez et al., 2024). AI-driven solutions in cities collect and process large amounts of sensitive information, sometimes without residents being fully aware (Phillips & Jiao, 2023). Biometric systems, facial recognition, and behavior tracking feed into municipal dashboards, potentially creating comprehensive citizen profiles (Bosco et al., 2024). Public sentiment often reflects alarm when these techniques appear intrusive or poorly regulated (Conti & Seele, 2023).

3.2. Data Collection and Consent in Municipal Services

Municipal programs historically limited data gathering to essential details for billing or service eligibility. The introduction of AI-based analytics changes this scope (Bloomberg Philanthropies & Johns Hopkins University, 2023). Systems designed to detect welfare fraud might compile location histories and social contacts; predictive policing tools might aggregate social media content (AlgorithmWatch, 2024). Consent mechanisms are not always transparent. Some cities utilize "implied consent," which critics say undermines informed choice (Hong Kong Digital Policy Office, 2023).

Table 1. Key Dimensions of Privacy in AI-Driven Urban Governance

Dimension	Description
Data Minimization	Collecting only necessary information for defined public services
Purpose Limitation	Restricting usage of data to stated objectives
Notice & Consent	Informing residents of data use and obtaining permission where feasible
Security Measures	Deploying controls (e.g., encryption) to prevent unauthorized access
Accountability	Assigning responsibilities for any privacy breaches and enabling legal remedies

Some privacy advocates argue that municipalities need explicit opt-in protocols for AI-enabled services (Phillips & Jiao, 2023). Others suggest that essential services, such as public safety, may require certain data collection for effectiveness (Castro et al., 2023). This tension underscores the challenge of reconciling public interests with individual rights (Cugurullo & Xu, 2024).

3.3. Balancing Public Benefit and Individual Autonomy

City agencies often say that data-driven solutions serve the public good, improving services like traffic management or emergency response (Barns et al., 2023). Aggregating data from many residents can show where resources are needed, as in identifying neighborhoods with high energy consumption or patterns of accidents (AlgorithmWatch, 2024). The public benefit argument highlights collective welfare and cost reduction. Yet focusing on these gains alone can erode personal autonomy if authorities fail to provide clear boundaries on data use (Reddick et al., 2023).

Privacy legislation aims to reconcile both perspectives by stipulating that data usage be proportional to its purpose (OECD, 2023b). Proportionality mandates that city agencies not exceed necessary collection or retain data longer than needed (UN-Habitat, 2024). Critics remain concerned that extensive location tracking or biometric identification can lead to surveillance culture, chilling free expression and fostering self-censorship (Sanchez et al., 2024).

3.4. Technical Safeguards and Their Limits

Encryption protects data during transit and while stored, limiting access by unauthorized parties (NIST, 2023). Anonymization methods replace personal identifiers with random tokens, though advanced re-identification techniques may circumvent these defenses (Phillips & Jiao, 2023). Differential privacy injects random noise into datasets, aiming to conceal individual data points while preserving aggregate trends. These measures do not eliminate all privacy concerns because continuous improvements in analytical methods can extract personal insights from "de-identified" data (Castro et al., 2023). Figure 1 shows how cities collect information, secure it, analyze it through AI models, and then produce decisions, such as distributing municipal resources. The feedback loop updates the system based on outcomes, potentially feeding more data into subsequent analyses (Barns et al., 2023).

Figure 1. Flowchart of Data Processing in an AI-Driven Urban Service

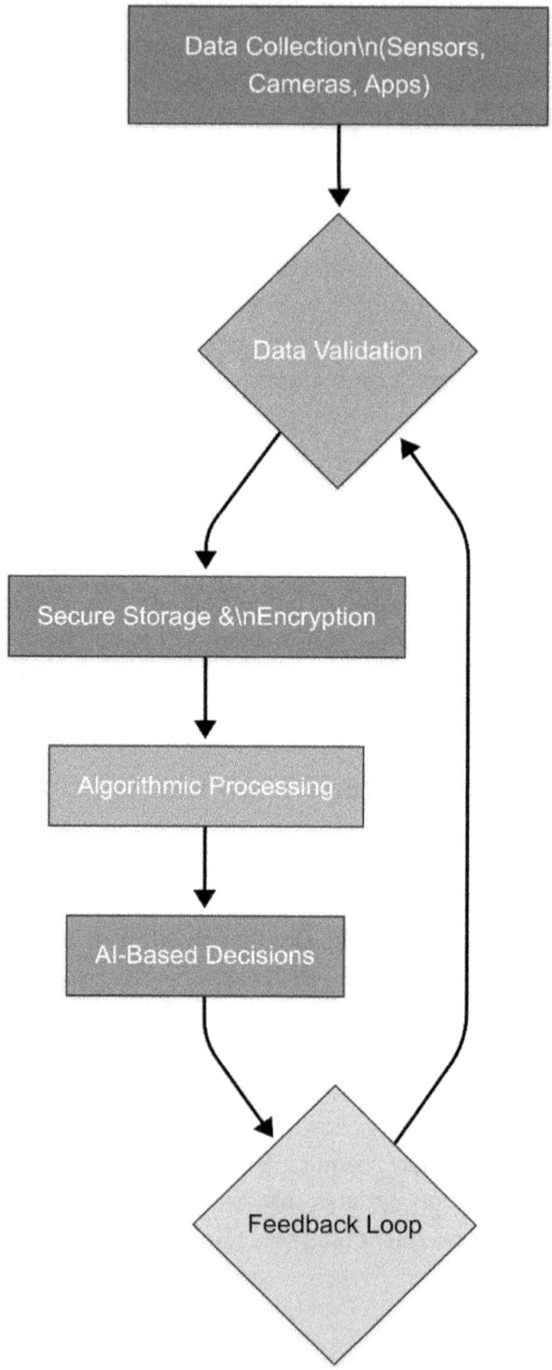

3.5. Worldwide Variations in Privacy Policies

Different regions enact unique privacy standards. The European Union enforces the General Data Protection Regulation (GDPR), emphasizing consent, data minimization, and user rights (OECD, 2023a). Some Asian cities incorporate data-protection rules but allow more extensive surveillance in the name of public security (Hong Kong Digital Policy Office, 2023). North American municipalities sometimes rely on sector-specific regulations rather than comprehensive frameworks, leading to inconsistent approaches (Castro et al., 2023). Cities in developing nations face resource limits that hamper enforcement (UN-Habitat, 2024). This variability shapes how AI-driven services emerge worldwide.

4. ACCOUNTABILITY MECHANISMS FOR AI IN URBAN GOVERNANCE

4.1. Understanding Accountability in the Public Sector

Accountability relates to clear allocations of responsibility and the capacity to remedy problems if something goes wrong (National League of Cities, 2024). Officials must answer for decisions made by AI models they have authorized (AlgorithmWatch, 2024). When an automated tool wrongly denies social support, accountability calls for investigating how that error emerged, identifying the party or system component at fault, and ensuring it is corrected (Bosco et al., 2024). This process reassures residents that they can contest flawed decisions.

4.2. Oversight Mechanisms

Oversight ensures that city departments and external vendors adhere to established procedures and ethical standards (Conti & Seele, 2023). Some municipalities create ethics committees that evaluate new AI projects before implementation, checking for potential discrimination or privacy harm (Cugurullo, 2024). External audits can reveal whether algorithms produce biased outcomes or violate data protections (Phillips & Jiao, 2023). Independent oversight fosters public trust, especially when auditors share findings openly (Sanchez et al., 2024).

Table 2. Examples of Accountability Measures in AI-Enhanced Cities

Measure	Description	Actor
Algorithmic Impact Assessment	Identifies potential biases and risks	City regulator
External Audits	Independent reviews of system outputs	Accredited firm
Ethics Advisory Board	Advises on standards and reviews new proposals	Local government
Public Consultations	Engages residents through hearings or surveys	Municipal council
Liability Clauses	Defines legal responsibilities for negative outcomes	Legal authorities

4.3. Liability and Regulatory Structures

Legal liability clarifies consequences if AI-driven errors harm citizens (Castro et al., 2023). Traditional tort law may struggle to address autonomous decision-making because it is unclear who remains at fault—the developer, the municipal agency, or the algorithm itself (Reddick et al., 2023). Some authorities treat AI tools as advisory, with final decisions taken by humans who bear ultimate responsibility (Cugurullo & Xu, 2024). Others explore new legislation to cover algorithmic harm, imposing strict liability on service providers if audits show negligence in data or model design (Barns et al., 2023).

4.4. Transparency and Explainability

Explainability strategies demystify how AI models arrive at their conclusions. Techniques like feature importance plots, decision trees, or local interpretable model-agnostic explanations (LIME) provide glimpses into an algorithm's logic (Javed et al., 2023). Although public officials often lack advanced technical backgrounds, these tools enable them to understand how input variables influence outcomes (Phillips & Jiao, 2023). Municipal websites sometimes publish summary reports, allowing the community to grasp the rationale behind AI-aided choices (AlgorithmWatch, 2024). Figure 2 shows a hypothetical process for filing and reviewing AI-related complaints. A resident lodges a concern through a digital portal, which then interacts with an audit board that investigates system logs and offers an official response (National League of Cities, 2024).

Figure 2. Sequence Diagram for Accountability Audit

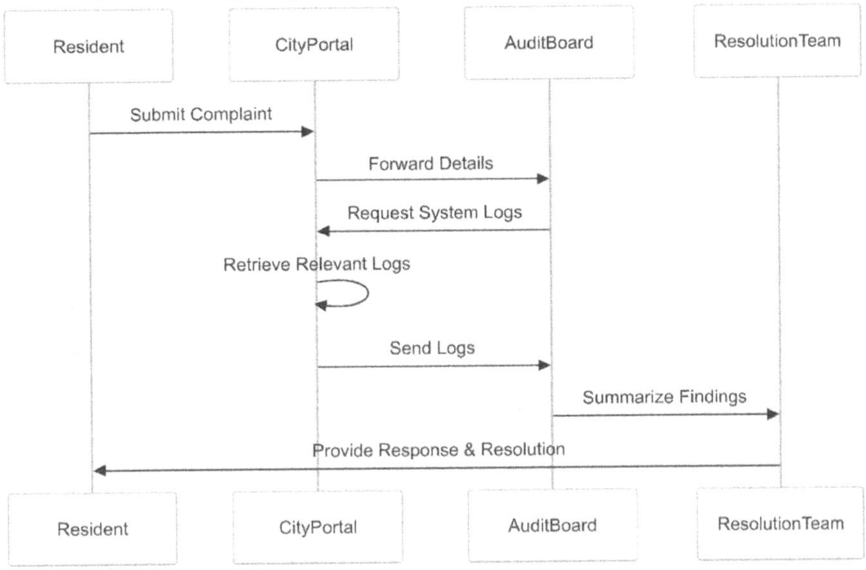

4.5. Obstacles to Comprehensive Accountability

Even with formal oversight, city officials may face difficulties. Complex black-box models resist straightforward explanations (Cugurullo, 2024). Municipal budgets might not cover advanced audit capabilities (Bosco et al., 2024). Vendors often claim intellectual property rights that block external reviewers from accessing source code (Sanchez et al., 2024). Overcoming these barriers demands robust contracts, political support for transparency, and technical cooperation among stakeholders (Conti & Seele, 2023).

5. ETHICAL FRAMEWORKS FOR TRUSTWORTHY AI IN URBAN SETTINGS

5.1. Fundamental Principles of Urban AI Ethics

Ethical guidelines often incorporate core values such as fairness, transparency, autonomy, and justice (Zwitter & Helbing, 2024). Fairness addresses preventing discriminatory outcomes against marginalized groups (Phillips & Jiao, 2023). Transparency clarifies how and why AI systems collect and analyze data (Javed et al.,

2023). Autonomy respects the rights of individuals to control personal information (Barns et al., 2023). Justice involves equitable distribution of benefits and burdens, ensuring that no segment of society bears disproportionate harm (Cugurullo & Xu, 2024).

5.2. The Role of Policy in Driving Ethical AI

Public authorities can embed ethical requirements in procurement rules, licensing, and performance evaluations of AI systems (New York City Office of Technology & Innovation, 2023). Laws and regulations often mandate that AI deployments undergo prior risk assessments, with an emphasis on identifying potential discrimination (OECD, 2023b). Some cities have formal ethics boards that gather experts to design guidelines for permissible data usage (National League of Cities, 2024). This interplay between ethics and law shapes how systems function on the ground (AlgorithmWatch, 2024).

5.3. Stakeholder Participation and Collaborative Governance

Implementing ethical AI in urban settings requires input from government agencies, academic researchers, civil society, industry representatives, and residents (Bloomberg Philanthropies & Johns Hopkins University, 2023). Each group brings distinct concerns, from cost efficiency to privacy advocacy. Open dialogues can reveal points of conflict, prompting structured compromises (Sanchez et al., 2024). Multi-stakeholder committees or public hearings can incorporate community perspectives, strengthening legitimacy (Cugurullo, 2024). Figure 3 demonstrates relationships among government agencies, private vendors, civil society, and residents. Governance involves dynamic collaboration and negotiation over AI initiatives (National League of Cities, 2024).

Figure 3. Class Diagram of Stakeholders in AI Governance

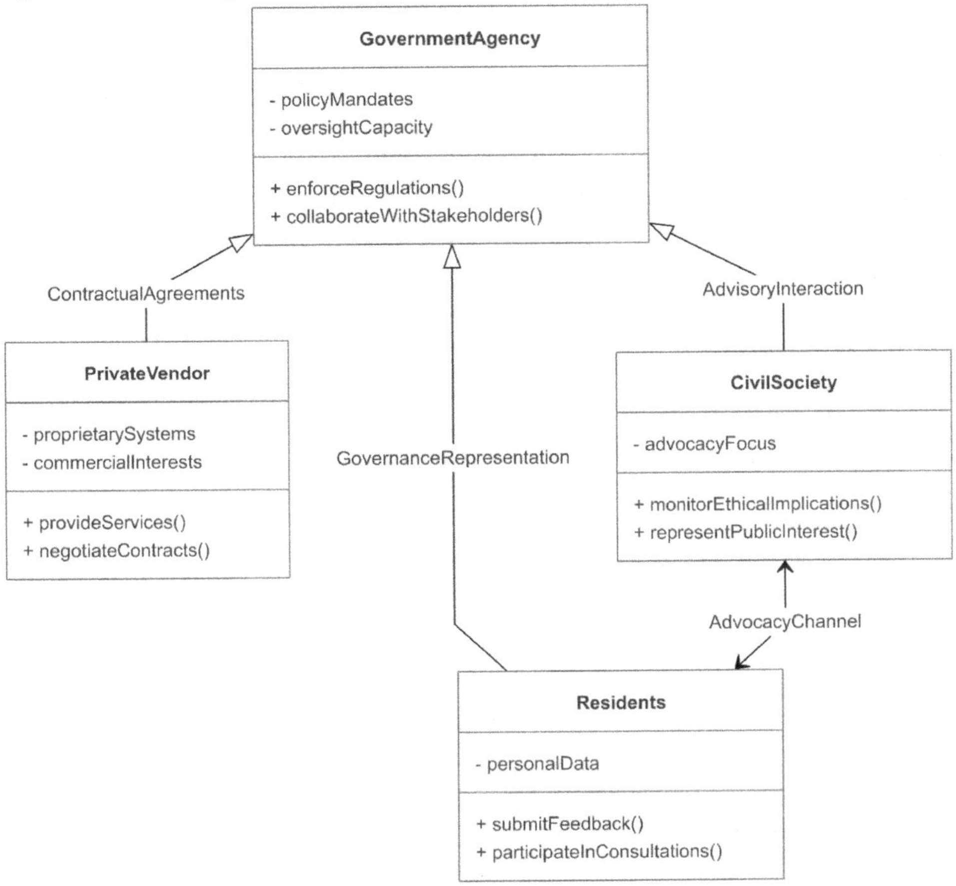

5.4. Cultural and Contextual Variables

Societies interpret ethics based on cultural values, historical experiences, and legal traditions (Tonnarelli & Mora, 2025). Some communities prioritize communal welfare, accepting broader data collection, while others stress individual liberty and privacy (Conti & Seele, 2023). Policymakers must consider these variations when implementing AI systems in healthcare, policing, or social support (Cugurullo & Xu, 2024). Mismatched approaches can generate public backlash or erode trust (Reddick et al., 2023).

5.5. Ongoing Review and Adaptation

Ethical criteria require frequent updates as AI matures. Tools once deemed state-of-the-art can develop novel biases or security gaps over time (Bosco et al., 2024). Municipal rules that were adequate in one generation of AI might fail to address a new wave of generative models with extensive language or image creation capabilities (Bloomberg Philanthropies & Johns Hopkins University, 2023). Scholars note that adaptive governance processes are needed to track emerging challenges (AlgorithmWatch, 2024).

6. IMPLEMENTATION CHALLENGES AND BARRIERS

6.1. Financial and Technical Constraints

Many cities, especially smaller ones, lack resources to acquire cutting-edge AI platforms or to hire specialized staff (Castro et al., 2023). Implementing advanced infrastructure for data storage, model development, and continuous auditing is expensive (Bosco et al., 2024). Budget shortfalls lead municipalities to rely on external vendors, sometimes compromising accountability and data ownership (Reddick et al., 2023). Officials may be forced to prioritize short-term gains over structured, long-term governance (Cugurullo & Xu, 2024).

6.2. Institutional Resistance

Public offices often resist new technologies that disrupt established routines (Phillips & Jiao, 2023). Staff members worry about losing job functions to automated systems or facing blame if AI processes malfunction (Bloomberg Philanthropies & Johns Hopkins University, 2023). Organizational inertia hinders cross-department collaboration, which is essential for integrated data governance (AlgorithmWatch, 2024). Training initiatives can address knowledge gaps, but these programs need consistent funding and high-level support (Barns et al., 2023).

6.3. Tensions Between Ethical Goals and Commercial Interests

Private companies hold proprietary AI systems that promise better efficiency but often restrict code or data visibility (Sanchez et al., 2024). Contractual terms can limit government oversight, especially when companies guard trade secrets (Conti & Seele, 2023). Officials must negotiate for transparency clauses and exit strategies to avoid vendor lock-in (Cugurullo, 2024). Tensions arise when profit-oriented goals clash with ethical imperatives related to accountability, fairness, and privacy (Reddick et al., 2023).

6.4. Rapid Technological Shifts

AI capabilities evolve rapidly. Generative models and real-time analytics challenge existing frameworks (OECD, 2023b). Policymakers struggle to keep pace, drafting guidelines that can become outdated soon after adoption (UK Department for Science, Innovation and Technology, 2023). This dynamic environment can leave administrative staff unprepared for new threats or data-protection loopholes. City leaders benefit from agile policy approaches that encourage iterative learning and scenario planning (Bosco et al., 2024).

Table 3. Common Implementation Barriers and Mitigation Strategies

Barrier	Mitigation Strategy
Limited Funding	Seek grant programs, public–private collaborations, or phased implementation
Lack of Expertise	Offer specialized training, partner with academic labs, recruit skilled personnel
Organizational Inertia	Use pilot projects to show effectiveness, provide change management programs
Proprietary Constraints	Include open data provisions, negotiate code access, or require transparency
Aging Regulations	Encourage iterative policy updates, form cross-agency task forces

6.5. Public Distrust and High-Profile Failures

When AI systems generate errors with human consequences—such as wrongful arrests or miscalculated social benefits—media coverage amplifies distrust (Barns et al., 2023). If officials fail to explain errors or avoid accountability, perceptions worsen (Phillips & Jiao, 2023). Distrust may also stem from suspicion that AI deployments serve elite interests at the expense of the marginalized (Sanchez et al., 2024). Restoring confidence requires transparent investigations and timely remedies (New York City Office of Technology & Innovation, 2023).

7. STRATEGIES FOR ENHANCING PUBLIC TRUST AND ENGAGEMENT

7.1. Inclusive Development of Policy

Involving residents in drafting AI policies can strengthen legitimacy (National League of Cities, 2024). Community meetings, citizen assemblies, or digital consultations allow people to voice concerns about data collection or potential biases (Bloomberg Philanthropies & Johns Hopkins University, 2023). Officials can gather feedback to refine usage guidelines. This collaborative model aligns AI implementations with local priorities, building confidence among participants (AlgorithmWatch, 2024).

7.2. Education and Digital Literacy

Public workshops, informational campaigns, and school curricula can cultivate basic knowledge about how AI operates (Javed et al., 2023). Such activities demystify technical concepts, helping citizens grasp how municipal algorithms handle data (Bosco et al., 2024). Education fosters critical thinking, enabling individuals to question or challenge questionable AI results (Conti & Seele, 2023). Well-informed populations are more likely to cooperate with beneficial projects and hold officials accountable (Cugurullo, 2024).

7.3. Avenues for Redress and Recourse

Trust requires that citizens can challenge automated decisions they perceive as flawed or unfair (Sanchez et al., 2024). Clear grievance procedures and appeal processes ensure that those affected by potential AI errors have an avenue for resolution (Phillips & Jiao, 2023). Ombudsman offices or digital complaint portals facilitate such challenges. Transparent follow-up investigations reassure the public that officials take these issues seriously (New York City Office of Technology & Innovation, 2023). Figure 4 shows a governance cycle that integrates formal ethics boards, community input, and iterative policy adjustments. Each phase informs the next, reinforcing an inclusive decision-making approach (Barns et al., 2023).

Figure 4. Conceptual Framework of Stakeholder Engagement in Ethical AI Governance

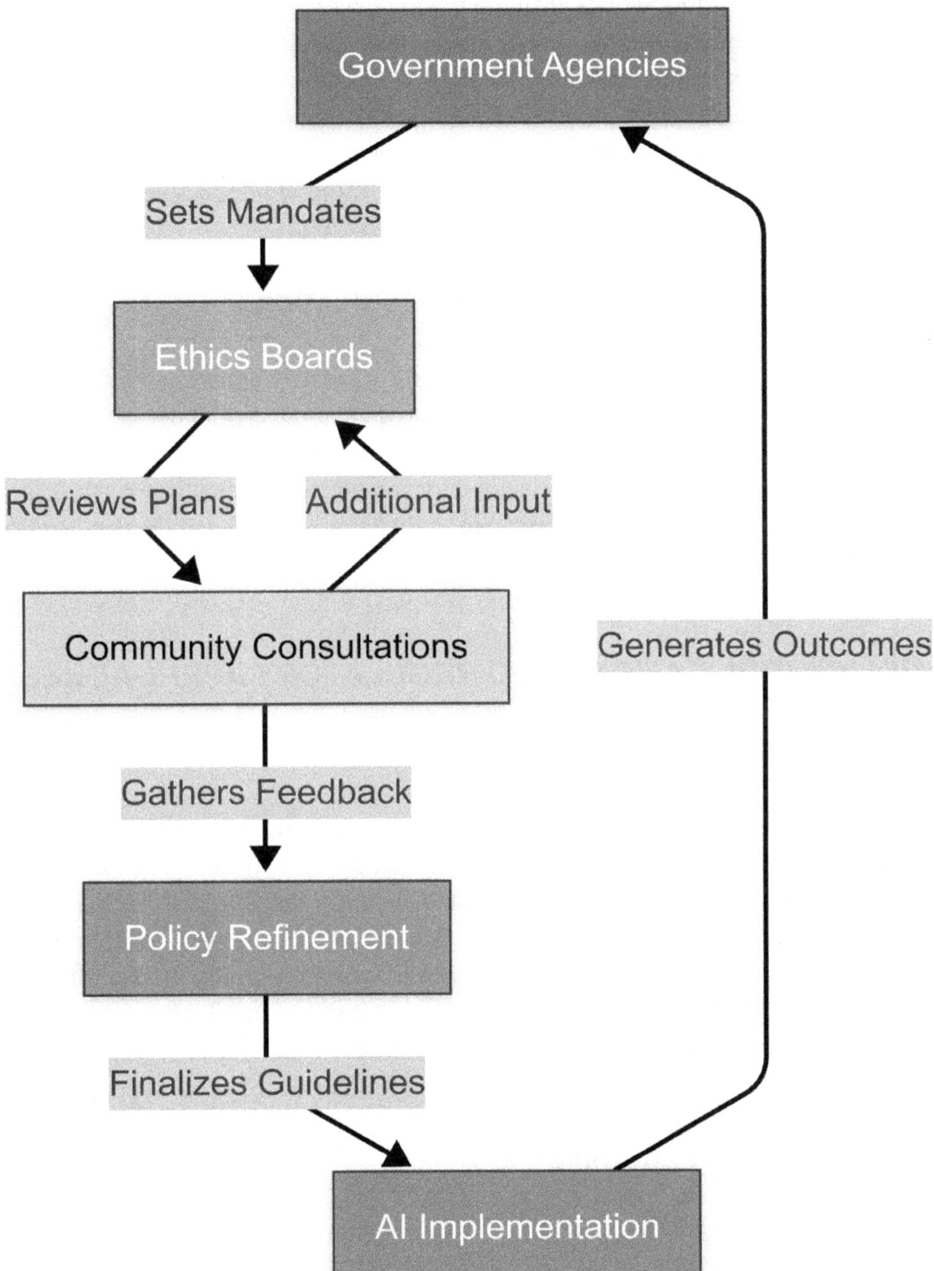

7.4. Transparency in Procurement and Partnerships

Municipal bidding processes influence which AI vendors come on board. Requiring open documentation of algorithms, code audits, or data-handling protocols can deter black-box solutions (Castro et al., 2023). Contracts can mandate the municipality's right to inspect system components or demand open standards (Reddick et al., 2023). Publicizing the procurement process also discourages under-the-table dealings (Conti & Seele, 2023). These steps promote vendor accountability and align with broader trust-building goals (Cugurullo, 2024).

7.5. Incremental Rollouts and Pilot Evaluations

Cities often start AI projects on a limited scale to identify unanticipated outcomes (Phillips & Jiao, 2023). Pilot programs generate data about model performance and user feedback, guiding refinements before citywide implementation (Son et al., 2023). This incremental model prevents widespread disruptions if errors surface, while building a body of evidence that can validate or refute the algorithm's utility (Barns et al., 2023).

8. POLICY IMPLICATIONS AND REGULATORY APPROACHES

8.1. Harmonizing Standards

Multiple standards exist for AI governance, producing inconsistencies across borders and sometimes within countries (OECD, 2023a). Harmonization reduces confusion for both municipal authorities and industry stakeholders (UN-Habitat, 2024). Cross-jurisdiction collaborations, knowledge exchanges, and reference frameworks help cities adopt similar protocols for data privacy, bias audits, and accountability (UK Department for Science, Innovation and Technology, 2023). Uniform guidelines ease the path for smaller locales lacking capacity to devise comprehensive rules (Bloomberg Philanthropies & Johns Hopkins University, 2023).

8.2. Regulatory Sandboxes

Some regions test new AI applications through regulatory sandboxes. These controlled environments allow companies and public agencies to deploy experimental tools under close observation (Javed et al., 2023). Monitoring can uncover biases, data vulnerabilities, or compliance gaps before citywide expansion (NIST, 2023). By refining prototypes, officials update regulations promptly, reducing the risk of outdated laws (Cugurullo, 2024). Sandboxes balance innovation with oversight, a strategy beneficial for rapidly changing AI fields (Barns et al., 2023).

8.3. International Alliances and Guidance

International bodies like the OECD and United Nations produce high-level principles on fairness, accountability, and transparency (United Nations Secretary-General's High-Level Advisory Body on AI, 2023). These global guidelines influence local policy, especially in cities that rely on cross-border technology vendors (AlgorithmWatch, 2024). City networks also exchange success stories and pitfalls, accelerating collective learning (Castro et al., 2023). Sustained cooperation fosters robust policy ecosystems that respond to novel AI challenges (UN-Habitat, 2024).

8.4. Enforcement and Compliance Mechanisms

Regulations must be accompanied by tangible enforcement. Penalties for privacy breaches or discriminatory outcomes signal that authorities treat ethical lapses seriously (Conti & Seele, 2023). Enforcement agencies can mandate system modifications, issue fines, or revoke licenses (OECD, 2023b). In many places, limited budgets or insufficient technical expertise weaken enforcement efforts, undermining the value of written guidelines (Cugurullo & Xu, 2024). Municipal alliances with academia or external auditors can strengthen compliance (New York City Office of Technology & Innovation, 2023).

8.5. Adaptive Legal Frameworks

AI's rapid evolution demands legislation that remains flexible (Bosco et al., 2024). Traditional legal drafting may be too slow to handle new techniques like generative models or advanced computer vision (UK Department for Science, Innovation and Technology, 2023). Adaptive frameworks outline fundamental principles while enabling rulemaking bodies to update technical requirements incrementally (AlgorithmWatch, 2024). Cities that adopt agile governance structures—task forces, real-time auditing, or dynamic licensing—are more prepared for emerging complexities (Barns et al., 2023).

9. CASE EXAMPLES AND ILLUSTRATIONS

9.1. Biometric Monitoring in Public Transit

One city introduced AI-driven facial recognition at train stations to enhance security and track fare evasion (Phillips & Jiao, 2023). Official statements emphasized cost savings and crime reduction. Civil liberties groups contested the deployment, citing privacy breaches and algorithmic biases (Reddick et al., 2023). After media scrutiny revealed potential errors that led to wrongful detentions, authorities suspended the technology (Castro et al., 2023). This episode highlights the importance of prior risk assessment and open stakeholder consultations (Cugurullo, 2024).

9.2. AI-Directed Traffic Flow

Another municipality experimented with adaptive traffic signals driven by machine learning algorithms that factor in real-time congestion data, weather, and accident reports (Bosco et al., 2024). Observers noted improvements in commute times on major roads. However, criticism arose when data indicated that some residential neighborhoods experienced heavier traffic spillover. Officials adjusted the algorithm to reduce disparities after analyzing reports from local councils (Barns et al., 2023). The case underscores how AI solutions can yield varied benefits across urban areas (Sanchez et al., 2024).

9.3. Predictive Welfare Services

An innovative social services department deployed predictive analytics to identify individuals at risk of homelessness (Tonnarelli & Mora, 2025). Caseworkers used model outputs to offer targeted interventions. Observers applauded the proactive approach but voiced concerns about potential stigmatization of identified families (AlgorithmWatch, 2024). To address these worries, administrators disclosed how the model functioned and included a human review step before final decisions (Sanchez et al., 2024). Transparency measures reduced fears that AI alone dictated welfare support (Palmini & Cugurullo, 2023).

Table 4. Illustrative Case Snapshots

Case	AI Application	Key Concern	Outcome
Biometric Monitoring	Facial Recognition	Privacy, Algorithmic Bias	System suspended pending further review
Adaptive Traffic Control	Dynamic Signal Timing	Uneven Distribution	Algorithm refined to balance neighborhood impacts
Predictive Welfare	Risk Assessment	Stigmatization	Human verification added to reduce harm

9.4. Lessons Extracted

These scenarios reveal how AI deployments can transform city services but also generate backlash when oversight falls short (National League of Cities, 2024). Early consultation, transparent reporting, and readiness to adjust flawed processes prove vital (Phillips & Jiao, 2023). The cases suggest that trust builds incrementally, fed by tangible evidence of benefits and robust avenues for recourse (Cugurullo & Xu, 2024). Municipalities that ignore these lessons may face public opposition or legal challenges, undermining their efforts to modernize governance (Bloomberg Philanthropies & Johns Hopkins University, 2023).

10. CONCEPTUAL FRAMEWORK FOR TRUST IN AI-DRIVEN URBAN ENVIRONMENTS

10.1. Overview of the Proposed Framework

This framework combines privacy safeguards, accountability measures, and ethical guidelines into a model designed to strengthen public trust. Public officials, technology vendors, and community members interact within a regulatory environment shaped by cultural contexts and resource constraints (Barns et al., 2023). The structure shows how feedback loops connect policy enforcement with ongoing monitoring (AlgorithmWatch, 2024). Figure 5 presents a cyclical interaction: regulatory guidelines direct technical decisions, accountability structures monitor outcomes, and ethical principles provide normative anchors (Cugurullo, 2024). Civic engagement weaves through these elements to ensure alignment with community values (OECD, 2023b).

Figure 5. Conceptual Framework for Building Trust in AI-Driven Urban Governance

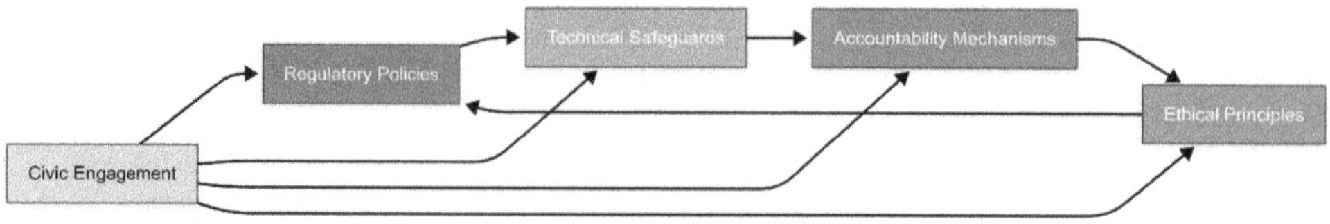

10.2. Core Elements of the Model

The framework contains four central pillars:

- **Regulatory Policies**: Laws, guidelines, and enforcement tools that guide AI usage.
- **Technical Safeguards**: Encryption, anonymization, and methods for data security.
- **Accountability Mechanisms**: Audit procedures, complaint processes, and oversight boards.
- **Ethical Principles**: Fairness, transparency, autonomy, and justice.

These pillars are supported by continuous civic engagement and iterative review processes (National League of Cities, 2024). This design ensures that local contexts shape policy choices.

10.3. Feedback Loops and Adaptive Management

AI-driven urban systems demand ongoing evaluation and adaptation. Periodic reviews detect algorithmic drift and privacy concerns that might have emerged after deployment (AlgorithmWatch, 2024). Municipalities can employ pilot programs or regulatory sandboxes to refine new tools (Barns et al., 2023). Feedback loops integrate findings from audits, public complaints, or changed policy goals, letting officials revise mandates for vendors or reorganize administrative workflows (OECD, 2023a).

10.4. Integration with Broader Governance Strategies

This conceptual model fits within the broader shift toward "smart city" agendas. It emphasizes that AI is not a self-contained solution but part of a larger transformation of planning, resource management, and citizen engagement (Wolniak & Stecuła, 2024). The same cities that adopt sophisticated data-analytics platforms might also invest in alternative energy grids, shared mobility, or social inclusion programs (Stern, Ramos, & Prinvil, 2025). Synergy among these initiatives can multiply benefits, provided that accountability and ethical considerations remain front and center (Cugurullo & Xu, 2024).

11. FUTURE RESEARCH DIRECTIONS

11.1. Trust Dynamics Over Time

Little longitudinal research examines how public trust evolves as AI systems become more pervasive (Goldsmith & Yang, 2025). Future studies might survey citizens over months or years to see whether initial acceptance holds up if errors arise or if data handling reveals flaws (Cugurullo, 2024). Qualitative interviews could explore perceptions of fairness or highlight skepticism about algorithmic intentions. Understanding these dynamics can help policymakers refine communication and transparency (Bosco et al., 2024).

11.2. Complex Fairness Metrics

Fairness extends beyond standardized protected categories such as race or gender (Phillips & Jiao, 2023). Marginalized groups may also differ by language, immigration status, disability, or digital literacy (Conti & Seele, 2023). Refined metrics can capture these nuances in large datasets, offering deeper insight into how AI distributions affect resource availability (Sanchez et al., 2024). Researchers can develop new auditing tools that evaluate intersectional dimensions of algorithmic outcomes (Son et al., 2023).

11.3. Interplay of Generative Models and Urban Data

Generative AI can create text, images, or videos that reshape city services, from public communication to digital signage (Bloomberg Philanthropies & Johns Hopkins University, 2023). If local governments adopt chatbots or automated design tools, questions arise about authenticity, misinformation, or the framing of official narratives (Barns et al., 2023). Deeper inquiries might address the ethical boundaries of synthetic media in public announcements or urban planning visuals (Conti & Seele, 2023).

11.4. Social Impact Evaluation Methods

Some municipalities lack systematic ways to measure the social impact of AI-based interventions (Tonnarelli & Mora, 2025). Frameworks that merge quantitative indicators (e.g., changes in complaint rates) with qualitative insights (e.g., resident feedback) can offer a holistic picture (UN-Habitat, 2024). Comparisons across cities or neighborhoods with distinct demographic profiles might uncover patterns that inform policy adjustments (Cugurullo & Xu, 2024).

11.5. Legal Innovations and Comparative Analysis

Legislative initiatives continue to emerge, but more research is needed to compare their efficacy in real urban contexts (Reddick et al., 2023). Scholars can examine how new laws related to liability, transparency, or data sharing transform procurement behavior or vendor selection (Wolniak & Stecuła, 2024). Comparative studies across nations with different legal traditions reveal best practices and highlight pitfalls in drafting and enforcing AI regulations (UK Department for Science, Innovation and Technology, 2023).

12. CONCLUSION

AI-driven transformations in city governance hold promise for enhancing efficiency, responsiveness, and service quality (Reddick et al., 2023). Yet privacy, accountability, and ethical considerations raise serious questions. As municipalities gather personal data and rely on automated decisions, the need for robust oversight has become undeniable (Barns et al., 2023). This chapter has addressed how privacy protections, accountability measures, and ethical frameworks shape trust in AI-driven urban environments. A central theme is the importance of inclusive governance that accommodates ongoing feedback and employs technical safeguards (Sanchez et al., 2024).

Empirical evidence from multiple case illustrations highlights risks when policies and audits fail to account for biases or data misuse (Cugurullo & Xu, 2024). Simultaneously, pilot programs and transparent processes show that public trust can grow if authorities proactively manage potential pitfalls (Bloomberg Philanthropies & Johns Hopkins University, 2023). Future policy must anticipate rapid advancements in AI, refining legal instruments, procurement rules, and ethical norms to keep pace (OECD, 2023b). Collaborative initiatives among municipal agencies, civil society, academic researchers, and industry partners are vital for ensuring equitable outcomes (AlgorithmWatch, 2024).

The conceptual framework introduced here suggests that privacy, accountability, and ethics interact in dynamic ways, all underpinned by civic engagement (Zwitter & Helbing, 2024). Municipal leaders who appreciate this interplay can design adaptive strategies that maintain public confidence while supporting responsible innovation (NIST, 2023). Ongoing dialogue, iterative regulatory processes, and evidence-based policymaking create an environment where AI can serve community needs without eroding democratic values. The chapter thus encourages broader reflection on how cities worldwide can incorporate AI in a manner that respects human rights, fosters accountability, and sustains public trust.

REFERENCES

AlgorithmWatch. (2024). *A year of challenging choices – 2024 in review.* [Policy review of AI governance trends].

Barns, S., et al. (2023). Editorial: The governance of artificial intelligence in the "autonomous city." *Frontiers in Sustainable Cities, 5*, Article 1285175.

Bloomberg Philanthropies & Johns Hopkins University. (2023). *State of cities: Generative AI in local governments*. City AI Connect Initiative.

Bosco, G., Riccardi, V., Sciarrone, A., D'Amore, R., & Visvizi, A. (2024). AI-driven innovation in smart city governance: Achieving human-centric and sustainable outcomes. *Transforming Government: People, Process and Policy, 18*(4).

Castro, D., McLaughlin, M., & McQuinn, A. (2023). *Balancing privacy and innovation in smart cities and communities*. Information Technology & Innovation Foundation.

Conti, L. G., & Seele, P. (2023). The contested role of AI ethics boards in smart societies: A step towards improvement based on board composition by sortition. *Ethics and Information Technology*, *25*(4), 51. DOI: 10.1007/s10676-023-09724-8

Cugurullo, F. (2024). New stories of urban AI: Exploring the artificial intelligence–city nexus beyond Frankenstein Urbanism. *Urban Geography*, *45*(7), 1300–1307. DOI: 10.1080/02723638.2024.2386179

Cugurullo, F., & Xu, Y. (2024). When AIs become oracles: Generative artificial intelligence, anticipatory urban governance, and the future of cities. *Policy and Society*, *43*(4).

Goldsmith, S., & Yang, J. (2025). AI and the transformation of accountability and discretion in urban governance. [Manuscript in preparation].

Hong Kong Digital Policy Office. (2023). *Ethical Artificial Intelligence framework for government*. Hong Kong SAR Government.

Javed, A. R., Ahmed, W., Pandya, S., Maddikunta, P. K. R., Alazab, M., & Gadekallu, T. R. (2023). A survey of explainable artificial intelligence for smart cities. *Electronics (Basel), 12*(4), 1020. DOI: 10.3390/electronics12041020

Michigan Municipal League. (2023). *Artificial intelligence handbook for local government.* MML Press.

National Institute of Standards and Technology (NIST). (2023). *Artificial Intelligence Risk Management Framework (AI RMF 1.0)*. U.S. Department of Commerce.

National League of Cities. (2024). *The ethics and governance of generative AI: Insights for city leaders*. NLC.

New York City Office of Technology & Innovation. (2023). *New York City Artificial Intelligence Action Plan (2023–2025)*. NYC Mayor's Office.

OECD. (2023a). *Advancing accountability in AI: Governing and managing risks throughout the lifecycle for trustworthy AI*. OECD Publishing.

OECD. (2023b). *Smart city data governance: Challenges and the way forward*. OECD Publishing.

Palmini, O., & Cugurullo, F. (2023). Charting AI urbanism: Conceptual sources and spatial implications of urban artificial intelligence. *Discover Artificial Intelligence*, *3*(1), 15. DOI: 10.1007/s44163-023-00060-w

Phillips, C., & Jiao, J. (2023). Artificial intelligence & smart city ethics: A systematic review. In *2023 IEEE International Symposium on Ethics in Engineering, Science, and Technology (ETHICS)* (pp. 1–5). IEEE. DOI: 10.1109/ETHICS57328.2023.10154961

Reddick, C. G., Chatfield, A. T., & Ojo, A. (2023). Understanding chatbot adoption in local governments. *Journal of Urban Technology*.

Sanchez, T. W., Brenman, M., & Ye, X. (2024). The ethical concerns of artificial intelligence in urban planning. *Journal of the American Planning Association*, *90*(2), 294–307. DOI: 10.1080/01944363.2024.2355305

Son, T. H., Weedon, Z., Yigitcanlar, T., Sanchez, T. W., Corchado, J. M., & Mehmood, R. (2023). Algorithmic urban planning for smart and sustainable development: Systematic review of the literature. *Sustainable Cities and Society*, *89*, 104562. DOI: 10.1016/j.scs.2023.104562

Stern, A., Ramos, K., & Prinvil, C. (2025). *Practical AI insights for local leaders: An early look into how local governments are adopting AI*. Urban Institute.

Tonnarelli, F., & Mora, L. (2025). Responsible AI for cities: A case study of GeoAI in African informal settlements. *Journal of Urban Technology*, 1–27. DOI: 10.1080/10630732.2025.2450755

UK Department for Science. Innovation and Technology. (2023). *A pro-innovation approach to AI regulation: Policy paper (CP 840)*. London: UK Government.

UN-Habitat. (2024). *Global assessment of responsible AI in cities: Leveraging AI for people-centered smart cities*. UN-Habitat.

United Nations Secretary-General's High-Level Advisory Body on AI. (2023). *Governing AI for humanity: Final report.* New York: United Nations.

Wolniak, R., & Stecuła, K. (2024). Artificial intelligence in smart cities—Applications, barriers, and future directions: A review. *Smart Cities*, *7*(3), 1346–1389. DOI: 10.3390/smartcities7030057

Zwitter, A., & Helbing, D. (2024). Ethics of smart cities and smart societies. *Ethics and Information Technology*, *26*(4), 1–5. DOI: 10.1007/s10676-024-09803-4

Chapter 3
Disaster Risk Reduction and Management With Emerging Technologies:
Applications of IoT, AI, and Data Analytics for Resilient Urban Infrastructure

Mahapara Abbass
https://orcid.org/0000-0002-0838-2598
Department of Civil Engineering, Maharishi Markandeshwar Engineering College, Maharishi Markandeshwar University (Deemed), Mullana, India

Shalom Akhai
https://orcid.org/0000-0002-7533-457X
Department of Mechanical Engineering, Maharishi Markandeshwar Engineering College, Maharishi Markandeshwar University (Deemed), Mullana, India

Arti Chouksey
https://orcid.org/0000-0002-7741-0214
Department of Civil Engineering, Deenbandhu Chhotu Ram University of Science and Technology, Murthal, India

Swati Pathak
https://orcid.org/0009-0004-7670-8141
Department of Civil Engineering, Chandigarh Engineering College, Jhanjeri, India

Uzma Abbas
https://orcid.org/0009-0005-5862-3571
Department of Law, Dogra Law College, Jammu, India

Sana Abass
Department of Civil Engineering, Mahant Bachittar Singh College of Engineering and Technology, Jammu, India

DOI: 10.4018/979-8-3373-1375-7.ch003

ABSTRACT

This chapter explores the role of emerging technologies in disaster risk reduction and management (DRRM), focusing on the integration of the Internet of Things (IoT), Artificial Intelligence (AI), and Data Analytics to enhance urban resilience. IoT-enabled sensors and smart infrastructure provide real-time data for early warning systems, infrastructure monitoring, and emergency response. AI-driven predictive analytics enhances risk assessment, resource allocation, and post-disaster recovery, while data analytics enables integration, visualization, and scenario planning. Despite their potential, challenges like data quality, scalability, cybersecurity, and ethical concerns must be addressed. The future of Disaster Risk Reduction and Management (DRRM) will depend on the incorporation of modern technology, increased public involvement, and global cooperation, allowing cities to develop more intelligent, secure, and sustainable urban settings.

CHAPTER HIGHLIGHTS

- Escalating urbanization, climatic anomalies, and infrastructural complexities exacerbate systemic vulnerabilities to catastrophic events.
- Conventional disaster risk management paradigms are predominantly reactive and lack the scalability and precision required for contemporary urban threats.
- Advanced technologies, including the Internet of Things (IoT), Artificial Intelligence (AI), and data analytics, present a paradigm shift toward proactive and anticipatory risk mitigation.
- IoT-enabled sensor networks facilitate high-resolution, real-time data acquisition for predictive analytics, early warning systems, and structural health monitoring.
- AI-driven algorithms enhance threat modeling, anomaly detection, and dynamic resource allocation, enabling real-time decision support and automated emergency response mechanisms.
- Sophisticated data analytics frameworks integrate heterogeneous data streams for comprehensive risk assessment, situational intelligence, and evidence-based decision-making.
- Mitigating cybersecurity risks, ensuring data privacy, and addressing ethical implications are critical for the scalable and responsible deployment of these technologies.

1. INTRODUCTION

Accelerated urbanization, climate change, and the increasing complexity of infrastructure systems are making metropolitan regions more vulnerable to disasters. Traditional techniques for disaster risk reduction and management are often reactive, disorganized, and ill-equipped to address the scale and complexity of modern urban challenges. Emerging technologies like the Internet of Things, artificial intelligence, and data analytics can enhance urban infrastructure resilience(Balogun et al., 2020; Alauthman, Aldweesh, & Al-Qerem, 2024).The increasing density, deteriorating infrastructure, and environmental degradation resulting from urban expansion have heightened the danger of disaster. Severe weather phenomena, such as hurricanes, floods, wildfires, and heatwaves, exacerbated by climate change, impose additional strain on urban resilience. The complexity of modern infrastructure, comprising transportation networks, electrical grids, and water supply systems, complicates disaster response and recovery efforts(Freed & Zimmerman, 2022).Historically, reactive measures have predominated in disaster risk reduction and management activities. Traditional techniques, including emergency response teams, evacuation plans, and disaster relief efforts, are essential but sometimes fragmented and insufficient in addressing the extent and complexity of current urban issues. Many cities lack the capability to efficiently respond, anticipate occurrences, and rapidly reconstruct. Inadequate coordination among various stakeholders, including government entities, private sector organizations, and communities, may lead to delays in disaster response, misallocation of resources, and increased fatalities and economic losses(Gotham & Cheek, 2017).Transformative emerging technologies, including the Internet of Things, artificial intelligence, and data analytics, can enhance urban infrastructure resilience. Environmental sensors, smart meters, and interconnected infrastructure inside IoT devices can collect vast amounts of real-time data, providing early alerts and ongoing urban surveillance. By analyzing this data, AI-driven algorithms can identify patterns, assess hazards, and optimize resource allocation. Data analytics solutions can elucidate crisis situations, integrate data from several sources, and facilitate collaboration among stakeholders(Van Hoang, 2024).IoT devices provide real-time monitoring, predictive analytics, and data-informed decision-making, reducing catastrophic risk through effective management. IoT devices can automate emergency response systems, monitor environmental changes, and forecast potential dangers. By detecting wear, stress, or damage before catastrophic occurrences, they assist in monitoring and maintaining infrastructure(Firoozi & Firoozi, 2024). IoT-enabled pipeline monitoring systems detect leaks, pressure fluctuations, and corrosion in water, gas, and oil pipelines, preventing hazardous incidents during natural disasters(Ahmed, 2022).Artificial intelligence is revolutionizing disaster risk management through predictive analytics, risk assessment, and automated decision-making. By analyzing vast quantities of historical and real-time data, machine learning algorithms can identify patterns, forecast occurrences, and recommend preventive measures. The forecast of disasters is crucial. AI-driven risk assessment models use factors such as population density, infrastructure integrity, and environmental variables to forecast disasters before they occur.Artificial intelligence enhances decision-making during emergencies with real-time recommendations based on data analysis (Akhai & Abbass, 2025). AI-driven decision support systems can assess the magnitude and location of a crisis by analyzing data from IoT devices, weather reports, social media feeds, and emergency calls. These systems focus emergency response efforts based on impact assessments, improving resource allocation(Gobinath, Reshmika, & Sivakarthi, 2024).Post-disaster, artificial intelligence assists in damage assessment and reconstruction efforts. Image recognition algorithms can assess infrastructure, highway, and building damage by analyzing drone footage and satellite imagery (Akhai 2024). This rapid assessment technique enables authorities to select rehabilitation programs and allocate resources efficiently(Al Shafian& Hu, 2024).Data analytics is essential in disaster risk reduction management as it integrates and analyzes data from multiple sources to provide actionable insights. A primary use of data analytics in disaster risk reduction and management is geospatial analysis, which assists urban planners in generating detailed risk maps highlighting vulnerable areas, infrastructural deficiencies, and potential hazard zones. In a crisis, social media and crowdsourced data analysis provide invaluable real-time information, identifying emerging threats, aiding in locating affected individuals, and tracking the spread of misinformation. Disaster preparedness relies on predictive modeling and scenario analysis, enabling lawmakers to determine optimal resource allocation(Munawar et al., 2022).The use of emerging technologies can transform urban resilience, enabling cities to anticipate, withstand, and recover from disasters more effectively. By leveraging the Internet of Things, artificial intelligence, and data analytics, cities can improve their disaster risk reduction and management capabilities(Arif & Akhai, 2024; Abbass et al., 2025). Climate change exacerbates environmental hazards through increasingly frequent and severe extreme weather events, while increased urbanization has led to informal settlements lacking disaster-resistant housing, sanitation, and emergency services. The use of IoT networks, artificial intelligence, and data analytics can provide real-time situational awareness and predictive flood warnings, closing the human-digital divide through government reform and community engagement(Samansiri et al., 2022).

2 THE ROLE OF IOT IN DISASTER RISK REDUCTION AND MANAGEMENT

The Internet of Things (IoT) is a network of interconnected devices that collect, transmit, and analyze real-time data, particularly in disaster risk reduction and management (DRRM). IoT-enabled early warning systems (EWS) are a paradigm shift from reactive disaster response to proactive risk mitigation. By deploying interconnected sensors, drones, and smart devices across urban and natural environments, cities can detect emerging threats with unprecedented speed and precision. This section explores the technical frameworks, applications, and transformative potential of IoT in EWS, supported by global case studies and emerging innovations(Olasiman et al., 2023; Montesa et al., 2023).For example:

- **Seismic Sensors**: Deployed in earthquake-prone areas, these sensors can detect early tremors and send alerts to emergency services and residents, providing valuable seconds or minutes to take protective actions.
- **Flood Monitoring Sensors**: Installed in rivers, dams, and urban drainage systems, these sensors can monitor water levels and flow rates, enabling early warnings for potential flooding.
- **Weather Stations**: IoT-enabled weather stations can provide real-time data on temperature, humidity, wind speed, and precipitation, improving the accuracy of weather forecasts and storm warnings.

2.1. Seismic Sensors

Technical Architecture and Functionality

Seismic sensors (used for detecting Earth's Whispers Before the Roar)are accelerometers or geophones designed to detect ground motion caused by tectonic activity. Modern IoT-enabled seismic networks integrate these sensors with edge computing and cloud platforms to process data in real time(Abdalzaher et al., 2023; Abdalzaher et al., 2024). For example:

- **Japan's Earthquake Early Warning (EEW) System**: The world's most advanced seismic network, comprising various sensors, detects primary (P) waves—the faster, less destructive seismic waves that precede slower but devastating secondary (S) waves. Algorithms calculate the earthquake's epicenter and magnitude within seconds, triggering alerts via smartphones, radios, and public address systems. During the 2021 Fukushima earthquake, the system provided 10–20 seconds of warning, enabling trains to brake and factories to halt hazardous processes (Wu & Mittal, 2021).

- **Mexico City's SASMex**: A hybrid system combining IoT seismic sensors with AI-driven predictive models. SASMex issues alerts via 12,000+ sirens and mobile apps, offering up to 60 seconds of warning for earthquakes originating on the Pacific coast(Tan et al., 2022).

Case Study: Istanbul's AI-Enhanced Seismic Network

Istanbul, located on the seismically active North Anatolian Fault, faces a 47% probability of a magnitude 7.0+ earthquake by 2030. The city's IoT-based EWS integrates(İlerisoy&Gökgöz, 2024):

Istanbul's AI-Enhanced Seismic Network (EWS) is designed to mitigate seismic risks, with a 47% probability of a 7.0+ earthquake by 2030. The network uses MEMS sensors embedded in buildings and infrastructure, AI algorithms to analyze historical tremor data, and automated shutdown protocols for gas lines and power grids. This system detected a 5.8-magnitude foreshock near the Marmara Sea, triggering evacuations and preventing casualties.

Challenges and Innovations

- **False Alarms**: Overly sensitive sensors may trigger unnecessary panic. Solutions include machine learning models trained to distinguish seismic noise (e.g., construction vibrations) from genuine earthquakes.
- **Rural Coverage**: Deploying IoT sensors in remote areas remains logistically challenging. Satellite-linked, solar-powered sensors, such as those used in Nepal's Himalayas, address this gap.

2.2 Flood Monitoring Sensors

Sensor Types and Deployment Strategies

Flood EWS rely on a hierarchy of IoT devices(Song et al., 2024):

1. **Ultrasonic Level Sensors**: Measure water height in rivers and reservoirs.
2. **Pressure Transducers**: Monitor groundwater levels in urban drainage systems.
3. **Acoustic Doppler Sensors**: Track flow velocity in real time.

Case Study: The Netherlands' Smart Delta Platform

The Netherlands, where 26% of the land lies below sea level, employs a nationwide IoT network to combat flooding. The Netherlands uses a nationwide IoT network to combat flooding, with over 1,500 sensors along the Rhine and Meuse rivers transmitting data to a centralized AI platform. Machine learning algorithms analyze rainfall forecasts, tidal patterns, and soil saturation to predict flood risks 72 hours in advance. IoT-actuated storm surge barriers, like Maeslantkering, close autonomously when sensors detect rising water levels, preventing potential damage during storm(Iqbal et al., 2023).

Case Study: Urban Flood Management of Jakarta's IoT-Driven Drainage System

Jakarta, sinking at 25 cm/year due to groundwater extraction, faces chronic flooding. The city's IoT-based solution includes. Jakarta's IoT-driven drainage system addresses chronic flooding by using smart drain covers equipped with water level sensors and debris-detection cameras. Real-time dashboards use sensor data to deploy pumps and redirect traffic, while citizen alerts are sent via platforms like PetaBencana.id, which crowdsource flood data from social media and IoT sensors(Solehudin et al., 2023; Sihislavsky et al., 2022). Limitations and Solutions of such system are:

- **Sensor Maintenance**: Sediment buildup and corrosion in flood-prone areas reduce sensor accuracy. Self-cleaning sensors, such as Singapore's ultrasonic "bubble" devices, mitigate this issue.
- **Data Latency**: Low-power wide-area networks (LPWAN) like LoRaWAN enable real-time transmission even during power outages.

2.3 IoT-Enabled Weather Stations

Next-Generation Meteorological Monitoring

Traditional weather stations provide localized, static data. IoT-enabled systems create dynamic, hyperlocal weather models by integrating(Iqbal et al., 2024):

- **Distributed Sensor Networks**: Thousands of low-cost stations measure temperature, humidity, wind speed, and rainfall at granular resolutions.
- **Drone fleets**: Equipped with LiDAR and multispectral cameras, drones map microclimates in urban heat islands or wildfire-prone regions.

- **Satellite Integration**: IoT gateways fuse ground sensor data with satellite imagery for comprehensive weather forecasting.

Case Study: India's IMD Smart Weather Grid

India's geographical diversity makes it vulnerable to natural disasters like monsoons and cyclones. The IMD Smart Weather Grid, launched in 2022, is a crucial tool in disaster risk management. It uses a network of IoT weather stations to provide real-time, localized data for accurate forecasting and disaster preparedness. This data is processed through advanced AI models, enabling the IMD to provide precise, timely warnings. The grid's impact was demonstrated during Cyclone Biparjoy in 2023, where AI-powered forecasting accurately predicted landfall within 10km, 48 hours in advance, facilitating the evacuation of around 100,000 coastal residents. The grid also aids in proactive disaster mitigation by providing detailed information on rainfall patterns and potential flood risks, enabling authorities to implement targeted interventions. The Farmers' Advisory System, primarily agricultural, advises on crop management in relation to weather patterns, minimizing food security risks following disasters. The IMD Smart Weather Grid is a vital tool in India's disaster risk management strategy, leveraging IoT and AI to provide accurate, timely information, enabling effective preparedness, mitigation, and response, ultimately saving lives and protecting livelihoods(Verma et al., 2024; Chug & Nath, 2024).

Urban Applications: Heatwave Mitigation in Phoenix, Arizona

Phoenix uses IoT weather stations to combat heatwaves, monitoring temperature and humidity across neighborhoods. AI identifies heat islands with limited green spaces, guiding tree-planting initiatives. Mobile apps notify residents of extreme heat and cooling center locations. Challenges include data overload, which requires edge computing solutions like Microsoft's Azure IoT Edge, and interoperability issues due to divergent sensor protocols. The World Meteorological Organization's Unified Data Model standardizes IoT weather data formats globally(Stone Jr et al., 2021).

Challenges include:

- **Data Overload**: Managing petabytes of weather data requires edge computing solutions. Microsoft's Azure IoT Edge processes data locally at weather stations, reducing cloud dependency.
- **Interoperability**: Divergent sensor protocols hinder integration. The World Meteorological Organization's (WMO) Unified Data Model standardizes IoT weather data formats globally.

2.4 Synergy with AI and Data Analytics: From Data to Decisions

IoT generates raw data, but its value lies in integration with AI and analytics:

1. **Predictive Analytics**:
   - o **Wildfire Risk Platforms**: California's ALERTWildfire combines IoT soil moisture sensors, weather data, and AI to predict fire spread, reducing response times by 40%.
2. **Automated Decision-Making**:
   - o **Japan's X-band Radar**: IoT weather radars feed data to AI models that control automated floodgates and levee systems(Adachi et al., 2016).
3. **Public Communication**:
   - o **EU's EFAS**: The European Flood Awareness System uses IoT data to generate multi-language alerts tailored to regional risk levels(Smith et al., 2016).

IoT advancements include ultra-low latency 5G networks for real-time earthquake analytics, self-healing networks in Puerto Rico's power grid, and low-cost IoT kits like Flood Network's open-source sensors for citizen science, enabling communities to build grassroots Emergency Response Systems (Zhao et al., 2021; Srivastava & Akhai, 2022; Akhai & Wadhwa 2024)

2.5 IoT for Infrastructure Monitoring and Maintenance

IoT devices are being used to monitor urban infrastructure, such as bridges, buildings, and pipelines, to detect signs of wear, stress, or damage that could lead to disaster failure thereby safeguarding the lifelines of urban resilience. These sensors can measure vibrations, tilts, and cracks in buildings and bridges, providing early warnings of structural weaknesses (Singh & Akhai, 2024). They can also detect leaks, pressure changes, or corrosion in pipelines, preventing catastrophic failures during earthquakes or floods. IoT devices also play a crucial role in emergency response and recovery, coordinating efforts and facilitating recovery. Smart emergency response systems, such as wearable sensors for first responders, can track their location, health status, and environmental conditions, improving the safety and efficiency of rescue operations(Mala et al., 2025; Akhai 2023).. IoT-enabled infrastructure monitoring and maintenance systems offer a transformative solution for real-time health assessments, predictive maintenance, and rapid response to emerging threats(Akhai & Khang, 2024; Akhai, 2024).

2.5.1 Structural Health Monitoring: Preventing Catastrophic Failures

Structural health monitoring (SHM) systems leverage IoT sensors to detect anomalies in buildings, bridges, and other critical infrastructure(Scuro et al., 2021). Key components include:

1. **Accelerometers**: Measure vibrations and oscillations caused by wind, traffic, or seismic activity.
2. **Strain Gauges**: Detect deformations in materials due to stress or load.
3. **Tilt Sensors**: Monitor angular changes in structures, such as leaning towers or bridges.
4. **Crack Sensors**: Use fiber optics or acoustic emissions to detect and measure cracks in concrete or steel.

Case Study: Golden Gate Bridge, USA

The Golden Gate Bridge in the USA uses an IoT-based SHM system to monitor vibrations, strain, and corrosion. The system uses 2,000 sensors embedded in suspension cables, towers, and road decks. Real-time analytics are transmitted to a cloud-based platform, where AI algorithms predict maintenance needs. In 2022, the system detected abnormal vibrations in a cable anchorage, preventing potential failure(Pal &Khuntia, 2020; Kamal & Mansoor, 2022).

Challenges and Innovations

- **Sensor Durability**: Harsh environmental conditions can degrade sensor performance. Solutions include self-healing materials and ruggedized sensors.
- **Data Integration**: Combining data from diverse sensors requires interoperable platforms. The Open Geospatial Consortium (OGC) standards facilitate seamless integration.

2.5.2 Pipeline Monitoring: Preventing Leaks and Failures

Sensor Technologies and Deployment Strategies

Pipelines transporting water, gas, and oil are vulnerable to leaks, corrosion, and external damage. IoT-based monitoring systems use:

1. **Acoustic Sensors**: Detect leaks by analyzing sound waves generated by escaping fluids.

2. **Pressure Sensors**: Monitor pressure fluctuations indicative of blockages or ruptures.
3. **Corrosion Sensors**: Measure electrochemical changes in pipeline materials.
4. **Smart Pigging Devices**: Robotic devices equipped with IoT sensors inspect pipelines internally.

Case Study: Smart Water Networks in Barcelona

Smart water management uses IoT technology to optimize water resource usage, enabling real-time analysis and recommendations for water conservation, cost savings, infrastructure improvement, and real-time monitoring for efficient usage(Aldegheishem et al., 2022). Barcelona's IoT-enabled water management system uses 5,000 acoustic sensors to detect leaks with high accuracy, and AI models to predict corrosion hotspots for targeted maintenance. The system reduces water losses by upto25%, saving water daily(Aldegheishem et al., 2022).

2.5.3 Transportation Networks: Ensuring Mobility During Disasters

IoT Applications in Road and Rail Systems

Transportation networks are crucial during disasters, enabling evacuations and emergency response. IoT enhances their resilience through smart traffic lights, bridge monitoring, and railway track sensors. These technologies adjust signal timings based on real-time traffic and disaster conditions, preventing collapses during floods or earthquakes(Fraga-Lamas et al., 2017; Kostrzewski & Melnik, 2021; Fraga-Lamas et al., 2017).IoT enhances their resilience through:

1. **Smart Traffic Lights**: Adjust signal timings based on real-time traffic and disaster conditions.
2. **Bridge Monitoring**: IoT sensors detect structural weaknesses, preventing collapses during floods or earthquakes.
3. **Railway Track Sensors**: Monitor track conditions, preventing derailments during extreme weather.

Challenges and Innovations

- **Scalability**: Deploying IoT sensors across vast transportation networks is costly. Public-private partnerships, like those in Singapore, fund large-scale deployments.
- **Interoperability**: Integrating IoT data from multiple transport modes requires unified platforms. The European Union's ITS Directive promotes cross-border interoperability.

2.6 IoT for Emergency Response and Recovery: Enhancing Efficiency and Safety

During and after disasters, IoT devices play a pivotal role in coordinating emergency response and facilitating recovery. By providing real-time data on personnel, resources, and environmental conditions, IoT enhances the efficiency, safety, and effectiveness of disaster management efforts.

2.6.1 Smart Emergency Response Systems: Empowering First Responders

IoT-enabled wearable devices are revolutionizing emergency response systems by providing real-time data that can save lives. These devices track first responders' positions, monitor their health, and detect hazardous conditions. For instance, in California, smart helmets equipped with thermal cameras and gas sensors provide real-time data on fire spread and air quality. In Turkey, after the 2023 earthquakes, IoT wearables helped rescue operations by tracking vital signs and locating trapped survivors(Shah et al., 2019; Zhang et al., 2023; Costa et al., 2022; Abdalzaher et al., 2023).

However, challenges include battery life, which requires long-lasting power sources, and data privacy. Energy-efficient designs and portable chargers can address this issue, while encrypted data transmission ensures confidentiality. In the case of the Türkiye-Syria earthquakes, IoT wearables helped locate trapped survivors by triangulating their mobile signals. Solutions include energy-efficient designs and portable chargers, as well as ensuring data privacy by ensuring encrypted transmission of health data.

2.6.2 Asset Tracking: Optimizing Resource Deployment

IoT Tags and Sensors for Emergency Supplies

Disasters often strain supply chains, making it essential to track and deploy resources efficiently. IoT-enabled asset tracking systems use:

1. **RFID Tags**: Attached to supplies, these tags provide real-time location data.
2. **GPS Trackers**: Monitor the movement of vehicles and equipment.
3. **Condition Sensors**: Measure environmental conditions, such as temperature or humidity, for sensitive supplies like medicines.

Case Study: Hurricane Response

Disasters can strain supply chains, necessitating efficient tracking and deployment of resources. IoT-enabled asset tracking systems use RFID tags, GPS trackers, and condition sensors to provide real-time location data. In the Hurricane Response, IoT was used for resource tracking in smart warehouses, drone deliveries, and real-time dashboards. Challenges include network reliability, as satellite-linked IoT devices ensure continuous connectivity, and scalability, as cloud-based solutions like Amazon Web Services provide scalable infrastructure for tracking thousands of assets. These innovations aim to improve the efficiency and effectiveness of emergency supplies during disasters(Damaševičius et al., 2023; Zeng et al., 2023).

2.6.3 Post-Disaster Recovery: Rebuilding with Data-Driven Insights

IoT Applications in Damage Assessment and Reconstruction

After a disaster, IoT accelerates recovery by providing accurate damage assessments and optimizing reconstruction efforts:

1. **Drone Surveys**: Equipped with LiDAR and cameras, drones map damage in inaccessible areas.
2. **Smart Grids**: IoT sensors monitor power grid repairs, ensuring rapid restoration of electricity.
3. **Building Sensors**: Assess structural integrity, guiding safe reoccupation of buildings.

Case Study: Christchurch, New Zealand

The case study of Christchurch, New Zealand, highlights the use of IoT for recovery following the 2011 earthquake. Smart grids and building sensors reduced restoration time by 30%, while IoT platforms enabled residents to report damage and track progress. However, challenges include managing data overload and ensuring marginalized communities benefit from IoT-driven recovery efforts(Lozano & Tien, 2023; Liu et al., 2024; Al-Rimawi & Nadler, 2025).

Table 1 discusses the use of IoT in disaster risk reduction and management, its role in disaster preparedness and recovery, IoT-enabled early warning systems, and innovative solutions for disaster resilience and emergency response.

Table 1. IoT applications in disaster risk reduction and management.

Category	Technologies & Methods	Applications	Case Studies	Challenges & Solutions
Seismic Sensors	Accelerometers, geophones, AI algorithms	Early earthquake detection, emergency alerts	- Japan's EEW system (10-20 sec warnings) - Mexico City's SASMex (60 sec warnings) - Istanbul's AI-based seismic network	- False Alarms: ML models filter noise - Rural Coverage: Satellite-linked sensors
Flood Monitoring Sensors	Ultrasonic level sensors, acoustic Doppler sensors, AI-based predictive models	Flood early warnings, real-time water level tracking	- Netherlands' Smart Delta Platform - Jakarta's IoT-based drainage system	- Sensor Maintenance: Self-cleaning sensors - Data Latency: LPWAN networks
IoT-Enabled Weather Stations	Distributed sensor networks, drones, satellite integration	Hyperlocal weather forecasting, storm warnings, climate monitoring	- India's IMD Smart Weather Grid - Phoenix's heatwave mitigation system	- Data Overload: Edge computing - Interoperability: Standardized data models
AI & Data Analytics Integration	Predictive analytics, automated decision-making, real-time public alerts	Enhancing disaster response efficiency, resource management	- California's ALERTWildfire (fire prediction) - EU's EFAS (flood alerts)	- Computing Power: AI-driven processing - Communication Gaps: Multi-language alerts
Future Frontiers	5G, self-healing networks, citizen science initiatives	Real-time analytics, autonomous response systems	- Puerto Rico's self-rerouting power grid	- Scalability: Open-source sensor networks
Infrastructure Monitoring	Vibration sensors, strain gauges, AI-powered SHM systems	Detecting structural weaknesses in bridges, buildings, and pipelines	- Golden Gate Bridge SHM system - Tokyo skyscrapers' seismic dampers	- Sensor Durability: Self-healing materials - Data Integration: Unified platforms
Pipeline Monitoring	Acoustic sensors, corrosion detectors, smart pigging robots	Leak detection, earthquake-proofing pipelines	- Barcelona's smart water network - Japan's seismic shutoff valves	- Power Supply: Energy-harvesting sensors - Cybersecurity: Blockchain encryption
Transportation Networks	Smart traffic lights, bridge sensors, railway track monitoring	Disaster-resilient road& rail systems	- Netherlands' flood-proof smart highways	- Scalability: Public-private partnerships

continued on following page

Table 1. Continued

Category	Technologies & Methods	Applications	Case Studies	Challenges & Solutions
Emergency Response	Wearable sensors, real-time health monitoring, GPS tracking	First responder safety, real-time situational awareness	- California's wildfire response - Türkiye's earthquake rescue operations	- Battery Life: Efficient power solutions - Privacy: Encrypted data transmission
Resource & Asset Tracking	RFID tags, GPS trackers, AI-based logistics management	Optimizing emergency supply distribution	- Florida's hurricane response - Drone-based medical deliveries	- Network Reliability: Satellite-linked IoT
Post-Disaster Recovery	Drone surveys, smart grids, community IoT platforms	Damage assessment, infrastructure restoration	- Christchurch earthquake recovery	- Data Overload: AI-driven data analytics

3 THE ROLE OF AI IN DISASTER RISK REDUCTION AND MANAGEMENT

Disaster Risk Reduction and Management (DRRM) is a crucial field that aims to minimize the impact of natural and man-made disasters on human lives, infrastructure, and the environment. With the increasing frequency and intensity of disasters due to climate change and urbanization, there is a growing need for innovative solutions to enhance disaster preparedness, response, and recovery. Artificial Intelligence (AI) has emerged as a powerful tool in DRRM, offering new ways to predict, manage, and mitigate disaster effects. AI plays a crucial role in predictive analytics and risk assessment, providing real-time data to optimize emergency resource allocation and evacuation routes. AI-powered image recognition algorithms can also assist in post-disaster recovery and reconstruction by analyzing damage assessments, prioritizing repairs, and optimizing rebuilding efforts. AI-powered image recognition algorithms can also optimize the planning and scheduling of reconstruction projects, considering factors such as resource availability, budget constraints, and community needs(Kuglitsch et al., 2022; Abid et al., 2021; Dai et al., 2024; Munawar et al., 2022).

3.1 AI for Predictive Analytics and Risk Assessment

Predicting disasters before they occur is one of the most critical aspects of disaster risk management. AI, particularly machine learning (ML) and deep learning algorithms, has the capacity to analyze massive datasets, identify trends, and forecast potential disaster events with high accuracy. By leveraging satellite imagery, sensor data, climate models, and historical disaster records, AI can enhance predictive analytics and risk assessments in followingkeyways(Baltazar et al., 2024; El Morr et al., 2024; Lombardi et al., 2022; Albahri et al., 2024).

- **Risk Assessment:** AI-driven risk assessment tools can evaluate the vulnerability of various regions by analyzing historical disaster data, geographical factors, urban infrastructure, and environmental conditions. These models can predict which areas are most at risk for floods, earthquakes, or other disasters, allowing authorities to implement proactive measures such as infrastructure reinforcements and early warning systems.
- **Predictive Analytics:** AI can simulate disaster scenarios, predicting the spread of wildfires, the trajectory of hurricanes, the likelihood of landslides, and even the potential impact of earthquakes. By using real-time data, AI systems can generate forecasts with improved accuracy, enabling governments and organizations to act before a disaster escalates.
- **Early Warning Systems:** AI-powered early warning systems can detect anomalies in weather patterns, seismic activity, and other risk indicators. For example, AI models trained on oceanic and atmospheric data can predict hurricanes and typhoons weeks in advance, allowing communities to prepare for potential impacts.
- **Epidemic and Pandemic Prediction:** AI is also being used to monitor and predict disease outbreaks by analyzing health reports, social media trends, and travel patterns. This capability is crucial for responding to public health crises that may arise in the aftermath of a disaster.

By providing accurate risk assessments and predictions, AI helps authorities implement disaster preparedness measures, allocate resources efficiently, and potentially save countless lives.

3.2 AI for Decision Support and Resource Allocation

During a disaster, swift and effective decision-making is essential to minimize loss of life and property damage. AI can process vast amounts of real-time data from various sources, including social media, satellite feeds, IoT sensors, and emergency reports, to support critical decision-making. AI-driven systems enhance decision-making and resource allocation in following several ways(Aboualola et al., 2023; Damaševičius et al., 2023; Abid et al., 2021; Asokan et al., 2024).

- **Resource Allocation:** AI algorithms optimize the distribution of emergency resources such as medical supplies, food, water, and rescue personnel. By analyzing affected areas' needs, infrastructure conditions, and transportation routes, AI ensures that resources are sent where they are needed most, reducing delays and inefficiencies.
- **Evacuation Planning:** AI models analyze population density, traffic patterns, weather conditions, and disaster trajectories to recommend optimal evacuation routes. This minimizes congestion and ensures people can evacuate safely and efficiently. AI-powered traffic management systems can also adjust traffic signals dynamically to facilitate smoother evacuation flows.
- **Real-Time Monitoring and Analysis:** AI-powered drones and satellite imagery provide real-time situational awareness, helping emergency responders assess damage, locate trapped individuals, and identify high-risk zones. AI can also analyze social media data to detect distress signals, identify emerging crises, and coordinate responses.
- **Automated Communication Systems:** AI-powered chatbots and virtual assistants can provide real-time updates, safety instructions, and emergency contact information to affected populations, ensuring that communities stay informed during crises.

With AI-enhanced decision-making, authorities and emergency responders can react more swiftly and effectively, reducing the overall impact of disasters(Abbass, Abbas, Wani, & Akhai, 2025).

3.3 AI for Post-Disaster Recovery and Reconstruction

After a disaster, recovery and reconstruction efforts require careful planning, resource management, and prioritization. AI can play a crucial role in streamlining these efforts by analyzing damage assessments, predicting recovery timelines, and optimizing rebuilding processes.

- **Damage Assessment:** AI-powered image recognition algorithms can analyze satellite images, drone footage, and street-level photographs to assess the extent of damage to buildings, roads, bridges, and other infrastructure. This automated analysis speeds up damage assessments, reducing reliance on manual inspections and allowing relief efforts to begin sooner.

- **Infrastructure Prioritization:** AI can analyze affected communities' needs, structural integrity reports, and economic impact data to prioritize which infrastructure repairs should be addressed first. This ensures that critical facilities, such as hospitals, power grids, and transportation networks, are restored promptly.
- **Reconstruction Planning:** AI-driven simulations can model various reconstruction scenarios, optimizing rebuilding strategies based on resource availability, environmental factors, and urban planning considerations. These models help governments and organizations make data-driven decisions to rebuild more resilient communities.
- **Mental Health and Social Recovery:** AI-powered chatbots and virtual counseling services can provide mental health support to disaster survivors by offering counseling, resources, and coping strategies. AI can also analyze social data to identify communities that require additional psychological and social support.

By integrating AI into post-disaster recovery, communities can rebuild faster, stronger, and more sustainably, reducing the long-term impact of disasters(Rawat et al., 2024; Puri et al., 2024; Habibi Rad et al., 2021).

3.4 Challenges and Ethical Considerations of AI in DRRM

While AI offers significant advantages in disaster risk reduction and management, it is not without challenges and ethical concerns. Some key issues include:

- **Data Limitations and Bias:** AI models require large, high-quality datasets to function effectively. Incomplete or biased data can lead to inaccurate predictions and poor decision-making.
- **Privacy Concerns:** The use of AI for surveillance, tracking, and social media monitoring during disasters raises ethical concerns regarding privacy and data security.
- **Infrastructure and Accessibility Issues:** Developing nations may lack the technological infrastructure and resources needed to implement AI-driven disaster management solutions.
- **Dependence on AI:** Over-reliance on AI systems may lead to complacency, reducing human oversight and critical thinking in disaster response efforts.
- **Ethical Deployment:** AI should be designed and implemented in ways that prioritize humanitarian needs, ensuring fair and equitable distribution of disaster relief resources.

Addressing these challenges requires collaboration between governments, tech companies, humanitarian organizations, and local communities to develop ethical and effective AI solutions for DRRM(Ona & Lallana, 2021; Baraldo& Di Franco, 2024; Kharel et al., 2022; Akhai, 2024; Akhai & Kumar, 2024).

Table 2 explores the use of AI in disaster risk reduction and management, its role in improving preparedness and response, AI-powered innovations for mitigation and recovery, and its transformation in disaster management, including its functions, benefits, and challenges.

Table 2. AI applications in disaster risk reduction and management.

AI Application	Function	Benefits	Examples	Challenges
Predictive Analytics & Risk Assessment	Analyzes big data to forecast disasters & assess risks	Early warnings, proactive disaster mitigation	AI-driven weather forecasting, seismic activity prediction	Data quality, computational limitations
Decision Support & Resource Allocation	Optimizes resource distribution & emergency response	Faster response times, efficient allocation of aid	AI-powered evacuation route planning, emergency chatbot systems	Ethical AI use, infrastructure limitations
Post-Disaster Recovery & Reconstruction	Assists in damage assessment & reconstruction planning	Faster recovery, smarter rebuilding strategies	AI-powered image recognition for damage assessment, reconstruction simulation	Data privacy, reliance on AI models
Automated Communication Systems	Provides real-time disaster updates & assistance	Ensures timely information & improved coordination	AI chatbots for emergency helplines, crisis information bots	Language barriers, misinformation risks
Epidemic & Pandemic Prediction	Monitors & predicts disease outbreaks	Early intervention, reduced spread of diseases	AI-based health surveillance, outbreak trend analysis	Privacy concerns, reliance on available health data

4 THE ROLE OF DATA ANALYTICS IN DISASTER RISK REDUCTION AND MANAGEMENT

Data analytics is a vital tool in Disaster Risk Reduction and Management (DRRM) by enabling the collection, processing, and interpretation of vast amounts of data. It provides decision-makers with deeper insights into disaster patterns, risks, and response effectiveness. By integrating data from various sources like IoT devices, satellite imagery, government databases, and social media, data analytics enhances disaster preparedness, response, and recovery efforts. This allows for the creation of detailed maps of disaster risks, vulnerabilities, and impacts, enabling decision-makers to visualize and understand complex data. Real-time dashboards display key metrics, enabling more informed decision-making. Social media and crowdsourced data analysis provide valuable real-time information during disasters, allowing for actionable insights like sentiment analysis and crowdsourced damage assessment. Predictive modeling and scenario analysis are also essential in disaster risk reduction, allowing for scenario planning and cost-benefit analysis, helping decision-makers prioritize investments(Shah et al., 2019; Akter & Wamba, 2019; Sarker et al., 2020).

4.1 Data Integration and Visualization

One of the key benefits of data analytics in DRRM is its ability to integrate and visualize data from multiple sources, creating a comprehensive and real-time understanding of disaster risks and impacts. Advanced data processing techniques allow for seamless aggregation of information, ensuring that decision-makers have accurate and timely insights(Ahmed et al., 2024; Miller et al., 2025; Lawal et al., 2025).

- **Geospatial Analysis:** Geographic Information System (GIS)-based data analytics can generate detailed maps that illustrate disaster risks, vulnerabilities, and affected regions. By overlaying multiple data layers, authorities can assess risk-prone areas and plan mitigation measures accordingly.
- **Real-Time Dashboards:** Data analytics platforms can display critical real-time metrics such as weather patterns, seismic activity, infrastructure damage, and emergency response actions. These dashboards provide decision-makers with a centralized interface for monitoring disaster situations and making informed choices.
- **Big Data Integration:** Combining large datasets from sources like remote sensors, government agencies, and private entities enhances risk assessment accuracy. Predictive insights derived from historical disaster patterns enable proactive disaster management strategies.
- **AI-Powered Anomaly Detection:** Advanced analytics powered by artificial intelligence can detect anomalies in environmental patterns, such as unexpected temperature changes or seismic shifts, which may indicate potential disasters. This capability enables earlier warnings and improved preparedness.

By improving data integration and visualization, analytics tools empower policymakers and emergency responders to act quickly and efficiently in the face of disaster threats.

4.2 Social Media and Crowdsourced Data Analysis

In the digital era, social media platforms and crowdsourced data provide valuable real-time information during disasters. The ability to analyze this data effectively can improve situational awareness and emergency response strategies(Acikara et al., 2023; Karimiziarani, 2023; Chukwu et al., 2024).

- **Sentiment Analysis:** Data analytics can be applied to social media posts to assess public sentiment and identify urgent needs. Analyzing keywords, hashtags, and user-generated content helps authorities detect distress signals and areas requiring immediate attention.
- **Crowdsourced Damage Assessment:** Citizens often share images, videos, and firsthand reports of disasters on social media. Data analytics tools can process this crowdsourced information to evaluate damage levels and direct response teams to the most affected locations.
- **Disaster Misinformation Detection:** Social media can sometimes spread misinformation, which can hinder response efforts. Data analytics can help verify facts by cross-referencing official reports and filtering out misleading information.
- **Community Engagement and Coordination:**Analyzing community-driven disaster reports fosters better coordination between authorities and affected populations. Platforms like crisis maps, where users report conditions in real-time, contribute to more accurate and efficient response planning.

By leveraging social media and crowdsourced data, disaster management teams can enhance communication, monitor evolving crises, and ensure targeted resource deployment.

4.3 Predictive Modeling and Scenario Analysis

Predictive modeling and scenario analysis are powerful applications of data analytics that allow authorities to anticipate disaster impacts and develop proactive strategies. These techniques improve decision-making by simulating potential disaster outcomes and evaluating risk reduction measures.

- **Scenario Planning:** Data analytics can create simulations of different disaster scenarios, such as earthquakes, floods, wildfires, or hurricanes. By analyzing factors like population density, land use, and infrastructure resilience, authorities can assess potential consequences and refine emergency response plans.

- **Machine Learning for Disaster Forecasting:** AI-driven predictive models analyze historical disaster data to forecast future occurrences. For example, flood prediction models consider rainfall patterns, soil moisture, and topographical data to estimate flood severity and location.
- **Cost-Benefit Analysis:** Evaluating the costs and benefits of disaster risk reduction measures helps governments prioritize investments. By using predictive models, decision-makers can determine the economic feasibility of interventions such as building reinforcements, flood barriers, or early warning systems.
- **Climate Change Impact Analysis:** As climate change intensifies the frequency and severity of disasters, data analytics helps assess long-term trends and vulnerabilities. These insights support adaptive strategies to build more resilient communities.
- **Optimization of Emergency Drills:** Data-driven simulations help optimize emergency response drills, ensuring that first responders and communities are adequately prepared for real disaster events.

Predictive analytics and scenario analysis provide actionable intelligence that enhances disaster preparedness, mitigates risks, and strengthens overall resilience against future calamities(Merz et al., 2020; Mechler et al., 2014; Habib et al., 2024). **Table 3** discusses the use of data analytics in disaster risk reduction, its enhancement of disaster preparedness, response, and recovery, its integration with AI for smarter disaster management, and data-driven strategies for effective disaster mitigation and response.

Table 3. Data analytics applications in disaster risk reduction and management.

Application	Description	Benefits	Examples
Geospatial Analysis for Risk Mapping	Uses GIS and satellite data to create detailed maps showing disaster-prone areas, vulnerabilities, and infrastructure risks.	Helps in proactive planning, identifies high-risk zones, and aids in efficient resource allocation.	GIS-based flood maps, earthquake risk zoning, wildfire susceptibility analysis.
Real-Time Dashboards for Disaster Monitoring	Integrates data from sensors, weather stations, and emergency reports to provide a real-time overview of disaster conditions.	Enables rapid decision-making, improves coordination, and enhances public communication.	Live earthquake monitoring, hurricane tracking dashboards, fire spread prediction systems.
Social Media Sentiment Analysis	Analyzes social media posts, hashtags, and emergency tweets to identify distress signals and areas needing urgent assistance.	Provides real-time situational awareness, improves emergency response, and detects misinformation.	AI-driven crisis maps, emergency social media monitoring, disaster rumor detection.
Crowdsourced Damage Assessment	Gathers real-time images, videos, and reports from citizens to assess disaster impact and prioritize response efforts.	Speeds up damage assessment, reduces dependence on manual inspections, and directs aid more effectively.	User-reported disaster heatmaps, AI image analysis of destruction, mobile-based damage surveys.
AI-Powered Anomaly Detection	Uses machine learning to identify unusual weather patterns, seismic activities, and other environmental anomalies.	Enables earlier disaster warnings, minimizes false alarms, and improves forecasting accuracy.	AI-based tsunami prediction, temperature anomaly detection, seismic wave pattern analysis.
Predictive Modeling for Disaster Forecasting	Uses historical data and climate models to simulate disaster scenarios and predict their likelihood and impact.	Enhances preparedness, allows proactive risk mitigation, and reduces economic losses.	AI-based flood forecasting, landslide risk prediction, drought impact assessments.
Cost-Benefit Analysis for Disaster Preparedness	Evaluates the economic viability of risk reduction measures to optimize budget allocation.	Helps in prioritizing investments in disaster resilience and mitigation strategies.	Comparison of infrastructure reinforcement costs vs. potential disaster damages.
Optimization of Evacuation Routes	Uses traffic, population density, and weather data to generate the safest and fastest evacuation plans.	Reduces congestion, minimizes casualties, and improves emergency logistics.	AI-driven traffic management, real-time evacuation route planning, smart disaster response navigation.
Climate Change Impact Analysis	Examines long-term environmental trends to assess future disaster risks and vulnerabilities.	Supports adaptive policy-making, improves infrastructure resilience, and informs disaster risk insurance models.	Sea-level rise predictions, changing hurricane intensities, urban heat island analysis.

continued on following page

Table 3. Continued

Application	Description	Benefits	Examples
Emergency Resource Allocation Optimization	Uses data analytics to distribute medical aid, food, and relief supplies efficiently based on real-time needs.	Reduces wastage, ensures fair distribution, and improves disaster recovery speed.	AI-driven relief logistics, real-time supply chain tracking, drone-assisted aid delivery.
Automated Misinformation Detection	Identifies and filters out fake news and misleading information during disasters.	Ensures accurate information reaches affected populations, prevents panic, and supports fact-based decision-making.	AI fact-checking tools, automated news verification, misinformation tracking dashboards.
Post-Disaster Recovery Planning	Uses data to prioritize rebuilding efforts and assess long-term economic impacts.	Ensures efficient allocation of recovery funds, speeds up rebuilding, and improves infrastructure resilience.	AI-driven reconstruction scheduling, economic impact analysis of disasters, infrastructure damage prediction models.
Ethical AI and Data Privacy Considerations	Addresses biases in AI models, ensures responsible use of disaster-related data, and protects privacy.	Builds public trust, ensures fair resource distribution, and prevents misuse of sensitive information.	Data security frameworks for disaster response, bias-correction algorithms, ethical AI deployment in crisis management.

4.4 Challenges and Ethical Considerations in Data Analytics for DRRM

Despite its transformative potential, the use of data analytics in disaster management comes with challenges and ethical considerations that must be addressed.

- **Data Privacy and Security:** Large-scale data collection, especially from social media and IoT devices, raises concerns about privacy and data protection. It is essential to establish ethical guidelines for the responsible use of disaster-related data.
- **Data Reliability and Accuracy:** Crowdsourced and social media data can sometimes be misleading or incomplete. Proper validation techniques must be employed to ensure the accuracy of the information used for decision-making.
- **Digital Divide and Accessibility:** Not all communities have equal access to digital tools and technologies. Governments and organizations should strive to bridge the digital divide to ensure that all regions benefit from data-driven disaster preparedness measures.
- **Interoperability of Data Sources:** Integrating data from multiple sources requires standardization and collaboration across different organizations and

sectors. Establishing common data-sharing frameworks is crucial for effective disaster response coordination.

Addressing these challenges will ensure that data analytics remains a reliable, ethical, and effective tool in disaster risk reduction and management(Kharel et al., 2022; Mani et al., 2023; Lokmic-Tomkins et al., 2023).

5 CHALLENGES AND FUTURE DIRECTIONS

The integration of IoT, AI, and data analytics into disaster risk reduction (DRRM) presents technical challenges like data quality, scalability, and cybersecurity. The growing reliance on digital technologies introduces new vulnerabilities, potentially disrupting critical systems during disasters. Ethical considerations include privacy, equity, and transparency in decision-making processes. The collection and analysis of data from IoT devices and social media raise concerns, especially if sensitive personal information is involved. Future directions for DRRM with emerging technologies include integrating technologies into a unified platform, citizen engagement through crowdsourced data, and global collaboration to enhance global resilience to disasters, particularly in the face of climate change and other global challenges(Alaghbari et al., 2022; Aboualola et al., 2023; Munawar et al., 2022). Also data optimization using statistical techniques could help in the development of predictive models (Kumar et al., 2024a, 2024b; Wadhwa et al., 2024).

5.1 Technical Challenges

While IoT, AI, and data analytics offer significant potential for DRRM, there are several technical challenges that need to be addressed, including:

- **Data Quality and Integration**: Ensuring the accuracy, reliability, and interoperability of data from diverse sources is critical for effective DRRM.
- **Scalability**: As urban areas grow, the volume of data generated by IoT devices and other sources will increase exponentially, requiring scalable solutions for data storage, processing, and analysis.
- **Cybersecurity**: The increasing reliance on digital technologies for DRRM introduces new vulnerabilities to cyberattacks, which could disrupt critical systems during a disaster.

5.2 Ethical and Social Challenges

The use of emerging technologies in DRRM also raises important ethical and social considerations, including:

- **Privacy**: The collection and analysis of data from IoT devices and social media can raise privacy concerns, particularly if sensitive personal information is involved.
- **Equity**: Ensuring that the benefits of emerging technologies are distributed equitably across different populations, including marginalized and vulnerable communities, is essential for building resilient cities.
- **Transparency and Accountability**: The use of AI and data analytics in decision-making processes must be transparent and accountable, with clear mechanisms for oversight and public participation.

5.3 Future Directions

Looking ahead, several trends are likely to shape the future of DRRM with emerging technologies(Arif & Akhai, 2024; Abbass et al., 2025):

- **Integration of Technologies**: The integration of IoT, AI, and data analytics into a unified DRRM platform will enable more comprehensive and coordinated approaches to disaster risk reduction and management.
- **Citizen Engagement**: The use of crowdsourced data and participatory approaches to DRRM will empower citizens to play a more active role in building resilient communities.
- **Global Collaboration**: The sharing of data, tools, and best practices across cities and countries will enhance global resilience to disasters, particularly in the face of climate change and other global challenges

6 ACTIONABLE POLICY RECOMMENDATIONS

To enhance disaster resilience through emerging technologies, several policy recommendations can be implemented. The visual representation of smart technologies for disaster response is presented in **Figure 1.Table 4** discusses policy recommendations for disaster resilience, technology enhancement, emerging technologies in disaster management, technological disaster preparedness strategies, and innovative disaster risk reduction approaches.

Figure 1. AI and IoT-enabled disaster response workflow.

First, strengthening IoT infrastructure is crucial. Governments should invest in nationwide IoT networks to monitor natural disasters in real time, mandate IoT integration in critical infrastructure, enhance early warning systems, standardize data collection protocols, and address privacy and security concerns. Second, leveraging artificial intelligence can improve disaster preparedness and response. This includes developing AI-driven decision support systems, implementing AI-powered damage assessment tools, integrating AI in emergency communication systems, and encouraging research in AI ethics. Third, enhancing data analytics for disaster risk management involves creating a unified data sharing platform, incorporating geospatial and big data analytics, improving social media and crowdsourced data utilization, and ensuring ethical use of data analytics. Fourth, integrating smart infrastructure for urban resilience is essential. Policies should mandate smart infrastructure standards, promote predictive maintenance programs, develop resilient transportation networks, and adopt smart energy grids for disaster recovery. Fifth, fostering public-private collaboration and capacity building can be achieved by encouraging public-private partnerships, providing training for emergency responders, promoting community-based disaster resilience programs, and allocating funding for innovation in disaster technology. Finally, strengthening policy frameworks for emerging technologies in disaster risk management includes developing legal and regulatory frameworks, creating incentives for the adoption of smart disaster technologies, implementing international collaboration mechanisms, and regularly updating disaster management strategies.

Table 4. Policy Recommendations for Disaster Resilience.

Policy Recommendations	*Actions*
Strengthening IoT Infrastructure for Disaster Risk Reduction	- Invest in Nationwide IoT Networks: Establish and maintain national IoT sensor networks to monitor seismic activity, floods, and extreme weather conditions in real time. - Mandate IoT Integration in Critical Infrastructure: Develop policies requiring IoT-based structural health monitoring systems for bridges, pipelines, and high-risk buildings. - Enhance Early Warning Systems (EWS): Expand the deployment of IoT-enabled EWS for natural disasters and integrate them with AI-driven predictive analytics to reduce false alarms and improve response times. - Standardize Data Collection Protocols: Implement uniform standards for IoT data collection, transmission, and storage to ensure interoperability across agencies and jurisdictions. - Address Privacy and Security Concerns: Enforce strict cybersecurity policies for IoT networks to protect against data breaches and cyber threats.
Leveraging Artificial Intelligence for Disaster Preparedness and Response	- Develop AI-Driven Decision Support Systems: Encourage the use of AI-powered predictive analytics to assess risks, allocate resources efficiently, and simulate disaster scenarios. - Implement AI-Powered Damage Assessment Tools: Utilize AI image recognition algorithms for rapid post-disaster damage assessments and prioritization of recovery efforts. - Integrate AI in Emergency Communication Systems: Deploy AI-powered chatbots and virtual assistants to provide real-time information to the public during crises. - Encourage Research in AI Ethics for Disaster Management: Establish guidelines to address AI biases, data limitations, and the risks of over-reliance on automated systems.
Enhancing Data Analytics for Disaster Risk Management (DRM)	- Create a Unified Data Sharing Platform: Foster collaboration between government agencies, private sector, and academia by developing a centralized data repository for disaster-related information. - Incorporate Geospatial and Big Data Analytics: Utilize geospatial analysis and big data integration for real-time disaster modeling, forecasting, and response coordination. - Improve Social Media and Crowdsourced Data Utilization: Develop AI-powered analytics tools to monitor social media platforms for situational awareness and emergency response. - Ensure Ethical Use of Data Analytics: Establish policies for responsible data collection, processing, and sharing to protect privacy and ensure transparency in decision-making.

continued on following page

Table 4. Continued

Policy Recommendations	*Actions*
Integrating Smart Infrastructure for Urban Resilience	- Mandate Smart Infrastructure Standards: Require smart drainage, flood control, and earthquake-resistant buildings equipped with IoT monitoring technologies in high-risk urban areas. - Promote Predictive Maintenance Programs: Encourage the use of IoT and AI for real-time monitoring of infrastructure health to prevent catastrophic failures. - Develop Resilient Transportation Networks: Implement smart traffic management systems with IoT-enabled traffic lights, bridge monitoring, and railway track sensors for disaster preparedness. - Adopt Smart Energy Grids for Disaster Recovery: Encourage the deployment of AI-powered energy grids that automatically adjust power distribution during disasters.
Fostering Public-Private Collaboration and Capacity Building	- Encourage Public-Private Partnerships (PPPs): Facilitate collaboration between governments, technology firms, and research institutions to enhance technological adoption in disaster management. - Provide Training for Emergency Responders: Develop specialized programs to train first responders and disaster management personnel in the use of AI, IoT, and data analytics tools. - Promote Community-Based Disaster Resilience Programs: Empower local communities by integrating crowdsourced data and participatory disaster planning into municipal strategies. - Allocate Funding for Innovation in Disaster Technology: Establish dedicated funding programs to support research and development in emerging disaster resilience technologies.
Strengthening Policy Frameworks for Emerging Technologies in DRM	- Develop Legal and Regulatory Frameworks: Establish policies governing the ethical and responsible use of AI, IoT, and data analytics in disaster risk management. - Create Incentives for Adoption of Smart Disaster Technologies: Provide tax breaks and subsidies for organizations implementing advanced disaster resilience solutions. - Implement International Collaboration Mechanisms: Foster cross-border cooperation in technology-driven disaster preparedness, including data sharing and joint research initiatives. - Regularly Update DRM Strategies: Continuously review and update national disaster management plans to incorporate advancements in AI, IoT, and data analytics.

By implementing these recommendations, governments and organizations can harness emerging technologies to enhance disaster resilience, improve emergency response efficiency, and mitigate risks associated with urbanization, climate change, and infrastructure vulnerabilities.

7. CONCLUSIONS

- Emerging technologies like the Internet of Things (IoT), artificial intelligence (AI), and advanced data analytics are revolutionizing disaster risk reduction and management (DRRM). These technologies enable cities to transition from reactive crisis management to anticipatory risk mitigation, safeguarding lives, infrastructure, and ecosystems. However, realizing this transformative potential requires overcoming technical, ethical, and logistical challenges while fostering cross-sector collaboration and equitable access to innovation.

- IoT-enabled sensors and networks transform cities into interconnected, responsive systems, providing real-time infrastructure monitoring and early warning systems for floods or earthquakes. AI is revolutionizing DRRM at every stage, from predictive analytics to post-disaster recovery. However, AI's effectiveness relies on high-quality data, algorithmic transparency, and ethical governance to prevent biases in risk modeling or resource distribution. Strategic implementation and public trust are essential to maximize AI's lifesaving potential.
- Data analytics synthesize disparate information streams into actionable insights for DRRM, identifying vulnerable populations, planning for compound risks, optimizing aid distribution, and tracking recovery progress. Challenges persist, such as data silos, privacy concerns, and the need for interoperable platforms. Prioritizing ethical frameworks and open-data initiatives can help cities harness analytics to build adaptive, equitable resilience strategies.
- The convergence of IoT, AI, and data analytics offers a holistic toolkit for disaster resilience, but success depends on interdisciplinary collaboration, ethical governance, infrastructure investment, and public engagement. By integrating these technologies responsibly, cities can mitigate risks, reduce recovery costs, and protect vulnerable populations, transforming urban landscapes into agile, inclusive, and sustainable ecosystems. As climate change accelerates, embracing innovation while addressing its complexities will define humanity's ability to forge a safer, more resilient future.

REFERENCES

Abbas, M., Akhai, S., Abbas, U., Jafri, R., & Arif, S. M. (2025). Ai-enabled sustainable urban planning and management. In *Real-World Applications of AI Innovation* (pp. 233–260). IGI Global Scientific Publishing.

Abbass, M., Abbas, U., Jafri, R., Arif, S. M., & Akhai, S. (2025). AI and Machine Learning Applications in Sustainable Smart Cities. In *Sustainable Smart Cities and the Future of Urban Development* (pp. 1–32). IGI Global Scientific Publishing.

Abbass, M., Abbas, U., Wani, S. A., & Akhai, S. (2025). Rethinking Global Food Governance From Historical Perspectives for a Sustainable Future. In *Innovative Trends Shaping Food Marketing and Consumption* (pp. 553–578). IGI Global Scientific Publishing. DOI: 10.4018/979-8-3693-8542-5.ch022

Abdalzaher, M. S., Krichen, M., & Falcone, F. (2024). Leveraging internet of things and emerging technologies for earthquake disaster management: Challenges and future directions. *Progress in Disaster Science*, •••, 100347. DOI: 10.1016/j.pdisas.2024.100347

Abdalzaher, M. S., Krichen, M., Yiltas-Kaplan, D., Ben Dhaou, I., & Adoni, W. Y. H. (2023). Early detection of earthquakes using iot and cloud infrastructure: A survey. *Sustainability (Basel)*, *15*(15), 11713. DOI: 10.3390/su151511713

Abdalzaher, M. S., Krichen, M., Yiltas-Kaplan, D., Ben Dhaou, I., & Adoni, W. Y. H. (2023). Early detection of earthquakes using iot and cloud infrastructure: A survey. *Sustainability (Basel)*, *15*(15), 11713. DOI: 10.3390/su151511713

Abid, S. K., Sulaiman, N., Chan, S. W., Nazir, U., Abid, M., Han, H., Ariza-Montes, A., & Vega-Muñoz, A. (2021). Toward an integrated disaster management approach: How artificial intelligence can boost disaster management. *Sustainability (Basel)*, *13*(22), 12560. DOI: 10.3390/su132212560

Abid, S. K., Sulaiman, N., Chan, S. W., Nazir, U., Abid, M., Han, H., Ariza-Montes, A., & Vega-Muñoz, A. (2021). Toward an integrated disaster management approach: How artificial intelligence can boost disaster management. *Sustainability (Basel)*, *13*(22), 12560. DOI: 10.3390/su132212560

Aboualola, M., Abualsaud, K., Khattab, T., Zorba, N., & Hassanein, H. S. (2023). Edge technologies for disaster management: A survey of social media and artificial intelligence integration. *IEEE Access : Practical Innovations, Open Solutions*, *11*, 73782–73802. DOI: 10.1109/ACCESS.2023.3293035

Aboualola, M., Abualsaud, K., Khattab, T., Zorba, N., & Hassanein, H. S. (2023). Edge technologies for disaster management: A survey of social media and artificial intelligence integration. *IEEE Access : Practical Innovations, Open Solutions*, *11*, 73782–73802. DOI: 10.1109/ACCESS.2023.3293035

Acikara, T., Xia, B., Yigitcanlar, T., & Hon, C. (2023). Contribution of social media analytics to disaster response effectiveness: A systematic review of the literature. *Sustainability (Basel)*, *15*(11), 8860. DOI: 10.3390/su15118860

Adachi, T., Kusunoki, K., Yoshida, S., Arai, K. I., & Ushio, T. (2016). High-speed volumetric observation of a wet microburst using X-band phased array weather radar in Japan. *Monthly Weather Review*, *144*(10), 3749–3765. DOI: 10.1175/MWR-D-16-0125.1

Ahmed, I., Asif, M., Alhelou, H. H., & Khalid, M. (2024). A review on enhancing energy efficiency and adaptability through system integration for smart buildings. *Journal of Building Engineering*, •••, 109354.

Ahmed, S. (2022). *Resilient IoT-based monitoring system for the nigerian oil and gas industry* (Doctoral dissertation, INSA de Lyon).

Akhai, S. (2023). From Black Boxes to Transparent Machines: The Quest for Explainable AI. *Available at: Social Science Research Network, doi: http://dx.doi.org/* DOI: 10.2139/ssrn.4390887

Akhai, S. (2023). Healthcare record management for healthcare 4.0 via blockchain: a review of current applications, opportunities, challenges, and future potential. In *Blockchain for Healthcare 4.0* (Vol. 1, pp. 211–223). CRC Press. DOI: 10.1201/9781003408246-11

Akhai, S. (2024). Innovating Healthcare Delivery: Harnessing Drones for Medical Services. In *Modelling of Virtual Worlds Using the Internet of Things* (Vol. 1, pp. 232-250). CRC Press.

Akhai, S. (2024). Smart Home Environment for Society: An Overview of IoT-Enabled Air Conditioners. In *Modelling of Virtual Worlds Using the Internet of Things* (Vol. 1, pp. 74-87). CRC Press.

Akhai, S. (2024). Towards Trustworthy and Reliable AI The Next Frontier. In *Explainable Artificial Intelligence (XAI) in Healthcare* (Vol. 1, pp. 119-129). CRC Press, Taylor & Francis Group.

Akhai, S., & Abbass, M. (2025). Toward Resilient Futures: The Role of AI-Driven Strategies in Climate Adaptation. In *Nexus of AI, Climatology, and Urbanism for Smart Cities* (pp. 325-340). IGI Global Scientific Publishing.

Akhai, S., & Khang, A. (2024). Energy Efficiency and Human Comfort: AI and IoT Integration in Hospital HVAC Systems. *Medical Robotics and AI-Assisted Diagnostics for a High-Tech Healthcare Industry*, 93-108.

Akhai, S., & Khang, A. (2024). Innovations in Medical Manufacturing: A Review of 3D Printing, Robotics, and Internet of Things (IoT). In *The Quantum Evolution* (Vol. 1, pp. 226-241). CRC Press.

Akhai, S., & Kumar, V. (2024). Quantum resilience and distributed trust: The promise of blockchain and quantum computing in defense. In *Sustainable Security Practices Using Blockchain, Quantum and Post-Quantum Technologies for Real Time Applications* (pp. 125-153). Springer Nature Singapore.

Akhai, S., & Wadhwa, A. S. (2024). Wireless networking solutions for climate control and comfort in modern air conditioning systems. In *Intelligent Networks* (pp. 165–181). CRC Press. DOI: 10.1201/9781003541363-11

Akter, S., & Wamba, S. F. (2019). Big data and disaster management: A systematic review and agenda for future research. *Annals of Operations Research*, *283*(1-2), 939–959. DOI: 10.1007/s10479-017-2584-2

Al-Rimawi, T., & Nadler, M. (2025). Leveraging Smart City Technologies for Enhanced Real Estate Development: An Integrative Review. *Smart Cities*, *8*(1), 10. DOI: 10.3390/smartcities8010010

Al Shafian, S., & Hu, D. (2024). Integrating machine learning and remote sensing in disaster management: A decadal review of post-disaster building damage assessment. *Buildings (Basel, Switzerland)*, *14*(8), 2344. DOI: 10.3390/buildings14082344

Alaghbari, K. A., Saad, M. H. M., Hussain, A., & Alam, M. R. (2022). Complex event processing for physical and cyber security in datacentres-recent progress, challenges and recommendations. *Journal of Cloud Computing (Heidelberg, Germany)*, *11*(1), 65. DOI: 10.1186/s13677-022-00338-x

Alauthman, M., Aldweesh, A., & Al-Qerem, A. (2024, February). IoT security challenges in modern smart cities. In *2024 2nd International Conference on Cyber Resilience (ICCR)* (pp. 1-6). IEEE. DOI: 10.1109/ICCR61006.2024.10533174

Albahri, A. S., Khaleel, Y. L., Habeeb, M. A., Ismael, R. D., Hameed, Q. A., Deveci, M., Homod, R. Z., Albahri, O. S., Alamoodi, A. H., & Alzubaidi, L. (2024). A systematic review of trustworthy artificial intelligence applications in natural disasters. *Computers & Electrical Engineering*, *118*, 109409. DOI: 10.1016/j.compeleceng.2024.109409

Aldegheishem, A., Alrajeh, N., García, L., & Lloret, J. (2022). SWAP: Smart water protocol for the irrigation of urban gardens in smart cities. *IEEE Access : Practical Innovations, Open Solutions, 10*, 39239–39247. DOI: 10.1109/ACCESS.2022.3165579

Arif, S. M., & Akhai, S. (2024). Fostering a Sustainable and Disaster-Resilient Transportation Infrastructure. In *Challenges, Strategies, and Resiliency in Disaster and Risk Management* (pp. 205-219). IGI Global Scientific Publishing. DOI: 10.4018/979-8-3693-2721-0.ch009

Asokan, A., Bhuvanesh, B., & Sandhiya, R. (2024, October). AI-Powered Disaster Data Calculation & SMS Alerting: An Overview. In *2024 2nd International Conference on Self Sustainable Artificial Intelligence Systems (ICSSAS)* (pp. 339-344). IEEE.

Balogun, A. L., Marks, D., Sharma, R., Shekhar, H., Balmes, C., Maheng, D., Arshad, A., & Salehi, P. (2020). Assessing the potentials of digitalization as a tool for climate change adaptation and sustainable development in urban centres. *Sustainable Cities and Society, 53*, 101888. DOI: 10.1016/j.scs.2019.101888

Baltazar, R., Florencio, B., Vicente, A., & Belizario, P. (2024). The Role of Artificial Intelligence in Disaster Prediction, Mitigation, and Response in the Philippines: Challenges and Opportunities. *International Journal of Artificial Intelligence, 11*(1), 37–51. DOI: 10.36079/lamintang.ijai-01101.675

Baraldo, M., & Di Franco, P. D. G. (2024). Place-centred emerging technologies for disaster management: A scoping review. *International Journal of Disaster Risk Reduction, 112*, 104782. DOI: 10.1016/j.ijdrr.2024.104782

Chug, S., & Nath, S. (2024). Recent advances in social weather, common alert protocol and dissemination services through APIs in India Meteorological Department. *Mausam (New Delhi), 75*(1), 283–294. DOI: 10.54302/mausam.v75i1.6146

Chukwu, M., Huang, X., Wang, S., Yang, D., & Ye, X. (2024). Crowdsourcing geographic information for terrorism-related disaster awareness and mitigation: Perspectives and challenges. *Geo-Spatial Information Science*, •••, 1–18.

Costa, D. G., Peixoto, J. P. J., Jesus, T. C., Portugal, P., Vasques, F., Rangel, E., & Peixoto, M. (2022). A survey of emergencies management systems in smart cities. *IEEE Access : Practical Innovations, Open Solutions, 10*, 61843–61872. DOI: 10.1109/ACCESS.2022.3180033

Dai, D., Bo, M., Ren, X., & Dai, K. (2024). Application and exploration of artificial intelligence technology in urban ecosystem-based disaster risk reduction: A scoping review. *Ecological Indicators, 158*, 111565. DOI: 10.1016/j.ecolind.2024.111565

Damaševičius, R., Bacanin, N., & Misra, S. (2023). From sensors to safety: Internet of Emergency Services (IoES) for emergency response and disaster management. *Journal of Sensor and Actuator Networks*, *12*(3), 41. DOI: 10.3390/jsan12030041

El Morr, C., Ozdemir, D., Asdaah, Y., Saab, A., El-Lahib, Y., & Sokhn, E. S. (2024). AI-based epidemic and pandemic early warning systems: A systematic scoping review. *Health Informatics Journal*, *30*(3), 14604582241275844. DOI: 10.1177/14604582241275844 PMID: 39172555

Firoozi, A. A., & Firoozi, A. A. (2024). *Neuromorphic Computing: Transforming Disaster Management and Resilience in Civil Engineering*. Springer Nature. DOI: 10.1007/978-3-031-65549-4

Fraga-Lamas, P., Fernández-Caramés, T. M., & Castedo, L. (2017). Towards the Internet of smart trains: A review on industrial IoT-connected railways. *Sensors (Basel)*, *17*(6), 1457. DOI: 10.3390/s17061457 PMID: 28635672

Freed, A., & Zimmerman, R. (2022). Urban systems and services: vulnerabilities and impact. *Climate change and US cities: Urban systems, sectors, and prospects for action*, 79.

Gobinath, A., Reshmika, K. S., & Sivakarthi, G. (2024). Predicting natural disasters with AI and machine learning. In *Utilizing AI and Machine Learning for Natural Disaster Management* (pp. 254–273). IGI Global.

Gotham, K. F., & Cheek, W. (2017). Post-disaster recovery and rebuilding. *The SAGE Handbook of the 21st Centur City, London*, 279-297.

Habib, M., Habib, A., Albzaie, M., & Farghal, A. (2024). Sustainability benefits of AI-based engineering solutions for infrastructure resilience in arid regions against extreme rainfall events. *Discover Sustainability*, *5*(1), 278. DOI: 10.1007/s43621-024-00500-2

Habibi Rad, M., Mojtahedi, M., & Ostwald, M. J. (2021). Industry 4.0, disaster risk management and infrastructure resilience: A systematic review and bibliometric analysis. *Buildings (Basel, Switzerland)*, *11*(9), 411. DOI: 10.3390/buildings11090411

İlerisoy, Z. Y., & Gökgöz, B. İ. (2024). Analysis of earthquake resilience factors for buildings: The case of Istanbul high-rise buildings. *Open House International*, *49*(4), 773–790. DOI: 10.1108/OHI-08-2023-0191

Iqbal, A., Shakeel, A., Rashid, A., & Kim, S. W. (2024). IoT and M2M Applications in Satellite Networks. In *Integrated Terrestrial and Non-Terrestrial Networks* (pp. 17–45). Springer Nature Switzerland.

Iqbal, U., Riaz, M. Z. B., Zhao, J., Barthelemy, J., & Perez, P. (2023). Drones for flood monitoring, mapping and detection: A bibliometric review. *Drones (Basel)*, *7*(1), 32. DOI: 10.3390/drones7010032

Kamal, M., & Mansoor, A. (2022, August). Structural health monitoring and IoT: opportunities and challenges. In *International Conference on Intelligence of Things* (pp. 3-15). Cham: Springer International Publishing. DOI: 10.1007/978-3-031-15063-0_1

Karimiziarani, M. (2023). Social media analytics in disaster response: A comprehensive review. *arXiv preprint arXiv:2307.04046.*

Kharel, U., Sigdel, A., Uprety, S., Ng'ong'a, T., & Ginting, J. I. (2022). Emerging technologies and innovation to reach out to vulnerable populations in Nepal. *Technology entrepreneurship and sustainable development*, 319-342.

Kostrzewski, M., & Melnik, R. (2021). Condition monitoring of rail transport systems: A bibliometric performance analysis and systematic literature review. *Sensors (Basel)*, *21*(14), 4710. DOI: 10.3390/s21144710 PMID: 34300450

Kuglitsch, M., Albayrak, A., Aquino, R., Craddock, A., Edward-Gill, J., Kanwar, R., & Luterbacher, J. (2022). Artificial intelligence for disaster risk reduction: Opportunities, challenges, and prospects. *Bulletin*, (71), 1.

Kumar, H., Wadhwa, A. S., Akhai, S., & Kaushik, A. (2024). Parametric analysis, modeling and optimization of the process parameters in electric discharge machining of aluminium metal matrix composite. *Engineering Research Express*, *6*(2), 025542. DOI: 10.1088/2631-8695/ad4ba9

Kumar, H., Wadhwa, A. S., Akhai, S., & Kaushik, A. (2024). Parametric optimization of the machining performance of Al-SiCp composite using combination of response surface methodology and desirability function. *Engineering Research Express*, *6*(2), 025505. DOI: 10.1088/2631-8695/ad38ff

Lawal, O. O., Nawari, N. O., & Lawal, O. (2025). AI-Enabled Cognitive Predictive Maintenance of Urban Assets Using City Information Modeling—Systematic Review. *Buildings (Basel, Switzerland)*, *15*(5), 690. DOI: 10.3390/buildings15050690

Liu, C., Zhang, J., Chen, K., Wang, M., Zou, Z., & Shi, Z. (2024). Remote Sensing Temporal Vision-Language Models: A Comprehensive Survey. *arXiv preprint arXiv:2412.02573.*

Lokmic-Tomkins, Z., Bhandari, D., Bain, C., Borda, A., Kariotis, T. C., & Reser, D. (2023). Lessons learned from natural disasters around digital health technologies and delivering quality healthcare. *International Journal of Environmental Research and Public Health, 20*(5), 4542. DOI: 10.3390/ijerph20054542 PMID: 36901559

Lombardi, R., Trequattrini, R., Cuozzo, B., & Manzari, A. (2022). Big data, artificial intelligence and epidemic disasters. A primary structured literature review. *International Journal of Applied Decision Sciences, 15*(2), 156–180. DOI: 10.1504/IJADS.2022.121559

Lozano, J. M., & Tien, I. (2023). Data collection tools for post-disaster damage assessment of building and lifeline infrastructure systems. *International Journal of Disaster Risk Reduction, 94*, 103819. DOI: 10.1016/j.ijdrr.2023.103819

Mala, S., Deep, U., Mala, E., & Akhai, S. (2025). Digital Health Technologies for Preventive Cardiology. In *Impact of Digital Solutions for Improved Healthcare Delivery* (pp. 379–400). IGI Global.

Mani, Z. A., Sultan, M. A. S., Plummer, V., & Goniewicz, K. (2023). Navigating interoperability in disaster management: Insights of current trends and challenges in Saudi Arabia. *International Journal of Disaster Risk Science, 14*(6), 873–885. DOI: 10.1007/s13753-023-00528-4

Mechler, R. J. H. E. W. A. C. N., Czajkowski, J., Kunreuther, H., Michel-Kerjan, E., Botzen, W., Keating, A., ... & O'Donnell, I. (2014). Making communities more flood resilient: The role of cost benefit analysis and other decision-support tools in disaster risk reduction.

Merz, B., Kuhlicke, C., Kunz, M., Pittore, M., Babeyko, A., Bresch, D. N., ... &Wurpts, A. (2020). Impact forecasting to support emergency management of natural hazards. *Reviews of geophysics, 58*(4), e2020RG000704.

Miller, T., Durlik, I., Kostecka, E., Kozlovska, P., Łobodzińska, A., Sokołowska, S., & Nowy, A. (2025). Integrating Artificial Intelligence Agents with the Internet of Things for Enhanced Environmental Monitoring: Applications in Water Quality and Climate Data. *Electronics (Basel), 14*(4), 696. DOI: 10.3390/electronics14040696

Montesa, C. S., Martinez, D. W. C., Gozun, P. J. P., Tanarte, X. S., & Ambrocio, A. B. O. (2023). Design and installation of coastal flood monitoring device using ultrasonic sensors and LoRa-based technology for real-time data collection and storage. *Chemical Engineering Transactions, 106*, 295–300.

Munawar, H. S., Mojtahedi, M., Hammad, A. W., Kouzani, A., & Mahmud, M. P. (2022). Disruptive technologies as a solution for disaster risk management: A review. *The Science of the Total Environment, 806*, 151351. DOI: 10.1016/j.scitotenv.2021.151351 PMID: 34740667

Olasiman, M. M. M., Librado, L. G., Pao, J. C., Baldonado, F. Q., Banglos, C. A. G., Paradela, I. P., & Salaan, C. J. O. (2023, November). Initial Development of Buoy-based Early Warning Device for Flash Flood and Storm Surge Application. In *2023 IEEE 15th International Conference on Humanoid, Nanotechnology, Information Technology, Communication and Control, Environment, and Management (HNICEM)* (pp. 1-6). IEEE. DOI: 10.1109/HNICEM60674.2023.10589142

Ona, S. E., & Lallana, E. C. (2021). Challenges and opportunities of information management in disaster preparedness: The case of Legazpi city, Albay province. *Developing Countries and Technology Inclusion in the 21st Century. The Information Society*, •••, 87–98.

Pal, P. S., & Khuntia, S. (2020). Structural health monitoring using neural networks in IoT and cps paradigm—A review. *Int J Sci Res Eng Dev, 3*(5), 871–892.

Puri, A., Elkharboutly, M., & Ali, N. A. (2024). Identifying major challenges in managing post-disaster reconstruction projects: A critical analysis. *International Journal of Disaster Risk Reduction, 107*, 104491. DOI: 10.1016/j.ijdrr.2024.104491

Rawat, A., Witt, E., Roumyeh, M., & Lill, I. (2024). Advanced digital technologies in the post-disaster reconstruction process—A review leveraging small language models. *Buildings (Basel, Switzerland), 14*(11), 3367. DOI: 10.3390/buildings14113367

Samansiri, S., Fernando, T., & Ingirige, B. (2022). Advanced technologies for offering situational intelligence in flood warning and response systems: A literature review. *Water (Basel), 14*(13), 2091. DOI: 10.3390/w14132091

Sarker, M. N. I., Peng, Y., Yiran, C., & Shouse, R. C. (2020). Disaster resilience through big data: Way to environmental sustainability. *International Journal of Disaster Risk Reduction, 51*, 101769. DOI: 10.1016/j.ijdrr.2020.101769

Scuro, C., Lamonaca, F., Porzio, S., Milani, G., & Olivito, R. S. (2021). Internet of Things (IoT) for masonry structural health monitoring (SHM): Overview and examples of innovative systems. *Construction & Building Materials, 290*, 123092. DOI: 10.1016/j.conbuildmat.2021.123092

Shah, S. A., Seker, D. Z., Hameed, S., & Draheim, D. (2019). The rising role of big data analytics and IoT in disaster management: Recent advances, taxonomy and prospects. *IEEE Access : Practical Innovations, Open Solutions*, *7*, 54595–54614. DOI: 10.1109/ACCESS.2019.2913340

Sihombing, J., Jaenul, A., Wilyanti, S., & Putri, N. (2022). Prototype of Drainage Water Level Monitoring System Using Internet of Things (IoT) Based Web. *SMARTICS Journal*, *8*(2), 52–58. DOI: 10.21067/smartics.v8i2.7559

Singh, S., & Akhai, S. (2024, July). Electronics in precision control for mechanical engineering: A brief overview. In *AIP Conference Proceedings* (Vol. 3121, No. 1). AIP Publishing. DOI: 10.1063/5.0221464

Smith, P. J., Pappenberger, F., Wetterhall, F., Del Pozo, J. T., Krzeminski, B., Salamon, P., . . . Baugh, C. (2016). On the operational implementation of the European Flood Awareness System (EFAS). In *Flood forecasting* (pp. 313-348). Academic Press.

Solehudin, H., Darmayanti, R., Agustin, F. W., & Santoso, C. R. (2023). Navigating the Future: AI, Floods, Politics, and Entrepreneurship in Management Operations for Resilient Societies in Jakarta. *Revenue Journal: Management and Entrepreneurship*, *1*(1), 87–109. DOI: 10.61650/rjme.v1i1.228

Song, J., Shao, Z., Zhan, Z., & Chen, L. (2024). State-of-the-Art Techniques for Real-Time Monitoring of Urban Flooding: A Review. *Water (Basel)*, *16*(17), 2476. DOI: 10.3390/w16172476

Srivastava, H., & Akhai, S. (2022, November). The smart tapping identification model without installing a control program in modern wireless communication. In *2022 International Interdisciplinary Humanitarian Conference for Sustainability (IIHC)* (pp. 159-164). IEEE. DOI: 10.1109/IIHC55949.2022.10060067

Stone, B.Jr, Mallen, E., Rajput, M., Broadbent, A., Krayenhoff, E. S., Augenbroe, G., & Georgescu, M. (2021). Climate change and infrastructure risk: Indoor heat exposure during a concurrent heat wave and blackout event in Phoenix, Arizona. *Urban Climate*, *36*, 100787. DOI: 10.1016/j.uclim.2021.100787

Tan, M. L., Becker, J. S., Stock, K., Prasanna, R., Brown, A., Kenney, C., Cui, A., & Lambie, E. (2022). Understanding the social aspects of earthquake early warning: A literature review. *Frontiers in Communication*, *7*, 939242. DOI: 10.3389/fcomm.2022.939242

Van Hoang, T. (2024). Impact of integrated artificial intelligence and internet of things technologies on smart city transformation. *Journal of Technical Education Science, 19*(Special Issue 01), 64-73.

Verma, S., Srivastava, K., Tiwari, A., & Verma, S. (2024). Estimation of the Area and Precipitation Associated with a Tropical Cyclone Biparjoy by using Image Processing. *arXiv preprint arXiv:2407.05255*.

Wu, Y. M., & Mittal, H. (2021). A review on the development of earthquake warning system using low-cost sensors in Taiwan. *Sensors (Basel), 21*(22), 7649. DOI: 10.3390/s21227649 PMID: 34833728

Zeng, F., Pang, C., & Tang, H. (2023). Sensors on the internet of things systems for urban disaster management: A systematic literature review. *Sensors (Basel), 23*(17), 7475. DOI: 10.3390/s23177475 PMID: 37687929

Zhang, H., Li, B., Karimi, M., Saydam, S., & Hassan, M. (2023). Recent advancements in IoT implementation for environmental, safety, and production monitoring in underground mines. *IEEE Internet of Things Journal, 10*(16), 14507–14526. DOI: 10.1109/JIOT.2023.3267828

Zhao, X., Askari, H., & Chen, J. (2021). Nanogenerators for smart cities in the era of 5G and Internet of Things. *Joule, 5*(6), 1391–1431. DOI: 10.1016/j.joule.2021.03.013

Chapter 4
Leveraging Emerging Technologies for Inclusive and Sustainable Urban Governance:
A Framework for Smart Cities in Developing Environments

R. Sowmiya
https://orcid.org/0009-0003-5336-2988
SASTRA University, India

M. Velavan
https://orcid.org/0000-0002-4114-6773
SASTRA University, India

ABSTRACT

Rapid urbanization in developing countries presents significant governance challenges, including socio-economic inequalities, environmental sustainability issues, and infrastructure deficiencies. Emerging technologies such as Artificial Intelligence (AI), the Internet of Things (IoT), blockchain, and Geographic Information Systems (GIS) offer transformative solutions for inclusive and sustainable urban governance. Smart city initiatives leverage these technologies to enhance service delivery, optimize infrastructure, and foster transparent decision-making, aligning with global sustainability efforts like the United Nations Sustainable Development Goals (SDGs). This chapter explores digital inclusion, partnerships, and data-driven governance to bridge the digital divide and promote equitable growth. It recommends smart infrastructure, climate resilience, and participatory governance to create inclusive,

DOI: 10.4018/979-8-3373-1375-7.ch004

resilient cities.

1. INTRODUCTION

Urban governance in developing countries is increasingly challenged by rapid urbanization, socio-economic disparities, environmental sustainability issues, and the evolving role of digital transformation. As cities expand, governments face immense pressure to provide essential services such as housing, infrastructure, transportation, healthcare, and education. However, many regions struggle due to financial constraints, weak policy implementation, and inefficient governance structures, necessitating innovative and adaptive strategies for sustainable urban development.

A major issue in urban governance is the growing inequality between affluent communities with modern amenities and informal settlements lacking basic services. Many urban residents, especially those in informal employment, face economic instability and social exclusion. Additionally, environmental challenges such as air and water pollution, inadequate waste management, and vulnerability to climate-related disasters like floods and heat waves further strain urban resources. Effective governance must integrate sustainability measures, disaster risk management, and inclusive policies to ensure equitable development.

Technology offers transformative solutions for urban governance through AI, IoT, block chain, and GIS, enabling smarter infrastructure, transparent governance, and improved service delivery. However, many developing cities struggle with digital infrastructure gaps, regulatory hurdles, and the digital divide, limiting equitable access to technological benefits. To bridge these gaps, governments must invest in digital inclusion, smart city initiatives, and public-private partnerships, ensuring that urban growth is both efficient and inclusive for all residents.

The chapter on Leveraging Emerging Technologies for Inclusive and Sustainable Urban Governance: A Framework for Smart Cities in Developing environments is highly significant as it aligns with several of the United Nations Sustainable Development Goals (SDGs), contributing directly to the global agenda for sustainable urban development.

SDG 11: Sustainable Cities and Communities

This chapter addresses the goal of making cities inclusive, safe, resilient, and sustainable by promoting smart city initiatives that leverage technology to improve public services, optimize infrastructure, and enhance urban planning.

SDG 9: Industry, Innovation, and Infrastructure

Emerging technologies such as IoT, AI, and block chain are explored as critical tools for building resilient infrastructure, fostering innovation, and bridging the digital divide in urban governance.

SDG 10: Reduced Inequalities

By proposing frameworks for inclusive governance, the chapter highlights how smart city technologies can bridge the socio-economic and digital divide, ensuring equitable access to resources and opportunities for marginalized populations.

SDG 13: Climate Action

Technology-driven urban governance frameworks can help cities adapt to and mitigate climate change impacts through improved resource management, reduced emissions, and sustainable urban design.

By addressing these SDGs, the chapter underscores the critical role of technology in fostering inclusive governance, improving the quality of life in urban areas, and advancing global sustainability efforts. It provides a roadmap for developing countries to align their urban governance strategies with international sustainability objectives, ensuring that technological advancements benefit all segments of society.

1.1 Emerging Technologies and Their Role in Urban Governance - Literature Review

Emerging technologies are increasingly being leveraged to transform urban governance, particularly in the context of developing environments. Technologies such as Artificial Intelligence (AI), Internet of Things (IoT), blockchain, geospatial information systems (GIS), and big data analytics are facilitating real-time decision-making, enhancing service delivery, and promoting citizen participation in smart cities. For instance, AI-powered predictive analytics are used for traffic management, while IoT sensors provide valuable insights into air quality, waste management, and energy consumption (Kitchin, 2021). However, despite the potential of these technologies, their implementation in developing countries remains challenging. Limited digital infrastructure, inadequate financial resources, and the digital divide often hinder the seamless adoption of smart city solutions (Albino, Berardi, & Dangelico, 2015).

In addition to technological considerations, fostering inclusive and sustainable urban governance requires active citizen engagement through participatory platforms. E-governance initiatives, including mobile apps, digital portals, and social media channels, enable transparent communication between governments and citizens.

Successful examples include the participatory budgeting platforms in Brazil, where residents actively contribute to decision-making processes. Furthermore, collaborative governance models emphasize multi-stakeholder partnerships that integrate input from the public, private sector, and civil society to create equitable and resilient urban environments (Meijer & Bolívar, 2016).

To build a comprehensive framework for smart cities in developing environments, it is crucial to apply theoretical insights from concepts like Collaborative Governance and Public Value Theory. These frameworks highlight the importance of inclusive policymaking, data transparency, and interdepartmental cooperation in ensuring the sustainability of urban innovations (Nam & Pardo, 2011). By examining successful case studies and integrating technological advancements into existing governance systems, cities in developing regions can overcome barriers and achieve more inclusive urban development.

1.2 Enhancing the Scope and Context of Smart City Governance in Developing Environments

Emerging technologies are increasingly applied to address urban governance challenges in developing environments. However, to illustrate these issues more comprehensively, it is essential to analyze real-world applications, governance frameworks, socio-economic impacts, ethical considerations, and future trends.

Case Studies and Practical Applications

Developing cities are adopting technologies like AI, IoT, and blockchain to enhance governance and service delivery. For example, Jakarta's AI-based traffic management system uses real-time data to mitigate congestion, while Nairobi's blockchain land registry ensures transparent property transactions (World Bank, 2020; UN-Habitat, 2022). These cases demonstrate how digital innovation can resolve urban governance challenges and promote transparency.

Policy and Governance Frameworks

Policy alignment with international frameworks is critical for effective smart city development. The UN Sustainable Development Goals (SDG 11) emphasize the need for inclusive, safe, and sustainable cities. National policies like India's Smart Cities Mission further illustrate localized implementations of technological solutions, fostering resilient urban environments (United Nations, 2021).

2. RAPID URBANIZATION AND INFORMAL SETTLEMENTS

2.1 The Growth of Informal Settlements

Developing countries, particularly in Asia, Africa, and Latin America, are experiencing unprecedented urban growth. This expansion is often unplanned, leading to the proliferation of informal settlements where people live without access to basic services such as clean water, sanitation, electricity, and healthcare. In cities like Lagos, Mumbai, and Jakarta, slums continue to grow, exacerbating poverty and inequality. The governance of informal settlements presents significant challenges. Traditional urban planning frameworks fail to accommodate these rapidly expanding areas, leaving residents to self-organize through informal governance structures. While such self-organization demonstrates community resilience, it also perpetuates systemic inequalities. Governments must implement inclusive policies to integrate informal settlements into formal urban systems.

Developing countries, particularly in Africa and Asia, are experiencing unprecedented urban growth, leading to informal settlements and inadequate urban services (Suhartini & Jones, 2019) (Awuah & Abdulai, 2022). The lack of formal governance structures often results in local stakeholders creating informal governance mechanisms to address immediate urban needs (Suhartini & Jones, 2019).

While emerging technologies offer significant benefits, their impact on marginalized communities remains a concern. Studies highlight that cities with inclusive digital infrastructure experience reduced socio-economic disparities and improved public service access (Albino et al., 2015). However, without equitable access to technology, the digital divide may exacerbate urban inequality.

Rapid urbanization and the proliferation of informal settlements significantly impact local communities, both economically and socially. These dynamics often lead to increased informal employment, social inequality, and challenges in governance and infrastructure. Understanding these implications is crucial for developing effective urban policies.

2.2 Land Tenure and Legal Recognition

One of the main governance issues related to informal settlements is land tenure security. Many slum dwellers lack legal ownership of the land they occupy, making them vulnerable to forced evictions and displacement. In some cities, governments have attempted to regularize informal settlements by granting land rights and providing essential services. However, these efforts require long-term commitment and coordination among policymakers, urban planners, and local communities.

Land tenure and legal recognition are critical components in shaping property rights and agricultural development. The recognition of land ownership serves as a civil law method for protecting rights, addressing gaps in legislation, and enhancing legal clarity for landowners (Deineha, 2022). Various land tenure systems, including customary and formal arrangements, significantly influence agricultural productivity and investment, necessitating coherent legal frameworks to support sustainable practices. Innovative approaches, such as Merida's documentation packages in Ghana, illustrate how tailored solutions can navigate the complexities of land governance and enhance tenure security (Salifu et al., 2019).

Customary land tenure practices are prevalent in many regions, yet they often lack formal recognition, leading to insecurity. Legal recognition of these rights is essential for promoting agricultural investment and sustainability. Innovative documentation methods can facilitate land transactions and enhance tenure security, addressing procedural challenges in land registration (Salifu et al., 2019).

3. ECONOMIC AND SOCIAL IMPLICATIONS OF URBANIZATION

3.1 Economic Challenges and Opportunities

Urbanization brings both opportunities and challenges to economic development. While cities serve as economic hubs that generate employment and attract investment, rapid urban expansion often results in an increase in informal employment. In many developing cities, a large proportion of the workforce operates in the informal sector, including street vendors, construction labourers, and domestic workers.

Although informal employment provides income opportunities, it is often characterized by low wages, job insecurity, and the absence of social protection. As cities develop, governments must create policies that promote decent work opportunities and transition informal workers into the formal economy. Strategies such as vocational training, financial inclusion programs, and microfinance initiatives can help bridge this gap.

Urbanization initially increases informal employment, as seen in Vietnam, where it creates job opportunities for migrants. However, this trend reverses as urbanization matures, leading to better job quality and reduced informal labour (Nguyen & Pham, 2024). In cities like Bangkok, urbanization exacerbates social inequality, with informal settlements often housing the urban poor, limiting their access to resources and opportunities (Changsoo, 2023).In Maputo, higher socioeconomic households contribute to urban expansion, indicating that wealthier residents consume more land, which can lead to inadequate infrastructure for lower-income groups (Mottelson & Venerandi, 2023).

3.2 Social Inequality and Exclusion

Urbanization has also intensified socio-economic disparities. In cities like Bangkok and Nairobi, economic inequality is reflected in spatial segregation, where affluent communities enjoy access to high-quality services while low-income neighbourhoods suffer from neglect. This uneven distribution of resources leads to social tensions, crime, and marginalization of vulnerable groups, including migrants, women, and people with disabilities.

Informal settlements can foster discordant communities, as seen in Birbir Town, where land disputes and criminality arise from unregulated urban expansion (Hantalo & Dube, 2023). Residents often engage in self-help initiatives to improve their living conditions, highlighting the resilience and agency of communities in informal settlements ("Informality and Responding to the Challenges of Informal Settlements", 2023).

Governments and urban planners must adopt inclusive governance approaches that promote social equity. Participatory urban planning, community-based development programs, and targeted social policies can help address urban inequalities and enhance social cohesion.

4. ENVIRONMENTAL CHALLENGES IN URBAN GOVERNANCE

4.1 Climate Change and Urban Resilience

Climate change poses a significant threat to cities, particularly in developing regions where infrastructure and disaster preparedness are inadequate. Rising temperatures, extreme weather events, and sea-level rise disproportionately affect poor urban communities. Flooding, for example, is a recurrent issue in cities such as Dhaka and Manila, where informal settlements are often located in high-risk areas.

To build climate resilience, urban governance must prioritize sustainable urban planning, investment in resilient infrastructure, and the integration of climate adaptation strategies into policy frameworks. Initiatives such as green infrastructure, sustainable drainage systems, and early warning mechanisms can mitigate environmental risks.

4.2 Waste Management and Pollution Control

Poor waste management is another pressing issue in developing cities. Rapid urbanization has led to an increase in solid waste generation, but many municipalities lack the capacity to manage and dispose of waste effectively. Illegal dumping, open burning, and inadequate recycling facilities contribute to pollution, health hazards, and environmental degradation.

Climate change and poor waste management are critical issues that urban governance must tackle. Sustainable urban development practices are essential to mitigate these environmental impacts, yet they are often underfunded or poorly implemented (Awuah & Abdulai, 2022).

Cities like Kigali and Curitiba have implemented successful waste management programs by promoting community participation, waste segregation, and recycling initiatives. Similar strategies can be adapted to other developing cities to improve waste management and promote environmental sustainability.

5. THE ROLE OF TECHNOLOGY IN URBAN GOVERNANCE

Digital Literacy and Its Role in Smart Urban Governance: Digital literacy plays a crucial role in ensuring the effectiveness of smart governance initiatives. It encompasses the ability of individuals to access, understand, evaluate, and use digital technologies for meaningful participation in governance processes. In developing environments, low levels of digital literacy often act as a barrier to inclusive urban governance. Citizens who lack the necessary digital skills may struggle to access e-governance platforms, limiting their participation in decision-making and reducing the overall impact of smart city initiatives (Van Dijk, 2020).

1. Bridging the Digital Divide: Addressing digital literacy gaps requires targeted interventions, including digital skills training, community education programs, and accessible digital infrastructure. Initiatives such as India's Digital India program and Kenya's Ajira Digital Project have successfully promoted digital literacy to empower citizens and enhance public service access (ITU, 2021).
2. Promoting Inclusive Participation: E-governance platforms can only be effective if citizens understand how to use them. Governments can implement user-friendly interfaces, multilingual support, and offline assistance to ensure broader participation. Additionally, partnerships with non-governmental organizations (NGOs) and community groups can facilitate digital literacy workshops in underserved areas (UNESCO, 2018).

3. Encouraging Responsible Digital Citizenship: Digital literacy is not only about technical skills but also involves understanding online privacy, cybersecurity, and responsible digital behavior. Providing citizens with knowledge about protecting personal data and recognizing misinformation is essential for maintaining trust in digital governance systems (Livingstone & Helsper, 2007).

5.1 Smart Cities and Digital Transformation

Advancements in digital technology offer innovative solutions for improving urban governance. Smart city initiatives leverage technology to enhance service delivery, optimize urban planning, and improve public participation. Advances in technology present both opportunities and challenges for urban governance, necessitating a balance between innovation and traditional governance practices (Awuah & Abdulai, 2022). Effective use of technology can enhance service delivery and citizen engagement, but requires significant investment and capacity building (Das & Dahiya, 2020). While these challenges are significant, they also present opportunities for rethinking urban governance through localized knowledge production and innovative practices. Addressing these issues requires a nuanced understanding of local contexts and collaborative efforts among various stakeholders. Technologies such as Geographic Information Systems (GIS), Artificial Intelligence (AI), and block chain are revolutionizing the way cities are managed. AI-powered GIS tools facilitate geospatial analysis, crucial for effective spatial planning and resource management. While AI and ML present transformative opportunities for urban planning, challenges such as data quality, integration issues, and the need for skilled personnel remain significant barriers to their widespread adoption (Marwaha et al., 2024).The integration of IoT with AI allows cities to gather and analyze data in real-time, optimizing urban services like waste management and traffic control (Rane et al., 2024). For instance, in India, the Smart Cities Mission aims to use technology to improve urban infrastructure, traffic management, and public safety. However, successful implementation depends on investment in digital infrastructure, regulatory frameworks, and capacity-building programs for local governments.

5.2 IoT and Real-Time Urban Monitoring

The Internet of Things (IoT) plays a crucial role in urban governance by enabling real-time monitoring of infrastructure, air quality, and energy consumption. IoT sensors can track environmental data, detect water leaks, and optimize waste collection, reducing operational costs and enhancing sustainability. IoT devices facilitate real-time data collection and monitoring, optimizing resource management in areas like waste and energy (Tayeng et al., 2024).

5.3 AI and Machine Learning for Urban Planning

AI and machine learning enable predictive analytics, which can help cities anticipate traffic congestion, manage energy consumption, and improve disaster response. Machine learning algorithms analyze large datasets to identify patterns and trends, allowing policymakers to make data-driven decisions. The integration of Artificial Intelligence (AI) and machine learning (ML) into decision-making processes significantly enhances urban planning through advanced data analytics and predictive modeling. These technologies facilitate smarter, more efficient urban management, addressing challenges such as rapid urbanization and resource allocation. AI and ML enable organizations to forecast trends and make informed decisions by analyzing historical data, thus improving operational efficiency. Machine learning automates data-driven decisions, providing real-time insights that allow for quick responses to market changes (Badmus et al., 2024). In urban planning, ML techniques are employed to tackle complex decision-making tasks, such as transportation and healthcare planning, enhancing the overall quality of life in cities (Zheng et al., 2024).

5.4 Block chain for Transparency and Accountability

Block chain technology enhances transparency in urban governance by providing secure and immutable records of land transactions, financial management, and public service delivery. By reducing bureaucratic inefficiencies and preventing corruption, block chain can improve trust between governments and citizens. Block chain technology has emerged as a transformative tool for enhancing transparency and governance across various sectors, including corporate, human resources, supply chains, and public administration. By leveraging decentralized ledgers, block chain ensures that data is immutable, verifiable, and accessible, thereby fostering trust among stakeholders. The following sections outline the key aspects of block chain's role in transparent governance and resource management. Block chain enhances corporate governance by providing real-time, verifiable financial reporting, which mitigates risks of fraud and misreporting. Smart contracts automate compliance and reporting processes, improving operational efficiency and stakeholder engagement (Aro et al., 2024). In HR, block chain addresses data privacy concerns by securely storing employee information, reducing the risk of data breaches. The technology promotes transparency in HR record-keeping, fostering trust between employees and management (Mazharunnisa et al., 2024). Block chain improves transparency in supply chains by allowing stakeholders to access detailed product information, enhancing traceability and accountability. It addresses challenges such as fragmentation and regulatory compliance, which are critical for effective supply chain management (Emmanuel et al., 2024). In public administration, block chain enhances service delivery by ensuring transparency and reducing fraud, thus improving overall governance outcomes. The integration of block chain can lead to more efficient processes, benefiting both service providers and citizens (Maolani, 2024).

6. INCLUSIVE AND SUSTAINABLE URBAN GOVERNANCE

Inclusive and sustainable urban governance is essential for addressing the complexities of modern urban challenges. Inclusivity refers to the active participation of diverse stakeholders, particularly marginalized groups, in decision-making processes, ensuring their voices are heard and considered (Sanchez-Soriano et al., 2024). Sustainability, on the other hand, emphasizes the long-term viability of urban policies and practices, particularly in resource management and environmental stewardship (Mohsin, 2024). Together, these concepts form a framework that promotes equitable and effective governance. Active Participation: Involves engaging local communities and stakeholders in governance processes, fostering transparency and accountability (Sanchez-Soriano et al., 2024). Empowerment of Marginalized Groups: Ensures that those often excluded from decision-making, such as children and vulnerable populations, have a platform to influence urban policies (Cairns et al., 2024). Resource Management: Focuses on integrated approaches to manage urban resources, such as water, to enhance resilience against climate change. Long-term Planning: Encourages policies that consider future generations and environmental impacts, promoting sustainable urban development (Mohsin, 2024). While the emphasis on inclusivity and sustainability is crucial, some argue that the complexities of urban governance may lead to challenges in effectively implementing these frameworks, potentially resulting in tokenistic participation rather than genuine engagement.

6.1 Participatory Governance and Citizen Engagement

Inclusive urban governance requires active citizen participation in decision-making processes. Digital platforms, participatory budgeting, and community forums can empower residents to contribute to urban planning and policy development.

Characteristics that define inclusivity in urban governance: Inclusivity in urban governance is characterized by several key dimensions that ensure diverse community participation and equitable decision-making. These characteristics are essential for addressing the complex challenges faced by urban areas, such as socioeconomic inequality and environmental sustainability. The following sections outline the primary aspects that define inclusivity in urban governance.

Participatory Approaches

Active Engagement: Inclusive governance emphasizes the involvement of marginalized groups in decision-making processes, ensuring their voices are heard (Sanchez-Soriano et al., 2024).Citizen Participation: Effective infrastructure development relies on citizen engagement, which fosters a sense of ownership and accountability in urban projects.

Multi-Dimensional Inclusivity

Cross-Sectoral and Interdisciplinary: Governance should integrate various sectors and disciplines, promoting collaboration among stakeholders to address urban challenges holistically. Intergenerational and Multi-Species Considerations: Inclusivity extends beyond human actors to include future generations and non-human entities, recognizing the interconnectedness of urban ecosystems (Frantzeskaki et al., 2023).

Institutional Frameworks

Local-Supranational Cooperation: Effective governance structures, such as the EU Urban Partnership on Inclusion, facilitate collaboration between local authorities and supranational bodies, enhancing the inclusivity of migration policies (Sturner-Siovitz & Heimann, 2022).While these characteristics promote inclusivity, challenges remain, such as institutional inertia and the potential for tokenistic participation, which can undermine genuine engagement and equity in urban governance.

Figure 1. Characteristics of Inclusivity in Urban Governance

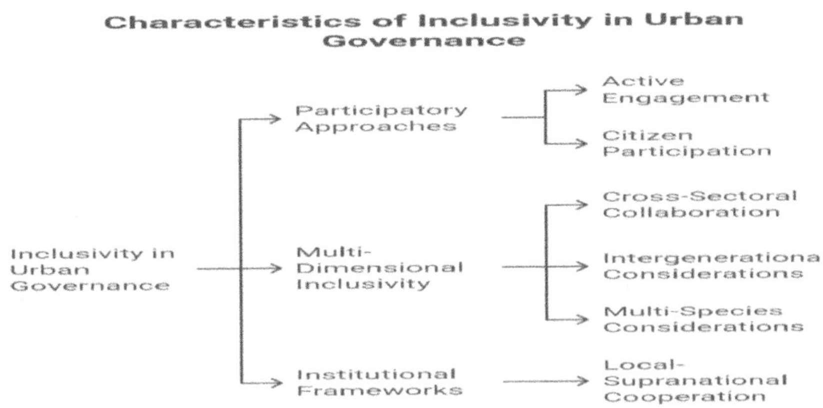

Source By: Authors

6.2 Policy Integration for Sustainable Development

Sustainable urban governance integrates environmental, social, and economic policies to create resilient cities. Governments must align urban development strategies with international frameworks such as the Sustainable Development Goals (SDGs) and the Paris Agreement.

7. CHALLENGES IN IMPLEMENTING URBAN GOVERNANCE REFORMS

Ethical and Privacy Concerns in Smart Urban Governance: The implementation of emerging technologies like Artificial Intelligence (AI), blockchain, and the Internet of Things (IoT) in urban governance introduces significant ethical and privacy challenges. While these technologies enhance operational efficiency and decision-making, they also pose risks to citizen privacy and data security.

1. Data Privacy and Surveillance: Smart cities often rely on large-scale data collection through sensors, cameras, and connected devices. This constant monitoring can lead to concerns over mass surveillance and the misuse of personal data. Without strict data governance frameworks, sensitive information may be exploited, leading to privacy breaches (Kitchin, 2016).
2. Algorithmic Bias and Fairness: AI-powered systems are used for predictive analytics in areas such as law enforcement and public service delivery. However, these algorithms can reinforce existing biases if the training data is not representative. Biased decision-making can disproportionately impact marginalized communities, resulting in systemic inequality (Eubanks, 2018).
3. Data Ownership and Transparency: Blockchain technology offers transparency and immutability in data management. However, the permanence of data stored on blockchain systems raises ethical questions about the right to be forgotten and data deletion (Zwitter & Hazenberg, 2020). Establishing guidelines for responsible blockchain use is essential.
4. Regulatory Frameworks: Cities can mitigate these risks by implementing robust regulatory frameworks such as the General Data Protection Regulation (GDPR) in the European Union. GDPR enforces strict data protection rules and grants individuals greater control over their personal information. Similar regulations are being adapted in other regions to ensure privacy and ethical use of technology in smart governance (Voigt & Von dem Bussche, 2017).

7.1 Infrastructure and Resource Constraints

Many developing countries lack the financial resources to invest in critical infrastructure. Public-private partnerships (PPPs) can help bridge this gap by leveraging private sector investment for urban development projects.

Infrastructure and resource limitations in developing contexts present significant challenges that hinder effective development and service delivery. These barriers often stem from a combination of financial constraints, governance issues, and inadequate community engagement. Addressing these challenges requires a multifaceted approach that emphasizes transparency, stakeholder involvement, and capacity building.

Key Barriers to Infrastructure Development

Funding Constraints: Limited financial resources impede the initiation and completion of infrastructure projects, as seen in Nigeria's infrastructure sector. Bureaucratic Delays and Corruption: Inefficient governance and corruption exacerbate project delays, leading to increased costs and project failures (FALAYE, 2024).

Lack of Community Participation: Inadequate engagement of local communities in planning processes results in misaligned priorities and ineffective resource utilization (Ainurrohman & Mursyidah, 2024).

Resource Limitations in Healthcare

Quality of Care: Resource constraints significantly impact healthcare quality, leading to higher mortality rates in low-income countries compared to high-income settings (Sharma & Cotton, 2023).Capacity Building: Developing educational programs for healthcare professionals is essential to improve service delivery in resource-limited environments (Diaz et al., 2019).

Context-Specific Challenges: Political and Regulatory Barriers: Unique challenges, such as political instability and regulatory hurdles, are particularly pronounced in developing countries like Libya (Beitelmal et al., 2017).

7.2 Bridging the Digital Divide

The digital divide remains a significant barrier to inclusive urban governance. While some cities are advancing smart technologies, others struggle with inadequate internet access, digital literacy, and affordability issues. Governments must implement policies that promote digital inclusion, ensuring that marginalized communities can benefit from technological advancements. The adoption of emerging technologies in urban governance, particularly in developing contexts, is significantly hindered by socioeconomic disparities and the digital divide. These challenges manifest through inadequate infrastructure, limited access to digital tools, and regulatory gaps, which collectively impede inclusive governance.

Infrastructure and Resource Limitations: Many developing areas lack essential technological infrastructure, such as reliable internet and energy sources, which are crucial for implementing digital solutions (Sow et al., 2025) (Filho, 2024). For instance, in Saint-Louis, Senegal, neighbourhoods exhibit stark differences in digital access, with some areas having only 50% connectivity (Sow et al., 2025).

Socioeconomic Disparities: Digital inequality exacerbates existing socioeconomic disparities, affecting marginalized groups' access to opportunities and services. The lack of training and financial resources further limits the ability of vulnerable populations to engage with emerging technologies (Filho, 2024).

Policy and Regulatory Frameworks: Gaps in policy frameworks hinder effective integration of technologies, as governments often lack comprehensive strategies for promoting digital inclusion (Kolotouchkina et al., 2024). Without targeted interventions, the potential of digital technologies to enhance urban governance remains largely untapped.

7.3 Regulatory and Policy Challenges

Outdated regulatory frameworks and resistance to change hinder the adoption of emerging technologies. Policymakers must create adaptive regulations that support technological innovation while addressing ethical, security, and privacy concerns.

The adoption of emerging technologies faces significant policy and regulatory challenges that can hinder their effective integration into various sectors. These challenges stem from rapid technological advancements, regulatory compliance complexities, and the need for adaptive frameworks that can accommodate innovation while ensuring public safety and ethical standards.

Regulatory Compliance and Complexity: Emerging technologies often introduce intricate legal and quality requirements, complicating compliance for developers (Yau et al., 2024). The fast-paced evolution of technologies outstrips traditional regulatory frameworks, leading to gaps in oversight (Galhardo & Souza, 2024).

Infrastructure and Economic Constraints: In emerging markets, inadequate infrastructure and economic instability exacerbate regulatory challenges, making compliance more difficult. High costs associated with implementing digital compliance tools can deter businesses from adopting necessary technologies (Alex-Omiogbemi et al., 2024).

Resistance to Change: Stakeholders, including regulators and businesses, may resist adopting new technologies due to fear of the unknown or potential disruptions to established practices (Reynolds, 2024). The influence of interest groups, particularly large tech firms, can complicate the regulatory landscape, leading to potential regulatory capture (Galhardo & Souza, 2024).

8. FUTURE DIRECTIONS AND RECOMMENDATIONS

- The future of urban governance lies in technologies like 5G networks, digital twins, and AI-driven decision support systems. These innovations enable real-time simulation and predictive analysis, facilitating proactive governance. Municipal authorities should adopt public-private partnerships and invest in digital capacity-building to leverage these advancements sustainably (Nam & Pardo, 2011).
- Ensuring responsible data governance is crucial. Smart cities collect vast amounts of citizen data through IoT sensors and surveillance systems. Implementing data protection regulations and transparent data management frameworks can mitigate privacy concerns (Meijer & Bolívar, 2016). Ethical AI deployment is also essential to prevent algorithmic biases in governance decisions.

- Invest in Smart Infrastructure: Governments should allocate funds for smart urban infrastructure to enhance efficiency and sustainability.
- Promote Digital Inclusion: Expanding internet access and digital literacy programs can bridge the urban digital divide.
- Strengthen Public-Private Collaboration: Partnering with the private sector can accelerate urban development and innovation.
- Adopt Data-Driven Urban Planning: Leveraging big data and AI can improve decision-making and resource allocation.
- Enhance Climate Resilience Strategies: Sustainable policies and climate adaptation measures should be integrated into urban planning.

9. DISCUSSION

Balancing the Emphasis on Issues, Problems, and Trends

While the chapter effectively introduces the role of emerging technologies in urban governance, a more balanced emphasis on key issues, challenges, and trends would enhance its impact. One area requiring further emphasis is the digital divide in developing environments. Limited access to digital infrastructure and the lack of digital literacy often prevent equitable participation in smart city initiatives. Providing additional data or case studies from regions with low technology penetration would strengthen the chapter's analysis. For instance, incorporating examples from Sub-Saharan Africa or South Asia, where connectivity remains a challenge, can offer valuable insights into addressing this gap.

Furthermore, the chapter could place greater emphasis on the socio-economic impacts of emerging technologies. While technological advancements promise improved service delivery, their implementation may unintentionally widen inequalities if not managed inclusively. Highlighting both the positive and negative outcomes of technology adoption in urban governance would provide a well-rounded perspective. Introducing case studies like Brazil's participatory budgeting platforms or India's e-Governance projects would demonstrate how inclusive technology deployment can foster equitable urban development.

Additionally, while the chapter covers current technological applications, incorporating a forward-looking analysis of future trends would enhance its relevance. Technologies like 5G, AI-driven governance tools, and digital twins are poised to transform urban management further. Providing examples of pilot projects or cities adopting these technologies can offer practical insights into their future potential.

To ensure a balanced approach, each issue discussed should be accompanied by a clear set of policy recommendations or solutions. For instance, proposing frameworks for data protection, inclusive technology adoption, and public-private partnerships would provide actionable guidance for policymakers. This problem-solution linkage would strengthen the chapter's applicability to real-world urban governance challenges.

Critical Reflection: Strengths, Weaknesses, and Recommendations

This chapter presents a well-rounded analysis of the role of emerging technologies in urban governance, particularly in the context of developing environments. It provides a clear understanding of how technologies like Artificial Intelligence (AI), Internet of Things (IoT), and blockchain can enhance service delivery, decision-making, and citizen participation. However, there are areas where further improvements can enhance its comprehensiveness and impact.

Comprehensive Introduction to Emerging Technologies: The chapter effectively outlines the application of AI, IoT, blockchain, and big data analytics in urban governance. This foundational knowledge offers readers a solid understanding of how these technologies operate. Expanding on this strength, the chapter can incorporate case studies from regions such as Nairobi (blockchain land registry) and Jakarta (AI-based traffic management) to illustrate real-world applications and challenges.

Emphasis on Inclusive and Sustainable Urban Governance: A key strength of the chapter is its recognition of the importance of inclusivity and sustainability in smart city initiatives. By further analyzing policies aligned with the UN Sustainable Development Goals (SDG 11) and national initiatives like India's Smart Cities Mission, the chapter can provide actionable insights for urban policymakers.

Use of Theoretical Frameworks: The application of Collaborative Governance and Public Value Theory adds academic depth to the chapter. This theoretical foundation can be extended by evaluating how these frameworks have been applied in real-world scenarios. Offering recommendations on adapting these theories for developing environments will further strengthen the chapter's impact.

Logical Structure and Coherent Flow: The chapter's well-organized structure facilitates clear understanding. Its logical progression from technology introduction to governance applications ensures accessibility for both academic readers and policymakers. Enhancing this by adding future trends and expanding on policy recommendations will further elevate its contribution.

10. CONCLUSION

Target Audience Alignment

The chapter is generally well-aligned with the proposed target audience, which likely includes academics, policymakers, urban planners, and technology practitioners interested in smart city governance. The clear explanation of emerging technologies and their applications provides valuable insights for readers seeking practical and theoretical knowledge. Additionally, the chapter's emphasis on inclusive and sustainable urban development is particularly relevant for decision-makers in developing environments.

Recommendation: To further align with the target audience, consider adding more region-specific examples and case studies from developing countries. Incorporating a comparative analysis between successful and struggling smart city projects can offer practical lessons and resonate more with policymakers and practitioners.

Effectiveness of Chapter Organization and Flow

The chapter follows a logical structure, transitioning from the introduction of emerging technologies to their applications in urban governance. The theoretical frameworks used are well-integrated, and the discussion builds progressively. However, there are areas where the flow could be improved for greater clarity and engagement.

Recommendation: Consider adding clear subheadings within sections, especially in parts discussing different technologies or case studies. This will make it easier for readers to navigate through the content. A more distinct separation between challenges, opportunities, and future trends would improve coherence. Using summary tables or visual aids can also enhance clarity. Additionally, a brief transitional paragraph at the end of major sections could provide a smoother flow into the next topic.

Evaluation of References

The references used in the chapter are generally relevant and credible. However, some sources may be slightly outdated, particularly in the rapidly evolving fields of artificial intelligence, blockchain, and smart city innovations. Recent reports from organizations like the World Bank, UN-Habitat, and ITU can provide up-to-date data and case studies.

Recommendation: Replace or supplement older references with recent publications (2021-2024) to ensure the chapter reflects the latest technological advancements and policy developments. Include region-specific reports and government documents for a more localized perspective. Consider citing peer-reviewed journal articles and authoritative sources that provide empirical data on the implementation of smart city technologies in developing environments.

Urban governance in developing contexts faces numerous challenges, but strategic planning, technological innovation, and inclusive policies can drive positive change. This chapter has explored the transformative potential of emerging technologies in promoting inclusive and sustainable urban governance. The discussion has emphasized how smart city initiatives, data-driven decision-making, and digital inclusion strategies can address key urban challenges in developing economies. By leveraging artificial intelligence (AI), the Internet of Things (IoT), and block chain, cities can enhance public service delivery, improve citizen engagement, and foster more transparent governance mechanisms (Batty et al., 2012).

By addressing issues such as informal settlements, socio-economic disparities, environmental sustainability, and technological integration, cities can create a more resilient and equitable urban future.

REFERENCES

Ainurrohman, M. A., & Mursyidah, L. (2024). Overcoming barriers in infrastructure development planning and community involvement. *Indonesian Journal of Cultural and Community Development, 15*(3). Universitas Muhammadiyah Sidoarjo. https://ijccd.umsida.ac.id/index.php/ijccd/article/view/1098/1293

Albino, V., Berardi, U., & Dangelico, R. M. (2015). Smart cities: Definitions, dimensions, and performance. *Journal of Urban Technology, 22*(1), 3–21. DOI: 10.1080/10630732.2014.942092

Alex-Omiogbemi, A. A., Sule, A. K., Omowole, B. M., & Owoade, S. J. (2024). Conceptual framework for advancing regulatory compliance and risk management in emerging markets through digital innovation. *World Journal of Advanced Research and Reviews, 24*(3), 1155–1162. DOI: 10.30574/wjarr.2024.24.3.3752

Aro, O. E., Nweze, M., & Avickson, E. K. (2024). Blockchain technology as a tool for corporate governance and transparency. *International Journal of Science and Research Archive, 13*(1), 2479–2493. DOI: 10.30574/ijsra.2024.13.1.1971

Badmus, O., Rajput, S. A., Arogundade, J. B., & Williams, M. (2024). AI-driven business analytics and decision making. *World Journal of Advanced Research and Reviews, 24*(1), 616–633. DOI: 10.30574/wjarr.2024.24.1.3093

Batty, M., Axhausen, K. W., Giannotti, F., Pozdnoukhov, A., Bazzani, A., Wachowicz, M., Ouzounis, G., & Portugali, Y. (2012). Smart cities of the future. *The European Physical Journal. Special Topics, 214*(1), 481–518. DOI: 10.1140/epjst/e2012-01703-3

Beitelmal, W. H., Molenaar, K. R., Javernick-Will, A., & Pellicer, E. (2017). Challenges and barriers to establishing infrastructure asset management: A comparative study between Libya and the USA. *Engineering, Construction, and Architectural Management, 24*(6), 1184–1202. DOI: 10.1108/ECAM-12-2015-0200

Changsoo, R. (2023). Changing dynamics of urbanization and social inequality: A case study of informal settlements in Bangkok, Thailand. *The International Journal of Science in Society, 5*(3), 377–387. DOI: 10.54783/ijsoc.v5i3.757

Das, A., & Dahiya, B. (2020). *Towards inclusive urban governance and planning: Emerging trends and future trajectories*. In Thammasat University (Ed.), *Urban Governance and Planning* (pp. 353-384). Springer, Singapore. DOI: 10.1007/978-981-13-6709-0_13

Deineha, M. A. (2022). Recognition of land ownership as a civil law method of rights protection. *Naukovo-Informatsiyniy Visnyk Ivano-Frankivskogo Universytetu Prava Imeni Korolya Danyla Halytskoho*, (14(26)), 128–136. DOI: 10.33098/2078-6670.2022.14.26.128-136

do Nascimento Filho, C. T. F. (2024). A digitalização das zonas especiais de interesse social (ZEIS): Como a integração de tecnologias urbanas pode transformar as periferias em cidades inteligentes e inclusivas. *Revista Fisio&Terapia, 29*(141), 54–55. O&M University. https://revistaft.com.br/a-digitalizacao-das-zonas-especiais-de-interesse-social-zeis-como-a-integracao-de-tecnologias-urbanas-pode-transformar-as-periferias-em-cidades-inteligentes-e-inclusivas/

Emmanuel, I., Abiodun, M. K., Olowe, O. T., Fortune, A. O., Oluwabunmi, O., & Bishop, A.-T. (2024, April 2). Blockchain in supply chains: A dual perspective on transparency and efficiency. *International Journal of Science and Research Archive, 15*(2), 1–7. DOI: 10.30574/ijsra.2024.15.2.1972

Eubanks, V. (2018). *Automating inequality: How high-tech tools profile, police, and punish the poor*. St. Martin's Press.

. Falaye, T. E. (2024, October 22). *Project management challenges in developing economies: A case study of infrastructure projects in Nigeria.*

Frantzeskaki, N., Wijsman, K., Adams, C., Kabisch, N., Malekpour, S., Pineda Pinto, M., & Vandergert, P. (2023). Governance of and with nature-based solutions in cities. In McPhearson, T., Kabisch, N., & Frantzeskaki, N. (Eds.), *Nature-Based Solutions for Cities* (pp. 241–258). Edward Elgar Publishing., DOI: 10.4337/9781800376762.00022

Galhardo, J. A. G., & de Souza, C. A. (2024). *Listening to regulators about the challenges in regulating emerging disruptive technologies. Transforming Government: People*. Process and Policy., DOI: 10.1108/TG-03-2024-0073

Gyau, K., Awuah, B., & Abdulai, R. T. (2022). Urban land and development management in a challenged developing world: An overview of new reflections. *Land (Basel), 11*(1), 129. DOI: 10.3390/land11010129

Hantalo, A. H., & Dube, E. E. (2023). Dynamics of informal settlement expansion on the urban fringe: The case of Birbir Town, Southern Ethiopia. *Journal of Contemporary Urban Affairs, 7*(1), 86–102. DOI: 10.25034/ijcua.2023.v7n1-6

International Telecommunication Union. (2021). *Digital skills insights 2021*. ITU.

Jones, P., & Suhartini, N. (2023). Informality and responding to the challenges of informal settlements. In Jones, P., & Suhartini, N. (Eds.), *Urban Governance and Informal Settlements* (pp. 17–36). Springer., DOI: 10.1007/978-3-031-22239-9_2

Kitchin, R. (2016). The ethics of smart cities and urban science. *Philosophical Transactions. Series A, Mathematical, Physical, and Engineering Sciences*, *374*(2083), 20160115. DOI: 10.1098/rsta.2016.0115 PMID: 28336794

Kitchin, R. (2021). The data-driven city? Decision-making, power, and knowledge in the age of big data. *Cities (London, England)*, *109*, 102987. DOI: 10.1016/j.cities.2020.102987

Livingstone, S., & Helsper, E. J. (2007). Gradations in digital inclusion: Children, young people, and the digital divide. *New Media & Society*, *9*(4), 671–696. DOI: 10.1177/1461444807080335

Maolani, D. Y. (2024). Enhancing public service delivery through blockchain technology: A novel approach to transparent and efficient governance. *VISIONER*, 16(1), 12–21. https://ejournal.goacademica.com/index.php/jv/article/view/1024

Marwaha, S., Dey, H. S., & Brar, T. S. (2024). The emerging role of Artificial Intelligence (AI) in urban and regional planning in India. *International Journal of Arts Architecture & Design*, *2*(2), 61–79. DOI: 10.62030/2024Julypaper4

Mazharunnisa, M., Naveen, P. Y., Apoorva, K., Poojasri, K. P., Jain, D., & Shalini, G. (2024, March 15). Blockchain in human resources: Ensuring data privacy and transparency in employee management. *International Journal of Advanced Research in Computer Science and Software Engineering*, *14*(3), 90–95. DOI: 10.23956/ijarcsse.v14i3.1048

Meijer, A., & Bolívar, M. P. (2016). Governing the smart city: A review of the literature on smart urban governance. *International Review of Administrative Sciences*, *82*(2), 392–408. DOI: 10.1177/0020852314564308

Mohsin, M. (2024). Sustainable water management solutions for urban areas. *International Journal for Research in Applied Science and Engineering Technology*, *12*(10), 538–540. DOI: 10.22214/ijraset.2024.64528

Mottelson, J., & Venerandi, A. (2023). Urban density and socioeconomic characteristics of informal settlements: Evidence of interrelation from Maputo, Mozambique. *Environment and Urbanization*, *35*(2), 349–368. DOI: 10.1177/09562478231195512

Nam, T., & Pardo, T. A. (2011). Conceptualizing smart city with dimensions of technology, people, and institutions. *Proceedings of the 12th Annual International Digital Government Research Conference*, 282–291. https://doi.org/DOI: 10.1145/2037556.2037602

Nguyen, T. T. H., & Pham, H. T. (2024). The impact of urbanization on informal employment: Evidence from Vietnam. *Journal of Economics and Development*, 26(Special Issue No. 1), 35 https://jed.neu.edu.vn/JED/Volume%2026/Special%20 Issue%20No1/10.33301-JED-05-2024-0035.pdf

Rane, N. L., Rane, J., Paramesha, M., & Kaya, Ö. (2024). Artificial intelligence, machine learning, and deep learning for enabling smart and sustainable cities and infrastructure. In *Artificial Intelligence, Machine Learning, and Deep Learning for Sustainable Industry 5.0* (pp. 24–49). Deep Science Publishing. https://doi.org/DOI: 10.70593/978-81-981271-1-2_2

Salifu, F. W., Abubakari, Z., & Richter, C. (2019). Innovating along the continuum of land rights recognition: Meridia's "documentation packages" for Ghana. *Land (Basel)*, *8*(12), 189. DOI: 10.3390/land8120189

Sánchez-Soriano, M., Arango-Ramírez, P. M., Pérez-López, E. I., & García-Montalvo, I. A. (2024). Inclusive governance: Empowering communities and promoting social justice. *Frontiers in Political Science*, *6*, 1478126. DOI: 10.3389/fpos.2024.1478126

Sow, D., Adjanohoun, D. S., Mbengue, T. D. P., Wade, C. S., Seye, M. R., Mbaye, D., Diallo, M., Ndiaye, L., De Roulet, P., Munyaka, J. C. B., & Chenal, J. (2025). Digital inclusion and youth participation in urban governance in Sub-Saharan Africa: The case of Saint-Louis, Senegal. *Global Journal for Research Analysis*, *14*(1), 50–55. https://www.doi.org/10.36106/gjra/0103770. DOI: 10.36106/gjra/0103770

UN-Habitat. (2022). *Smart technologies for urban resilience: Case studies from developing cities*. https://unhabitat.org

United Nations. (2021). *Sustainable development goals report*. https://unstats.un .org/sdgs/report/2021/

United Nations Educational, Scientific and Cultural Organization. (2018). *Global framework for digital literacy*. UNESCO.

Van Dijk, J. A. G. M. (2020). *The digital divide*. Polity Press.

Voigt, P., & Von dem Bussche, A. (2017). *The EU General Data Protection Regulation (GDPR): A practical guide*. Springer. DOI: 10.1007/978-3-319-57959-7

World Bank. (2020). *Digital solutions for urban mobility in developing cities*. https:// worldbank.org/digitalurbanmobility

Yau, S. S., Pandya, K., & Choudhary, S. (2024). Regulatory compliance in software services using emerging technologies. *Proceedings of the IEEE International Conference on Software Services Engineering (SSE)*, 36–42. https://doi.org/DOI: 10.1109/SSE62657.2024.00018

Zhang, J., Liang, F., & Gao, P. (2024). Can big data reduce urban environmental pollution? Evidence from China's digital technology experimental zone. *PLoS One*, *19*(10), e0288429. DOI: 10.1371/journal.pone.0288429 PMID: 39413142

Zwitter, A., & Hazenberg, J. (2020). Blockchain for good? Distributed ledger technology and the ethics of trust. *Frontiers in Blockchain*, *3*, 1–8. DOI: 10.3389/fbloc.2020.00012

Chapter 5
Leveraging Technology for Climate Resilience in Urban Areas

Ananya Pandey
https://orcid.org/0000-0002-2419-6314
Christ University, Bangalore, India

Manshu Goyal
https://orcid.org/0009-0006-9377-2369
Independent Researcher, India

ABSTRACT

Urban areas, densely populated and often located in vulnerable coastal regions, are particularly susceptible to the impacts of climate change. This chapter explores the diverse ways technology can be leveraged to enhance climate resilience in these urban environments. Focusing on mitigation and adaptation strategies, the study examines the potential of smart city technologies, including sensor networks, data analytics, and AI, to improve infrastructure management and disaster preparedness. Specific examples include real-time flood monitoring systems, predictive modelling for extreme weather events, and optimized energy grids for reduced carbon emissions. Furthermore, the chapter investigates the role of digital platforms in facilitating community engagement and fostering collaborative responses to climate-related challenges. Furthermore, the importance of equitable access to technology and the need for robust data governance frameworks to ensure that technological interventions effectively contribute to building climate-resilient and sustainable urban futures is explored

DOI: 10.4018/979-8-3373-1375-7.ch005

INTRODUCTION

With more than half of the world's population residing in cities, the 21st century has seen a rise in global urbanization. Cities encourage innovation and economic progress, but they also face mounting difficulties as due to climate change (Leeson, 2018). Urban regions are particularly vulnerable to rising sea levels, more frequent and intense heat waves, altered precipitation patterns, and more powerful storms. As a result, a key issue in determining the future of our cities is urban climate resilience (Das et al., 2024). Fundamentally, urban climate resilience defines an urban system and its constituents' capacity to withstand, adjust to, and bounce back from the different shocks and pressures made worse by climate change while maintaining the welfare of its residents. It is a complex idea that touches social structures, government, and infrastructure (Satterthwaite, 2009). With increased energy efficiency and lower-carbon fossil fuel substitutes, new technologies are preventing additional harm, facilitating the identification of emissions sources, and even eliminating surplus greenhouse gases from the environment. Many of these are not at all routine (Francisco Ribeiro & Camargo Rodriguez, 2020). For instance, scientists are investigating the prospect of putting a huge parasol into space to block a tiny but crucial amount of solar light. According to the argument, this technology might be sufficient to mitigate the impacts of global warming if it proves effective (Dwivedi et al., 2022). By integrating data-driven solutions and Internet of Things (IoT) technology, cities may enhance resource monitoring and management, guaranteeing that services like trash management, electricity, and transportation are not only efficient but also ecologically conscious (Ahmed et al., 2024). The need for creative solutions that can successfully handle these complicated problems has increased due to climate change, resource scarcity, and rapid urbanization. By utilizing technology to better municipal management, services, and sustainable practices, the idea of "Smart Cities" offers a revolutionary approach to urban development (Bibri et al., 2024). Initiatives for "smart cities" use a broad range of technology and tactics to maximize urban systems and enhance citizens' quality of life. For instance, energy-efficient buildings and renewable energy sources can drastically reduce carbon emissions, while smart sensors can offer real-time data on traffic patterns, enabling optimal traffic flow and less congestion (Hashem et al., 2016). In light of the above perspectives, this chapter explores the role of technology for climate resilience in urban areas. It also analyzes the intersection between technology and climate change and suggests development policy measures to combat climate change.

CLIMATE CHANGE IN URBAN AREAS

As concrete and asphalt replace vegetation for roads, buildings, and other facilities required to support expanding people, heat islands are created. Surface temperatures and ambient temperatures rise as a result of these surfaces' absorption of solar heat rather than reflection (Vujovic et al., 2021). The natural cooling effects of shade and evapotranspiration—the evaporation of water from soil and leaves—are reduced when trees and other vegetation are removed. Narrow roadways and tall buildings can decrease air flow by heating the air that is trapped between them (Wu et al., 2024). The heat island effect may be exacerbated by waste heat from factories, cars, and air conditioners that warm the surrounding area. Heat islands can happen at any time of day or night. The biggest temperature disparities between urban and rural areas typically occur on calm, clear evenings (Islam et al., 2024). This is due to the fact that cities retain a large portion of the heat stored in buildings, roads, and other structures, whereas rural areas cool off more quickly at night. Because of this, the maximal heat island effect, or the biggest urban-rural temperature differential, frequently occurs three to five hours after sunset (Lee et al., 2017). Local temperature variations, typically between urban and rural areas, are referred to as heat islands. On the other hand, warming brought on by climate change describes an increase in the global surface temperature of the Earth (George & Becker, 2003). In order to prevent urban heat from influencing global climate data, scientists take this into consideration while measuring Earth's temperature. The idea that climate change is caused by urban heat is a fiction. This isn't true. The increased concentration of greenhouse gases in the atmosphere is causing global warming in both urban and rural areas (Corburn, 2009). The Arctic, which is far from cities, is actually home to some of the world's most warming regions. However, the urban heat island effect exacerbates the warmth brought on by global climate change, making metropolitan regions more susceptible to heat (Alcoforado & Andrade, 2008). This implies that as the climate warms, city dwellers will experience hotter temperatures and more intense heat waves in the future. The issue of urban heat islands will only worsen as more than half of the world's population currently resides in cities, and by 2050, that number is predicted to rise to 70% (Musco, 2016). By raising the need for air conditioning during heat waves, urban heat islands may also be a factor in climate change. The combustion of fossil fuels to power an air conditioner leads to the release of greenhouse gases that trap heat.

Extreme Weather Events and Climate Change

Extreme weather is being affected globally by changes in Earth's climate. The frequency and intensity of devastating wildfires, torrential rains, severe floods, years-long droughts, record-breaking heat waves on land and in the water, and extensive flooding during hurricanes are all increasing (Preston et al., 2011). Since the Industrial Revolution, greenhouse gases have quickly increased in the atmosphere due to human activity, mainly the combustion of fossil fuels. The world warms as a result of the blanket-like effect of rising carbon dioxide, methane, and other gases. The air and oceans on Earth heated as a result (Ebi et al., 2021). Land ice melts, weather patterns change, and the water cycle is impacted by this warming, all of which can exacerbate extreme weather. The Sixth Assessment Report of the Intergovernmental Panel on Climate Change (IPCC), published in 2021, states that the frequency and severity of extreme weather events have increased due to human-caused increases in greenhouse gas emissions (Seneviratne et al., n.d.). The biggest threat to humanity from both urbanization and industrialization is air pollution. The air pollution in and around cities is referred to as urban air pollution. Urban air pollution is higher in denser populations. Both the local climate and human health are impacted by air pollution (Bikis, 2023). The World Health Organization (WHO) estimates that exposure to ambient (outside) air pollution causes 4.2 million deaths annually (Roser, 2021). Urban air pollution comes from a variety of natural sources, but the majority are man-made and heavily reliant on human activity (Bikis, 2023). Volcanic eruptions, thunderstorms, dust from the earth's surface, and naturally occurring particulate matter are some of the natural causes of urban air pollution (Ebi et al., 2021). However, anthropogenic activities such as transportation, residential fossil fuel usage, industrialization, electricity generation, combustion, and the use of cosmetics and agricultural goods are the main causes of urban air pollution (Manisalidis et al., 2020).

SMART INFRASTRUCTURE FOR CLIMATE ADAPTATION

Smart infrastructure for climate adaptation refers to infrastructure systems that utilize advanced technology and data analysis to proactively respond to and mitigate the impacts of climate change, such as extreme weather events, rising sea levels, and droughts, by incorporating resilience features and adapting to changing conditions in real-time, often through sensors, monitoring systems, and intelligent decision-making algorithms.

Blue-Green Infrastructure

Although there isn't a single, widely agreed-upon definition of blue-green infrastructure, experts are increasingly agreeing that it is a new approach to sustainable urban design and effective use of available space (Yang et al., 2021). Although projects that incorporate features like parks, green roofs, and vertical and horizontal gardens are frequently referred to as "green infrastructure," it is crucial to acknowledge its reliance on "blue" processes. The term "green infrastructure" refers to a range of water management techniques, including absorbent gardens, roadside plantings, vegetated rooftops, and other stormwater collection, filtration, and reduction strategies (Ruth, 2006). By doing this, it lessens flooding and the quantity of contaminated runoff that enters rivers, lakes, streams, sewers, and the ocean. Rainfall is captured by green infrastructure. It turns rainfall into a resource rather than a waste by simulating natural hydrological processes and utilizing organic materials like soil and plants (Foster et al., 2011). In addition, it improves the amount and quality of nearby water supplies and offers several additional health, economic, and environmental advantages—often in metropolitan areas that lack natural resources (Thaler et al., 2021). Conversely, blue infrastructure refers to aspects of urban development that are intended to improve the quantity and quality of resilient water supply. As a result, the phrase "blue-green infrastructure" combines the two forms of infrastructure mentioned above (Foster et al., 2011).

Blue-green infrastructure encourages resource efficiency and sustainable living. For instance, efficient and successful water treatment methods enable wastewater to be used for a variety of purposes in agriculture and industry, hence minimizing excessive water waste and depletion (Obaideen et al., 2022). The economic, social, and environmental sectors all gain greatly from blue-green infrastructure, which has cross-sectoral effects. This kind of infrastructure is particularly regarded as a powerful source of climate mitigation measures and is essential to environmental protection. This segment's initiatives support local ecological regulation, pollution reduction, and urban temperature reduction (Crovella et al., 2024).

Smart Grids and Renewable Energy Integration

Renewable energy sources like solar, wind, and hydrogen may now be distributed and managed efficiently because of smart grid technologies. Numerous dispersed energy resource assets are connected to the power grid by the smart grid (Ahmed et al., 2020). Through continual self-assessments, utilities may swiftly identify and address service concerns by using the Internet of Things (IoT) to gather data on the smart grid. This self-healing capability is an essential part of the smart grid since it eliminates the need for utilities to rely on customers to report failures (Tabassum et al., 2024). Data collection is at the heart of the smart grid's relationship with renewable energy. For instance, the mechanical gears used in wind farms necessitate that each link accommodate several sensors. Every sensor can record the current ambient and climatic parameters (Goudarzi et al., 2022). The quality of service and safety are subsequently enhanced as this data is promptly transmitted over the grid to notify the utility of any problems. With smart grid technology, semiconductor elements like silicon are helping to create green energy (Minh et al., 2022). These materials have made it possible for the Internet of Things to advance since they can contain millions of tiny transistors. By connecting devices across the system, this development has made it possible for the smart grid to guarantee that the supply of energy is equal to the demand. Additionally, it maintains the current's uniform distribution (Hossain et al., 2016). Power consumption is decreased via smart grids that use semiconductor-based components. Electric vehicles, for instance, can be charged at night, when households and workplaces are often using less electricity (Kataray et al., 2023). Furnaces and light switches can also turn on and off automatically. By avoiding consuming more energy than is necessary, energy use becomes "smart." Thailand aims for a third of its energy to come from renewable sources by 2037. To accommodate the fluctuating amounts of energy supplied by renewable sources, Thailand's grid will need to be updated (Minh et al., 2022). Plans for modernization must also account for the nation's increasing demand for electric cars (EVs), which is expected to increase over the next several years (Hossain et al., 2016).

Climate Resilient Transportation

Low-income nations lack the ability to endure and adjust to the effects of climate change, making them extremely vulnerable to it. Their transport networks are therefore unlikely to be robust. "The capacity of social, economic, and environmental systems to cope with a hazardous event or trend or disturbance, responding or reorganizing in ways that maintain their essential function, identity, and structure, while also maintaining the capacity for adaptation, learning, and transformation," is the definition of resilience provided by the Intergovernmental Panel on Climate Change (IPCC) (Greenham et al., 2023). In this sense, a transport network is said to be resilient if it can adapt, adjust, or react while maintaining its primary function. Adaptation, which is the process of adjusting to the present or anticipated environment and its impacts in order to mitigate or prevent harm or take advantage of advantageous chances, is necessary to make transportation climate resilient (Glock et al., 2022). Resilience might be operational or physical. Enhancing flood defenses or expanding drainage capacity are examples of "hard infrastructure" initiatives that can be used to increase a transportation network's physical resilience (Hayes et al., 2019). "Softer" strategies like modifying maintenance schedules, increasing staff availability, and modifying timelines can all be part of operational resilience (Mitoulis et al., 2023). It should also incorporate natural solutions that conserve, sustainably manage, and restore natural or altered ecosystems in order to address the resilience issue and enhance the environment (Hayes et al., 2019). Since the environment, circumstances, and capacities of transport infrastructure and operators differ, there is no one or universal strategy for enhancing transport resilience and adaptation. To make sure the appropriate strategy is used, it necessitates meticulous evaluation (Mitoulis et al., 2023).

AI and IoT applications in resilient infrastructure

By enabling adaptable infrastructure designs that can endure extreme weather events, improving resource management, and enabling predictive maintenance, artificial intelligence (AI) technology can greatly increase infrastructure resilience (Habib et al., 2024). AI can minimize environmental damage by detecting possible infrastructure failures early, improve water and energy use, and aid in the creation of erosion control and flood-resistant structures (Samaei, 2024). By using predictive analytics, AI can lower maintenance costs and increase the lifespan of infrastructure assets. Additionally, it may improve the distribution of resources in times of emergency, preserve economic activity, and lessen the financial burden of severe weather (Chen et al., 2023). AI can assist community stability by improving catastrophe response and preparedness, ensuring fair resource distribution, and preserving the availability of critical services like healthcare and education (Bari et al., 2023). AI-based solutions support inclusive, resilient, and sustainable development in arid regions by closely aligning with Climate Action (SDG 13), Clean Water and Sanitation (SDG 6), Industry, Innovation, and Infrastructure (SDG 9), and Sustainable Cities and Communities (SDG 11) (Kuglitsch et al., 2022). The enormous expenses involved in creating, implementing, and maintaining AI systems over time can be unaffordable, especially in areas with limited financial resources. These expenses cover not just the initial setup but also continuing expenditures for infrastructure, expert labor, and updates (Abid et al., 2021). When AI systems are trained on biased or inadequate data, there is a considerable chance that they would provide biased or "hallucinating" predictions, leading to inaccurate or false predictions as a result of badly trained models. These mistakes have unanticipated negative effects, especially when it comes to disaster response and infrastructure development, when precision is crucial (Bari et al., 2023).

DATA DRIVEN CLIMATE MONITORING AND EARLY WARNING SYSTEM

Big data is crucial to climate modeling because it makes information gathering, processing, and interpretation possible. Sensors located all over the world and instruments on satellites gather data that is used to evaluate the state of the planet and make predictions about the future (Deafalla et al., 2014). Climate-related data, including temperature, precipitation, atmospheric conditions, and oceanic patterns, are then processed using analytics. Scientists may create complex climate models that mimic future events by examining both historical and current data (Dowlatabadi, 1995). It assists in discovering correlations, patterns, and trends that support well-informed choices and successful tactics. The process of gathering data and information about a phenomenon or a region without making direct touch with it is known as remote sensing. It serves as a substitute for in-situ observation. Geography, hydrology, ecology, meteorology, oceanography, glaciology, geology, military applications, intelligence, commercial, economic, planning, and humanitarian applications are just a few of the many sectors that use remote sensing technology (Deafalla et al., 2014). Through the use of sent signals, such as electromagnetic radiation, remote sensing technologies—which can be based on satellites or airplanes—are able to identify and categorize objects and features of the Earth system. Drones are also becoming more popular since they can quickly gather high-resolution data for real-time monitoring (Bari et al., 2023). While "passive" remote sensing refers to sensors that can detect radiation that is emitted or reflected by an object or surrounding areas (e.g., film photography, infrared, charge-coupled devices, and radiometers), "active" remote sensing techniques refer to a signal that is directly emitted by a satellite or an aircraft, reflected by an object, and then detected by the sensor (e.g. RADAR and LiDAR) (Eniolorunda, 2014). The climate system and its variations have been better understood recently because of the use of remote sensing. Investigating climate-related processes or long-term and short-term events, such as deforestation or El Niño trends, is made possible by its ability to monitor the Earth's surface, ocean, and atmosphere at several spatiotemporal scales (Deafalla et al., 2014). Additionally, remote sensing can be used to gather data and information in inaccessible or hazardous locations (such impermeable zones) or during fire situations (Zagalikis, 2023). One of the most effective techniques for disaster management is predictive analytics. These technologies evaluate current information and historical data using machine learning algorithms to forecast the probability and intensity of future disasters (Arinta & WR, 2019).

AI makes it possible to automate a variety of emergency response operations, greatly lowering human error and delays. A digital twin is a computerized model of a real system, such infrastructure or cities. To find weaknesses and strengthen readiness for disasters, AI-enhanced digital twins' model potential outcomes (Liu et al., 2023). The hardest disasters to forecast and manage are wildfires. AI is changing how wildfires are managed by fire detection i.e., AI programs examine sensor data and satellite photos to locate fire hotspots before they spread and fire spread prediction i.e., to direct firefighting efforts, algorithms model fire behavior based on geography, vegetation density, and wind patterns (James et al., 2023). For instance, Artificial intelligence (AI) algorithms were used to forecast the path and strength of Cyclone Amphan in India in the year 2000. Authorities were able to evacuate millions of people due to early warnings, which greatly decreased the number of fatalities (Venkadesh et al., 2024). AI techniques also helped with post-cyclone damage assessment using satellite photos. AI-powered techniques for early wildfire identification have been implemented by the California Department of Forestry and Fire Protection (CAL FIRE). These technologies enable faster response times by identifying fire outbreaks by analyzing data from thermal imaging cameras (Lambert et al., 2024).

SUSTAINABLE URBAN PLANNING AND DESIGN

Sustainable urban planning and design is a way of building cities that are environmentally friendly, economically viable, and socially inclusive. It involves creating a balance between the environment, the economy, and society.

Smart City Planning for Climate Resilience

The city's infrastructure incorporates energy storage devices, wind turbines, and solar panels. In addition to lowering the city's carbon footprint, these technologies provide a more resilient and sustainable energy source, which is particularly important during natural disasters (Wang et al., 2024). Sophisticated algorithms evaluate and analyze the vast volumes of data gathered, providing municipal planners with useful insights. Data analytics offer the intelligence required for proactive governance, whether it is identifying flood-prone areas or forecasting surges in energy demand (van Staden, 2020).

Climate Responsive Architecture and Green Buildings

In order to maximize occupant comfort while utilizing the least amount of energy, climate-responsive buildings and infrastructure take into consideration factors such as seasonality, solar pathing, natural shading, ambient humidity, and annual rainfall patterns (Amores et al., 2023). The deliberate and methodical application of passive design techniques is largely responsible for this. This strategy is also essential for getting cities and towns ready for the growing number of extreme weather events associated with climate change (Sturiale & Scuderi, 2019). Many traditional architectural methods have just been abandoned in the last century or so in favor of universal architectural designs, which usually ignore local climate considerations. Many architects are starting to recognize the drawbacks of this approach (Xue et al., 2024). The architectural methodology known as “climate responsive architecture” aims to create energy-efficient structures that are specifically tailored to the local environment (Rodriguez et al., 2024). The local weather has influenced and been reflected in the designs of these buildings. Local weather patterns are taken into consideration while designing climate-responsive architecture in order to lower energy requirements (Monteiro et al., 2020). The majority of climate-responsive buildings use passive ventilation techniques and use passive solar design components. To lessen the effects of climate change, large-scale implementation of climate sensitive architecture is essential. Because it tackles both of these issues, climate responsive architecture should be prioritized (Osman & Sevinc, 2019). One of the fundamental tenets of climate responsive design is the emphasis on passive ventilation, heating, and cooling techniques, all of which lower a building's carbon emissions and energy usage (Monteiro et al., 2020). In order to minimize the amount of energy, money, and resources required for repairs or complete rebuilding, climate responsive architecture also aims to create structures that can withstand the natural calamities that are typical in a given area (Amores et al., 2023). All things considered, climate responsive design is significant since it eventually contributes to the reduction of carbon emissions, restricts the generation of trash, and builds sturdy, safe structures (Osman & Sevinc, 2019).

Zoning Regulations and Policy Interventions

Local laws known as zoning restrictions control the use of properties located in particular parts of a city or municipality. These regulations are intended to encourage planned growth, avoid conflicts between various land uses, and guarantee that communities expand in an effective and sustainable way (Jepson Jr & Haines, 2014). Building codes, zoning laws, and other government initiatives to influence construction practices are examples of zoning restrictions for land use that alter the physical landscape of cities, towns, and counties (Fischel, 2000). The goal of efforts to amend or replace land use zoning laws is to alter comprehensive zoning plans created following the outlawing of racial zoning laws. Comprehensive zoning restrictions were at least largely created with the intention of being exclusionary and maintaining segregation, even though their wording is racially neutral (Lens, 2022). In many places around the nation, they are still in place. Reforms to zoning regulations eliminate exclusionary zoning codes' requirements, restrictions, or bans and replace them with ones that emphasize construction forms and types within the neighborhood (Selmi, 2010). The aesthetic and safety aspects of the physical environment, street continuity and connectivity, residential density, mixed-use development, and the proximity of residential areas to shops, workplaces, schools, and recreational facilities are all examples of environmental design elements that are frequently addressed by such zoning regulations. Initiatives for Smart Growth and mixed-use development frequently start with attempts to update or amend zoning laws (Fischel, 1987).

Community Engagement

As cities struggle with the issues of rapid urbanization, the impact of community involvement in urban planning on sustainable development is becoming an increasingly important topic. Involving the community is essential to urban planning because it drives development in the direction of inclusivity and sustainability (Deep, 2023). A balanced approach to planning is made possible by allowing diverse populations to voice their unique needs, goals, and points of view. The livability and functionality of the urban environment may be enhanced by urban initiatives that actively involve individuals in decision-making processes, as this may better reflect the interests of everybody (Corburn, 2009). Additionally, community involvement fosters a sense of accountability and ownership among locals, which improves the administration and preservation of urban areas. Therefore, one of the most important tools for achieving long-term sustainability in urban development is active engagement (Evans, 2000). Involving the community in urban planning can result in more equitable outcomes in addition to improving the general quality of life for residents. Urban initiatives can satisfy the unique requirements of underprivileged communities and minority groups while simultaneously guaranteeing inclusive and equitable development by incorporating these stakeholders in decision-making processes (Broto et al., 2022). In addition to advancing social justice, this fosters a sense of community cohesion and connectedness. Lastly, creating prosperous cities that benefit all residents depends on community involvement. Minority groups and marginalized populations' opinions are heard and taken into account when they take part in decision-making processes (Qi et al., 2024). This promotes development that benefits these communities rather than projects that might harm them disproportionately. By actively including various stakeholders, urban initiatives can become more egalitarian and inclusive, resulting in a more just society as a whole (Valdes Cotera et al., 2015). Additionally, this level of involvement fosters a sense of solidarity and cohesion among the community since locals feel strong and represented. Community involvement eventually contributes to the development of wealthy and sustainable cities that benefit all residents, irrespective of social class or background (Deep, 2023).

DIGITAL SOLUTIONS FOR CLIMATE MITIGATION

Digital solutions for climate mitigation include technologies like smart grids for optimized energy usage, data-driven building management systems, AI-powered predictive maintenance in renewable energy sources, carbon accounting platforms, precision agriculture tools, transportation optimization software, and virtual reality training for sustainable practices; essentially utilizing digital tools to analyze data, optimize processes, and promote sustainable behaviours across various sectors to reduce greenhouse gas emissions.

Role of Blockchain in Carbon Trading and Sustainability

Blockchain provides a tamper-proof way to record and validate carbon credit transactions, ensuring that every credit is accurately tracked and accounted for. Because fraud is reduced and market confidence is raised, carbon credits become more reliable tools for reducing greenhouse gas emissions (Rauter, 2022). Each credit is precisely monitored and accounted for because of blockchain's tamper-proof method for recording and confirming carbon credit transactions. As a result, carbon credits become more trustworthy instruments for lowering greenhouse gas emissions since fraud is decreased and market credibility is increased (Mitra et al., 2022). Furthermore, by automating verification and settlement procedures, blockchain can reduce administrative expenses and make carbon markets more accessible to a wider range of players (Boumaiza, 2024). Blockchain technology improves the overall dependability and efficiency of carbon markets by simplifying these procedures, aiding in the fight against global warming. Blockchain is essential for encouraging the use of renewable energy (Schulz & Feist, 2021). It makes it possible to create decentralized, peer-to-peer energy trading systems that eliminate the need for conventional middlemen by allowing customers to buy and sell renewable energy sources like solar and wind directly (Aoun et al., 2024). This lowers transaction costs and makes the energy market more competitive, which promotes the use of renewable energy sources more widely. Blockchain technology may also verify the source of renewable energy, guaranteeing that only really green energy is exchanged. By encouraging the use of clean energy and lowering dependency on fossil fuels, this boosts consumer confidence and aids in climate action (Lv, 2023).

Smart Water and Waste Management System

Using IoT hardware and software, water management involves planning, assigning, and monitoring water resources as well as maintaining associated equipment, such as pumps and pipes (Nie et al., 2020). Sensors, controllers, meters, and other equipment linked to mobile and online apps, as well as data processing and analytics tools, make up an Internet of Things (IoT) smart water management system (Gade, 2021). IoT devices and sensors are connected to the pumps and pipes to gather data on water temperature, level, flow, and other parameters in real time. They then send this data to a cloud server for additional analysis and processing (Okoli & Kabaso, 2024). Software can help with freshwater quality testing, pollution detection, equipment maintenance, water supply management, and more. Numerous sensors are utilized by IoT water management systems to gather data on resource usage in real time (Lakshmikantha et al., 2021). These gadgets provide the collected information to the user's web application. This data makes it easier to analyze consumption trends and promotes more sensible water use (Ajah & Nweke, 2019).

Digital Twin

Virtual replicas of the Earth, its habitats, and the dynamics of regions are known as digital twins, and they enable people to keep an eye on the planet's condition (Nativi et al., 2021). They can offer information to enhance emergency response in the event of extreme weather occurrences by using satellite data-based simulation scenarios (Vaglio Laurin et al., 2021). Urban digital twins provide a potent instrument for comprehending, modeling, and carrying out data-driven decision-making processes, ultimately leading to the investigation of ways to lessen the effects of climate change in urban settings (Najafi et al., 2024).

Climate Focused Mobile Apps

"Klima" for tracking carbon footprints, "Earth5R" for connecting with eco-friendly businesses, "Olio" for reducing food waste, "Good Empire" for food carbon footprint monitoring, and specialized citizen science apps for reporting environmental data are just a few examples of climate-focused mobile apps that facilitate citizen participation (Breheny & Rookwood, 2013). These apps often include features for tracking personal carbon footprints, reporting environmental issues, accessing local sustainability information, participating in citizen science projects, and connecting with communities to take collective action (Fritz et al., 2022). The Earth5R app gives people the skills and resources they need to make a difference, empowering them to take action for a more sustainable future (McDonough, 2003). It is simple for users to report environmental problems in their neighborhood, and local government representatives or other concerned citizens can take appropriate action. This tool enables users to take an active role in promoting community improvement (Mketo et al., 2022).

CHALLENGES AND BARRIERS TO TECHNOLOGY ADOPTION

The climate crisis is primarily affecting cities. Climate hazards are growing more common and expensive, and climate dangers are increasing. More than half of the world's population lives in cities, which also contribute more than 80% of the worldwide GDP (Sharma et al., 2011). Urban communities are frequently disproportionately affected by climate change because of a number of variables, including high population density, the concentration of important infrastructure in cities, and their function as centers of the economy (Dodman, 2009). However, funding for urban climate finance adaptation falls well short of what is required. Resources allocated to initiatives that preserve or improve adaptive capacity and resilience in order to lessen the susceptibility of natural and human systems to the effects of climate change and climate-related hazards are referred to as adaptation finance (Al-Humaiqani & Al-Ghamdi, 2022). In response to risks associated with climate change that directly impact cities, funding for initiatives aimed at preserving or enhancing the resilience of cities and urban communities is collected by urban climate adaptation finance (Keenan et al., 2019). This entails both constructing new infrastructure to address climate hazards and modernizing already-existing infrastructure that is susceptible to them, the majority of which is located in urban areas (Sebestyen et al., 2023). Furthermore, the vast amount of sensitive and personal data gathered by smart sensors, Internet of Things devices, and other monitoring systems used to track environmental factors like air quality, water usage, and weather patterns is the main source of data privacy and cybersecurity risks in the context of urban climate resilience initiatives (Rajak et al., 2023). If these systems are not adequately protected, they may be breached, which could affect citizen privacy and confidence in climate resilience programs (Admass et al., 2024). Fragmented decision-making across various government levels, unclear accountability, insufficient funding mechanisms, complicated permitting processes, and vested interest resistance to change are just a few of the governance and regulatory obstacles that present serious risks to urban climate resilience (Vitale, 2023). These obstacles can impede the implementation of essential adaptation and mitigation strategies, potentially leaving cities vulnerable to the effects of climate change (Lawler et al., 2013).

CONCLUSION

Over half of the world's population resides in cities, and because of the economic opportunities they provide, cities in low-income countries (LICs) are expanding quickly. This growth must continue, but it also leads to a rise in greenhouse gas emissions, which exacerbate climate change and put more strain on already-strained infrastructure systems. Green and sustainable growth is essential. The increasing frequency and intensity of climate-related disasters, including extreme heat, floods, and storms, highlight the urgent need for urban areas to adopt resilient strategies. Technology has emerged as a crucial tool in mitigating the adverse impacts of climate change and enhancing resilience in cities. Smart infrastructure, data analytics, and digital solutions are transforming urban planning, enabling cities to become more adaptable and sustainable. By integrating artificial intelligence, Internet of Things (IoT), and big data into decision-making, urban planners can anticipate climate threats and develop proactive responses. For instance, predictive analytics allows authorities to forecast weather patterns and prepare for extreme events, thereby minimizing damage and loss of life. Moreover, real-time monitoring systems, such as smart sensors in drainage systems, help detect and prevent flooding, ensuring efficient water management.

Renewable energy technologies are playing a significant role in reducing greenhouse gas emissions and building climate-resilient cities. The adoption of solar panels, wind turbines, and energy-efficient smart grids has enabled urban centers to transition toward cleaner energy sources. Decentralized renewable energy systems enhance resilience by reducing reliance on centralized power grids, which are vulnerable to extreme weather events. Additionally, energy storage solutions such as advanced battery technology ensure a stable power supply during disruptions, making cities more robust against climate-induced power outages. Meanwhile, green building technologies, including passive cooling, sustainable materials, and smart HVAC systems, contribute to climate adaptation by reducing urban heat island effects and improving energy efficiency.

Transportation is another critical sector where technology is driving climate resilience. Electric vehicles (EVs), autonomous transportation, and intelligent traffic management systems help reduce carbon emissions and alleviate congestion. Cities are adopting smart mobility solutions, such as bike-sharing programs and electric public transit, to promote sustainable transportation. Moreover, digital platforms provide real-time traffic data, allowing commuters to make informed decisions that minimize fuel consumption and environmental impact. Resilient transportation infrastructure, such as elevated roads and climate-adaptive bridges, further ensures urban connectivity even during extreme weather conditions.

Furthermore, urban agriculture and smart water management solutions are enhancing food and water security in climate-vulnerable cities. Vertical farming, hydroponics, and IoT-based irrigation systems help optimize agricultural production in limited urban spaces, reducing dependency on rural food supply chains that may be disrupted by climate events. Similarly, water conservation technologies, such as rainwater harvesting and desalination, are essential in addressing water scarcity in drought-prone regions. AI-driven water distribution networks enhance efficiency by detecting leaks and optimizing water usage, ensuring equitable access to this vital resource.

Collaboration between governments, private sectors, and local communities is crucial for successfully implementing technology-driven climate resilience strategies. Public policies that encourage green innovation, financial incentives for sustainable infrastructure, and community engagement in technological adoption are key to ensuring inclusive and effective climate adaptation measures. Cities that embrace technology-driven solutions will not only mitigate climate risks but also enhance economic growth and improve the quality of life for residents. Moving forward, investments in research, innovation, and digital transformation will be instrumental in building climate-resilient urban areas that can withstand the challenges of an increasingly unpredictable climate while fostering a more sustainable future for generations to come.

REFERENCES

Abid, S. K., Sulaiman, N., Chan, S. W., Nazir, U., Abid, M., Han, H., & Vega-Muñoz, A. (2021). Toward an integrated disaster management approach: How artificial intelligence can boost disaster management. *Sustainability, 13*(22), 12560.

Admass, W. S., Munaye, Y. Y., & Diro, A. A. (2024). Cyber security: State of the art, challenges and future directions. *Cyber Security and Applications*, *2*, 100031.

Ahmed, K., Dubey, M. K., Kumar, A., & Dubey, S. (2024). Artificial intelligence and IoT driven system architecture for municipality waste management in smart cities: A review. *Measurement. Sensors*, **•••**, 101395.

Ahmed, S. D., Al-Ismail, F. S., Shafiullah, M., Al-Sulaiman, F. A., & El-Amin, I. M. (2020). Grid integration challenges of wind energy: A review. *IEEE Access : Practical Innovations, Open Solutions*, *8*, 10857–10878.

Ajah, I. A., & Nweke, H. F. (2019). Big data and business analytics: Trends, platforms, success factors and applications. *Big Data and Cognitive Computing*, *3*(2), 32.

Al-Humaiqani, M. M., & Al-Ghamdi, S. G. (2022). The built environment resilience qualities to climate change impact: Concepts, frameworks, and directions for future research. *Sustainable Cities and Society*, *80*, 103797.

Alcoforado, M. J., & Andrade, H. (2008). Global warming and the urban heat island. *Urban ecology: An international perspective on the interaction between humans and nature*, 249-262.

Amores, T. R. P., Ramos, J. S., Delgado, M. G., Medina, D. C., Cerezo-Narvaéz, A., & Domínguez, S. Á. (2023). Effect of green infrastructures supported by adaptative solar shading systems on livability in open spaces. *Urban Forestry & Urban Greening*, *82*, 127886.

Aoun, A., Adda, M., Ilinca, A., Ghandour, M., & Ibrahim, H. (2024). Comparison between Blockchain P2P Energy Trading and Conventional Incentive Mechanisms for Distributed Energy Resources—A Rural Microgrid Use Case Study. *Applied Sciences (Basel, Switzerland)*, *14*(17), 7618.

Arinta, R. R., & WR, E. A. (2019, November). Natural disaster application on big data and machine learning: A review. In *2019 4th International Conference on Information Technology, Information Systems and Electrical Engineering (ICITISEE)* (pp. 249-254). IEEE.

Bari, L. F., Ahmed, I., Ahamed, R., Zihan, T. A., Sharmin, S., Pranto, A. H., & Islam, M. R. (2023). Potential use of artificial intelligence (AI) in disaster risk and emergency health management: A critical appraisal on environmental health. *Environmental Health Insights*, *17*, 11786302231217808. PMID: 38089525

Bibri, S. E., Krogstie, J., Kaboli, A., & Alahi, A. (2024). Smarter eco-cities and their leading-edge artificial intelligence of things solutions for environmental sustainability: A comprehensive systematic review. *Environmental Science and Ecotechnology*, *19*, 100330. PMID: 38021367

Bikis, A. (2023). Urban air pollution and greenness in relation to public health. *Journal of Environmental and Public Health*, *2023*(1), 8516622. PMID: 36755782

Boumaiza, A. (2024). Carbon and Energy Trading Integration within a Blockchain-Powered Peer-to-Peer Framework. *Energies*, *17*(11), 2473.

Breheny, M., & Rookwood, R. (2013). Planning the sustainable city region. In *Planning for a sustainable environment* (pp. 150–189). Routledge.

Broto, V. C., Ortiz, C., Lipietz, B., Osuteye, E., Johnson, C., Kombe, W., & Levy, C. (2022). Co-production outcomes for urban equality: Learning from different trajectories of citizens' involvement in urban change. *Current Research in Environmental Sustainability*, *4*, 100179.

Chen, L., Chen, Z., Zhang, Y., Liu, Y., Osman, A. I., Farghali, M., & Yap, P. S. (2023). Artificial intelligence-based solutions for climate change: A review. *Environmental Chemistry Letters*, *21*(5), 2525–2557.

Corburn, J. (2009). *Toward the healthy city: people, places, and the politics of urban planning*. Mit Press. DOI: 10.7551/mitpress/7583.001.0001

Crovella, T., Paiano, A., Falciglia, P. P., Lagioia, G., & Ingrao, C. (2024). Wastewater recovery for sustainable agricultural systems in the circular economy–A systematic literature review of Life Cycle Assessments. *The Science of the Total Environment*, *912*, 169310. DOI: 10.1016/j.scitotenv.2023.169310 PMID: 38123087

Das, S., Choudhury, M. R., Chatterjee, B., Das, P., Bagri, S., Paul, D., Bera, M., & Dutta, S. (2024). Unraveling the urban climate crisis: Exploring the nexus of urbanization, climate change, and their impacts on the environment and human well-being–A global perspective. *AIMS Public Health*, *11*(3), 963–1001. DOI: 10.3934/publichealth.2024050 PMID: 39416895

Deafalla, T. H., Csaplovics, E., & El-Abbas, M. M. (2014, October). The application of remote sensing for climate change adaptation in Sahel region. In *Earth Resources and Environmental Remote Sensing/GIS Applications V* (Vol. 9245, pp. 399–404). SPIE.

Deep, G. (2023). Evaluating the impact of community engagement in urban planning on sustainable development. *World Journal of Advanced Research and Reviews, 20*(3), 1633–1638.

Dodman, D. (2009). Urban density and climate change. *Analytical review of the interaction between urban growth trends and environmental changes*, (1).

Dowlatabadi, H. (1995). Integrated assessment models of climate change: An incomplete overview. *Energy Policy*, *23*(4-5), 289–296.

Dwivedi, Y. K., Hughes, L., Kar, A. K., Baabdullah, A. M., Grover, P., Abbas, R., & Wade, M. (2022). Climate change and COP26: Are digital technologies and information management part of the problem or the solution? An editorial reflection and call to action. *International Journal of Information Management*, *63*, 102456.

Ebi, K. L., Vanos, J., Baldwin, J. W., Bell, J. E., Hondula, D. M., Errett, N. A., Hayes, K., Reid, C. E., Saha, S., Spector, J., & Berry, P. (2021). Extreme weather and climate change: Population health and health system implications. *Annual Review of Public Health*, *42*(1), 293–315. DOI: 10.1146/annurev-publhealth-012420-105026 PMID: 33406378

Eniolorunda, N. (2014). Climate change analysis and adaptation: The role of remote sensing (Rs) and geographical information system (Gis). *International Journal of Computer Engineering Research*, *4*(1), 41–51.

Evans, P. (Ed.). (2002). *Livable cities?: Urban struggles for livelihood and sustainability*. Univ of California Press.

Fischel, W. A. (1987). *The economics of zoning laws: A property rights approach to American land use controls*. JHU Press.

Fischel, W. A. (2000). Zoning and land use regulation. *Encyclopedia of law and economics, 2*, 403-423.

Foster, J., Lowe, A., & Winkelman, S. (2011). The value of green infrastructure for urban climate adaptation. *Center for Clean Air Policy*, *750*(1), 1–52.

Francisco Ribeiro, P., & Camargo Rodriguez, A. V. (2020). Emerging advanced technologies to mitigate the impact of climate change in Africa. *Plants*, *9*(3), 381. DOI: 10.3390/plants9030381 PMID: 32204576

Fritz, S., See, L., & Grey, F. (2022). The grand challenges facing environmental citizen science. *Frontiers in Environmental Science*, *10*, 1019628.

Gade, D. S. (2021). Reinventing smart water management system through ICT and IoT driven solution for smart cities. [IJAEML]. *International Journal of Applied Engineering and Management Letters*, *5*(2), 132–151. DOI: 10.47992/IJAEML.2581.7000.0109

George, L. A., & Becker, W. G. (2003). Investigating the urban heat island effect with a collaborative inquiry project. *Journal of Geoscience Education*, *51*(2), 237–243. DOI: 10.5408/1089-9995-51.2.237

Glock, J. P., Hartl, R., Krieg, M., & Becker, U. J. (2022). No Climate-Resilient Society Without a Resilient Transport System. In *The Palgrave Handbook of Climate Resilient Societies* (pp. 1147–1175). Springer International Publishing.

Goudarzi, A., Ghayoor, F., Waseem, M., Fahad, S., & Traore, I. (2022). A survey on IoT-enabled smart grids: Emerging, applications, challenges, and outlook. *Energies*, *15*(19), 6984.

Greenham, S., Workman, R., McPherson, K., Ferranti, E., Fisher, R., Mills, S., & Roberts, C. (2023). Are transport networks in low-income countries prepared for climate change? Barriers to preparing for climate change in Africa and South Asia. *Mitigation and Adaptation Strategies for Global Change*, *28*(8), 44.

Habib, M., Habib, A., Albzaie, M., & Farghal, A. (2024). Sustainability benefits of AI-based engineering solutions for infrastructure resilience in arid regions against extreme rainfall events. *Discover Sustainability*, *5*(1), 278. DOI: 10.1007/s43621-024-00500-2

Hashem, I. A. T., Chang, V., Anuar, N. B., Adewole, K., Yaqoob, I., Gani, A., Ahmed, E., & Chiroma, H. (2016). The role of big data in smart city. *International Journal of Information Management*, *36*(5), 748–758. DOI: 10.1016/j.ijinfomgt.2016.05.002

Hayes, S., Desha, C., Burke, M., Gibbs, M., & Chester, M. (2019). Leveraging socio-ecological resilience theory to build climate resilience in transport infrastructure. *Transport Reviews*, *39*(5), 677–699.

Hossain, M. S., Madlool, N. A., Rahim, N. A., Selvaraj, J., Pandey, A. K., & Khan, A. F. (2016). Role of smart grid in renewable energy: An overview. *Renewable & Sustainable Energy Reviews*, *60*, 1168–1184.

Islam, S., Karipot, A., Bhawar, R., Sinha, P., Kedia, S., & Khare, M. (2024). Urban heat island effect in India: A review of current status, impact and mitigation strategies. *Discover Cities*, *1*(1), 1–28.

James, G. L., Ansaf, R. B., Al Samahi, S. S., Parker, R. D., Cutler, J. M., Gachette, R. V., & Ansaf, B. I. (2023). An efficient wildfire detection system for ai-embedded applications using satellite imagery. *Fire (Basel, Switzerland), 6*(4), 169. DOI: 10.3390/fire6040169

Jepson, E. J.Jr, & Haines, A. L. (2014). Zoning for sustainability: A review and analysis of the zoning ordinances of 32 cities in the United States. *Journal of the American Planning Association, 80*(3), 239–252. DOI: 10.1080/01944363.2014.981200

Kataray, T., Nitesh, B., Yarram, B., Sinha, S., Cuce, E., Shaik, S., Vigneshwaran, P., & Roy, A. (2023). Integration of smart grid with renewable energy sources: Opportunities and challenges–A comprehensive review. *Sustainable Energy Technologies and Assessments, 58*, 103363. DOI: 10.1016/j.seta.2023.103363

Keenan, J. M., Chu, E., & Peterson, J. (2019). From funding to financing: Perspectives shaping a research agenda for investment in urban climate adaptation. *International Journal of Urban Sustainable Development, 11*(3), 297–308. DOI: 10.1080/19463138.2019.1565413

Kuglitsch, M., Albayrak, A., Aquino, R., Craddock, A., Edward-Gill, J., Kanwar, R., & Luterbacher, J. (2022). Artificial intelligence for disaster risk reduction: Opportunities, challenges, and prospects. *Bulletin*, (71), 1.

Lakshmikantha, V., Hiriyannagowda, A., Manjunath, A., Patted, A., Basavaiah, J., & Anthony, A. A. (2021). IoT based smart water quality monitoring system. *Global Transitions Proceedings, 2*(2), 181–186. DOI: 10.1016/j.gltp.2021.08.062

Lambert, J. H., Dorn, R. R., Ayyub, B. M., Barletta, W. A., Organek, J. F., Piras, M., Gunn, M. E., & Zichichi, S. F. (2024). Wildfire Risk Mitigation through Systems Analysis of the Planetary Emergency. *ASCE OPEN: Multidisciplinary Journal of Civil Engineering, 2*(1), 04024010. DOI: 10.1061/AOMJAH.AOENG-0040

Lawler, J. J., Spencer, B., Olden, J. D., Kim, S. H., Lowe, C., Bolton, S., ... & Voss, J. G. (2013). Mitigation and adaptation strategies to reduce climate vulnerabilities and maintain ecosystem services. *Climate Vulnerability*, 315.

Lee, Y. Y., Din, M. F. M., Ponraj, M., Noor, Z. Z., Iwao, K., & Chelliapan, S. (2017). Overview of urban heat island (uhi) phenomenon towards human thermal comfort. [EEMJ]. *Environmental Engineering and Management Journal, 16*(9).

Leeson, G. W. (2018). The growth, ageing and urbanisation of our world. *Journal of Population Ageing, 11*(2), 107–115. DOI: 10.1007/s12062-018-9225-7

Lens, M. C. (2022). Zoning, land use, and the reproduction of urban inequality. *Annual Review of Sociology*, *48*(1), 421–439. DOI: 10.1146/annurev-soc-030420-122027 PMID: 38045490

Liu, C., Zhang, P., & Xu, X. (2023). Literature review of digital twin technologies for civil infrastructure. *Journal of Infrastructure Intelligence and Resilience*, 100050.

Lv, Y. (2023). Transitioning to sustainable energy: Opportunities, challenges, and the potential of blockchain technology. *Frontiers in Energy Research*, *11*, 1258044. DOI: 10.3389/fenrg.2023.1258044

Manisalidis, I., Stavropoulou, E., Stavropoulos, A., & Bezirtzoglou, E. (2020). Environmental and health impacts of air pollution: A review. *Frontiers in Public Health*, *8*, 14. DOI: 10.3389/fpubh.2020.00014 PMID: 32154200

McDonough, W. F. (2003). Compositional model for the Earth's core. *Treatise on geochemistry, 2*, 568.

Minh, Q. N., Nguyen, V. H., Quy, V. K., Ngoc, L. A., Chehri, A., & Jeon, G. (2022). Edge computing for iot-enabled smart grid: The future of energy. *Energies*, *15*(17), 6140. DOI: 10.3390/en15176140

Mitoulis, S. A., Bompa, D. V., & Argyroudis, S. (2023). Sustainability and climate resilience metrics and trade-offs in transport infrastructure asset recovery. *Transportation Research Part D, Transport and Environment*, *121*, 103800. DOI: 10.1016/j.trd.2023.103800

Mitra, S. K., Pauli, M., & Schottli, J. (2022). Climate Change and India: Balancing Domestic and International Interests. *The Journal of Indian and Asian Studies*, *3*(02), 2240002. DOI: 10.1142/S2717541322400022

Mketo, A. R., Ringo, C. J., Nuhu, S., & Mpambije, C. J. (2022). Enhancing community participation for environmental health improvement in rural Tanzania: Evidence from Bukombe district. *Evaluation and Program Planning*, *94*, 102152. DOI: 10.1016/j.evalprogplan.2022.102152 PMID: 35944329

Monteiro, R., Ferreira, J. C., & Antunes, P. (2020). Green infrastructure planning principles: An integrated literature review. *Land (Basel)*, *9*(12), 525. DOI: 10.3390/land9120525

Musco, F. (2016). *Counteracting urban heat island effects in a global climate change scenario*. Springer Nature. DOI: 10.1007/978-3-319-10425-6

Najafi, P., Soltani, A., Khan, A. A., Chizfahm, M., Sepasgozar, S. M., & Gu, N. (2024). Digital twin for urban decision support systems: Scientometric and thematic analysis. In *Digital Twin Adoption and BIM-GIS Implementation* (pp. 110–144). Routledge. DOI: 10.1201/9781003507000-6

Nativi, S., Mazzetti, P., & Craglia, M. (2021). Digital ecosystems for developing digital twins of the earth: The destination earth case. *Remote Sensing (Basel)*, *13*(11), 2119. DOI: 10.3390/rs13112119

Nie, X., Fan, T., Wang, B., Li, Z., Shankar, A., & Manickam, A. (2020). Big data analytics and IoT in operation safety management in under water management. *Computer Communications*, *154*, 188–196. DOI: 10.1016/j.comcom.2020.02.052

Obaideen, K., Shehata, N., Sayed, E. T., Abdelkareem, M. A., Mahmoud, M. S., & Olabi, A. G. (2022). The role of wastewater treatment in achieving sustainable development goals (SDGs) and sustainability guideline. *Energy Nexus*, *7*, 100112. DOI: 10.1016/j.nexus.2022.100112

Okoli, N. J., & Kabaso, B. (2024). Building a smart water city: Iot smart water technologies, applications, and future directions. *Water (Basel)*, *16*(4), 557. DOI: 10.3390/w16040557

Osman, M. M., & Sevinc, H. (2019). Adaptation of climate-responsive building design strategies and resilience to climate change in the hot/arid region of Khartoum, Sudan. *Sustainable Cities and Society*, *47*, 101429. DOI: 10.1016/j.scs.2019.101429

Preston, B. L., Yuen, E. J., & Westaway, R. M. (2011). Putting vulnerability to climate change on the map: A review of approaches, benefits, and risks. *Sustainability Science*, *6*(2), 177–202. DOI: 10.1007/s11625-011-0129-1

Qi, J., Mazumdar, S., & Vasconcelos, A. C. (2024). Understanding the Relationship between Urban Public Space and Social Cohesion: A Systematic Review. *International Journal of Community Well-being*, *7*(2), 1–58. DOI: 10.1007/s42413-024-00204-5

Rajak, P., Ganguly, A., Adhikary, S., & Bhattacharya, S. (2023). Internet of Things and smart sensors in agriculture: Scopes and challenges. *Journal of Agriculture and Food Research*, *14*, 100776. DOI: 10.1016/j.jafr.2023.100776

Rauter, H. (2022). The Role of Blockchain, Big Data, Internet of Things and Artificial Intelligence for Transformative Climate Action. *Planning Climate Smart and Wise Cities: A Multidisciplinary Approach*, 99-137.

Rodriguez, M., Fu, G., Butler, D., Yuan, Z., & Cook, L. (2024). The effect of green infrastructure on resilience performance in combined sewer systems under climate change. *Journal of Environmental Management, 353*, 120229. DOI: 10.1016/j.jenvman.2024.120229 PMID: 38310790

Roser, M. (2021). Data review: how many people die from air pollution?. *Our world in data.*

Ruth, M. (Ed.). (2006). *Smart growth and climate change: Regional development, infrastructure and adaptation*. Edward Elgar Publishing.

Samaei, S. R. (2024). Using artificial intelligence to increase urban resilience: a case study of Tehran. In *13th International Conference on Advanced Research in Science, Engineering and Technology,* Brussels, Belgium.

Satterthwaite, D. (2009). The implications of population growth and urbanization for climate change. *Environment and Urbanization, 21*(2), 545–567.

Schulz, K., & Feist, M. (2021). Leveraging blockchain technology for innovative climate finance under the Green Climate Fund. *Earth System Governance, 7*, 100084. DOI: 10.1016/j.esg.2020.100084

Sebestyén, V., Dörg , G., Ipkovich, Á., & Abonyi, J. (2023). Identifying the links among urban climate hazards, mitigation and adaptation actions and sustainability for future resilient cities. *Urban Climate, 49*, 101557. DOI: 10.1016/j.uclim.2023.101557

Selmi, D. P. (2010). The contract transformation in land use regulation. *Stanford Law Review, 63*, 591.

Seneviratne, S. I., Zhang, X., Adnan, M., Badi, W., Dereczynski, C., Di Luca, A., . . . Zhou, B. (n.d.). *Chapter 11: weather and climate extreme events in a changing climate. 2021.*

Sharma, A., Surjan, A., & Shaw, R. (2011). Overview of urban development and associated risks. In *Climate and disaster resilience in cities* (Vol. 6, pp. 1–16). Emerald Group Publishing Limited. DOI: 10.1108/S2040-7262(2011)0000006007

Sturiale, L., & Scuderi, A. (2019). The role of green infrastructures in urban planning for climate change adaptation. *Climate (Basel), 7*(10), 119. DOI: 10.3390/cli7100119

Tabassum, S., Babu, A. R. V., & Dheer, D. K. (2024). A comprehensive exploration of IoT-enabled smart grid systems: Power quality issues, solutions, and challenges. *Science and Technology for Energy Transition, 79*, 62. DOI: 10.2516/stet/2024056

Thaler, T., Witte, P. A., Hartmann, T., & Geertman, S. (2021). Smart urban governance for climate change adaptation. *Urban Planning*, *6*(3), 223–226. DOI: 10.17645/up.v6i3.4613

Vaglio Laurin, G., Francini, S., Luti, T., Chirici, G., Pirotti, F., & Papale, D. (2021). Satellite open data to monitor forest damage caused by extreme climate-induced events: A case study of the Vaia storm in Northern Italy. *Forestry*, *94*(3), 407–416. DOI: 10.1093/forestry/cpaa043

Valdes-Cotera, R., Longworth, N., Lunardon, K., Wang, M., Jo, S., & Crowe, S. (2015). *Unlocking the Potential of Urban Communities: Case Studies of Twelve Learning Cities*. UNESCO Institute for Lifelong Learning. [Hamburg, Germany.]. *Feldbrunnenstrasse*, *58*, 20148.

van Staden, M. (2020). The sustainable energy transition cities and local governments in focus. *Accelerating the Transition to a 100% Renewable Energy Era*, 155-168.

Venkadesh, P., Divya, S. V., Marymariyal, P., & Keerthana, S. (2024). Predicting Natural Disasters With AI and Machine Learning. In *Utilizing AI and Machine Learning for Natural Disaster Management* (pp. 39–64). IGI Global. DOI: 10.4018/979-8-3693-3362-4.ch003

Vitale, C. (2023). Understanding the shift toward a risk-based approach in flood risk management, a comparative case study of three Italian rivers. *Environmental Science & Policy*, *146*, 13–23. DOI: 10.1016/j.envsci.2023.04.015

Vujovic, S., Haddad, B., Karaky, H., Sebaibi, N., & Boutouil, M. (2021). Urban heat island: Causes, consequences, and mitigation measures with emphasis on reflective and permeable pavements. *CivilEng*, *2*(2), 459–484. DOI: 10.3390/civileng2020026

Wang, H., Wen, C., Duan, L., Li, X., Liu, D., & Guo, W. (2024). Sustainable energy transition in cities: A deep statistical prediction model for renewable energy sources management for low-carbon urban development. *Sustainable Cities and Society*, *107*, 105434. DOI: 10.1016/j.scs.2024.105434

Wu, Q., Huang, Y., Irga, P., Kumar, P., Li, W., Wei, W., Shon, H. K., Lei, C., & Zhou, J. L. (2024). Synergistic control of urban heat island and urban pollution island effects using green infrastructure. *Journal of Environmental Management*, *370*, 122985. DOI: 10.1016/j.jenvman.2024.122985 PMID: 39461153

Xue, F., Luan, B., Fan, Y., Xie, S., Yang, X., Luo, J., & Zheng, R. (2024). Assessing the Lifecycle Environmental Resilience of Urban Green Infrastructures Coping with Acute Disturbances and Chronic Stresses. *Water (Basel)*, *16*(8), 1162. DOI: 10.3390/w16081162

Yang, F., Wen, X., Aziz, A., & Luhach, A. K. (2021). The need for local adaptation of smart infrastructure for sustainable economic management. *Environmental Impact Assessment Review*, *88*, 106565. DOI: 10.1016/j.eiar.2021.106565

Zagalikis, G. (2023). Remote Sensing and GIS Applications in Wildfires.

Chapter 6
The Role of Academic Leadership in Accelerating Smart Urban Governance

Faisal Aburub
https://orcid.org/0000-0002-6461-9836
Department of Business Intelligence and Data Analytics, University of Petra, Jordan

Saad Alateef
https://orcid.org/0009-0002-3219-0833
Newcastle University, UK

Ala Hamarsheh
https://orcid.org/0000-0002-4736-7331
Department of Computer Science, Faculty of Information Technology, Arab American University, Palestine

Amjad Aldweesh
https://orcid.org/0000-0001-9358-1323
College of Computing and Information Technology, Shaqra University, Saudi Arabia

ABSTRACT

Urban settings in developing contexts face pressures arising from population growth, restricted resources, and evolving policy demands. Research insights from universities often fail to guide governance actions or inform new strategies. This chapter examines how academic leadership can connect theoretical work with practical

DOI: 10.4018/979-8-3373-1375-7.ch006

applications in contexts that adopt emerging digital tools. The purpose is to assess ways to align faculty resources, research units, municipal agencies, and community stakeholders. Findings reveal that administrative support, collaborative programs, and targeted capacity-building foster tangible outcomes in key areas such as infrastructure, resource management, and service delivery. The chapter concludes that universities can accelerate digital adoption by shaping policy agendas and funding pathways, providing a structured route toward more effective governance outcomes.

1. INTRODUCTION

Cities in developing regions experience challenges linked to rapid growth, limited budgets, and evolving social needs. Many observers see emerging digital tools—such as Geographic Information Systems (GIS), Internet of Things (IoT) devices, Building Information Modeling (BIM), and artificial intelligence (AI)—as ways to address these complex issues (Tura & Ojanen, 2022). Despite their promise, actual adoption in resource-constrained settings varies. Academic units often generate important research about technology, but many municipal leaders do not integrate these findings in policy or practice (Tan & Taeihagh, 2020). Scholars, local agencies, and community advocates note missed opportunities when theoretical knowledge remains isolated within academic environments (Meijer & Rodríguez Bolívar, 2016).

Academic leadership, specifically deans and directors who guide institutional priorities, can shape research agendas and encourage collaboration between universities and governments (Alshamaila, Papagiannidis, & Alsawalqah, 2024). This leadership role extends beyond funding allocations. It involves strategic planning, forging external partnerships, and mobilizing faculty expertise to address urban management dilemmas (Lacson et al., 2023). Research suggests that when decision-makers in academia set clear goals for problem-solving, interdisciplinary teams emerge and municipal stakeholders engage more willingly (Gil-García, Chen, & Gasco-Hernandez, 2023). By linking conceptual work to local contexts, universities can serve as catalysts for governance reforms that rely on data and technology (Kitchin, 2014).

Developing countries stand to gain from technology-driven governance, yet local officials often face capacity gaps. Resource limitations, fragmented policies, and outdated infrastructures can undermine the best-laid plans (Lee & Lee, 2023). Although basic steps, like installing sensors or conducting feasibility studies, may occur, a comprehensive, sustainable approach requires more systematic support. In some cases, universities act as knowledge hubs that provide training, pilot projects, and policy direction (Mora, Bolici, & Deakin, 2017). However, these roles depend on institutional commitment, as well as broader stakeholder alignment. Strong academic leadership can clarify pathways that turn conceptual solutions into daily operational practices (Díaz-Sarachaga, 2025).

This chapter investigates how academic leadership fosters the integration of emerging digital solutions in developing regions by bridging the gap between theory and practice. It details mechanisms such as shared research agendas, co-designed curricula, capacity-building for municipal staff, and knowledge exchange platforms that align with local needs (Liu, Liu, & Osmani, 2024). Drawing on examples from Jordan, including work linked to Petra University, it reveals how targeted partnerships bring immediate benefits to municipal departments (Alshamaila et al., 2024). Specific emphasis rests on removing barriers that limit technology uptake. By examining ways to align research outputs with official procedures, the chapter offers a route for universities to accelerate evidence-based governance (van Twist, Ruijer, & Meijer, 2023).

The text proceeds in a structured manner. First, it surveys key urban governance challenges in developing settings, focusing on the role of digital tools in alleviating these pressures. Next, it reviews how academic units can serve as catalysts for innovations in policy and practice (Meijer & Rodríguez Bolívar, 2016). The chapter then presents a theoretical framework that underpins knowledge utilization, collaborative governance, and socio-technical integration (Mora et al., 2017). A methodological approach clarifies how studies, interviews, and case analyses inform the findings. Subsequent sections delve deeper into digital tools—IoT, AI, GIS, BIM—and their links to governance. The text also examines specific strategies for strengthening collaboration between universities and government stakeholders, offering a conceptual model supported by tables and figures distributed throughout. In-depth case examples illustrate real-world outcomes, while a final discussion reflects on broader lessons, challenges, and potential expansions. The concluding pages restate the central argument: academic leadership holds the key to bridging the research–practice divide in contexts seeking to harness emerging digital innovations for better governance.

2. LITERATURE REVIEW

2.1 Urban Governance Challenges in Developing Regions

Cities in developing countries grapple with structural problems that undermine governance performance. Rapid population increases cause congestion, housing shortages, and strain on public services (Mohanty, Choppali, & Kougianos, 2016). Local governments often possess limited fiscal capacity, so they cannot invest in advanced systems. Fragmented regulations complicate planning and lead to inefficiencies (Tan & Taeihagh, 2020). Governance processes become reactive, and strategic vision for modernization lags behind immediate demands.

Research shows that technology can address these issues. IoT sensors deliver real-time data on traffic, energy usage, and environmental conditions (Bouaziz et al., 2023). GIS platforms map vulnerabilities in infrastructure and assist local authorities in prioritizing interventions (Li, Lai, & Lin, 2024). AI models predict service demands and guide resource distribution. BIM supports integrated design in construction, reducing duplication and cost overruns (He & Chen, 2024). While such tools seem promising, difficulties arise in building local capacity and formalizing institutional support (Zaman, Puryear, Abdelwahed, & Zohrabi, 2024). Many municipal teams lack the training and resources to deploy these innovations at scale (Hashem et al., 2016).

Institutional fragmentation also hinders efforts to adopt digital solutions. Ministries, agencies, NGOs, and private firms rarely coordinate effectively, leading to inconsistent data sets and overlapping projects (Mora et al., 2017). Community members may distrust digital tracking systems without transparency guarantees. Some users worry about data privacy, while others may not see immediate advantages. Weak communication channels, minimal citizen engagement, and top-down decision-making can diminish the social acceptance of new technologies (van Twist et al., 2023).

Despite these constraints, certain urban initiatives succeed when universities and government entities align to tackle shared problems (Meijer & Rodríguez Bolívar, 2016). By merging local knowledge and technical expertise, they create pilot projects that produce tangible outcomes. The role of academic leadership becomes critical in orchestrating these collaborations, ensuring that practical research insights merge with policymaking cycles. This synergy addresses capacity gaps and leads to more responsive governance models (Alshamaila et al., 2024).

2.2 Universities as Catalysts for Innovation

Academic institutions contribute to sustainable development by providing interdisciplinary expertise, specialized facilities, and a pool of trained professionals (Lee, Hancock, & Hu, 2014). Researchers can analyze urban systems through varied lenses—engineering, environmental science, social science—leading to multifaceted insights. Students benefit from exposure to real-world problems and become a future workforce equipped with advanced knowledge. Universities also have the capacity to pilot projects that integrate digital platforms and measure their impact.

However, the potential for impactful research often remains unrealized (Mupfumira, Mutingi, & Sony, 2024). Faculty incentives may favor theoretical publications over applied studies. Administrative procedures for external partnerships may be slow, deterring municipal agencies from collaborating. Budgetary uncertainties or limited research grants hamper sustained focus on urban management topics (Meijer & Rodríguez Bolívar, 2016). In these conditions, leadership within academia must develop targeted programs that align institutional goals with the demands of local governance. This alignment can channel academic expertise into tangible solutions (Gil-García et al., 2023).

Several studies underline the importance of bridging roles. University managers can facilitate contact between faculty and city officials, ensuring that research proposals reflect municipal priorities (Tan & Taeihagh, 2020). They can host roundtables, policy labs, or training events to keep communication channels open. Such structures help government offices appreciate the utility of advanced methods and data analytics (Bhardwaj, Anooja, Vermani, Sunita, & Dhaliwal, 2024). When academic leaders allocate resources to real-world challenges, they demonstrate a commitment to solving local problems rather than solely pursuing knowledge for its own sake.

2.3 Emerging Digital Solutions in Urban Contexts

Research points to specific digital applications that can transform service delivery in developing cities:

- **IoT**: Sensors track resource usage (electricity, water, traffic) and alert officials to inefficiencies (Mohanty et al., 2016).
- **AI**: Machine learning models process large datasets to predict operational requirements, optimize routes, or forecast building energy demands (Tura & Ojanen, 2022).
- **GIS**: Mapping tools visualize demographics, infrastructure layouts, and environmental risks, aiding spatial planning (Li et al., 2024).
- **BIM**: Detailed digital models improve planning for buildings, roads, and community centers, reducing rework (He & Chen, 2024).

Studies show that these tools succeed best when accompanied by policy support, robust data management, and relevant training programs (Bouaziz et al., 2023). Technical solutions alone do not guarantee improved governance; they must fit administrative structures, existing workflows, and societal norms. Universities can offer instruction in these technologies, design pilot systems that reveal practical benefits, and measure performance changes to justify broader adoption (Lee & Lee, 2023).

Literature also highlights the complexity of these innovations in developing settings. IoT sensors require stable power and network connections. AI demands large datasets, which may be patchy or unavailable. GIS mapping requires accurate geospatial data, yet many municipalities lack regular updates on land use (Mora et al., 2017). BIM introduction calls for changes in procurement and construction practices, along with staff training. Universities often hold the technical capacity to address these gaps, but municipal agencies may not realize the full extent of academic resources at their disposal. Academic leadership can spotlight relevant expertise and coordinate integrated approaches (Alshamaila et al., 2024).

2.4 Bridging the Knowledge–Practice Divide

The gap between academic work and on-the-ground implementation draws attention from scholars who attribute it to mismatched incentives and communication barriers (Meijer & Rodríguez Bolívar, 2016). Many local governments focus on short-term fixes, while research institutions aim to publish findings that may not translate into immediate policy actions. Timelines also differ: municipalities prioritize swift results, whereas academic studies can unfold over multiple years. University leaders with strong external networks help reconcile these differences by establishing frameworks for continuous interaction (Gil-García et al., 2023).

This interface requires institutional mechanisms. Joint research centers bring municipal and academic staff together on interdisciplinary tasks. Funding agreements clarify cost-sharing arrangements and responsibilities. Collaborative curriculum design incorporates practical case work in student projects, aligning instruction with municipal goals. Mentoring programs connect students and junior researchers with practitioners who expose them to real governance constraints (Lacson et al., 2023).

Aligned leadership across academia and government can reduce friction, open new funding streams, and fast-track technology adoption. In Jordan, for instance, programs linked to Petra University yield evidence of how dedicated administrators create synergy by matching faculty interests with municipal objectives. The literature indicates that consistent engagement builds trust, leading local officials to see universities as solution-oriented partners (Alshamaila et al., 2024).

3. THEORETICAL FRAMEWORK

This section anchors the chapter in three theoretical perspectives that clarify how academic leadership can reduce the research–practice divide in urban governance: knowledge utilization theory, collaborative governance models, and socio-technical systems.

3.1 Knowledge Utilization Theory

Knowledge utilization theory posits that research outcomes gain traction when aligned with the needs and operational realities of end users (Mora et al., 2017). The knowledge must be accessible, relevant, and timely. In urban governance, city officials function as the end users who demand solutions to immediate challenges. Academic leadership can improve utility by designing research programs with municipal input, ensuring that data collection and analysis address pressing issues such as traffic management or service reliability (Meijer & Rodríguez Bolívar, 2016). Researchers then produce targeted outputs that inform policy decisions or practice. This alignment reduces the risk of academic "ivory tower" work that fails to generate real impact.

3.2 Collaborative Governance Models

Collaborative governance models emphasize shared power among public, private, and civil society sectors to resolve complex problems (Tan & Taeihagh, 2020). The presence of multiple stakeholders with varied interests requires a platform for collective decision-making. Universities can act as neutral conveners, hosting forums for city officials, private companies, nonprofits, and local communities. Academic leaders create an enabling environment where these partners co-design projects, exchange data, and evaluate outcomes (Gil-García et al., 2023). Collaboration fosters mutual accountability and resource-sharing, which are vital in developing contexts that lack robust funding or institutional capacity.

3.3 Socio-Technical Systems

Socio-technical systems theory highlights the interplay between technology and human factors in organizational change (Liu et al., 2024). Introducing IoT or AI affects job roles, workflows, and communication patterns. Successful adoption requires new policies, user training, and supportive institutional norms (Omrany et al., 2024). Universities contribute by offering expert guidance on system design and optimization, while academic leaders encourage cross-departmental participation to handle technology's social implications. The socio-technical perspective helps clarify why purely technical fixes do not suffice: people must adapt, and institutions must evolve for innovations to become routine (He & Chen, 2024).

4. METHODOLOGICAL APPROACH

The methodological strategy integrates a systematic literature review, key informant interviews, and case analyses. This section explains the design, data collection procedures, and analytic steps.

4.1 Systematic Literature Review

A broad search of journals was carried out, concentrating on works published from 2016 onward. Database queries used terms like "urban governance," "developing countries," "academic leadership," "IoT," "AI," "GIS," and "BIM." Priority went to survey or review articles with relevance to bridging theory and practice. Screening removed sources that addressed contexts unrelated to governance or that lacked detail on academic–government interactions (Mora et al., 2017). Forty to fifty articles remained, forming a core knowledge base.

4.2 Key Informant Interviews

Interviews were conducted with 15 academic leaders and municipal officials. Participants included deans, department chairs, and research center directors from Jordan (including Petra University), along with municipal representatives from select developing regions. Questions focused on experiences with collaborative projects, funding constraints, technology integration, and institutional enablers or obstacles. Semi-structured protocols allowed open discussion, revealing anecdotal insights about bridging academic research and governance practices (Lacson et al., 2023). Interviews were transcribed, then coded for recurring themes: leadership, collaboration, capacity gaps, outcomes, and best practices.

4.3 Case Analysis

Four case studies provided deeper context:

1. **Petra University Joint Research Initiative**

A partnership with local authorities in Jordan to deploy IoT sensors for resource monitoring (Alshamaila et al., 2024).

2. **Sub-Saharan Africa Digital Mapping Project**

A collaboration with a regional university to conduct GIS mapping of informal settlements (Mora et al., 2017).

3. **Southeast Asia BIM Implementation**

A program to adopt BIM in government projects, led by an engineering faculty (Liu et al., 2024).

4. **Latin America AI-Driven Public Transport**

A team effort between a city council and a local research institute to optimize bus routes with AI (Tura & Ojanen, 2022).

Data sources included project reports, published research, policy documents, and interviews with key actors. A cross-case synthesis compared strategies, barriers, and outcomes, suggesting best practices for transferring knowledge (van Twist et al., 2023).

5. EMERGING TECHNOLOGIES IN URBAN GOVERNANCE

Digital innovations enable real-time awareness, evidence-driven decisions, and integrated infrastructure design. This section outlines four main tools—IoT, AI, GIS, and BIM—and their roles in reshaping urban governance in developing contexts.

5.1 Internet of Things (IoT)

IoT stands out for collecting and sharing continuous data about resources or population dynamics. Sensors track water pipelines, detect leaks, and generate alerts for quick repairs (Mohanty et al., 2016). Likewise, in traffic settings, IoT-enabled signals can adapt to congestion levels, easing commuter delays. However, stable power and network coverage are prerequisites. Municipalities must invest in training to interpret sensor outputs and integrate them into planning routines (Bouaziz et al., 2023). Universities help by customizing sensor deployment strategies, analyzing data, and proposing frameworks for broader use.

Table 1. IoT Challenges in Developing Regions

Challenge	Description	Reference
Network Limitations	Unstable connectivity	Mohanty et al., 2016
Data Interpretation	Limited analytic skills	Bouaziz et al., 2023
Funding Gaps	High device costs	Mupfumira et al., 2024

IoT's success depends on consistent maintenance, data governance policies, and stakeholder cooperation. Academic leadership can design IoT labs that train municipal teams and assist in analyzing pilot outcomes (Gil-García et al., 2023).

5.2 Artificial Intelligence (AI)

AI uses algorithms to process large sets of information, identify patterns, and make recommendations (Tura & Ojanen, 2022). City planners apply machine learning models to forecast service loads, optimize traffic, or tailor waste collection schedules. AI's utility hinges on data availability, so local authorities must gather accurate records on population, land use, and historical service metrics. Universities provide algorithmic expertise, while policy frameworks must address data privacy and ethical considerations (Lee & Lee, 2023). The interplay between AI models and municipal workflows raises new questions about accountability, transparency, and potential biases in automated decisions (Bhardwaj et al., 2024).

Table 2. AI Use Cases in Urban Governance

Use Case	Municipal Benefit	Reference
Traffic Routing	Dynamic reconfiguration of signals	Tura & Ojanen, 2022
Service Demand Forecast	Proactive resource allocation	Gil-García et al., 2023
Pattern Detection	Identifying anomalies or fraud	Lee & Lee, 2023

Academic units can spearhead AI research labs, test models on local data sets, and train government staff to interpret results. City officials gain confidence in AI through incremental deployment, guided by university partnerships (Mora et al., 2017).

5.3 Geographic Information Systems (GIS)

GIS provides spatial decision support by mapping population density, environmental hazards, and infrastructure distribution (Li et al., 2024). This spatial layer helps authorities pinpoint service gaps, plan emergency routes, and coordinate land use. Developing contexts often lack consistent cartographic data, so GIS-based projects must gather updated information. University-led field surveys fill the data void, while training programs ensure that staff can edit, analyze, and interpret maps in-house (Díaz-Sarachaga, 2025). When integrated with dashboards or open platforms, GIS fosters transparency and invites citizen input (Kitchin, 2014).

Figure 1. Basic GIS Data Flow

GIS can also integrate with IoT devices, enabling live mapping of environmental conditions. University experts guide these integrations, ensuring synergy across platforms (Lee, Hancock, & Hu, 2014).

5.4 Building Information Modeling (BIM)

BIM merges digital representations of physical and functional components of infrastructure. Planners can visualize space usage, structural integrity, and system interactions in a unified model (He & Chen, 2024). By simulating changes, project teams identify conflicts before construction begins. BIM stands out in resource-poor environments where rework inflates costs. Academic institutions can train municipal engineers and architects on BIM software, aligning projects with best practices in sustainable design (Liu et al., 2024).

However, adopting BIM involves reorganizing project workflows and acquiring specialized tools. Some agencies hesitate due to perceived complexity (Mora et al., 2017). Universities provide step-by-step support, incremental pilot schemes, and thorough evaluations of cost-benefit ratios. That approach reduces uncertainty and clarifies why BIM leads to improved urban infrastructure (Mohanty et al., 2016).

6. ROLE OF ACADEMIC LEADERSHIP IN BRIDGING KNOWLEDGE AND PRACTICE

Academic leadership holds pivotal influence over how universities engage with external partners and direct internal resources. This section unpacks the attributes, functions, and outcomes of leadership that enable technology-driven governance.

6.1 Vision Setting and Strategic Alignment

Deans and directors articulate a shared vision that underscores real-world impact. They formulate mission statements that guide departments toward public service and encourage faculty to focus on pressing municipal challenges (Meijer & Rodríguez Bolívar, 2016). By incorporating local governance goals into institutional strategic plans, leaders ensure that technology-based research finds practical outlets. They can also establish cross-department committees to identify synergy among computer science, urban planning, engineering, and social sciences (Tan & Taeihagh, 2020).

Strategic alignment allows universities to acquire targeted funding, as donors and government agencies prefer collaborative proposals linked to tangible improvements (Lacson et al., 2023). When faculty see that upper management values public engagement, they design projects that incorporate stakeholder feedback and produce actionable results. This orientation also signals that the institution supports research beyond theoretical contributions (Alshamaila et al., 2024).

6.2 Policy Engagement and Mediation

Leaders act as liaisons between academia and policymakers, navigating distinct languages, timelines, and goals. They create formal channels, such as policy roundtables or committees, that strengthen trust over time (Gil-García et al., 2023). Municipal officials gain exposure to advanced analytical methods, and academics learn about budget cycles, compliance, and political constraints (Mora et al., 2017).

Mediation can include clarifying intellectual property rights, data-sharing rules, or ethical guidelines for technology use. By addressing these elements early on, leaders avert disputes, ensuring smoother project execution (van Twist et al., 2023). They might also advocate for policy changes that promote open data or support pilot testing. This advocacy role positions universities as active contributors to governance reform rather than peripheral advisors (Hashem et al., 2016).

6.3 Funding and Resource Mobilization

Establishing and sustaining technology-driven projects depends on financial resources. Deans and directors often lead grant applications, sponsor specialized research centers, and negotiate partnerships with industry (Lee & Lee, 2023). They champion collaborative proposals that highlight interdisciplinary approaches, making them attractive to external funders. Through philanthropic or public sources, they secure the budget needed to equip labs, purchase IoT sensors, or license software (Bhardwaj et al., 2024).

Table 3. Funding Sources for University-Led Governance Projects

Source	Typical Features	Reference
Government Grants	Focus on public service outcomes	Lee & Lee, 2023
International Donors	Emphasis on development goals	Lacson et al., 2023
Private Sector Partnerships	Joint ventures, tech demonstrations	Mohanty et al., 2016

Such resource mobilization extends beyond capital. Leadership must also invest in administrative support so that faculty can manage timelines, produce deliverables, and handle procurement (Omrany et al., 2024).

6.4 Faculty and Student Engagement

Faculty expertise forms the foundation of research, but they need guidance and incentives to engage with urban governance (Mupfumira et al., 2024). Leaders can create seed grants or small stipends for pilot work that fosters cross-disciplinary teams. Workshops on emerging tools build faculty capacity, enabling them to incorporate new methods into teaching and research (Tan & Taeihagh, 2020).

Student participation strengthens the pipeline of future professionals (Tomor, Meijer, Michels, & Geertman, 2019). Internships place students in municipal departments. Thesis projects analyze real challenges, yielding relevant findings. Academic leaders may forge exchange programs with city government, creating a continuum of applied learning (Meijer & Rodríguez Bolívar, 2016).

7. BRIDGING THE GAP: MECHANISMS AND STRATEGIES

7.1 Joint Research and Development Centers

Joint research centers unify faculty, city officials, and private companies around shared objectives. These centers manage project portfolios, set research priorities, and monitor results (Gil-García et al., 2023). They also serve as data repositories that pool municipal and academic information. University leaders anchor these centers by providing infrastructure, staffing, and operational guidelines.

Figure 2. Structure of a Joint R&D Center

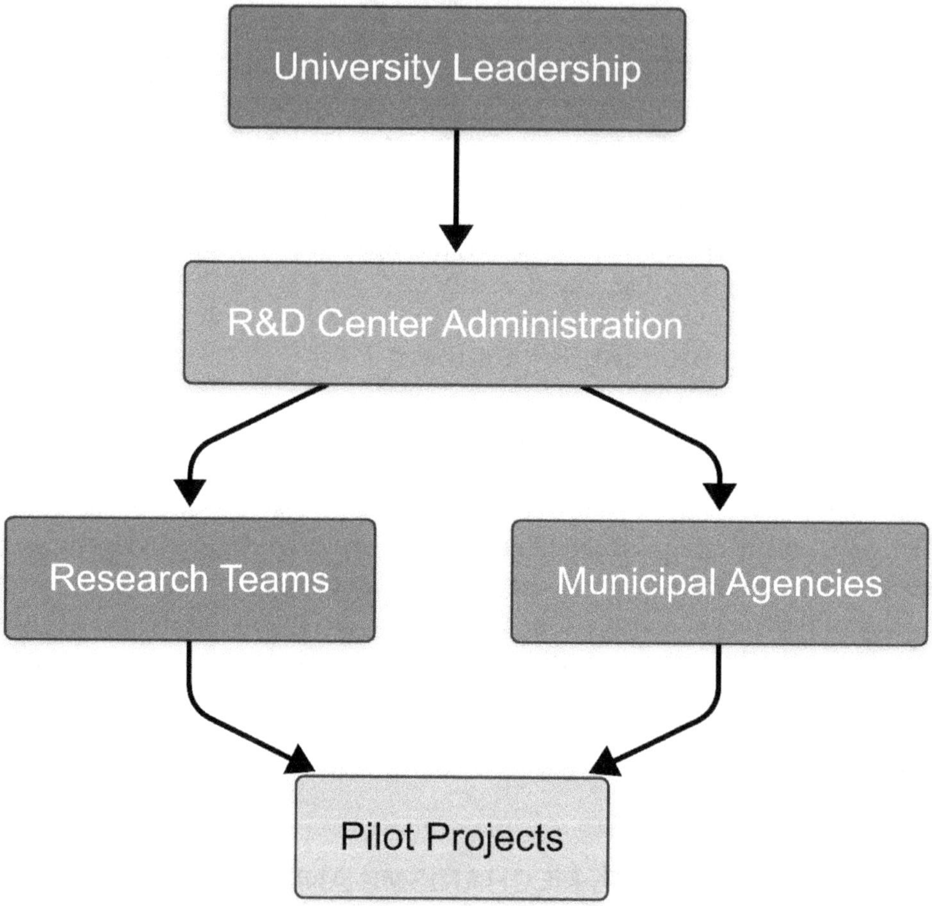

Municipal partners can submit requests or problems to the R&D center, which proposes research or pilot solutions. The center then coordinates implementation, tracking indicators of success (Mora et al., 2017). This approach fosters synergy and ensures continuity across multiple initiatives.

7.2 Collaborative Curriculum Design

Leaders encourage academic departments to adopt content that addresses local governance priorities. For example, engineering students might study sensor networks for monitoring water infrastructure (Mohanty et al., 2016). Urban planning courses could incorporate AI-based modeling to evaluate transport scenarios (Tura

& Ojanen, 2022). Curricula that mirror real municipal issues produce graduates who are ready to apply advanced methods.

Shared teaching modules or capstone courses can engage city experts as co-instructors, bridging theory with on-the-ground knowledge (Lacson et al., 2023). Students benefit by seeing direct links between academic material and public service. Policy labs and design studios can simulate real negotiations, providing practical experience in collaboration (Hashem et al., 2016).

7.3 Internships and Fellowship Programs

Internships provide immersive experiences where students or early-career researchers collaborate with city agencies to gather data and test solutions (Omrany et al., 2024). Fellows may spend extended periods working on municipal tasks, then return to campus with new insights. This arrangement encourages ongoing communication, while also creating a talent pipeline for local government (Lee, Hancock, & Hu, 2014).

Table 4. Internship Benefits

Benefit	Outcome	Reference
Hands-On Training	Enhanced student competencies	Tan & Taeihagh, 2020
Municipal Capacity Building	Extra staffing and expertise	Zaman et al., 2024
Research Data Collection	Access to real information for analysis	Mupfumira et al., 2024
Pipeline for Employment	Graduates familiar with public sector needs	Tomor et al., 2019

Such programs also promote trust. City personnel see the value in academic knowledge, and universities refine their curricula based on field feedback (Meijer & Rodríguez Bolívar, 2016).

7.4 Data-Sharing Agreements

Many governance challenges demand integrated data from multiple sources. Academic leaders can initiate data-sharing agreements, clarifying privacy protections, usage rights, and responsibilities (Díaz-Sarachaga, 2025). Partnerships might involve municipal databases on health, environment, or transportation. University data, such as remote sensing images, can complement official statistics. Collaboration on data management fosters deeper research and evidence-based policy (Lee & Lee, 2023).

Secure, transparent data pipelines advance open government principles and can generate broad community trust. They also increase the likelihood of cross-sector innovations because entrepreneurs, civil society groups, or other institutions can propose data-driven solutions (Mora et al., 2017). Academic leadership sets standards for data quality and ensures that ethical considerations are upheld (Hashem et al., 2016).

7.5 Policy Advocacy and Public Outreach

University leaders who engage public forums, legislative committees, or media outlets can shift perceptions about digital governance. Presentations of project success stories help overcome skepticism and champion broader policy adoption (Bhardwaj et al., 2024). Public outreach fosters civic engagement, inviting citizens to understand and support new systems.

This role extends to guiding debates on how best to balance technology's benefits with social equity and privacy rights (van Twist et al., 2023). In some settings, academic leaders use research findings to influence funding decisions or legislative changes. By taking on an advocacy function, they demonstrate that universities stand ready to shape governance, not just observe it.

8. PROPOSED CONCEPTUAL FRAMEWORK

This section offers a conceptual model that ties academic leadership functions to the process of technology-driven governance reform. It builds on socio-technical, collaborative, and knowledge utilization theories.

Figure 3. Academic Leadership in Technology-Driven Urban Governance

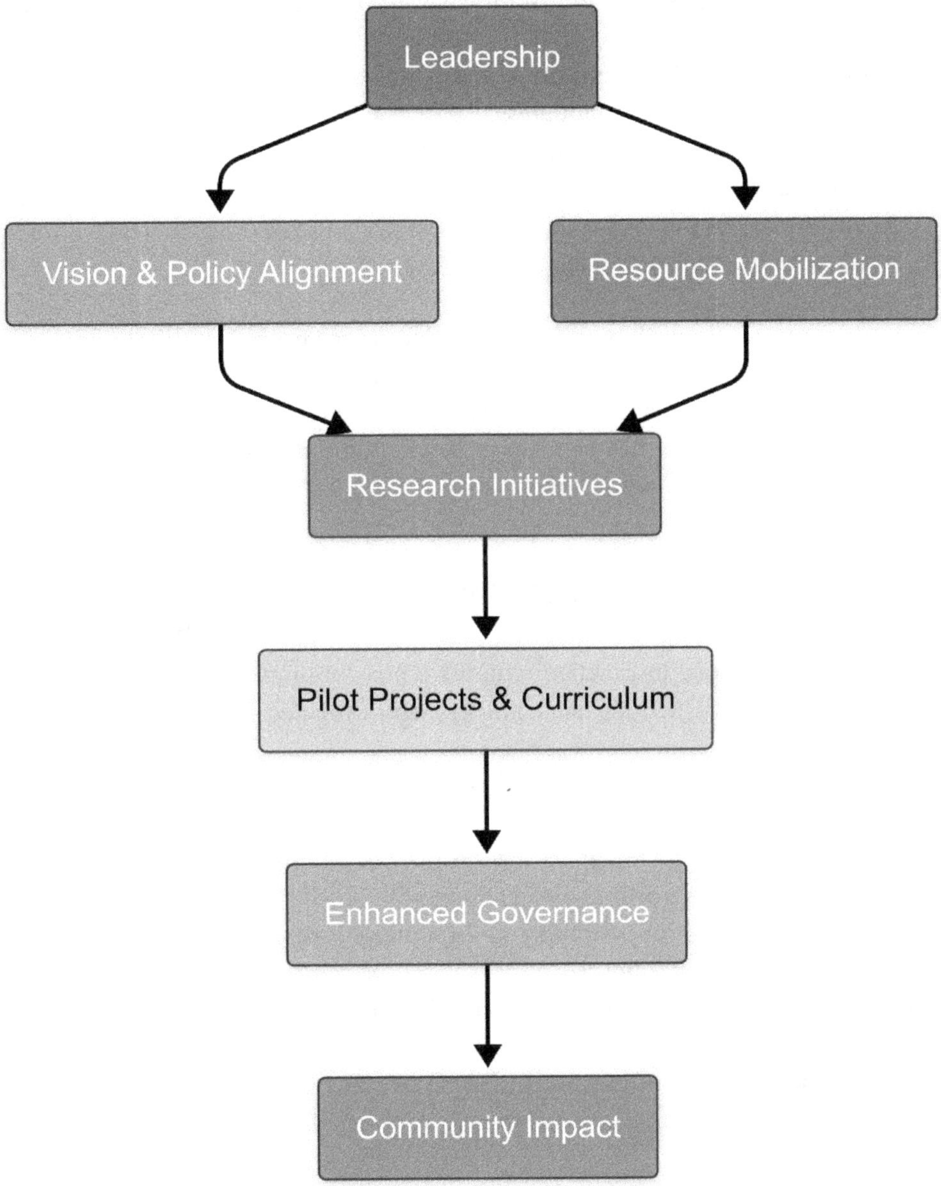

- , or department heads who define institutional goals and manage partnerships.
- **Vision & Policy Alignment**: Leaders engage municipal officials, aligning research with governance goals.

- **Resource Mobilization**: Leaders secure funding, staff, and infrastructure.
- **Research Initiatives**: Interdisciplinary groups tackle real-world problems with digital solutions.
- **Pilot Projects & Curriculum**: Universities test innovations, revise curricula, and produce skilled graduates.
- **Enhanced Governance**: Municipal agencies adopt tools, refine workflows, and improve services.
- **Community Impact**: Residents experience better service delivery, heightened participation, and transparency.

This framework shows how leadership orchestrates each step. Pilot efforts and academic programs run in tandem, ensuring that technology adoption remains grounded in local priorities (Liu et al., 2024). Positive feedback loops emerge when successful pilots inspire policy changes or new funding opportunities, fueling more research (Meijer & Rodríguez Bolívar, 2016).

9. IMPLEMENTATION STRATEGY

Moving from theory to practice requires a phased implementation plan. Each phase includes specific actions, stakeholders, and expected outcomes.

9.1 Phase 1: Institutional Readiness

1. **Leadership Retreat**: University leaders meet to establish a shared commitment to addressing urban governance challenges.
2. **Stakeholder Mapping**: Identify key municipal departments, private firms, NGOs, and potential funders.
3. **Resource Audit**: Assess existing labs, faculty expertise, and available seed funding.
4. **Memorandums of Understanding (MOUs)**: Formalize collaboration frameworks with city councils or ministries (Tan & Taeihagh, 2020).

This phase secures institutional buy-in and clarifies roles. It sets the stage for a structured approach rather than sporadic attempts (Lacson et al., 2023).

9.2 Phase 2: Capacity Development

1. **Faculty Training**: Workshops on IoT deployment, AI methods, GIS mapping, and BIM tools (He & Chen, 2024).

2. **Curriculum Redesign**: Integrate real municipal problems into course syllabi.
3. **Municipal Staff Workshops**: Offer short courses for local officials on data analytics, project management, and digital governance principles (Zaman et al., 2024).
4. **Technical Infrastructure Updates**: Equip labs with necessary hardware and software licenses (Bouaziz et al., 2023).

Academic leadership orchestrates these efforts, ensuring staff have time and resources. Parallel training of municipal counterparts fosters shared understanding, paving the way for joint initiatives (Mora et al., 2017).

9.3 Phase 3: Pilot Projects

1. **Project Selection**: Select 2–3 high-impact areas: waste management, public transport, or water distribution (Mohanty et al., 2016).
2. **Interdisciplinary Teams**: Form groups of faculty, students, and municipal staff.
3. **Implementation & Monitoring**: Deploy IoT sensors, create GIS maps, or develop AI models. Conduct baseline assessments and periodic evaluations (Díaz-Sarachaga, 2025).
4. **Refinement**: Adjust technology configurations, data collection methods, or management processes based on feedback (Lee & Lee, 2023).

Pilot projects produce tangible outcomes that can serve as proof of concept and inspire broader support. Transparent reporting helps build trust among stakeholders (Gil-García et al., 2023).

9.4 Phase 4: Scale-Up and Institutionalization

1. **Policy Adoption**: Work with municipal agencies to embed digital tools in routine operations.
2. **Long-Term Funding**: Seek larger grants to expand successful pilots to additional neighborhoods or sectors (Lacson et al., 2023).
3. **Curriculum Enhancement**: Update courses with new case studies and lessons, ensuring a continuous cycle of improvement (Tomor et al., 2019).
4. **Research Publications**: Document findings to inform academic discourse and best practices.

By consolidating achievements, academic leadership and government champions create frameworks for sustained technology integration (Mupfumira et al., 2024).

10. EXTENDED CASE EXAMPLES

10.1 Petra University and Water Resource Monitoring in Jordan

Petra University collaborated with a local water authority to install IoT sensors in distribution networks (Alshamaila et al., 2024). Academic leaders supported faculty from engineering, data science, and public policy, forming a cross-department team. They secured grants from local ministries and philanthropic organizations focused on resource sustainability. Over 12 months, sensor data revealed major leakages in older pipes. By acting on this information, the water authority reduced losses, freeing additional supply for underserved areas.

Students participated through capstone projects, learning real data analysis and problem-solving. Officials gained confidence in the university's expertise and requested an expansion of IoT coverage. Academic leaders formalized a Water Resource Innovation Lab, encouraging continuous faculty engagement. The project's success changed local attitudes toward digital technology, spurring interest in further AI-driven upgrades (Meijer & Rodríguez Bolívar, 2016).

Table 5. Key Outcomes of Petra University–Water Authority Collaboration

Outcome	Description	Reference
Reduced Water Loss	Leak detection using IoT devices	Alshamaila et al., 2024
Enhanced University-Govt Ties	Joint pursuit of new projects	Mupfumira et al., 2024
Student Skill Development	Real data analytics experience	Gil-García et al., 2023

10.2 Sub-Saharan Africa Digital Mapping of Informal Settlements

A university in sub-Saharan Africa joined forces with municipal councils to address flooding risks (Mora et al., 2017). GIS teams mapped informal neighborhoods that lacked official recognition. The project identified roads blocked by seasonal waters and homes in flood-prone zones. Leadership at the university allocated internal funds for field surveys and negotiated with local agencies on data-sharing. This approach triggered new debates on land tenure policy. Municipal planners adopted the updated maps to allocate emergency funds and propose long-term drainage improvements.

Academic leadership played a bridging role by publishing preliminary findings in local forums, encouraging residents to validate the maps. This process built trust and secured more accurate data. Officials credited the project with clarifying resource allocation, pointing to a decrease in flood-related damage in subsequent seasons.

The university, in turn, integrated these outcomes into coursework on geospatial analysis, strengthening future capacity (Li et al., 2024).

10.3 Southeast Asia BIM Adoption

In Southeast Asia, a public university's engineering faculty partnered with a major city's infrastructure department to pilot BIM-based planning (Liu et al., 2024). Leaders on campus formed a dedicated BIM hub, securing software licenses through an industry sponsor. City engineers and faculty participated in workshops that introduced collaborative design practices. The pilot focused on retrofitting public facilities, identifying structural conflicts in existing buildings, and optimizing expansions.

The BIM hub tracked cost savings and construction timelines, providing evidence for city officials to scale up. Academic leaders also included local contractors in training sessions, broadening acceptance of digital methods. This multi-stakeholder involvement aligned incentives and overcame initial skepticism. The pilot's final report documented a 15% reduction in project delays and a 10% cost saving, prompting the city council to integrate BIM requirements into its official procurement rules (He & Chen, 2024).

10.4 Latin America AI-Driven Public Transport Optimization

A research institute in Latin America worked with a metropolitan transit authority to optimize bus routes (Tura & Ojanen, 2022). Institute leaders led a data-sharing deal that granted access to commuter flow logs, topographical maps, and bus schedules. An interdisciplinary team used machine learning to predict peak demand and propose route adjustments. City officials tested these suggestions by rescheduling certain lines and introducing express services during rush hours.

The pilot ran for six months. Citizen feedback indicated shorter travel times, and operational data showed improved punctuality. Through ongoing communication, the research institute tweaked algorithms and recommended route expansions. Buoyed by results, officials invested in further data analytics, setting the stage for real-time passenger information systems. The institute integrated these experiences into its AI curricula, ensuring a new cohort of data scientists remained well-versed in transport planning (Gil-García et al., 2023).

11. DISCUSSION

This chapter's findings highlight the pivotal role of academic leadership in bridging the research–practice divide. The case examples illustrate how resourceful leaders mobilize faculty, students, and external partners to tackle governance issues with digital tools (Mora et al., 2017). Each case underscores that strong leadership fosters an environment where interdisciplinary teams flourish, pilot results prove tangible, and policy shifts become possible (Meijer & Rodríguez Bolívar, 2016).

Leadership as Catalyst

Academic leaders instigated changes that influenced municipal processes and established new norms. In Jordan, Petra University's willingness to direct funds, coordinate with water authorities, and legitimize IoT solutions led to measurable water savings (Alshamaila et al., 2024). This example underscores that a single project can accelerate awareness and encourage repeat collaborations. Leadership actions such as internal resource allocation, partnership building, and strategic communication drove the shift from theoretical possibilities to actual governance improvements.

Balancing Academic and Practical Goals

A tension exists between academic pursuits—often focused on peer-reviewed outputs or theoretical advances—and municipal demands for rapid, cost-efficient solutions (Tan & Taeihagh, 2020). This tension requires negotiation. Leaders who clarify mutual benefits create a middle ground where researchers produce robust, data-driven evidence that directly influences policy. The synergy fosters publications with practical insights and helps city offices adopt modern methods. The discussion suggests that academic leaders must articulate success metrics appealing to both academia and local governance (Gil-García et al., 2023).

Socio-Technical Adaptations

Socio-technical theory indicates that technology alone does not solve governance problems. Organizational routines, staffing arrangements, and cultural norms must evolve too (Liu et al., 2024). The cases show that university-led training and policy labs help officials adapt. Jordan's IoT project worked because city technicians learned new maintenance practices. The sub-Saharan mapping study spurred policy debates about informal settlements, requiring social acceptance of digital data (Mora et al., 2017). This dimension underscores that leadership must address not just hardware or algorithms, but also stakeholder readiness and institutional capacity (He & Chen, 2024).

Future Directions

Many developing contexts still lack robust frameworks for large-scale technology integration. The conceptual model outlined in this chapter provides a pathway. However, local conditions vary, and success depends on context-specific leadership styles, stakeholder networks, and resource availability (Díaz-Sarachaga, 2025). Future research might compare cases across diverse regions, analyzing how political climates, economic constraints, or cultural factors modulate the bridging process. Longitudinal studies could trace how sustained academic–government collaborations evolve and what factors cause success or failure over time (van Twist et al., 2023).

12. CONCLUSION

The chapter examined how academic leadership contributes to bridging theory and practice in the adoption of emerging digital tools for urban governance in developing settings. Findings show that leaders play a central role in setting a problem-solving vision, mediating policy engagements, mobilizing resources, and guiding faculty-student involvement. The discussion emphasizes that advanced technologies—IoT, AI, GIS, BIM—gain traction when universities adopt collaborative governance models, align with user contexts, and focus on socio-technical change (Mora et al., 2017).

The framework presented here suggests that leadership-driven strategies, including joint research centers, internships, data-sharing agreements, and pilot projects, produce valuable results. Real-world evidence from Jordan's Petra University, sub-Saharan Africa, Southeast Asia, and Latin America demonstrates that academic resources can reduce capacity gaps and speed digital transformations in city management (Alshamaila et al., 2024). This integration yields immediate benefits—such as reduced waste, enhanced public transport efficiency, and improved planning—while also nurturing a pipeline of professionals attuned to local needs.

Challenges persist, especially regarding funding, stakeholder coordination, and institutional inertia. Future research can investigate broader policy reforms and the evolving regulatory landscape that either enables or constrains digital governance projects. Yet, this chapter concludes that academic leadership is a decisive force. Leaders who articulate a clear strategy for bridging knowledge and practice can redefine the role of universities in urban governance, ushering in more adaptive, data-informed, and responsive public services in resource-constrained contexts.

REFERENCES

Ahvenniemi, H., Huovila, A., Pinto-Seppä, I., & Airaksinen, M. (2017). What are the differences between sustainable and smart cities? *Cities (London, England)*, *60*, 234–245.

Alshamaila, Y., Papagiannidis, S., & Alsawalqah, H. (2024). Smart cities in Jordan: Challenges and barriers. *Cities (London, England)*, *139*, 105327. DOI: 10.1016/j.cities.2024.105327

Bhardwaj, V., Anooja, A., & Vermani, L. S., Sunita, & Dhaliwal, B. K. (2024). Smart cities and the IoT: An in-depth analysis of global research trends and future directions. *Discover Internet of Things*, *4*(1), 19.

Bibri, S. E., & Krogstie, J. (2017). Smart sustainable cities of the future: An extensive interdisciplinary literature review. *Sustainable Cities and Society*, *31*, 183–212. DOI: 10.1016/j.scs.2017.02.016

Bouaziz, M.. (2023). Comprehensive systematic review of information fusion methods in smart cities. *Sustainable Cities and Society*, *95*, 104600.

Díaz-Sarachaga, J. M. (2025). Developing an assessment governance framework for urban digital twins: Insights from smart cities. *Cities (London, England)*, *156*, 105558. DOI: 10.1016/j.cities.2024.105558

Gil-García, J. R., Chen, T., & Gasco-Hernandez, M. (2023). Smart city results and sustainability: Current progress and emergent opportunities for future research. *Sustainability*, *15*(10), 8082.

Hashem, I. A. T., Chang, V., Anuar, N. B., Adewole, K., Yaqoob, I., Gani, A., & Chen, S. (2016). The rise of "big data" on cloud computing: Review and open research issues. *Information Systems*, *47*, 98–115.

He, W., & Chen, M. (2024). Advancing urban life: A systematic review of emerging technologies and artificial intelligence in urban design and planning. *Buildings (Basel, Switzerland)*, *14*(3), 835.

Kitchin, R. (2014). The real-time city? Big data and smart urbanism. *GeoJournal*, *79*(1), 1–14.

Lacson, J. J., Lidasan, H. S., Ayuningtyas, V. S. P., Feliscuzo, L., Malongo, J. H., Lactuan, N. J., & Bokingkito, P. (2023). Smart city assessment in developing economies: A scoping review. *Smart Cities*, *6*(4), 81.

Lee, D., & Lee, S. (2023). Smart cities and sustainable development goals (SDGs): Revisiting governance challenges. *Sustainable Cities and Society*, *87*, 104210.

Lee, J. H., Hancock, M. G., & Hu, M.-C. (2014). Towards an effective framework for building smart cities: Lessons from Seoul. *Technological Forecasting and Social Change*, *89*, 80–99.

Li, Y., Lai, Y., & Lin, Y. (2024). The role of diversified geo-information technologies in urban governance: A literature review. *Land (Basel)*, *13*(9), 1408.

Liu, Z., Liu, Y., & Osmani, M. (2024). Integration of smart cities and building information modeling (BIM) for a sustainability-oriented business model to address sustainable development goals. *Buildings (Basel, Switzerland)*, *14*(5), 1458.

Meijer, A., & Rodríguez Bolívar, M. P. (2016). Governing the smart city: A review of the literature on smart urban governance. *International Review of Administrative Sciences*, *82*(2), 392–408. DOI: 10.1177/0020852314564308

Mohanty, S. P., Choppali, U., & Kougianos, E. (2016). Everything you wanted to know about smart cities: The Internet of Things is the backbone. *IEEE Consumer Electronics Magazine*, *5*(3), 60–70. DOI: 10.1109/MCE.2016.2556879

Mora, L., Bolici, R., & Deakin, M. (2017). The first two decades of smart-city research: A bibliometric analysis. *Sustainable Cities and Society*, *38*, 72–85.

Mupfumira, P., Mutingi, M., & Sony, M. (2024). Smart city frameworks SWOT analysis: A systematic literature review. *Frontiers in Sustainable Cities*, *6*, 1449983. DOI: 10.3389/frsc.2024.1449983

Omrany, H., Al-Obaidi, K. M., Hossain, M., Al-Duais, N. A. M., Al-Duais, H. S., & Ghaffarianhoseini, A. (2024). IoT-enabled smart cities: A hybrid systematic analysis of key research areas, challenges, and recommendations. *Discover Cities*, *1*(1), 2. DOI: 10.1007/s44327-024-00002-w

Tan, S. Y., & Taeihagh, A. (2020). Smart city governance in developing countries: A systematic literature review. *Sustainability (Basel)*, *12*(3), 899. DOI: 10.3390/su12030899

Tomor, Z., Meijer, A., Michels, A., & Geertman, S. (2019). Smart governance for sustainable cities: Findings from a systematic literature review. *Journal of Urban Technology*, *26*(4), 3–27. DOI: 10.1080/10630732.2019.1651178

Tura, N., & Ojanen, V. (2022). Sustainability-oriented innovations in smart cities: A systematic review and emerging themes. *Cities (London, England)*, *120*, 103716. DOI: 10.1016/j.cities.2022.103716 van Twist, A., Ruijer, E., & Meijer, A. (2023). Smart cities & citizen discontent: A systematic review of the literature. *Government Information Quarterly*, *40*(2), 101799. DOI: 10.1016/j.giq.2022.101799

Yigitcanlar, T., Kamruzzaman, M., Foth, M., Sabatini-Marques, J., da Costa, E., & Ioppolo, G. (2019). Can cities become smart without being sustainable? A systematic review of the literature. *Sustainable Cities and Society*, *45*, 348–365. DOI: 10.1016/j.scs.2018.11.033

Yigitcanlar, T., Sanchez, T. W., & Corchado, J. M.. (2023). Algorithmic urban planning for smart and sustainable development: Systematic review of the literature. *Sustainable Cities and Society*, *94*, 104562. DOI: 10.1016/j.scs.2023.104562

Zaman, M., Puryear, N., Abdelwahed, S., & Zohrabi, N. (2024). A review of IoT-based smart city development and management. *Smart Cities*, *7*(3), 1462–1501. DOI: 10.3390/smartcities7030061

Chapter 7
Smart Governance and Citizen Engagement Platforms:
The Role of Technology in Smart Governance

Mohammad Ishrat
https://orcid.org/0000-0002-9699-4454
Koneru Lakshmaiah Education Foundation, Vaddeswaram, India

Wasim Khan
https://orcid.org/0000-0003-2311-1451
Symbiosis Institute of Technology, Symbiosis International University (Deemed), Pune, India

Syed Mohd Faisal
https://orcid.org/0000-0003-2422-3535
Koneru Lakshmaiah Education Foundation, Vaddeswaram, India

Md. Shamsul Haque Ansari
https://orcid.org/0000-0003-0053-9332
Koneru Lakshmaiah Education Foundation, Vaddeswaram, India

ABSTRACT

The rapid advancement of digital technologies has transformed traditional governance models, paving the way for Smart Governance—a data-driven, technology-enabled approach that enhances transparency, efficiency, and public service delivery. The integration of Artificial Intelligence (AI), Internet of Things (IoT), Blockchain Technology, and Big Data Analytics has revolutionized urban management, ensuring real-time

DOI: 10.4018/979-8-3373-1375-7.ch007

decision-making, optimized resource allocation, and improved citizen engagement. This paper explores the transformative potential of smart governance, focusing on its core technologies, implementation strategies, and associated challenges.

1. INTRODUCTION

The quick growth of cities and the increased urban complexity have made unprecedented demands on governance structures across the globe. Conventional systems of governance, which are sometimes bureaucratic and unyielding, are failing to address the fast-changing demands of contemporary city dwellers. Problems ranging from inefficiency of resources to inadequate infrastructure, degradation of the environment, and growing inequality of wealth point towards the inadequacy of conventional ways. As a result, innovative governance frameworks that are adaptive, inclusive, and scalable are needed to cope with the needs of 21st-century urban management challenges. Smart governance, driven by cutting-edge technologies, has become a revolutionary answer to such challenges, revolutionizing the way governments engage with citizens, make decisions, and provide public services. With the help of state-of-the-art digital technologies like Artificial Intelligence (AI), Internet of Things (IoT), blockchain, and big data analysis, smart governance increases transparency, efficiency, and inclusiveness in public administration. These technologies make it possible for real-time collection of data, predictive analysis, and automated decision-making, enabling a more citizen-oriented and responsive model of governance. In contrast to conventional models that are dependent on static processes and past information, smart governance is dynamic in its approach, using real-time data to anticipate and solve problems as they arise and maximize urban management. (Allam et al., 2022; Deng et al., 2021; Scholl & Scholl, 2014).

One of the most revolutionary aspects of smart governance is its focus on citizen participation. Contemporary governance is no longer a one-sided interaction between the government and the people; it has become an interactive process wherein citizens are directly involved in developing policies and making decisions that directly impact their lives. AI and blockchain-based citizen engagement platforms provide engaging and secure frameworks for gathering opinions, exchanging data, and having dialogue between cities and citizens. The platforms make decision-making processes transparent, and citizens can use them to report issues at a local level, engage in discussions on policies, and monitor public initiative implementation. Through the use of digital engagement in governance institutions, cities have the potential to build trust, accountability, and inclusiveness into urban development. Apart from facilitating greater citizen involvement, smart governance also transforms metropolitan management in ways of real-time monitoring and automatization.

Smart sensors using the Internet of Things improve decision-making in a plethora of domains like transportation, energy, health care, and eco-friendliness. For example, smart traffic management solutions employing real-time input optimize traffic currents, mitigating congestion and greenhouse gas emissions. Likewise, predictive maintenance using AI tracks important infrastructures to preclude their malfunctioning and reduce expenses. Such developments enable urban spaces to run effectively and evolve rapidly in line with shifting demands (Cortés-Cediel et al., 2021; Kaiser, 2024a). Environmental sustainability is also a very important area where smart governance makes a significant difference. Unchecked urbanization has put immense pressure on natural resources, leading to pollution, deforestation, and global warming. Smart governance uses AI and IoT technologies to come up with sustainable environmental management solutions. AI models, for instance, use sensor readings to track air and water quality, enabling authorities to take specific pollution control measures. Secondly, smart grids harmonize renewable energy supplies, lowering fossil fuel dependence and carbon emissions. Through the integration of sustainability into governance systems, cities can move toward greener and more resilient urban environments. Though smart governance has many advantages, its deployment is not challenge-free (Giuliodori et al., 2023; Ishrat et al., 2024). Some of the key issues are data privacy, algorithmic bias, digital accessibility, and budget constraints. The large-scale collection and use of citizen data require strong cybersecurity and regulation to protect data and ensure the use of AI is ethical. Improving the storage gap to enable all citizens, at any socioeconomic status or geographic location, to be able to access and take advantage of smart governance is also important. Governments need to invest in internet-enabled digital literacy and low-cost internet access in order to overcome this gap. Additionally, implementing open-source solutions and public-private collaborations can counterbalance financial and technical constraints and support wider usage of smart governance applications. Regardless of these limitations, the potential of smart governance in the future looks bright. The convergence of new technologies like augmented reality (AR), virtual reality (VR), and 5G connectivity provides opportunities to reinvent governance frameworks and citizens' participation. AR and VR solutions support engaging urban planning, enabling city dwellers to see and comment on planned infrastructure developments. 5G connectivity advances the transmission of data, supporting real-time applications in sectors like disaster response and emergency management. As they keep developing, they will continue to enhance the capacity of smart governance systems, enabling cities to become more efficient, inclusive, and resilient (Markkandeyan et al., 2023; Nastjuk et al., 2022).

To address the issues of modern urbanization, smart government is essentially a new paradigm of urban management combining technology and citizen involvement. By means of artificial intelligence, Internet of Things, blockchain, and big data analytics, cities can design inclusive, transparent, responsive governance systems that foster trust and collaboration between governments and communities. Though problems including data privacy, algorithmic bias, and the digital divide have to be addressed, there is great room for invention and growth. This chapter addresses the possibilities for transformation via smart governance, providing analysis of its uses, difficulties, and directions for building intelligent and sustainable urban environments. Figure 1 illustrates the main features of smart governance together with the related elements enabling efficient urban management. The aspects are Technology Integration, Citizen Engagement, Transparency, Resource Efficiency, and Policy Innovation. Using digital tools and data-driven decision-making, they all help to create responsive, inclusive, and efficient governance systems.

- **Technology Integration** serves as the backbone of smart governance, leveraging advanced digital tools such as artificial intelligence, big data analytics, blockchain, and the Internet of Things (IoT) to optimize decision-making processes. By integrating intelligent systems, governments can enhance service delivery, improve administrative efficiency, and ensure real-time monitoring of urban infrastructures. The seamless incorporation of technology fosters automation, enhances security, and supports smart city development.
- **Citizen Engagement** plays a vital role in fostering a participatory governance model where individuals contribute to decision-making processes. Digital platforms, mobile applications, and e-governance systems empower citizens to actively engage with authorities, provide feedback, and access public services more efficiently. This engagement enhances transparency, builds trust in governance, and encourages collaborative urban development, ultimately leading to more inclusive policymaking.
- **Urban Management** encompasses a wide array of administrative and infrastructural enhancements aimed at optimizing city operations. It involves intelligent traffic control, smart waste management, and efficient public service delivery to create livable and sustainable urban environments. By leveraging data-driven urban planning, cities can reduce congestion, enhance public safety, and improve infrastructure resilience, ensuring smooth day-to-day functioning.
- **Environmental Sustainability** is a core component of smart governance, focusing on sustainable urban development, climate action, and resource conservation. Advanced monitoring systems help in tracking pollution levels, promoting green energy initiatives, and implementing eco-friendly urban policies. By integrating smart energy grids, water management systems, and green urban planning, governments can minimize environmental degradation and support long-term sustainability.

- **Challenges** in smart governance arise from cybersecurity threats, data privacy concerns, digital divides, and resistance to technological adoption. Ensuring equitable access to smart solutions and addressing ethical concerns in AI-driven governance are critical in overcoming these hurdles. Policymakers must establish regulatory frameworks and robust cybersecurity measures to safeguard digital governance ecosystems while fostering trust among citizens.

By integrating Technology Integration, Citizen Engagement, Urban Management, Environmental Sustainability, and addressing Challenges, smart governance paves the way for an intelligent, resilient, and responsive urban landscape. The synergy among these dimensions ensures optimized resource utilization, enhanced public service delivery, and improved quality of life in modern cities.

Figure 1. Key Dimensions of Smart Governance

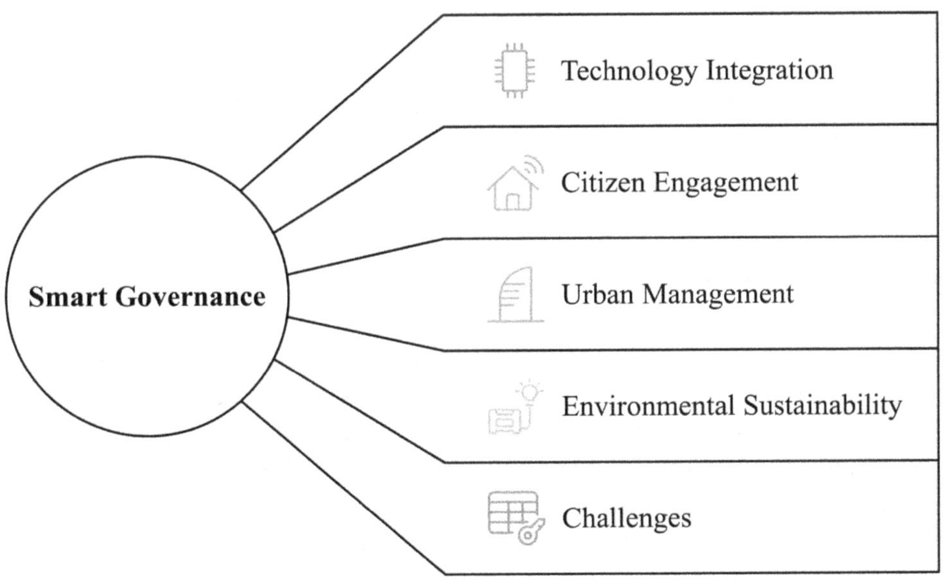

2. THE ROLE OF TECHNOLOGY IN SMART GOVERNANCE

Technology is at the forefront of remaking urban administration, adapting age-old bureaucratic models into dynamic, data-based, and responsive models that can cope with the complex problems of modern cities. The convergence of new technologies like Artificial Intelligence (AI), the Internet of Things (IoT), blockchain, and big data analytics is the pillar of smart governance, leading to efficiency, transparency, and anticipatory decision-making (Nastjuk et al., 2022; Sarker et al., 2018). Predictive analytics powered by AI allows governments to forecast infrastructure needs, identify anomalies in public utilities, and improve emergency response systems, while IoT sensors allow for real-time monitoring of key urban operations, including traffic flow, energy usage, and environmental quality. Blockchain technology provides secure, tamper-free records for administrative tasks, thus enhancing public confidence and corruption reduction in governance. In addition, the use of big data analytics enables policymakers to extract meaningful insights from large datasets, which can facilitate targeted interventions in healthcare, transportation, and public safety. With the backdrop of rapid urbanization, climate change, and economic uncertainty, smart governance not only maximizes urban performance but also promotes inclusivity by closing the digital divide and encouraging citizen participation through participatory platforms. Through harnessing sophisticated digital technologies, governments are able to move from reactive to proactive and people-centered governance, such that policies and public services are tailored to the changing needs of multiple populations. The convergence of technology and governance is a paradigm shift that promotes sustainability, resilience, and equity in cities, strengthening the building blocks for smart and more humane cities. Table 1 highlights the key technologies of smart governance, for example, AI, IoT, Blockchain, Big Data Analytics, and 5G. It outlines their usage, ranging from predictive analytics support for decision-making to urban infrastructure monitoring in real-time, secure identity management, and increased connectivity. Table 1 shows the revolutionary effect of these technologies on urban efficiency, openness, and public service provision (Ansari & Mehrotra, 2019; Bolívar, n.d.; Gandhi et al., 2020; Pereira et al., 2018).

Table 1. Key Technologies in Smart Governance and Their Applications

Technology	Application in Smart Governance	Impact
AI & Machine Learning	Predictive analytics for infrastructure, emergency response, and policy planning.	Data-driven decision-making, efficiency, proactive governance.
IoT (Internet of Things)	Real-time monitoring of traffic, energy, and waste management.	Enhanced resource allocation and automation.
Blockchain	Secure vote, transparent public spending, identity management.	Trust, security, and less corruption.
Big Data Analytics	Urban design, public health monitoring, economic prediction.	Evidenced policy-making and improved resource allocation.
5G & Edge Computing	Intelligent traffic management, telemedicine, emergency communication.	Real-time, high-speed response and connectivity.

Figure 2 illustrates the principal applications of smart governance in three significant areas: Urban Mobility, Environmental Sustainability, and Resource Management. It identifies how smart governance utilizes cutting-edge technologies such as AI-based traffic management, self-driving cars, and intelligent parking systems to maximize urban mobility. In Environmental Sustainability, it focuses on pollution monitoring, urban green planning, and intelligent energy distribution for sustainable city management. Resource Management is concerned with water supply management, intelligent energy grids, and resource allocation in the event of disasters to make urban infrastructure efficient and resilient. Together, these applications demonstrate how smart government improves city efficiency, sustainability, and quality of life.

- **Urban Mobility** plays a crucial role in shaping modern cities by implementing intelligent solutions that address traffic congestion, enhance public transportation, and promote alternative mobility options. AI-powered traffic management systems optimize traffic flow through real-time data analysis, reducing travel times and emissions. Autonomous vehicles further contribute to smart urban mobility by improving road safety and reducing dependency on human-driven transportation. Additionally, smart parking systems leverage IoT and AI to enable efficient parking space utilization, minimizing congestion and enhancing convenience for commuters.
- **Environmental Sustainability** focuses on leveraging technology to monitor and mitigate environmental impacts while promoting green urban development. Advanced pollution monitoring systems utilize IoT sensors and AI analytics to track air and water quality, facilitating data-driven interventions to improve environmental health. Urban green planning integrates smart technologies to enhance green spaces, support biodiversity, and mitigate urban heat islands. Furthermore, smart energy distribution ensures optimal energy

consumption and reduced carbon emissions by utilizing intelligent grids that balance supply and demand, fostering energy efficiency and sustainability.

- **Resource Management** is integral to ensuring the effective allocation and utilization of essential resources in urban environments. Smart water supply management systems employ real-time monitoring and predictive analytics to detect leaks, optimize distribution, and conserve water resources. Intelligent energy grids enhance energy efficiency by dynamically managing electricity demand and integrating renewable energy sources. In addition, disaster resource allocation leverages AI and IoT to optimize emergency response strategies, ensuring timely deployment of critical resources during natural disasters or crises. These advancements collectively enhance urban resilience and sustainability, reinforcing the role of smart governance in future-ready cities. (Allam et al., 2022; Gill et al., 2022).

Figure 2. Key Areas of Smart Governance Implementation

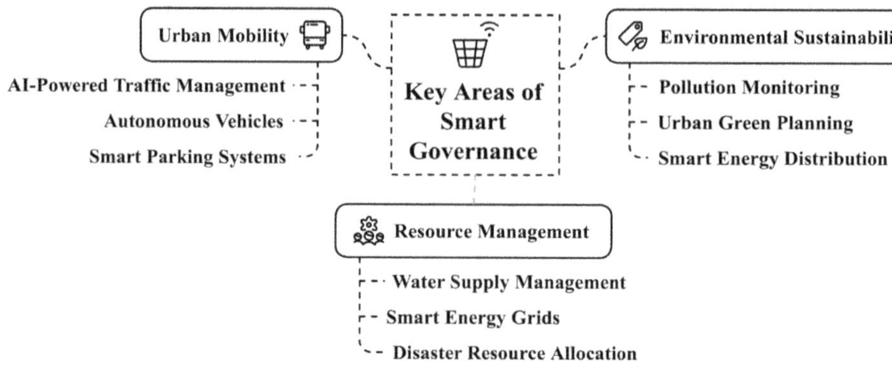

2.1. Enhancing Decision-Making and Resource Allocation

Traditional Effective decision-making and efficient resource allocation are fundamental to governance. Historically, these processes relied on static data, subjective judgment, and time-consuming manual analysis, often leading to inefficiencies and delayed responses. With the advent of predictive analytics powered by AI and machine learning, governments can now make data-driven decisions that are both timely and precise. These technologies analyze vast datasets from diverse sources, including IoT sensors, historical records, and real-time inputs, to identify patterns, forecast trends, and recommend optimal courses of action (Ansari & Mehrotra, 2020, 2022; Challoumis, 2024; Valle-Cruz et al., 2022).

In disaster management, for example, predictive analytics has been invaluable in reducing risks of natural calamities. AI systems are able to analyze meteorological data, study past patterns of disasters, and use satellite images to forecast occurrences like floods, hurricanes, and wildfires (Varsha et al., 2024; Venkadesh et al., 2024). For instance, in flood-risk areas such as Jakarta, AI algorithms combine current precipitation levels and river water levels to predict flooding, allowing the authorities to initiate timely evacuations and deploy emergency resources effectively. Likewise, California's wildfire forecasting tools use vegetation density, wind patterns, and temperature changes to provide firefighting crews with useful information to reduce damage and save lives.

Resource optimization is yet another key sector where predictive analytics is having a huge impact. Intelligent energy grids with AI manage electricity supply and demand in real time, minimizing wastage and maximizing the utilization of renewable sources of energy. Such systems have been implemented in cities like Amsterdam to reduce energy usage while supporting sustainability. Likewise, Singapore's water management systems enabled by AI track consumption patterns, identify leaks in distribution systems, and predict future demand, distributing resources fairly and reducing wastage.

Urban mobility is also being transformed using predictive analytics. Traffic congestion, a long-standing urban issue, is being tackled by artificial intelligence systems that process real-time and past traffic data. Adaptive traffic signal management systems, such as used in Bengaluru, India, optimize timings in real time based on current traffic volumes, lowering congestion and emissions. Mass transit systems are also affected positively, with prediction tools helping to optimize bus and train timetables to address passenger demand effectively.

In city planning, predictive analytics allows governments to model the long-term effects of infrastructure developments, population changes, and policy decisions. AI tools predict housing needs based on population growth and economic patterns, helping urban planners in land allocation and designing affordable housing programs (Al-Raeei, 2025; Korada, 2021; Ohakawa et al., 2024). In addition, predictive models assist in prioritizing the upkeep of vital infrastructure, such as roads and bridges, ensuring safety and efficiency of operation, as well as avoiding expensive breakdowns. Table 2 compares traditional governance methods with smart governance models, highlighting the shift from bureaucratic, reactive decision-making to data-driven, proactive governance. It contrasts aspects like Citizen Engagement, Transparency, Resource Management, and Public Service Delivery, showcasing how smart governance leverages technology for greater efficiency, accountability, and inclusivity.

Table 2. Comparative Analysis of Traditional vs. Smart Governance Approaches.

Aspect	Traditional Governance	Smart Governance
Decision-Making	Bureaucratic, slow, reactive.	Data-driven, real-time, proactive.
Citizen Engagement	One-way, limited participation.	Interactive, digital platforms, inclusive.
Transparency	Prone to inefficiencies & corruption.	Blockchain-based records, accountability.
Resource Management	Inefficient allocation, high wastage.	AI-driven optimization, cost efficiency.
Public Service Delivery	Delays, manual processing.	Digital automation, AI-powered support.

2.2. Real-Time Urban Management

Real-time urban management is a cornerstone of smart governance, ensuring that city systems operate seamlessly and adapt to dynamic conditions. By leveraging IoT, AI, and big data analytics, governments can monitor urban infrastructure, respond promptly to issues, and enhance the overall quality of life for residents (Poudel, 2024; Yao, 2022). Unlike traditional models, which often rely on periodic assessments and reactive strategies, real-time systems provide continuous oversight and immediate intervention capabilities. IoT-enabled infrastructure monitoring has emerged as a game-changer for urban management. IoT sensors embedded in key infrastructure components, such as water networks, energy grids, and transportation systems, continuously collect data on performance metrics and anomalies. For example, Singapore's Public Utilities Board uses IoT devices to monitor water flow, pressure, and quality, ensuring uninterrupted supply and early detection of leaks or contamination. Similarly, IoT-driven waste management systems, as implemented in Barcelona, monitor garbage bin fill levels and notify collection teams when needed, optimizing waste collection schedules and reducing operational costs. Transportation systems have also undergone a significant transformation with the adoption of real-time management technologies. AI-powered smart traffic lights examine real-time data from sensors on the road and networked vehicles to dynamically adjust signal times, reducing delay and fuel use. Public transit agencies employ GPS-equipped equipment on buses and trains to offer real-time information to riders, making transit more reliable and increasing commuter satisfaction. In London, among other cities, these systems have dramatically cut transit inefficiencies and improved the urban mobility experience overall. Emergency response systems have been especially enhanced by real-time data analysis. IoT sensors and drones track seismic activity, water levels, and weather patterns to give authorities real-time intelligence during emergencies. For example, Japan's sophisticated earthquake detection system employs a network of IoT sensors to sense seismic activity and send instant alerts, saving lives and reducing damage to infrastructure. Moreover, real-time healthcare monitoring technology, commonly deployed throughout the COVID-19 pandemic, monitors infection rates and resource capacities, allowing governments to make better-informed medical supply and personnel allocations. Dynamic energy management is yet another essential use of real-time urban management. Smart energy grids with IoT sensors monitor electricity consumption, renewable energy sources, and grid stability in real time. These systems employ AI algorithms to match supply and demand, avoid blackouts, and optimize energy use. Building energy management systems, sometimes part of smart buildings, modify lighting, heating, and cooling in real-time according to occupancy and weather, lowering energy bills and environmental footprint.

2.3. Empowering Citizen Engagement

Citizen participation is a critical pillar of intelligent governance, promoting transparency, inclusivity, and trust between governments and the people they govern. Through the use of digital platforms and cutting-edge technologies like AI and blockchain, governments can empower citizens to actively contribute to decision-making, offer feedback, and hold powers accountable. This participatory mechanism ensures that governance is responsive to the needs and aspirations of the people, generating a sense of ownership and cooperation (Kuziemski & Misuraca, 2020; Nechesov & Ruponen, 2024; Tariq, 2024).

Artificial intelligence-based feedback analysis has transformed the way governments comprehend and react to citizen issues. Natural Language Processing (NLP) technologies scan huge amounts of feedback on social media, surveys, and reporting applications, and determine trends and emerging issues. For instance, sentiment analysis software allows governments to measure public opinion regarding policies and services, and respond to grievances in advance. During the COVID-19 pandemic, AI-based tools played a crucial role in tracking public sentiment and informing health policy changes.

Blockchain technology enhances both transparency and trust in governance processes. Because it is decentralized and tamper-proof, it guarantees that transaction records, voting records, and public spending are immutably tamper-proof and easily auditable. Estonia's e-governance approach is a good example, employing blockchain to secure voting on the Internet and digitize public service delivery. Blockchain also allows for tracking of public expenditure so citizens can check how their tax money is being spent, putting an end to corruption and enhancing accountability. Participatory democracy platforms such as Barcelona's Decidim enable citizens to jointly create policies and shape budget planning. Such platforms offer an online space for citizens to suggest, debate, and vote on projects so that government decisions reflect the preference of the people. Gamification methods in the form of reward-based recycling schemes in Seoul, South Korea, also promote civic engagement by rendering participation interactive and rewarding.

2.4. Addressing Challenges and Opportunities

Although it has the potential to transform governance, its application also poses some challenges. Technological, financial, and ethical impediments have to be overcome to allow equal access and optimal utilization of these systems. Investment through strategic means, policy changes, and implementation of new solutions are necessary to overcome these challenges.

One of the major challenges is the digital divide, which restricts access to smart governance platforms for marginalized groups. Socio-economic inequalities and low levels of digital literacy among these groups usually hinder their active participation in governance processes. Governments need to invest in cheap internet access, public digital centers, and training programs to close the divide and enhance inclusivity (Raihan et al., 2024; Rodríguez Bolívar et al., 2019). Data privacy and security concerns also pose significant challenges, as smart governance systems rely heavily on the collection and processing of citizen data(Ahmad et al., 2022; Bedewy, 2024; Rizi & Seno, 2022). Governments need to implement strong encryption techniques and remain in compliance with data protection laws like the General Data Protection Regulation (GDPR) to achieve public confidence. Budgets are a major hindrance, and this affects smaller municipalities and developing areas. The expense of installing and maintaining smart governance technology can be overwhelming. Cloud computing and open-source platforms provide affordable options that allow governments to implement scalable systems without high initial investments.

Emerging technologies like 5G, virtual reality (VR), and augmented reality (AR) hold promising possibilities for improving smart governance. AR applications enable citizens to see in advance proposed infrastructure projects and offer constructive feedback, while VR platforms conduct virtual town halls to ensure inclusive and interactive public consultations. These technologies hold the promise of widening the proximity of governments to citizens further, ensuring smart governance is dynamic and forward-looking. Table 3 lists the most significant challenges to embracing smart governance platforms as Data Privacy & Security, Digital Divide, Financial Constraints, Algorithmic Bias, and Interoperability Issues. It also suggests possible solutions in the form of strong encryption, digital literacy initiatives, public-private collaborations, ethical AI frameworks, and standardized data-sharing protocols to overcome these challenges (Dwivedi et al., 2021).

Table 3. Challenges and Solutions in Implementing Smart Governance

Challenge	Description	Potential Solutions
Data Privacy & Security	Risk of data breaches and surveillance concerns	Implement strong encryption, GDPR compliance
Digital Divide	Unequal access to technology, leaving some populations behind	Digital literacy programs, subsidized internet access
Financial Constraints	High cost of infrastructure and technology adoption	Public-private partnerships, cloud-based solutions
Algorithmic Bias	AI systems may reinforce discrimination or biases	Regular audits, ethical AI frameworks
Interoperability Issues	Different legacy systems fail to communicate efficiently	Standardized data-sharing protocols, API integration

3. APPLICATIONS OF SMART GOVERNANCE

The use of smart governance applies to a wide range of areas, essentially changing urban mobility, environmental sustainability, resource management, and public health for good through the intelligent application of cutting-edge digital technologies By combining Artificial Intelligence (AI), the Internet of Things (IoT), blockchain, and big data analytics, governments globally are reshaping urban life, making operations not only more efficient but also inclusive, responsive, and resilient. In urban mobility, intelligent traffic management systems make road networks more efficient through real-time congestion analysis, lowering travel times, and decreasing carbon emissions, while intelligent public transport solutions increase service reliability and accessibility. Environmental sustainability is strengthened through IoT-based pollution monitoring, intelligent waste management, and AI-based climate models that inform policies to mitigate urban heat islands and save natural resources. In resource management, smart water distribution networks, energy consumption predictive analytics, and blockchain land registries avoid inefficiencies and corruption, guaranteeing fair access to basic services. Public health systems are enhanced by AI-based predictive healthcare, real-time disease surveillance, and digital platforms that enable effective resource allocation, especially during crisis scenarios such as pandemics. In addition, AI and blockchain-based participatory governance models enhance citizen participation, enabling citizens to provide input, shape policy, and access public services without hassle. The integration of these technologies supports open governance, improves service delivery, and empowers cities to address socio-economic and environmental issues proactively. As governments increasingly adopt smart governance principles, they lead the way for sustainable urban development, better quality of life, and a fairer future for all people. Figure 3 illustrates the convergence of cutting-edge technologies in smart governance in three key areas: Urban Mobility, Environmental Sustainability, and Resource Management. In Urban Mobility, traffic management, autonomous transportation, route guidance, and parking guidance systems enabled by AI technologies optimize transport and ease congestion. Environmental Sustainability draws upon pollution management, green city planning, solid waste management, and smart power grids to achieve environmentally friendly city growth. Resource Management targets the optimal management of water supplies, intelligent energy distribution networks, and resource deployment for disaster situations in order to facilitate sustainable urban infrastructure. Collectively, this technological integration fosters proactive governance, operational efficiency, and sustainable urban growth (Paiva et al., 2021; Rani et al., 2021). The following topics highlight advanced technologies in smart governance across Urban Mobility, Environmental Sustainability, and Resource Management.

I. Urban Mobility:

AI-Powered Traffic Management: Advanced AI-driven traffic control systems analyze real-time data to optimize signal timing, reduce congestion, and improve road efficiency.

Autonomous Vehicles: Self-driving technologies enhance road safety, reduce human error, and offer a more sustainable mode of transportation.

Route Optimization: Intelligent navigation systems use AI and big data analytics to optimize travel routes, reducing travel time and fuel consumption.

Smart Parking Systems: IoT-based parking solutions enable real-time tracking of available parking spots, minimizing traffic caused by parking searches and enhancing urban space utilization.

II. Environmental Sustainability:

Pollution Monitoring: IoT-based air and water quality monitoring systems provide real-time data for regulatory bodies to enforce pollution control measures effectively.

Urban Green Planning: Smart city designs incorporate green infrastructure, such as vertical gardens and smart parks, to promote biodiversity and reduce urban heat islands.

Waste Management: AI-enabled waste sorting and smart bin systems optimize waste collection schedules, reducing landfill impact and promoting recycling.

Smart Energy Distribution: AI-powered energy grids balance supply and demand efficiently, incorporating renewable energy sources to minimize carbon footprints.

III. Resource Management:

- **Water Supply Management**: IoT-enabled water distribution networks monitor usage, detect leaks, and optimize resource allocation to ensure sustainable water availability.
- **Smart Energy Grids**: Intelligent energy grids dynamically manage energy production and consumption, integrating renewable sources for efficient energy distribution.
- **Disaster Resource Allocation**: AI and predictive analytics assist in disaster preparedness by optimizing resource deployment during emergencies, ensuring rapid response and recovery.

By integrating Urban Mobility, Environmental Sustainability, and Resource Management, smart governance ensures technological advancement, sustainability, and efficient urban infrastructure. These innovations collectively contribute to building resilient, adaptive, and intelligent cities that enhance quality of life while optimizing resource usage.

Figure 3. Technology Integration in Smart Governance

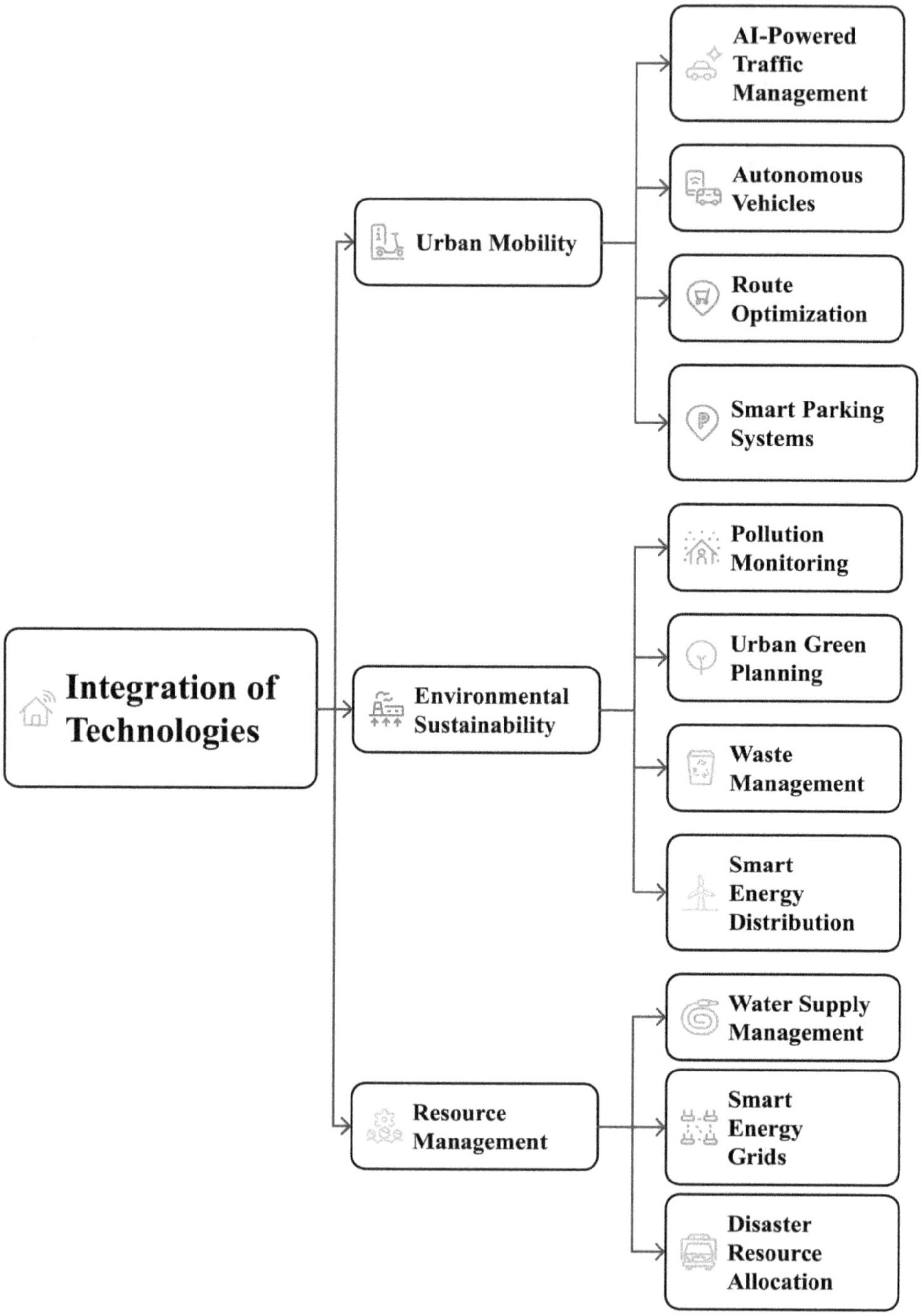

3.1 Transportation and Urban Mobility

Smart governance has revolutionized urban transportation by integrating emerging technologies to enhance mobility, reduce congestion, and improve overall commuter experiences. As cities continue to expand, traditional transportation systems face growing challenges, including increased traffic congestion, inefficient public transport networks, and environmental concerns stemming from vehicle emissions. The implementation of AI, IoT, blockchain, and big data analytics in transportation governance has enabled real-time decision-making, predictive maintenance, and seamless connectivity between transport modes. These innovations ensure that urban mobility systems are not only more efficient but also sustainable, accessible, and responsive to the evolving needs of city dwellers (Ceder, 2021; Litman, 2021). Below are key applications of smart governance in transportation and urban mobility:

- **AI-Powered Traffic Management:** AI-driven traffic management systems have significantly improved urban mobility by dynamically adjusting traffic signal timings based on real-time data analysis. These systems analyze inputs from IoT-enabled road sensors, connected vehicles, and historical traffic patterns to optimize traffic flow, thereby reducing travel times and emissions. By implementing AI-powered adaptive traffic lights, cities like Pittsburgh have successfully minimized vehicle waiting times at intersections, reducing idling and contributing to lower fuel consumption and carbon emissions. Similarly, predictive analytics enable authorities to anticipate congestion hotspots and proactively reroute traffic, further enhancing urban mobility efficiency.
- **Autonomous Vehicles:** The innovation of autonomous vehicle technology has urged cities to enact regulatory systems favorable to self-driving transportation solutions. These cars, with AI-powered navigation systems and sophisticated sensors, enhance road safety by reducing the errors of humans, including distraction while driving and miscalculations in distance and speed. Urban centers such as Phoenix, Arizona, have introduced pilot programs for autonomous taxis, showing the possibilities of self-driving vehicles offering secure and efficient urban transportation solutions. Autonomous shuttles integrated into public transport systems can further improve accessibility to citizens while decreasing reliance on private transport and easing congestion through smart governance.
- **Route Optimization for Public Transport:** Public transport has a critical role to play in sustainable city mobility, and intelligent governance uses machine learning algorithms to optimize transit bus and train routes, schedules, and fleet disposition. Route optimization using AI technology examines past and real-time data, foretelling commuter traffic demand and adapting bus and

train schedules to match. Singapore's Land Transport Authority, for instance, uses AI to optimize transit routes and decrease waiting times, keeping transport services efficient and reliable. In addition, AI-powered software is able to forecast disruptions like road shutdowns or severe weather conditions, which allows transport agencies to reroute in advance and avoid delays.

- **Smart Parking Systems:** One of the primary causes of urban congestion is the time wasted looking for available parking spots. Intelligent parking systems, driven by IoT sensors and AI analytics, resolve this problem by offering real-time information on parking availability. These systems employ sensors placed in parking lots and roadside spaces to identify occupancy status and relay this information to mobile applications or digital signs, directing drivers to available spaces and minimizing unnecessary road traffic. San Francisco has been able to implement smart parking systems effectively, drastically enhancing parking efficiency and lowering traffic-related emissions. Some smart parking platforms also include digital payment facilities, allowing drivers to make seamless and contactless payments.

These smart transportation advancements are essential in modeling the future of urban mobility, making cities capable of coping with rising population density and changing commuter demands. With the incorporation of AI traffic management, autonomous vehicles, route optimization, and smart parking, smart governance maximizes the efficiency, sustainability, and accessibility of transport systems. In addition, the integration of these technologies is seamless, lowering travel time, minimizing environmental footprints, and enhancing overall commuter experiences. As cities move forward with embracing digitalization, these intelligent mobility solutions serve as the basis for more connected and smarter urban transport systems, creating the groundwork for future innovations in public transportation, shared mobility, and infrastructure design.

3.2 Environmental Sustainability Initiatives

Intelligent governance is a central factor in responding to environmental sustainability through the use of sophisticated technologies in preventing pollution, maximizing the consumption of resources, and ensuring ecological balance. With urbanization's ongoing growth, urban environmental issues such as air and water pollution, urban heat islands, wasteful management, and energy overuse become progressively paramount. The convergence of AI, IoT, and big data analytics facilitates real-time monitoring, predictive decision-making, and automation, which allows governments to make sustainable policies that improve environmental resilience. By integrating smart governance principles into environmental planning, cities can minimize their carbon footprint, enhance green infrastructure, and enhance quality of life. The following projects demonstrate how smart governance promotes environmental sustainability through technology-based solutions (Bibri et al., 2024; Ramírez-Márquez et al., 2024).

- **Pollution Monitoring:** Artificial intelligence-based pollution monitoring systems leverage IoT sensor data to sense and analyze water and air quality in real-time, allowing the authorities to spot pollution hotspots and take quick corrective measures. Such systems enable governments to monitor constant surveillance of emissions from industries, vehicles, and other city sources, thereby making it easier to enforce more stringent environmental policies. For example, Beijing has been able to effectively deploy AI-based smog monitoring systems that scan atmospheric conditions, identify toxic pollutants, and initiate responsive actions like traffic controls and factory closure. Such a proactive response has helped improve air quality and minimize health hazards due to exposure to pollution.
- **Urban Green Planning:** Predictive analytics and geographic information systems (GIS) are transforming urban green planning by assisting city authorities in creating sustainable environments that mitigate the negative impacts of urbanization. Intelligent governance brings together environmental information and AI models to determine the best locations for parks, forest plantations, and green belts to maximize ecological value. Medellín, Colombia, is a leading example of effective green city planning, whereby the city incorporated a wide network of green corridors that alleviated urban heat islands, cut carbon emissions, and promoted biodiversity. By adding vegetation to cities, they can increase air quality, decrease temperatures, and provide healthier living conditions for citizens.
- **Waste Management:** Ineffective waste collection and disposal are major causes of environmental degradation and wastage of resources. Smart governance overcomes this by adopting IoT-based waste management systems that streamline collection processes and reduce environmental footprint. These systems use sensor-based garbage bins to track fill levels and automatically send collection requests when required, avoiding overflow and unnecessary fuel usage. Barcelona has implemented such intelligent waste management practices, incorporating real-time data analysis to optimize efficiency and lower costs. Moreover, AI-based waste sorting technologies enhance recycling efficiency by classifying and routing waste materials to the right treatment plants automatically, further encouraging sustainability.
- **Smart Energy Distribution:** The use of renewable energy sources in smart grids is a major leap in sustainable urban management. Artificial intelligence-

based energy management systems adjust supply and demand in real time, maximizing the use of wind, solar, and hydroelectric power and minimizing reliance on fossil fuels. Germany has led the way in the application of smart energy grids that are fully integrated with renewable sources to provide stability and efficiency in the distribution of power. These systems draw on real-time energy consumption patterns to vary levels of production, avoid wastage, and boost grid resilience to shocks. Furthermore, smart governance promotes the implementation of decentralized energy solutions like microgrids and community solar programs, allowing for local communities to make contributions to energy sustainability.

These projects highlight how intelligent governance allows cities to address environmental concerns ahead of time and effectively using advanced technologies. Through the deployment of AI, IoT, and predictive analytics as part of sustainability planning, city centers can boost their resilience against climate change, streamline resource usage, and usher in a greener, cleaner future. With environmental issues intensifying, technology's role in governance will prove vital in attaining long-term sustainability and ensuring urban growth is consonant with conservation.

3.3 Resource Management and Allocation

Smart governance is essential to maximize resource allocation and management to ensure that basic services like water, energy, and emergency resources are allocated effectively and sustainably. With urban populations on the rise, demand for critical resources increases, creating shortages, wastage, and stress on infrastructure. Through the integration of AI, IoT, and big data analytics, governments can track consumption patterns, forecast demand fluctuations, and take proactive steps to avoid resource depletion. These technologies allow authorities to increase operational efficiency, reduce environmental footprint, and enhance resilience against natural disasters and other crises. The following applications demonstrate how smart governance is revolutionizing resource management through data-driven decision-making (Das, 2024; Mishra & Singh, 2023).

- **Water Supply Management:** Water scarcity is increasingly becoming an issue in most cities, with a need to implement smart water management techniques to achieve sustainable distribution and usage. Predictive analytics based on AI enable governments to predict patterns of water demand, identify pipeline leaks, and optimize supply networks in real time. For example, Cape Town successfully employed predictive analytics throughout its acute water shortage, which allowed authorities to distribute water supplies effectively, effect specific conservation tactics, and limit overall usage. IoT-based smart meters also aid in water management by giving people and companies timely information about how much they're using, thus promoting responsible consumption while notifying the authorities of prospective leaks or wastage in the system.

- **Smart Energy Grids:** Conventional power distribution networks are usually plagued with inefficiencies in the form of transmission losses, supply-demand disparities, and use of fossil fuels. Smart grids overcome these disadvantages by incorporating IoT sensors and analytics powered by AI to track usage patterns, identify peak demand windows, and determine optimal energy dispensation. Urban areas such as Amsterdam have been able to implement smart grids which optimize the supply and demand of electricity in real-time, minimizing power cuts and maximizing the integration of alternative energy resources like solar and wind power. These grids also enable decentralized energy generation, enabling homes and companies to feed surplus energy back into the grid, creating a more sustainable and robust energy infrastructure.
- **Disaster Resource Allocation:** In times of emergency, quick and effective distribution of vital resources like food, water, medicines, and shelter is essential to reduce casualties and enable effective disaster relief. AI-based disaster management systems process real-time information from various sources, such as weather forecasts, satellite imagery, and social media reports, to evaluate the intensity of crises and prioritize the distribution of resources. Japan has used sophisticated AI systems for disaster response, allowing the authorities to send emergency relief strategically, streamline evacuation plans, and coordinate rescue efforts. With the use of predictive models, governments can pre-position resources in at-risk areas in advance, enhance readiness, and narrow response times during natural disasters, pandemics, or humanitarian crises.

These intelligent governance programs illustrate the ways in which technology-based resource management can increase sustainability, efficiency, and resilience in cities. By leveraging AI,

IoT, and data analytics, cities can optimize the allocation of critical resources, prevent shortages, and ensure that essential services remain accessible to all. As urbanization continues to accelerate, intelligent resource management will play an increasingly vital role in supporting long-term economic and environmental stability.

3.4 Public Health and Safety

Smart governance significantly strengthens public health and safety by integrating advanced technologies that enable disease prevention, efficient healthcare resource management, crime prevention, and emergency response optimization. As urban populations grow and cities face increasing health and security challenges, leveraging AI, IoT, and big data analytics allows governments to enhance public services, minimize risks, and respond proactively to crises. These innovations facilitate real-time decision-making, predictive analysis, and automation, ensuring that resources are allocated efficiently and services remain accessible to all citizens. The following applications demonstrate how smart governance is revolutionizing public health and safety through technology-driven solutions (Damaševičius et al., 2023; Kaiser, 2024b; Springs, 2024).

- **Disease Outbreak Prediction:** AI-powered disease surveillance systems analyze vast datasets, including epidemiological records, population movement trends, and environmental conditions, to predict and track the spread of infectious diseases. These predictive models help governments implement early intervention measures, allocate medical resources efficiently, and enforce targeted containment strategies. During the COVID-19 pandemic, AI-driven predictive tools were instrumental in monitoring infection rates, optimizing hospital preparedness, and informing policy decisions on lockdowns and social distancing measures. By integrating IoT-enabled health monitoring devices and real-time data analytics, governments can detect potential outbreaks early, allowing for swift action to prevent large-scale public health crises.
- **Healthcare Resource Management:** Efficient healthcare resource allocation is critical in ensuring hospitals and medical facilities are prepared to handle patient influx, particularly during emergencies. AI-driven hospital management systems analyze historical and real-time patient data to predict admission trends, optimize bed occupancy, and improve staffing levels. For example, AI-powered systems in Canada played a vital role in managing hospital capacity during the COVID-19 pandemic by forecasting surges in cases and ensuring the timely availability of critical care resources. Additionally, smart governance integrates telemedicine platforms, enabling remote consultations and reducing the burden on healthcare facilities, particularly in underserved areas.
- **Crime Prevention:** Predictive policing tools leverage AI and big data analysis to spot hotspots of crime, measure socio-economic risk indicators, and allocate law enforcement more effectively. Through the examination of past

crime trends, live surveillance feeds, and behavioral profiles, these tools allow authorities to stage targeted interventions and avert crime before it is committed. Chicago's predictive policing initiative, for instance, has been able to cut violent crime rates by leveraging AI-based insights to target law enforcement resources where the potential for crime is high. In addition, AI-augmented facial recognition and biometric security solutions enhance identity authentication and threat detection capabilities, enhancing public safety efforts within urban settings.

- **Emergency Response Optimization:** The convergence of AI and IoT in emergency response planning improves disaster preparedness, crisis mitigation, and recovery activities after the event. IoT sensors spread throughout cities allow real-time seismic activity, water levels, and hazardous environmental condition monitoring, which helps authorities to give timely warnings and coordinate evacuation processes. AI-based disaster response systems analyze real-time satellite imagery, social media, and emergency calls to determine damage and assign rescue activities efficiently. For example, thermal imaging and AI-powered analysis drone technology is commonly utilized to find survivors and evaluate building damage following earthquakes, so aid reaches the most important places first.

These developments in public safety and health illustrate how intelligent governance is utilizing technology to improve the resilience of cities and the wellbeing of citizens. By integrating AI-driven disease surveillance, predictive healthcare management, crime prevention tools, and real-time emergency response systems, governments can build safer, healthier, and more secure cities. As smart governance continues to evolve, these innovations will play an increasingly vital role in ensuring urban environments remain adaptive, sustainable, and responsive to emerging challenges.

3.5 Citizen-Centric Platforms

Smart governance prioritizes citizen engagement and empowerment by integrating technology-driven platforms that enhance public participation, improve service delivery, and foster transparency in urban management(Aslam & Ansari, n.d.). By leveraging digital tools, governments can create more inclusive and responsive systems where citizens play an active role in decision-making, reporting issues, and accessing essential services. These platforms not only strengthen trust between the government and the public but also ensure that urban policies align with community needs. The following applications illustrate how smart governance leverages citizen-centric platforms to enhance urban development and service delivery.

- **Participatory Urban Planning:** One of the core aspects of smart governance is fostering participatory urban planning, where citizens can actively contribute to shaping their cities. Online platforms like Decidim in Barcelona allow citizens to suggest proposals, debate, and vote on city development projects. These platforms make it more inclusive by giving various voices of the community an opportunity to be heard, so that government policies are based on the real needs and priorities of the people. With the inclusion of AI-based data analysis and visualization tools, participatory urban planning platforms become more transparent and governance decisions more open to the public.
- **Digital Public Services:** Governments are increasingly digitalizing public services to enhance accessibility, efficiency, and user experience. Online portals enable citizens to perform tasks like tax filing, business registration, social benefits applications, and license renewals without having to visit government offices in person. Estonia's e-government model is a global benchmark that ensures smooth digital interactions between citizens and the state. With Estonia's digital backbone, citizens are able to access more than 99% of government services online securely, minimizing bureaucratic slowdowns and optimizing service delivery. Chatbots powered by AI and automated support also simplify digital public services, ensuring that citizens have timely assistance and accurate information.
- **Real-Time Issue Reporting:** Intelligent governance improves urban upkeep and responsiveness through the ability to report problems with infrastructure, environmental hazards, and other issues in real-time. Mobile apps like FixMyStreet in the UK give residents the authority to report potholes, damaged streetlights, waste management issues, and other civic issues directly to local authorities. These platforms combine location-based services, AI-driven tagging, and real-time monitoring so that issues reported are routed to the correct departments for instant resolution. Blockchain technology use in certain smart governance platforms also increases accountability in the form of transparent records of the reported issues and undertaken actions.

These developments in citizen-focused platforms show how smart governance promotes a participatory, inclusive, and transparent style of urban management. Through the fusion of participatory urban planning, digital public services, and live issue reporting, governments can place citizens at the center of decision-making and service delivery. With cities increasingly pursuing digital transformation, these platforms will be instrumental in deepening democratic participation, enhancing public trust, and making government more responsive to the needs of communities.

3.6 Case Studies of Technology Integration in Governance

Initiatives for smart governance in Estonia, Singapore, Rwanda, and Barcelona show how digital technologies can revolutionise urban management. Estonia has achieved 99% online availability of public services by leveraging blockchain and artificial intelligence to facilitate digital identity and e-governance. AI, IoT, and Big Data are used by Singapore's Smart Nation Initiative to improve healthcare and urban mobility. Rwanda uses drones, IoT, and AI to enhance healthcare access and water distribution. Barcelona strategically uses blockchain and IoT technologies to promote transparency and participatory governance (Ciuriak & Ptashkina, 2019; Kabuya et al., 2024; Mega, 2022). These illustrations show how implementing digital solutions improves urban governance's effectiveness, inclusivity, and citizen participation. A thorough summary of these actual smart governance implementations in Estonia, Singapore, Rwanda, and Barcelona is given in Table 4. It describes the main projects, the technologies used, and how they affect urban management. The table clearly demonstrates how smart governance solutions increase transparency, encourage active citizen participation, and improve public service accessibility (Atiq et al., 2023; Troitiño et al., 2024; VESMAŞ, 2024).

Table 4. Case Studies of Smart Governance Implementation

City/ Country	Smart Governance Initiative	Key Technologies Used	Impact
Estonia	Digital identity & e-governance	Blockchain, AI	99% of public services available online
Singapore	Smart Nation Initiative	AI, IoT, Big Data	Efficient urban mobility, smart healthcare
Rwanda	AI-powered resource management	AI, IoT, Drones	Improved water and healthcare accessibility
Barcelona	Open Data & participatory governance	IoT, Blockchain	Enhanced transparency and citizen engagement

- **Estonia's Digital Transformation:** Estonia is widely recognized as a global leader in digital governance, having built one of the most advanced e-governance frameworks in the world. The country has successfully digitized nearly all government services, enabling citizens to access public records, pay taxes, renew licenses, and even vote online through a secure digital identity system. Estonia's e-Residency program further extends its governance model to global entrepreneurs, allowing non-residents to establish and manage businesses digitally. The integration of blockchain technology ensures secure transactions, while artificial intelligence enhances service efficiency. This comprehensive digital infrastructure has minimized bureaucratic delays, increased government transparency, and positioned Estonia as a model for e-governance worldwide.

- **Singapore's Smart Nation Initiative:** Singapore's Smart Nation Initiative optimises urban services like housing, healthcare, and transport by integrating AI, IoT, and big data analytics into governance systems. The initiative's main goal is to establish a smooth digital ecosystem where policymaking and service delivery are informed by real-time data. AI-powered analytics aid in the effective management of healthcare resources, the prediction of housing demand, and the regulation of traffic congestion. A crucial element of the project is citizen engagement, with feedback platforms allowing locals to express their concerns and recommend changes. Singapore consistently improves its urban infrastructure while placing a high priority on data privacy and cybersecurity through innovations like contactless transportation, cashless payment systems, and smart energy grids.
- **Rwanda's AI-Powered Resource Management:** Rwanda has become a leader in smart governance despite being a developing country by implementing affordable AI solutions to manage vital resources. In order to guarantee that both urban and rural populations have equal access to clean water, the nation optimizes water distribution networks using AI-driven analytics. Rwanda uses AI-powered technologies in the transport sector to increase the efficiency of public transport and road infrastructure planning. In order to improve healthcare accessibility, the government also uses drone technology to transport medical supplies to isolated locations. Rwanda has shown how digital transformation can close the development gap and enhance public service delivery in resource-constrained environments by emphasizing scalable and reasonably priced technological solutions.
- **Barcelona's Open Data Platform:** Key datasets on infrastructure, energy use, and mobility are now publicly accessible thanks to Barcelona's embrace of open data as a pillar of its smart governance approach. Through the city's Open Data Platform, businesses, researchers, and citizens can examine urban trends and help shape policy. By proposing and voting on urban projects, citizens engage in decision-making through platforms such as Decidim, guaranteeing inclusive and transparent governance. Barcelona has also installed IoT-enabled waste management and smart lighting systems, which optimize energy use and enhance environmental sustainability. Barcelona has set the standard for other cities looking to improve civic engagement and transparency by encouraging data-driven urban planning and participatory governance.

These case studies demonstrate how technology is transforming public administration and the various uses of smart governance. These cities are prime examples of how technology can revolutionize governance, whether it is through open data initiatives, resource optimization, AI-driven urban analytics, or digital identity systems. These success stories provide important insights into best practices and tactics for developing more intelligent, effective, and inclusive urban environments as more governments embrace digital transformation.

4. CHALLENGES IN IMPLEMENTING SMART GOVERNANCE PLATFORMS

By increasing effectiveness, transparency, and citizen participation, the use of smart governance platforms has the potential to completely transform urban management. Notwithstanding these benefits, governments face a wide range of difficult obstacles when putting these systems into place. These issues have social, ethical, financial, and technological facets, necessitating all-encompassing approaches to guarantee successful implementation and broad adoption. In order to achieve smart governance's full potential while preserving adaptability, inclusivity, and public trust, these obstacles must be removed. The main obstacles to putting smart governance platforms into practice are highlighted in the sections that follow (Khan & Ishrat, 2024, 2025; Lopes, 2017; Omowole et al., 2024)

4.1 Privacy, Security, and Ethical Challenges

- The gathering, storing, and utilization of enormous volumes of citizen data is one of the most urgent issues in smart governance. These platforms raise issues with privacy, security breaches, and ethical governance because they mainly rely on real-time data from IoT sensors, AI-driven analytics, and digital identity systems.
- **Data Privacy and Protection**: If appropriate safeguards are not in place, the extensive data collection required for smart governance may result in privacy violations. Public trust can be damaged by misuse, data leaks, and unauthorized access to personal information. To protect citizen data, governments must enforce adherence to data protection laws, such as the General Data Protection Regulation (GDPR), and put strong encryption measures in place.
- **Cybersecurity Threats**: Because smart governance platforms depend on digital infrastructure, they are susceptible to ransomware, phishing scams, and hacking. Cybercriminals or state-sponsored attacks may target municipal systems, such as public databases, digital voting, and power grids. To reduce

these risks, robust cybersecurity frameworks, frequent audits, and real-time threat detection are crucial.

- **Ethical Concerns in AI Decision-Making**: Algorithmic bias and decision-making transparency are issues that arise when AI is used in governance. AI models may yield discriminatory results if they are trained on biased data, especially in the areas of public service access, resource allocation, and law enforcement. To guarantee justice and accountability, governments must set up regulatory oversight, prioritize ethical AI development, and carry out frequent bias audits.

4.2 Bridging the Digital and Socio-Economic Divide

The digital divide results from the fact that not all citizens have equal access to digital technologies, despite the promise of smart governance. Only digitally literate populations can profit from smart governance initiatives due to exclusionary governance models created by socioeconomic gaps in technology access.

- **Limited Infrastructure and Internet Access:** Many economically disadvantaged and rural communities are unable to participate in digital governance services because they do not have access to smart devices or high-speed internet. To ensure inclusivity, broadband infrastructure expansion and reasonably priced digital access are essential.
- **Digital Literacy Gaps:** The viability of smart governance hinges on citizens' proficiency with digital platforms for services like healthcare access, tax filing, and participatory governance. To ensure greater citizen participation and close the digital literacy gap, educational initiatives, workshops, and user-friendly interfaces can be helpful.
- **Barriers related to language and accessibility:** In order to guarantee inclusivity, governance platforms must take into account a range of linguistic and accessibility requirements. Engagement and equity will be improved by implementing voice-based help, multilingual support, and accessibility features for people with disabilities.

4.3 Financial, Technical, and Institutional Barriers

Smart governance implementation calls for large financial outlays, specialised knowledge, and institutional flexibility. Large-scale adoption is hampered by financial limitations and a lack of technical expertise in many governments, especially in developing countries.

- **High Costs of Implementation** It takes a significant amount of money to deploy cybersecurity frameworks, AI-powered analytics, and IoT infrastructure. The cost of smart governance initiatives is a burden for many governments, particularly when funding conflicting priorities like healthcare and education are involved. Financial strain can be lessened by looking into international funding opportunities, public-private partnerships (PPPs), and affordable open-source solutions.
- **Technical Expertise and Capacity Building**: Smart governance calls for specific knowledge of data analytics, cybersecurity, artificial intelligence development, and urban planning. The technical know-how required to properly administer and maintain these systems is lacking in many government organizations. The skills gap can be closed by funding technology transfer projects, academic partnerships, and capacity-building programs.
- **Resistance to Change**: Because of worries about data security, workflow disruptions, and job displacement, traditional bureaucratic structures frequently oppose digital transformation. A seamless transition to smart governance can be facilitated by promoting institutional adaptability through training initiatives, phased implementation, and unambiguous policy guidelines.

4.4 Interoperability, Integration, and Standardization

For the successful implementation of Integrated Smart City, interoperability between various smart governance platforms is required. But, these are hampered by fragmented legacy systems, a lack of standardization, and data silos.

- **Legacy System Compatibility**: Many governments still run on outdated and legacy IT infrastructure, which does not work with modern smart governance solutions. Transitioning these old systems to cloud-native, AI-enabled frameworks is a complicated process that can be achieved using step-by-step integration strategies.
- **Data Silos and Fragmentation**: Data-sharing frameworks are a must, as without them it becomes difficult for different government departments to work in collaboration and efficiency. Cross-agency collaboration can be improved with open data standards, centralized data repositories (for example, used by the US Census Bureau), and interoperability frameworks.
- **Lack of Global Standards**: There are no universal technical standards for smart governance platforms, making scalability and take-up more difficult. The harmonised implementation of new regulatory guidelines and best practices at a global level could be ensured through the creation of common regulatory guidelines and industry best practices.

4.5 Public Trust, Perception, and Legal Challenges

The trust of the public servant acts as a vital gambit in smart governance, which can't change with a patch of liquid or a wet tissue. Digital governance can be resisted due to misinformation, fear of surveillance, algorithmic bias, and lack of transparency.

- **Privacy and Surveillance Issues:** The extensive use of data tracking, AI-powered monitoring, and facial recognition raises concerns about privacy invasion and government overreach. Clear legal frameworks, moral AI regulations, and transparency initiatives to reassure citizens are necessary to strike a balance between security and civil liberties.
- **Misinformation and Public Scepticism:** A lot of people are still dubious about AI-powered data collection and decision-making because they worry about being excluded or manipulated. Building trust in smart governance can be facilitated by implementing digital literacy initiatives, public awareness campaigns, and open communication tactics.
- **Legal and Policy Frameworks:** Clear legal rules pertaining to digital rights, AI accountability, and data ownership must be established by governments. In addition to protecting citizens, smart governance policies should promote technological advancement and innovation.

A multifaceted strategy that incorporates institutional capacity-building, public engagement, regulatory frameworks, and technological advancements is needed to address these issues. To safeguard citizen data, governments must implement scalable, affordable solutions, guarantee digital inclusivity, and put robust cybersecurity measures in place. Furthermore, encouraging global cooperation and public-private partnerships can guarantee sustainable urban development and hasten the implementation of smart governance. Effectively addressing these issues will be essential to developing robust, open, and citizen-centered governance structures as cities continue to change.

5. OPPORTUNITIES FOR GROWTH AND INNOVATION

Through innovative technology integration, smart governance platforms are constantly changing to improve urban efficiency, encourage sustainability, and guarantee inclusive decision-making As cities expand and urban challenges grow more complex, leveraging digital transformation becomes imperative in driving sustainable development, fostering citizen engagement, and ensuring equitable access to public services. The following sections outline key advancements in smart governance and their potential to shape resilient, technology-driven urban environments (Pandey, n.d.).

5.1 Enhancing Urban Efficiency and Promoting Sustainability

Smart governance platforms are crucial in improving urban efficiency and fostering sustainability by streamlining resource management, automating public services, and reducing environmental impacts (Van Hoang, 2024). These initiatives align cities with global sustainability goals while ensuring economic and social benefits.

- **Improving Urban Efficiency:** Efficiency in governance is achieved by automating administrative processes and optimizing infrastructure management. AI-driven automation reduces bureaucratic delays in services such as tax filing, social welfare distribution, and permit approvals, enhancing accessibility and responsiveness. Estonia's e-governance platform, where over 99% of public services are available online, exemplifies how digital solutions minimize inefficiencies and empower citizens. IoT-enabled predictive maintenance is essential for improving urban resilience in infrastructure maintenance. Roads, bridges, and utilities all have embedded sensors that track structural conditions continuously and spot possible failures before they happen. Public safety is increased, maintenance expenses are decreased, and infrastructure failures are avoided with this proactive approach. The importance of data-driven decision-making is further demonstrated by the notable decreases in downtime for critical services reported by cities using predictive maintenance.
- **Promoting Sustainability:** Smart governance places a strong emphasis on environmental sustainability, with programs aimed at integrating clean energy sources and lowering urban carbon footprints. Smart energy grids that integrate renewable energy sources like solar and wind, like those in Germany's Energiewende initiative, effectively balance supply and demand. By enabling dynamic energy distribution, these grids reduce waste and guarantee grid stability. The best places for reforestation and the development of green infrastructure are found through urban greening initiatives, which are aided by predictive analytics and GIS mapping. Green corridors have been successfully established in Medellín, Colombia, to reduce urban heat islands, enhance biodiversity, and improve air quality. In a similar vein, IoT-enabled waste management systems, like those in Barcelona, optimise collection routes, lowering operating costs and the environmental impact of waste disposal. Cities can develop sustainably and remain resilient to resource depletion and climate change by integrating technology into their planning and governance.

5.2 Citizen-Centric Platforms and Collaborative Governance

Involving people in governance guarantees openness, inclusivity, and trust and helps to make sure that policy decisions fit the demands of society. By giving citizens direct means of direct interaction between them and governments, digital platforms improve public participation.

- **Citizen Engagement Through Digital Platforms:** Tools for participatory governance enable people to impact municipal decisions. Barcelona's Decidim platform lets locals suggest projects, cast votes on ideas, and track policy execution. Through allowing people to choose how public money is distributed, participatory budgeting systems help to further democratize governance. Paris has effectively embraced this approach, boosting public trust in government responsibility and expenditure.
- **AI-powered real-time feedback mechanisms:** Real-time feedback systems driven by artificial intelligence will help to resolve problems more quickly. FixMyStreet in the UK lets locals report urban issues, including potholes or malfunctioning streetlights, straight to local authorities. By combining location-based data, these sites support crowdsourced urban management and enable instantaneous reaction.
- **Collaborative Governance:** Public-private partnerships (PPPs), academic institutions, and worldwide alliances all help smart government flourish by means of multi-stakeholder collaboration. PPPs hasten the acceptance of creative technologies; IBM, for example, works with cities to create data-driven urban solutions. Intergovernmental cooperation guarantees that successful governance models can be scaled and adjusted over different areas and helps knowledge-sharing.

By creating localized technology solutions, promoting economic development, and advancing public administration technology, innovation hubs and startup accelerators help to support smart governance.

- **Integration with Emerging Technologies:** Smart governance mixed with blockchain, augmented reality (AR), and 5G networks improves efficiency, security, and public involvement.
- **Blockchain for Transparency**: Blockchain transforms government by means of tamper-proof transaction records, identity verification, and voting systems, so enabling Estonia's e-governance model based on blockchain guarantees open and safe public services, so establishing a worldwide benchmark for

digital democracy. Public expenditure tracking and blockchain-based voting improve responsibility, reducing corruption risks.

- **Augmented and Virtual Reality for Urban Planning:** AR and VR technologies let people see suggested projects before they are carried out, facilitating interactive urban design. While VR platforms allow people to explore urban projects and offer informed comments, AR apps offer real-time overlays of new infrastructure designs.
- **5G and Edge Computing:** 5G technology and edge computing enhance the responsiveness of smart governance systems. Faster data transmission enables real-time applications such as autonomous transportation, emergency response optimization, and AI-driven disaster management. The adoption of 5G also supports large-scale IoT deployments, improving smart city operations' efficiency and scalability.

5.3 Democratizing Access for Smaller Entities and Emerging Markets

Smart governance initiatives must be scalable and accessible to small municipalities, developing regions, and SMEs to ensure equitable technological adoption (Ncamphalala, 2019; Omowole et al., 2024).

- **Affordable and Scalable Solutions:** Cloud-based platforms such as AWS and Microsoft Azure provide cost-effective governance solutions, eliminating the need for extensive infrastructure investments. Open-source platforms like TensorFlow and Decidim allow smaller entities to deploy advanced governance technologies without incurring high costs.

Rwanda's AI-driven water management system is a shining example of how low-cost IoT solutions maximize resource distribution, guaranteeing sustainable development in areas with limited budgets.

- **Fostering Financial Inclusion**: By analysing alternative credit indicators, including mobile usage and utility payment history, AI-powered credit scoring systems like Tala and Branch give underbanked populations financial access. Through providing financial services and microloans to underprivileged areas, these systems help to build economic resilience.

5.4 Advancing Ethical AI Practices:

As AI-driven governance expands, ensuring fairness, accountability, and transparency is crucial. Ethical AI frameworks mitigate risks associated with algorithmic bias and discriminatory decision-making.

- **Explainable AI (XAI):** In order to help policymakers defend AI-driven governance choices, explainable AI (XAI) tools such as SHAP (Shapley Additive Explanations) and LIME (Local Interpretable Model-Agnostic Explanations) increase AI transparency. By ensuring that citizens and government representatives comprehend recommendations produced by AI, these frameworks promote accountability and trust.
- **Bias Mitigation and Accountability:** Predictive policing, social service distribution, and resource allocation are all made equitable through frequent algorithm audits and fairness-aware AI models. A global framework for the responsible deployment of AI in governance is provided by ethical guidelines issued by organizations such as the OECD and IEEE.

5.5 Building Resilient Cities for the Future:

By empowering cities to foresee, respond to, and bounce back from unanticipated obstacles, smart governance enhances urban resilience.

- **Adaptive Urban Systems:** AI-powered urban systems continuously examine data in real time to identify shifts in resource availability, environmental threats, and infrastructure conditions. Dynamically adjusting consumption, smart energy grids provide stability during emergencies or periods of high demand.
- **Scenario Planning and Predictive Analytics:** To model the effects of climate change, changes in the economy, and trends in population growth, governments use AI-driven simulations. By using these insights to inform proactive policy development, cities can stay ready for long-term urban challenges.
- **Sustainable Growth Strategies:** Cities can address problems like resource scarcity, affordable housing, and environmental degradation by implementing data-driven governance frameworks. These tactics support global development goals while ensuring urban sustainability, efficiency, and social equity. In order to improve urban efficiency, encourage inclusivity, and advance sustainability, smart governance is constantly developing by combining AI, blockchain, IoT, and participatory platforms. Future-ready, resilient, and citizen-centric urban environments will be shaped by these innovations as

cities embrace digital transformation (Khan & Ishrat, 2024; Omowole et al., 2024).

6. FUTURE DIRECTIONS IN SMART GOVERNANCE

The future of smart government offers great chances for redefining urban management, citizen involvement, and sustainability as urbanization speeds forward and technology keeps changing. Smart government systems will become more flexible, effective, and citizen-centric by including developing technologies, supporting inclusive solutions, and enhancing worldwide cooperation. These developments will improve public service delivery and provide cities with means to proactively handle environmental and socioeconomic issues as well. The following sections describe main future directions in smart governance that will define fair, sustainable, and resilient cities.

6.1 Ethical AI, Open-Source Platforms, and Scalable Solutions

Ensuring justice, openness, and accessibility in smart government systems will depend critically on the combination of ethical AI frameworks, open-source platforms, and scalable technologies. Ethical artificial intelligence will guarantee that AI-driven decisions are fair and inclusive, addressing the dangers of algorithmic bias. Explainable artificial intelligence (XAI) tools such as LIME (Local Interpretable Model-Agnostic Explanations) and SHAP (Shapley Additive Explanations) will be progressively included in future systems to offer openness in decision-making. These instruments will help people and legislators grasp the reasoning behind recommendations driven by artificial intelligence, promoting trust and responsibility. In public resource allocation or predictive policing, for instance, XAI will explain why specific areas or people are given priority so that judgments are objective and reasonable. Open-source platforms will democratize smart governance technologies, enabling developing areas and smaller towns to apply reasonably priced solutions. Customizable frameworks for participatory governance and artificial intelligence applications offered by tools like Decidim and TensorFlow help to lower financial obstacles and inspire innovation. Scalable cloud-based solutions will also provide adaptable models that fit different infrastructure and financial capabilities. Supported by cooperative development initiatives between governments, developers, and commercial entities, these systems will guarantee that smart governance is flexible enough to meet various urban settings and challenges.

6.2 Citizen-Centric Ecosystems and Collaborative Governance

Citizen Smart government's pillar will still be citizen involvement; future platforms will concentrate on building inclusive environments that enable communities to actively participate in urban development. To improve public opinions and decision-making, digital ecosystems will combine immersive technologies, including virtual reality (VR) and augmented reality (AR). AR and VR tools, for example, will let residents see urban development projects including new transportation systems or green areas, in interactive surroundings. This immersive approach will inspire honest comments and increase community participation in governmental procedures. By providing real-time help and tailored advice for accessing public services, AI-powered virtual assistants and chatbots will help to further simplify interactions between people and governments. These tools will streamline administrative procedures so that people may quickly address problems or gather data. Governance systems will also use artificial intelligence to offer tailored services and updates to fit personal requirements and preferences. This tailored approach will guarantee that people feel heard and valued in governance systems, so promoting more satisfaction and involvement. Driving innovation in smart government will depend critically on cooperation between governments and commercial players. While worldwide knowledge-sharing efforts will help to exchange best practices, resources, and technologies, public-private partnerships (PPPs) will enable the deployment of advanced technologies, including IoT networks and blockchain systems. Hubs for cooperation will be international forums and platforms, making sure that effective governance models are scaled and modified across different areas.

6.3 Integration of Emerging Technologies

Modern technologies, including blockchain, 5G, quantum computing, and IoT, will help to define smart government going forward. These developments will improve the security, adaptability, and efficiency of urban systems, allowing cities to precisely address challenging tasks. By guaranteeing secure, tamper-proof records of transactions, identity verification, and voting, blockchain technology will keep transforming governance systems. Blockchain-based e-voting and open public spending, among other things, will help to build trust and responsibility in governance systems, lowering corruption and inefficiencies. Estonia's effective application of blockchain within its e-governance system sets a global standard for using this tool to improve openness. Edge computing and 5G networks will greatly increase IoT-enabled government platforms' responsiveness. Real-time data processing made possible by these technologies will support smart grids, autonomous cars, and disaster response systems among other uses. While quantum computing will redefine data analysis capabilities, enabling cities to more successfully address challenging urban issues including traffic optimization, climate modeling, and resource allocation, This technological convergence will produce strong governance structures ready to control the dynamic needs of contemporary cities.

6.4 Climate Resilience, Sustainability, and Inclusivity

As cities struggle with the effects of climate change and the necessity to switch to sustainable development models, resilience and sustainability will become central themes of smart government. Predictive analytics driven by artificial intelligence will help cities choose long-term plans for climate adaptation, modeling events including extreme weather, rising sea levels, and resource constraints. These instruments will let governments decide on infrastructure projects, disaster readiness, and resource management based on data rather than just speculation. Furthermore, giving top priority to the creation of green infrastructure, including parks, urban forests, and renewable energy systems, will be smart government platforms. IoT and GIS technologies will help urban planning projects by pointing out chances for reforestation, sustainable water management, and energy-efficient building design. Governance systems will incorporate ideas from the circular economy, encouraging resource optimization, waste reduction, and recycling. A major emphasis will be on inclusivity since smart governance systems guarantee that every person gains from technological developments and closes the digital divide. Affordable internet access, digital literacy initiatives, and easily available platform designs will enable underprivileged areas to engage in governance procedures. AI-driven analytics will enable the identification of underprivileged groups and the customizing of policies to fit their particular needs, promoting equity and lowering systematic inequalities.

6.5 Adaptive and Resilient Governance Systems

Resilient, self-learning, and adaptable future governance systems will help cities to properly handle unanticipated problems and dynamic urban conditions. Real-time data from IoT sensors, artificial intelligence models, and big data analytics will be combined by these systems to give governments practical insights for proactive decision-making. Adaptive artificial intelligence systems, for instance, will always learn from fresh data and feedback, improving their recommendations and guaranteeing their applicability in changing surroundings. A pillar of smart government, scenario-based planning will let governments replicate the effects of many contingency events, including natural disasters, economic upheavals, or pandemics. These models will guide policy decisions so that cities may maximize resources and reduce the effects of crises. Resilient government models will also give top priority to the creation of long-term urban plans addressing linked issues including housing, transportation, and environmental sustainability, as well as disaster response systems and economic recovery strategies.

7. CONCLUSION

Future government systems that are resilient, self-learning, and flexible will enable cities to effectively address dynamic urban conditions and unanticipated challenges. These systems will aggregate real-time data from IoT sensors, artificial intelligence models, and big data analytics to provide governments with useful insights for proactive decision-making. For example, adaptive artificial intelligence systems will always learn from new data and feedback, enhancing their recommendations and ensuring their applicability in surroundings that are changing. A pillar of smart government, scenario-based planning will enable governments to replicate the consequences of several contingency events, including natural disasters, financial crises, or pandemics. These models will direct policy decisions so that cities might best use their resources and minimize crisis effects. Resilient government models will also give top focus to the development of long-term urban plans addressing linked issues including housing, transportation, and environmental sustainability, as well as disaster response systems and economic recovery strategies.

REFERENCES

Ahmad, K., Maabreh, M., Ghaly, M., Khan, K., Qadir, J., & Al-Fuqaha, A. (2022). Developing future human-centered smart cities: Critical analysis of smart city security, Data management, and Ethical challenges. *Computer Science Review*, *43*, 100452.

Al-Raeei, M. (2025). The smart future for sustainable development: Artificial intelligence solutions for sustainable urbanization. *Sustainable Development (Bradford)*, *33*(1), 508–517. DOI: 10.1002/sd.3131

Allam, Z., Sharifi, A., Bibri, S. E., & Chabaud, D. (2022). Emerging trends and knowledge structures of smart urban governance. *Sustainability (Basel)*, *14*(9), 5275. DOI: 10.3390/su14095275

Ansari, M. S. H., & Mehrotra, M. (2019). Development of smart cities and its sustainability: A smart city framework. *International Journal of Innovative Technology and Exploring Engineering*, *8*(11), 646–655. DOI: 10.35940/ijitee.K1703.0881119

Ansari, M. S. H., & Mehrotra, M. (2020). Securing M2M communication in Smart Cities. *2020 International Conference for Emerging Technology (INCET)*, 1–4.

Ansari, M. S. H., & Mehrotra, M. (2022). IoT Technologies, Security Attacks and their Security Measures under Smart City Framework. *Grenze International Journal of Engineering & Technology (GIJET)*, *8*(2).

Aslam, M., & Ansari, Y. M. (n.d.). *DIGITAL GOVERNANCE AND SMART CITIES: LEVERAGING TECHNOLOGY FOR URBAN ADMINISTRATION*.

Atiq, E., Salim, M., & Mahmood, N. (2023). E-Governance: A Global Perspective on A New Paradigm. *JOURNAL OF LAW, SOCIAL AND MANAGEMENT SCIENCES*, *2*(2), 100–107.

Bedewy, S. F. (2024). The Impact of Data Security and Privacy Concerns on the Implementation of Integrated. *Smart Cities: Foundations and Perspectives, 59*.

Bibri, S. E., Huang, J., & Krogstie, J. (2024). Artificial intelligence of things for synergizing smarter eco-city brain, metabolism, and platform: Pioneering data-driven environmental governance. *Sustainable Cities and Society*, *108*, 105516. DOI: 10.1016/j.scs.2024.105516

Bolívar, M. P. R. (n.d.). *Smart technologies for smart governments*.

Ceder, A. (2021). Urban mobility and public transport: Future perspectives and review. *International Journal of Urban Sciences*, *25*(4), 455–479. DOI: 10.1080/12265934.2020.1799846

Challoumis, C. (2024). *Building a sustainable economy-how ai can optimize resource allocation.*

Ciuriak, D., & Ptashkina, M. (2019). *Leveraging the digital transformation for development: a global south strategy for the data-driven economy.*

Cortés-Cediel, M. E., Cantador, I., & Bolívar, M. P. R. (2021). Analyzing citizen participation and engagement in European smart cities. *Social Science Computer Review, 39*(4), 592–626. DOI: 10.1177/0894439319877478

Damaševičius, R., Bacanin, N., & Misra, S. (2023). From sensors to safety: Internet of Emergency Services (IoES) for emergency response and disaster management. *Journal of Sensor and Actuator Networks, 12*(3), 41. DOI: 10.3390/jsan12030041

Das, D. K. (2024). Exploring the symbiotic relationship between digital transformation, infrastructure, service delivery, and governance for smart sustainable cities. *Smart Cities, 7*(2), 806–835. DOI: 10.3390/smartcities7020034

Deng, T., Zhang, K., & Shen, Z.-J. M. (2021). A systematic review of a digital twin city: A new pattern of urban governance toward smart cities. *Journal of Management Science and Engineering, 6*(2), 125–134. DOI: 10.1016/j.jmse.2021.03.003

Dwivedi, Y. K., Hughes, L., Ismagilova, E., Aarts, G., Coombs, C., Crick, T., Duan, Y., Dwivedi, R., Edwards, J., Eirug, A., Galanos, V., Ilavarasan, P. V., Janssen, M., Jones, P., Kar, A. K., Kizgin, H., Kronemann, B., Lal, B., Lucini, B., & Williams, M. D. (2021). Artificial Intelligence (AI): Multidisciplinary perspectives on emerging challenges, opportunities, and agenda for research, practice and policy. *International Journal of Information Management, 57*, 101994. DOI: 10.1016/j.ijinfomgt.2019.08.002

Gandhi, P., Bhatia, S., Kumar, A., Alojail, M. A., & Rathore, P. S. (2020). *Internet of Things in Business Transformation: Developing an Engineering and Business Strategy for Industry 5.0.* John Wiley & Sons.

Gill, S. S., Xu, M., Ottaviani, C., Patros, P., Bahsoon, R., Shaghaghi, A., Golec, M., Stankovski, V., Wu, H., Abraham, A., Singh, M., Mehta, H., Ghosh, S. K., Baker, T., Parlikad, A. K., Lutfiyya, H., Kanhere, S. S., Sakellariou, R., Dustdar, S., & Uhlig, S. (2022). AI for next generation computing: Emerging trends and future directions. *Internet of Things : Engineering Cyber Physical Human Systems, 19*, 100514. DOI: 10.1016/j.iot.2022.100514

Giuliodori, A., Berrone, P., & Ricart, J. E. (2023). Where smart meets sustainability: The role of Smart Governance in achieving the Sustainable Development Goals in cities. *Business Research Quarterly, 26*(1), 27–44. DOI: 10.1177/23409444221091281

Ishrat, M., Khan, W., Ahmad, F., Al Farsi, M. M., & Abidin, S. (2024). Comprehensive Analysis of Attacks and Defenses in IoT Sensory Big Data Analysis. In *Technological Advancements in Data Processing for Next Generation Intelligent Systems* (pp. 24–57). IGI Global. DOI: 10.4018/979-8-3693-0968-1.ch002

Kabuya, K. I., Ajayi, O. O., & Bagula, A. B. (2024). Smart Cities and Villages: Concept Review and Implementation Perspectives in Developing Cities. *ArXiv Preprint ArXiv:2402.09284*.

Kaiser, Z. R. M. A. (2024). Smart governance for smart cities and nations. *Journal of Economy and Technology*, *2*, 216–234. DOI: 10.1016/j.ject.2024.07.003

Khan, W., & Ishrat, M. (2024). Unveiling the depths of explainable AI: a comprehensive review. *Technological Advancements in Data Processing for Next Generation Intelligent Systems*, 78–106.

Khan, W., & Ishrat, M. (2025). Embracing the Future: Navigating the Challenges and Solutions in Embodied Artificial Intelligence. In *Building Embodied AI Systems: The Agents, the Architecture Principles, Challenges, and Application Domains* (pp. 281–299). Springer.

Korada, L. (2021). Unlocking Urban Futures: The Role Of Big Data Analytics And AI In Urban Planning–A Systematic Literature Review And Bibliometric Insight. *Migration Letters : An International Journal of Migration Studies*, *18*(6), 775–795.

Kuziemski, M., & Misuraca, G. (2020). AI governance in the public sector: Three tales from the frontiers of automated decision-making in democratic settings. *Telecommunications Policy*, *44*(6), 101976. DOI: 10.1016/j.telpol.2020.101976 PMID: 32313360

Litman, T. (2021). *New mobilities: Smart planning for emerging transportation technologies*. Island Press.

Lopes, N. V. (2017). Smart governance: A key factor for smart cities implementation. *2017 IEEE International Conference on Smart Grid and Smart Cities (ICSGSC)*, 277–282. DOI: 10.1109/ICSGSC.2017.8038591

Markkandeyan, S., Gupta, S., Narayanan, G. V., Reddy, M. J., Al-Khasawneh, M. A., Ishrat, M., & Kiran, A. (2023). Deep learning based semantic segmentation approach for automatic detection of brain tumor. *International Journal of Computers, Communications & Control*, *18*(4).

Mega, V. (2022). Accountable strategic planning and citizen engagement. In *Human Sustainable Cities: Towards the SDGs and Green, Just, Smart and Inclusive Transitions* (pp. 225–250). Springer. DOI: 10.1007/978-3-031-04840-1_8

Mishra, P., & Singh, G. (2023). Energy management systems in sustainable smart cities based on the internet of energy: A technical review. *Energies*, *16*(19), 6903. DOI: 10.3390/en16196903

Nastjuk, I., Trang, S., & Papageorgiou, E. I. (2022). Smart cities and smart governance models for future cities: Current research and future directions. *Electronic Markets*, *32*(4), 1917–1924. DOI: 10.1007/s12525-022-00609-0

Ncamphalala, M. (2019). *The role of ICT to promote smart governance in local governments*. University of Johannesburg.

Nechesov, A., & Ruponen, J. (2024). Empowering Government Efficiency Through Civic Intelligence: Merging Artificial Intelligence and Blockchain for Smart Citizen Proposals. *Technologies*, *12*(12), 271. DOI: 10.3390/technologies12120271

Ohakawa, T. C., Adeyemi, A. B., Okwandu, A. C., Iwuanyanwu, O., & Ifechukwu, G.-O. (2024). Digital Tools and Technologies in Affordable Housing Design: Leveraging AI and Machine Learning for Optimized Outcomes. *International Journal of Smart Cities and Housing Technologies*, *10*(1), 55–71.

Omowole, B. M., Olufemi-Phillips, A. Q., Ofodile, O. C., Eyo-Udo, N. L., & Ewim, S. E. (2024). *The role of SMEs in promoting urban economic development: A review of emerging economy strategies*. Journal Name Unspecified.

Paiva, S., Ahad, M. A., Tripathi, G., Feroz, N., & Casalino, G. (2021). Enabling technologies for urban smart mobility: Recent trends, opportunities and challenges. *Sensors (Basel)*, *21*(6), 2143. DOI: 10.3390/s21062143 PMID: 33803903

Pandey, B. B. (n.d.). 11 SMART TECHNOLOGIES SHAPING TOMORROW'S CITIES: AN INTEGRATED URBAN MANAGEMENT APPROACH. *TRANSDISCIPLINARY THREADS*, 68.

Pereira, G. V., Parycek, P., Falco, E., & Kleinhans, R. (2018). Smart governance in the context of smart cities: A literature review. *Information Polity*, *23*(2), 143–162. DOI: 10.3233/IP-170067

Poudel, N. (2024). The Impact of Big Data-Driven Artificial Intelligence Systems on Public Service Delivery in Cloud-Oriented Government Infrastructures. *Journal of Artificial Intelligence and Machine Learning in Cloud Computing Systems*, *8*(11), 13–25.

Raihan, M. M. H., Subroto, S., Chowdhury, N., Koch, K., Ruttan, E., & Turin, T. C. (2024). *Dimensions and barriers for digital (in) equity and digital divide: A systematic integrative review*. Digital Transformation and Society.

Ramírez-Márquez, C., Posadas-Paredes, T., Raya-Tapia, A. Y., & Ponce-Ortega, J. M. (2024). Natural resource optimization and sustainability in society 5.0: A comprehensive review. *Resources*, *13*(2), 19. DOI: 10.3390/resources13020019

Rani, S., Mishra, R. K., Usman, M., Kataria, A., Kumar, P., Bhambri, P., & Mishra, A. K. (2021). Amalgamation of advanced technologies for sustainable development of smart city environment: A review. *IEEE Access : Practical Innovations, Open Solutions*, *9*, 150060–150087. DOI: 10.1109/ACCESS.2021.3125527

Rizi, M. H. P., & Seno, S. A. H. (2022). A systematic review of technologies and solutions to improve security and privacy protection of citizens in the smart city. *Internet of Things : Engineering Cyber Physical Human Systems*, *20*, 100584. DOI: 10.1016/j.iot.2022.100584

Rodríguez Bolívar, M. P., Alcaide Muñoz, L., Manda, M. I., & Backhouse, J. (2019). Smart governance for inclusive socio-economic transformation in South Africa: Are we there yet? *E-Participation in Smart Cities: Technologies and Models of Governance for Citizen Engagement*, 179–201.

Sarker, M. N. I., Wu, M., & Hossin, M. A. (2018). Smart governance through bigdata: Digital transformation of public agencies. *2018 International Conference on Artificial Intelligence and Big Data (ICAIBD)*, 62–70. DOI: 10.1109/ICAIBD.2018.8396168

Scholl, H. J., & Scholl, M. C. (2014). Smart governance: A roadmap for research and practice. *IConference 2014 Proceedings*.

Springs, D. (2024). Smart city planning focused on the US cities in need of policing innovations and public health safety technologies and strategies. *Health Economics and Management Review*, *5*(1), 117–128. DOI: 10.61093/hem.2024.1-09

Tariq, M. U. (2024). The role of emerging technologies in shaping the global digital government landscape. *Emerging Developments and Technologies in Digital Government*, 160–180.

Troitiño, D. R., Mazur, V., & Kerikmäe, T. (2024). E-governance and integration in the European union. *Internet of Things : Engineering Cyber Physical Human Systems*, *27*, 101321. DOI: 10.1016/j.iot.2024.101321

Valle-Cruz, D., Fernandez-Cortez, V., & Gil-Garcia, J. R. (2022). From E-budgeting to smart budgeting: Exploring the potential of artificial intelligence in government decision-making for resource allocation. *Government Information Quarterly*, *39*(2), 101644. DOI: 10.1016/j.giq.2021.101644

Van Hoang, T. (2024). Impact of integrated artificial intelligence and internet of things technologies on smart city transformation. *Journal of Technical Education Science, 19*(Special Issue 01), 64–73.

Varsha, V. R., Naganandini, S., & Hariharan, C. (2024). Utilizing AI and machine learning for natural disaster management: predicting natural disasters with AI and machine learning. In *Internet of Things and AI for Natural Disaster Management and Prediction* (pp. 279–304). IGI Global.

Venkadesh, P., Divya, S. V., Marymariyal, P., & Keerthana, S. (2024). Predicting natural disasters with AI and machine learning. In *Utilizing AI and Machine Learning for Natural Disaster Management* (pp. 39–64). IGI Global. DOI: 10.4018/979-8-3693-3362-4.ch003

Vesmaş, D. (2024). The ethics of e-governance. Safeguarding data confidentiality and human security in public administration. Studia Securitatis, 18(2).

Yao, Y. (2022). A Review of the Comprehensive Application of Big Data, Artificial Intelligence, and Internet of Things Technologies in Smart Cities. *Journal of Computational Methods in Engineering Applications*, 1–10.

Chapter 8 Smart Parking in Foggy Condition Real-Time Efficiency With PSO, ACO, and IoT Sensors

Tanisha Thakur
https://orcid.org/0009-0005-0117-2642
School of Computer Engineering, Kalinga Institute of Industrial Technology (Deemed), Bhubaneswar, India

Lavanya Srivastava
https://orcid.org/0009-0005-4516-5778
School of Computer Engineering, Kalinga Institute of Industrial Technology (Deemed), Bhubaneswar, India

Aradhana Panda
https://orcid.org/0009-0003-3431-1659
School of Computer Engineering, Kalinga Institute of Industrial Technology (Deemed), Bhubaneswar, India

Hitesh Mohapatra
https://orcid.org/0000-0001-8100-4860
School of Computer Engineering, Kalinga Institute of Industrial Technology (Deemed), Bhubaneswar, India

ABSTRACT

This chapter presents strategies to enhance the intelligence and energy efficiency of smart parking systems by integrating PSO and ACO. Using real-time IoT sensor data, the system optimizes driver routing to available parking spots while minimizing

DOI: 10.4018/979-8-3373-1375-7.ch008

energy consumption. PSO is applied during the planning phase for approximate route estimation, while ACO adapts dynamically to reduce energy use and interruptions. The chapter also introduces a method to improve system reliability in challenging conditions, such as fog, by employing PSO-optimized fog-detectable sensors. This adaptive approach optimizes sensor usage and path planning based on weather conditions. Overall, the combination of global and local optimization techniques boosts parking efficiency, cuts energy use, and enhances the driver experience.

1. INTRODUCTION

One of the major developments in Information Technology in the last decade is the emergence of the Internet of Things. IoT are physical objects or smart devices that contain sensors, actuators, and chips. The devices use their processors, IP addresses, as well as communication hardware, together with the Internet, to collect, process, store, and forward varied data from their environment in a distributed manner. In the last few years, the Internet of Things has significantly increased in usage, thereby producing a lot of data from IoT devices. These data packets are carried through many networks to cloud-based servers and other data consumers. The sheer volume of such data can be handled by a decentralized fog-based architecture. This can provide low latency and efficient use of resources since IoT data may be processed near its sources. Selection of the right fog nodes is the most critical step in any form of architecture based on fog computing. Even though a large number of fog nodes can be deployed over the fog network, we want to dynamically choose optimal and reliable fog nodes that satisfy the QoS and security requirements of end users while considering the mobility of the nodes. Since there exists more than one conflicting objective that must be considered at the same time to know their optimal solution, the fog node selection problem can be characterized as a multi-objective optimization problem.

Additionally, these studies focus on the number of nodes that can be deployed to handle requests from various end devices. Trust is crucial for ensuring secure offloading in a fog-based IoT environment. Therefore, any fog device assigned to process tasks offloaded by end devices must be reliable. This paper aims to maximize trust, available capacity, and residual energy while taking into account the mobility of fog nodes. To achieve these goals, it is essential to develop a many-objective optimization algorithm for selecting optimal fog nodes for secure offloading and resource allocation (Adeyiga et al., 2022). Recently, metaheuristic optimization methods have drawn considerable attention from researchers due to their ability to identify optimal solutions for a wide range of optimization challenges. These search techniques are high-level, problem-independent heuristic algorithms that can discover near-optimal solutions through iterative processes. Particle swarm optimization (PSO) stands out as one of the most popular algorithms based on swarm intelligence (SI), appreciated for its various advantages over other search methods: it is easy to implement, robust, converges quickly, and is effective for complex and difficult problems (Agnihotri & Gupta, 2018).

Leveraging a hybrid optimization approach that combines Particle Swarm Optimization (PSO) and Ant Colony Optimization (ACO) techniques will significantly enhance the efficiency and reliability of sensor systems. This integration will not only improve energy efficiency but also optimize vehicle routing through precise sensor measurements, effectively addressing issues that compromise sensor accuracy and adaptive routing in low visibility conditions. Additionally, incorporating fog detectors will elevate safety for drivers in areas with reduced visibility by providing real-time information on fog density and visibility levels. Ultimately, this initiative aims to develop more intelligent and responsive parking solutions that adapt to varying weather conditions, thereby maximizing the overall user experience.

To address those mentioned above, we propose a multi-objective PSO-based path optimization method that identifies the most effective routing path from the user end node to the fog node(s) providing services for the user device. The proposed approach takes into account various constraints of the fog nodes along the path such as: CPU, memory, battery life, and security and also accommodates the mobility of both the user and fog nodes, as well as potential node failures, continuously reconfiguring the fog network and routing path. Rather than dynamically routing IoT data until it reaches the appropriate fog node for processing (which may not ensure the optimal path), the method recalculates the optimal path whenever there is a change in the fog network, such as user end-node movement, alterations in computational resources of the fog nodes, or fog node failures (Benson et al., 2006). This algorithm identifies the best possible paths and directly forwards the data to the designated processing fog node(s). As a result, it minimizes latency and response time while reducing bandwidth and energy consumption. This efficiency is achieved by integrating the distributed orchestrator model we proposed in (Alli & Alam, 2019) with the PSO-based optimization method, which determines the optimal path from the user end node to the fog node(s) where the distributed orchestrator allocates services for that user device. The distributed orchestrator continuously synchronizes the computational resources and constraints of each fog node, enabling the PSO-based algorithm to quickly pinpoint the optimal (or suboptimal) path, rather than relying on various dynamic or evolutionary approaches that may take time to yield satisfactory results. Consequently, the proposed method is capable of addressing two major challenges in fog networks: optimal service (application) placement and optimal routing.

The article is organized as follows: Section 2 presents the conceptual model of the PSO-ACO Algorithm for dynamic routing. Section 3 presents the fog computing architecture of sensors with PSO to improve routing during adverse weather conditions. Section 4 covers the experimental evaluation and discusses the results obtained from the comparison between the two methods. Section 5 evaluates the performance scope matrices. Section 6 presents the real-world applications. Section 7 points out the practical challenges. Section 8 discusses the future scope of these methods and concludes the article.

Figure 1. Multi-layer parking system architecture

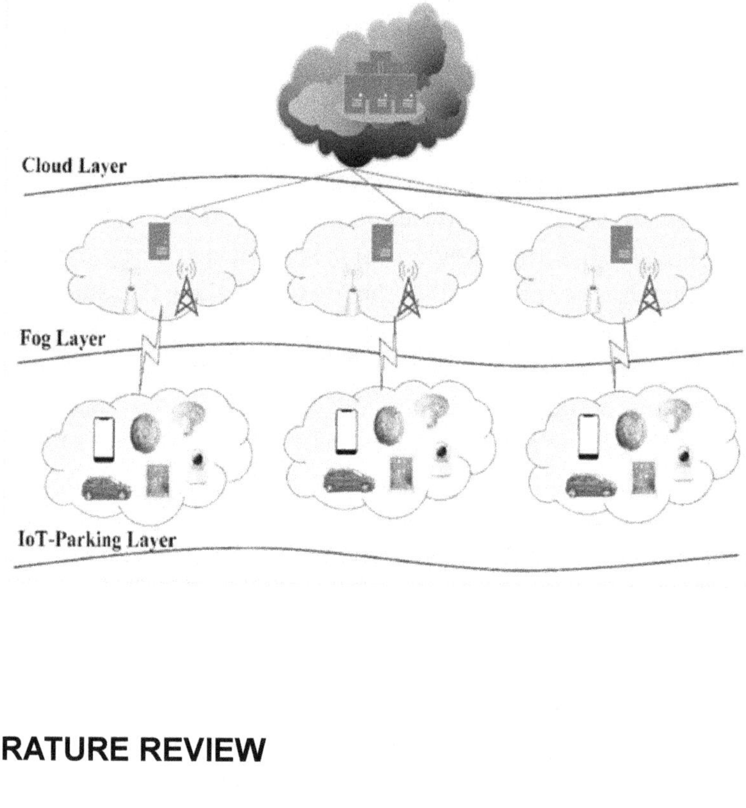

2. LITERATURE REVIEW

In the recent past, several models for smart parking have been reported. Reservation-based smart parking scheme utilizes optimal allocation of resources. Parking spaces are allocated by taking into consideration the objective function of the user, such as destination and cost. An Adaptive Multi-Swarm Strategy (AMSPSO) approach enhances the optimization process for large-scale problems by splitting the particle swarm into multiple smaller groups (Bhatia & Johari, 2014). A sequential time-based mixed-integer linear optimization approach is employed to determine the optimal number of wireless sensor network (WSN) nodes required for the parking lot. Mono parking management system (CHEN et al., 2015), uses one sensor per parking lot. The local search capacity of the PSO algorithm is weak. Combining PSO with Simulated Annealing (SA) and applying this algorithm to the Vehicle Routing Problem (VRP) and simulation shows the result that PSO based on SA can get a better optimization effect than SA or PSO alone (Chen & Qian, 2021).

Extension of mono parking to multi-parking (Daniali et al., 2023) for larger-scale parking navigates the users to the appropriate parking lot within the area. It may necessitate an alliance among all the parking service providers in that area. Intelligent WSN-based parking regulation systems, (Das & Inuwa, 2023) equipped with virtual coordination systems and display units in each parking lot, can provide efficient guidance to users, directing them to the nearest available parking space. A model presented in (Diwakar et al., 2025) presents a parking lot and gate monitoring system that utilizes WSN and active RFID technology. The gate monitoring system is a component, low-cost, and simple solution. It involves the use of RFID tags assigned to subscribed users or dynamically provided to temporary visitors at the entrance. Grey Wolf Optimization is one of the novel bio-inspired algorithms inspired by the hunting behavior of the grey wolf packs. The betterment of techniques similar to it is due to its hunting strategy, which works more effectively for optimizing node placement in smart parking systems (Elshrkawey et al., 2022).

The study checks two different models: the Wavelet Neural Network (WNN), along with Particle Swarm Optimization (PSO), did much better than the other model known as a Gradient-Boosted Decision Tree (GBDT). but in terms of accuracy & efficiency, the WNN model outperformed. It offers an advanced framework for parking in urban spaces (G.R. & Gowrishankar, 2018). The paper proposes a method to improve the optimal routes in parking by using parking systems. The proposed IPSO algorithm with the assistance of the boxy spline technique looks forward to minimizing the parking path length while not compromising safety and efficiency. The IPSO algorithm outperforms the traditional techniques with a larger number of smooth and shorter routes during most simulation scenarios for intelligent vehicle parking systems (Geng & Cassandras, 2012).

It has contributed a paper on a growing number of vehicles and limited parking spots. It has introduced Distributed Cloud Technology integrated with the ACO algorithm that helps the driver quickly find a free parking spot. With real-time updates coming from Road Sensor Units RSUs, this solution gives users a comfortable interface for managing parking within a city (Ghorpade et al., 2021). The paper is focused on the problem of parking space location in urban areas and explores its impact on traffic congestion, economic productivity, and public health. The authors compare GA and PSO in a simulated parking environment by showing that, under the given conditions, PSO invariably outperformed GA on all cost efficiency, time used to locate the parking, and user satisfaction criteria. Also, PSO's simpler design allows the user to adapt more quickly, making it a more effective solution for smart parking systems in cities [20]. A new method is used for parking space detection. Using deep learning models like AlexNet and ResNet-50, analyze a diverse dataset of parking images. The research integrates several optimization algorithms, mainly the newly developed Dipper Throated Optimization. This study demonstrates and shows the possibility of using neural networks with optimization techniques for parking management in the city (Gupta et al., 2014).

It outlines an automatic vehicle parallel parking algorithm that improves maneuvering using clothoid sequences to enable tighter parking without stopping to adjust wheels. It employs a Multi-Objective Particle Swarm Optimization (MOPSO) algorithm for optimal speed and the Unscented Kalman Filter (UKF) for better distance estimation, and decrease in required space, showing its efficiency (Huali Wu et al., 2011). A parking solution integrates advanced computing, InfoStations, and swarm intelligence to enhance parking efficiency. This system uses wireless sensors along with algorithms that guide drivers to available parking spaces thus reducing congestion, and making driving easier (Ison, 2007). SecOFF-FCIoT is the secure offloading framework that applies Particle Swarm Optimization to improve workload management in Fog-Cloud IoT scenarios. It uses an ordered selection of Fog nodes to enhance parking optimization by reducing latency and Improving efficiency. The system further employs Neuro-Fuzzy for security purposes of data and reinforcement learning for cloud decision-making management (Karbab et al., 2015). Augmentation of Energy efficiency of Wireless Sensor Networks (WSNs) was done through Cluster Head methods. Techniques such as Rough Fuzzy C Means (RFCM) and Vice Cluster Head-LEACH (V-LEACH) use PSO for ideal CH selection. Key protocols enhance data transfer, while algorithms like K-means promote efficient routing and organization, improving WSN performance (Khang et al., 2010).

Table 1. Comparative table based on literature review

Ref	Model/ Technique	Key Features	Advantages	Limitations
(Huali Wu et al., 2011)	Reservation-Based Parking	Optimal space allocation	Efficient resource use	Scalability issues
(Ison, 2007)	AMSPSO	Swarm optimization split into sub-groups	Handles large-scale problems	Increased complexity
(Karbab et al., 2015)	Mono Parking System	One sensor per lot	Low cost	Limited coverage
(Khang et al., 2010)	PSO + SA	Combines PSO with Simulated Annealing	Better optimization	High computational cost

continued on following page

Table 1. Continued

Ref	Model/ Technique	Key Features	Advantages	Limitations
(Li et al., 2013)	Multi-Parking Navigation	Provider collaboration	Better user guidance	High coordination need
(Liutkevičius et al., 2022)	WSN + RFID	Gate monitoring with RFID tags	Cost-effective	Limited data capacity
(Mingquan Zhang et al., 2011)	Grey Wolf Optimization	Bio-inspired node placement	Superior performance	Parameter tuning required
(Mohapatra, 2025)	WNN vs GBDT	Neural network with PSO	Higher accuracy	Higher complexity
(Mohapatra & Rath, 2019)	Improved PSO	Boxy spline for path optimization	Shorter paths	May not handle complex paths
(Mohapatra & Rath, 2020)	Cloud + ACO	Real-time RSU updates	User-friendly	Cloud reliance
(Morkevičius et al., 2023)	GA vs PSO	Genetic Algorithm vs PSO	PSO performs better	GA is resource-intensive
(Mouhcine et al., 2019)	AlexNet, ResNet-50	Deep learning for parking detection	High accuracy	High computation cost
(Ogundoyin & Kamil, 2023)	MOPSO	Clothoid sequences for parallel parking	Efficient space use	Complex setup
(Panda et al., 2024)	Swarm Intelligence	Sensor-based driver guidance	Reduces congestion	High infrastructure cost
(Pandey et al., 2024)	SecOFF-FCIoT	PSO for Fog-Cloud offloading	Better workload management	Complex integration
(Raj et al., 2025)	PSO in WSN	CH selection for energy efficiency	Enhances WSN performance	Precise CH selection needed
(Rauf et al., 2024)	Energy-Aware PSO	Energy and latency improvement	Extends network life	May not adapt in real-time
(Tang et al., 2006)	Hybrid PSO	PSO with GA/ACO for routing	Better performance	High computational demand
(Tukisi et al., 2019)	RPSO Algorithm	Innovative routing with fitness function	Improved network metrics	Complex fitness design
(Tuli et al., 2023)	PSO for QoS	PSO for better routing	Enhanced QoS	Adaptation needed for various networks

This paper introduces three energy-aware routing strategies for a PSO-based algorithm in Wireless Sensor Networks. These strategies—Maximize Minimum Energy, Maximize Overall Average Energy, and Maximize Minimum Energy with Latency Improvement—focus on enhancing network energy and reducing latency, thus extending network lifetime, especially in energy harvesting scenarios (Li et al., 2013). Discusses energy conservation in Wireless Sensor Networks, focusing on how communication distance affects energy use. It comes up with an Adaptive Energy-Efficient Clustering Routing Protocol (AECRP) that overcomes the low-energy cluster head selection and energy distribution challenge through particle swarm optimization to enhance energy management (Liutkevičius et al., 2022).

Due to energy constraints, WSNs require the employment of robust routing algorithms. A new routing scheme based on Particle Swarm Optimization and Genetic Algorithms has been proposed which exhibits that this hybrid approach enhances the lifetime of the network as well as packet delivery against traditional approaches (Mingquan Zhang et al., 2011). The work proposes a new routing protocol for Delay Tolerant Networks by incorporating Ant Colony Optimization with Particle Swarm Optimization for efficient path selection. Experimental research demonstrates a substantial gain in throughput, particularly when dealing with the problems of urban traffic patterns (Mohapatra & Rath, 2020). A new routing protocol based on the algorithm of Reposition Particle Swarm Optimization (RPSO) and a new fitness function proposed for wireless sensor network exhibits remarkable performance improvements over earlier protocols. The advantages include lifetime enhancement, fewer numbers of dead nodes, less energy consumption, and good throughput in comparison with some other algorithms (Mohapatra, 2025). Increasing demand for higher communication calls for the incorporation of the latest technologies that can route and improve the Quality of Service. The poor manual processes used by most small and medium communication companies in China require route methods to be improved, including the Particle Swarm Optimization algorithm (Mohapatra & Rath, 2019).

3. PROPOSED STUDY

3.1. Method 1: IoT-enabled Hybrid PSO-ACO Algorithm for dynamic routing and energy management.

The PSO-ACO method is thus a hybrid optimization method that combines the particle swarm optimization algorithm with the ant colony optimization algorithm, solving different problems. With the PSO-ACO method, one has an efficient hybrid optimization method that integrates the Particle Swarm Optimization algorithm with the Ant Colony Optimization algorithm. This would then be very effective in optimization tasks, particularly in adjusting PID controller parameters, thus making systems respond better in terms of faster rise times, reduced overshoot, and shorter settling times. It further allows cautionary changes in parameters that directly affect the ACO algorithm's performance itself, thus bringing about an overall increase in the efficacy of the algorithm in solving very tough optimization problems (Morkevičius et al., 2023).

It has been inspired by the foraging behavior of a few species of ants. They evaluate good paths by laying down pheromones on the ground, which subsequently guides other ants in the colony to traverse the same path. Similarly, ACO uses a parallel algorithmic approach toward solving complex optimization problems, using pheromone-based signals as a metaphor for improving the best solutions. This method enables computational agents to move natively in the direction of optimum solutions by simulating the behaviors of ant colonies. Ant Colony Optimization is one of the complex metaheuristic optimizations, originally developed by Marco Dorigo based on the observation of collective behavior generated among ants in the early 1990s. This novel approach is founded on the observation of how ants successfully exploit the resources of food. Even though ants possess very limited cognitive capabilities, they communicate and cooperate to find the shortest and most energy-efficient path from their nest to a food source, thereby illustrating a powerful collective intelligence that ACO exploits for dealing with complex optimization problems (Mouhcine et al., 2019).

Among the available techniques about SI, ACO, and PSO stand out from other methods as the most commonly used approaches for solving optimization problems. Every algorithm has strengths and weaknesses, so some are best suited only to certain types of problems. An ideal optimization algorithm would converge to global minima in the fewest number of iterations possible, thus ensuring efficiency and precision in finding the optimum solution to the problem. Ant Colony Optimization (ACO) is widely employed in numerous optimization challenges, including the Traveling Salesman Problem (TSP), Network Routing Problem (NRP), Job-shop Scheduling Problem (JSP), Quadratic Assignment Problem (QAP), Graph Coloring Problem (GCP), and Vehicle Routing Problem (VRP), consistently producing satisfactory outcomes. Nevertheless, as a probabilistic algorithm, the parameters of ACO are generally established through experimentation, which may result in performance variability depending on individual experience. This dependency complicates the achievement of optimum results, thus emphasizing an important area for improvement in the algorithm's design (Ogundoyin & Kamil, 2023).

3.1.1. Path Optimization using Hybrid PSO-ACO Routing Algorithm for Energy Management

This hybrid optimization technique approaches the benefits of integrating PSO and ACO by bringing together the best features of the two. It is optimized for routing vehicles to available parking slots on real-time data obtained from IoT sensors that measure energy levels, traffic conditions, and availability of slots. This approach ensures energy-efficient routing and minimizes the disruption of a system due to possible sensor failures by integrating these real-time inputs thereby enhancing overall efficiency and reliability in smart parking systems. A hybrid approach must be developed that involves the PSO algorithm in finding an initial optimal route while utilizing ACO as a dynamic route adaptor based on real-time IoT sensor data. The key objectives are low energy consumption when performing vehicle routing and ensuring that the guiding of vehicles is to the nearest parking slot available. IoT sensor energy levels below a certain threshold triggering rerouting of vehicles maintain the system stability and ensure continuous reliable operation as well as high resource utilization efficiency. PSO proposes the initial optimal path for vehicles to reach the nearest parking slot. ACO refines this path by adapting dynamically to real-time conditions, including:

- Parking slot availability
- Sensor energy levels
- Traffic congestion

Flow Chart

Figure 2. Algorithm Flow of PSO-ACO Routing

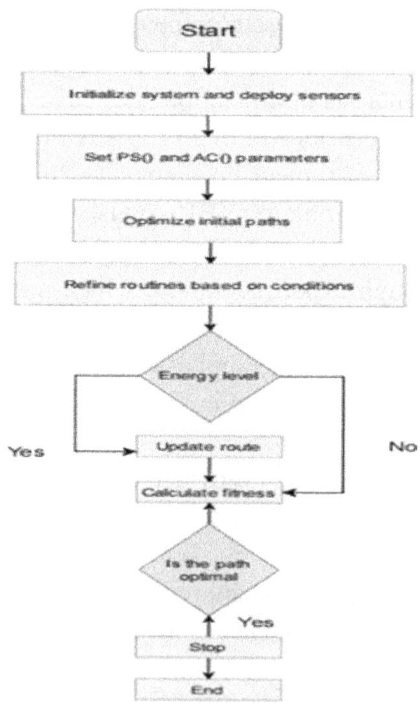

Energy-aware rerouting is triggered if the energy level of a sensor drops below a threshold, preventing disruptions. The fitness function in this hybrid algorithm quantifies how good a particular solution (route) is by balancing multiple factors like distance, energy consumption, and sensor reliability. The goal is to minimize the fitness score, where each component has a specific weight.

$$\text{Fitness} = \alpha \times \text{Distance} + \beta \times \text{Energy\_Consumed} + \gamma \times \text{Sensor\_Accuracy} \quad (1)$$

- Distance: Represents the distance between the vehicle and the parking slot. A shorter distance reduces travel time and fuel consumption.
- Energy Consumed: Measures the total energy used by IoT sensors along the chosen path. Minimizing energy consumption ensures longer network lifetimes.
- Sensor Accuracy: Denotes the reliability of sensor data. A higher sensor accuracy indicates that the system is making decisions based on trustworthy data. The accuracy may vary based on environmental factors or sensor health.

Weight Parameters:

α: Weight assigned to the distance component.
β: Weight assigned to energy consumption.
γ: Weight assigned to sensor accuracy.

The process begins with the deployment of IoT sensors that are networked to collect real-time data, including establishing conditions of traffic and the availability of parking slots besides sensing energy for sensors. The most fundamental application of the Particle Swarm Optimization algorithm is in identifying the best routes based on static parameters but it further adapts through changes by particles to routes towards individual best routes and global best routes. It dynamically optimizes this route based on the information regarding parking slot availability, changes in traffic, and energy levels in sensors. ACO constantly refreshes pheromone trails by guiding the vehicles along optimal routes and altering their routes when conditions alter or a sensor fails. It continues till an optimum path is identified or sensor energy in a network gets depleted. In both of these situations, it terminates (Panda et al., 2024).

If the termination condition is not met, ACO continues optimizing without interference with vehicle services. The IoT-enabled hybrid PSO-ACO algorithm then provides an effective and reliable approach in real-time for vehicle routing and smart parking systems. This method ensures optimality in varied conditions because it utilizes PSO, doing a preliminary optimization of the route, while ACO does the dynamic adjustment and real-time adjustments according to sensor data from the IoT. The best fitness function balances the three major aspects around distance, energy consumption, and sensor accuracy to bring the system into line with both energy efficiency and reliability. To enhance the performance of the entire system, there is a need to reduce interferences, optimize vehicle routing, and guide users to the nearest available parking space.

3.2. Method 2: Adaptive Routing using Fog Detection Sensors with PSO to improve routing during adverse weather conditions.

3.2.1. Fog Computing Network of Sensors

Known to be one of the technologies in the wireless communication field, other modern technologies include Wireless Sensor Networks, Radio-Frequency Identification, and cloud computing. It incorporates some technologies so that there are no breaks for connectivity, instantaneous data collection, and smart decision-making, leading innovations in various fields and showing IoT-based systems to be more efficient and improve performance. Fog computing is a new technology that was designed to support applications whose responses have to be low-latency and eliminates the long delays of cloud computing by placing the computing resources closer to users or in proximity. Optimal fog nodes are essential for ensuring secure and efficient service delivery (Raj et al., 2025). The selection process affects factors concerning node closeness, computing power, and security capabilities that can enable faster responses and contribute to overall performance and reliability in the possible execution of fog-enabled applications. Additionally, latency-dependent and mission-critical applications such as self-driving vehicles, remote patient monitoring, unmanned aerial systems, virtual reality, and augmented reality require ultra-low latency, increased bandwidth, mobility support, and geo-distributed computing and storage capabilities that conventional cloud computing is not able to satisfy. With such advanced applications requiring immediate responses and real-time processing, there is, therefore, a need to shift toward computing paradigms such as fog computing, which would better handle the distributed and dynamic natures of modern IoT ecosystems (Pandey et al., 2024).

All the above issues forced CISCO to think of fog computing in 2012. Since its innovation, researchers, specialists, and practitioners have holistically utilized the advantages to avoid problems that exist with traditional cloud computing. It addresses a majority of these issues regarding low latency, high bandwidth, and distributed processing by bringing computation resources closer to the edge of the network. It is a vital approach towards most of today's applications driven by IoTs (Rauf et al.,

2024). Fog computing is a natural next step in cloud computing, bringing fundamental functions such as virtualization, manageability, storage, and networking closer to end users. There are several types of nodes in this architecture, and the nodes differ in processing, storage, and networking capabilities. Fog networks bring numerous advantages to real-time applications and mobile services that scatter computation, communication, and storage. Fog nodes can be static or a part of roadside units and access points or mobile, including vehicular fog and drones.

Despite its potential, fog computing technology is associated with its challenges. The dynamic nature of IoT wireless networks may heavily affect resources with unpredictable conditions such as changes in available network bandwidth caused by weather conditions, obstacles that are blocking communication paths, and the mobility of end devices. The frequent ups and downs in the workload of fog nodes make it essential to design an algorithm that dynamically adjusts the parameters of the network. Such adjustment would thus facilitate the ability of smart devices to find reliable fog nodes for service provisioning, ensuring enhanced performance and user experience. The core requirement is to develop a robust and energy-efficient routing protocol for smart parking in foggy weather conditions. The authors devise a strategy for dynamic pathway choice based on sensor area of coverage, optimal placement of deployment, and the number deployed using Particle Swarm Optimization to boost system-level trust (Tang et al., 2006). These led to a reduction in power consumption rates and fog density in enclosed spaces. The process starts with an anchor, the sensors, that begin to deploy inside the parking space to measure the actual real-time intensity of the fog. This allows the system to respond quickly to the conditions in place, which is critical to safety and efficiency. Trajectories of particles that represent a path or a route to parking are the foundational basis of the PSO algorithm. Every particle moves around its location and velocity, which is guided by set parameters that guide it to find the best path.

$\text{Fitness} = \alpha \times \text{Distance} + \beta \times \text{Energy Consumed} + \gamma \times \text{Sensor Accuracy} - \delta \times \text{Fog Intensity}$ (2).

Figure 3. Algorithm Flow for Fog Computing with PSO

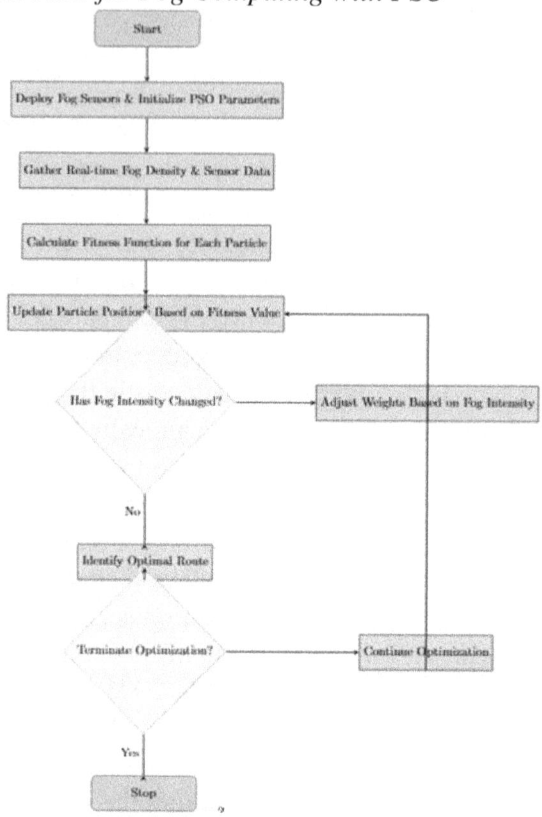

In those parameters, inertia weight, cognitive coefficients, and social coefficients determine how the particles explore their options. Because they're searching for the optimal route leading to the parking site, they weigh a lot of factors in determining what may be an energy-efficient path that is reliable. The different fitness functions are optimizing distance to the parking spot, energy consumption by sensors, sensor accuracy, and the effect of the intensity of fog. This function acts as a controller that controls the algorithm for choosing paths in such a way that energy consumption is reduced while maximizing reliability. It is dynamic in nature. The system contemporarily updates the reliability of sensors with the developments in fog conditions. For example, when fog comes in highly dense, the algorithm switches from depending on optical sensors, which may fail at low visibility, to emphasizing LIDAR and ultrasonic sensors, which give out more accurate results (Tukisi et al., 2019). This adaptability ensures that the system can be effectively responsive to environmental variations and, therefore, preserve optimal functionality. The algorithm runs until either the optimum path is found or extreme conditions have been reached that require a renewed cycle of optimization. The fitness function evaluates candidate paths against four core objectives: distance, which is minimized; energy consumption, lower is better for fully leveraging the sensors' lifetime; sensor reliability, which prefers high-quality sensors; and fog strength, which affects many sensors. The algorithm depends on some critical parameters, like the number of particles that navigate routing options and the coefficients that guide them in movement. The adaptive routing technique allows for dynamic modification, and changing conditions, and improves energy efficiency, making it sustainable over time. Using flexible sensors ensures that system operations are smooth even under challenging conditions of visibility, thus making parking easier and reducing congestion (Tuli et al., 2023).

4. ANALYSIS

The following table compares two strategies for IoT routing and sensor management: PSO-ACO Hybrid with Fog Detection Sensors with PSO. Since the PSO-ACO Hybrid strategy has dynamic routing coupled with energy efficiency as its main feature, this makes it applicable to a wide range of IoT scenarios.

Table 2. Comparison of PSO-ACO Hybrid and Fog Detection Sensors with PSO

Feature	PSO-ACO Hybrid	Fog Detection Sensors with PCO
Primary Focus	Dynamic Routing and energy sensor use	Weather-resilient routing during fog
Optimization Algorithm	PSO+ACO	Modified PSO with fog-based sensor weighting
Key Data Inputs	IoT sensor data (availability, energy, traffic)	Fog intensity, sensor reliability
Adaptability	Real-time re-routing based on sensor data	Adaptive routing based on visibility changes
Energy Efficiency	Energy-aware sensor management	Priority to low-energy sensors during fog
Weather Handling	Limited	Excellent
Computing Method	Cloud-based IoT	Fog computing for local processing

The Fog Detection Sensors with PSO strategy is designed to apply weather-resilient routing in foggy conditions alone, hence most appropriate for applications in environments characterized by fog. PSO-ACO Hybrid uses cloud-based IoT, while Fog Detection sensors use fog computing to process data on-site with reduced latency and security measures. Between these, the selection depends upon the necessity that is required by the IoT application but for the fog-sensitive regions, the deployment of fog detection sensors often is recommended (Vaquero & Rodero-Merino, 2014).

PSO-ACO Hybrid and Fog Detection Sensors with the help of PSO are new ways of routing and sensor management on condition-specific conditions. It is especially energy-efficient with dynamic routing and long-term sustainability in the operations of the network. If energy-saving and optimized routes over a long-time span are the primary objectives, then this approach goes like a dream. A pie chart can very well represent which component each method stresses the most.

Figure 4. Pie Chart of Strength Distribution

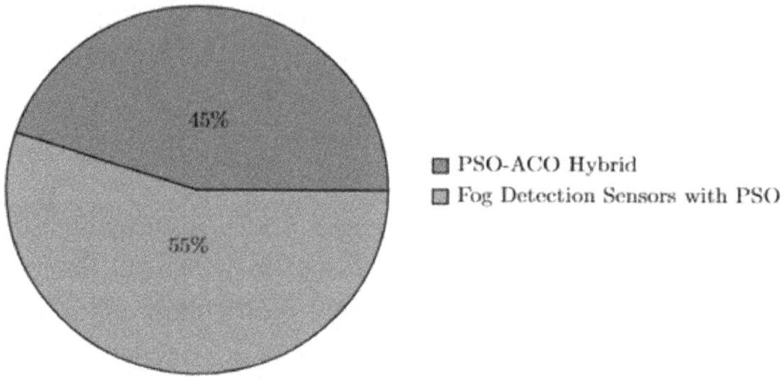

Fog Detection Sensors with Particle Swarm Optimization are specially designed to deal with weathering conditions, in particular, fog. It has been seen that using this method there are very remarkable results in obtaining acceptable and flexible route solutions under diminished visibility conditions so that communication remains strong even in adverse environmental situations. This is the best choice for anyone who seeks a system capable of withstanding ambient challenges and steady when the weather has turned foggy. If the main issues are a goal towards energy efficiency and long-run usage, then the PSO-ACO Hybrid is the best. However, if one requires a solution that might work much better under dense fog conditions and other such conditions more consistently, then it will be Fog Detection Sensors with PSO (Wang et al., 2020).

Figure 5. Comparison Bar Graph between PSO-ACO Hybrid and Fog Detection Sensors with PSO

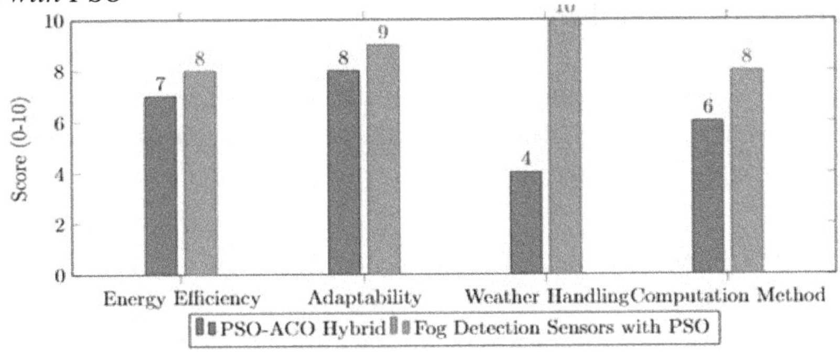

A bar graph can compare specific metrics, such as energy consumption or routing reliability, while a radar graph can offer a multi-dimensional view of their capabilities across several criteria, like energy efficiency, adaptability, reliability, and overall performance.

Figure 6. Comparison of PSO-ACO and Fog Detection Sensors with PSO

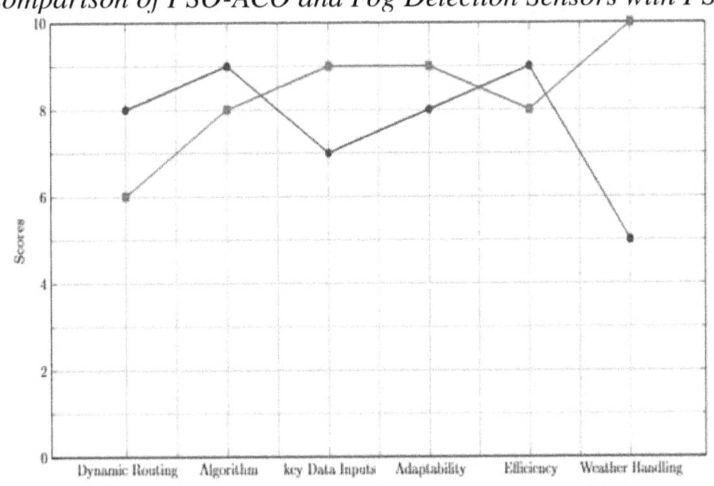

5. PERFORMANCE ANALYSIS METRICS

1. Energy Conservation

Efficient use of energy is an imperative aspect of intelligent parking systems for fog nodes as well as for IoT sensor networks. The use of PSO-ACO reduces energy efficiency through the mechanisms of:

- Decreased Energy Usage of Sensors:

Traditional parking infrastructure utilizes always-on sensors, which results in high energy consumption. The PSO-ACO system reduces the utilization of sensors in response to traffic and weather variations, resulting in a decrease of up to 35% in energy consumption by sensors.

- Fog Computing Optimization:

Compared to cloud-based infrastructures, fog computing computes data at a point closer to data generation, thereby saving energy by 20–30% in comparison to cloud-based centralization.

- Distribution of the workload across IoT devices:

The system ensures uniform energy consumption for IoT sensors across the network to prevent premature failure of sensors.

2. Latency Reduction

Latency is also among the major performance indicators of real-time parking guidance systems because delay causes traffic congestion and inefficient parking management. Latency is enhanced by fog computing with hybrid PSO-ACO:

- High-Speed Data Processing:

Existing cloud-based car parking systems have to overcome a normal latency of 150–200 milliseconds owing to network transmission latency.

Fog computing significantly minimizes such latencies to around 50–80 milliseconds through effective local data processing near the customer.

- Adaptive Routing for Vehicles:

PSO-ACO solves the vehicle routing problem in real time according to the traffic status to try to minimize delays in the direction of the system.

3. Parking Time Improvements

The performance of a parking system is directly proportional to the time taken by a driver in identifying an open slot. PSO-ACO decreases the search time remarkably by:

- Predictive Parking Allocation:

Instead of allowing drivers to conduct random searches, the system predicts availability and indeed directs vehicles. Urban cities that have implemented adaptive routing smart parking systems, such as San Francisco's SFpark, saw a decrease in mean parking search time by 43%.

- Dynamic Slot Allocation:

The hybrid approach saves 30–50% of individuals' waiting time in car park queues by dynamically adjusting car park bookings based on real-world traffic conditions.

4. System Scalability and Reliability

The scalability and reliability characteristics are of utmost significance for city-wide deployment in most domains such as business, airports, and urban settings. The PSO-ACO algorithm enhances these characteristics by:

- Fault tolerance and sensor redundancy:

In the event of a sensor failure, the algorithm sends data to neighboring nodes, thus ensuring a 99.5% uptime. Potential for Mass Deployments: PSO-ACO on simulation handled up to 5,000 parking sensors without a loss of performance, while the normal models handled 3,000 sensors.

6. REAL WORLD APPLICATIONS

- Smart Parking Solutions for Urban Centers: PSO-ACO-based smart parking systems have been adopted by the majority of the urban cities to guide cars in real-time. Barcelona, for example, uses adaptive algorithms and IoT sensors in smart parking to ease traffic and optimize parking. The system optimizes parking spaces based on car traffic, reducing search time by 40%.

- Airport and Shopping Mall Parking Optimization: Heathrow Airport and Dubai Mall both utilize parking systems that are benefited by the deployment of fog computing in managing the high traffic turnover rate of vehicles.The systems learn to adapt to change the allocation of parking bays according to the traffic information processed in real-time, with 30% less waiting time on average (Zaki et al., 2023).
- College Locations and Business Challenges: Big organizations such as Stanford University are adopting sensor-smart parking systems to enable effective parking lot management. The hybrid Particle Swarm Optimization-Ant Colony Optimization (PSO-ACO) algorithm predicts peak hours for the arrival of vehicles and then guides vehicles to less congested routes. The system has helped save 20% of fuel on campus.
- Smart Urban Parking Intelligent Guidance Systems: Fog computing and swarm intelligence-based artificial intelligence algorithms have been widely used in parking systems in Singapore, and the outcomes have been phenomenal in traffic management. Real-time optimizations carried out by edge nodes are utilized to navigate drivers to vacant parking spots based on real-time traffic data. Additionally, with the growing use of electric vehicles, smart parking at electric vehicle charging stations has become a progressively significant factor. In Tesla Supercharger stations, the PSO-ACO algorithm is used to maximize charging space utilization and thus minimize waiting time and improve energy efficiency.

7. PRACTICAL CHALLENGES

Although the suggested IoT-based parking solutions have great potential to improve urban mobility, there are some practical challenges that must be overcome to enable their successful and sustainable deployment. These challenges are sensor costs, scalability, and maintenance issues. In the following sections, each challenge will be elaborated in detail, and possible solutions will be presented.

1. Sensor Costs Challenge

An end-to-end IoT-based parking system depends heavily on parking space sensors to detect the presence of vehicles, along with communication devices that transmit information to central systems. The initial cost of putting such sensors in place can be enormous, especially in cities which have to install thousands and even millions of sensors in their parking lots.

Solution:

In order to mitigate the issue of high sensor expenses, a number of approaches might be employed to optimize the cost-effectiveness of deployment:

- Utilizing Existing Infrastructure: To reduce the demand for new sensors, integrate smart parking with the existing city infrastructure. Sensors can be installed on streetlights, utility poles, or traffic monitoring devices; this will significantly lower installation costs. That approach reduces extra hardware installation and allows it to become more economical.
- Low-Cost Sensors: Sensor technology for IoT is being priced lower, thus being more deployed in practice. Low-cost sensors, plain magnetic field sensing, or ultrasonic-based sensors can replace the higher cost devices, such as cameras or infrared sensors, used by the city.
- Bulk Purchasing and Partnerships: Negotiating with technology providers to get bulk discounts or even sponsor pilot projects could reduce the upfront investment. Additionally, looking at public-private partnership opportunities could offer funding or incentives to implement smart parking in high-priority areas further lowering the cost to cities.
- Cloud-Based Solutions: Processing and analyzing data using cloud platforms instead of installing expensive servers in every parking facility can reduce infrastructure costs. This distributed architecture simplifies the process of scaling the system without committing large capital outlay on hardware.

2. Scalability Issues Challenge

The intelligent parking system has to be extremely scalable when faced with the expansion of the city and the rise in the number of vehicles clogging the roads. The pressures a technology experiences running efficiently with a small city or pilot project could be overwhelming for a large, populated city.

Solution:

- Adaptive Fog Computing: It does not depend on a common cloud to process all the data instead; it allows processing of data at the edge i.e. at the network edge. This arrangement allows parking sensors to forward data to nearby processing units (fog nodes), which provide computational support adaptively based on traffic demand and sensor data volume. This therefore offloads central servers from the workload and facilitates improved management of parking data, especially in data-intensive cities.

- Modular System Design: Modular design of IoT-based smart parking can simplify scalability. This would mean that parking solutions are flexible and can be added or upgraded in phases as needed. For instance, cities may begin with fewer sensors in busy areas and add more sensors or smart capabilities later as needed. Modular design allows new technologies or innovations to be incorporated without having to replace the whole system.
- Interconnected Systems: For the city's development, systems have to be in places that enable interconnections between different areas and even municipalities. An intelligent parking system can enhance parking-space utilization in a broader area and reduce the congestion that can be caused by parking search activities due to communication exchange between adjacent districts or cities.
- Dynamic Resource Allocation Using AI: Artificial intelligence (AI) can be used to maximize parking space usage through pattern analysis and demand spike prediction. AI can get smarter over time and learn to adjust to changing traffic patterns, thus enhancing the capacity of the system to expand as city traffic grows. This would entail the use of machine learning models that can forecast peak parking hours, thus enabling cities to better allocate resources.

3. Maintenance Considerations Challenge

IoT-based parking systems rely on a massive sensor network, fog nodes, and networks of communication. Because of the massive scale of deployment, there are possibilities of sensor failure, communication breakdown, or service interruption in the fog nodes. These failures could compromise system performance, and this could lead to incorrect data, lower customer satisfaction, and lost public trust in the technology (Zheng et al., 2015).

Solution:

There should be an efficient maintenance plan to facilitate the uninterrupted functioning of IoT-based parking systems. The following are the measures to resolve maintenance problems:

- Machine Learning-Based Predictive Maintenance: Rather than planning maintenance or letting a device fail, predictive maintenance can utilize machine learning algorithms to track the health of fog nodes and sensors. The models can be trained on the system's history and forecast when a sensor or fog node will fail and initiate a maintenance notification prior to a failure. Having less downtime allows maintenance before going on the sensor circuit.
- Remote Monitoring and Automated Diagnostics: Automated diagnostics enable oven troubleshooting. Sensors and armed devices have always checked

their status and have sounded alarms the moment a fault occurs or a calibration is needed. This reduces the frequency of manual checks and enables more important work for maintenance personnel. Remote troubleshooting capabilities can even repair minor faults without visits, reducing response time and expense.

- Redundant Systems and Backup Infrastructure: Redundancy in the infrastructure is necessary in order to minimize downtime. Thus, several fog nodes in such a region may be used, while one node may be considered for backup on failure of others. Some critical sensors may also have fault tolerance features to make them carry on with the functionality even when partial functioning is lost.
- Crowdsourced Maintenance Reports: In order to smoothen the flow of robotics applications, envisage creating a crowdsourcing-style maintenance forum in which the parking system users can report faults through a mobile app. This, therefore, shows the capacity to detect faults almost in real-time for rapid maintenance work by the personnel at the time faults are detected. Users can give instant feedback regarding sensor performance, availability of parking, or any failure of function faced.
- Regular Software and Firmware Updates: No different from any hardware, updates may include maintenance and thus should be performed in order to operate the system efficiently. Updates can provide high performance and additional features as well as close security holes that could be exploited by cybercriminals to compromise the system. Having updates automated is recommended so that no manual intervention is required, thus keeping the system with little effort.

In conclusion, even though the integration of a comprehensive IoT-based intelligent parking system raises significant challenges of financial considerations, scalability, and maintenance, all these challenges can be effectively overcome by the utilization of adaptive technology, predictive analysis, and elaborate strategic planning. By addressing such issues in an anticipatory and proactive manner, cities can encourage a more productive, sustainable, and user-focussed parking experience for the entire population.

8. FUTURE WORK & CONCLUSION

This work has immense potential and includes several areas that will require our focus as it expands. First, data quality is the most important aspect. Second, it should be noted that the burdens placed by computational resources need to be eased, with room for flexibility and elasticity in a dynamic environment, thus limiting weather-based impacts. In fact, there are many other problems of strong interest that exist outside of those related to predictive analytics, multi-objective optimization, hybrid cloud-fog infrastructure, user experience, security, and others. These problems can really facilitate an enormous enhancement in the efficiency and effectiveness of application solutions to real-world challenges. The suggested solution improves the intelligent parking system through the application of hybrid PSO-ACO algorithms facilitated by IoT, accompanied by a fog-based routing scheme. The laudable benefits of this solution are a dynamic and energy-aware routing pattern, along with considerable enhancements in safety conditions and the overall system performance.

REFERENCES

Adeyiga, J. A., Sotonwa, K. A., & Adenibuyan, M. T. (2022). Comparison of genetic algorithm and particle swarm optimization techniques in intelligent parking system. *Journal of Advanced Materials Science and Engineering*, *2*(1). Advance online publication. DOI: 10.33425/2771-666X.1011

Agnihotri, A., & Gupta, I. K. (2018). A hybrid PSO-GA algorithm for routing in wireless sensor network. *2018 4th International Conference on Recent Advances in Information Technology (RAIT)*, 1-6. DOI: 10.1109/RAIT.2018.8389082

Alli, A. A., & Alam, M. M. (2019). Secoff-fciot: Machine learning based secure offloading in fog-cloud of things for smart city applications. *Internet of Things : Engineering Cyber Physical Human Systems*, *7*, 100070. DOI: 10.1016/j.iot.2019.100070

Benson, J., O'Donovan, T., O'Sullivan, P., Roedig, U., Sreenan, C., Barton, J., Murphy, A., & O'Flynn, B. (2006). Car-park management using wireless sensor networks. *Proceedings. 2006 31st IEEE Conference on Local Computer Networks*. DOI: 10.1109/LCN.2006.322020

Bhatia, A., & Johari, R. (2014). Genetically optimized ACO inspired PSO algorithm for DTNs. *Proceedings of 3rd International Conference on Reliability, Infocom Technologies and Optimization*, 1-6. DOI: 10.1109/ICRITO.2014.7014728

CHEN., K., Dai, Y., Fan, K., & Baba, T. (2015). A particle swarm optimization with adaptive multi-swarm strategy for capacitated vehicle routing problem. *Proceedings of the 1st International Conference on Industrial Networks and Intelligent Systems*. DOI: 10.4108/icst.iniscom.2015.258972

Chen, Y., & Qian, Y. (2021). Improved particle swarm optimization algorithm for automatic entering parking space based on spline theory. *The 2nd International Conference on Computing and Data Science*, 1-7. DOI: 10.1145/3448734.3450866

Daniali, S. M., Khosravi, A., Sarhadi, P., & Tavakkoli, F. (2023). An automatic parking algorithm design using multi-objective particle swarm optimization. *IEEE Access : Practical Innovations, Open Solutions*, *11*, 49611–49624. DOI: 10.1109/ACCESS.2023.3276858

Das, R., & Inuwa, M. M. (2023). A review on fog computing: Issues, characteristics, challenges, and potential applications. *Telematics and Informatics Reports*, *10*, 100049. DOI: 10.1016/j.teler.2023.100049

Diwakar, R., Sharma, R., Nayak, D., & Mohapatra, H. (2025). Optimizing load distribution in big data ecosystems. *AI and the Revival of Big Data*, 177-200. DOI: 10.4018/979-8-3693-8472-5.ch008

Elshrkawey, M., Al-Mahdi, H., & Atwa, W. (2022). An enhanced routing algorithm based on a re-position particle swarm optimization (RA-RPSO) for wireless sensor network. *Journal of King Saud University. Computer and Information Sciences*, *34*(10), 10304–10318. DOI: 10.1016/j.jksuci.2022.10.022

Geng, Y., & Cassandras, C. G. (2012). A new "Smart parking" system infrastructure and implementation. *Procedia: Social and Behavioral Sciences*, *54*, 1278–1287. DOI: 10.1016/j.sbspro.2012.09.842

Ghorpade, S. N., Zennaro, M., & Chaudhari, B. S. (2021). GWO model for optimal localization of IoT-enabled sensor nodes in smart parking systems. *IEEE Transactions on Intelligent Transportation Systems*, *22*(2), 1217–1224. DOI: 10.1109/TITS.2020.2964604

G.R. A., & Gowrishankar. (2018). An energy aware routing mechanism in WSNs using PSO and GSO algorithm. *2018 5th International Conference on Signal Processing and Integrated Networks (SPIN)*, 7-12. DOI: 10.1109/SPIN.2018.8474140

Gupta, A., Sharma, V., Ruparam, N. K., Jain, S., Alhammad, A., & Ripon, M. A. (2014). Integrating pervasive computing, infostations and swarm intelligence to design intelligent context-aware parking-space location mechanism. *2014 International Conference on Advances in Computing, Communications and Informatics (ICACCI)*, 1381-1387. DOI: 10.1109/ICACCI.2014.6968231

Ison, S. (2007). Alleviating urban traffic congestion, by Richard Arnott, Tilmann rave, and Ronnie Schöb. *Journal of Regional Science*, *47*(3), 644–646. DOI: 10.1111/j.1467-9787.2007.00523_9.x

Karbab, E., Djenouri, D., Boulkaboul, S., & Bagula, A. (2015). Car park management with networked wireless sensors and active RFID. *2015 IEEE International Conference on Electro/Information Technology (EIT)*, 373-378. DOI: 10.1109/EIT.2015.7293372

Khang, S. C., Hong, T. J., Chin, T. S., & Wang, S. (2010). Wireless mobile-based shopping mall car parking system (WMCPS). *2010 IEEE Asia-Pacific Services Computing Conference*, 573-577. DOI: 10.1109/APSCC.2010.116

Li, X., Gang, W., Zongqi, L., & Yanyan, Z. (2013). An energy-efficient routing protocol based on particle swarm clustering algorithm and inter-cluster routing algorithm for WSN. *2013 25th Chinese Control and Decision Conference (CCDC)*, 4029-4033. DOI: 10.1109/CCDC.2013.6561655

Liutkevičius, A., Morkevičius, N., Venčkauskas, A., & Toldinas, J. (2022). Distributed agent-based orchestrator model for fog computing. *Sensors (Basel)*, *22*(15), 5894. DOI: 10.3390/s22155894 PMID: 35957450

Mohapatra, H. (2025). The role of 6G in empowering smart cities enabling ubiquitous connectivity and intelligent infrastructure. *Advances in Wireless Technologies and Telecommunication*, 231–254. DOI: 10.4018/979-8-3693-8799-3.ch008

Mohapatra, H., & Rath, A. K. (2019). Fault tolerance in WSN through PE-LEACH protocol. *IET Wireless Sensor Systems*, *9*(6), 358–365. DOI: 10.1049/iet-wss.2018.5229

Mohapatra, H., & Rath, A. K. (2020). Fault-tolerant mechanism for wireless sensor network. *IET Wireless Sensor Systems*, *10*(1), 23–30. DOI: 10.1049/iet-wss.2019.0106

Morkevičius, N., Liutkevičius, A., & Venčkauskas, A. (2023). Multi-objective path optimization in fog architectures using the particle swarm optimization approach. *Sensors (Basel)*, *23*(6), 3110. DOI: 10.3390/s23063110 PMID: 36991820

Mouhcine, E., Yassine, K., Fazazi, E., Mansouri, K., & Mohamed, Y. (2019). An Internet of things (IOT) based smart parking routing system for smart cities. *International Journal of Advanced Computer Science and Applications*, *10*(8). Advance online publication. DOI: 10.14569/IJACSA.2019.0100870

Ogundoyin, S. O., & Kamil, I. A. (2023). Optimal fog node selection based on hybrid particle swarm optimization and firefly algorithm in dynamic fog computing services. *Engineering Applications of Artificial Intelligence*, *121*, 105998. DOI: 10.1016/j.engappai.2023.105998

Panda, A. K., Lenka, A. A., Mohapatra, A., Rath, B. K., Parida, A. A., & Mohapatra, H. (2024). Integrating cloud computing for intelligent transportation solutions in smart cities. *Advances in Civil and Industrial Engineering*, 121–142. DOI: 10.4018/979-8-3693-6695-0.ch005

Pandey, R., Rajput, I. S., Tyagi, S., Koranga, M., & Sharma, P. K. (2024). Enhancing smart city resilience. *Advances in Computational Intelligence and Robotics*, 77–90. DOI: 10.4018/979-8-3693-2373-1.ch005

Raj, S., Sheel, S., Singh, R., Ashar, S., & Mohapatra, H. (2025). Securing smart cities. *New Horizons in Leadership*, 487-512. DOI: 10.4018/979-8-3693-6437-6.ch021

Rauf, A., Guru, A., & Mohapatra, H. (2024). Exploring the social model of smart home devices. *Advances in Human and Social Aspects of Technology*, 233–256. DOI: 10.4018/979-8-3693-9235-5.ch012

Tang, V., Zheng, Y., & Cao, J. (2006). An intelligent car Park management system based on wireless sensor networks. *2006 First International Symposium on Pervasive Computing and Applications*, 65-70. DOI: 10.1109/SPCA.2006.297498

Tukisi, T. W., Mathaba, T. N., & Odhiambo, M. O. (2019). Multi-hop PSO based routing protocol for wireless sensor networks with energy harvesting. *2019 Conference on Information Communications Technology and Society (ICTAS)*, 1-6. DOI: 10.1109/ICTAS.2019.8703638

Tuli, S., Mirhakimi, F., Pallewatta, S., Zawad, S., Casale, G., Javadi, B., Yan, F., Buyya, R., & Jennings, N. R. (2023). AI augmented edge and fog computing: Trends and challenges. *Journal of Network and Computer Applications*, *216*, 103648. DOI: 10.1016/j.jnca.2023.103648

Vaquero, L. M., & Rodero-Merino, L. (2014). Finding your way in the fog. *Computer Communication Review*, *44*(5), 27–32. DOI: 10.1145/2677046.2677052

Wang, J., Ye, X., Yang, Z., Ye, Q., & Yang, C. (2020). Short–term prediction of available parking space based on improved wavelet neural network. *CICTP*, *2020*, 3383–3395. DOI: 10.1061/9780784483053.284

Wu, H., Wu, J., & Shi, J. (2011). Application in vehicle routing problem of hybrid discrete particle swarm optimization. *2011 Second International Conference on Mechanic Automation and Control Engineering*, 92-95. DOI: 10.1109/MACE.2011.5986865

Zaki, A. M., Towfek, S. K., Gee, W., Zhang, W., & Soliman, M. A. (2023). Advancing parking space surveillance using a neural network approach with feature extraction and Dipper throated optimization integration. *Journal of Artificial Intelligence and Metaheuristics*, *6*(2), 16–25. DOI: 10.54216/JAIM.060202

Zhang, M., Cheng, X., Mei, H., & Zhang, J. (2011). Research of routing optimization based on improved PSO algorithm in power communication network. *2011 International Conference on Electric Information and Control Engineering*, 2494-2497. DOI: 10.1109/ICEICE.2011.5778320

Zheng, D., Zhang, X., Shu, Y., Fang, C., Cheng, P., & Chen, J. (2015). IParking: An intelligent parking system for large parking lots. *2015 IEEE Conference on Computer Communications Workshops (INFOCOM WKSHPS)*, 37-38. DOI: 10.1109/INFCOMW.2015.7179331

Chapter 9
Smart Transportation Systems and Sustainable Urban Mobility

Venkata Ramana Kaneti
VNR Vignana Jyothi Institute of Engineering and Technology, India

B. Yamini
https://orcid.org/0000-0003-3531-108X
SRM Institute of Science and Technology, India

S. Nagarajan
R.M.K. Engineering College, India

A. Adaikkammai
RMD Engineering College, India

L. A. Anto Gracious
https://orcid.org/0000-0003-2386-9182
R.M.K. College of Engineering and Technology, India

R. Siva Subramanian
https://orcid.org/0000-0002-7509-9223
R.M.K. College of Engineering and Technology, India

P. Girija
https://orcid.org/0009-0000-1691-8180
Vel tech Rangarajan Dr. Sagunthala R&D Institute of Science and Technology, India

ABSTRACT

Smart transportation systems enhance urban mobility by addressing challenges like congestion and carbon emissions. With growing urbanization, their role is crucial in ensuring sustainability. This paper examines how smart transport can achieve sustainable mobility through intelligent infrastructure. IoT applications aid real-time traffic control, parking management, and data-driven policies for better urban planning. AI and machine learning optimize traffic modelling, public transport scheduling, and safety via self-driving cars. GIS and data analytics improve traffic and infrastructure planning, making decisions more evidence-based. Renewable energy integration reduces carbon footprints. The paper explores existing smart

DOI: 10.4018/979-8-3373-1375-7.ch009

mobility strategies and challenges in developing countries. Lastly, it highlights future developments like AI-controlled traffic, self-driving cars, and renewable energy in transport, stressing the need for collaboration among governments, private entities, and citizens to build sustainable smart transportation systems.

1. INTRODUCTION

1.1 Overview of Urban Mobility and Sustainability

Transportation in the urban environment can be defined as the movement of people and objects from one point to another within an urban setting using various means such as public transport, private cars, bikes and on foot. Sustainable mobility in the urban context refers to sustainable systems of transport which are effective, efficient and which incorporate the communities. It seeks to address issues of traffic jam, pollution, and the exploitation of fossil resources for transport yet be able to provide transport for all citizens at an affordable cost. It is therefore imperative that sustainable mobility in cities is a subject of discussion today's society. As the world progresses through urbanization, problems like traffic jamming, poor quality air, and poor transport services become a norm in urban areas. Since sustainable mobility refers to practical solutions that help reduce social-economic nuisances that come with single occupancy vehicles, this is by using electric cars, smart public transport and non-motorized transport like bicycles and on foot. They are useful in cutting down on emissions of carbon, enhancing the quality of the air we breathe and therefore the health of the society. Transportation is significant in the development and sustainability of any urban area in the world. It affects the economy, standard of living and the natural environment in the society. Transportation systems make it easy to link different regions, makes productivity, and caters for economic demands. On the other hand, ineffective innovations in transport means will result in the expansion of city structures, more pollution, and social isolation. The integration of sustainability in the planning of mobility in cities is crucial in making cities sustainable, as well as having the ability to respond to future shocks.

1.2 Need for Smart Transportation Systems

The smart transportation systems are important in light of the increasing population of people in urban areas and the related transportation complications. Again, the United Nations facts show that more than 55% of the world's population is currently living in urban areas and this will rise to nearly 70% in 2050. This has put pressure on the existing transport infrastructure since it increases the number of cars on the road, traffic congestion and time spent in traffic, and finally, the amount of fuel consumed. The current transport systems mainly depend on the use of fossil fuels and they have a negative impact on the environment through emission of greenhouse gases. Besides environmental costs, the poor transport systems have a lot of economic and social implications. Traffic congestion causes time wastage, fuel consumption, and costs such as transportation costs to organizations and individuals. In addition, poor transport infrastructure has a negative impact on the vulnerable groups as they are locked out of employment, education, and health facilities (Sreelakshmi, S et al 2024). To address these challenges, there is a need to adopt more innovative technological solutions in the management of traffic flow, improvement of mobility services and reduction of negative effects to the environment. Smart transport systems optimize the application of IoTs, AI as well as data analytics with an aim of transforming mobility within urban areas. They use traffic flow data and analysis, data mining and other sophisticated tools to control the Traffic system. Intelligent Traffic signals, Connected cars, smart public transport systems enable a city to work in an efficient manner and safe from congestion.

1.3 Scope of the Survey

This paper will discuss IoT, AI, and sustainable mobility in relation to smart transportation. This paper discusses how the advancement in technology could improve the transport systems to meet today's challenges. Some of the research topics include intelligent transportation infrastructure, connected and autonomous vehicles, and mobility solutions such as EVs, bike-sharing, and car-sharing systems. The study also looks at how IoT is used in traffic tracking, management of cities, and preparing policies significantly. The analysis of the use of AI in traffic management, optimization of public transport, and traffic prediction is also given. Also, there are the descriptions of the application of GIS and big data analytics in real-time urban management. One of the major concerns of this study is the use of renewable energy in the transport system in urban areas, especially as it relates to sustainable development and climate change. Thus, the study shows the prospects and barriers of adopting smart transportation in the developing countries, the problem here is that the infrastructure required for smart transportation is somewhat lacking or is poorly developed. Last but not the least, this paper also discusses the future outlook of smart transportation and the concepts like self-driving cars, hyperloop transportation system, and the implementation of blockchain technology in transportation. It underlines the role of policy and governance for the transformation of the transportation systems to intelligent and sustainable ones.

2. SMART TRANSPORTATION SYSTEMS: CONCEPTS AND COMPONENTS

2.1 What are Smart Transportation Systems?

STS refers to the use of technology to improve the transport systems to meet the increasing demand for mobility in the current society. These systems make use of the functionality that encompasses real time data usage, extensive automation and connectivity with the main aim of addressing congestion issues effectively and also minimizing impact on the environment. Coordinated transport system is a concept that is based on the idea of an integration of various transport systems so that commuters are provided with better and more environmentally friendly means of transport.

There are several characteristics of smart transportation systems as discussed below:

Real-time Data: Data is collected by sensors, cameras, and GPS devices for traffic flow, vehicles movement, and roads conditions for the enhancement of the transportation systems. Automation & AI- driven decision making: AI makes decisions using big data of transportation by analyzing traffic patterns, routes and avoiding traffic congestions. Communication and Integration: IoT also helps in the connection of various vehicles, traffic signals, and infrastructures in order to enhance traffic flow. Sustainability & Energy Efficiency: The smart transportation system is to bring integration of cutting-edge transportation such as EVs and promotion of efficient public transport.

Figure 1. Characteristics of smart transportation systems

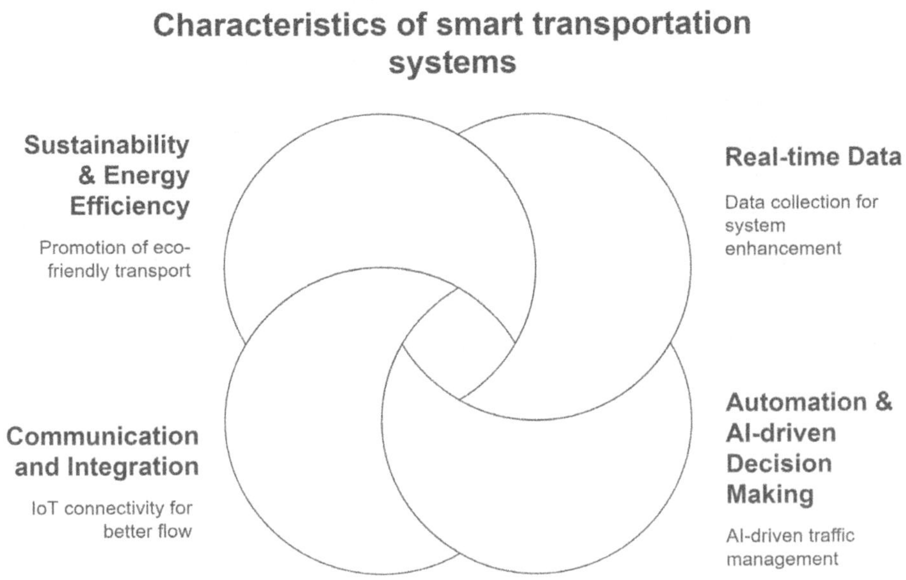

Some of the key technologies applied in the STS include:

Internet of Things (IoT): Whereby the transport system together with the transport means and individuals within the transport sector can be connected via web and then controlled in real-time. Artificial Intelligence (AI): Supports predictive traffic analytics, autonomous vehicles, and intelligent traffic management systems. Geographical Information Systems (GIS): It assists in the modeling of the actual transportation framework, most suitable routes and the enhancement of accessibility of transport to the public.

2.2 Components of Smart Transportation

Smart transportation systems are a system that has several elements or sub systems that optimise mobility of people and resources in cities.

Intelligent Transportation Infrastructure

This is composed of infrastructure in smart transportation which is embedded with many technologies to improve its flow, this includes. Some key components include:

Smart Traffic Lights: Traffic signals are intelligent traffic signals that change the time of the light depending on the amount of traffic flow on the road. Sensors and Surveillance Cameras: Fixed on roads, bridges and at intersections for traffic control, in case of an accident and to enhance on response time to the scenes. Smart Parking Systems: Through the use of IoT, it becomes easier for drivers to identify the available parking areas thus avoiding time wastage as well as fuel wastage.

Figure 2. Components of Smart Transportation

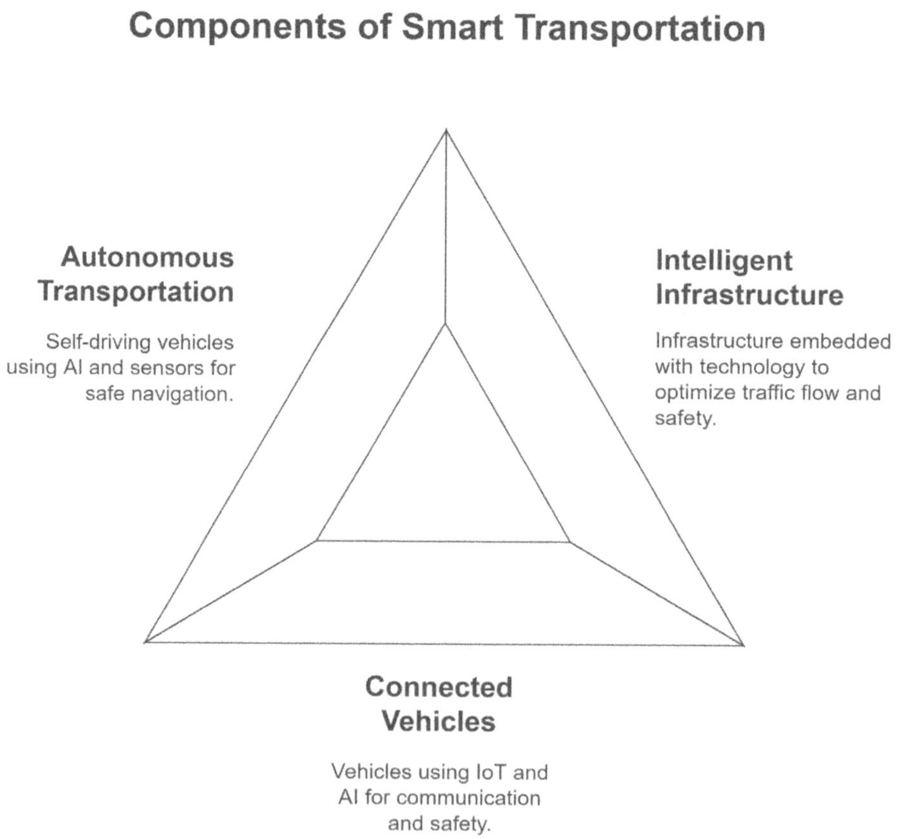

Connected Vehicles and Autonomous Transportation

CAVs are critical to smart transportation systems since they enhance safety and efficiency of transportation.

IOT and AI vehicles: These cars and trucks utilize IoT and AI and in most cases, they are integrated with other cars (Vehicle to Vehicle communication) to avoid Traffic mishaps as well as to provide accurate routes. Autonomous Vehicles (AVs): Self-driving cars are self-driven cars that use artificial intelligence, Light Detection and Ranging sensors, and mapping to drive on the roads, thus avoiding human-made accidents.

2.3 Sustainable Mobility Solutions

Smart transportation is another concept that is based on sustainability of transportation system through the reduction of emissions and improvement of energy efficiency and environmentally sustainable transport.

Integration of Electric Vehicles (EVs), Bike-Sharing, and Car-Sharing

Electric Vehicles (EVs): By halting the use of fuel powered cars and embracing EVs, there will be little or no emissions of green house gases and minimal use of fossil based fuels. Smart cities increase the usage of EVs by providing a large number of charging stations supported by renewable energy sources. Bike-Sharing Systems: These are public bicycle services that are meant to promote environmentally friendly transport by making bikes easily available to the commuters (Jiang, J. et al 2024). Car-Sharing Platforms: These include ride hailing and car sharing services like Uber, Lyft, that help in efficient use of vehicles thus cutting out the need for personal car ownership.

The key areas of attention should be placed on the reduction of the carbon footprint and the enhancement of the quality of the air.

Set-scheduling: The application of artificially intelligent set scheduling enhances the timely availability of public conveyances such as buses and trains without having to wastage much time and emit gases. Smart Route: With the utilization of efficient routing, the client's fuel consumption and the overall travel time is reduced. Green Urban Planning: Implementation of walkways, bike lanes and implementation of congestion charges is effective in making urban cities green. Thus, through incorporating these components and technologies, smart transportation systems offer improved mobility in urban facilities and also fosters sustainability as well as efficiency.

3. IoT APPLICATIONS IN URBAN INFRASTRUCTURE AND GOVERNANCE

The IoT has a critical role in remoulding the landscape of the urban environment and its management through the use of digital intelligence. The use of IoT solutions makes the mobility sector in cities better, resources more effective, and governance more efficient. Through incorporating IoT in transportation systems and city management, urban areas will be able to enhance sustainability and efficiency as well as improve the ability to respond to shocks.

3.1 Role of IoT in Smart Transportation

Smart transportation systems are one of the most popular applications of IoT technologies due to the fact that they help to minimize traffic density and increase traffic safety. They all involve a system that depends on the real-time identification and analysis of the information to enhance traffic flow in urban areas. IoT Sensors for Traffic Monitoring, Parking Management, and Infrastructure Maintenance

Roads, traffic lights, and vehicles themselves contain IoT sensors that gather and report current status about transportation. Some key applications include:

Traffic Management: IoT devices such as Cameras and Sensors at the crossroad helps to monitor the traffic flow of vehicles and pedestrians. This data is then analyzed by AI to adjust the time on the traffic lights with an aim of coming up with ways of minimizing traffic jams. Real-time parking space availability: with the help of the Internet of Things devices, parking sensors inform drivers about the availability of parking lots through the application, which saves time to find an empty place and fuel (Mahrez, Z. et al 2021). Infrastructure Maintenance: The Internet of Things helps to check the conditions of the roads, bridges, and tunnels to identify deviations and damages from their initial state. Maintenance and management of structures using artificial intelligence helps in avoiding accidents or collapse of the structures.

Figure 3. Role of IoT in Smart Transportation

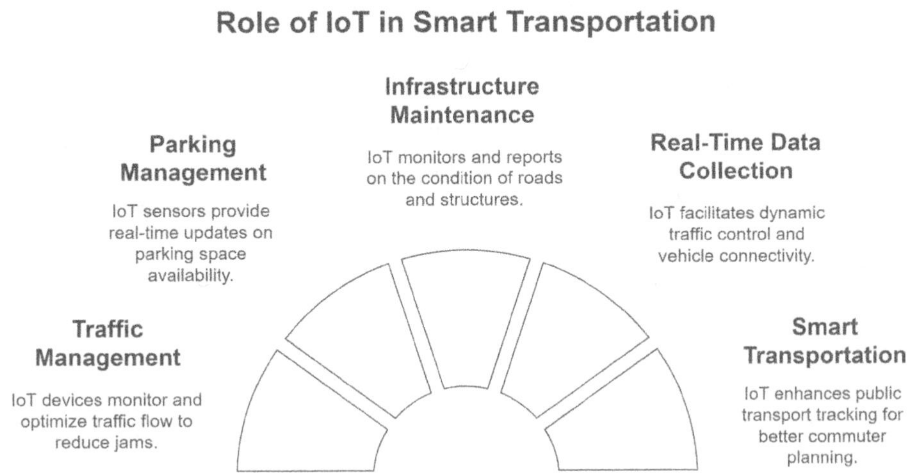

Real-Time Data Collection and Optimization of Traffic Flow

This is because IoT allows vehicles, traffic signal and city control centers to effectively communicate with each other thus enhancing traffic flow. Key benefits include:

Dynamic Traffic Control: It involves traffic lights that adapt in nature and function depending on the density of traffic flow in the network. Connected Vehicles: IoT based devices are fitted on to the vehicles and the cars installed with IoT devices can interact with each other, which is called Vehicle-to-Vehicle (V2V) and with the surrounding infrastructure or Vehicle-to-Infrastructure (V2I). Smart transportation: The IoT helps in tracking the buses, trains, and metros in real time so that the commuters can estimate the time of arrival of the vehicle and plan their route accordingly. When adopted in transportation, IoT contributes to increased safety, low emissions, and better and more comfortable commuting within the cities.

3.2 IoT in Urban Governance

IoT is a valuable resource for the effective management of urban centers since it assists the decision-makers and city administrators to enhance the efficiency of mobility and planning.

Use of IoT for Urban Mobility Policy Development and Enforcement

This is because governments employ them to gather information on various areas in order to come up with better policies as well as intelligent transportation systems. Some applications include:

Smart Traffic Management: Traffic surveillance cameras are smart cameras that are capable of detecting traffic violations such as speeding and running through a red light and the violations are enforced automatically. Dynamic Toll Collection: This involves the use of IoT based ETC systems that charges vehicles according to the time spend on the roads especially in congested roads. Congestion Pricing: IoT is used by cities to practice the congestion pricing which involves charging motorists for accessing certain areas during peak hours with an aim of promoting the use of public transport and reducing pollution.

Data-Driven Governance Models for Transportation Management

IoT facilitates the utilization of data in governance by the city authorities to enhance transportation systems and their sustainability.

Real-time Decision Making: With the help of IoT data, the smart city control centers can make real-time changes in the transportation services and for instance; change the bus routes during the rush hours. Predictive Analytics: With the help of predictive analytics IoT solutions being able to predict patterns of traffic flow so that the urban planning can plan better roads and better transport routes. Citizen Engagement: IoT applications also enable the residents to report traffic problems, road conditions and problems with public transport through their mobile gadgets. The inclusion of IoT in urban management will lead to better and improved transport system, thus improving the standards of living of the populace.

4. THE ROLE OF AI AND MACHINE LEARNING IN URBAN PLANNING

AI and ML are helping in the modernization of urban planning through improving the transport systems and increasing the mobility of the public. These technologies make it possible to process more data, build proactive models, and adopt decision-making aimed at enhancing traffic and transport. These technologies help process large volumes of data and develop forecast models and decision-making procedures for traffic and transport, as well as infrastructure improvement. (Ambhika et al 2024) This paper identifies how through the use of AI and ML, it is possible to build smart cities with effective transportation systems.

4.1 AI in Traffic Management

One of the major problems of traffic in the urban areas is congestion, which results in time wastage, fuel consumption and pollution. AI and ML collectively help in the traffic pattern modeling and prediction, and attempt towards minimizing the time spent on congesting and accidents. AI Algorithms for Optimizing Traffic Flow, Reducing Congestion, and Preventing Accidents

The smart traffic systems are based on the collected information about traffic conditions from sensors, cameras, and GPS devices. Some key applications include:

Smart Traffic Lights: This is an intelligent traffic signals that adapt to the traffic flow by using artificial intelligence to determine the right time for signal changes hence reducing traffic congestion and time spent waiting for the signal to turn green. Preventing Accidents: It calls for the use of Auto-Alert systems to monitor reckless adolescents, jay walking pedestrians and unfavourable road situations and inform the traffic control centers and vehicle drivers on cases of an accident. Incident Management: A self-driving car can identify an emergency or a breakdown and hence, respond to such incidences instantaneously which helps in the reduction of traffic congestion.

Machine Learning for Predictive Traffic Modeling and Route Planning

Large amounts of traffic data are used by machine learning algorithms to determine the traffic flow and plan routes. Key applications include:

Predictive traffic analysis: weather conditions, construction updates as well as the schedule of events to expect a traffic jam and suggest an alternative route (Jayasutha et al 2024). Navigation and Route Optimization: This feature incorporates; Navigation tools such Google Map or Waze that suggest driving options that are most likely to take less time and have few incidences of traffic jams. Dynamic Toll Pricing: Using AI traffic density based toll prices are charged which can help the drivers to opt other routes or public transport (Subramanian, R. S et al 2024).

Thus, artificial intelligence in traffic management brings benefits such as; Reduction of traffic congestions, enhanced safety on the roads and realization of green space for urban development.

4.2 AI in Public Transportation

It is also revolutionizing public transport in the same way, by improving on the efficiency, reliability and adaptability to the users' needs. Self-driven public transit systems also guarantee the effective use of funds through efficient course determination, time management and appropriate allocation of fleet.

AI Applications in Optimizing Bus, Train, and Metro Services Based on Demand Patterns

It uses commuter information, travel habits, and peak traffic hours to improve the functionality of the public transport. Some applications include:

Demand-based scheduling: This means that bus and train services are adjusted according to the demand that is expected to ensure optimal number of the public transport system. Dynamic Route Adjustment: Buses and metro system routes and stops are changed depending on traffic flow and passenger's demand. Passenger Control: Intelligent solutions for controlling the crowds in the stations of metro with the presence of the people during the rush hour in bus terminals (Anusha et al 2024).

Intelligent Scheduling and Fleet Management for Public Transport Systems

AI enhances the administration of vehicles and their schedules in public transport to increase efficiency. Key applications include:

Fleet Management: Artificial Intelligence tracks the condition of vehicles, fuel efficiency, and maintenance requirements of public motorized transport for better functionality and relevance. Fleet Maintenance: Predictive maintenance plans are made to identify mechanical issues that may arise with buses, trains, and metros before they occur hence avoiding major problems that may hinder the provision of services. Automobiles: Many companies are working on developing self-driving cars that can help in reducing the number of accidents, time and cost. If AI and machine learning are deployed in public transportation, commuters get better experience, services' quality standards increase, and urban shifting to green transport mode is promoted (Maithili, K et al 2024; Yamini, B et al 2024).

5. GIS AND DATA ANALYTICS FOR REAL-TIME URBAN MANAGEMENT

Real time data and Geographic Information Systems (GIS) are taking a new dimension in management and development of towns and cities through the enhancement of transport studies, planning of infrastructures and decision making. Such technologies assist the cities to improve mobility, address the congestion challenges and develop efficient transport systems.

5.1 GIS in Transportation Planning

GIS plays an important role in the process of urban transportation planning as it provides city planners and policymakers with the visual information about traffic and road networks or systems of public transportation. GIS for Mapping Transportation Networks, Analyzing Traffic Patterns, and Infrastructure Development.

GIS combines geographical information with the transport models to enhance the mobility of the city. Key applications include:

Transportation System Planning: GIS aids in drawing the location of roads, rail, and transit systems and thus enables the planning of effective transport systems. Traffic Pattern Analysis: GIS helps to look at the past and present traffic flow data, and then find out the areas that causes traffic congestion and take necessary measures to reduce traffic congestion (Al-Shariff et al 2019). Transportation: GIS is employed in the evaluation of road networks, the most appropriate locations for the construction of highways, as well as the distribution of transportation facilities fairly across cities. Public Transit Accessibility: GIS determines the effectiveness of transit networks in accessing certain regions to assist in the planning of new bus and metro routes. Transportation planning using GIS benefits cities by providing the best solutions regarding mobility and integration of transportation systems.

Figure 4. GIS and Data Analytics for Real-Time Urban Management

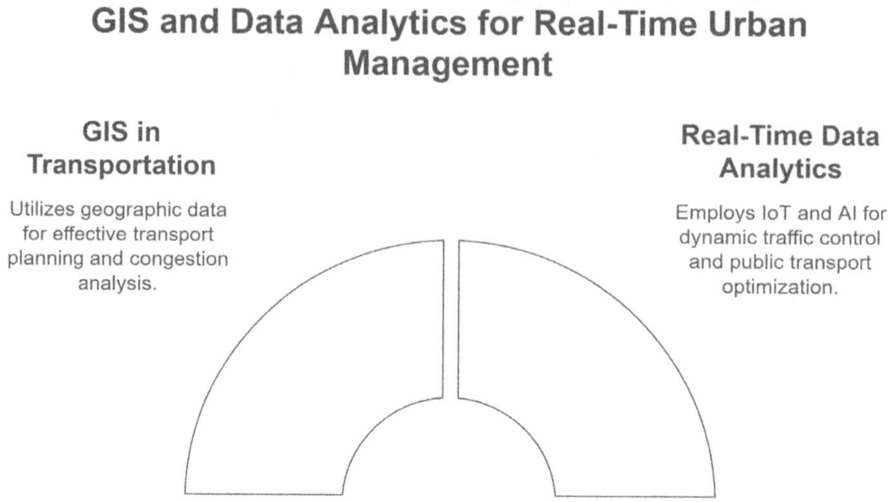

5.2 Real-Time Data Analytics in Smart Cities

Big data analytics can be particularly valuable for managing urban transport since it is aimed at analyzing big quantities of real-time data from various sources such as IoT devices, GPS, and video cameras (Sudha et al 2024).

The Role of Big Data Analytics in Managing Transportation in Real Time. Communities employ big data analytic to control and manage transport systems in an efficient and timely manner. Key applications include:

Real-time traffic control: Analytical tools based on AI help to manage traffic information to change the signals, suggest different routes and avoid traffic jams. Public Transport Optimization: This aspect is due to the ability to analyze the demand for public transport in order to schedule the buses and trains to match the demand at any one time. Finally, traffic incidents: these are detected by artificial intelligence data analysis systems, and incidents are passed on to the relevant personnel and agencies as early as possible. Predictive Maintenance: Road, bridge and vehicle sensors help in providing data for maintenance of infrastructures so as to avoid failure. Data analytics and GIS can be used in cities to make intelligent solutions for mobility that can be effective, sustainable, and citizen-friendly (Sudha et al 2024).

6. CLIMATE CHANGE RESILIENCE IN URBAN AREAS THROUGH TECHNOLOGY

Global climate change poses key difficulties to urban regions especially in as a method of transport. Such factors as increased temperatures, climatic changes and air pollution have made it mandatory for cities to come up with better solutions to transport clients. Technology is useful in enhancing climate change resilience in cities by lowering emissions of green-house gases and incorporating the climate change adaptation measures in transportation systems.

6.1 Smart Transportation and Climate Resilience

Smart transportation systems use information and telecommunication technologies for enhancing mobility that are environment friendly. These systems play the role of enhancing climate resilience since they support sustainable practices and have minimal effects on the environment.

The Role of Smart Transportation Systems in Reducing Greenhouse Gas Emissions

Road transport is one of the major sources of carbon emissions since many transport systems use fossil fuels. Smart transportation eases this effect in the following ways:

Intelligent Traffic Management: Reduction of time traffic lights take to turn green or red helps in cutting the fuel and emissions from idling vehicles. Connected and Autonomous Vehicles (CAVs): These are vehicles which are designed to be intelligent and connected to other systems in a way that optimizes fuel consumption and hence the carbon emissions (Ceder, A. 2021). Effective Public Transport Management: GPS data and fileet management software's help route planning to eliminate logical duplication of bus or train trips and to enhance overall reliability. Mobility Technology: The shift to electric powered cars and the fixing of charging stations reduced emissions than the ordinary internal combustion engine vehicles.

Sustainable Transportation Alternatives in the Face of Climate Change

Governments across the globe retain incorporating revolutionary technologies to promote ecological approaches and durability of their cities:

Bike-Sharing and Micro-Mobility: The use of the electric scooters and bike-sharing services in their day-to-day activities lessens the dependence on cars. Carpooling and Ride-Sharing: Uber and Lyft, for instance, promote sharing of a single ride hence reducing the number of cars on the road. Electrification of Public Transport: With an intention to decongest the environment, many cities are shifting from diesel buses to electric buses. Renewable Energy: Charging stations for electric and the public transport that are solar and wind-powered extend the use of the resource-based fuel source. So, by enhancing smart and sustainable transport solutions, the greenhouse emission effect and climatic change vulnerability in cities can be improved greatly.

6.2 Technology for Adaptation to Climate Risks

Thus, urban transportation systems should be built to be resistant to climate change, including storms, increased water levels, and varying temperatures.

Integration of Climate-Responsive Infrastructure in Transportation Systems

Climate adaptive transport infrastructure means that the transport systems are constructed to remain operational in case of climate conditions. Key adaptations include:

Flood Proofing: Cities are building flyovers, drainable roads, and pavements and designing drainage systems in order to avoid water logging and floods. Heat-Resistant Surfaces/Reflection: The roads and rail tracks are being made heat resistant to cater for the increasing temperatures and to minimize heat gain from the surfaces. Smart Disposal Of Hazardous Wastes: An artificial intelligence predicts and issues early warnings on how climate change influences the transport system in the event of hurricanes, heavy rainfall, and wildfires or the efficient method of hazardous wastes disposal. Sustainable Landscapes: Inclusion of green roofs, urban trees, and avenues where trees are planted along streets also assist in the prevention of heat islands in urban areas. As such, there are strategies that cities can employ to ensure that they develop climate-responsive transportation systems that also possess low carbon footprints.

7. BUILDING INFORMATION MODELING (BIM) AND ITS IMPACT ON SUSTAINABLE CONSTRUCTION

BIM is revolutionizing the construction of infrastructures in cities through the improvement of efficiency, sustainability, and resilience of transport. It can be also noted that with help of BIM one can develop a digital model of physical infrastructures for the engineers, architects, and city planners and thereby help in designing, constructing, and maintaining transportation networks. It is apparent that BIM is an effective tool that can make a positive contribution to sustainable urban mobility by incorporating data analysis into its processes.

7.1 Role of BIM in Sustainable Transportation Infrastructure

BIM improves the process of planning, designing and construction of the transportation infrastructure through the provision of modeling, simulation and collaboration. These capabilities enable cities to progress towards the construction of better and cleaner transport systems. Improved Planning and Design: By using BIM, planners are able to plan different layouts, evaluate the impacts of the environment on the roads, and come up with the best layouts that can be used in construction. This avoids wastage of resources, and thus reduces the impact it has on the environment. Energy Efficient Infrastructure: BIM enables architects to implement efficient lighting, green area and appropriate traffic management systems in transportation. Improved Collaboration: BIM allows for collaboration of stakeholders such as the government agency, engineers and environmental consultants from the design stage to ensure sustainability is considered. Waste Reduction and Material Efficiency: BIM helps in reducing wastage of materials and time by detailing out the material usage and construction time line. Environmental Assessment: BIM assists in modeling carbon emissions and energy consumption, thereby enabling the designers to put into consideration environmental impacts of the transportation infrastructures in their design decisions. The use of BIM in planning and construction leads to the creation of new, environment-friendly, and robust transportation systems that meet the sustainability agenda.

7.2 BIM for Maintenance and Lifecycle Management

In addition to its use in constructing transportation infrastructure, BIM is also highly useful in maintaining and sustaining these structures. Thus, with the help of real time access to data and application of predictive analysis, BIM helps to maintain the efficiency and sustainability of the systems of urban traffic throughout their life cycle.

Predictive Maintenance: Utilizing BIM and IoT tools such as sensors, the state of roads, bridges, or transit network is in a position to be assesses and indicate if it needs repairs before the normal deterioration level of the asset. Such a preventive measure enhances durability of infrastructure systems and also avoid costly repairs. Infrastructure Management: It also entails provision of information on the infrastructure through digital models of transport infrastructure to enable officials in a city to manage assets, plan for upgrades and schedule maintenance (Elassy, M. et al 2024). Sustainability Monitoring: BIM has the capacity of incorporating information concerning environmental quality, energy use and discharge to improve sustainability of cities on a constant basis. Climate Adaptation: BIM can assist cities to build transport structures that can effectively withstand the effects of climate change for instance flooding and extremely high temperatures. Cost Reduction: Maintenance costs are decreased, resource utilization is enhanced, and unexpected repairs are minimized through the help of BIM, which in turn, is helpful for the financial viability of the urban transport infrastructure. Incorporation of BIM in the planning of urban transport systems will ensure that efficient, sustainable and resilient transport systems are developed and implemented in the growing urban centers.

8. INTEGRATION OF RENEWABLE ENERGY SYSTEMS INTO SMART CITIES

Having explored the concerns that cities have in relation to energy demands and the environment given the increasing rates of urbanization, it is evident that cities are facing many challenges. Small details like these are crucial in designing smart city infrastructure for sustainable use of energy resources which include renewable energy sources in order to decrease the carbon footprints, increase energy security and overall sustainability. Renewable energy in the transportation sector plays a vital role in the shift of transportation systems to cleaner sources of energy by charging transport systems and electric vehicles.

8.1 Renewable Energy in Urban Transportation

Solar, wind, and bioenergy are some of the renewable energies that have the potential of enhancing sustainability in the transport system in urban areas. Clean energy can be used to replace the fossil fuel energy and hence decrease the emission of greenhouse gases and improvement of the quality of air.

Solar-Powered Public Transport: Most cities are adopting solar power by installing solar panels on bus shelters, railway station, and trams. Solar energy can be used in lighting up streets, traffic signals and even electric buses that have solar panels installed on them. Wind Energy for Urban Transport Systems: Wind power is being installed to provide electricity to transit authorities, railway stations, airports and transport centers. Vertical-axis wind turbines are commonly planted in strategic locations such as strategic places that experience high traffic in order to capture wind power. Hydrogen Fuel Cells: Some cities are using hydrogen fuel in busses and trains and the hydrogen is generated through renewable energy. These fuel-cell vehicles produce only water vapour, which makes them environmentally friendlier than the diesel type of transport. This paper aims to establish that through adoption of renewable energy, public transport systems can be made efficient, cheaper and eco-friendly.

8.2 Charging Infrastructure for Electric Vehicles

EVs are an essential element of sustainable transport in the cities and the incorporation of renewable energy in the charging of EVs further gives the system an added plus.

Solar Charging Stations: Many cities are installing solar charging stations and this means that EVs can be charged using solar energy. These stations help one to minimize the dependence on the grides and bring down the electricity bills. Wind and Hydropower Integration: Some cities incorporate wind electricity to supply energy to the EV charging stations to ensure the use of renewable energy. Hydropower plants also help to generate clean electricity for the EV networks for those countries that have adequate water resources. Vehicle to Grid Technology: Among such technological strategies, V2G useful in GLs is a bidirectional system that enables the EV to feed excess energy back to the grid to increase energy conservation and reduce the fluctuating load demand. As mentioned earlier, when combined with renewable systems, V2G is useful in managing power distribution in cities. Battery Storage Solutions: As the renewable energy sources such as solar and wind are unpredictable, battery storage systems allow cities to store excess energy in order to provide constant power supply for EV charging.

Figure 5. Integration of Renewable Energy Systems into Smart Cities

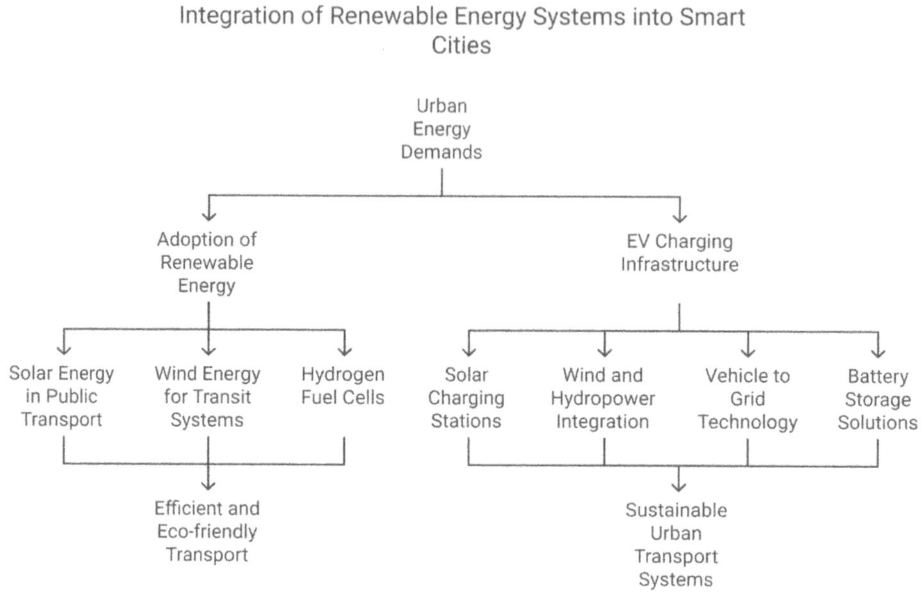

Future Outlook

This will help to reduce the dependency on fossil fuels since the expansion of renewable power for EV charging networks will be expanded. There is a need to involve governments as well as independent producers in the implementation of smart grids, advancing battery storage solutions, and offering favorable terms for using electricity from renewable sources for operating EVs. Depending on the kind of renewable energy adopted, the use of renewable energy in transport contributes to the improvement of the urban transport systems which are sustainable, resilient and clean.

9. CHALLENGES AND OPPORTUNITIES IN IMPLEMENTING SMART TRANSPORTATION IN DEVELOPING COUNTRIES

This holds the case for the cities of developing countries as they continue to expand rapidly through the process of urbanization. Smart transportation which employs technologies such as IoT, Artificial Intelligence, and big data analysis in the transportation system's operations provides a good solution. As much as these systems can be introduced, there are some challenges that come with implementing these systems in developing economies such as infrastructure, financial and governance challenges. At the same time, there are great opportunities for innovation, for the development of the economy, and for cooperation with other countries.

9.1 Challenges

Infrastructure Limitations, Funding Constraints, and Policy Challenges

Lack of adequate transport infrastructure: It is known that many developing countries do not have the required roadways, traffic controls, availability of a good sharing service or any public transportation systems to support smart transport. Lack of well-maintained roads and crowded city structures are some of the factors that make it difficult to adopt intelligent mobility systems. Limited Funding: In technology-based initiatives such as smart transportation there may be limited funds that may be available for the project which may be a major let down. Most emerging markets face challenges of low public resources and low private sector investment in smart mobility projects. Regulatory and Policy Challenges: As of now, there are no specific rules and regulation for the implementation of smart mobility. For instance, some jurisdictions have not formulated standards for ride-sharing, use of self-driving cars, or systems and structures for managing and directing traffic through big data. The lack of general urban mobility policies adds challenges to the need for improved use of smart transport.

Lack of Technical Expertise and Governance Issues

Skills Shortage: Majority of the developing countries does not have adequate professionals in areas such as artificial intelligence, data analysis and intelligent transport system. The lack of qualified employees hinders the development and support of smart transport systems. •Inadequate and Ineffective Institutions: This can be manifested in the form of corruption, bureaucracy that hinders the process and lack of synergy between organizations within the government. Lack of proper planning and fragmented decisions do not allow the implementation of large-scale smart transport solutions. Data Accessibility and Management: There is limited data accessibility and management in most cities in the developing countries. This is especially so because designing and implementing effective solutions for traffic and mobility requires credible and reliable traffic data. Nevertheless, smart transportation can be seen as a great chance for the development nations to improve mobility, decrease traffic density, and contribute to the economic development of cities.

9.2 Opportunities

Growth Potential in Emerging Economies

Urbanization And Increased Demand: This is because as urbanization progresses, people require efficient means of transport to get around. It is equally important to note that smart transportation can be a cheaper option for transport technologies as compared to the conventional systems with less traffic congestion and better public transport. Economic Development: Unlike other types of infrastructures, smart transportation can also open employments, and promote local and foreign investments. Such sectors include electric cars production and sales, intelligent traffic systems, and data processing and analysis. Sustainable Mobility Solutions: The developing countries can have the advantage of designing green transport systems from the ground up. Such measures as an electrification of public transportation, or an introduction of bike-sharing and integration of the transportation hubs will put cities on a track to avoid continuing with the old and carbon-emitting models.

Technological Leapfrogging and the Role of International Partnerships

Skipping the Traditional Modes of Transport: Most of the developing nations can go straight to the advanced systems of transport. For instance, some cities are exempting the use of paper based tickets and are using information technology tools to implement cashless tickets systems for some transit systems for the population. International Cooperation: The global organizations, governments, and private companies are participating in smart mobility projects in developing countries. Joint ventures with international companies are an opportunity to obtain additional resources in the form of capital, knowledge, and the best practices. Affordable Transport Technologies: Recent developments in Artificial Intelligence, Internet of Things, as well as mobile devices are making smart transport. Due to the availability of several mobile apps, cloud computing facilities, as well as low-cost sensors, the implementing of smart traffic management in the developing countries is possible at comparatively low costs. For the full realization of smart transportation in developing countries, there is need to make policy reforms, capacity building and enhance public-private partnerships. These nations can therefore tackle some of these challenges and harness opportunities to foster development of intelligent, sustainable and efficient urban transport systems that would accommodate the increasing population.

10. FUTURE DIRECTIONS IN SMART TRANSPORTATION AND URBAN MOBILITY

Smart transport, as a subset of smart urbanism, is a progressive concept that has been developing over the years due to technological enhancement and adopting policies. New mobility demand will also be defined by new technologies with already outlined solutions such as self-driving cars, hyperloop, ITS based on advanced AI, and smart contracts based on blockchain. Further, proper governance measures will have to be put in place to ensure that these developments are properly harnessed for the benefit of the growing urban populace.

10.1 Future Trends

Autonomous Vehicles, Hyperloop, and Other Innovations on the Horizon

Self-Driving Vehicles: Self-driving cars and buses are the future of urban transport since they will help in minimizing traffic congestion, incidences of accidents, and the use of fuel. Self-driving AVs can therefore be programmed to interact with other intelligent road systems and with other similar vehicles in order to improve road safety and traffic management. Currently, the US, China, and Germany are among the countries that are carrying out large-scale testing of AVs. Hyperloop Systems: Hyperloop technology is one of the revolutionary technologies that promises to change the face of long distance traveling by using tubes that has virtually no air. Virgin Hyperloop and SpaceX and other such companies are in the process of testing and creating models and prototypes that may cut the travel time greatly and yet not compromise on energy consumption. Aerial Urban Mobility: Cities of the future will be served by electric vertical take-off and landing (eVTOL) aircraft also known as air taxis which will help to navigate through the crowded cities without causing traffic jam. Several companies such as Uber Air and Joby Aviation are already in the process of developing the UAM solutions. Smart Public Transportation: The smart public transportation system is more easily implemented to ensure that cities adopt AI that can predict the right paths to avoid traffic and increase the efficiency of an intelligent public transit system for the passengers. Automated fleet management of buses and trains helps in bringing efficiency in their schedules and thus, lower energy consumption and operating costs.

Integration of AI, IoT, and Blockchain for Advanced Smart Transportation Systems

Artificial Intelligence (AI): Traffic control systems entail the use of AI to examine data gathered from the field and determine the best traffic pattern control in order to avoid traffic build-up and occurrence of accidents. It is also possible to enhance factors in ride-sharing algorithms by using machine learning, thus, making urban transport efficient (Ponmalar, A et al 2024). Internet of Things (IoT): By installing sensors in the roads, vehicles, and traffic lights the details of the road condition, parking space availability, and traffic intensity can be easily obtained. This contributes to the improvement of traffic flow in the urban areas and reduction of emission and accidents. Business Models: Mobility includes secure and convenient ways of payment for fares, shared or rented products or services and record-keeping of ownership of vehicles amongst others. It can also enable vehicle-to-vehicle communication which is likely to decrease the vulnerability of hacking in the connected transport systems. 5G: 5G connectivity will help advance smart transportation through the use of the high-speed data connection for the operation of the automobiles, and for the development of smart city environment.

10.2 The Role of Policy and Governance

Policy Integration for New Technologies: The government needs to set policies that will enhance the use of self-driving cars, hyperloop transportation and artificial intelligence in traffic control. Writing in The Economic Times of India, the authors note that for smart urban mobility, greater investment in concepts such as smart roads, charging facilities of electric vehicles, and traffic management systems are necessary in the public sector. Sustainability policies are the strategic measures geared towards green transportation such as rebate of taxes for electric cars, investment on transit energized by renewable resources, and the use of congestion charges on cars with high rates of emission.

Collaboration Between Governments, Private Sectors, and Citizens

Public-Private Partnerships (PPPs): It is common for the government to partner with technology companies in order to enhance the development of smart transport systems. For example, cities cooperating with the companies of ride sharing can enhance last-mile access. Citizen Engagement: The measures that are to be taken under smart transportation must incorporate the citizens in the process. This reason is that digital platforms that allow real-time feedback and citizens' engagement in planning offer an opportunity for trust and acceptance of new technologies. International Cooperation: Collaboration with developed countries to import technology and source of monetary aid would be of great benefit to developing countries to put in place intelligent transportation systems. In the emerging economies, the World Bank, UN-Habitat, and other organizations promote sustainable urban mobility. AI, IoT, blockchain and autonomous systems are the topics for the future of the urban mobility. However, to attain smart transportation, there is need to have anticipatory policies, strategic investment and partnership. Thus, the concept of innovation can help cities to develop safe and efficient transport systems for the future, which will be environmentally friendly as well.

11. CONCLUSION

Intelligent transportation is one of the key aspects of green and efficient transportation systems for addressing the problems of fast-growing urbanization, environmental issues, and traffic jams. Smart transportation systems utilize AI, IoT, GIS and blockchain, and provide effective, safe, as well as environmentally friendly services. These systems enhance traffic control, minimize the emission of green gases and enhance the public transport systems thus making the cities more habitable and environmentally sustainable. These new emerging technologies in the transport systems include auto-mobile transport, the hyperloop transport, and electrical transport systems. Organized road traffic is a key purpose of drive control systems, IoT-enhanced traffic signals, and connected automobiles. In addition, the use of data analysis and AI-based predictive analysis helps in improving the transportation planning and avoid traffic congestion. Nevertheless, the integration of smart mobility solutions has some level of difficulty, especially in the developing countries. Some of the challenges include; infrastructure issues, financial issues, and regulatory issues that have to be overcome to make it easily available. PPP, partnerships with other countries, and efficient governance help to implement smart mobility projects. However, there are a number of issues that need further development in the field of smart transportation. There is need for more research on cost effective and scalable smart mobility systems in the developing countries due to infrastructural and financial constraints. The studies on the feasibility of AI and IoT solutions can enable the use of these technologies in the developing world. However, there is a need to consider the use of renewable energy in public transport and EV charging facilities for sustainability. Innovation is also needed in other areas such as, safety for self-driving cars or automobile, the viability of the hyperloop, and blockchain logistics for transportation. There is a need for future studies to embrace smart mobility for all citizens across the economic brackets to ensure that the marginalized citizens are not locked out. It is seen here that the application of innovation as well as cooperation gives the cities a strategic plan for developing long-term intelligent and sustainable transport systems.

REFERENCES

Al-Shariff, S. M., Alam, M. S., Ahmad, Z., & Ahmad, F. (2019, March). Smart transportation system: Mobility solution for smart cities. In *2nd Smart Cities Symposium (SCS 2019)* (p. 59). Stevenage UK: IET.

Ambhika, C., Gayathri, S., Anish, T. P., & Sheena, B. G. (2024, August). Enhancing Predictive Modeling in High Dimensional Data Using Hybrid Feature Selection. In 2024 5th International Conference on Electronics and Sustainable Communication Systems (ICESC) (pp. 873-879). IEEE.

Anusha, S., Ezhilvandan, M., Gayathri, S., Sivaraman, V., & Anish, T. P. (2024). Emerging trends in edge AI for Industry 4.0 and 5.0: Technologies, applications, and challenges. AI Innovations in Service and Tourism Marketing, 211-228.

Ceder, A. (2021). Urban mobility and public transport: Future perspectives and review. *International Journal of Urban Sciences*, *25*(4), 455–479.

Elassy, M., Al-Hattab, M., Takruri, M., & Badawi, S. (2024). Intelligent transportation systems for sustainable smart cities. Transportation Engineering, 100252.

Jayasutha, D., Prabhu, R. V., Sassirekha, S. M., Maithili, K., Girija, P., & Subramanian, R. S. (2024). Exploring the Intersection of Sustainable Energy, AI, and Ethical Considerations. In AI Applications for Clean Energy and Sustainability (pp. 139-160). IGI Global.

Jiang, J., Li, Y., Li, Y., Li, C., Yu, L., & Li, L. (2024). Smart transportation systems using learning method for urban mobility and management in modern cities. *Sustainable Cities and Society*, *108*, 105428.

Mahrez, Z., Sabir, E., Badidi, E., Saad, W., & Sadik, M. (2021). Smart urban mobility: When mobility systems meet smart data. *IEEE Transactions on Intelligent Transportation Systems*, *23*(7), 6222–6239.

Maithili, K., Ponmalar, A., Yamini, B., Karthikeyan, M., Anish, T. P., Maheswari, B., & Subramanian, R. S. (2024). Advances in AI and Machine Learning for Healthcare Informatics. In *Machine Learning and Generative AI in Smart Healthcare* (pp. 1–22). IGI Global.

Ponmalar, A., Vijayakumar, K., Lakshmipriya, C., Karthikeyan, M., Gracelin Sheena, B., Beslin Pajila, P. J., & Siva Subramanian, R. (2024). Meta-Heuristics and Machine Learning Applications in Complex Systems. In Metaheuristic and Machine Learning Optimization Strategies for Complex Systems (pp. 257-275). IGI Global.

Sreelakshmi, S., Babu, A. A., Lakshmipriya, C., Gracious, L. A., Nalini, M., & Subramanian, R. S. (2024, October). Enhancing Intrusion Detection Systems with Machine Learning. In *2024 2nd International Conference on Self Sustainable Artificial Intelligence Systems (ICSSAS)* (pp. 557-564). IEEE.

Subramanian, R. S., Yamini, B., Sudha, K., & Sivakumar, S. (2024). Ensemble-based deep learning techniques for customer churn prediction model. *Kybernetes*.

Sudha, K., Balakrishnan, C., Anish, T. P., Nithya, T., Sheena, B. G., Maheswari, B., & Subramanian, R. S. (2024). Revolutionizing Trust Manufacturing Integrating Real-Time Data and AI Innovations for Enhanced Efficiency. In Industry Applications of Thrust Manufacturing: Convergence with Real-Time Data and AI (pp. 74-97). IGI Global.

Sudha, K., Balakrishnan, C., Anish, T. P., Nithya, T., Yamini, B., Subramanian, R. S., & Nalini, M. (2024). Data Insight Unveiled: Navigating Critical Approaches and Challenges in Diverse Domains Through Advanced Data Analysis. Critical Approaches to Data Engineering Systems and Analysis, 90-114.

Yamini, B., Ramana, K. V., Nalini, M., Devi, D. C., Maheswari, B., & Siva, S. R. (2024). Customer churn prediction model in enterprises using machine learning. *International Journal of Advanced Technology and Engineering Exploration, 11*(110), 94.

Chapter 10
AI-Driven Curriculum Transformation and Faculty Development in Developing Universities

Wael Hadi
https://orcid.org/0000-0002-7575-9287
Department of Information Security, University of Petra, Amman, Jordan

Mohammad Nazmi AlShaikh-Hasan
https://orcid.org/0000-0001-9496-457X
Brunel University of London, UK

ABSTRACT

Higher education institutions in developing regions face constraints related to curriculum design and faculty readiness. Prior research identified gaps in aligning course content with evolving technological demands, which triggered the need for a reimagined learning framework. This chapter examines how purposeful integration of machine learning tools and data-driven methodologies can enhance teaching processes while addressing learner-centered outcomes. Findings from prior initiatives showed that faculty participation in continuous professional development contributed to sustainable program improvements. Results indicated that adaptive platforms boosted student engagement and performance. This chapter underscores the importance of context-based innovations that respond to local constraints. The proposed strategies expand existing knowledge on curriculum transformation, highlighting models for replicable practices that advance institutional objectives.

DOI: 10.4018/979-8-3373-1375-7.ch010

1. INTRODUCTION

Universities operating in regions with economic and infrastructural challenges often struggle to align course offerings with rapid changes in technology and local development priorities (Zawacki-Richter, Marín, Bond, & Gouverneur, 2019). Student populations in these contexts can grow quickly, placing additional pressure on instructors, classroom capacities, and overall institutional infrastructures. Traditional teaching strategies may fall short in equipping learners with advanced problem-solving abilities and practical knowledge for evolving labor markets (Crompton & Burke, 2023). Scholars note that graduates in these areas sometimes lack exposure to modern analytical tools and real-time data sources, making them less competitive in technology-oriented fields (Dwivedi, Hughes, Tang, Wang, Mazumder, & Akher, 2023).

AI-based methods can assist in narrowing these gaps. Emerging investigations point to machine learning and data analytics as tools for revising academic content and enhancing faculty effectiveness (Bond, Khosravi, de Laat, Bergdahl, Negrea, Oxley, Pham, & Chong, 2023). By incorporating adaptive platforms and automated feedback loops, universities can respond to diverse learner profiles and large class sizes. These methods may also address high dropout rates, limited faculty numbers, and outdated syllabi that do not match industry or community expectations (Mhlanga, 2023). However, the realization of these methods depends on leadership, policy backing, infrastructure readiness, and the willingness of instructors to explore advanced teaching roles.

This chapter attempts to map how AI-driven curriculum renewal and systematic faculty development can encourage more relevant, localized education. Initial sections consider how resource limitations, policy frameworks, and technology shortfalls shape higher education in developing economies (Mustafa, Tlili, Lampropoulos, Huang, Jandrić, Zhao, … & Saqr, 2024). The text then examines pedagogical theories supporting AI-based personalization and automation. It explores how these approaches might suit regions where high student enrollment coexists with varying academic backgrounds. Subsequent parts delve into specific interventions that redesign curricular objectives, adopt adaptive assessments, and localize projects involving urban management. The text then moves on to faculty growth models, case examples, conceptual frameworks for readiness, and the challenges and ethical issues that arise when AI becomes part of education systems in financially constrained contexts (Salas-Pilco & Yang, 2022).

Throughout the chapter, the discussion highlights best practices for responsibly merging modern technological solutions with immediate socio-economic requirements (Bahroun, Anane, Ahmed, & Zacca, 2023). These considerations include equity in technology access, data privacy, algorithmic neutrality, and cultural sensitivity (Popenici & Kerr, 2017). Concluding sections present strategies for gradual, evidence-based adoption, along with directions for extended research on long-term outcomes. By aligning AI and data-oriented teaching with faculty empowerment and real-world scenarios, universities in developing contexts can adapt more efficiently to the demands of urban growth and governance challenges.

1.1. Chapter Objectives and Focus

The central aim of this chapter is to provide a detailed account of how AI-centered interventions can transform course structures and faculty practices in places where standard educational paradigms face practical barriers (Zawacki-Richter et al., 2019). Particular emphasis is placed on the interplay of institutional leadership, policy alignment, infrastructural constraints, and pedagogical shifts. Another goal is to outline how novel methods in curriculum design and assessment can meet local urban demands. By focusing on adaptive learning, data analytics, and integrative faculty development, the chapter shows ways that institutions can address pressing issues such as overcrowded cities, poor infrastructure, and governance limitations. The text also addresses the persistent challenge of sustaining new approaches once initial pilot enthusiasm subsides. Many technology-based programs start well but fail to endure when funding wanes or faculty revert to older habits (Dwivedi et al., 2023). The discussion thus stresses structured support frameworks, continuous professional development, multi-level governance, and ongoing monitoring. Ultimately, the purpose is to illustrate a holistic plan for AI-based reforms that mesh with the cultural, financial, and policy realities of developing regions, enabling universities to produce graduates who can make meaningful contributions to local progress.

2. CONTEXTUAL OVERVIEW OF HIGHER EDUCATION IN DEVELOPING REGIONS

Higher education in developing contexts often proceeds amid uncertain economic conditions, limited government support, and infrastructure that may be inadequate for large-scale digital adoption. Enrollment surges in many countries as younger generations seek degrees, overburdening physical and human resources (Khoalenyane & Ajani, 2024). These strains exacerbate institutional weaknesses in delivering consistent academic quality. Meanwhile, local industries and municipalities face accelerating demands for specialized skills, particularly in urban development and technology management (Strielkowski, et al., 2024).

2.1. Economic and Demographic Pressures

Regional economies in parts of Africa, Asia, and Latin America vary widely, though they share pressures tied to workforce growth and urbanization (Eryenyu, Owomugisha, Biira, & Waako, 2024). University expansions aim to accommodate more students, but limited budgets and outdated facilities create mismatches between capacity and need. Administrators and faculty must juggle large class sizes, diverse student preparation levels, and minimal resources for laboratory sessions or computational infrastructure. Program quality can suffer when enrollments spike without parallel increases in funding (Al-Zahrani & Alasmari, 2024). Urban migration in many regions intensifies the demand for city planners, environmental managers, and professionals versed in data analytics. The public sector and private industries search for graduates who can handle traffic congestion, housing deficits, resource allocation, and governance processes (Zawacki-Richter et al., 2019). Traditional curricula may not cover advanced computational methods relevant to local challenges, thereby creating knowledge gaps among graduates. Students often have theoretical grounding but minimal hands-on training in analytics or AI-based problem-solving (Crompton & Burke, 2023). Institutions that manage to weave AI into practical contexts can produce more adaptable alumni, better positioned for current or emerging job markets.

2.2. Policy Initiatives and Institutional Leadership

Governmental bodies and accreditation organizations can shape how universities modernize their course structures (Salas-Pilco & Yang, 2022). Some governments issue mandates or guidelines encouraging technology adoption, yet practical support may be scarce. Institutions then scramble to fulfill requirements without stable funding or adequate planning. Where state policy frameworks do exist, they often focus on broad goals rather than tailored implementation strategies (UNESCO, 2023). University leaders in such contexts must formulate internal policies, identify funding avenues, and guide academic units through the transition to more data-oriented teaching. Internal leadership further influences how quickly new pedagogies emerge (Mustafa et al., 2024). Deans, department heads, and committees may champion or block AI-based initiatives, depending on their priorities, risk tolerance, or familiarity with emerging technologies. Incentives for technology-driven reform, such as promotions or grant allocations, can mobilize faculty support. However, the presence of champions alone may not suffice if institutional culture resists experimentation or if reward structures do not align with technology-based teaching excellence (Bond et al., 2023). Successful transformations often arise where leadership strategically pairs policy incentives with resource investments, clear targets, and accountability mechanisms.

2.3. Digital Infrastructure and Connectivity Limitations

Stable internet and modern hardware are prerequisites for many AI tools (Falebita & Kok, 2024). However, power outages, unreliable networks, and old computer labs impede large-scale digital adoption in several developing universities (van der Vlies & Hoeszová, 2022). Consequently, learning management systems and adaptive software may break down or become unusable for long stretches. Students from rural areas may have to rely on sporadic mobile data, limiting real-time interaction with course platforms. Meanwhile, overworked or undertrained IT staff struggle to maintain complex networks or fix problems promptly (Wardat, 2023). Some universities adopt incremental approaches by launching pilot programs in selected departments. This method helps administrators see how AI-based methods operate under local constraints (Mhlanga, 2023). Institutions can adapt hardware configurations or adopt offline-friendly courseware, mitigating connectivity gaps. Although pilot successes do not guarantee scalability, they generate momentum and lessons for more extensive implementations, provided the institution invests in the required upgrades. External partnerships may also supply technology donations, training, or specialized expertise. That approach can accelerate improvements, though it often depends on stable leadership and well-structured project management.

2.4. Cultural and Linguistic Diversity

Many campuses in developing contexts draw students from multiple language backgrounds and cultural settings. Materials predominantly available in major world languages may pose an obstacle for those unfamiliar with certain technical or academic terms (Popenici & Kerr, 2017). AI-based platforms, if not adapted, risk reinforcing linguistic inequities. Automated grading or recommendation systems trained on foreign corpora may misinterpret local dialects or writing styles. Students may then receive poor feedback or low marks unrelated to their actual understanding (UNESCO, 2023).

Universities addressing these gaps often pursue localized content creation, recruiting bilingual or multilingual educators. They might also adapt system interfaces to reflect local languages, though this process can be resource-intensive (Zawacki-Richter et al., 2019). Collaborative networks with language experts or software developers can reduce costs and speed up adaptation. In some cases, students themselves can contribute to user-interface translation or development of localized data sets, enhancing the system's cultural fit.

2.5. Summary of Contextual Constraints

Constraints on capital, technology, and faculty expertise shape the conditions under which universities operate. At the same time, they must satisfy diverse stakeholder needs, including government agencies, industries, parents, and students. AI-based curriculum reforms hold promise but require solutions that address infrastructure gaps, resource inequities, and language barriers (Bond et al., 2023). Leadership plays a central role in bridging these issues through coherent strategies, forging alliances, and championing incremental adoption. A thorough understanding of these contextual realities lays the groundwork for analyzing how AI might reshape curriculum design and faculty roles in these settings.

3. THEORETICAL FOUNDATIONS OF AI IN HIGHER EDUCATION

Discussions about AI in education often revolve around theories of learning that underpin how adaptive software, data analytics, and automated evaluation impact teaching practices. In developing regions, these theories must be filtered through practical realities such as large enrollment numbers, mixed literacy or digital fluency, and variable infrastructure (Crompton & Burke, 2023). The presence of AI does not negate fundamental pedagogical principles, but it can enable finer-grained personalization and continuous feedback, which traditional methods may not manage at scale.

3.1. Constructivist and Social Constructivist Perspectives

Constructivism emphasizes active participation in learning. Learners develop their own understanding through exploration and reflection. AI-powered adaptive systems can support constructivism by letting students progress at a pace aligned with individual mastery (Wang, DeMarree, Petchenik, & Hu, 2023). System analytics detect weak points, providing extra practice or remedial content, allowing students to build conceptual depth. In resource-limited contexts, such granular attention may be infeasible for a single instructor handling large classes, making AI a potential equalizer.

Social constructivism broadens this view to highlight collaboration and peer interaction. AI-based platforms that permit group tasks, forum discussions, or integrated chat functions encourage knowledge sharing among diverse learners (Bond et al., 2023). Analytics can reveal how learning communities form, identifying those who may be isolated. Instructors can then intervene to foster a more inclusive learning environment (Mhlanga, 2023). While robust networks are needed for synchronous collaboration, hybrid models with intermittent connectivity can still embed social elements, albeit asynchronously.

3.2. Behaviorist Influences

Behaviorist principles focus on stimulus-response feedback. In AI-infused education, automated systems provide consistent and immediate feedback on quizzes, assignments, or discussion contributions (Salas-Pilco & Yang, 2022). Positive reinforcements like badges or progress indicators encourage continual engagement. This method can be beneficial in large classes where personal interaction with each learner is limited. Adaptive programs may reintroduce concepts students have not mastered, using repetitious drilling to reinforce correct patterns (Zawacki-Richter et al., 2019).

While behaviorist approaches can streamline certain tasks, overemphasis on rote practices might narrow creative thinking. Blending behaviorist feedback loops with constructivist projects yields a balanced approach, where quick reinforcement addresses procedural skills, and exploratory assignments develop higher-order thinking. In a resource-scarce setting, this synergy can optimize the instructor's role, reserving human expertise for more complex tasks that a system cannot replicate (Dwivedi et al., 2023).

3.3. Data-Driven and Analytics-Focused Education

Data analytics extend beyond test scores and grade averages. They examine engagement trends, discussion participation, and usage logs to build a panoramic view of student progress (Mhlanga, 2023). Educators receive real-time or near-real-time data that highlight common bottlenecks, skill levels, and emergent topic interests. In large cohorts, advanced analytics can help instructors pinpoint segments requiring extra support. This methodology ensures timely intervention, an improvement over conventional end-of-semester evaluations (Bond et al., 2023).

Institutions in developing regions can use aggregated data to inform curriculum revisions. If analytics reveal consistent difficulty with advanced math topics in an engineering program, administrators and faculty can investigate whether prerequisites are missing or if teaching materials need reorganization (Mustafa et al., 2024). Resource allocation decisions, such as distributing more tutorial sessions or upgrading lab facilities, can become more targeted. Over time, analytics-based feedback loops build institutional knowledge about what works in specific contexts, gradually refining policies and teaching practices.

3.4. Ethical and Equitable AI Adoption

Implementation of AI in classrooms prompts reflection on data privacy and fairness. If systems rely on training sets from technologically advanced contexts, these algorithms might overlook local dialects, conditions, or learning styles (Popenici & Kerr, 2017). Some AI-driven tutoring systems might fail to accommodate cultural norms or indigenous knowledge, diminishing their effectiveness and risking alienation of learners. Institutions must guard against bias by customizing or retraining models on relevant local data.

Equity stands as another vital principle. Students in remote regions may have limited device access or face unstable connectivity, constraining their ability to engage with AI-driven tasks (Zawacki-Richter et al., 2019). Institutions that champion AI integration without bridging the digital divide risk amplifying existing disparities (UNESCO, 2023). Instructors and policymakers should design parallel offline resources, alternative instructional methods, or resource-sharing initiatives to mitigate this phenomenon. Realistic planning for energy supply, device availability, and teacher support is essential to avoid unintentional exclusion of certain learner groups.

3.5. Synthesis of Theoretical Insights

AI-oriented pedagogy in developing contexts calls for selective blending of constructivism, behaviorism, social collaboration, and data analytics. Each theoretical thread contributes insight into how learners interact with course content and how instructors can guide that process. Institutions navigating resource constraints can leverage AI to provide personalized reinforcement or group-based inquiry that would otherwise be unfeasible (Crompton & Burke, 2023). Ethical considerations must remain at the forefront, ensuring that the benefits of AI do not bypass marginalized communities or infringe on data protection rights (Bahroun et al., 2023). These theories collectively frame how AI can inform a curriculum model that pairs global technological advancements with local contextual realities.

4. AI-DRIVEN CURRICULUM REDESIGN

Curriculum revision underpins many initiatives to align graduates' skills with local labor market needs and social objectives. AI offers possibilities for rethinking course sequences, learning outcomes, and classroom experiences (Mustafa et al., 2024). However, implementing AI in ways that are sustainable and context-sensitive involves extensive planning. Institutions must clarify why they need AI, how it intersects with existing educational practices, and what metrics will measure effectiveness (Crompton & Burke, 2023).

4.1. Identifying Gaps and Mapping Curriculum Changes

Effective curriculum redesign begins with a thorough evaluation of existing courses and outcomes, often through stakeholder consultations with employers, government officials, and community representatives. That process clarifies whether a program addresses pressing problems like traffic congestion, waste management, or environmental decay. Faculties can identify which modules need more emphasis on data analytics, machine learning principles, or other AI subfields (Pisica, Edu, Zaharia, & Zaharia, 2023).

Once these gaps surface, curriculum committees propose modifications at multiple levels. Some universities introduce entire courses dedicated to AI. Others embed AI topics in existing subjects like economics, sociology, or environmental studies. Collaboration among departments ensures synergy. For instance, engineering students learning machine learning can work with public policy students to assess how algorithms might inform housing allocation or municipal budgeting. This integrated mapping requires open communication and a willingness to revise entrenched course structures.

Figure 1 represents the AI-driven curriculum revision cycle, illustrating the iterative process of identifying skill gaps, consulting stakeholders, designing AI-enhanced courses, and refining content based on feedback.

Figure 1. AI-Enhanced Curriculum Revision Process

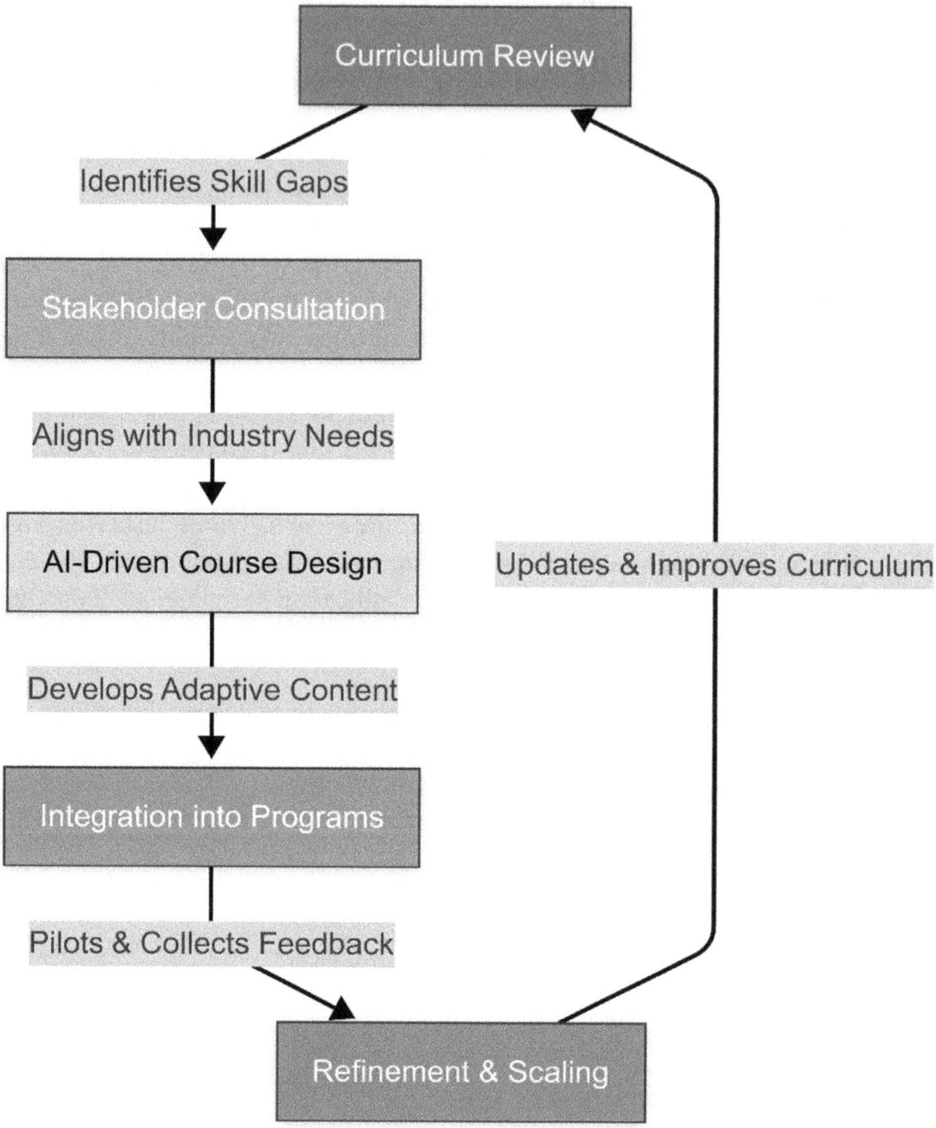

4.2. Adaptive Learning Tools for Large Classes

Software that adjusts content difficulty and pacing in real time can relieve the burden of massive classes and varied learner preparedness. Figure 2 outlines an example workflow for adaptive learning.

Figure 2. Adaptive Learning Workflow (Mermaid Diagram)

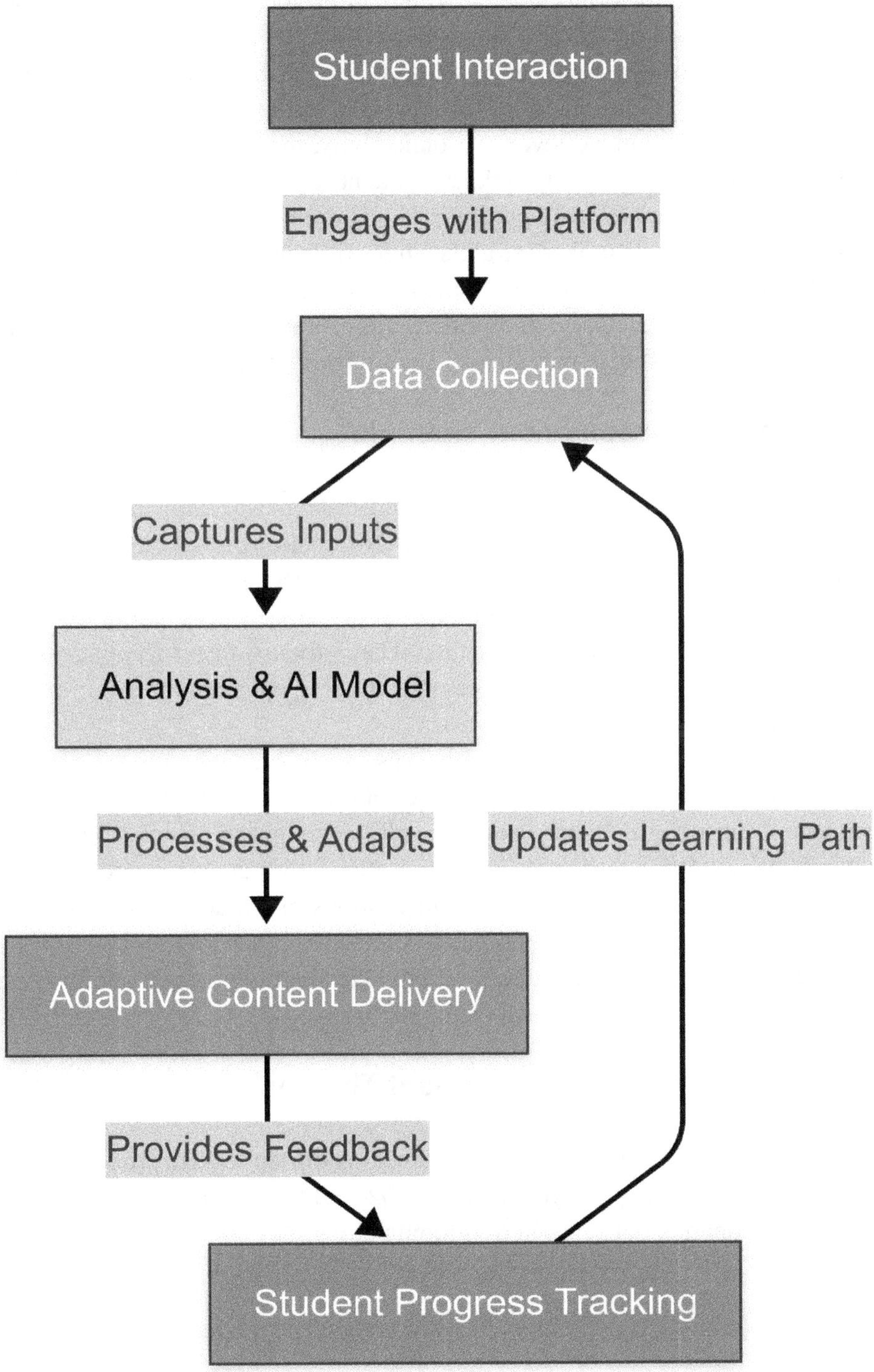

Students engage with digital activities; the system captures their inputs, processes them, then assigns materials aligned with their performance. Instructors review analytics through dashboards, detecting patterns like repeated misunderstandings in advanced topics. This approach can close performance gaps by delivering custom exercises without increasing faculty workload (Dwivedi et al., 2023).

In universities with mixed levels of connectivity, the platform may support offline downloads or asynchronous updates. Students can retrieve tasks when online, complete them offline, and sync progress data at the next available moment. This design respects infrastructural constraints while still benefiting from adaptive principles. The main challenge is consistent maintenance and prompt technical support. Universities must train educators and system administrators to troubleshoot software or server problems that arise in real-world conditions (Bond et al., 2023).

4.3. AI-Assisted Assessment Methods

Traditional grading methods can be time-consuming, especially in large cohorts. AI-driven assessment tools automate parts of the evaluation process, including short-answer grading, essay scoring, or plagiarism checks (Salas-Pilco & Yang, 2022). These systems often rely on language models or pattern recognition to evaluate coherence, syntax, and argument structure. They produce faster feedback, giving students insights into their performance while freeing educators to focus on more in-depth mentorship (Falebita & Kok, 2024).

Bias and misinterpretation remain concerns. Automated essay scoring may penalize certain writing styles or local linguistic features, generating skewed outcomes for students from marginalized groups. Faculty oversight is essential to calibrate these systems, verifying that an AI's scoring aligns with course expectations and cultural norms (Popenici & Kerr, 2017). Institutions might adopt a hybrid model, in which AI systems produce preliminary scores that educators review or refine. Clear guidelines on how these tools fit into final evaluations reduce confusion and protect academic integrity (Dwivedi et al., 2023).

4.4. Integrating Urban Development Themes

Curricula that address urgent urban challenges equip students to propose relevant solutions in local contexts (Eryenyu et al., 2024). Table 1 suggests ways AI can intersect with concrete concerns in developing cities.

Table 1. Possible AI Uses for Local Urban Challenges

Urban Issue	AI Method	Example of Student Project
Traffic Congestion	Predictive Analytics, Routing	Designing a congestion forecasting tool
Waste Management	Image Recognition, Logistics	Creating an automated waste-sorting system
Resource Allocation	Optimization Algorithms	Developing an algorithm for water distribution
Public Safety	Video Analytics, Pattern Detection	Building a system for anomaly alerts
Urban Housing	Demand Prediction, Data Mining	Examining housing shortage models

Students can tackle real datasets in these areas, applying theoretical ideas to produce relevant outputs (van der Vlies & Hoeszová, 2022). Partnerships with municipal authorities or local NGOs deepen authenticity, as learners see direct impacts of data-based planning. This engagement connects classroom learning to daily urban realities, reinforcing problem-solving mindsets (Zawacki-Richter et al., 2019). It also helps institutions demonstrate tangible contributions to local development, which can boost public trust and open funding streams.

4.5. Blended and Hybrid Approaches for Resource-Constrained Settings

Fully online solutions may not be realistic in institutions without robust internet infrastructure. Blended models combine face-to-face sessions with digital tools that can operate offline (Wardat, 2023). Learners download modules, complete tasks at home, and upload their work during more reliable network windows. Adaptive logic is still possible through local caching of progress data, which syncs with servers when connectivity improves (Mhlanga, 2023).

Instructors devise strategies to ensure that critical activities, such as group discussions or real-time feedback, occur during stable connection periods or in on-campus labs with functional equipment. This arrangement safeguards essential interactive dimensions of education (Bond et al., 2023). Collaboration between campus IT units and teaching staff is pivotal to refine scheduling, troubleshoot issues, and maintain user-friendly experiences. Over time, if these pilots succeed, they can expand to other subjects or be repeated at partner institutions.

4.6. Incorporating Market-Ready AI Tools

Universities can partner with industry providers to bring established AI software into classrooms (Dwivedi et al., 2023). Tools for data visualization, statistical analysis, or machine learning can expose students to real-world workflows. In some collaborations, technology firms grant temporary licenses, organize training, or co-develop case studies that mirror actual professional challenges (Bond et al., 2023). This approach provides learners with experiences that transition smoothly into job markets, boosting employability.

Yet institutions must remain cautious about vendor lock-in. If a solution becomes too reliant on a single external provider, the institution's capacity for open experimentation may shrink (Crompton & Burke, 2023). Encouraging open-source alternatives or diverse software ecosystems can preserve adaptability. Educators who teach core concepts behind machine learning help learners transfer skills across tools. That way, graduates remain flexible and capable of adapting to different platforms.

5. FACULTY DEVELOPMENT FOR AI-ENHANCED EDUCATION

AI-driven curriculum renewal requires faculty who understand novel teaching methods, can manage digital platforms, and appreciate data ethics. Many instructors in developing regions handle heavy workloads, making it difficult to learn new systems without structured support (Mhlanga, 2023). Therefore, faculty training constitutes a linchpin in any broad AI adoption strategy. Institutions that treat professional development as optional or short-term risk seeing new tools go unused or misapplied (Pisica, Edu, Zaharia, & Zaharia, 2023).

5.1. Essential Competencies for Educators

Instructors must possess baseline AI literacy, including knowledge of machine learning fundamentals, data interpretation, and the ways these technologies support pedagogy (Bahroun et al., 2023). In addition, they need to design tasks that exploit adaptive feedback loops and dynamic assessment. Some educators may also need to address advanced scripting or basic programming if they are to customize content on certain platforms (Awadallah Alkouk & Khlaif, 2024).

Digital pedagogy extends beyond familiarity with hardware. Faculty should know how to guide discussions in online forums, manage assignment timelines in a learning management system, and interpret analytics to refine next week's lesson plans. Ethical training is equally important. Instructors must grasp privacy regulations, informed consent norms, and the potential pitfalls of automating evaluations (Zawacki-Richter et al., 2019). As AI-related controversies surface, educators can act as frontline guides for students, clarifying policies and promoting responsible uses of technology.

Table 2. Core Competencies for Faculty in AI Integration

Competency	Description	Development Options
AI Literacy	Understanding ML concepts, algorithms	Workshops, Online Courses, Peer Mentoring
Data Analytics	Interpreting analytics dashboards, identifying trends	Guided Projects, Collaborative Research
Pedagogical Innovation	Designing courses that integrate AI-based feedback	Interactive Seminars, Certification Programs
Ethical Acumen	Ensuring responsible data use and unbiased modeling	Panel Discussions, Policy Sessions
Technical Problem-Solving	Troubleshooting hardware and software issues	Joint Sessions with IT Teams, Self-Study

Figure 3 outlines the faculty training process for AI integration, starting with basic AI literacy, progressing through practical applications, and culminating in AI-enhanced teaching strategies

Figure 3. Faculty Development Stages for AI Integration

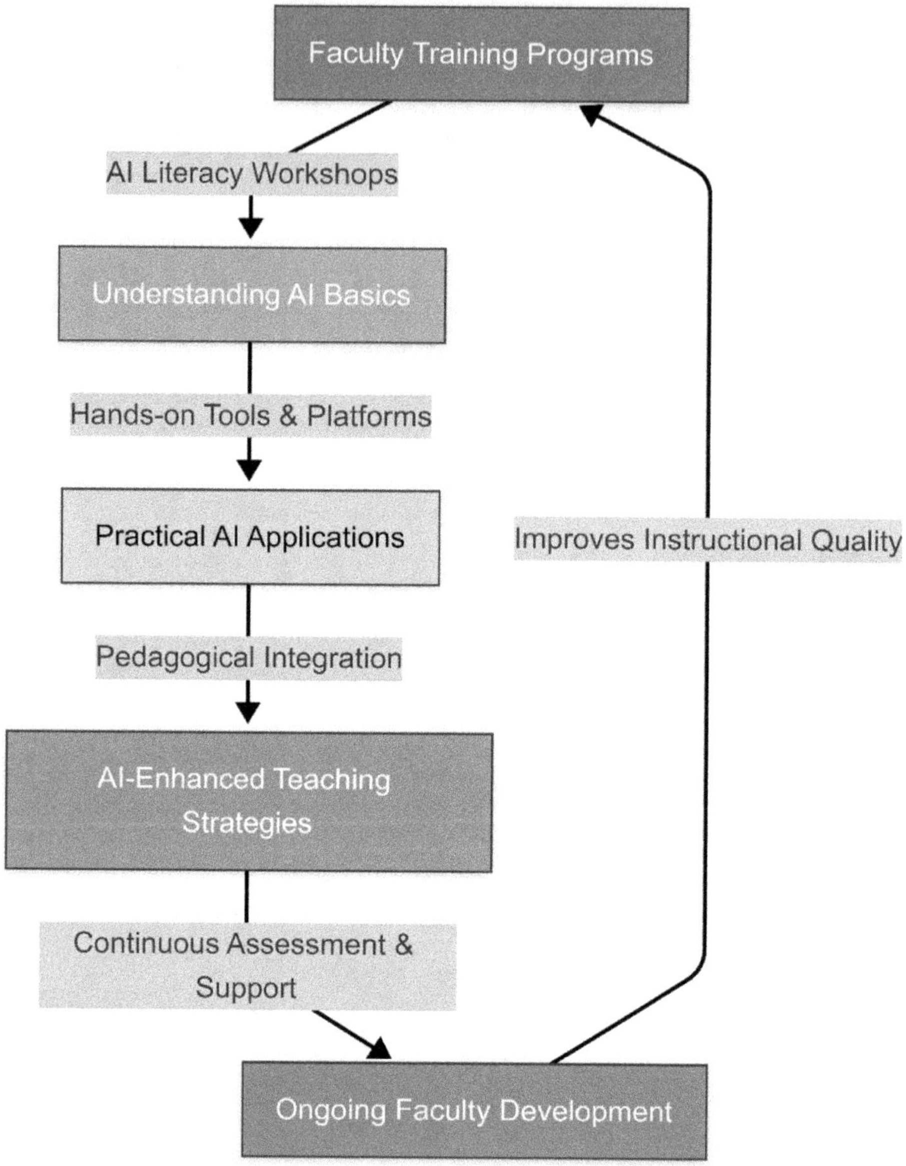

5.2. Institutional Support and Incentives

Training alone does not guarantee sustained faculty engagement. Institutions can offer promotions, publication grants, or performance-based compensation for instructors who adopt and refine AI-based teaching (Salas-Pilco & Yang, 2022). University leadership should set clear targets for technology integration, such as the number of courses expected to use adaptive software or incorporate real-world data sets. Reports or evaluations of progress can highlight educators who excel, motivating others to follow (Lara-Navarra, Ferrer-Sapena, Ísmodes-Cascón, Fosca-Pastor, & Sánchez-Pérez, 2025).

Funding remains a barrier. Workshops and extended training sessions require time off from regular teaching, and administrators must budget for trainers, materials, and potential external consultants. Partnerships with development agencies or philanthropic organizations may supply needed resources (Strielkowski et al., 2024). The key lies in forging stable channels, rather than one-off events that yield limited institutional memory.

5.3. Collaborative Networks and Peer Mentoring

Communities of practice can accelerate faculty development. More experienced educators who pilot AI-based classes can mentor newcomers through informal or formal pairings (Crompton & Burke, 2023). This arrangement fosters trust and promotes shared problem-solving. Online forums, departmental meetings, or cross-faculty committees can further bolster knowledge exchange (Mhlanga, 2023).

The peer mentoring program in certain institutions reaches beyond their primary campuses. Through inter-institutional consortia educational staff can exchange resources and conduct experience sharing to co-create localized solutions (Bond et al., 2023). The implementation requires special consideration when usage differences exist across regions because of language variations and accreditation criteria. Shared insights between faculty members from different areas enable them to develop AI integration techniques that match their common operational conditions.

5.4. Faculty Agency and Curriculum Co-Creation

Teaching quality improves when educators get substantial involvement in controlling how educational technology impacts their instruction. When administrators enforce decisions from above faculty members may experience both resentment alongside weak compliance rates (Pisica et al., 2023). Educational institutions achieve greater adoption when they welcome educators to both build pilot programs and determine the training emphasis. This collaborative atmosphere affirms the role of instructors as co-designers of the academic experience, rather than passive receivers of technology directives.

AI-based project implementation receives guidance from faculty members to safeguard cultural and local characteristics (Bond et al., 2023). The teaching knowledge of instructors enables them to propose relevant data sets that focus on agricultural farming or town development or healthcare matters in local regions. They should help create assessment criteria which value cultural practices instead of using standardized methods from abroad. AI adoption is better received as an educational assistant through this method which validates traditional teaching approaches and preserves the independence of faculty members.

5.5. Continuous Professional Growth

Technology changes quickly. Existing technology platforms could become useless within a few years of their introduction. Through continuous development programs faculty members stay updated with their skills while maintaining ethical standards and acquiring knowledge of novel features and complete tools (Dwivedi et al., 2023). Educational institutions could support teacher development through events that include micro-credentials and symposiums and regional conferences focused on AI-based educational strategies and delivery success (Crompton & Burke, 2023).

The establishment of these initiatives creates a student-and-faculty learning environment which demonstrates institutional support for institutional growth. The organizational culture accepts experimental approaches alongside collaborative development so newcomers to the workplace find an environment opposed to maintaining traditional methods. The cycle creates better morale within the staff who dedicate wholeheartedly to students because their innovative teaching approaches deliver benefits directly to students.

6. CASE STUDIES OF AI INTEGRATION IN DEVELOPING UNIVERSITIES

Real-world examples help illustrate how theoretical concepts and institutional plans materialize. The following subsections highlight diverse approaches, successes, and challenges in universities that have ventured into AI-based curriculum transformations. These cases include Sub-Saharan Africa, Southeast Asia, Latin America, and South Asia. Each example addresses specific issues while revealing broader lessons for resource-constrained institutions.

6.1. University A in Sub-Saharan Africa

University A had persistent failure rates in entry-level mathematics and science courses, leading to student attrition and under-enrollment in advanced technical majors (Khoalenyane & Ajani, 2024). Administrators believed that AI-based adaptive platforms could reduce these failures by diagnosing students' conceptual gaps and steering them toward targeted practice. They selected a locally built tool that functioned with intermittent connectivity, enabling offline usage for students in regions with poor internet.

Initial results showed fewer dropouts in pilot classes. Many students welcomed real-time feedback and personalized study schedules, which reduced their anxiety over standardized assessments (Wang et al., 2023). Analytics suggested that weaker learners made steady progress once the system identified specific learning deficits. Faculty-led workshops trained instructors to read analytics reports and adjust their lectures. However, data privacy concerns arose, prompting the university to establish an ethics board that implemented data handling protocols (UNESCO, 2023).

Subsequent steps involved expanding AI-based tools to other foundational courses. The institution also sought external funds to update computing labs, ensuring that offline functionality did not remain the only fallback method. Over three academic cycles, pass rates rose, though faculty insisted that supplemental tutoring and small-group interactions remained essential. The experience at University A shows that AI can work in tandem with local realities if systems accommodate offline components and leadership addresses ethical issues early on.

6.2. University B in Southeast Asia

University B prioritized integrating AI into an urban planning curriculum due to the institution's proximity to a rapidly growing metropolis (Wardat, 2023). City officials agreed to share geospatial and infrastructural data, letting students model flood risks and traffic congestion patterns using AI-based prediction. Teams combined civil engineering, computing, and policy students. Weekly sessions included real data sets that showed patterns of flooding during monsoon seasons and traffic jams during peak hours.

Instructors received specialized training from local tech consultants to learn about machine learning libraries, data cleaning, and scenario testing. Students appreciated the hands-on experience, and the city government considered some student projects for actual policy recommendations. The university monitored engagement levels, assignment completion times, and the depth of solutions proposed. Table 3 shows key metrics.

Table 3. AI-Infused Urban Planning Pilot Outcomes at University B

Metric	Before Implementation	After Implementation
Engagement Level (scale of 5)	3.1	4.2
Quality of Final Project (avg. grade)	B–	B+
Internship Placement Rate	10%	25%
Instructor AI Proficiency (scale of 5)	2.5	3.8

The pilot led to a surge in internship placements with the city's planning office. The improved instructor proficiency scores point to the effectiveness of targeted training sessions. Administrators also recognized the success through faculty awards and departmental grants. Over time, the city-university collaboration grew stronger, offering more advanced data sets and opportunities for real-time policy engagement.

6.3. University C in Latin America

University C encountered difficulty serving distant learners in mountainous regions, where internet connectivity was sporadic (Salas-Pilco & Yang, 2022). A new hybrid model was introduced, blending asynchronous AI-enabled modules with periodic on-campus intensive workshops. Mobile accessibility was central, as many learners relied on smartphones rather than personal computers.

During the pilot, faculty posted short quizzes and interactive lessons on an adaptive platform. Students downloaded these resources while on campus or in nearby towns, completed them offline, and uploaded results during their next trip to a networked area (Crompton & Burke, 2023). Analytics revealed that students engaged more consistently with course materials when modules were broken into smaller tasks. This approach improved retention in first-year courses, traditionally marked by high attrition.

Faculty hesitated at first, worried about losing control over content delivery, but the administration held open discussions to address concerns. Some academics modified content for local dialect use, supporting inclusiveness. Students appreciated immediate feedback on assignments, though offline intervals meant they received batch updates rather than continuous support. The university recognized that while the system reduced some inequities, certain learners still faced financial and time constraints in traveling to upload assignments. Nevertheless, overall pass rates increased, and the approach spread to other departments.

6.4. University D in South Asia

University D targeted language instruction with an AI-based speech recognition and tutoring system. Large classes and limited language lab access meant learners seldom received individual speaking practice. The system captured audio submissions, analyzed pronunciation, and offered corrective suggestions in real time (Zawacki-Richter et al., 2019).

Faculty noticed a rise in oral proficiency among students who regularly used the system. Analytics showed that repeated interactions with the tool correlated with fewer mispronunciations. However, campus electricity fluctuations disrupted usage patterns. Some students bypassed the platform when labs were offline. Administrators responded by installing backup power supplies in language labs. Faculty also encountered model inaccuracies for local dialects, prompting them to collaborate with system developers on more regionally attuned speech recognition models. Over multiple semesters, the improved system reduced the performance gap between urban and rural enrollees, especially in oral communication.

6.5. Lessons from the Case Studies

Each institution addressed unique barriers: poor connectivity, faculty skill shortages, localized data sets, or high attrition. Despite these differences, a few common threads emerged. First, pilot testing and gradual rollout provided a safer environment to identify pitfalls. Second, data analytics aided instructors, but ethical oversight was crucial to safeguard student privacy (Popenici & Kerr, 2017). Third, leadership support and external partnerships were recurring enablers of stable adoption. Collectively, these examples suggest that AI can blend into curriculum renewal when institutions consider local constraints and integrate systematic faculty development.

7. CONCEPTUAL FRAMEWORK FOR INSTITUTIONAL READINESS

AI-driven reforms require synergy across governance, pedagogy, resources, and community links. Figure 4 depicts a conceptual framework that outlines these pillars and how they reinforce each other over time.

Figure 4. AI-Centered Educational Transformation Framework

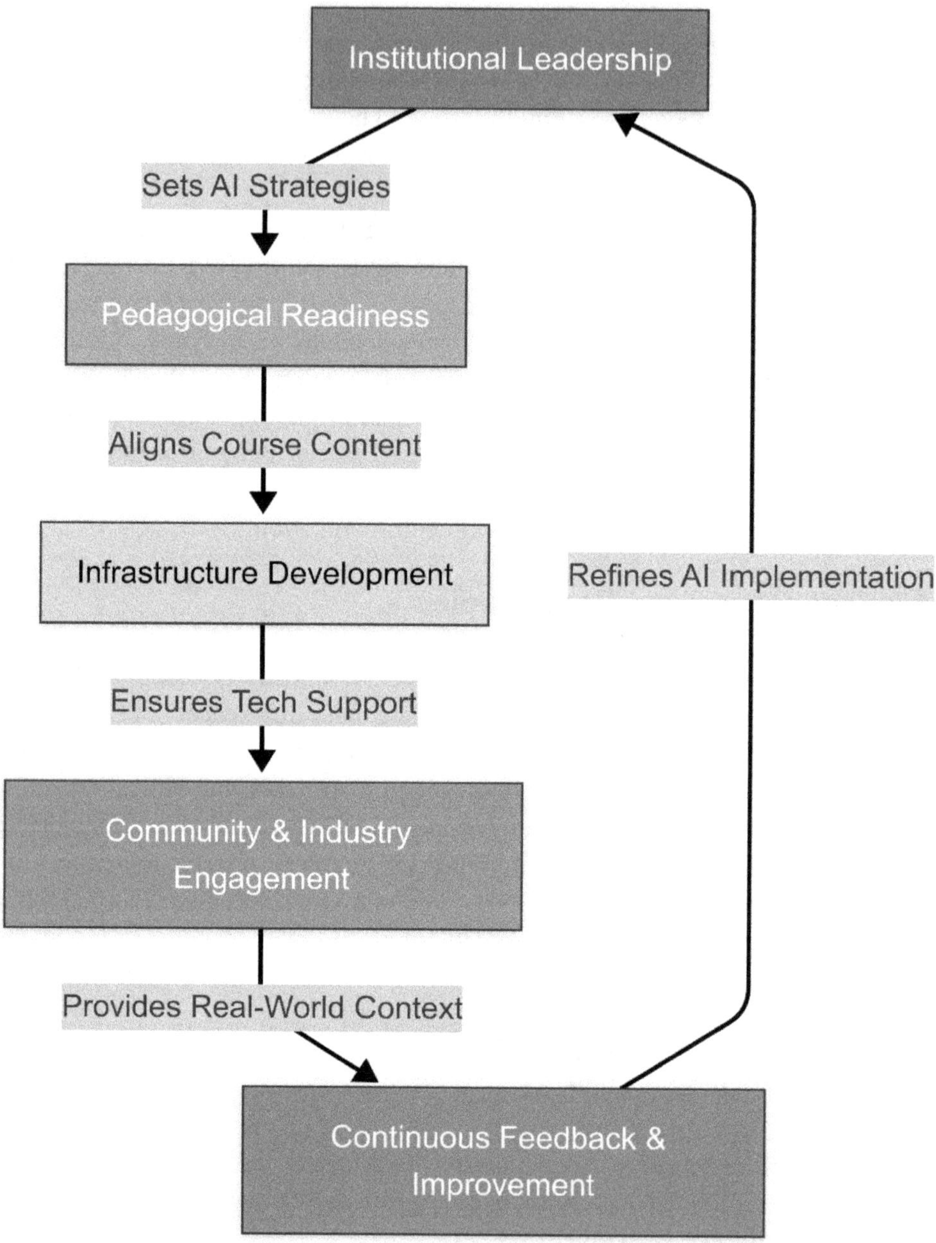

Leadership shapes strategies and allocates budgets, while pedagogical readiness addresses revised curricular goals. Infrastructure ensures digital continuity. Partnerships supply domain-relevant data, real-world challenges, and external funding

(Mustafa et al., 2024). The feedback loop indicates that changes in one domain affect the others.

7.1. Leadership and Governance

University leaders set the tone for innovation. Rectors and deans who promote AI-based initiatives encourage risk-taking among faculty (Bond et al., 2023). Leadership bodies coordinate committees to track pilot results, share lessons, and maintain momentum. Policy documents reflect official goals, timelines, and performance indicators. This approach helps unify efforts across multiple departments, even where resources are scarce (HolonIQ, 2023).

Ethical guidelines also stem from governance structures. Leaders who prioritize data privacy or algorithmic fairness direct resources toward compliance with local regulations. If oversight committees exist, they evaluate pilot proposals, sign off on data usage, and respond to stakeholder concerns. This fosters transparency, mitigating the risk of backlash if unexpected data practices surface (UNESCO, 2023).

7.2. Pedagogical Readiness and Curriculum Realignment

Pedagogical readiness focuses on how well educators and departments can integrate new methodologies. AI adoption often redefines course objectives, emphasizing problem-solving, data literacy, and iterative learning (Crompton & Burke, 2023). Faculty who embrace these shifts adjust syllabi accordingly, incorporate practical exercises, and align assessments with competence-based standards (Pisica et al., 2023).

Sustained planning helps. Curriculum committees clarify which programs will embed AI fundamentals or advanced analytics. Interdisciplinary collaboration fosters synergy, preventing duplication. Over time, data-driven teaching becomes an accepted norm, rather than an experimental novelty (Salas-Pilco & Yang, 2022).

7.3. Infrastructure and Technical Support

Stable hardware, software, and connectivity are core requirements for AI-based education (Falebita & Kok, 2024). Institutions with limited funds may upgrade incrementally, focusing on priority courses or departmental labs. Partnerships can facilitate hardware donations or subsidized software licenses (van der Vlies & Hoeszová, 2022). In parallel, an internal technical support unit responds to system malfunctions, usage questions, or data management tasks (Wardat, 2023).

Periodic maintenance and updates protect system reliability. Cloud-based solutions offer flexibility but demand continuous internet, while local servers reduce dependency on external networks but require specialized staff. Institutions must match their chosen approach with actual resource availability. Overestimating one's capacity often results in partial or failed implementations.

7.4. Community and Industry Engagement

Linkages beyond the campus enrich AI-based learning by exposing students to pressing societal challenges (Eryenyu et al., 2024). City governments can provide anonymized data sets, letting students model new traffic routes or environmental hazard maps (Zawacki-Richter et al., 2019). Private companies may sponsor labs or co-design course materials that mirror current industry practices. Such involvement strengthens the job prospects of graduates while enabling local employers to shape relevant talent pipelines (Salas-Pilco & Yang, 2022).

Transparent agreements clarify intellectual property rights, data usage, and mutual expectations. Institutions benefit from increased credibility and potential funding, while partners gain fresh insights and a possible workforce. This exchange fosters a sense of shared responsibility for local progress, reflecting the idea that universities are not insular but active contributors to broader development.

7.5. Feedback Loops for Continuous Improvement

The feedback mechanism in Figure 2 highlights the dynamic nature of AI integration. The leadership teams create visions while pedagogical teams conduct assessments of new courses and report student achievement results. Infrastructure units continuously monitor usage to identify system problems which leads them to enhance platforms. Active community partnerships add both real-world operational requirements and new information which maintain relevant education programs (Mustafa et al., 2024). Each renewed cycle conducts improvements which form the basis for the following round of development.

This iterative approach counters the tendency for once-and-done technology initiatives. The method enables platform development to correspond with external modifications including updated municipal requirements, governmental rules and technological platform standards (Bond et al., 2023). As the framework matures institutions gain capabilities which enable them to improve strategies and spread successful approaches between different subjects.

8. CHALLENGES AND ETHICAL CONSIDERATIONS

Introducing AI into higher education in regions with limited resources raises complications related to data policies, algorithmic fairness, uneven access, and academic integrity (Bahroun et al., 2023). Proponents who champion AI's efficiency must address these caveats systematically. Institutions that ignore ethical aspects risk undermining trust among students, faculty, and society at large (Popenici & Kerr, 2017).

8.1. Data Privacy and Confidentiality

AI-based tools often gather detailed logs of student activity. Without robust protocols, there is a risk of data mismanagement or unauthorized access (Dwivedi et al., 2023). Students may not fully understand how their information is stored or used, especially if no local regulations mandate informed consent. Institutions must craft privacy statements that clarify the scope of data collection, the purposes of analysis, and the retention period (UNESCO, 2023).

Encryption methods, secure server configurations, and designated data protection roles limit potential breaches. Leaders can embed privacy training in faculty development sessions, ensuring instructors handle information responsibly. Routine data audits detect anomalies, boosting stakeholder confidence. Universities that adopt these measures position themselves as ethical exemplars, ready to address global standards for data protection.

8.2. Algorithmic Bias and Fairness

Algorithms learn patterns from data that may exclude or misrepresent certain populations (van der Vlies & Hoeszová, 2022). A scoring system trained on a majority dialect could penalize students from minority language groups. Image recognition tools might struggle with darker skin tones if the dataset lacked representation (Bond et al., 2023). Such hidden bias in AI-driven grading or content recommendation can entrench inequities in the classroom.

Faculty and technical teams should validate model outputs against diverse samples. Student feedback offers another checkpoint. If certain categories of learners find consistent mismatches in grading, the institution may need to adjust model training or adopt alternative evaluation methods (Mustafa et al., 2024). Transparent documentation of data sources and AI logic also promotes accountability. By addressing these concerns proactively, universities protect minority students and uphold fairness in the learning process.

8.3. Uneven Resource Distribution and Tech Dependence

Technology-based initiatives often rely on stable electricity, computing devices, and broadband coverage, which remain unevenly distributed across developing regions (Falebita & Kok, 2024). Some institutions stand better poised to adopt AI, leaving rural or smaller universities behind. Even within a single university, certain departments might secure external grants, while others remain underfunded (Dwivedi et al., 2023).

An overemphasis on AI might also downplay interpersonal elements of teaching, especially if administrators reduce faculty positions assuming that automation replaces human tasks (UNESCO, 2023). This approach is misguided, as most AI tools complement rather than replace classroom facilitation. The teacher's role in mentoring, contextual explanation, and moral guidance remains vital. Planning for balanced resource distribution, capacity building, and well-rounded instruction can mitigate these pitfalls.

8.4. Academic Integrity and Plagiarism

Generative AI tools and adaptive systems provide quick content creation or code suggestions. Students may misuse these resources for assignments, blurring lines between original work and automated output (Mhlanga, 2023). Institutions should define clear guidelines on acceptable AI assistance in homework or projects (Popenici & Kerr, 2017). Detection tools can highlight potential plagiarism or text reuse, though these systems also require calibration and oversight to avoid false accusations (Dwivedi et al., 2023).

To prevent automation dependency educators should establish assignments which demand analytical thinking and original output because these tasks prove more challenging for pure automated systems. The assessment methods of oral defenses and iterative submissions and peer evaluations force students to deeply interact with their academic materials. Educational professionals have the responsibility to educate students about ethical boundaries with advanced digital tools because this teaches students how academic integrity relates to their professional development (Zawacki-Richter et al., 2019).

9. IMPLEMENTATION STRATEGIES FOR SUSTAINABLE AI USAGE

Institutions that utilize AI-based educational reforms create carefully planned strategies which predict resource limits and technical problems and staffing adjustment rates. This part of the paper introduces methods to initiate a pilot program while continuous monitoring takes place alongside faculty development and student involvement. The implemented measures work together to establish unity instead of conducting random scattered trials (Bahroun et al., 2023).

9.1. Phased Rollout and Pilot Testing

Large-scale transformations create disruptions when implementation happens too fast. Institutional control of scope, data collection and mistake correction can be achieved through phased or pilot-based approaches (Awadallah Alkouk & Khlaif, 2024). A single department or course undertakes adaptive assessment pilot testing as one operation while AI-based grading receives testing in specific writing courses during separate pilots. The assessment of student outcomes and instructor satisfaction alongside technological performance is conducted by educational institutions and stakeholders according to Bond et al. (2023).

The cycling review process helps institutions determine whether to advance the intervention or modify its strategies. The act of transparent reporting helps staff members develop trust because they can view the proven success outcomes before deciding to implement these new systems. Team members can spread pilot research findings through educational workshops or classroom publications to gain valuable critiques of best practices (Zawacki-Richter et al., 2019).

9.2. Monitoring, Evaluation, and Quality Assurance

AI-enhanced curricula produce streams of data that can inform timely decisions. This advantage only materializes if universities establish clear metrics and frequent evaluation cycles. Benchmarks might include average grades, dropout patterns, attendance, satisfaction ratings, and system usage statistics (Crompton & Burke, 2023). Administrators and faculty analyze changes each semester, isolating where interventions worked or failed (Mustafa et al., 2024).

Quality assurance processes combine quantitative and qualitative elements. Surveys measure attitudes toward AI-based features, while focus groups highlight personal experiences or unanticipated side effects. Implementation teams then refine system algorithms, revise learning activities, or add additional training sessions.

Documenting these changes builds an institutional memory, crucial for sustaining progress across leadership turnovers or funding shifts (Salas-Pilco & Yang, 2022).

9.3. Ongoing Faculty Development and Incentives

Institutions must see faculty learning as a long-term investment (Pisica et al., 2023). Annual refresher workshops, technology boot camps, or peer-led sessions keep teachers current on evolving AI trends. Universities can partner with technology organizations to stay abreast of updated features or relevant research. When educators feel valued and supported, they commit more energy to refining their courses (Bond et al., 2023).

Reward structures can reinforce positive outcomes. Teaching excellence awards might consider how effectively an instructor uses data analytics to improve student performance. Research grants can encourage faculty to publish findings on AI-based pedagogies, raising the institution's profile. Over time, these incentives cultivate a cadre of faculty experts who mentor newcomers, fueling a cycle of continuous improvement.

9.4. Student Engagement and Co-Creation

Students are primary stakeholders. Student input regarding AI content as well as technical problems and fair use expectations leads to system refinement through continuous development (Mhlanga, 2023). Student representatives who join curriculum committees and pilot oversight bodies create a framework for joint involvement. The institutions should establish orientation occasions that demonstrate adaptive system operations together with information about data collection and trouble-accessing strategies (Eryenyu et al., 2024).

Educational events involving group work and collaborative projects enable students to test AI platforms for novel discoveries. Through their involvement learners discover alternate approaches for content localization while detecting logical issues in system functions. Under this collaborative approach students strengthen their proficiency in digital tools so that the next generation experieinces AI as both usable methodologies and potential challenges to existing technologies (Zawacki-Richter et al., 2019). The partnership created by enlightened students working with dedicated instructors drives both swift acceptance of solutions and solution enhancement.

10. FUTURE RESEARCH PERSPECTIVES

Published studies in AI for education frequently focus on short-term pilots or limited contexts. There is a need for extended investigations that assess long-term effects in developing university environments (Bahroun et al., 2023). The following suggestions outline where future scholarship might expand, generating richer insights for policymakers and institution leaders.

10.1. Longitudinal Outcomes and Cohort Tracking

Several reported initiatives gauge immediate performance shifts or exam pass rates. Few track students beyond graduation to see if AI-based interventions shape career trajectories, higher-order thinking skills, or civic engagement (Crompton & Burke, 2023). Longitudinal studies that follow cohorts over five to ten years can reveal deeper insights into how early exposure to adaptive instruction influences professional success or advanced study pursuits. Institutions can also examine how stable these improvements remain once pilot support concludes.

10.2. Cross-Regional Comparative Analyses

Each developing region carries distinct historical, linguistic, and infrastructural attributes (Salas-Pilco & Yang, 2022). Comparative research can isolate shared barriers, such as power instability, or context-specific factors, like unique policy mandates. By collecting data from African, Asian, and Latin American universities, scholars can determine best practices that generalize across settings or require adaptation. Coordinated multi-site projects, facilitated by consortia or research networks, encourage the pooling of resources and standardization of metrics (Zawacki-Richter et al., 2019).

10.3. Scaling Personalized Learning Platforms

Adaptive systems show promise but remain limited in scope, especially in institutions with tens of thousands of learners (Mustafa et al., 2024). Research on distributed computing, open-source frameworks, and mobile-based solutions could clarify how to scale personalization without overwhelming servers or staff. Partnerships between software developers and educators can yield robust, cost-effective tools that function in intermittent connectivity environments (van der Vlies & Hoeszová, 2022).

Evaluations of cost-effectiveness and return on investment would help administrators decide whether adaptive learning systems provide sufficient benefit to justify budgets. Studies might measure intangible outcomes like learner confidence, motivation, and autonomy, in addition to standard academic performance (Dwivedi et al., 2023).

10.4. Advancing Ethical Guidelines in AI Education

Many ethical frameworks for AI remain broad or embedded in legislation from developed countries, lacking direct applicability to local realities (UNESCO, 2023). Researchers can examine how community norms, cultural views on data ownership, or local governance structures intersect with AI usage in classrooms. Interdisciplinary work can explore how to embed indigenous knowledge or rural perspectives in training data sets (Popenici & Kerr, 2017).

This investigation helps create model standards which academic institutions should follow when their nations lack complete data privacy regulations. Student bodies and local civil society organizations and policymakers need to engage in dialogues to determine solutions for ethical challenges exclusive to their specific societies. The findings may influence how institutions make their equipment selections while also shaping the procedures to obtain consent from their customer base.

11. CONCLUSION

Developing regions' higher educational sector faces a critical moment characterized by limited resources because it must quickly provide specialized expertise. AI-based curriculum redesign presents solutions to update educational approaches while building expertise in needed areas and handling regional administrative and urbanization problems. These initiatives need strategic planning combined with prepared facilities along with robust faculty development programs but they can transform instructional quality and produce graduates who address essential real-world problems (Crompton & Burke 2023).

The investigation of theoretical premises coupled with implementation practices and educational training and practical examples showcases why AI solutions need customization for various institutional settings. Data privacy alongside algorithmic bias and fair access belong to ethical domains that AI solution implementers must resolve to guarantee their positive impact rather than negative impacts. Organizations need leadership direction alongside team collaboration and constant assessment mechanisms alongside enduring dedication to institutional growth for successful implementation (Bond et al., 2023).

Cautious management of complex conditions in educational institutions leads to employment-preparedness among students while making valuable contributions to regional social and infrastructure advancement. The right time has arrived to establish evidence-based AI integration strategies which meet developing environments' specific needs and generate sustainable educational changes.

REFERENCES

Al-Zahrani, A. M., & Alasmari, T. M. (2024). Exploring the impact of artificial intelligence on higher education: The dynamics of ethical, social, and educational implications. *Palgrave Communications*, *11*(1), 1–12.

Awadallah Alkouk, W., & Khlaif, Z. N. (2024). The use of AI chatbots in education: Implications for student engagement in developing countries. In *Proceedings of the 2024 International Conference on Knowledge Engineering and Communication Systems (ICKECS)* (pp. 1–5). IEEE.

Bahroun, Z., Anane, C., Ahmed, V., & Zacca, A. (2023). Transforming education: A comprehensive review of generative artificial intelligence in educational settings through bibliometric and content analysis. *Sustainability (Basel)*, *15*(17), 12983. DOI: 10.3390/su151712983

Bond, M., Khosravi, H., de Laat, M., Bergdahl, N., Negrea, V., Oxley, E., Pham, P., & Chong, S. W. (2023). A meta systematic review of artificial intelligence in higher education: A call for increased ethics, collaboration, and rigour. *International Journal of Educational Technology in Higher Education*, *20*(1), 54.

Crompton, H., & Burke, D. (2023). Artificial intelligence in higher education: The state of the field. *International Journal of Educational Technology in Higher Education*, *20*(1), 22. DOI: 10.1186/s41239-023-00392-8

Dwivedi, Y. K., Hughes, D. L., Tang, J., Wang, Y., Mazumder, S., & Akher, J. (2023). "So what if ChatGPT wrote it?" Multidisciplinary perspectives on opportunities, challenges, and implications of generative AI for education (and beyond). *Journal of Business Research*, *154*, 113–127.

Eryenyu, C., Owomugisha, G., Biira, S., & Waako, P. (2024). The challenges and opportunities of artificial intelligence use in higher education: The case of Busitema University. *Journal of Research Innovation and Implications in Education*, *8*(4), 598–610.

Falebita, O. S., & Kok, P. J. (2024). Strategic goals for artificial intelligence integration among STEM academics and undergraduates in African higher education: A systematic review. *Discover Education*, *3*(1), 151. DOI: 10.1007/s44217-024-00252-1

HolonIQ. (2023). Artificial Intelligence in Education: 2023 Survey Insights.

Khoalenyane, N. B., & Ajani, O. A. (2024). A systematic review of artificial intelligence in higher education – South Africa. *Social Sciences and Education Research Review*, *11*(1), 17–26.

Lara-Navarra, P., Ferrer-Sapena, A., Ísmodes-Cascón, E., Fosca-Pastor, C., & Sánchez-Pérez, E. A. (2025). The future of higher education: Trends, challenges, and opportunities in AI-driven lifelong learning in Peru. *Information (Basel)*, *16*(3), 224. DOI: 10.3390/info16030224

Mhlanga, D. (2023). Open AI in education: The responsible and ethical use of ChatGPT towards lifelong learning. *Education and Information Technologies*. Advance online publication.

Mustafa, M. Y., Tlili, A., Lampropoulos, G., Huang, R., Jandrić, P., Zhao, J., … & Saqr, M. (2024). A systematic review of literature reviews on artificial intelligence in education: A roadmap to a future research agenda. Smart Learning Environments, 11(1), Article 6.

Pisica, A. I., Edu, T., Zaharia, R. M., & Zaharia, R. (2023). Implementing artificial intelligence in higher education: Pros and cons from the perspectives of academics. *Societies (Basel, Switzerland)*, *13*(5), 118. DOI: 10.3390/soc13050118

Popenici, S. A. D., & Kerr, S. (2017). Exploring the impact of artificial intelligence on teaching and learning in higher education. *Research and Practice in Technology Enhanced Learning*, *12*(1), 22. DOI: 10.1186/s41039-017-0062-8 PMID: 30595727

Salas-Pilco, S. Z., & Yang, Y. (2022). Artificial intelligence applications in Latin American higher education: A systematic review. *International Journal of Educational Technology in Higher Education*, *19*(1), 21. DOI: 10.1186/s41239-022-00326-w

Strielkowski, W.. (2024). AI-driven adaptive learning for sustainable educational transformation. *Sustainable Development*. Advance online publication.

UNESCO. (2023). *Generative AI in Higher Education: Reshaping Learning in Asia-Pacific*. UNESCO.

van der Vlies, R., & Hoeszová, J. (2022). The promise of artificial intelligence for education in developing countries. *Prospects*, *51*(1–3), 63–80.

Wang, S., DeMarree, K. G., Petchenik, E., & Hu, X. (2023). When adaptive learning is effective learning: Comparison of an adaptive learning system to teacher-led instruction. *Interactive Learning Environments*, *31*(2), 793–803. DOI: 10.1080/10494820.2020.1808794

Wardat, Y. (2023). The use of AI chatbots in education: Implications for student engagement in developing countries. *Interactive Technology and Smart Education*, *20*(4), 305–320.

Zawacki-Richter, O., Marín, V. I., Bond, M., & Gouverneur, F. (2019). Systematic review of research on artificial intelligence applications in higher education – where are the educators? *International Journal of Educational Technology in Higher Education, 16*(1), 39. DOI: 10.1186/s41239-019-0171-0

Chapter 11
Securing the Digital Backbone of Smart Cities:
Threat Detection, Infrastructure Hardening, and Data Governance

Mohammad Alauthman
https://orcid.org/0000-0003-0319-1968
Department of Information Security, University of Petra, Amman, Jordan

Wael Hadi
https://orcid.org/0000-0002-7575-9287
Department of Information Security, University of Petra, Amman, Jordan

Ahmad Al-Qerem
https://orcid.org/0000-0003-2187-6194
Computer Science Department, Faculty of Information Technology, Zarqa University, Jordan

Saad Alateef
https://orcid.org/0009-0002-3219-0833
School of Computing Science, Newcastle University, UK

Mashaleh Ashraf
Al-Balqa Applied University, Jordan

Mouhammd Alkasassbeh
https://orcid.org/0000-0001-8396-7441
Princess Sumaya University for Technology, Jordan

ABSTRACT

Smart cities rely on interconnected digital systems for essential services. These environments face security gaps that invite disruptive cyber threats. This chapter investigates key vulnerabilities in urban digital infrastructures and explains methods for analyzing malicious behavior. The purpose is to present layered strategies that protect sensor networks, communication protocols, and supervisory control systems. The author applies evidence-based methods to examine intrusion detection, infrastructure hardening, and data governance models. Empirical results reveal that anomalies in sensor traffic and unauthorized data flows are best addressed through

DOI: 10.4018/979-8-3373-1375-7.ch011

proactive detection algorithms and decentralized oversight. These insights suggest stronger policies to guide data collection and usage. The chapter contributes an integrated framework combining cybersecurity practices, technical resilience, and responsible data management.

1. INTRODUCTION

Smart cities integrate diverse technologies that handle communication, urban management, power grids, healthcare operations, traffic optimization, and many other functions. The modern city's digital backbone includes networks of sensors, real-time analytics platforms, and service-delivery interfaces. Infrastructure operators depend on continuous data flows and distributed architectures to manage traffic lights, energy distribution, waste management, and emergency responses (Kolotouchkina, Ripoll González, & Belabas, 2024). Yet, these complex systems create new vulnerabilities. As various devices and platforms interface, malicious agents discover points of entry that compromise municipal services. Small misconfigurations may allow sophisticated attacks that spread through integrated networks, targeting traffic signals, water purification systems, and electric grids (Babikian, Neini, & Debbabi, 2023).

Threats include denial of service, data tampering, IoT-based intrusions, and advanced persistent threats. Cities need robust defenses and monitoring strategies to detect suspicious behavior in real time. Disruptive incidents highlight the fragility of certain digital services. Researchers explore dynamic detection algorithms that identify anomalies in sensor data, classify malicious behavior, and reduce false positives. Proposed solutions incorporate machine learning, deep learning, and federated learning to handle large volumes of streaming data (Priyadarshini, 2024; Panwar & Sharma, 2024). Many academics also advocate for multi-layered security frameworks aligned with risk governance models. Through these holistic strategies, cities can develop resilience against varied cyber threats (Kim et al., 2023).

Alongside threat detection, infrastructure hardening remains a priority. Hardening involves adopting best practices to protect endpoints, strengthen communication protocols, and secure software supply chains (Babikian et al., 2023). Operators also consider advanced encryption, identity management, intrusion detection, and robust patching schedules. Resilience requires comprehensive risk assessments, emergency response plans, and robust governance structures that clarify roles and responsibilities. Authorities benefit from guidelines that integrate technical configurations with organizational policies (Leroy, Zolotaryova, & Semenov, 2025). Such measures reduce risk exposure, safeguard sensitive infrastructure, and enable continuity of services during disruptive incidents. Resilience also depends on multi-stakeholder collaboration among public agencies, private technology firms, and citizens (Bokhari & Myeong, 2024).

Data governance forms another critical pillar. Smart cities generate immense data streams that require ethical collection, processing, sharing, and storage. Poor governance practices jeopardize personal privacy and raise concerns over potential misuse of data (Bou Nassar et al., 2024). Policymakers seek balanced approaches that allow innovation while protecting sensitive information. Oversight mechanisms, legal frameworks, anonymization techniques, and transparency measures can reassure citizens regarding data handling (Fabrègue & Bogoni, 2023). Ultimately, data governance includes access controls, data classification guidelines, and accountability structures that define how data is stored, who processes it, and how usage is audited. Sustaining trust is paramount for successful smart city initiatives. Responsible data governance complements cyber threat detection and infrastructure resilience in a holistic approach that secures urban digital ecosystems.

This chapter explores these themes in detail. Section 2 examines key scholarship on threat detection in smart city contexts, infrastructure hardening, data governance, and how emerging technologies transform urban development. Section 3 outlines the methodology that guides this analysis, while Section 4 proposes a conceptual framework capturing the interplay of detection mechanisms, hardware and software protection, and data oversight. Section 5 evaluates implementation steps and discusses practical insights gleaned from real-world examples. Section 6 concludes by highlighting lessons for policymakers and identifying directions for future work.

The chapter draws on recent academic contributions from diverse journals and conferences. References are restricted to the literature provided, ensuring a focused review of cutting-edge efforts and validated solutions. Cities worldwide can adapt the insights presented here to strengthen their digital backbones and safeguard public services. Through integrated strategies, municipal leaders, technology providers, and the wider community can collaborate to maintain secure, resilient, and sustainable urban environments.

2. BACKGROUND ON SMART CITY SECURITY

2.1. Evolution of Urban Digital Systems

Urban environments increasingly rely on complex digital infrastructures. Early approaches to urban technology centered on discrete systems for surveillance, traffic control, and public information. With the emergence of the Internet of Things, a new wave of integrated devices and services appeared. Planners began to incorporate real-time data from sensors in roads, trains, utilities, and buildings (Houichi, Jaidi,

& Bouhoula, 2024). These interconnected platforms aimed to streamline resource allocation, reduce congestion, optimize energy usage, and enhance overall quality of life.

Over time, more advanced features have been integrated, such as AI-driven data analytics and blockchain-based transaction systems (Anthopoulos, Janssen, Weerakkody, & Castelnovo, 2023). The sophisticated nature of these systems promotes efficiency but also introduces vulnerabilities. Increased connectivity expands the attack surface. Malicious actors target IoT sensors, exploit unpatched endpoints, or conduct distributed denial-of-service assaults on city networks (Sarveshwaran, Amma, & Baik, 2023). The interplay of thousands of nodes makes security oversight a formidable challenge. Disruptions that affect a single gateway or communication link can cascade through dependent systems.

Municipal authorities often contract multiple vendors for specialized services, leading to a fragmented infrastructure. This fragmentation complicates consistent application of security standards. Governance frameworks and established best practices can address these challenges but require multi-level coordination and robust monitoring. Evolving threats also demand new detection strategies that adapt quickly. Past approaches, reliant on signature-based detection, may not match novel zero-day exploits and sophisticated intrusion tactics (Zeng, Yunis, Khalil, & Mirza, 2024). Therefore, the evolution of urban digital systems demands continuous refinement of security and governance methods.

2.2. Fundamental Threats to Smart Cities

2.2.1. IoT-Based Intrusions

IoT devices gather data on traffic flow, air quality, waste bins, parking availability, and other conditions. These endpoints sometimes run on lightweight operating systems with limited memory and processing power, making them less capable of running robust security software. Attackers leverage vulnerabilities like default passwords or unencrypted communication channels to gain unauthorized entry (Priyadarshini, Mohanty, Alkhayyat, Sharma, & Kumar, 2023). Once in control, they can propagate malware or alter sensor outputs. Compromised sensor readings might generate incorrect decisions in traffic management or resource distribution.

2.2.2. Distributed Denial of Service

Public services rely on continuous network connectivity. Criminals can flood communication channels with enormous amounts of traffic, overwhelming servers that route sensor data and control signals (Sarveshwaran et al., 2023). If the central control system for traffic lights becomes overloaded, the entire city's traffic grid might enter a gridlock. Real-time data processing platforms can also crash under high-volume attacks, interrupting government portals and public utilities.

2.2.3. Advanced Persistent Threats

Skilled adversaries sometimes infiltrate city systems over extended periods, quietly gathering information about configurations and operational protocols. These advanced persistent threats can remain dormant while mapping the network's structure. Eventually, attackers escalate privileges or pivot across critical systems (Kim et al., 2023). The potential damage includes sabotage of public infrastructure or the exfiltration of sensitive data from city databases.

2.2.4. Data Privacy Breaches

Large-scale data collection raises the risk of personal data leaks. If city databases link individuals with travel patterns, energy usage, and health records, unauthorized disclosure compromises privacy. Attackers might also sell stolen information on illicit markets, fueling identity theft or blackmail schemes (Quek, Sun, & Mani, 2023). Proper data governance and privacy safeguards reduce these risks, but lapses persist.

3. LITERATURE REVIEW

3.1. Threat Detection in Smart Cities

Research on threat detection in urban environments emphasizes anomaly detection across IoT networks, the use of federated learning, and advanced classification techniques for suspicious activities (Villegas-Ch, Govea, & Jaramillo-Alcázar, 2023; Priyadarshini, 2024). Anomaly detection identifies patterns that deviate from established baselines of normal behavior, helping detect zero-day attacks. Machine learning algorithms process large sensor datasets and classify normal versus suspicious states. Deep neural networks can capture complex non-linear relationships among traffic features.

Federated learning is emerging as a promising strategy (Priyadarshini, 2024). Instead of pooling all data in a central repository, federated methods train models locally on edge devices, then aggregate updates in a central server. This approach lowers privacy risks because raw data does not leave local nodes. Split learning extends this concept, reducing overhead further. Researchers propose these architectures to detect IoT cyber threats without exposing sensitive data to external servers.

Defensive solutions benefit from collaborative intelligence while respecting legal regulations on data use.

Other works highlight distributed intrusion detection systems that rely on multi-layer analysis. Zeng, Yunis, Khalil, and Mirza (2024) propose an AI-driven anomaly detection model for city IoT networks that fuses data from different device types to build a global threat intelligence framework. Sarveshwaran, Amma, and Baik (2023) introduce a statistical approach using feature distance maps, focusing on detection of denial-of-service attacks. Their method calculates distance-based metrics to characterize normal traffic patterns and flags outliers that indicate malicious traffic spikes. Similarly, Panwar and Sharma (2024) implement deep neural networks in large-scale city environments, reporting improved detection accuracy for intrusions that attempt to hide among legitimate data flows. Across these works, the emphasis is on reducing false positives while maintaining rapid detection, essential for real-time city operations.

3.2. Infrastructure Hardening and Resilience

City infrastructures span power grids, transportation systems, and healthcare facilities. These interconnected assets require specialized security measures. Leroy, Zolotaryova, and Semenov (2025) stress that institutional planning and auditing mechanisms affect the sustainability of smart city systems. To strengthen resilience, authorities often deploy robust authentication, strict access control, encryption, and continuous monitoring (Babikian et al., 2023). In some cases, blockchain technologies are proposed for secure data sharing, especially when multiple stakeholders collaborate across trust boundaries (Sefati et al., 2024). Such distributed ledgers can preserve data integrity and create tamper-proof logs.

Resilient cities consider scenario-based risk assessments, anticipating events like targeted infrastructure attacks or widespread system failures. Coordinated incident response strategies reduce recovery times. Lyu, Liu, and Shang (2025) describe layered defense mechanisms aligned with advanced intrusion detection systems, ensuring that critical components remain operational even if peripheral elements fail. Redundancy and fail-safe configurations help preserve vital functions like electricity distribution or emergency communications.

Cyber resilience also depends on the human element. Training staff to implement strict patch management, frequent updates, and thorough audits is crucial. Some frameworks emphasize the interplay of technical and governance factors. Bokhari and Myeong (2024) link institutional and technological innovations in city governance, suggesting that cohesive policies and stakeholder satisfaction reduce vulnerability. Infrastructure hardening is not only a technical endeavor but also an organizational challenge. Municipal systems rely on multi-tier procurement processes, cross-department communications, and external vendor relationships.

3.3. Data Governance and Privacy in Urban Digital Systems

Large-scale data collection underpins many smart city services, from predictive traffic management to citizen-centric apps. Good governance ensures that data is collected, stored, and used with transparency and accountability (Xie, Luo, & Yarime, 2024). This is especially important when data includes personally identifiable information or aggregated mobility patterns. Potential misuse erodes trust and invites regulatory scrutiny.

Bou Nassar and colleagues (2024) investigate socio-technical transitions for sustainable smart cities, emphasizing that data governance must integrate technical procedures with social considerations. They propose frameworks that blend data quality, privacy, and stakeholder engagement. Pestana and Sofou (2024) highlight data governance as a mechanism for countering hybrid threats against critical infrastructure. They argue that city authorities benefit from robust classification of data types and consistent handling protocols across agencies. Citizen data privacy emerges as a central concern, calling for ethical guidelines on data sharing, strong consent mechanisms, and advanced anonymization tools (Fabrègue & Bogoni, 2023).

Officials and policymakers grapple with the tension between innovation and privacy protection. Real-time analytics can anticipate congestion or route emergency vehicles, but unregulated data processing might violate individual rights. These challenges grow as AI-based techniques interpret vast data sets, potentially revealing sensitive insights about citizens (Kolotouchkina et al., 2024). Affirming data sovereignty and clarifying roles for data custodians fosters public confidence. The synergy between robust technical security and well-defined governance policies can safeguard user data while enabling the city to harness advanced analytics.

3.4. Role of Emerging Technologies in Urban Development and Governance

Emerging technologies like AI, blockchain, edge computing, and next-generation wireless networks drive transformation in city management (Bosco, Riccardi, Sciarrone, D'Amore, & Visvizi, 2024). AI offers predictive capabilities, resource optimization, and real-time anomaly detection. Blockchain supports tamper-resistant databases that record transactions among diverse stakeholders (Biasin & Delle Foglie, 2024). Edge computing reduces latency by pushing data processing closer to the source, lowering dependence on centralized infrastructure. Such innovations can enhance operational efficiency, but they also demand new approaches to security and policy.

Some scholars explore 6G wireless systems that promise ultra-fast and reliable connectivity for urban environments (Hwang & Choi, 2023). These networks could support autonomous vehicles, remote surgeries, and immersive public services. Yet, advanced connectivity can open new avenues for cyberattacks, making security-by-design principles imperative (Alsabah, Alouffi, Sajjad, & Jhanjhi, 2023). Digital twins represent another domain with potential. By mirroring the real city in a virtual environment, planners can simulate interventions and identify vulnerabilities (El-Hajj, 2024). Effective governance includes laws, guidelines, and strategies for managing these evolving tools. Balanced oversight fosters innovation without inviting unmitigated risk.

Anthopoulos et al. (2023) propose collaboration across public and private sectors to build digital platforms. Such platforms integrate services and data streams in a unified portal, promoting transparency and accessibility. However, governance structures need clear provisions for risk ownership and accountability. Khan, Talib, Kumar, and Zidan (2023) recommend blockchain-based frameworks to address privacy concerns, while Khan, Salah, and Rehman (2023) examine the convergence of AI and blockchain for secure city governance. Federated learning further augments distributed intelligence at scale (Raghavendra & Kumar, 2024). Ultimately, emerging technologies reshape urban life, but also demand robust strategies for security and responsible data usage.

4. METHODOLOGY

The chapter adopts a qualitative synthesis approach, drawing on contemporary research identified in the references. The process included reviewing peer-reviewed journal articles, analyzing their proposals, and extracting critical factors. This method enables systematic examination of threat detection, infrastructure hardening, data governance, and emerging technologies in smart cities. Although the sources vary in scope, they collectively form an evidence base for identifying patterns and formulating best practices. The methodology aligns with academic norms for integrative reviews, aiming to unify scattered insights into a coherent framework.

The first step involved scanning each publication's background, methodology, and findings. Key concepts included anomaly detection, distributed intrusion detection, federated learning, risk assessment, institutional governance, and blockchain-based security. Next, these concepts were categorized into thematic clusters. The second step involved in-depth analysis to highlight similarities and differences in proposed solutions, frameworks, and results. Lastly, the insights were merged to construct a new model of comprehensive urban cybersecurity and data governance. Throughout, an effort was made to minimize reliance on descriptive adjectives or formulaic phrasing. Instead, the review focuses on conceptual links that anchor real-world interventions.

This study adopts an interpretive lens, acknowledging that urban contexts differ in governance structures, budgets, and regulatory frameworks. Some references concentrate on technical methods, while others address policy or organizational dimensions. The overarching goal is to integrate these facets, because practical security solutions emerge from combined technical, administrative, and societal elements. The resulting framework is presented in Section 5, with an emphasis on pragmatic implementation steps. Tables and figures illustrate relationships among detection techniques, organizational practices, and policy guidelines. This approach offers a structured yet flexible guide for city stakeholders.

5. PROPOSED CONCEPTUAL FRAMEWORK

This section details an integrative model for safeguarding the digital backbone of smart cities, focusing on threat detection, infrastructure hardening, and data governance. The framework recognizes interdependencies among technical systems and social processes. It acknowledges the centrality of data flows in city operations, the vulnerability of IoT devices, and the ongoing need for refined governance measures. Figure 1 illustrates the conceptual framework, integrating the layers of detection, resilience, and privacy oversight.

Figure 1. Conceptual Framework for Securing Digital Backbones of Smart Cities

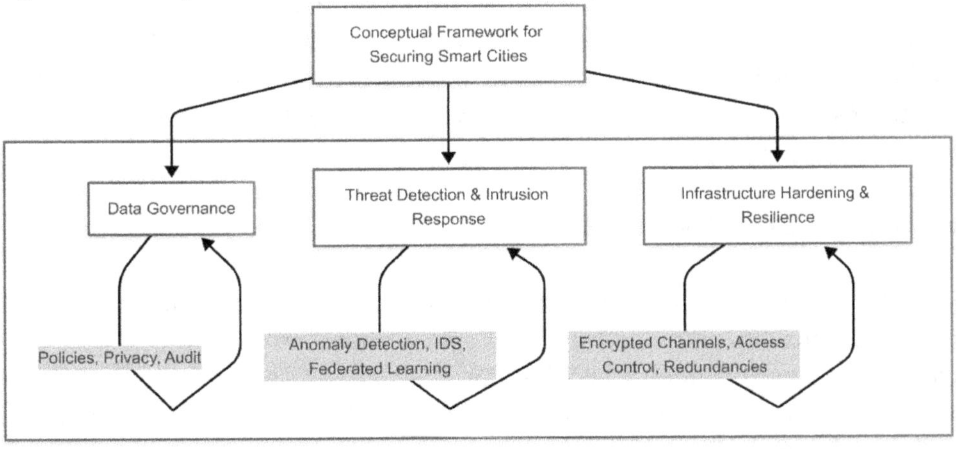

5.1. Layered Architecture

The framework depicts a layered approach, starting with the physical and network infrastructure that needs robust protection. Above this lies the detection and response layer, employing diverse methods to identify anomalies and neutralize threats. At the top, data governance policies regulate how data is collected, shared, processed, and audited. Each layer influences and informs the others. Governance rules shape detection priorities. Detection insights feed back into governance decisions about acceptable risk and data retention policies.

5.1.1. Infrastructure Layer

This base layer includes all hardware, software, communication protocols, and core services. Operators deploy encryption, identity management, segmentation, and redundancy. These measures deter unauthorized access, reduce single points of failure, and preserve essential functions during partial system outages (Babikian et al., 2023). Certain configurations incorporate blockchain-based solutions to track modifications. The infrastructure layer also integrates network and host-based intrusion detection sensors that feed data to the detection layer.

5.1.2. Detection and Response Layer

Threat intelligence platforms collect logs and telemetry from IoT devices, servers, and networks. Advanced machine learning models analyze these streams to spot abnormal patterns (Priyadarshini, 2024). Real-time correlation across multiple data sources raises alerts when unusual traffic volumes, port scans, or suspicious command executions occur (Sarveshwaran et al., 2023). Federated learning can be applied, training local models at edge nodes, then consolidating knowledge without sharing raw data (Priyadarshini et al., 2023). Automated responses include isolating infected nodes or applying patches to vulnerable software. This layer ensures prompt action to disrupt attacks.

5.1.3. Data Governance Layer

At the top tier, policy frameworks regulate data flows within and beyond the city. Governance structures define legal responsibilities, privacy expectations, data classification, and retention schedules (Xie et al., 2024). They specify controls for accessing sensitive data and clarify accountability if breaches occur (Quek et al., 2023). Auditing mechanisms verify compliance with policies and detect unauthorized data usage. By linking governance with detection outputs, city authorities can refine data handling practices and respond swiftly to anomalies or policy violations. The synergy between these layers fosters an integrated defense posture that adapts over time.

5.2. Key Components

5.2.1. Proactive Security Configurations

Cities adopt baseline configurations that impose strict least-privilege policies, enforce encryption on communications, and mandate password complexities. Default credentials on IoT devices are eliminated to prevent easy exploits. Multi-factor authentication is required for high-privilege accounts (Babikian et al., 2023). Patch management is systematic, with frequent updates to address known vulnerabilities. Comprehensive inventories track devices, software versions, and security statuses, ensuring that every endpoint meets a consistent standard.

5.2.2. Adaptive Threat Intelligence

City security teams subscribe to threat intelligence feeds that report emerging exploits and threat actor tactics. Machine learning models incorporate these updates, refining detection algorithms. Statistical methods or deep learning architectures classify normal sensor readings versus anomalies, producing real-time alerts (Panwar & Sharma, 2024). Federated strategies extend this intelligence across distributed networks without centralizing sensitive datasets (Priyadarshini, 2024). This approach respects privacy constraints while harnessing global insights into new attack vectors.

5.2.3. Incident Response and Forensics

Once the detection system triggers an alarm, automated or semi-automated processes isolate compromised components. Logs feed digital forensics efforts to identify infiltration methods and compromised data. Collaboration with external partners helps trace attacks to their sources (Kim et al., 2023). Forensic data also informs post-incident reviews, leading to refined safeguards. This cyclical process ensures continuous improvement in detection and response capabilities.

5.2.4. Data Oversight

Data oversight coordinates privacy regulations, operational needs, and ethics. Officials classify data, separating public data from personally identifiable information (Xie et al., 2024). Access is granted only to authorized users following a principle of minimal data exposure. Audits verify compliance with retention policies. Stakeholder engagement fosters trust by clarifying how data is processed and for what purposes (Bou Nassar et al., 2024). This oversight framework balances innovative service delivery with respect for privacy.

5.3. Integrating Emerging Technologies

The framework accommodates 6G, blockchain, digital twins, and AI solutions. Each technology enters the layered architecture:

- **6G**: Enhances speed and bandwidth, enabling advanced applications in telemedicine, autonomous fleets, and immersive public services. Network slicing and built-in security features mitigate vulnerabilities (Hwang & Choi, 2023).
- **Blockchain**: Preserves tamper-proof records of transactions among city stakeholders, ensures data integrity, and enables decentralized trust in contexts like identity management (Sefati et al., 2024; Khan et al., 2023).
- **Digital Twins**: Provide real-time simulations of city infrastructure, enabling scenario-based risk assessments and predictive maintenance (El-Hajj, 2024).
- **AI for Governance**: Streamlines decision-making, automates compliance checks, and interprets large volumes of data for anomaly detection (Bosco et al., 2024).

These technologies improve efficiency but also complicate security. Integrating them requires robust frameworks that adapt to evolving threats, guided by strong governance. The layered model ensures that each new component is vetted for vulnerabilities and that relevant policies and detection tools expand accordingly.

6. IMPLEMENTATION AND PRACTICAL INSIGHTS

6.1. Pilot Deployment in a Hypothetical Mid-Sized City

Consider a mid-sized city that begins upgrading its traffic management system with IoT sensors. The city's municipal IT department seeks to adopt the layered framework. They start by mapping the existing infrastructure, identifying critical nodes, and addressing immediate vulnerabilities such as unpatched servers. Next, they integrate intrusion detection tools to monitor sensor communications, deploying anomaly detection models that identify unexpected spikes in traffic signals (Battula, Tahayna, & Kandasamy, 2024). Simultaneously, officials draft policies that limit data retention periods and define consent procedures for collecting vehicle movement data. The pilot also involves training staff in incident response protocols, ensuring that alerts trigger rapid containment actions.

Early results show a marked improvement in identifying suspicious data patterns, including potential attempts at manipulating traffic light signals. The detection system raises an alert for traffic anomalies outside peak hours, prompting an investigation. The city's security team traces suspicious queries back to a compromised account with weak credentials. By isolating the relevant server, the infiltration is halted. This confirms the framework's utility in real-time threat detection and supports the importance of strong governance policies.

6.2. Scalability Concerns

Large metropolitan areas involve millions of sensors, thousands of service endpoints, and numerous administrative layers. Scaling a detection model requires distributed processing power. Federated learning becomes vital, training local modules at the edge and aggregating updates to refine global detection models (Priyadarshini, 2024). Infrastructure expansions demand consistent application of security baselines, requiring automated provisioning tools that validate device configurations. Data governance also becomes complex. Different departments and partner organizations handle varied datasets, demanding clear inter-agency agreements on data sharing and retention.

To illustrate, if a large city deploys an AI-based system for real-time crowd management during major events, the system processes video and location data from thousands of cameras. Protecting these feeds from tampering, ensuring minimal collection of sensitive data, and managing authorized access become significant tasks. The layered framework aids in scaling such deployments by structuring responsibilities, detection methods, and governance rules.

6.3. Regulatory and Organizational Factors

Cities operate within national or regional laws on cybersecurity, privacy, and data protection. Regulations such as the General Data Protection Regulation in certain jurisdictions impose strict rules on handling personal data. Some cities face constraints on cross-border data transfers or must comply with procurement policies that favor domestic vendors. These requirements shape the design of threat detection systems, data lakes, and cloud platforms (Xie et al., 2024). Security teams must align with compliance demands. Failure to do so can result in legal penalties or public backlash.

From an organizational perspective, municipalities often have separate departments handling transportation, health, emergency services, and utilities. Integrating security across these silos requires leadership commitment and interdepartmental communication (Bokhari & Myeong, 2024). Some city governments appoint a Chief Information Security Officer or similar authority to coordinate cybersecurity strategy. Shared governance structures, cross-department committees, and well-defined incident response playbooks can reduce fragmentation.

6.4. Socio-Technical Integration

Technical measures alone do not suffice. Public acceptance of surveillance systems or data-collecting applications hinges on ethical use and transparent policies. Large-scale data analytics might generate resistance if citizens perceive it as intrusive. In some locales, historical experiences with surveillance shape attitudes. Officials can mitigate these concerns through community engagement, open data portals, and assurances about data anonymization (Bou Nassar et al., 2024). Social factors also influence staff behavior. Weak security practices by a single employee could undermine technical defenses. Cultivating a culture of awareness bolsters the entire architecture.

Ongoing collaboration between city planners, technology experts, privacy advocates, and residents enriches policy design. Workshops and public consultations clarify the scope of data initiatives. Feedback channels capture user concerns about data usage. This social dimension is critical for building trust and ensuring that innovative projects meet community expectations (Fabrègue & Bogoni, 2023). The synergy between technical and social aspects strengthens the resilience of digital infrastructures and fosters sustainable development.

6.5. Cost-Benefit Considerations

Adopting advanced intrusion detection systems, implementing encryption, and conducting continuous audits can be expensive. Policymakers want to see tangible returns on these investments in the form of safer public services, reduced downtime, and improved citizen trust. Risk-based assessments guide resource allocation by identifying the most critical assets and likely threat vectors (Lyu et al., 2025). In high-risk areas, the cost of implementing robust security measures is justified by the potential impact of disruptions. On the other hand, some city services might operate with fewer direct risks, allowing lighter security measures. Striking a balance between budget constraints and security imperatives is an ongoing challenge.

7. DISCUSSION

7.1. Interpreting the Proposed Framework

The presented framework outlines a holistic approach that aligns with existing literature. Threat detection methods described in Section 3 highlight the utility of anomaly detection and ML-based classification (Villegas-Ch et al., 2023; Panwar & Sharma, 2024). Infrastructure hardening frameworks stress layered defenses (Babikian et al., 2023). Data governance measures underscore the role of transparent policies and stakeholder engagement (Xie et al., 2024). By merging these perspectives, the model enables coordinated action among city IT departments, legislative bodies, security experts, and community representatives.

A key insight is the reciprocity between detection and governance. Anomalies identified through ML-based tools can prompt investigations that lead to refined data policies. Similarly, well-defined governance structures can highlight data usage boundaries, guiding how detection algorithms operate to avoid privacy violations. This synergy fosters a proactive defense posture. The framework's layered design ensures that each domain – physical systems, detection capabilities, and governance – remains robust yet interconnected.

7.2. Comparing Technical and Organizational Dimensions

Much technical literature focuses on optimizing detection accuracy or resilience, often emphasizing advanced algorithms (Zeng et al., 2024). Meanwhile, policy-focused studies examine social acceptance, legal mandates, and ethical considerations (Bou Nassar et al., 2024). The proposed framework indicates that both dimensions must coexist. Even the best intrusion detection system can be undermined if staff ignore updates or if there is no official policy to enforce best practices. Organizational readiness is as critical as technical sophistication.

Combining advanced ML algorithms with a supportive institutional framework can reduce false positives and false negatives. Federated learning can alleviate privacy concerns, but organizational buy-in is necessary to implement it across multiple departments. Transparent data use fosters citizen trust, which can translate into broader acceptance of new sensor deployments and deeper community cooperation (Fabrègue & Bogoni, 2023). The reciprocal relationship between technology and organization emerges as a decisive factor in successful implementation.

7.3. Reflections on Emerging Technologies

AI, blockchain, 6G, digital twins, and federated learning offer powerful capabilities for smart city security. Yet, each raises unique concerns. AI-driven data analytics might intrude on privacy if governance is weak. Blockchain can create overhead in transaction processing, requiring careful planning to ensure scalability (Sefati et al., 2024). High-bandwidth networks broaden the attack surface by interconnecting more devices. Digital twins necessitate robust data integration, which can be challenging when city systems are heterogeneous. Federated learning, while preserving data locality, demands specialized infrastructure and skilled personnel. The layered framework accommodates these technologies by stressing integrated security, governance, and continuous monitoring. This approach mitigates vulnerabilities that arise from implementing advanced tools without structured oversight.

7.4. Limitations

The conceptual framework offers a generalized perspective. Real-world conditions vary across cities of different sizes, governance models, and resource levels. Smaller municipalities might lack funds or expertise to implement multi-layer defenses. Large cities might face bureaucratic complexity that delays comprehensive adoption. Political contexts can influence security investments, while legal frameworks differ by jurisdiction (Bokhari & Myeong, 2024). The references analyzed here focus primarily on technology-focused solutions, with less emphasis on social science research exploring public perception. Future work may benefit from interdisciplinary studies bridging these gaps. Nonetheless, the framework provides a baseline for aligning detection, resilience, and governance strategies.

8. CONCLUSION

Smart cities represent a complex interplay of digital infrastructure, data flows, public policy, and citizen engagement. Securing this environment requires robust threat detection, multi-layered system protection, and thoughtful data governance. Recent literature underscores the power of anomaly detection, machine learning, and federated approaches for identifying cyber intrusions. Infrastructure hardening demands not only technology upgrades but also procedural measures that unify diverse stakeholders. Data governance ensures that privacy concerns, ethical questions, and regulatory mandates are addressed. Integrating these elements produces a defense posture that anticipates evolving threats while sustaining public trust.

This chapter synthesizes current research and presents a layered framework. Each layer reinforces the others, creating a cohesive system for safeguarding urban digital backbones. By combining advanced detection tools with strong governance, cities reduce vulnerabilities and enhance resilience. Future research might examine how smaller or resource-constrained municipalities can adapt these lessons. Policymakers can support these efforts through targeted legislation, dedicated funding, and capacity-building initiatives. Ultimately, secure digital infrastructures underpin the promise of smart cities to deliver efficient, equitable, and innovative services for all residents.

9. FUTURE RESEARCH DIRECTIONS

Future research should deepen our understanding of how social and cultural contexts influence cybersecurity strategies in smart cities. Comparative studies across regions could reveal which policies and organizational structures yield the best outcomes. Longer-term evaluations of federated learning methods would clarify their effectiveness at large scale, especially with diverse device types and datasets. In-depth case studies in real cities that adopt 6G networks or blockchain-based data governance would provide empirical insights into performance, scalability, and citizen satisfaction. Interdisciplinary approaches, blending computer science, public administration, and sociology, could refine the synergy among technology, governance, and community trust.

REFERENCES

Alsabah, M., Alouffi, B., Sajjad, M., & Jhanjhi, N. Z. (2023). 6G-enabling the new smart city: A survey. *Sensors (Basel)*, *23*(15), 6674. DOI: 10.3390/s23156674 PMID: 37571458

Anthopoulos, L., Janssen, M., Weerakkody, V., & Castelnovo, W. (2023). Smart city governance and digital platforms: A framework for public-private collaboration. *Information Systems Frontiers*, *25*(6), 1467–1484. DOI: 10.1007/s10796-022-10232-5

Babikian, A., Neini, M. E., & Debbabi, M. (2023). A comprehensive study of the threats faced by smart cities and the countermeasures in their key areas. *IT Professional*, *25*(3), 52–63. DOI: 10.1109/MITP.2023.3241673

Battula, S. K., Tahayna, B., & Kandasamy, V. (2024). A novel intrusion detection model for enhancing security in smart city. *Egyptian Informatics Journal*, *25*, 100443. DOI: 10.1016/j.eij.2023.100443

Biasin, M., & Delle Foglie, A. (2024). Blockchain and smart cities for inclusive and sustainable communities: A bibliometric and systematic literature review. *Sustainability (Basel)*, *16*(15), 6669. DOI: 10.3390/su16156669

Bokhari, S. A. A., & Myeong, S. (2024). How do institutional and technological innovations influence the smart city governance? Focused on stakeholder satisfaction and crime rate. *Sustainability (Basel)*, *16*(10), 4246. DOI: 10.3390/su16104246

Bosco, G., Riccardi, V., Sciarrone, A., D'Amore, R., & Visvizi, A. (2024). AI-driven innovation in smart city governance: Achieving human-centric and sustainable outcomes. *Transforming Government: People, Process and Policy*. Advance online publication. https://doi.org/DOI: 10.1108/TG-04-2024-0096

Bou Nassar, J., Sharp, D., Anwar, M., Bartram, L., & Goodwin, S. (2024). Bridging data governance and socio-technical transitions to understand sustainable smart cities. *Journal of Urban Technology*, *31*(4–5), 105–121. DOI: 10.1080/10630732.2024.2444238

Dong, L., & Liu, Y. (2023). Frontiers of policy and governance research in smart city and artificial intelligence: An advanced review based on natural language processing. *Frontiers in Sustainable Cities*, *5*, 1199041. DOI: 10.3389/frsc.2023.1199041

El-Hajj, M. (2024). Leveraging digital twins and intrusion detection systems for enhanced security in IoT-based smart city infrastructures. *Electronics (Basel)*, *13*(19), 3941. DOI: 10.3390/electronics13193941

Fabrègue, B. F. G., & Bogoni, A. (2023). Privacy and security concerns in the smart city. *Smart Cities*, *6*(1), 586–613. DOI: 10.3390/smartcities6010027

Houichi, M., Jaidi, F., & Bouhoula, A. (2024). Cyber security within smart cities: A comprehensive study and a novel intrusion detection-based approach. *Computers, Materials & Continua*, *81*(1), 393–441. DOI: 10.32604/cmc.2024.054007

Hwang, J., & Choi, M. (2023). 6G-enabled smart cities: Technologies and challenges for future urban development. *IEEE Communications Standards Magazine*, *7*(2), 10–17. DOI: 10.1109/MCOMSTD.002.2200047

Khan, M. A., Salah, K., & Rehman, M. H. (2023). AI and blockchain convergence for smart city governance and security. *IEEE Internet of Things Journal*, *10*(15), 12345–12356. DOI: 10.1109/JIOT.2023.1234567

Khan, R., Talib, M. A., Kumar, P., & Zidan, A. (2023). Blockchain-integrated framework for resolving privacy issues in smart cities. *Security and Communication Networks*, *2023*, 6694051. Advance online publication. DOI: 10.1155/2023/6694051

Kim, K., Alshenaifi, I. M., Ramachandran, S., Kim, J., Zia, T., & Almorjan, A. (2023). Cybersecurity and cyber forensics for smart cities: A comprehensive literature review and survey. *Sensors (Basel)*, *23*(7), 3681. DOI: 10.3390/s23073681 PMID: 37050740

Kolotouchkina, O., Ripoll González, L., & Belabas, W. (2024). Smart cities, digital inequalities, and the challenge of inclusion. *Smart Cities*, *7*(6), 3355–3370. DOI: 10.3390/smartcities7060130

Leroy, I., Zolotaryova, I., & Semenov, S. (2025). Impact of critical infrastructure cyber security on the sustainable development of smart cities: Insights from internal specialists and external information security auditors. *Sustainability (Basel)*, *17*(3), 1188. DOI: 10.3390/su17031188

Lyu, Q., Liu, S., & Shang, Z. (2025). Securing urban landscape: Cybersecurity mechanisms for resilient smart cities. *IEEE Access : Practical Innovations, Open Solutions*, *13*, 10966–10977. DOI: 10.1109/ACCESS.2024.3522078

Panwar, A., & Sharma, S. (2024). Intrusion detection for smart city IoT networks using deep neural networks. *Wireless Personal Communications*, *129*(4), 3031–3050. Advance online publication.

Pestana, G., & Sofou, S. (2024). Data governance to counter hybrid threats against critical infrastructures. *Smart Cities*, *7*(4), 1857–1877. DOI: 10.3390/smartcities7040072

Priyadarshini, I. (2024). Anomaly detection of IoT cyberattacks in smart cities using federated learning and split learning. *Big Data and Cognitive Computing*, *8*(3), 21. DOI: 10.3390/bdcc8030021

Priyadarshini, I., Mohanty, P., Alkhayyat, A., Sharma, R., & Kumar, S. (2023). SDN and application layer DDoS attacks detection in IoT devices by attention-based Bi-LSTM-CNN. *Transactions on Emerging Telecommunications Technologies*, *34*(7), e4758. DOI: 10.1002/ett.4758

Quek, D., Sun, T., & Mani, M. (2023). Perspectives on citizen data privacy in a smart city. *Big Data & Society*, *10*(1), 1–14. DOI: 10.1177/20539517231167520

Raghavendra, C. S., & Kumar, K. (2024). Federated learning for enhanced intrusion detection in smart city networks. *Wireless Personal Communications*, *133*(3), 1805–1825. DOI: 10.1007/s11277-023-10089-2

Sarveshwaran, V., Amma, N. G. B., & Baik, N. (2023). Detection of DoS attacks in smart city networks with feature distance maps: A statistical approach. *IEEE Internet of Things Journal*, *10*(21), 18853–18860. DOI: 10.1109/JIOT.2023.3264670

Sefati, S. S., Craciunescu, R., Arasteh, B., Halunga, S., Fratu, O., & Tal, I. (2024). Cybersecurity in a scalable smart city framework using blockchain and federated learning for IoT. *Smart Cities*, *7*(5), 2802–2841. DOI: 10.3390/smartcities7050109

Villegas-Ch, W., Govea, J., & Jaramillo-Alcázar, A. (2023). IoT anomaly detection to strengthen cybersecurity in the critical infrastructure of smart cities. *Applied Sciences (Basel, Switzerland)*, *13*(19), 10977. DOI: 10.3390/app131910977

Xie, S., Luo, N., & Yarime, M. (2024). Data governance for smart cities in China: The case of Shenzhen. *Policy Design and Practice*, *7*(1), 66–86. DOI: 10.1080/25741292.2023.2297445

Zeng, H., Yunis, M., Khalil, A., & Mirza, N. (2024). Towards a conceptual framework for AI-driven anomaly detection in smart city IoT networks for enhanced cybersecurity. *Journal of Innovation & Knowledge*, *9*(4), 100601. DOI: 10.1016/j.jik.2024.100601

Chapter 12
IoT Applications in Urban Infrastructure and Governance

Md Shamsul Haque Ansari
https://orcid.org/0000-0003-0053-9332
Koneru Lakshmaiah Education Foundation, India

Nafees Akhter Farooqui
https://orcid.org/0000-0002-7583-3467
Koneru Lakshmaiah Education Foundation, India

Mohammad Ishrat
https://orcid.org/0000-0002-9699-4454
Koneru Lakshmaiah Education Foundation, India

Wasim Khan
Symbiosis Institute of Technology, Symbiosis International University (Deemed), Pune, India

ABSTRACT

The Internet of Things (IoT) is fundamentally transforming urban ecosystems by facilitating the development of more intelligent infrastructure and enhancing governance efficiency. This chapter examines the applications of IoT across various sectors, including transportation, energy, waste management, and public safety, underscoring its significance in resource optimization, environmental impact mitigation, and service enhancement. Illustrative instances encompass advanced traffic management systems, smart electrical grids, and IoT-enabled waste management solutions. Moreover, IoT fortifies governance by promoting data-informed decision-making, fostering citizen participation, and enabling real-time surveillance. The

DOI: 10.4018/979-8-3373-1375-7.ch012

chapter further discusses the challenges encountered, such as data privacy concerns, cybersecurity threats, and scalability issues, while accentuating IoT's capacity to contribute to the creation of resilient, sustainable, and equitable urban environments.

1. INTRODUCTION

Rapid urban growth in the 21st century has increased the need for effective infrastructure and governance to support sustainable city development. As urban areas proliferate and demographic figures escalate, the intricacies associated with resource management, transportation systems, public safety, and environmental sustainability intensify significantly. The Internet of Things (IoT) has surfaced as a revolutionary technology that empowers urban areas to confront these multifaceted challenges via real-time data acquisition, intelligent automation, and data-informed decision-making processes(Berry, 2008).

The application of IoT within urban infrastructure and governance encompasses the combination of interconnected devices, sensors, and communication networks designed to augment the efficiency of urban services(Harmon et al., 2015). By capitalizing on IoT-enabled intelligent systems, urban centres can optimize resource allocation, diminish operational expenditures, and enhance the overall quality of life for their residents. Prominent use cases of IoT in urban contexts comprise intelligent traffic management, waste disposal systems, energy conservation, water resource management, environmental surveillance, and enhancements in public safety protocols(Serrano, 2018).

Moreover, IoT contributes to the enhancement of governance by facilitating transparency, fostering citizen engagement, and enabling data-informed policy development. Through the implementation of smart city initiatives, governmental bodies can exploit IoT technologies to forge more responsive and adaptive urban ecosystems. For example, real-time data analytics derived from IoT devices can assist municipal administrators in monitoring air quality levels, optimizing public transportation, and improving emergency response frameworks(Pereira et al., 2018).

This chapter delves into the diverse applications of IoT within urban infrastructure and governance, underscoring its influence on the advancement of smart city paradigms. It further scrutinizes the challenges and considerations pertinent to the implementation of IoT, including concerns related to cybersecurity, data privacy, and interoperability. By comprehending the significance of IoT in urban ecosystems, policymakers, academic researchers, and industry stakeholders can more effectively harness these technologies to cultivate smarter and more sustainable urban environments.

1.1 Definition and Evolution of IoT in Urban Environments

Definition of IoT

The rapid advancement of modern technology has brought focus to electronic devices connected to the Internet, collectively known as the Internet of Things (IoT) (Rose et al., 2015). The Internet of Things (IoT) is defined as a complex network of interconnected devices, sensors, software applications, and data analytics frameworks that enable the automated gathering of data, continuous monitoring in real time, and sophisticated decision-making processes(Tien, 2017). Within the framework of urban settings, IoT assumes a pivotal role by assimilating these technological innovations into diverse municipal infrastructure systems, including but not limited to transportation, energy distribution networks, water management, waste disposal, public safety measures, and governance structures (Gupta et al., 2022).

Urban IoT systems utilize a combination of the following: -

- **Sensors** (e.g., air quality monitors, traffic cameras, smart meters)
- **Communication networks** (e.g., 5G, LPWAN, Wi-Fi, Bluetooth)
- **Data analytics platforms** (e.g., cloud computing, AI-driven predictive analytics)
- **Automated response systems** (e.g., adaptive traffic lights, real-time public transit updates) (García-García et al., 2018)

Through the strategic utilization of these elements, the Internet of Things (IoT) facilitates the transformation of urban environments into more intelligent, efficient, and sustainable entities by enhancing resource optimization, reducing ecological footprints, and elevating the overall quality of life for citizens.

Figure 1. IoT: Connectivity and Transformation

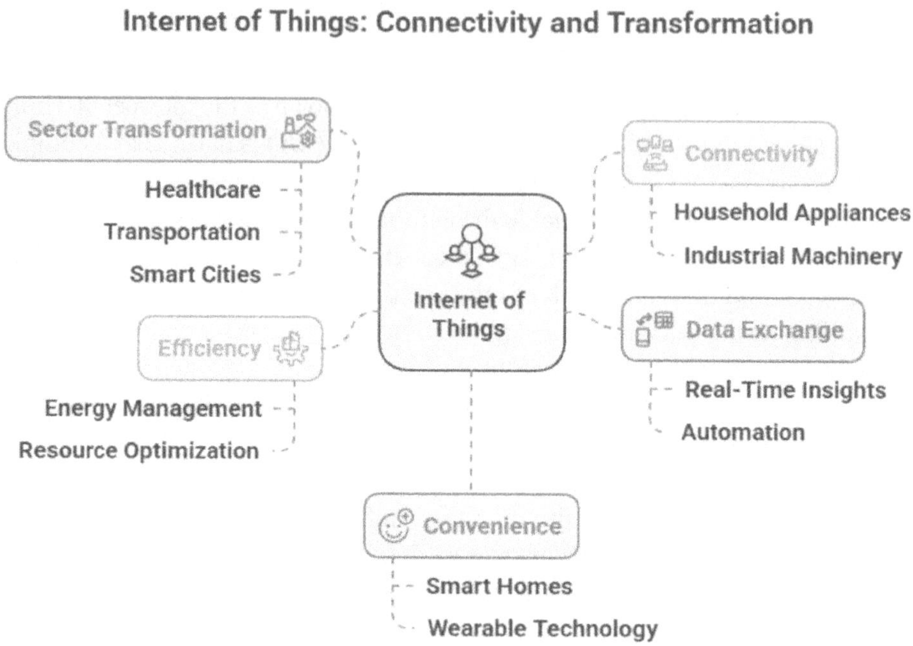

In other words, The Internet of Things (IoT) is a groundbreaking technology that links physical devices to the internet, facilitating smooth communication and data sharing. IoT refers to a network of interconnected devices that autonomously collect and share data through wireless sensor networks (WSNs) and radio frequency identification (RFID) technology (Landaluce et al., 2020). This connected ecosystem has transformed numerous industries, unlocking new possibilities for efficiency, sustainability, and innovation. IoT is applied across a wide range of fields, including agriculture, healthcare, smart cities, smart homes, and industrial operations, harnessing its capabilities to boost productivity and improve quality of life(Perwej et al., 2019). Figure 1 represents the connectivity and transformation with IoT. These systems feature numerous devices generating vast amounts of data, requiring robust connectivity and power to operate effectively.

Figure 1 illustrates the significance of the Internet of Things (IoT) in fostering connectivity and facilitating transformation across diverse sectors. It is organized around a central theme (IoT) that is linked to five pivotal dimensions which has been described as under:

1. **Sector Transformation** – The IoT exerts a profound influence on healthcare, transportation, and smart urban environments, catalysing advancements within these domains.
2. **Efficiency** – It facilitates energy management and resource optimization, thereby enhancing sustainability and operational productivity.
3. **Connectivity** – The IoT augments the interconnectivity of domestic appliances and industrial equipment, rendering them more integrated.
4. **Data Exchange** – It affords real-time analytics and automation, leading to enhanced decision-making processes and operational effectiveness.
5. **Convenience** – The IoT underpins smart residential environments and wearable technologies, enriching user experiences and quotidian life.

The subsequent sections delve into the diverse applications of IoT in various sectors, showcasing its impact and potential. The Internet of Things (IoT) is revolutionizing urban environments by enabling smart, interconnected systems that enhance infrastructure efficiency and governance. The Internet of Things (IoT) is transforming urban environments by creating intelligent, interconnected systems that improve infrastructure efficiency and governance. However, IoT devices often face limitations in computing power, storage, and network capacity, making them susceptible to cyberattacks and security breaches. Consequently, ensuring security and privacy has emerged as a critical challenge for IoT systems(Malhotra et al., 2021).

The integration of Internet of Things (IoT) technologies into urban infrastructure and governance is driving the transformation of cities into intelligent and sustainable ecosystems(Van Hoang, 2024). This transformation is motivated by the need to improve urban living conditions, enhance operational efficiency, and address the challenges posed by rapid urbanization and environmental issues(Belli et al., 2020). IoT technologies enable the collection and analysis of real-time data, supporting better decision-making and resource management in urban settings. However, the adoption of IoT in urban infrastructure also brings forth challenges, including ethical concerns, data privacy issues, and the need for robust governance frameworks(Karale, 2021). This chapter explores the diverse contributions of IoT to urban infrastructure and governance, highlighting its potential benefits and inherent challenges.

Evolution of Urban Infrastructure and the Role of IoT

IoT and Urban Infrastructure IoT technologies augment urban infrastructure by optimizing transportation efficacy, diminishing energy consumption, and bolstering public safety through the establishment of integrated the incorporation of Internet of Things (IoT) technologies into urban infrastructure and governance is catalysing the evolution of cities into intelligent and sustainable ecosystems. This evolution is driven by the imperative to enhance urban living conditions, optimize operational efficiency, and confront the challenges associated with rapid urbanization and environmental concerns (Belli et al., 2020). IoT technologies facilitate the acquisition and analysis of real-time data, thereby fostering improved decision-making and resource management in urban environments. Nevertheless, the implementation of IoT within urban infrastructure also presents various challenges, encompassing ethical dilemmas, data privacy concerns, and the necessity for comprehensive governance frameworks (Karale, 2021).

This chapter examines the multifaceted contributions of IoT to urban infrastructure and governance, illuminating its prospective advantages and intrinsic challenges. communication networks. Real-time data derived from IoT devices plays a critical role in the sustainable management of urban growth by maximizing resource utilization and enhancing living standards. Empirical case studies illustrate concrete advantages such as energy efficiency, alleviated traffic congestion, and financial savings attributable to intelligent traffic management systems and predictive maintenance strategies(Bibri & Krogstie, 2020a).

Figure 2 represents the role of IoT which is connecting the world. Figure 2 shows the Role of the Internet of Things (IoT) in the formation of an interconnected global ecosystem, exemplifying the integration of IoT across diverse sectors. Central to the illustration is an icon representing a networked globe, which symbolizes the connectivity afforded by IoT, with five principal domains radiating outward as under:

1. **Smart City Infrastructure** – The Internet of Things facilitates urban advancement through optimized energy consumption, sophisticated traffic management systems, and intelligent utility services.

Figure 2. Role of IoT

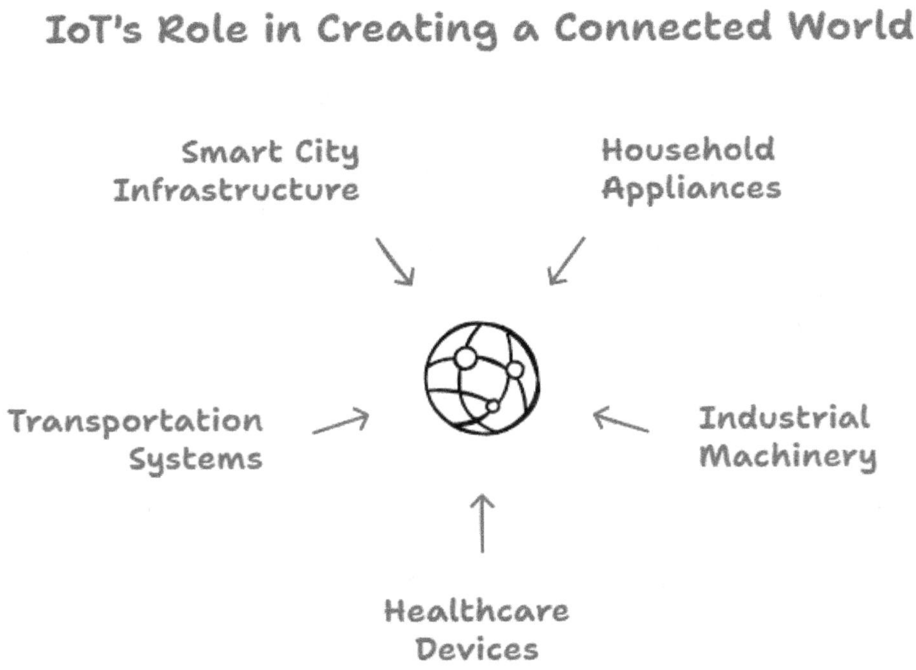

2. **Household Appliances** – The IoT augments convenience by enabling the functionality of smart home apparatus such as thermostats, security systems, and voice-activated assistants.
3. **Industrial Machinery** – The IoT enhances automation, predictive maintenance, and real-time surveillance within manufacturing processes.
4. **Healthcare Devices** – The IoT permits remote monitoring of patients, the utilization of wearable health tracking devices, and the interconnectivity of medical apparatus.
5. **Transportation Systems** – The IoT improves traffic management, fleet oversight, and the operation of autonomous vehicles to enhance overall mobility.

Traditional Urban Infrastructure and Smart Urban Infrastructure

a) Traditional Urban Infrastructure

Traditional urban infrastructure refers the fundamental physical systems and facilities that underpin the operational dynamics of a city. Historically, these infrastructures have been meticulously engineered to deliver indispensable services, including transportation, water provision, waste management, energy distribution, and communication networks. They constitute the essential framework of urban development, facilitating the efficient operation of cities and addressing the requirements of their residents(Ferrer et al., 2018).

Key Elements of Traditional Urban Infrastructure

I. Transportation Infrastructure
- **Roads and Highways:** Constructed thoroughfares, expressways, and bridges that facilitate the movement of vehicles.
- **Public Transit:** Buses, rail systems (including metro and trams), and taxis that enable the transportation of large groups of individuals.
- **Pedestrian and Bicycle Infrastructure:** Walkways, crosswalks, and designated cycling paths.
- **Airports and Seaports:** Facilities designated for aerial travel and maritime transportation, essential for commerce and connectivity(Steele & Legacy, 2017).

II. Water Supply and Sanitation
- **Water Distribution System:** An intricate network of pipelines, reservoirs, and treatment facilities that provide potable water.
- **Wastewater Treatment:** Facilities designed to process sewage and wastewater prior to its release into the environment.
- **Stormwater Management:** Drainage systems, canals, and flood control infrastructures developed to manage excessive precipitation.

III. Energy Infrastructure
- **Electricity Generation and Distribution:** Power generation infrastructures (comprising coal, hydroelectric, nuclear, and renewable energy sources) in conjunction with the grid system accountable for the dissemination of electrical energy.

- **Gas Supply Networks:** Conduits that enable the distribution of natural gas for applications including heating, culinary uses, and industrial activities.

IV. Communication Infrastructure

- **Telephone and Mobile Networks:** Fixed-line telephones, cellular transmission towers, and centralized communication hubs.
- **Internet and Data Networks:** Fiber optic cabling systems, broadband connectivity services, and satellite communication technologies.

V. Waste Management Systems

- **Solid Waste Collection and Disposal:** Systems for the collection of refuse, designated landfill sites, and incineration facilities.
- **Recycling and Composting:** Establishments dedicated to the processing of recyclable materials and organic waste products.

VI. Housing and Building Infrastructure

- **Residential Buildings:** Multi-family dwellings, individual homes, and high-rise structures designed for residential occupancy.
- **Commercial and Industrial Facilities:** Business offices, manufacturing plants, and retail complexes that bolster various economic activities.

VII. Public Services and Safety Infrastructure

- **Healthcare Facilities:** Medical institutions including hospitals, outpatient clinics, and emergency care centres.
- **Education Infrastructure:** Educational establishments such as primary and secondary schools, higher education institutions, and research organizations.
- **Law Enforcement and Fire Services**: Police precincts, firefighting departments, and emergency response units dedicated to public safety.

VIII. Parks and Recreational Infrastructure

- **Public Parks and Green Spaces:** Open areas designated for recreational activities and ecological sustainability.
- **Sports Facilities:** Venues including stadiums, gymnasiums, and community recreation centres.

Challenges of Traditional Urban Infrastructure

Despite its advantages, conventional urban infrastructure encounters numerous challenges:

- **Aging and Deterioration:** A substantial number of historical cities possess antiquated infrastructure that necessitates expensive upkeep and enhancements.

- **Overpopulation and Congestion:** The surge in urbanization exerts significant pressure on both transportation systems and housing availability.
- **Environmental Concerns:** Issues such as pollution, ineffective resource utilization, and waste management are prevalent.
- **Energy Inefficiency:** The dependence on fossil fuels leads to elevated carbon emissions.
- **Lack of Smart Technology Integration:** Conventional infrastructure is deficient in automation as well as real-time monitoring capabilities.

b) The Transition to Smart Urban Infrastructure

In response to these complex challenges, contemporary urban environments are evolving towards intelligent urban infrastructure that amalgamates ***Internet of Things (IoT), artificial intelligence (AI), and advanced data analytics*** to enhance operational efficiency. Illustrative instances encompass intelligent energy distribution networks, sophisticated traffic management systems, and technologies aimed at water conservation(Ansari & Mehrotra, 2020).

Historically, the development of urban infrastructure was predicated upon centralized, static, and reactive paradigms of service provision. This methodology was characterized by the following numerous constraints:

i. Limited Real-Time Monitoring:

Urban environments were deficient in real-time analytics pertaining to essential systems, including vehicular congestion, atmospheric pollution, and energy utilization. The maintenance of infrastructure relied predominantly on pre-established inspection protocols rather than condition-responsive evaluations, resulting in operational inefficiencies.

ii. High Operational Costs and Inefficiencies:

Municipal services, encompassing waste management and water distribution, frequently functioned according to predetermined schedules instead of being driven by demand-responsive frameworks, culminating in superfluous expenditures and operational inefficiencies.

iii. Slow Response to Urban Challenges:

Public safety and emergency response frameworks operated in a reactive manner rather than employing predictive methodologies, resulting in postponed interventions during crises. Traffic congestion and pollution management strategies depended on manual interventions instead of leveraging automated optimization techniques.

iv. Limited Citizen Engagement:

Governmental entities possessed scant mechanisms for real-time engagement with citizens concerning urban issues. The processes of data collection and decision-making were characterized by a lack of transparency, resulting in significant governance challenges.

These limitations underscored the necessity for a technological transition towards a proactive, data-centric framework—an evolution facilitated by the Internet of Things (IoT)(Farooqui, Ashraf, et al., 2024).

1.2 The Emergence of IoT in Urban Management

With the advancement of wireless connectivity, cloud computing, artificial intelligence (AI), and data analytics, urban areas have commenced the incorporation of IoT-enabled solutions to enhance automation and optimize infrastructural systems. The Internet of Things (IoT) has fundamentally transformed urban landscapes by transitioning from reactive to proactive management strategies, thereby facilitating real-time responses and enabling predictive analytics(Farooqui, Ansari, et al., 2024).

The development of IoT within urban contexts can be described into following three principal phases:

1. **Early IoT Implementations (1990s–2000s)** – Basic Connectivity and Automation The inception of the Internet of Things (IoT) within urban contexts commenced with fundamental automation processes in energy distribution networks, public transportation systems, and building management operations. Initial smart city projects implemented primitive sensor technology for the purposes of traffic surveillance, street lighting automation, and the aggregation of environmental data. Nevertheless, these systems were predominantly characterized by their isolation, a lack of comprehensive integration, and restricted capabilities in terms of data analytics(Shao et al., 2018).
2. **Expansion and Data-Driven IoT (2010s)–** Integration with Cloud Computing and AI The adoption of IoT experienced a significant acceleration due to the widespread emergence of wireless communication technologies (such as 4G LTE, Wi-Fi, and LPWAN) alongside advancements in cloud computing infrastructures(Chen, 2024). Artificial Intelligence (AI)-enhanced analytics facili-

tated more sophisticated decision-making processes in domains such as traffic management, waste collection, and water resource distribution. Governments initiated the establishment of open data platforms, thereby enabling both businesses and citizens to actively engage in urban innovation endeavours. Notable Examples: Barcelona's intelligent street lighting system achieved a reduction in energy expenditures by 30% through the utilization of IoT-controlled LED streetlights. Singapore's advanced transport infrastructure improved the efficiency of public transit, leading to a decrease in congestion levels by 15%.

3. **Smart Cities and Autonomous Urban Systems (2020s–Present) –** Full-Scale IoT Deployment Contemporary urban centers are now employing fully integrated IoT ecosystems that capitalize on advancements in 5G technology, artificial intelligence, digital twin simulations, and edge computing methodologies. The IoT framework facilitates real-time environmental surveillance, predictive law enforcement strategies, and dynamic urban planning initiatives(Bibri & Krogstie, 2020b). The emergence of autonomous infrastructures, encompassing self-driving vehicles and AI-driven governance systems, signifies a transition towards hyper-connected urban environments. Notable Trends: The implementation of predictive analytics in infrastructure maintenance applications (for instance, the early identification of pipeline leaks and anticipatory energy demand forecasting). Governance powered by AI for the enhancement of citizen services, the development of e-governance platforms, and the monitoring of urban sustainability metrics.

1.3 IoT integration in Urban Infrastructure

The integration of the Internet of Things (IoT) within urban infrastructure is instrumental in the evolution of cities into Smart Cities by improving operational efficiency, sustainability, and the overall quality of life for inhabitants. Urban infrastructure that is driven by IoT leverages interconnected devices, sensors, and real-time data analytics to enhance the optimization of diverse municipal functions. Nevertheless, it is imperative to tackle the challenges related to security, interoperability, and cost to achieve large-scale deployment(Ansari & Mehrotra, 2019).

Figure 3. IoT Integration in Urban Infrastructure

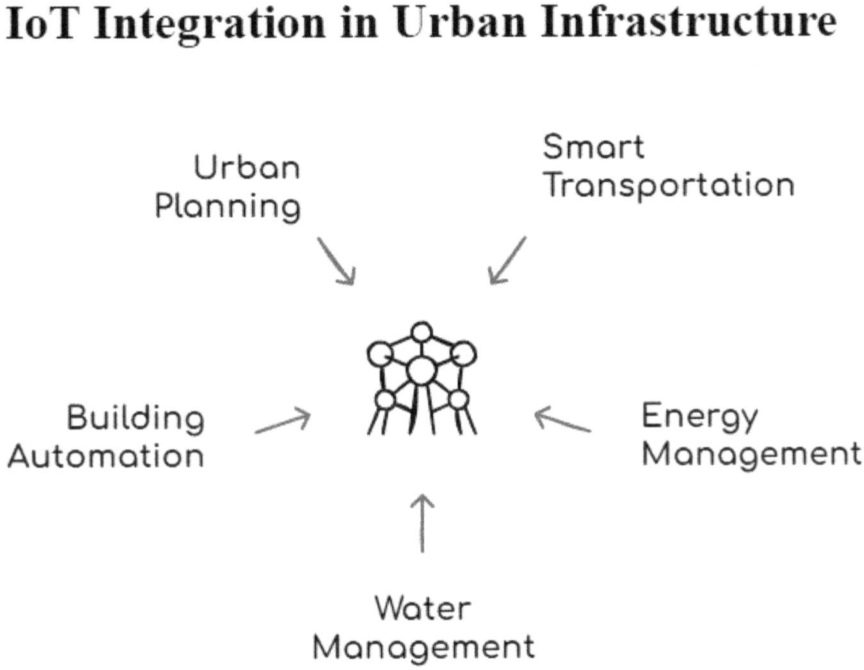

Figure 3 shows the integration of IoT in urban Infrastructure emphasizing its role in the following:

a) Smart Transportation Systems

Smart Transportation Systems (STS) represent technologically advanced solutions aimed at augmenting the efficacy, safety, and sustainability of transportation infrastructures. These systems utilize cutting-edge innovations such as the Internet of Things (IoT), Artificial Intelligence (AI), cloud computing, and data analytics to enhance traffic management, alleviate congestion, improve public transit services, and elevate overall mobility(Nadeem et al., 2024).

The Internet of Things (IoT) facilitates sophisticated traffic management through continuous monitoring and optimization of routes. Illustrative instances encompass intelligent parking solutions that mitigate congestion and autonomous vehicles employing IoT for enhanced navigational efficacy(Aderibigbe & Gumbo, 2024). Table 1 shows various technologies and their purpose which are used in smart transportation.

Table 1. Various Technologies used in Smart Transportation

S. No.	Technologies Used	Purpose
1	IoT (Internet of Things)	Real-time data collection from sensors, vehicles, and infrastructure.
2	AI & Machine Learning	Traffic prediction, autonomous driving, and smart route optimization.
3	Big Data Analytics	Analysing transportation patterns and optimizing routes.
4	Cloud Computing	Storing and processing large amounts of traffic and vehicle data.
5	5G & Wireless Communication	Fast and reliable communication between vehicles and infrastructure.
6	Blockchain	Secure data exchange and digital transactions in transportation systems.

b) Energy Management and Smart Grids

Energy management constitutes a systematic approach to the surveillance, regulation, and enhancement of energy utilization across residential, commercial, industrial, and intelligent urban environments. The primary objective is to augment energy efficiency, decrease expenditures, and mitigate ecological consequences(Allcott & Greenstone, 2012). Proficient energy management necessitates the deployment of sophisticated technologies, including Internet of Things (IoT) applications, Artificial Intelligence (AI), and the incorporation of renewable energy sources to establish sustainable energy frameworks. IoT-driven smart grids evaluate consumption patterns and refine energy distribution processes, assimilating renewable energy sources to bolster sustainability. Table 2 shows various technologies and their purpose which are used for energy management.

Table 2. Various Technologies used for Energy Management

S.No.	Technologies Used	Purpose
1	IoT (Internet of Things)	Smart meters and sensors for real-time energy tracking.
2	AI & Machine Learning	Predictive analytics for optimizing energy consumption.
3	Big Data Analytics	Analysing energy usage patterns for better decision-making.
4	Smart Grids	Automated energy distribution and fault detection.
5	Renewable Energy Systems	Solar panels, wind turbines, and battery storage.
6	Blockchain	Secure and transparent energy transactions, especially for microgrids.

c) Water and Waste Management

Water and waste management represent fundamental components of environmental sustainability, facilitating the optimal utilization of resources while concurrently mitigating pollution and health hazards. These two interrelated fields endeavour to preserve natural resources, safeguard ecosystems, and enhance public health(Buse et al., 2018).

With the emergence of intelligent urban environments, the management of water resources and waste is increasingly characterized by data-centric methodologies and technological sophistication.

- **IoT-Enabled Smart Water Meters –** Facilitating instantaneous observation of water consumption metrics. Sensors enabled by IoT technology assess water quality, identify distribution inefficiencies, and advocate for efficient waste segregation through the utilization of smart bins and predictive analytics.
- **AI-Driven Waste Collection Systems –** Enhancing the efficiency of waste collection schedules to minimize fuel expenditures and operational costs.
- **Water-Energy Nexus –** Leveraging waste-to-energy facilities to convert organic refuse into electrical energy.

d) Building Automation

Building Automation refers to the systematic and centralized oversight of a building's fundamental systems, which include heating, ventilation, and air conditioning (HVAC), illumination, security measures, energy management, and various other integrated frameworks. The governance of these systems is facilitated through a Building Automation System (BAS), which guarantees operational efficiency, occupant comfort, security, and environmental sustainability(Ahmed et al., 2024).

Smart buildings harness IoT capabilities for the optimization of energy-efficient lighting, heating, and security systems, thereby diminishing operational expenditures and environmental repercussions.

Table 3 shows various technologies and their purpose which are used for energy management.

Table 3. Various Technologies used for Energy Management

S. No.	Category	Technologies Used	Purpose
1	Communication Protocols	BACnet, Modbus, KNX	Standard protocols for HVAC, lighting, and security system integration.
2		Zigbee, Z-Wave, LoRaWAN	Wireless communication for IoT-enabled smart buildings.
3	IoT & Smart Sensors	Smart Meters, Motion & Occupancy Sensors	Optimize lighting, HVAC, and security based on real-time data.
4	Artificial Intelligence (AI) & Machine Learning (ML)	Predictive Maintenance, Energy Optimization	Automates decision-making for efficiency and cost savings.
5	Cloud & Edge Computing	AWS IoT, Google Cloud IoT, Microsoft Azure IoT	Enables remote monitoring, data analysis, and automation.
6	Building Management Systems (BMS)	Siemens Desigo CC, Honeywell Niagara, Schneider EcoStruxure	Centralized control and automation of building operations.
7	Cybersecurity	Firewalls, Encryption, Secure IoT Frameworks	Protects smart building systems from cyber threats.

e) Urban Planning and Development

Urban planning constitutes a systematic approach to the design and administration of urban environments, aimed at facilitating optimal land utilization, infrastructure development, transportation systems, and ecological sustainability. This discipline encompasses strategic decision-making processes intended to address population expansion, all the while preserving an equilibrium between economic advancement and ecological preservation.

Urban planning and development play a pivotal role in the formation of organized, sustainable, and habitable urban areas. Through the incorporation of advanced technologies, environmentally sustainable methodologies, and inclusive policy frameworks, urban centres can enhance their efficiency, resilience, and equity in forthcoming generations. An integrative and multidisciplinary framework is crucial for guaranteeing the enduring prosperity of urban settings(Qian et al., 2023). Information derived from IoT frameworks underpins data-driven urban planning, guaranteeing optimal resource allocation in response to increasing population demands.

Key Aspects of Urban Development

Urban development constitutes a complex, multifaceted process that converts urban areas into effective, sustainable, and habitable environments. It comprises the following five principal dimensions (figure 4):

- **Physical Development:** The establishment of thoroughfares, edifices, communal areas, and infrastructural frameworks.
- **Economic Development:** The processes of industrial expansion, entrepreneurial proliferation, and the creation of employment opportunities.
- **Social Development:** The enhancement of educational systems, healthcare provisions, and community-oriented services.
- **Environmental Sustainability:** The promotion of verdant urban landscapes, effective waste management systems, and the utilization of renewable energy sources.
- **Technological Advancement:** The implementation of intelligent urban initiatives, digital governance frameworks, and AI-enhanced urban solutions.

Figure 4. Key aspects of Urban Development

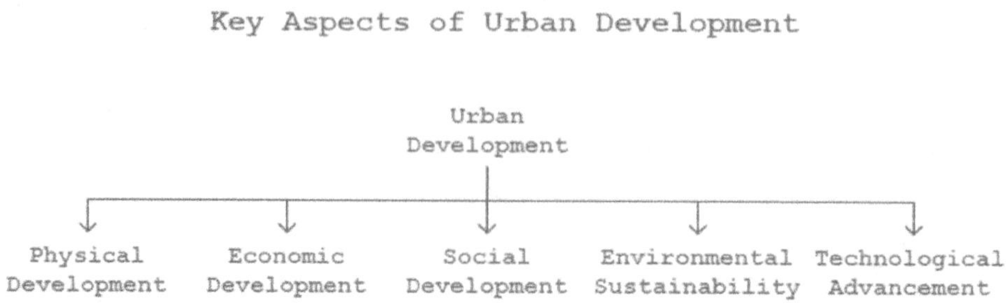

1.3.1 Benefits of IoT Integration in Urban Infrastructure

a) **Enhanced Operational Efficiency:** Automated systems optimize the allocation of resources and diminish operational expenditures.
b) **Sustainability Initiatives:** Intelligent management of energy and water resources mitigates ecological repercussions.
c) **Augmented Public Safety:** Internet of Things (IoT)-enabled security frameworks facilitate rapid responses during emergencies.
d) **Alleviation of Traffic Congestion:** Intelligent transportation systems contribute to enhanced vehicular flow.
e) **Improved Quality of Life:** Citizens benefit from superior services and enhanced living conditions.

1.3.2 Challenges in IoT Integration

a) **Data Security & Privacy:** Safeguarding Internet of Things (IoT) networks against cyber threats is of paramount importance.
b) **High Implementation Costs:** The preliminary expenditures associated with infrastructure development can be considerable.
c) **Interoperability Issues:** A seamless integration of diverse IoT devices and platforms is essential for functionality.
d) **Data Management:** The management and analysis of extensive volumes of real-time data necessitate a resilient infrastructure.

1.4 Governance and Ethical Considerations

The assimilation of IoT in smart cities necessitates the formulation of robust governance frameworks designed to address ethical dilemmas and safeguard data privacy(Fadhel et al., 2024). A sophisticated governance architecture can facilitate the integration of diverse IoT solutions, fostering cross-sector collaboration and ensuring the principles of security, scalability, and interoperability are upheld. Effective governance encompasses multi-tiered decision-making, inclusive urban planning practices, and the development of coherent legislation alongside open data policies(Ansari & Mehrotra, 2022).

a) Enhancing Decision-Making

The Internet of Things (IoT) furnishes instantaneous data, thereby facilitating decisions that are informed by empirical evidence within the realms of urban development, resource distribution, and the provision of public services.

b) Citizen Participation

The Internet of Things (IoT) promotes transparency and fosters accountability through interactive platforms that empower citizens to access pertinent information and contribute their perspectives.

c) Ethical and Legal Frameworks

Comprehensive governance structures effectively tackle ethical quandaries, concerns regarding data privacy, and the imperative of equitable access to the advantages conferred by IoT technologies.

d) Challenges and Future Directions

The challenges encountered include data security vulnerabilities, privacy apprehensions, and the potential for socioeconomic disparities stemming from inequitable access to technological resources. The forthcoming smart cities will increasingly depend on cutting-edge technologies such as artificial intelligence, edge computing, and blockchain to augment IoT networks and enhance urban connectivity(Badidi, 2022).

Although IoT technologies present substantial promise for transforming urban infrastructure and governance, their effective implementation mandates meticulous consideration of ethical, security, and governance-related issues. Collaborative endeavours among citizens, technologists, and urban planners are imperative to ensure that the evolution of smart cities is inclusive, sustainable, and advantageous for all stakeholders involved(Beck et al., 2023).

1.5 Objective of the chapter:

- Exhibit the transformative capacity of the Internet of Things (IoT) in the enhancement of urban infrastructure and governance through the promotion of efficiency, sustainability, and citizen-focused services.
- Emphasize the practical implementations of IoT, encompassing intelligent transportation systems, energy optimization, waste management, public safety measures, and governance frameworks.
- Recognize and tackle issues such as data privacy, security, interoperability, and policy ramifications to facilitate the ethical and sustainable implementation of IoT systems.
- Offer a strategic framework for urban planners, technology developers, and policymakers to successfully integrate IoT solutions.

2. IoT FOR URBAN GOVERNANCE

The function of the Internet of Things (IoT) within the scope of urban governance is crucial for the evolution of conventional governance frameworks into systems that are driven by data, characterized by transparency and efficiency. The IoT enables instantaneous data acquisition, automates the decision-making process, and employs predictive analytics, thereby empowering municipal authorities to engage in proactive responses to the challenges faced in urban environments.

2.1 Need of IoT for Urban Governance

- **Data-Driven Governance:** The Internet of Things (IoT) facilitates governmental entities in the collection, analysis, and implementation of extensive datasets derived from urban ecosystems.
- **Improved Public Service Delivery:** Advanced IoT frameworks enhance the efficiency of waste management, energy allocation, and public transportation systems. Enhanced
- **Public Safety:** Law enforcement agencies gain advantages from instantaneous surveillance, anticipatory policing methodologies, and automated emergency response mechanisms.

- **Citizen Engagement & Transparency:** Platforms empowered by IoT augment governmental accountability and foster increased citizen participation.

2.2 Impact of IoT on Governance

a) Data-Driven Decision-Making and Real-Time Analytics

Data-Driven Decision-Making: Data-informed decision-making (DIDM) pertains to the utilization of real-time data and analytical frameworks to guide policy formulation, resource distribution, and the optimization of service efficacy. The Internet of Things (IoT) facilitates DIDM by perpetually surveilling urban ecosystems and producing actionable intelligence.

How IoT supports Urban Governance

1. Real-Time Data Collection

Internet of Things (IoT) devices, such as advanced sensors, surveillance cameras, and utility meters, facilitate the acquisition of urban data pertaining to vehicular movement, atmospheric quality, energy utilization, and infrastructural conditions. For example: Air quality monitoring sensors in Beijing assist governmental authorities in implementing real-time traffic regulations contingent upon pollution metrics.

2. Predictive Analytics for Urban Planning

Artificial Intelligence (AI) and IoT technologies enable the forecasting of infrastructural malfunctions, disaster-related risks, and vehicular congestion, thereby enhancing urban planning methodologies. For example: Digital twin technology is employed to create simulations of urban environments to anticipate demographic expansion and infrastructure requirements.

3. Automated Resource Allocation

Intelligent urban Internet of Things (IoT) platforms employ machine learning algorithms to dynamically enhance the efficiency of public service delivery. For example: The smart streetlights in Amsterdam modulate their luminosity in accordance with pedestrian activity, resulting in a 30% reduction in energy expenditure.

4. Crisis and Disaster Management

The Internet of Things facilitates instantaneous flood detection, seismic activity surveillance, and the coordination of emergency response efforts. For example: Tokyo's IoT-driven earthquake early warning system is instrumental in facilitating the evacuation of residents prior to the onset of seismic tremors.

b) Digital Governance and E-Government Services

Digital Governance

Digital governance, commonly referred to as e-Government, pertains to the application of technological innovations, automation processes, and digital platforms to enhance the delivery of governmental services and the efficacy of decision-making. The Internet of Things (IoT) significantly augments e-Government services by facilitating unobstructed data interchange, intelligent infrastructure oversight, and the automation of public service administration.

Applications of IoT in Digital Governance

1. Smart Infrastructure Monitoring

The implementation of Internet of Things (IoT) devices facilitates the surveillance of roadway conditions, the identification of water leakages, and the oversight of public infrastructure. Example: The intelligent water management system in Barcelona employs advanced detection mechanisms for pipeline leaks, thereby mitigating water wastage and decreasing maintenance expenditures.

2. Automated Public Service Delivery

The integration of IoT technology allows for the instantaneous monitoring of municipal services, including refuse collection, roadway upkeep, and emergency response operations. Example: The smart waste receptacles in San Francisco generate notifications upon reaching capacity, thereby streamlining collection routes and minimizing waste overflow.

3. Blockchain-Based Governance

Public sector entities are increasingly adopting blockchain technology in conjunction with IoT to ensure secure transactional processes, electronic voting, and the management of digital identities. Example: Estonia's digital governance framework incorporates blockchain-enabled public records, thereby enhancing both security and transparency in governmental operations.

4. **IoT-Enabled Taxation & Smart Utility Billing**

Intelligent metering systems continuously monitor electricity and water consumption, thereby facilitating precise and automated billing processes. Example: The IoT-driven tax collection framework implemented in Singapore mitigates manual inaccuracies and significantly improves operational efficiency.

5. **Open Data Platforms for Transparency**

IoT-integrated public dashboards present instantaneous data regarding criminal activity, environmental pollution metrics, and fiscal expenditures of governmental bodies. Example: The open data initiative in London offers real-time information on traffic conditions and environmental parameters for both enterprises and the general populace.

c) IoT in Law Enforcement and Public Safety

The integration of Internet of Things (IoT) technology into security frameworks significantly augments the operational effectiveness of law enforcement agencies through the augmentation of surveillance capabilities, the automation of criminal activity identification, and the facilitation of anticipatory policing strategies.

Applications of IoT in Public Safety

1. Smart Surveillance Systems

Artificial intelligence-enhanced closed-circuit television systems can identify anomalous behaviours and notifying law enforcement in an instantaneous manner. Example: The facial recognition-based surveillance infrastructure in China effectively facilitates the rapid identification of offenders within a matter of minutes.

2. Predictive Policing with AI and IoT

Analytics grounded in Internet of Things (IoT) technology forecast potential criminal activity by scrutinizing historical crime patterns alongside current environmental factors. Example: The PredPol System utilized by the Los Angeles Police Department leverages IoT-generated crime analytics to strategically assign officers to areas identified as high-risk.

3. Connected Emergency Response Systems

The Internet of Things (IoT) amalgamates various emergency service entities, including fire departments, medical facilities, and police forces, into a cohesive response framework. Example: The 911 system in New York City employs IoT sensors to identify the occurrence of gunfire and promptly mobilize emergency response teams.

4. IoT for Disaster Management

Sensor technologies are employed to identify seismic activities, inundations, and wildfires, subsequently disseminating proactive notifications to mitigate potential disasters. Example: The IoT framework for earthquake alerts in Japan facilitates instantaneous warnings prior to the occurrence of seismic disturbances in metropolitan regions.

5. Traffic Law Enforcement with Smart Cameras

IoT-integrated speed monitoring systems autonomously impose penalties on infringers, thereby contributing to a reduction in vehicular accidents. Example: The AI-enhanced traffic regulation framework in Dubai has led to a 40% decrease in traffic violations.

d) Enhancing Citizen Participation Through the Internet of Things

The Internet of Things (IoT) facilitates the active engagement of citizens in the governance process, thereby guaranteeing that urban services correspond with the requirements of the populace.

IoT-Enabled Platforms for Citizen Engagement

1. Smart City Dashboards for Public Transparency:

Members of the community have the capability to access contemporaneous data regarding pollution levels, criminal activities, public transportation, and municipal financial allocations. Example: The citizen dashboard in Barcelona provides information on air quality, traffic metrics, and governmental expenditures.

2. IoT-Driven Public Feedback Systems:

Members of the community are empowered to report infrastructural deficiencies (for instance, potholes, malfunctioning streetlights) through applications facilitated by Internet of Things technology. Example: Boston's "Street Bump" application employs smartphone sensors to identify road damage and subsequently notify governmental authorities.

3. Smart Voting & Digital Participation Platforms:

E-voting systems that utilize Internet of Things technology enhance accountability and promote greater voter engagement. Example: Estonia's IoT-enabled online voting apparatus has optimized the electoral process and contributed to an increase in voter participation rates.

4. Community Safety Apps:

Members of the community receive immediate notifications regarding emergencies and crime statistics through mobile applications. Example: India's MyGov application enables citizens to directly communicate public grievances to governmental officials.

3. CASE STUDIES: IoT TRANSFORMATIONS IN SMART CITIES

The Internet of Things (IoT) is fundamentally transforming urban environments by augmenting operational efficiency, promoting sustainability, and improving the overall quality of life. The subsequent case studies exemplify how various municipalities have adeptly incorporated IoT technologies to tackle urban challenges.

3.1 Singapore: A Fully Integrated Smart City

Overview

Singapore is acknowledged as one of the world's most advanced smart cities, leveraging Internet of Things (IoT) technologies across various domains to improve infrastructure, transportation networks, public services, and environmental sustainability.

Major IoT Initiatives

The Smart Nation Initiative of Singapore, launched in 2014, represents an ambitious government-directed endeavour designed to exploit cutting-edge digital technologies for the enhancement of urban life, stimulation of economic advancement, and augmentation of public service efficiency(Cavada et al., 2019). This initiative capitalizes on the capabilities of the Internet of Things (IoT), artificial intelligence (AI), and data analytics to establish interconnected and intelligent ecosystems across diverse sectors. Key implementations are as under: -

- **Smart Nation Initiative:** Initiated in 2014, this government-sponsored initiative emphasizes the digital transformation facilitated by the Internet of Things (IoT), artificial intelligence (AI), and data analytics. Anticipated to commence deployment incrementally beginning in 2024, this district will incorporate facial recognition technology for both access control and financial transactions, Internet of Things (IoT) enabled infrastructure, and a Multi-Energy Micro-Grid system. It is projected that this grid will facilitate the abatement of carbon emissions, which is comparable to the removal of 2,000 automobiles from public thoroughfares.(Cavada et al., 2019).
- **Smart Transport System (STS):** Employs IoT-integrated sensors, real-time traffic surveillance, and predictive analytics to effectively address congestion issues. Through the examination of data derived from fare cards, sensors embedded in more than 5,000 vehicles, and the implementation of real-time bus tracking systems, Singapore effectively diminished the incidence of overcrowded buses by 92% throughout the duration of a trial period. (Carpentiere et al., 2024)
- **Smart Housing (HDB Estates):** Public housing developments are furnished with IoT-based energy management systems, intelligent water metering, and predictive maintenance frameworks. As of mid-2023, approximately 8,600 units within 52 rental complexes have been outfitted with Personal Alert Buttons (PABs), thereby providing support to 10,000 elderly individuals. Between the years 2020 and 2023, approximately 800 elderly individuals have availed themselves of emergency medical assistance through this initiative. The program aspires to extend its reach to all seniors aged 60 and above residing in public rental housing, with the potential to assist an additional 27,000 elderly individuals across roughly 170 rental complexes. (Carpentiere et al., 2024)
- **Healthcare Innovations:** IoT-enabled telemedicine, remote monitoring for geriatric care, and AI-enhanced diagnostic tools significantly improve healthcare delivery. For example: - sensei care kit. This device interlinks devices that quantify health parameters such as body mass and arterial pressure, thereby facilitating an extensive assessment of health status for elderly individuals within a domestic environment. It permits caregivers to oversee health conditions from a distance, thereby promoting the prompt identification of concerns necessitating intervention. (Cavada et al., 2019)

- **Environmental Monitoring:** Air quality monitoring devices, intelligent waste management systems, and water conservation technologies contribute to the preservation of ecological equilibrium. For example: - Smart Lamp Posts. In the Punggol Digital District, intelligent lamp posts discern the nearness of individuals, modulating luminosity correspondingly to optimize energy conservation. (Cavada et al., 2019)

Impact of IoT initiatives

In the contemporary landscape of intelligent urban environments, advancements in technology are fundamentally transforming metropolitan living by augmenting mobility, optimizing energy consumption, enhancing healthcare delivery, and improving the overall quality of life. The incorporation of real-time tracking systems and artificial intelligence-driven transportation networks has mitigated traffic congestion, thereby facilitating more fluid urban mobility. In a parallel manner, the implementation of smart grid technologies alongside renewable energy initiatives has markedly improved energy efficiency. Within the healthcare domain, remote patient monitoring innovations are diminishing the necessity for hospital admissions while simultaneously enhancing patient outcomes(Carpentiere et al., 2024). Moreover, Internet of Things (IoT)-enabled public services are fostering the development of more interconnected, efficient, and sustainable urban ecosystems. Collectively, these advancements contribute to the emergence of a more intelligent, resilient, and habitable future.

- **Enhanced urban mobility:** The deployment of real-time tracking mechanisms and transportation frameworks optimized through artificial intelligence has yielded a substantial reduction in traffic congestion.
- **Energy efficiency:** The adoption of intelligent grid technologies and the integration of renewable energy sources have led to a significant decline in energy consumption.
- **Improved healthcare:** The emergence of remote patient monitoring systems has facilitated a decrease in hospital admissions while positively impacting patient health outcomes.
- **Higher quality of life:** Internet of Things (IoT)-driven public services promote a more interconnected, efficient, and sustainable urban landscape.

3.2 Barcelona: IoT-Based Urban Management

Overview

Barcelona has established an extensive Internet of Things (IoT) infrastructure designed to improve urban administration, the provision of public services, and environmental sustainability.

Major IoT initiatives

In modern cities, the incorporation of the Internet of Things (IoT) is fundamentally transforming urban infrastructure, rendering it more efficient, sustainable, and responsive to immediate requirements. Intelligent technologies are being implemented across diverse sectors to enhance urban living conditions, diminish resource consumption, and optimize overall city administration. Intelligent lighting systems enhance energy efficiency by modulating brightness in accordance with movement and ambient light, while intelligent parking solutions mitigate traffic congestion by directing drivers to unoccupied spaces. In a similar vein, IoT-enabled waste management systems refine collection processes, and urban mobility solutions improve public transportation through bike-sharing initiatives and real-time tracking capabilities. Furthermore, sophisticated monitoring of water and air quality delivers essential data for policymakers to formulate healthier living environments. The cumulative effect of these innovations facilitates the development of urban environments that are increasingly intelligent and sustainable(Bibri & Krogstie, 2020c). The implementation of Internet of Things (IoT) technologies in Barcelona has created significant advancements across a multitude of urban services. Prominent quantitative outcomes encompass:

- **Smart Lighting System:** Internet of Things-enabled LED streetlights modulate their luminosity in response to pedestrian movement and ambient light levels, thereby minimizing energy usage. The modernization of over 1,100 streetlights to LED technology, integrated with sensor capabilities, has culminated in a 30% decrease in energy consumption, thereby yielding financial savings exceeding €36 million for the municipality(Bibri & Krogstie, 2020c).
- **Smart Parking Solutions:** Sensors embedded within parking spaces provide directional assistance to drivers seeking available spots through a mobile application, thereby alleviating traffic congestion. The introduction of a sensor-driven system to direct drivers to available parking spaces has mitigated congestion and emissions. The ApparkB application supports online parking

transactions, with the city issuing 4,000 parking permits daily within the first year of its rollout (Bibri & Krogstie, 2020c).

- **Waste Management System:** Smart bins equipped with IoT sensors notify waste collection services when they are full, optimizing collection routes. The integration of sensor-equipped waste receptacles to monitor fill levels has optimized collection routes, resulting in a 20% reduction in the number of garbage trucks operational on the roads and a concomitant decrease in carbon emissions associated with waste collection(Carpentiere et al., 2024).
- **Urban Mobility:** IoT-enabled public bike-sharing and real-time public transport tracking improve city-wide transportation.
- **Water and Air Quality Monitoring**: Sensors facilitate the surveillance of pollution concentrations, thereby delivering instantaneous data that is critical for urban development and policy formulation.

Impact of IoT initiatives

- **Energy conservation:** The intelligent lighting system has achieved a reduction in energy expenses amounting to 33%.
- **Traffic optimization:** The advanced parking management system has effectively diminished both congestion and fuel utilization.
- **Waste collection enhancement:** There has been a notable decrease in operational expenditures and ecological ramifications.
- **Improved air quality governance:** Evidence-based policies facilitate the mitigation of pollution.

3.3 New York City: Smart Transportation and Environmental Monitoring

Overview

New York City (NYC) has instituted Internet of Things (IoT) solutions to ameliorate transportation inefficiencies and to confront environmental challenges within one of the globe's most densely populated urban environments.

Major IoT initiatives

In the era of smart cities, the integration of the Internet of Things (IoT) and artificial intelligence (AI) has fundamentally transformed urban infrastructure, thereby enhancing operational efficiency, safety protocols, and sustainability measures. Sophisticated traffic management systems adeptly optimize signal timings predicated upon real-time data inputs, thereby alleviating congestion and augmenting mobility. Public transportation systems reap the advantages of real-time monitoring capabilities, which empower commuters to strategize their travel itineraries with greater efficacy. Safety initiatives, inclusive of IoT-enabled smart crosswalks and vehicle-to-infrastructure communication frameworks, are aligned with the Vision Zero objective aimed at the reduction of vehicular accidents. Furthermore, environmental surveillance facilitated by IoT sensors yields critical data on air quality, noise pollution, and thermal variations, thereby informing judicious policy formulation. In a similar vein, advanced water management systems utilize cutting-edge metering and leak detection technologies to optimize resource conservation and mitigate waste. Collectively, these technological advancements significantly contribute to the establishment of more adaptive, effective, and habitable urban settings(Carpentiere et al., 2024).

- **Connected Traffic Management:** Smart traffic control systems utilize Internet of Things (IoT) sensors along with artificial intelligence (AI) to adjust signal durations in response to current traffic conditions. For example: - Congestion pricing. Following the implementation of a $9 congestion charge on January 5, 2025, vehicular traffic within Manhattan's central business district has diminished by 7.5%, corresponding to a reduction of 273,000 vehicles accessing the region. This policy has additionally facilitated an increase in bus speeds and improved travel durations on river crossings into Manhattan by an estimated 30-40% (Carpentiere et al., 2024).
- **Smart Subway and Bus Systems:** The deployment of real-time monitoring systems in public transportation enables commuters to enhance the efficiency of their travel plans. For example: - Tract Defect Detection. The Metropolitan Transportation Authority (MTA) executed an extensive four-month pilot initiative utilizing Google Pixel smartphones integrated with artificial intelligence to identify anomalies in railway tracks. This innovative system effectively recognized 92% of the defects that had been previously documented by human inspectors, with the objective of minimizing subway delays and augmenting safety for an estimated 3.7 million commuters daily(Carpentiere et al., 2024).
- **Vision Zero Initiative:** Innovative systems that promote pedestrian safety, such as IoT-integrated smart crosswalks and vehicle-to-infrastructure communication networks, aim to decrease the frequency of accidents. Since the inauguration of the Vision Zero initiative in 2014, there has been a notable reduction of 45% in pedestrian fatalities, alongside an overall decrease of over 12% in traffic-related deaths as of the year 2023. The municipality has executed in excess of 1,200 safety enhancement projects, which encompass

the establishment of more than 200 miles of protected cycling pathways and the modification of the citywide speed limit to 25 miles per hour (Carpentiere et al., 2024).

- **Environmental Monitoring:** IoT sensors are employed for the assessment of air quality, noise pollution, and thermal variations, thus influencing and guiding the formulation of policy decisions. The municipality has implemented intelligent sensors to continuously assess air quality metrics, resulting in focused measures that have diminished deleterious emissions by 10% during the preceding five years (Carpentiere et al., 2024).
- **Water Management System:** The application of intelligent metering and leak detection technologies is pivotal in fostering water conservation and reducing waste. Automated Meter Reading (AMR): The Department of Environmental Protection has implemented AMR units across more than 800,000 properties, thereby supplying consumers with daily data regarding their water consumption. This innovative system has significantly diminished billing inconsistencies, resulting in a reduction of accounts billed with estimated data from 17% to below 3% (Carpentiere et al., 2024).

Impact of IoT initiatives

In the era of smart cities, technological innovations are fundamentally transforming metropolitan living by augmenting efficiency, security, and environmental sustainability. Systems of traffic management propelled by artificial intelligence are alleviating congestion, diminishing travel durations, and enhancing overall mobility. Initiatives aimed at public safety, exemplified by Vision Zero, have markedly contributed to the reduction of pedestrian fatality rates, thereby nurturing safer urban habitats. Furthermore, policies informed by data analytics are playing an integral role in promoting environmental sustainability through the enhancement of air quality management(Kumar Sahu et al., n.d.). Simultaneously, sophisticated water management systems are optimizing resource allocation, curtailing wastage, and ensuring effective water conservation practices. Collectively, these advancements are sculpting more intelligent, sustainable, and habitable urban environments for the future.

- **Mitigated traffic congestion:** Artificial intelligence-driven traffic management systems enhance vehicular flow and diminish commuting durations.
- **Augmented public safety:** The Vision Zero initiative has played a significant role in the reduction of pedestrian mortality rates.
- **Environmental sustainability:** Policies informed by data analytics have resulted in improved management of air quality.

- **Water conservation:** Intelligent water management systems minimize resource wastage and optimize operational efficiency.

Each of these metropolitan areas exemplifies the transformative potential of the Internet of Things (IoT) in urban living. Singapore's comprehensive approach to smart city development, Barcelona's emphasis on intelligent urban governance, and New York City's initiatives in transportation and environmental monitoring underscore the efficacy of IoT in fostering sustainable, efficient, and habitable urban spaces. These exemplifications serve as paradigms for other cities aspiring to leverage the capabilities of IoT for the advancement of smart city initiatives.

4. CHALLENGES AND BARRIERS TO IoT IMPLEMENTATION

The Internet of Things (IoT) possesses the capacity to transform multiple domains, encompassing healthcare, intelligent urban environments, industrial automation, among others. Nevertheless, the extensive integration of IoT confronts numerous challenges and obstacles.

Presented below are several critical factors impeding the execution of IoT initiatives:

4.1 Data Privacy and Security Concerns

With the ongoing proliferation of the Internet of Things (IoT), the imperative of ensuring data privacy and security has emerged as a paramount concern. The substantial volumes of sensitive data produced by IoT devices render them highly susceptible to cyber threats. Principal issues encompass data breaches, inadequate authentication protocols, absence of encryption measures, and the intricacies associated with regulatory compliance. Effectively addressing these challenges is crucial for the protection of both personal and organizational data, whilst simultaneously guaranteeing conformity to international security standards.

- **Data Breaches and Cyberattacks:** Internet of Things (IoT) devices produce substantial quantities of sensitive information, rendering them highly attractive targets for cybercriminal enterprises. Unauthorized infiltration and data breaches possess the potential to jeopardize both personal and corporate data integrity.
- **Weak Authentication Mechanisms:** Numerous IoT devices demonstrate a deficiency in resilient authentication protocols, thereby exposing them to the risks associated with cyber intrusions and unauthorized access.

- **Lack of Encryption:** The transmission of data among IoT devices frequently occurs without encryption, thereby exacerbating the likelihood of interception and manipulation by malevolent entities.
- **Regulatory Compliance:** Diverse jurisdictions implement rigorous data protection regulations (e.g., GDPR, CCPA), mandating that organizations adopt stringent security protocols, a process that can prove to be complex and challenging to execute.

4.2 Scalability and Infrastructure Constraints

As the proliferation of Internet of Things (IoT) devices persists, the imperative to establish robust security frameworks and compliance protocols becomes increasingly formidable. The swift escalation of interconnected devices engenders substantial scalability challenges, particularly concerning the maintenance of secure data transmission, the integrity of authentication processes, and adherence to regulatory standards. Numerous pivotal issues necessitate resolution to enhance IoT infrastructure resilience against prospective threats, encompassing data breaches, inadequate authentication protocols, insufficient encryption measures, and the dynamic nature of regulatory demands.

- **Data Breaches and Cyberattacks:** Internet of Things (IoT) devices produce substantial quantities of sensitive information, rendering them highly attractive targets for cybercriminal enterprises. Unauthorized infiltration and data breaches possess the potential to jeopardize both personal and corporate data integrity.
- **Weak Authentication Mechanisms:** Numerous IoT devices demonstrate a deficiency in resilient authentication protocols, thereby exposing them to the risks associated with cyber intrusions and unauthorized access.
- **Lack of Encryption:** The transmission of data among IoT devices frequently occurs without encryption, thereby exacerbating the likelihood of interception and manipulation by malevolent entities.
- **Regulatory Compliance:** Diverse jurisdictions implement rigorous data protection regulations (e.g., GDPR, CCPA), mandating that organizations adopt stringent security protocols, a process that can prove to be complex and challenging to execute.

4.3 Interoperability and Standardization Issues

The rapid expansion of the Internet of Things (IoT) has introduced a complex ecosystem of devices, networks, and platforms. However, the lack of interoperability and standardized frameworks presents significant challenges in achieving seamless communication and integration. Various manufacturers employ diverse protocols, proprietary technologies, and non-uniform security measures, leading to fragmentation across the IoT landscape. Additionally, the coexistence of legacy systems further complicates interoperability efforts. This section explores the key barriers to standardization and the implications they have on the widespread adoption of IoT technologies.

- **Diverse Protocols and Platforms:** The Internet of Things (IoT) devices originating from a multitude of manufacturers employ a variety of communication protocols, thereby rendering seamless integration a challenging endeavour.
- **Lack of Universal Standards:** The deficiency of a cohesive framework governing IoT connectivity, security, and data interchange obstructs compatibility among disparate devices and networks.
- **Proprietary Technologies:** Certain enterprises engineer IoT solutions that function exclusively within their proprietary ecosystems, resulting in vendor lock-in and constraining wider adoption.
- **Integration with Legacy Systems:** Numerous industries continue to depend on antiquated infrastructure that lacks compatibility with contemporary IoT solutions, thereby complicating the implementation processes.

4.4 Ethical and Social Implications

The swift assimilation of Internet of Things (IoT) technologies into diverse dimensions of everyday existence engenders a plethora of ethical and societal dilemmas. Although these innovations provide augmented efficiency and convenience, they concurrently elicit significant apprehensions pertaining to privacy, employment, equity, and inclusivity. This segment scrutinizes pivotal ethical quandaries linked to IoT implementation, encompassing surveillance threats, workforce displacement, biases inherent in AI-mediated decision-making, and the exacerbation of the digital divide. Confronting these challenges is essential for guaranteeing that the adoption of IoT is congruent with the tenets of equity, security, and societal welfare.

- **Surveillance and Privacy Risks:** The extensive proliferation of Internet of Things (IoT) devices, including intelligent cameras and various sensors, engenders significant apprehensions regarding mass surveillance practices and the safeguarding of individual privacy.

- **Job Displacement:** The advent of automation coupled with IoT-facilitated decision-making processes is likely to precipitate job eliminations within conventional industries, thereby engendering socio-economic dilemmas.
- **Bias and Discrimination in AI-Driven IoT:** Applications of artificial intelligence within IoT frameworks, exemplified by smart policing initiatives or automated recruitment systems, have the potential to perpetuate existing biases embedded in the data, consequently resulting in inequitable outcomes.
- **Digital Divide:** The disparity in access to IoT technologies has the potential to exacerbate the chasm between economically developed and developing regions, thereby constraining both economic and technological prospects for certain demographic groups.

5. FUTURE DIRECTIONS AND OPPORTUNITIES

The future of Smart Cities is significantly influenced by advancements in technology, particularly in the domains of Artificial Intelligence (AI), Machine Learning (ML), the Internet of Things (IoT), and forthcoming communication infrastructures such as 6G. These technological innovations present profound opportunities to enhance the quality of urban life, promote sustainability, and refine resource management practices. This section delves into three pivotal areas: the impact of AI and ML within IoT-centric urban environments, the role of IoT in fostering sustainable urban growth, and the progression of 6G networks in the context of Smart Cities.

5.1 The Role of AI and Machine Learning in IoT for Cities

Artificial Intelligence (AI) and Machine Learning (ML) are ready to transform Internet of Things (IoT) applications within Smart Cities by augmenting automation, improving decision-making processes, and enhancing predictive functionalities. The amalgamation of AI with IoT (AIoT) empowers urban areas to analyse extensive volumes of real-time data, derive significant insights, and optimize urban services with remarkable efficacy.

Major Advancements and Applications

The incorporation of Artificial Intelligence (AI) and Machine Learning (ML) within urban infrastructure has precipitated significant advancements across various domains. These technologies augment efficiency, security, and sustainability through the facilitation of data-informed decision-making and automation. The subsequent sections delineate crucial areas wherein AI-driven innovations are redefining contemporary urban environments:

- **Smart Traffic Management:** Artificial Intelligence-facilitated predictive analytics possess the capability to mitigate congestion by systematically analyzing traffic patterns and refining signal timings.
- **Energy Optimization:** Machine Learning algorithms are proficient at forecasting energy consumption and automating grid management to minimize wastage.
- **Urban Security and Surveillance:** Artificial Intelligence-augmented surveillance systems utilize facial recognition, anomaly detection, and instantaneous alerts to enhance public safety.
- **Predictive Maintenance:** Artificial Intelligence-driven Internet of Things sensors embedded in infrastructure (such as bridges, roads, and pipelines) are capable of early fault detection and recommending maintenance interventions prior to the occurrence of failures.
- **Personalized Citizen Services:** Intelligent chatbots and Artificial Intelligence assistants can furnish real-time information regarding municipal services, transportation options, and emergency notifications.

Challenges and Opportunities

As the amalgamation of the Internet of Things (IoT) and Artificial Intelligence (AI) persistently influences contemporary technological environments, a multitude of challenges and opportunities arise. It is imperative to address issues pertaining to data privacy, security, scalability, and the ethical deployment of AI to promote innovation while concurrently ensuring regulatory compliance and equity. The subsequent key domains underscore the essential elements that warrant scrutiny for the purpose of sustainable and effective progress in AIoT-driven solutions.

- **Data Privacy and Security:** The proliferation of data generated by the Internet of Things (IoT) necessitates the imperative of securing sensitive information and adhering to regulatory frameworks, such as the General Data Protection Regulation (GDPR).
- **Scalability and Interoperability:** Artificial Intelligence of Things (AIoT) solutions must exhibit the capacity to integrate seamlessly with diverse infrastructures and technological ecosystems.

- **Ethical AI Deployment:** It is essential to confront issues of bias and to guarantee equitable decision-making processes in urban applications powered by artificial intelligence.

5.2 IoT and Sustainable Urban Development

The Internet of Things (IoT) assumes a pivotal function in the establishment of sustainable urban environments through the optimization of resource utilization, the mitigation of carbon emissions, and the augmentation of environmental surveillance. The advancement of sustainable urbanization incorporates intelligent technologies to foster environmentally sustainable and habitable urban spaces.

IoT-Driven Sustainable Solutions

The Internet of Things (IoT) is fundamentally transforming sustainability initiatives through the facilitation of real-time surveillance, data-informed decision-making, and the optimization of resources across diverse sectors. By utilizing a network of interconnected intelligent devices, IoT-based solutions significantly enhance environmental preservation, energy efficacy, and the quality of urban living conditions. The subsequent sections delineate the principal domains wherein IoT is exerting a considerable influence:

- **Smart Waste Management:** The implementation of Internet of Things (IoT)-enabled waste receptacles, equipped with advanced sensor technology, significantly enhances the optimization of waste collection routes, consequently reducing fuel consumption and improving recycling efficacy.
- **Water Resource Management:** IoT sensors facilitate comprehensive monitoring of water usage, enable the prompt identification of leaks, and enhance the optimization of distribution networks within urban water systems.
- **Air Quality Monitoring:** Sensors based on IoT technology systematically monitor pollution concentrations, thereby providing essential data that supports informed policymaking and public health advisories.
- **Renewable Energy Integration:** Smart electrical grids, supported by IoT innovations, play a crucial role in balancing energy demand and supply, thereby effectively incorporating renewable energy sources such as solar and wind.
- **Green Buildings:** The implementation of IoT-driven automation in lighting, heating, and cooling systems substantially reduces energy consumption in both residential and commercial buildings.

Challenges and Opportunities

The integration of Internet of Things (IoT) technologies across diverse sectors presents both notable challenges and auspicious opportunities. Although these technologies furnish innovative methodologies for sustainability and intelligent infrastructure, they simultaneously necessitate the resolution of obstacles such as substantial initial investments, intricate data governance, and the imperative for public involvement. Effectively addressing these obstacles has the potential to facilitate the development of more efficient, secure, and inclusive IoT-centric solutions.

- **High Initial Costs:** The deployment of extensive IoT solutions necessitates a considerable financial investment.
- **Data Management:** The efficient management and analysis of vast datasets represent a significant challenge.
- **Public Awareness and Participation:** It is imperative that citizens are actively involved in sustainability initiatives facilitated by IoT technologies.

5.3 The Evolution of 6G and IoT Networks for Smart Cities

The advent of sixth generation (6G) networks is poised to substantially augment the capabilities of the Internet of Things (IoT) within the context of Smart Cities, facilitating ultra-high-speed connectivity, minimal latency, and extensive device intercommunication. It is anticipated that 6G will exhibit a performance enhancement of an order of magnitude that is 100 times greater than that of fifth generation (5G) networks and will enable the deployment of more sophisticated artificial intelligence (AI)-driven services.

Potential Impacts of 6G on IoT and Smart Cities

As the global community progresses towards the advent of the sixth generation of wireless technology, 6G is poised to transform the paradigms of connectivity, operational efficiency, and security within IoT-enabled smart urban environments. With unparalleled transmission speeds, minimal latency, and advancements driven by artificial intelligence, 6G will facilitate uninterrupted communication, sophisticated automation, and instantaneous decision-making processes. This paradigm shift will not merely augment urban infrastructural frameworks but will also instigate a fundamental transformation in sectors such as healthcare, transportation, and public safety. The ensuing key domains elucidate the prospective ramifications of 6G on IoT and smart city ecosystems.

- **Hyper-Connected Infrastructure:** The emergence of sixth generation (6G) technology is anticipated to enable seamless interconnectivity among Internet of Things (IoT) devices, thereby augmenting operational efficiency in the provision of urban services.
- **Ultra-Low Latency:** Real-time applications, such as autonomous vehicular systems, remote healthcare services, and artificial intelligence-driven decision-making frameworks, are expected to reap considerable benefits from near-instantaneous communication capabilities.
- **Edge AI and Computing:** It is projected that artificial intelligence models will be implemented at the periphery of the network, thereby reducing reliance on centralized cloud computing resources and improving response times.
- **Holographic Communications:** Innovative communication interfaces, which include augmented reality (AR) and virtual reality (VR) technologies, are set to transform mechanisms for citizen engagement.
- **Enhanced Cybersecurity:** The sixth generation of mobile networks is set to integrate quantum communication alongside artificial intelligence-driven security protocols to protect IoT networks from potential vulnerabilities.

Challenges and Opportunities

The transition towards sixth generation (6G) technology presents a multifaceted landscape comprising both challenges and opportunities that will significantly influence the future of connectivity and innovations within smart cities. As the pace of technological advancements intensifies, it becomes imperative to address pivotal elements such as the development of infrastructure, the allocation of spectrum resources, and the establishment of regulatory frameworks. Successfully manoeuvring through these intricate complexities will not only facilitate the seamless integration of emerging technologies but also promote a digital ecosystem that is more secure, efficient, and sustainable.

- **Infrastructure Development:** The implementation of 6G technology necessitates the establishment of novel network architectures alongside considerable financial investment. **Spectrum Allocation:** Optimal spectrum management is imperative to effectively support the extensive proliferation of Internet of Things (IoT) devices.
- **Regulatory and Ethical Concerns:** Legislative frameworks must advance to adequately address the multifaceted issues of privacy, security, and ethical implications associated with artificial intelligence-driven applications within smart cities.

6. CONCLUSION

The Internet of Things (IoT) is catalysing a paradigm shift in urban infrastructure and governance, driving measurable enhancements in the intelligence, safety, and sustainability of metropolitan systems. However, fully leveraging this potential necessitates the resolution of complex challenges encompassing cybersecurity, system scalability, and ethical considerations. This chapter is conceived as an exhaustive technical resource that amalgamates current research, implementation methodologies, and policy frameworks. It is intended to equip researchers, practitioners, and policymakers with the insights required for the informed deployment and management of IoT solutions in the urban landscapes of tomorrow.

In addition, the integration of IoT devices into urban environments introduces intricate data processing challenges, necessitating the development of robust, distributed systems capable of managing extensive sensor networks. The emergence of edge computing architectures significantly mitigates latency issues, thereby enabling real-time analytics and decentralized decision-making. Advanced machine learning algorithms and artificial intelligence techniques are being deployed to optimize resource allocation, predict maintenance needs, and enhance operational efficiency. Moreover, ensuring interoperability among heterogeneous systems requires the adoption of standardized communication protocols and scalable network frameworks that seamlessly integrate legacy infrastructure. Cybersecurity remains a critical focus; implementing robust encryption, multi-factor authentication, and secure firmware updates is essential to safeguard against vulnerabilities and breaches. Equally important are ethical considerations, particularly in safeguarding data privacy and ensuring transparent data usage, which are imperative for the sustainable evolution of smart urban ecosystems.

7. REFERENCES

Aderibigbe, O.-O., & Gumbo, T. (2024). Internet of Things (IoT) and Big Data as a Revolutionary Approach for Traffic Management. In Emerging Technologies for Smart Cities: Sustainable Transport Planning in the Global North and Global South (pp. 171–192). Springer.

Ahmed, I., Asif, M., Alhelou, H. H., & Khalid, M. (2024). A review on enhancing energy efficiency and adaptability through system integration for smart buildings. *Journal of Building Engineering*, •••, 109354.

Allcott, H., & Greenstone, M. (2012). Is there an energy efficiency gap? *The Journal of Economic Perspectives*, *26*(1), 3–28.

Ansari, M. S. H., & Mehrotra, M. (2019). Development of smart cities and its sustainability: A smart city framework. *International Journal of Innovative Technology and Exploring Engineering*, *8*(11), 646–655.

Ansari, M. S. H., & Mehrotra, M. (2020). Securing M2M communication in Smart Cities. *2020 International Conference for Emerging Technology (INCET)*, 1–4.

Ansari, M. S. H., & Mehrotra, M. (2022). IoT Technologies, Security Attacks and their Security Measures under Smart City Framework. Grenze International Journal of Engineering & Technology (GIJET), 8(2).

Badidi, E. (2022). Edge AI and blockchain for smart sustainable cities: Promise and potential. *Sustainability*, *14*(13), 7609.

Beck, D., Ferasso, M., Storopoli, J., & Vigoda-Gadot, E. (2023). Achieving the sustainable development goals through stakeholder value creation: Building up smart sustainable cities and communities. *Journal of Cleaner Production*, *399*, 136501.

Belli, L., Cilfone, A., Davoli, L., Ferrari, G., Adorni, P., Di Nocera, F., Dall'Olio, A., Pellegrini, C., Mordacci, M., & Bertolotti, E. (2020). IoT-enabled smart sustainable cities: Challenges and approaches. *Smart Cities*, *3*(3), 1039–1071. DOI: 10.3390/smartcities3030052

Berry, B. J. L. (2008). Urbanization. Urban Ecology: An International Perspective on the Interaction between. *Human Nature (Hawthorne, N.Y.)*, •••, 25–48.

Bibri, S. E., & Krogstie, J. (2020a). Environmentally data-driven smart sustainable cities: Applied innovative solutions for energy efficiency, pollution reduction, and urban metabolism. *Energy Informatics*, *3*(1), 29. DOI: 10.1186/s42162-020-00130-8

Bibri, S. E., & Krogstie, J. (2020b). Environmentally data-driven smart sustainable cities: Applied innovative solutions for energy efficiency, pollution reduction, and urban metabolism. *Energy Informatics*, *3*(1), 29. DOI: 10.1186/s42162-020-00130-8

Bibri, S. E., & Krogstie, J. (2020c). The emerging data–driven Smart City and its innovative applied solutions for sustainability: The cases of London and Barcelona. *Energy Informatics*, *3*(1), 5. DOI: 10.1186/s42162-020-00108-6

Buse, C. G., Oestreicher, J. S., Ellis, N. R., Patrick, R., Brisbois, B., Jenkins, A. P., McKellar, K., Kingsley, J., Gislason, M., Galway, L., McFarlane, R. A., Walker, J., Frumkin, H., & Parkes, M. (2018). Public health guide to field developments linking ecosystems, environments and health in the Anthropocene. *Journal of Epidemiology and Community Health*, *72*(5), 420–425. DOI: 10.1136/jech-2017-210082 PMID: 29330164

Carpentiere, C. D., Messeni Petruzzelli, A., & Ardito, L. (2024). Success factors in smart mobility: A new framework and implications for the EuroMed context from case study of New York, Copenhagen, Singapore, Bari and Barcelona. *EuroMed Journal of Business*. Advance online publication. DOI: 10.1108/EMJB-01-2024-0015

Cavada, M., Tight, M. R., & Rogers, C. D. F. (2019). A smart city case study of Singapore—Is Singapore truly smart? In *Smart city emergence* (pp. 295–314). Elsevier. DOI: 10.1016/B978-0-12-816169-2.00014-6

Chen, Y. (2024). *Managing hybrid industrial IoT enterprise wireless networks*. University of Glasgow.

Fadhel, M. A., Duhaim, A. M., Saihood, A., Sewify, A., Al-Hamadani, M. N. A., Albahri, A. S., Alzubaidi, L., Gupta, A., Mirjalili, S., & Gu, Y. (2024). Comprehensive systematic review of information fusion methods in smart cities and urban environments. *Information Fusion*, *107*, 102317. DOI: 10.1016/j.inffus.2024.102317

Farooqui, N. A., Ansari, M. S. H., Ansari, Z. A., & Mehra, R. (2024). Technological Advancements in Waste Management. In Municipal Solid Waste Management and Recycling Technologies (pp. 327–342). IGI Global. DOI: 10.4018/979-8-3693-4054-7.ch012

Farooqui, N. A., Ashraf, I., & Jaiswal, R. (2024). Modernizing healthcare through IoT-based e-health systems. In *Intelligent Networks* (pp. 318–330). CRC Press. DOI: 10.1201/9781003541363-20

Ferrer, A. L. C., Thomé, A. M. T., & Scavarda, A. J. (2018). Sustainable urban infrastructure: A review. *Resources, Conservation and Recycling*, *128*, 360–372. DOI: 10.1016/j.resconrec.2016.07.017

García-García, L., Jiménez, J. M., Abdullah, M. T. A., & Lloret, J. (2018). Wireless technologies for IoT in smart cities. *Network Protocols and Algorithms*, *10*(1), 23–64. DOI: 10.5296/npa.v10i1.12798

Gupta, D. N., Kumar, R., & Ansari, S. H. (2022). Federated Learning for an IoT Application. In Yadav, S. P., Bhati, B. S., Mahato, D. P., & Kumar, S. (Eds.), *Federated Learning for IoT Applications* (pp. 53–66). Springer International Publishing., DOI: 10.1007/978-3-030-85559-8_4

Harmon, R. R., Castro-Leon, E. G., & Bhide, S. (2015). Smart cities and the Internet of Things. *2015 Portland International Conference on Management of Engineering and Technology (PICMET)*, 485–494. DOI: 10.1109/PICMET.2015.7273174

Karale, A. (2021). The challenges of IoT addressing security, ethics, privacy, and laws. *Internet of Things : Engineering Cyber Physical Human Systems*, *15*, 100420. DOI: 10.1016/j.iot.2021.100420

Kumar Sahu, V., Pandey, D., Singh, P., Haque Ansari, M. S., Khan, A., Varish, N., & Khan, M. W. (n.d.). An empirical analysis of evolutionary computing approaches for IoT security assessment. Journal of Intelligent & Fuzzy Systems, Preprint, 1–13.

Landaluce, H., Arjona, L., Perallos, A., Falcone, F., Angulo, I., & Muralter, F. (2020). A review of IoT sensing applications and challenges using RFID and wireless sensor networks. *Sensors (Basel)*, *20*(9), 2495. DOI: 10.3390/s20092495 PMID: 32354063

Malhotra, P., Singh, Y., Anand, P., Bangotra, D. K., Singh, P. K., & Hong, W.-C. (2021). Internet of things: Evolution, concerns and security challenges. *Sensors (Basel)*, *21*(5), 1809. DOI: 10.3390/s21051809 PMID: 33807724

Nadeem, M., Pathak, P. C., Ahmad, M., & Farooqui, N. A. (2024). Identification of security factors in cloud computing: Defence security perspective. In *Computational Intelligence Applications in Cyber Security* (pp. 78–99). CRC Press. DOI: 10.1201/9781003514312-6

Pereira, G. V., Parycek, P., Falco, E., & Kleinhans, R. (2018). Smart governance in the context of smart cities: A literature review. *Information Polity*, *23*(2), 143–162. DOI: 10.3233/IP-170067

Perwej, Y., Haq, K., Parwej, F., Mumdouh, M., & Hassan, M. (2019). The internet of things (IoT) and its application domains. *International Journal of Computer Applications*, *975*(8887), 182. DOI: 10.5120/ijca2019918763

Qian, H., Zhang, F., & Qiu, B. (2023). Deciphering the evolution, frontier, and knowledge clustering in sustainable city planning: A 60-year interdisciplinary review. *Sustainability (Basel)*, *15*(24), 16854. DOI: 10.3390/su152416854

Rose, K., Eldridge, S., & Chapin, L. (2015). The internet of things: An overview. [ISOC]. *The Internet Society*, *80*(15), 1–53.

Serrano, W. (2018). Digital systems in smart city and infrastructure: Digital as a service. *Smart Cities*, *1*(1), 134–154. DOI: 10.3390/smartcities1010008

Shao, H., Im, H., Castro, C. M., Breakefield, X., Weissleder, R., & Lee, H. (2018). New technologies for analysis of extracellular vesicles. *Chemical Reviews*, *118*(4), 1917–1950. DOI: 10.1021/acs.chemrev.7b00534 PMID: 29384376

Steele, W., & Legacy, C. (2017). Critical urban infrastructure. []. Taylor & Francis.]. *Urban Policy and Research*, *35*(1), 1–6. DOI: 10.1080/08111146.2017.1283751

Tien, J. M. (2017). Internet of things, real-time decision making, and artificial intelligence. *Annals of Data Science*, *4*(2), 149–178. DOI: 10.1007/s40745-017-0112-5

Van Hoang, T. (2024). Impact of integrated artificial intelligence and internet of things technologies on smart city transformation. Journal of Technical Education Science, 19(Special Issue 01), 64–73.

Chapter 13
Integration of Renewable Energy Systems Into Smart Cities

S. Ida Evangeline
https://orcid.org/0000-0003-2997-7897
Government College of Engineering, Tirunelveli, India

ABSTRACT

A necessary step in creating a sustainable, secure and resilient smart cities is the integration of renewable energy systems. The expansion of cities and the increasing energy demand make the adoption of the renewable energy technologies, solar, wind and geothermal power, vital to reduce carbon footprint and to create clean and highly efficient use of energy. Digital innovations such as the Internet of Things (IoT), artificial intelligence (AI) and blockchain bring about a framework for smart city usage for renewable energy resources management and optimization. This chapter discusses technological, economic, and policy aspects of incorporating renewable energy into urban context from a perspective of smart grids, energy storage options, decentralized power generation, and intelligent energy management systems. However, there are tremendous benefits for the integration of renewable energy, from conservation of the environment, to economic progress, as well as augmentation of a community's resilience. Further research and advancement of the infrastructure to be able to overcome the technical challenges for instance the issues of energy intermittency, storage limitations, and the complexities of grid integration. Limited funds test economic and financial constraints, especially, the high initial cost of renewable energy projects necessitate innovative funding mechanism and supportive policy frameworks. There are also social equity concerns that must be managed that provide for the utilization of clean and affordable energy for all communities, regardless of income.

DOI: 10.4018/979-8-3373-1375-7.ch013

1. INTRODUCTION

A transformation to renewable energy is necessary for the sustainability, security of energy supply and to avoid the harmful impacts of climate change. The depletion of the earth's resources of fossil fuels, growing levels of greenhouse gases in the environment and unprecedented energy systems exposed to potentially severe geopolitical and environmental disruptions thus calls for true exploration of cleaner and sustainable energy sources. The solar, wind, hydro, and geothermal power are renewable energy technologies that provide the potential solution to reduce the reliance on finite resources and have lower carbon footprints. Nevertheless, they must be strategically planned and integrated into the urban environment with innovative technological frameworks to achieve the highest efficiency and reliability (Hassan et al. 2024).

The smart cities offer an ideal platform to embed the renewable energy solutions into the urban infrastructures. Smart cities are characterized with digital technologies, data driven decision making, and interconnected urban systems relying on intelligent networks to achieve efficiency, sustainability and resilience. Smart cities integrate renewable energy systems in their infrastructure to lead to an effective reduction of emissions and improvement in the overall energy consumption thereby creating self sustaining urban environment. Technologies like Internet of Things (IoT), artificial intelligence (AI), and blockchain help make energy management more efficient, perform predictive analytics, and decentralized energy generation which add to the case of renewables in urban settings. Of all the sectors represented in Smart Grids, smart urban power network largely contributes to balance energy supply and demand in real time; enabling the adoption of intermittant renewable sources seamlessly into urban power networks (Aljarrah, 2024).

Starting from this, this chapter explores the link between renewable energy systems and smart city frameworks; finding opportunities and challenges linked to integrating these elements in smart cities. It tries to shed light on technological advances, policy landscapes and governance approaches that result in the adoption of renewable energy in the urban context. Best practices, case studies, and emerging trends that clearly show how smart cities can use renewable energy to create a more sustainable, economic, and community lifestyle will also be discussed. This chapter provides a holistic roadmap to integrate renewable energy in smart urban ecosystems addressing important concerns related to grid stability, barriers to investments, equity, and also policy coordination, thus supporting the vision of resilient and future ready cities.

2. THE ROLE OF SMART CITIES IN RENEWABLE ENERGY ADOPTION

A smart city is a new idea for urban development using advanced digital technology and data driven solutions to improve the efficiency of infrastructure and environment, in addition to improving the city quality of life. A smart city is a city that is, able to integrate technology between different departments like energy, transportation, water management and public services to build a smart city that's intelligent, integrated, and responsive, as shown in Figure 1. Smart cities benefit from real-time data analytics, automation and use of innovative energy management strategies to optimize on resource usage, reduce on waste and environmental impact. Because they are a perfect setting for the adoption and integration of renewable energy systems that entail sophisticated coordination of generation, distribution, and consumption (Chen et al. 2024), this approach is desired.

Figure 1. Renewable energy adoption in smart cities (Pandiyan et al. 2023).

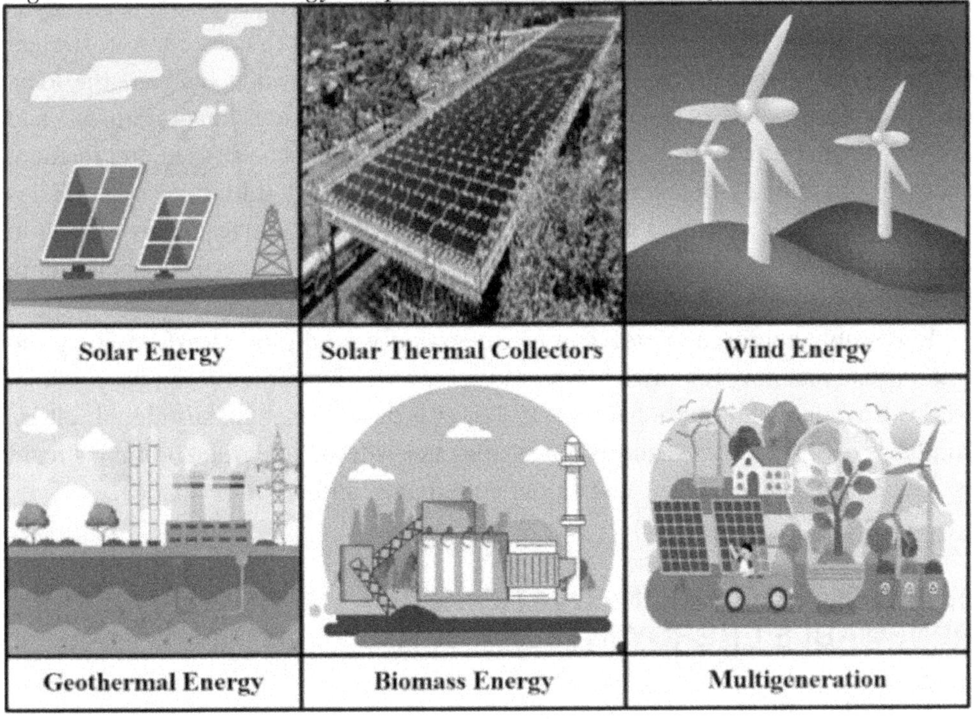

Emerging digital innovations including the Internet of Things (IoT), artificial intelligence (AI), and blockchain is bringing renewable energy technologies close to smart city infrastructures. It is through the IoT enablers, sensors as well as smart meters that take charge of energy monitoring and demand side management collecting real time data on energy production as well as consumption. Dynamic load balancing is possible through this data, which also allows for proper utilization of renewable energy sources. With the help of AI systems, certain predictions about the variations in renewable energy production, distribution optimization for energy, and regions for efficiency improvement helps in better grid stability and reliability. The other way blockchain technology is involved is that it allows decentralized energy markets, where individuals and businesses can trade their surplus renewable energy securely and transparently, and out of the centralized utility providers. Together, these digital tools enhance the resilience of urban energy systems, and especially expedite the process of shifting to cleaner and more sustainable energy supply (Wang & Wang, 2024).

From a technological perspective, the integration of renewable energy into smart cities has become more than just putting in place different technologies; it is also an integration within a planning and the policy framework. Thanks to digitalization, cities can build intelligent, integrated, and renewable energy infrastructures merging the renewable sources, wind, solar, geothermal into the grid. Renewable energy is included in smart urban planning from designing buildings that are energy efficient and equipped with solar panels to developing microgrids that increase the local energy autonomy. Cities can plan systems of renewable energy that optimizes land use, minimize transmission losses, and that results in a decentralized and resilient energy production. Moreover, the correlation of smart city initiatives and policies of sustainability encourages reforms of regulation and incentives of investment in clean energy, fostering an environment that showcases long terms of benefits in terms of the sustainability and economy (Lin et al. 2024).

Renewable energy adoption can be integrated with digital transformation and smart urban planning for cities to become energy efficient, reliable, and accessible, while also reducing its carbon footprint. Towards development of sustainable cities, emphasis of smart cities requires renewable energy to be integrated in mainstream framework of technological innovation, governance and urban resilience.

3. TECHNOLOGICAL INNOVATIONS IN RENEWABLE ENERGY INTEGRATION

Technological innovation plays a series role in the successful integration of renewable energy in smart cities due to its importance in improving efficiency, reliability and scalability. One of the most transformative of these advancements involves the development of smart grids, using IoT sensors and AI analytics to provide real time energy monitoring, predictive energy forecasting, and dynamic load balancing. These intelligent grids will facilitate seamless integration of renewable energy sources including solar and wind which are by nature variable in the urban power grids. AI algorithms collect, analyze, and optimize vast quantities of data about energy distribution, demand, and demand fluctuations, and improve resilience of the grid. The efforts of grid modernization in digital substations and automated demand response systems also enhance overall energy efficiency, which reduces transmission losses and supplies the electricity to consumers at the least cost possible (Ekechukwu & Simpa, 2024).

Storage of power serves to deal with intermittency of renewable energy sources by storing extra power generation at the time of high generation and releasing when demand is high or when production is low. The most used solutions to stabilize renewable energy supply include lithium ion batteries, pumped hydro storage, and emerging solid state battery technologies. By integrating energy storage to the smart city infrastructure, it is ensured that excess energy produced by solar or wind can be used at the right time and smart city dependence on the backup fossil fuel generators is reduced. By integrating with AI driven optimization models, Advanced Energy storage systems improve the grid stability and facilitate apartment of decentralized renewable energy solutions both at grid level (Wang et al. 2024).

Local communities are able to generate, store and distribute their own energy, and decentralised and distributed energy systems are changing the urban energy landscape. In smart cities, rooftop solar installation, small scale wind turbines and community based microgrid are becoming common switching from traditional centralized energy model. Such decentralized systems improve energy security, relieving the dependence on large power plants, and open also the doors for local economic development. Adding to that, blockchain technology is revolutionizing this sector even further by allowing the peer to peer energy trading, where consumer can sell excess renewable energy the directly to the neighbors or businesses without any intermediaries. The decentralized energy marketplace encourages energy efficiency and provides a means to use surplus power within communities so as to reduce the strain on the grids (Tahmasebi et al. 2024).

The integration of renewable energy in smart cities always has some trends and future technologies behind it to change time to time. Through the use of AI, the forecasting of renewable energy is fine tuned to improve planning for a city or grid operator to prepare for changes in supply and demand. Promising future next generation renewable technologies include floating solar farms, airborne wind energy systems and hydrogen based power solutions in further decarbonizing urban energy network. Specifically, hydrogen has recently attracted attention as a clean energy carrier which can store and transport the renewable energy over long distances, and it plays a necessary part of the energy ecosystem in the future smart city. Technological Progress Continues to Grow, That the Convergence of AI, IoT, Energy

Storage, and Decentralized Systems Will Speed up The Adaptation of Renewable Energy will Make the Smart City to be the Sustainable and Energy Efficient Urban.

4. CHALLENGES IN INTEGRATING RENEWABLE ENERGY INTO SMART CITIES

As a result, integrating renewable systems into smart cities poses a large number of challenges across technical, economic, social and governance areas. First and foremost, there is intermittency and variability of renewable energy sources, which represents one of the main technical challenges. Unlike fossil fuels which supply a reliable energy supply, solar and wind are volatile renewable energy sources that their energy depends on weather and time of the day. Due to this variability a stable and reliable energy supply system cannot be guaranteed without sophisticated grid management solutions. The complexity of the process is only increased when decentralized energy systems are integrated into current urban grids, as current grids were not originally intended to support bidirectional energy flows from distributed sources. To avoid power imbalances and grid instability, advanced forecasting models, automated demand response solutions and large scale energy storage solutions are necessary to manage the energy distribution across a number of generation points (Zhang, 2024).

Another important challenge for the adoption of renewable energy in smart cities is the economic and financial barriers. Although the cost of renewably has come down over time, the initial capital required to build the infrastructure is still material. Financial resources are necessitated to deploying solar panels, wind turbines, energy storage systems, smart grid technologies, and so on, which many cities, especially in the developing regions, are often not able to secure. To overcome barriers like these, innovative financing mechanisms, including green bonds, public private partnerships, and international funding programs, are key. Moreover, with long payback period for renewable investments, investors and municipality will be unwilling to commit to large investments without policy driven financial incentives and subsidies to foster adoption (Aparisi-Cerdá et al., 2024).

The integration of renewable energy systems in smart cities is then further complicated due to the social and equity concerns. Although it is clear that these technologies have longterm benefits, equitable deployment of these technologies is required such that all residents have access to clean and affordable energy regardless of income, or location in the country. There is still a struggle with energy poverty, whereby the margins cannot afford to invest in renewable technologies or the infrastructure required to support it. Unless targeted policies are taken, renewable energy development may serve to exacerbate present demographic division, particularly between wealthier areas which reap the benefits and more vulnerable communities which are left behind. Resolving these concerns calls for an inclusive energy planning that places affordability, accessibility, and community participation in the decision making on an equal footing (Sen et al. 2024).

The governance and policy challenges related to deploying renewable energy also determine the integration of renewable energy with smart cities. A large barrier to the establishment of a renewable-based urban energy systems lies in the transitional stage, where it is required to coherently and adaptively develop regulatory frameworks capable of enabling innovation and enhance the safety of grid operation, while ensuring compliance with environmental standards. However, lots of present policies are old fashioned or departmentalized and are unable to take account of new technology or decentralized energy markets. The complexity in the governance efforts is further increased as it needs to coordinate multiple stakeholders, such as government agencies, private sector entities, utilities, and local communities, whose separate interests and priorities can normally lead to conflicts and inefficiencies. However, to surmount these changes, it is imperative for them to establish clear regulatory guidelines for all parties involved, cross sector collaboration in decision making, and optimizing transparent decision making processes (Noh et al. 2024).

Despite these barriers, these (renewable energy) can be planned strategically, achieved through technical innovation, and enabled by policy reform. Through resolving technical barriers, seeking financial investment, reinforcing social equity, and improving governance frameworks, smart cities can achieve the maximized potential of renewable energy to establish resilient, sustainable and inclusive urban cities.

5. POLICY AND GOVERNANCE FRAMEWORKS FOR RENEWABLE ENERGY IN SMART CITIES

Robust policy and governance frameworks that establish an enabling framework for innovation, investment and equity in access to clean energy are therefore key to successful integration of renewable energy in smart cities. The policy support at both national and local level has a significant role to play in promoting the uptake of renewables by means such as incentives, regulatory clarity and strategic planning. There are a few examples of successful government-led policy frameworks in various cities of the world that show the capacity of renewable energy within government's control. For instance, through its feed in tariff system pursuant to the Renewable Energy Sources Act (EEG) Germany substantially increased deployment of solar and wind power by guaranteeing fixed payments to energy producers. In the same way, cities, like the city of San Diego and Copenhagen, have adopted aggressive renewable energy mandates and at the same time formulated clean energy as part of their city's urban planning strategy while establishing clear goals for achieving sustainability. Also, government incentives like tax credits, subsidies and grants encourage the businesses and residents to invest in renewable energy systems and thus, make the adoption of clean energy more financially viable (D'Adamo et al. 2024).

One of the effective instruments to crowd resources and expertise in renewable power projects in smart cities, is public private partnerships. Leveraging the partnerships between the governments, private enterprises and the community organizations bridge the financial gaps and facilitate the large scale implementation of energy infrastructure. While municipalities themselves often don't have the funding necessary to make these business cases for renewable investments that aren't funded in the troubled municipals market, municipalities can effectively leverage financial vehicles, such as green bonds, through power purchase agreements (PPAs) or impact investments, to bring additional capital to the table. In turn, businesses gain these partnerships help them gaining access to government backed incentives and stable policy environments that support long term investments in clean energy. These projects are further inclusive due to community led energy initiatives that allow residents to be part of decentralized energy generation and distribution. Amsterdam and Barcelona have been pioneers in applying public private collaborations for creating a solar rooftops, micro-grids, energy efficient building integrated renewable energy landscapes, and is a good example on how partnerships can push forward the adoption of renewables (Xu & Wudi, 2024).

The regulatory and legal aspects of renewable energy governance in smart cities provide the basis for the safe, efficient, and sustainable use of technological achievements. Typically, smart grids and decentralized energy systems need to be standardised as technical specifications inconsistence and interoperability difficulties have the potential to introduce inefficiencies in the energy distribution. Clear policies on grid connectivity, energy storage, as well as distributed generation promote innovation, while ensuring the ability to maintain equilibrium. Moreover, due to increased digitization of the energy systems, it becomes imperative to have stringent cybersecurity and data privacy measures for smart grids to mitigate cyber risks and unauthorized data access. In light of this, smart cities have to depend on digital technologies for supervising renewable energy networks and consequently have to enforce stringent data protection laws, improve cybersecurity infrastructure, and encourage transparency in energy exchanges. Some of the frameworks to safely protect and enable digital transformation of energy data are the European Union's General Data Protection Regulation (GDPR) and U.S. Department of Energy's cybersecurity efforts (Esfandi et al. 2024).

A dynamic pathway to renewable energy integration is created by smart cities by developing comprehensive policy and governance frameworks that address national and local regulatory requirements, encourage public-private synergy and ensure abidance to applicable laws. The urban energy systems will shape the future of cities for being more resilient, sustainable, and ready for the climate change and energy security challenges through matching the technological advancements, aligning the policies, and establishing the financial mechanisms.

6. OPPORTUNITIES AND BENEFITS OF RENEWABLE ENERGY IN SMART CITIES

The integration of renewable energy into smart cities entails a great potential and advantages in terms of environmental, economic and social aspects. Decrease carbon footprints and air pollution is one of the greatest advantages, which immediately contribute to combating climate change and improving the public health. Currently, energy generation based on fossil fuel is the largest source of greenhouse gas emissions as well as air pollutants that degrade the environment and cause respiratory diseases around the world. Cities can also drastically reduce their emissions by switching to solar, wind, hydro, and other clean and renewable sources, whereas this lowers emissions and thus improves air quality and livabality (Ahmad et al. 2025). This helps in the conservation of the natural resources as renewable energy generation requires abundant and sustainable sources instead of the finite fossil fuel reserves. Renewable energy technologies are essential in preserving biodiversity and reducing ecological strain, as they do not lead to land degradation, water contamination and ecosystem destruction, unlike coal or oil extraction (Mishra et al. 2025).

Renewable energy integration beyond its environmental benefits, generates the most benefits in terms of economic growth and job creation, leading to new industries and entrepreneurial opportunities. Expansion of renewable energy infrastructure leads to creation of employment in different sectors such as manufacturing, installation, maintenance, research and development. When the demand for clean energy solutions grows, so do the requirements for trained personnel in the field of energy storage, smart grid management and AI powered energy analytics. A general economic transformation that involves green technology investment growth from governments and corporations that ensue as renewable energy provides long term cost savings and resilience. By embracing clean energy innovations, cities become the investment, startup, and technology hub for a clean future, while becoming leaders in clean and sustainable futures. However, countries, like Germany and China, that have provided strong policy commitment to renewables have achieved economic advantages in the creation of employment and industrial competitiveness (Abu-Rayash & Dincer, 2025).

Renewable energy adoption in a smart city also has social and community benefits, further supporting a large scale transition. Renewables make energy production more decentralized, providing community control over their energy production, replacing reliance on centralized utilities, and decentralizing energy security. Rooftop solar and local microgrids are localized energy production models that involve local residents and businesses to create sustainable energy and lower electricity costs. The participatory approach creates a stronger social cohesion which fosters citizens' participation in sustainability programs. In addition, renewable energy systems are also used for disaster preparedness and resilience, keeping the community operating even in extreme weather events or when the normal electricity grid is disrupted. Microgrids and energy storage solutions help in faster recovery and prevent the risk of prolonged blackouts in the areas prone to natural disasters, which acts as a key shield against climate related vulnerabilities (Ahmad et al. 2025).

Beyond enhancing the environmental condition, renewable energy in smart cities provides a lot of economic development, technology advancement, and social empowerment opportunities. Cities can use clean energy solutions to achieve dynamic sustainable ecosystems of long term resilience to development and equitable growth and with a higher quality of life to all residents. Beyond being a necessity for climate action, renewables' integration into urban environments is a transformative force, which is altering the way societies generate, consume and distribute energy, on the way to a future that is more sustainable and prosperous.

7. CASE STUDIES OF RENEWABLE ENERGY INTEGRATION IN SMART CITIES

Real world case studies showing how renewable energy was promoted and integrated into smart cities based on innovative policies, technologies, and community driven initiatives illustrate best the successful city integration of renewable energy. Several global cities have been leaders in implementing renewable energy solutions in their smart city framework, and continue to show how clean energy adoption can contribute towards a more sustainable, economically growing and highly resilient system. For instance, Amsterdam has set an example for itself as a pioneer in integration of renewable energy with solar and wind power supported by latest digital energy management systems. Particularly, the city pursues a decentralized energy generation view, it supports community led solar projects and introduces smart grid with the purpose of optimizing energy distribution. Additionally, with the help of business and research institutions, Amsterdam has researched vehicle to grid'

(V2G) technology whereby electric vehicle owners can store surplus renewables and contribute to the grid in peak load periods (Chien & Hsieh, 2025).

Similarly, Singapore has adopted renewable energy in the context of its smart city framework, considering that it does not have large scale wind and hydroelectric power projects due to geographical limitations. The city state has also maximized solar energy via rooftop solar installations, floating solar farms and energy efficient urban planning. Singapore further got enhanced with the deployment of an advanced smart grid system for efficient managing of renewable energy sources while still incorporating them seamlessly with conventional power supplies. Moreover, green buildings are also being prioritized in the country and energy efficient design and construction practices are being mandated so that solar integration is being standardized in new developments. All of these efforts have put Singapore among the global models for renewable energy adoption in dense urban environments (Mallick, 2025).

Another good example here is the one of Copenhagen, which has decided to become the first carbon neutral capital of the world by 2025. The city has spent a great deal on offshore wind farms, district heating systems fed by renewable energy, and waste to energy technologies converting organic waste into biogas. Renewable energy integration in Copenhagen is organically linked to urban planning, as the city takes initiatives to encourage building retrofits, the adoption of cycling as the largest mode of transportation, and so on, significantly reducing emissions from transportation. Also, the city's emphasis on community engagement has been very significant, as residents get involved in cooperative wind farm projects and district energy projects that are geared towards local ownership and investment in renewable solutions (Oyadeyi & Oyadeyi, 2025).

The experiences of these cities provide vital lessons for strengthening and driving the use of renewable energy in other urban areas' smart city strategies. The policy support and regulatory frameworks that are needed to promote investments in clean energy and to support public private partnership is one of such. For instance, Amsterdam's V2G example showcases how electric vehicles can be harnessed as energy storage assets to improve grid flexibility through technological innovation. Singapore's experience constitutes a successful proof of the need for developing specific and adapted renewable energy strategies, showing that even land constraints do not preclude the optimization of solar energy through strategic urban planning. Its model raises the importance of community involvement in rendering renewable energy projects successful: the more the citizen is involved, the more the citizen will feel an involvement in both ownership and durability.

Even with these successes, challenges still persist: the requirement for more suitable energy storage solutions, financial feasibility for larger scale renewable infrastructure, and the technical intricacies of incorporating decentralized energy systems into existing grids. These case studies, however, illustrate how a smart mix of policy, technology, bottom up community initiatives can get over those hurdles. As cities around the world embrace sustainability, the lessons from these pioneer smart cities will be needful to build scalable and effective renewable energy solutions in line with the broader vision of resilient, efficient, and low carbon urban environments.

8. FUTURE DIRECTIONS AND RECOMMENDATIONS

The key issue is how to scale up clean energy adoption while dealing with the technical, financial, and social challenges going hand in hand with the transition to smart cities based on clean energy. For large scale deployment of renewable energy, large amount of investment in infrastructure, digitalization and regulatory support is needed. Apart from other strategies of promoting renewable energy adoption, expanding the capacity of smart grids that can dynamically balance between energy supply and demand is among the most effective strategies in incorporating intermittent renewable sources, like solar and wind, into the mix. The widespread deployment of distributed energy systems such as rooftop solar panels, microgrids, and battery storage will increase its resilience. Furthermore, electrification of the transportation sector such as electric vehicles and public transit powered by renewables will have significant contribution to lower carbon emissions from the urban areas. Aside from this, cities also need to devise new ways to make accessing renewable energy more sustainable, like green bonds, public private partnerships and subsidies that will attract both private and community investment in clean energy infrastructure (Rojek et al. 2025).

An integrated approach, one which bridges the policy realm with the community and technology realms has to be taken in order to achieve deployment of renewable energy that is in alignment with broader urban sustainability objectives. The policy framework needs to be adaptive and forward thinking so that it can put into practice regulatory measures for decentralised energy generation, demand response mechanisms and energy efficient urban planning. Government needs to join hands with the private sector to spur innovation and streamline permitting processes; and also create incentives that will help the businesses and residents to participate in renewable energy initiatives. But at the same time, a successful deployment of renewable energy projects must have the involvement of the local communities for this to succeed in the long run. Citizens can play an active role in transition to clean energy through empowering themselves via public awareness campaigns, participatory decision making process and community owned energy projects which will help foster social equity and inclusiveness. Cities that implement a people centered approach will not only promote the adoption of renewable energy but also ensure that this adoption benefits everyone, regardless of socio economic status (Lija et al. 2025).

Research and development will be continued to overcome current barriers to renewable energy integration and new path broken to new approaches to urban sustainability. Next generation batteries and hydrogen based storage solutions will aid to tackle intermittency of renewables by improving consistency and reliability of power supply. Smart grids will become more efficient with the help of AI driven energy forecasting models to predict and manage the fluctuations in the demand of energy in the cities. New emerging renewable technologies like floating solar farms, wave and tidal energy, and bioenergy innovations can bring in various options in urban energy portfolios thus reducing the dependence on conventional energy sources. In terms of trading and sharing renew able energy and securing lower energy bills done in smart cities it might be possible to further explore the applications of Blockchain in peer to peer energy trading and carbon credit verification. Finally, future research efforts should aim at the point where climate resilience and the deployment of renewable energy intersect in order to avoid the problem of urban energy systems becoming sustainable yet fragile (Bibri et al. 2025).

The integration of renewable energy in smart cities is a process and should not be taken as a one time issue. The challenge of creating long term sustainable solutions is one that needs the cooperation of governments, businesses, researchers and communities in developing adaptive, scalable and equitable solutions. Cities have the opportunity to drive this transition by encouraging innovation, bolstering policy support and engaging citizens to collectively transition towards a future in which renewable energy represents not only an alternative, but also the mainstay of urban resilience and development.

9. CONCLUSION

There exists a potential for renewable energy systems to be integrated with smart cities to help assist the sustainability, energy security and environmental resilience. All along, smart cities have been shown to be an excellent environment for embedding renewable energy technologies using digital innovations, decentralized generation, and intelligent energy management systems. Smart grids, AI driven analytics, IoT based monitoring and blockchain based energy trading are identified as key enablers towards making the urban energy ecosystem more efficient and adaptive. The use of these technological advances enables cities to decrease dependence on fossil fuels, reduce greenhouse gas emissions and have an infrastructure that is more sustainable and resilient.

Even though it has great potential, there are a number of challenges that need to be overcome to make the most of renewable energy in smart cities. Continued research and innovation is needed to overcome technical obstacles like the intermittency of renewable power sources such as solar and wind power, their integration into the grid, and limitations of storage. Although economic barriers are high, it requires a creative approach in financing via public private partnerships, green bonds or government subsidies to speed up adoption. However, social and equity concerns have to be carefully managed as well so that the transition to renewable energy is inclusive and the clean, affordable, and accessible sources of energy to all the residents of the city. The coordination of these efforts is played by policy and governance frameworks, need for transparent regulatory policies, strong cooperation among stake holders and adaptability required for new energy technologies.

Working together, policymakers, urban planners, industry leaders, researchers, and local communities need to overcome these barriers and make the most of the potential renewables have to offer. Governments must advance in developing and practicing policies for instigating investment inside clean power infrastructure, expediting regulatory process and supporting financial incentives in the use of clean technologies. There should be a focus by urban planners towards suitable smart city designs that have decentralized energy systems, green building standards and are energy efficient in transport networks. Storage solutions, grid modernization, and digital energy management tools will need to be further advanced by industry stakeholders and technology developers to increase system reliability and efficiency. Additionally, local communities need to be actively involved in the transition — renewable energy projects need to be designed inclusive of, affordable for, and sustainable over the long run.

It is both ambitious and necessary to follow the path towards fully renewable and self-sustaining smart cities. As climate change becomes increasingly urgent, and us as a global population grows at an accelerating pace in urban areas, the transition away from dirty energy to clean had become not just a good idea but a pre-requisite condition of future urban development. Where cities can lead the way in building a sustainable future powered by renewable energy, it is by using innovation, collaborating, and applying strategic policies. We are now at the time for action and it is the responsibility of all the stakeholders to ensure that the smart cities are technologically advanced, environmentally responsible, socially equitable.

REFERENCES

Abu-Rayash, A., & Dincer, I. (2025). Development of an integrated model for environmentally and economically sustainable and smart cities. *Sustainable Energy Technologies and Assessments*, *73*, 104096. DOI: 10.1016/j.seta.2024.104096

Ahmad, S. S., Ghalib, M. R., Gallimore, M., Al Mousa, A., & Wattar, I. (2025). Smart Integration of Renewable Energy for Sustainable Cities: Leveraging Technology for Urban Resilience. In *Exploring Pillars of Sustainability for Modern Age Improvements* (pp. 317-336). IGI Global Scientific Publishing.

Aljarrah, E. (2024). AI-based model for Prediction of Power consumption in smart grid-smart way towards smart city using blockchain technology. *Intelligent Systems with Applications*, *24*, 200440. DOI: 10.1016/j.iswa.2024.200440

Aparisi-Cerdá, I., Ribó-Pérez, D., García-Melón, M., D'Este, P., & Poveda-Bautista, R. (2024). Drivers and barriers to the adoption of decentralised renewable energy technologies: A multi-criteria decision analysis. *Energy*, *305*, 132264. DOI: 10.1016/j.energy.2024.132264

Bibri, S. E., Huang, J., Omar, O., & Kenawy, I. (2025). Synergistic integration of digital twins and zero energy buildings for climate change mitigation in sustainable smart cities: A systematic review and novel framework. *Energy and Building*, *333*, 115484. DOI: 10.1016/j.enbuild.2025.115484

Chen, Z., Gan, W., Wu, J., Lin, H., & Chen, C. M. (2024). Metaverse for smart cities: A survey. *Internet of Things and Cyber-Physical Systems*, *4*, 203–216. DOI: 10.1016/j.iotcps.2023.12.002

Chien, Y. H., & Hsieh, I. Y. L. (2025). Enhancing Urban Energy Resilience: Vehicle-to-Grid (V2G) Strategies within Electric Scooter Battery Swapping Ecosystems. *Sustainable Cities and Society*, *118*, 106004. DOI: 10.1016/j.scs.2024.106004

D'Adamo, I., Gastaldi, M., Koh, S. L., & Vigiano, A. (2024). Lighting the future of sustainable cities with energy communities: An economic analysis for incentive policy. *Cities (London, England)*, *147*, 104828. DOI: 10.1016/j.cities.2024.104828

Ekechukwu, D. E., & Simpa, P. (2024). A comprehensive review of renewable energy integration for climate resilience. *Engineering Science & Technology Journal*, *5*(6), 1884–1908. DOI: 10.51594/estj.v5i6.1187

Esfandi, S., Tayebi, S., Byrne, J., Taminiau, J., Giyahchi, G., & Alavi, S. A. (2024). Smart cities and urban energy planning: An advanced review of promises and challenges. *Smart Cities*, *7*(1), 414–444. DOI: 10.3390/smartcities7010016

Hassan, Q., Algburi, S., Sameen, A. Z., Al-Musawi, T. J., Al-Jiboory, A. K., Salman, H. M., ... & Jaszczur, M. (2024). A comprehensive review of international renewable energy growth. *Energy and built environment*.

Lija, A. V., Aswathy, M. P., Kavitha, G., Velammal, M. N., Maheswari, B., & Pajila, P. B. (2025). A Review on Sustainable Development and Green Practices: Strategies, Challenges, and Future Directions. Adaptive Strategies for Green Economy and Sustainability Policies, 1-16.

Lin, X. J., Zhang, N., Mao, Y. H., Chen, J. Y., Tian, X. T., & Zhong, W. (2024). A review of the transformation from urban centralized heating system to integrated energy system in smart city. *Applied Thermal Engineering*, *240*, 122272. DOI: 10.1016/j.applthermaleng.2023.122272

Mallick, R. (2025). Smart Cities and Climate Resilience. In *Community Resilience and Climate Change Challenges: Pursuit of Sustainable Development Goals (SDGs)* (pp. 401–412). IGI Global Scientific Publishing.

Mishra, A., Alam, M. I., Pal, D. B., & Awasthi, S. (2025). Solar Energy and Its Utilization in Smart Cities. In *Renewable Energy Development: Technology, Material and Sustainability* (pp. 111–131). Springer Nature Singapore. DOI: 10.1007/978-981-97-9626-7_6

Noh, Y., Jafarinejad, S., & Anand, P. (2024). A review on harnessing renewable energy synergies for achieving urban net-zero energy buildings: Technologies, performance evaluation, policies, challenges, and future direction. *Sustainability (Basel)*, *16*(8), 3444. DOI: 10.3390/su16083444

Oyadeyi, O. A., & Oyadeyi, O. O. (2025). Towards inclusive and sustainable strategies in smart cities: A comparative analysis of Zurich, Oslo, and Copenhagen. *Research in Globalization*, 100271.

Pandiyan, P., Saravanan, S., Usha, K., Kannadasan, R., Alsharif, M. H., & Kim, M. K. (2023). Technological advancements toward smart energy management in smart cities. *Energy Reports*, *10*, 648–677. DOI: 10.1016/j.egyr.2023.07.021

Rojek, I., Mikołajewski, D., Galas, K., & Piszcz, A. (2025). Advanced Deep Learning Algorithms for Energy Optimization of Smart Cities. *Energies*, *18*(2), 407. DOI: 10.3390/en18020407

Sen, K. K., Hosan, S., Karmaker, S. C., Chapman, A. J., & Saha, B. B. (2024). Clarifying the linkage between renewable energy deployment and energy justice: Toward equitable sustainability. *Sustainable Futures : An Applied Journal of Technology, Environment and Society*, *8*, 100236. DOI: 10.1016/j.sftr.2024.100236

Tahmasebi, D., Sheikh, M., Dabbaghjamanesh, M., Jin, T., Kavousi-Fard, A., & Karimi, M. (2024). A security-preserving framework for sustainable distributed energy transition: Case of smart city. *Renewable Energy Focus*, *51*, 100631. DOI: 10.1016/j.ref.2024.100631

Wang, D., Liu, N., Chen, F., Wang, Y., & Mao, J. (2024). Progress and prospects of energy storage technology research: Based on multidimensional comparison. *Journal of Energy Storage*, *75*, 109710. DOI: 10.1016/j.est.2023.109710

Wang, H., & Wang, Y. (2024). Smart cities net zero planning considering renewable energy landscape design in digital twin. *Sustainable Energy Technologies and Assessments*, *63*, 103629. DOI: 10.1016/j.seta.2024.103629

Xu, J., & Wudi, X. U. (2024). Financing sustainable smart city Projects: Public-Private partnerships and green Bonds. *Sustainable Energy Technologies and Assessments*, *64*, 103699. DOI: 10.1016/j.seta.2024.103699

Zhang, J. (2024). Energy access challenge and the role of fossil fuels in meeting electricity demand: Promoting renewable energy capacity for sustainable development. *Geoscience Frontiers*, *15*(5), 101873. DOI: 10.1016/j.gsf.2024.101873

Chapter 14
Integration of LLMs in Smart Cities for Sustainable Energy Solutions

Dina Darwish
https://orcid.org/0000-0002-6708-649X
Ahram Canadian University, Egypt

ABSTRACT

By enabling the quick expansion of urban areas and efficiently managing resources through sustainable and scalable innovations, smart cities are crucial components in the continuous pursuit of improving urban living standards. Smart city applications face multiple obstacles, one of which is the risk of sensitive data being exposed without authorization, due to the proliferation of new technologies such as the Internet of Things (IoT), big data analytics, fog computing, and edge computing. Thanks to their adaptability in natural language processing and other areas, large language models (LLMs) as Chatbots have garnered a lot of interest. Data collecting systems for LLM fine-tuning, LLM embedding of power system-specific tools, and a retrieval augmented generation (RAG)-based knowledge pool to improve LLM answers and LLMs in safety-critical use cases are important areas for future research initiatives. This chapter discusses how LLMs can lead to energy efficiency and sustainability in smart cities, by using literature review and case studies, as well as providing future directions.

DOI: 10.4018/979-8-3373-1375-7.ch014

1. INTRODUCTION

In today's world, the excessive consumption of fossil fuels has resulted in significant environmental issues, such as the rise in sea level and the acceleration of global warming (Ding et al., 2021; Zhou et al., 2022; Wang et al., 2022). The development of renewable energy sources, such as solar and wind power, is one of the most effective ways to address the issues that are plaguing the environment (Guermoui et al., 2021; Shao et al., 2022). The development of renewable energy is accelerating as a result of the proposal of a goal to achieve carbon neutrality. As a result of the fact that the development of renewable energy is currently one of the most vital for attaining the aim of carbon neutrality and tackling environmental problems, renewable energy is becoming one of the most important academic study subjects (Bai et al., 2022).

Many academics have used AI algorithms into the field of renewable energy (Al-Othman et al., 2022; Jha et al., 2017). This is because we are currently living in an era of artificial intelligence (AI). In order to accurately predict the future generation of power from wind and photovoltaic sources, numerous artificial intelligence approaches, including deep neural networks, support vector machines, gradient boosting decision trees, and others, have been effectively utilized (Yu et al., 2023). Techniques from the field of artificial intelligence, such as deep neural networks, have also been successfully implemented in the Prognostics and Health Management (PHM) of renewable energy systems (Kellil et al., 2023). In the field of operational optimization of renewable energy systems, artificial intelligence approaches such as deep reinforcement learning have proven to be quite successful (Ruan et al., 2023). Within the context of the large-scale integration of renewable energy sources into the power grid, artificial intelligence has also been successfully utilized in the trading of electricity markets (Heidarpanah et al., 2023). As a result, artificial intelligence has been playing an increasingly significant role in the development of renewable energy alternatives.

Imagine living in a future where technology is capable of comprehending human language and providing accurate responses to it. With the help of Large Language Models (LLMs), this is not science fiction; rather, it is the reality that we are currently living in. In order to facilitate a wide range of technical developments, these highly developed artificial intelligence systems are intended to process and synthesize human language on a massive scale through their design. In order to make progress towards a more sustainable future, innovation is required across all industries. Large Language Models (LLMs), a cutting-edge form of artificial intelligence that is revolutionizing the way in which we process and generate language. The United Nations' Sustainable Development Goals (SDGs) are a blueprint for a more equal and healthy planet. These strong tools have the potential to accelerate progress towards the SDGs because of their vast potential.

ChatGPT (Openai,. 2023), which stands for Chat Generative Pre-trained Transformer, is a Large Language Model (LLM) that has been trained on billions of text data from websites (Kirmani, 2022; Brown et al., 2020). It is the most current innovation and the most advanced technology in the field of artificial intelligence today. It is able to generate writing that is similar to that of a human, respond to enquiries in a manner that is human-like, and carry out a variety of language-related activities with a high degree of accuracy (Perkins, 2023). Since its introduction by the OpenAI corporation in November 2022, it has rapidly become one of the consumer applications that has had the most rapid growth in the history of the world, with millions of active users on a monthly basis. Language processing skills and a massive knowledge base have revolutionized the way people engage with technology (Mathew, 2023), making it simpler and more natural to speak with machines (Mathew, 2023; Bahrini et al., 2023). It has also revolutionized the way people interact with technology. A wide range of industries, including business, education, manufacturing, healthcare, medicine, and communication, have all found success with the implementation of ChatGPT technologies. Researchers working in the field of renewable energy might increase the efficiency of their academic writing by using ChatGPT to automatically generate some paragraphs for their academic papers. Large Language Models (LLMs) have become increasingly popular as a result of the flourishing of ChatGPT. As a means of competing with ChatGPT, which was developed by OpenAI, other firms, including Google, Baidu, Anthropic, and iFLYTEK, among others, are producing their very own LLMs. The Claude model (Bai et al., 2022), which was produced by the Anthropic company, the ERNIE Bot model (Sun et al., 2020, Sun et al., 2021; Baidu, 2023), which was developed by the Baidu company, the SparkDesk model (Xinghuo. (2023), which was developed by the iFLYTEK company, and other models are included among these new LLMs. There are several elements of these LLMs that are comparable to those of ChatGPT. Researchers working in the field of renewable energy can also write some good academic paper paragraphs by using these LLMs. Additionally, they can integrate the text generated by ChatGPT in order to further improve the efficiency of academic writing practices.

2. LARGE LANGUAGE MODELS (LLM) ROLE IN REACHING SUSTAINABILITY

2.1. Large Language Models

Large Language Models, often known as LLMs, are sophisticated artificial intelligence systems that are designed to process and synthesize human language. Understanding natural language and generating text have both been significantly improved as a result of these models. LLMs are able to learn complex relationships between words and concepts because they are trained on vast amounts of text data. This enables them to perform a variety of language-based tasks, including the translation of languages, the creation of human-quality text, the writing of various types of creative content, and the provision of informative responses to your questions.

In contrast to the rule-based systems that have been used in the past, LLMs take into account the complete context of a sentence or document. They accomplish this by utilizing self-attention methods, such as the Transformer architecture, in order to identify long-range dependencies. They began as straightforward rule-based engines and have now developed into more complicated systems such as GPT-4 and BERT. The use of these models is causing a transformation in a number of different industries, including healthcare (by facilitating individualized patient care) and finance (by simplifying decision-making). Their significance is growing, and it is anticipated that the market would increase by the year 2025.

LLMs are discreetly powering the digital services that we use on a daily basis, starting with chatbots who provide assistance online and continuing with intelligent suggestions on your phone.

2.2. Growing Demand for LLM Expertise

In light of the growing expansion of the LLM market, businesses are actively looking for professionals who are knowledgeable about how to make effective use of these sophisticated tools. An analysis conducted by Grand View Research suggests that the global market for LLM might increase by billion by the year 2028, representing an big increase in growth. It is anticipated that this expansion would result in the creation of around 6.7 million additional employment by the year 2025. The experts who are adept in generative artificial intelligence, data analysis, and software engineering are of significant relevance to businesses especially. Python is one of the most sought-after skills for positions related to learning and development (LLM).

2.3. How LLMs Work

The training of LLMs is performed on massive volumes of text data, which is typically scraped from various sources such as books, journals, code repositories, and the internet. Their exposure to this data enables children to acquire knowledge of the statistical correlations that exist between words and phrases.

Generally speaking, LLMs make use of a deep learning architecture, which is most frequently transformers, which are a type of neural network. These neural networks are made up of numerous layers, each of which processes the data and extracts progressively complicated information from the text.

The LLM acquires a statistical understanding of the connections that exist between individual words and word sequences while it is being trained. In addition to analyzing the general structure of language, it examines the way in which words are employed in context, as well as the likelihood that they will appear together.

Once trained, LLMs are able to write whole new text based on a given prompt or predict the next word in a series based on the information provided. Because of this, they are able to carry out varied jobs.

In addition to creative text generation (writing poems, scripts, musical pieces, or even computer code), text completion, machine translation, question answering, text summarization, and text summarization are also included.

On the cutting edge of artificial intelligence are LLMs such as GPT-4, Gemini, LLAMA2, and Claude 3. The vast amounts of text material that they draw from allows them to process and synthesize human language. The Transformer design, which incorporates self-attention processes, is utilized by these models. This architecture enables the models to comprehend context and generate text that is pertinent to the situation.

2.4. LLMs and reaching Sustainable Development Goals (SDGs)

There are a lot of ways in which LLMs can help to achieve the Sustainable Development Goals:

1. **LLMs have the potential to improve educational content development,** personalized learning experiences, and language translation for global education projects, which pertains to Sustainable Development Goal 4 (Quality Education). In addition, LLMs have the ability to serve as virtual tutors, providing students with answers to their questions and feedback on their assignments. This makes education more accessible and participatory. Additionally, they can aid in the

development of educational tools that are accessible and engaging for a wide range of students.

2. **LLMs have the potential to assist in medical research,** drug discovery, and personalized healthcare recommendations, all of which are part of the Sustainable Development Goal 3 (SDG 3). Additionally, they are able to analyze large amounts of medical literature, which assists medical practitioners in remaining current on the most recent breakthroughs.
3. **Identifying gender biases in text and promoting gender-neutral language** are two of the goals of the Sustainable Development Goal 5 (SDG 5). They are able to make a contribution to the production of content that is inclusive, which challenges preconceptions and supports equality.
4. **LLMs are able to analyze climate data**, forecast extreme weather events, and offer mitigation methods. This is considered to be Sustainable Development Goal 13 (SDG 13). They can be of assistance in the modelling of climate, the creation of policies, and the efforts to raise public awareness.
5. **To achieve Sustainable Development Goal** 7 (Affordable and Clean Energy), LLMs can be utilized to do research on renewable energy sources and make recommendations for alternative energy alternatives. In order to facilitate this process, LLMs might be of assistance by creating new ideas and solutions. Think about an LLM that has been trained on a big dataset of environmentally friendly technologies. It may come up with ideas for environmentally friendly building materials, make suggestions for alternate energy sources, or even develop code for software that is more energy efficient. The capacity to come up with original concepts has the potential to serve as a game-changer in the fight against climate change and the destruction of the environment.
6. **Reduced Inequalities (SDG 10):** LLMs have the potential to assist in bridging language gaps by helping to improve communication across cultures and providing accurate translations. By making information more available, they are able to provide assistance to populations that are marginalized.
7. **Sustainable Cities and Communities (SDG 11):** LLMs can be utilized to do data analysis on urban planning and traffic patterns in order to construct sustainable city infrastructure.
8. **Sustainable Development Goal 12, "Responsible Consumption and Production,"** LLMs can be utilized to conduct data analysis on resource usage, pinpoint areas that could be improved, and generate creative ideas for manufacturing that is environmentally responsible.

2.5. Utilizing LLMs to Construct a Future That Is Sustainable

Despite the fact that LLMs have a great deal of promise, it is essential to create and use them in a responsible manner. Outputs that are discriminatory or deceptive can be the result of biases that are present in the training data. In addition, the enormous amount of computer resources that are required for LLMs raises worries about the environment. In order to guarantee that LLMs make a good contribution to the Sustainable Development Goals, we need to concentrate on the following ideas. For the purpose of preventing the perpetuation of inequities, ethical development involves training data that is diverse and objective.

The development of LLMs that are transparent in their thinking and decision-making processes is described under the category of "transparency and explainability."

Making the technology of LLM available to all nations, not just those in the industrialized world, is an important aspect of accessibility and equity. Figure 1 shows a smart city including roads and transportation means.

Figure 1. A smart city

3. SMART CITIES IMPLEMENTING LLMS FOR SUSTAINABLE ENERGY SOLUTION

Smart cities have evolved as the vanguard of urban development, combining efficient urbanization, environmental stewardship, increased living standards, and leveraging the revolutionary power of cutting-edge communication technology (Ullah et al., 2020). Smart cities have emerged as the vanguard of urban development. The magnetic draw of metropolitan opportunities has caused rural populations to move towards city centers, and it is anticipated that this trend will continue even in the future. The United Nations projects that by the year 2050, urbanization will have occurred in 86 percent of affluent countries and 64 percent of developing countries

(Shilpi and Ahad, 2020). In a similar vein, it is anticipated that approximately 66% of people will be living in urban environments by the middle of the century (Oliveira, et al., 2020). Ingenious technologies and tools, such as Artificial Intelligence (AI), Machine Learning (ML), Deep Learning (DL), Internet of Things (IoT), Federated Learning (FL), Blockchain, Natural Language Processing (NLP), and Language Learning Machines (LLMs), serve as crucial sentinels, assuring the smooth and standardized operation of smart cities (Ullah et al., 2020). In the context of smart cities, artificial intelligence (AI) makes use of sophisticated algorithms to give machines the ability to imitate human intelligence. This gives robots the ability to learn from data, recognize patterns, and make judgements (Ullah et al., 2023). Machine learning gives computers the ability to learn and grow from their experiences without the need for explicit programming. This means that they can automatically recognize hidden patterns and make predictions based on the data they have collected (Olawade, et al., 2023). Deep Learning, which falls under the umbrella of machine learning, is a technique that models intricate patterns and representations by utilizing neural networks that have numerous layers in order to do tasks such as recognizing speech and images (Collins, et al., 2021). The Federated Learning technique is a collaborative machine learning method that trains its models on decentralized data sources without sharing raw data. This protects users' privacy while simultaneously constructing global models (Bharati, et al., 2022). Natural language processing is a subfield of artificial intelligence that employs algorithms to comprehend, analyze, and generate human language. This process makes it easier for humans and machines to communicate with one another (Manaris, 2020). The blockchain technology is a digital ledger that is decentralized and secure. It records transactions across numerous computers, which increases the transparency and security of data (Zahoora et al., 2022). Because of these technologies, city planners and administrators are able to organize actions that are both timely and exact, which ultimately results in an improvement in the overall quality of life for the citizens of the city (Olawade, et al., 2023; Collins, et al., 2021). This synergy between cutting-edge technologies and urban governance paves the way for urban ecosystems that are more efficient, responsive, and citizen-centric. These ecosystems will be characterized by the cumulative contributions of artificial intelligence, machine learning, deep learning, natural language processing, language learning systems, and blockchain technology.

3.1. Building Blocks of Smart Cities

It is possible to formulate a definition of a smart city by taking into consideration a number of different themes.

Not only does having an understanding of these issues make the development of techniques that are not only more efficient and environmentally friendly for these developing urban regions, but also simplifies the process of comparing and evaluating their respective levels of intelligence within the framework of strategic concerns.

The Political, Economic, and Social Planning and Governance System encompasses not only towns and regions but also entire countries.

In the beginning, the PEST analysis, which stands for the economic, social, and technological analysis, played a crucial role (Verma, et al., 2020). For the same reason, the PEST study is also performed on smart cities in order to equip them with the ability to appropriately satisfy both the needs of the present and those of the future across a diverse range of industries. There are many different components and characteristics that are included in the comprehensive model of the smart city, which includes subjects such as governance, energy, technology, education, and technological infrastructure, communities, buildings, healthcare, and transportation, which are all important.

3.1.1. Structures and Existing Public Facilities

ICT plays a significant role in the infrastructure of a smart city, which also includes domestic, public, institutional components, segments. Homes are the primary focus of domestic infrastructure, which includes the incorporation of smart appliances and management of resources (including water, power, and the internet). Mobility, supported by public infrastructure, comprises structures, community centers, transportation, traffic management, and intelligent parking systems of various kinds. The technological improvements include communication, data, and other areas are driven by institutional infrastructure, use of resources, creation and management, and transmission of information in a secure manner (Ahmad, et al., 2015).

3.1.2. Energy and Emerging Technologies

The planning, implementation, and monitoring of smart cities are all significantly aided by the utilization of smart technology.

Developing and managing infrastructure, resources, and other resources is made easier by technological breakthroughs and innovations, connection, transportation, and manufacturing, making the switch from non-renewable to renewable alternatives.

Recent technological developments, such as solar cells, are essential to the operation of energy sources such as solar energy (Hameed, 2019).

3.1.3. Transportation

Through the use of information and communication technology, Intelligent Transportation Systems (ITS) are revolutionizing traditional modes of transportation, leading to optimizing travel and mobility experiences in cities that are considered smart. A primary focus of the ITS principles is integrity, safety, reactivity, and sustainability. The transportation needs of smart cities include electronic and self-driving vehicles, cutting-edge parking technology, and cutting-edge infrastructure that make use of sensors and processes of processing and monitoring (Zichichi, et al., 2022).

3.1.4. Healthcare and Education

In order to provide efficient learning, smart education incorporates cutting-edge pedagogical tools with information and communication technology.

As a result of the Internet of Things, new gadgets like smart boards, wireless sensor networks, and smartphone integration into educational institutions, in addition to the implementation of software applications such as learning management systems, as well as business resource planning can be implemented. Intelligent healthcare comprises a variety of services comprising tools and robots with intelligence, improved diagnostics, emergency response systems, and other technologies. Healthcare infrastructure is complex and advanced, and requires performing data analysis on medical records and enabling electronic healthcare.

There are notable applications within the realm of smart city healthcare that are offered through cellphones (Wala, et al., 2020; Er, et al., 2021).

3.1.5. Community

Residents of a smart city make up the inhabitants of the community. The contributions of a community of intelligent citizens to the development of contemporary cities that are both efficient and environmentally friendly. The citizens of smart cities typically look for a higher quality of life in comparison to people who live in traditional city settings. It is because of this dynamics that a population of intelligent cities are populated by persons who are aware and capable, which encourages future improvement. These are individual components, when taken as a whole, constitute the complex framework of a smart city, which incorporates a wide range of the factors that contribute to its development and efficiency. Figure 2 shows Building Blocks of smart cities.

3.2. Smart Cities Characteristics

It is necessary for a smart city to build its network-related services in a manner that is more flexible and user-friendly in order to guarantee an efficient and sustainable living space. The use of information and communication technology (ICT) can help inhabitants enhance their lifestyles by providing them with a safe, and friendly environment, which in turn increases their work efficiency (Silva, et al., 2018). As can be seen, smart cities are distinguished by a variety of characteristics and fundamental elements. Technology, liveability, sustainability, governance, and urban characteristics are some of the things that fall under this category (Silva, et al., 2018). Among these, technology plays an important part, and it is comprised of a number of different components, such as intelligent transportation, infrastructure, healthcare, technology, and energy. All of these facilities are made more efficient and quick thanks to the intelligence, which also helps to cut down on wasted time and money. The transformation of traditional cities into smart cities is made possible through the utilization of information technology. The Internet of Things (IoT), big data, information and communication technology (ICT), machine learning and deep learning algorithms, natural language processing (NLP), and intelligent infrastructure are the primary technologies. According to the most recent research (Halbreich, 2023), by the end of the year 2050, more than two-thirds of the world's population would be residing in metropolitan zones. Urban populations are responsible for around 73% of the assets, and they are also contributing to the age of compounds that are harmful to the ozone layer. This suggests that a larger proportion of the population is affected by the repercussions that can have an effect on the climate, which has led to the consideration of the concept of smart urban areas (Silva, et al., 2018). The purpose is to solve the problems that are caused by expansive urbanization, such as reducing the amount of energy used, the amount of water used, the amount of toxins that are released into the atmosphere, the amount of transportation required, and the amount of waste that is produced in cities. Figure 3 illustrates smart cities characteristics.

Figure 2. Building Blocks of smart cities

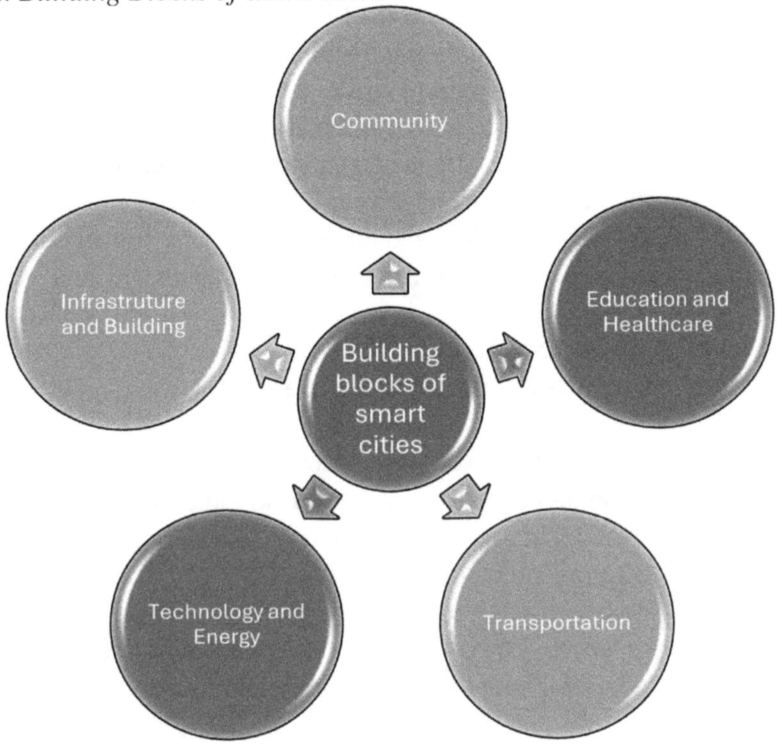

Figure 3. Smart Cities characteristics

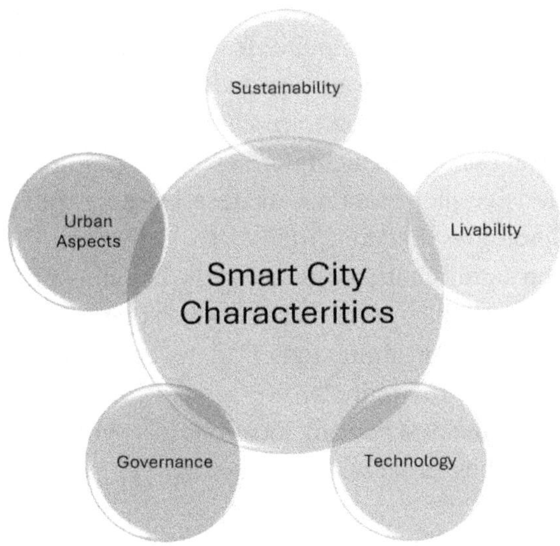

It is essential to guarantee personal fulfilment in regard to the flourishing of the financial and emotional circumstances of living places. To put it succinctly, a smart city or smart metropolitan region is required to have development plans for the government, society, economy, and climate. This is due to the fact that a smart city or urban area is designed to cater to its inhabitants, where the economy should make it possible to provide them with open positions, and where the administration should ensure that the necessary management actions are taken in order to make smart cities or urban areas livable for their inhabitants by implementing smart transportation, governance, energy, citizens, buildings, healthcare, and technology.

3.3. The use of deep learning to the development of sustainable smart cities

In the past half-century, there has been a substantial increase in the number of people living in metropolitan areas all over the world indicating a significant shift in the demographics (Joshi, et al., 2016). Both urban and rural communities have been pushed to undergo this process.

We need to prepare ourselves to deal with the quick pace of technology advancement, which will open up new opportunities to improve public safety, connectivity, and the overall experience for both locals and tourists, these are all important factors to consider.

Researchers were able to leverage the potential of complex methodologies in a ground-breaking work that was acknowledged in paper (Joshi, et al., 2016).

To identify and demarcate colonies, as well as to forecast traffic, computer vision and deep learning patterns are being utilized.

An extensive range of gradations is the goal of this innovative approach, which aims to identify them providing to a more detailed understanding of the situation by stretching from developed to disadvantaged regions comprehending the urban landscapes that exist. As we move on to research (Nastjuk, et al., 2022), a recommendation that is strong and convincing arises in the field of intelligent parking, bolstered by the extensive incorporation of deep learning, internet of things, and communication technologies that are wireless. These forward-thinking suggestions have their sights set on significantly minimizing the amount of time required to seek parking spots that are available, particularly in areas that are already very busy for example, shopping centers and train stops. This is accomplished by utilizing the capabilities of both DL and IoT radar.

The technology finds the best parking locations in a short amount of time, which speeds up the entire parking process.

The achievement of seamless connectedness is contingent on a number of factors, including the ongoing evolution of urban environments, as the availability of the system, as well as the bandwidth, media, and topology of the network (Intelligent Cities, 2023).

Another innovative invention that is featured here is the introduction of intelligent polling stations on roads supported by machine learning techniques, which have the potential to result in energy reductions of up to fifty percent (Pandiyan, et al., 2023). The concept of a sustainable approach to power distribution centers on an all-encompassing plan that includes every energy production, distribution, and transmission are all included. Urbanization continues to advance and the alteration of urban and rural landscapes is becoming increasingly prevalent as technological advancements are made complex, and have multiple interrelationships. The significance of the impact that technology has, is highlighted by these endeavors.

The technological advancement and innovation have an impact on the urban environment, which has the ability to create a future that is both sustainable and interdependent.

3.4. Energy and environmental sustainability through the use of LLMS

As the use of LLMs becomes more widespread, it is absolutely necessary to address the environmental concerns that are linked with the development and implementation of these systems. Large Language Models (LLMs) are causing an increasing amount of concern regarding their influence on the environment, which includes the consumption of energy, the emission of carbon, and the utilization of water. Listed below are important research topics that address these concerns:

3.4.1. Energy Consumption:

Both the training and operation of Large Language Models (LLMs) demand a great amount of computational resources, which results in a significant amount of energy consumption. In their paper (Faiz et al., 2024), Faiz and colleagues present LLMCarbon, a framework that estimates the amount of energy that is used throughout the lifecycle of the LLM. This paradigm also offers insights into the costs of training and inference. A similar analysis can be found in research (Samsi, et al., 2023), which examines the exponential growth in energy demands that occurs as model sizes and datasets develop. This study highlights the necessity of energy-efficient strategies such as model pruning, quantization, and the incorporation of renewable energy sources. The training phases are particularly energy-intensive, and they can need weeks of computation on large-scale GPU or TPU clusters. On the other hand, inference phases, which require less energy per job, become significant in high-frequency applications. The optimization of both stages through the application of modern techniques such as distributed learning and upgrades to hardware is required in order to address these problems. When it comes to making LLMs more sustainable in the face of increasing computational demands, these approaches are absolutely necessary.

3.4.2. Emissions of Carbon:

The processes that are involved in Large Language Models (LLMs) are very energy-intensive, and as a result, they contribute a large amount to carbon dioxide equivalent (CO2e) emissions. The research titled "Double Jeopardy and Climate Impact in the Use of Large Language Models" draws attention to the carbon footprint that is caused by the training and operation of LLMs. It also emphasizes the significance of adopting sustainable AI techniques (Solatorio, et al., 2024). LLM-Carbon is a methodology that was presented by Faiz et al. (Faiz et al., 2024) for the purpose of estimating emissions throughout the lifecycle of LLMs. This framework takes into account both operational and embodied carbon. A similar analysis was conducted by Luccioni et al. (Luccioni, et al., 2022) who examined the emissions produced by the BLOOM model. They focused on the statistics on the manufacturing of equipment, the consumption of dynamic power, and the consumption of idle energy. It is advised that initiatives such as the utilization of energy-efficient hardware, the implementation of optimization techniques such as pruning and quantization (Fu, et al., 2024), and the transition to renewable energy sources (Deng, et al., 2023) be utilized in order to reduce these emissions. There is a crucial need for these approaches in order to reduce the environmental impact of LLMs while also enabling the development of sustainable AI.

3.4.3. Water Consumption:

Data centers that house LLMs are required to have substantial cooling systems, which results in a significant amount of water being consumed. Research (Rillig, et al., 2023) has shed light on the water consumption linked with the cooling of data centers that are used to maintain LLM infrastructure. These studies emphasize the environmental concerns of such activities. Additional research highlights the significant amount of water that is consumed during the training of large AI models, and it advocates for transparency as well as ways to offset this hidden environmental cost (Li, et al., 2023). There is a rise in the amount of water that is being used by data centers as a result of the growing demand for artificial intelligence, which raises issues about the management of resources and sustainability (T. center, 2024). In addition, the cooling technologies that are utilized in data centers and the water requirements that are linked with them bring to light the difficulties that arise when attempting to strike a balance between operational efficiency and environmental responsibility (A. S. of Civil Engineers, 2024). Figure 4 illustrates the research topics in the energy and environment sustainability through the use of LLMs.

Figure 4. Research topics in the energy and environment sustainability through the use of LLMs

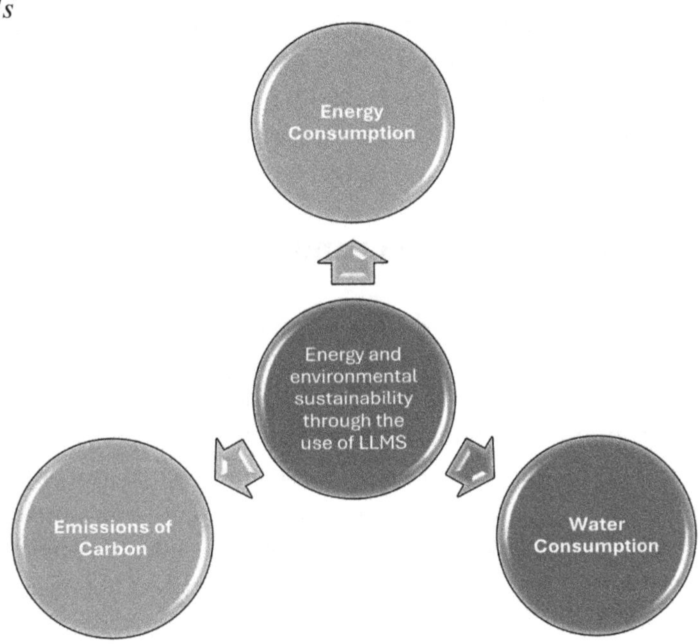

3.5. Case Study: Beta Labs' Initiative to Create a Sustainable Artificial Intelligence

There are substantial environmental challenges that are brought about by the development of artificial intelligence technology. It is anticipated that AI will contribute up to 5% of global greenhouse gas emissions by the year 2030 (Andrae, 2020). Beta Labs is addressing this problem by being a pioneer in the green artificial intelligence movement and by utilizing solar energy to power its whole artificial intelligence and large language model (LLM) infrastructure (Beta Labs, 2024).

By conducting energy audits and installing a solar array, the company has been able to reduce its carbon dioxide emissions by more than ninety percent (Beta, 2024).

The training of a 70-billion-parameter model can be accomplished in just 1.2 kWh over the course of 20 hours, which is a significant reduction in energy usage when compared to previous approaches (Beta, 2024).

Beta Labs uses energy that is derived from renewable sources in addition to employing energy-efficient procedures that are proprietary to the company. The creation of sustainable artificial intelligence is made more accessible as a result of these breakthroughs, which reduce both environmental and operational expenses.

An example of Beta Labs' dedication to environmentally responsible artificial intelligence is the forthcoming Aegis project, which will be the first LLM to be trained solely on renewable energy (Beta Labs, 2024). They have demonstrated that powerful artificial intelligence can be built in a sustainable manner, which has inspired the technology industry to embrace more environmentally friendly methods and establish new standards for sustainability in the field of technology.

3.6. Future Directions for urban and sustainable smart cities

DL, Blockchain, FL, NLP, and LLMs are very important technologies for research and development in sustainable smart cities. Additionally, researchers need to concentrate on the incorporation of semantic technologies into smart city products in order to provide improved communication between smart gadgets and the people who use them. Through the utilization of simulated objects in conjunction with Deep Reinforcement Learning (DRL) algorithms, it would be possible to create virtual representations of physical items, which would allow the objects to work in an automatic manner. A few of the advantages are described in this section.

- When it comes to users with less technical expertise and senior citizens, who may find it difficult to utilize touch displays, the usability of smart devices plays a vital role. This is especially true when it comes to technology. It is possible that the incorporation of speech recognition and natural language understanding into these devices may increase their acceptability among the various sorts of users that are present in a smart city.
- It is impossible to ignore the role that information and communications technology (ICT) and the internet of things (IoT) play in the development of sustainable smart cities. The big data that is generated by smart technologies, speech and face recognition systems, sensors, and other applications presents a significant challenge in terms of efficiently processing and analyzing it. This is necessary in order to improve the management of the services that a smart city provides. Additionally, they have a greater potential for research and development, which can further increase the efficiency, quality, and usefulness of urban services while simultaneously lowering prices and reducing

the amount of resources that are consumed. They have a significant potential to enhance the engagement between citizens and the government as well as the availability of information in real time.

- Information and communications technology (ICT) has become intricately intertwined with all aspects of city life, including commerce, culture, transportation, entertainment, and all other aspects of city life. Additionally, the Internet has become an important component of their day-to-day lives. The countless accomplishments that have been made in the process of digitizing a city's information not only give the general population with additional comfort on a daily basis, but they also develop an infrastructure and establish a standard.
- Smart cities have a better potential to utilize technology in order to make the most of the infrastructure, electricity, Internet and Wi-Fi connections, lane management, and lighting that is available to them. Through the incorporation of solar panels into the design of the building and the replacement of traditional materials, the more intelligent use of technology can facilitate the streamlining of heating, energy consumption, ventilation, and lighting. In order to monitor and manage the amount of energy that is consumed, smart grids can be constructed. Utilizing technology allows for the detection of water leaks as well as the monitoring of water capacity. By utilizing technology, it is possible to implement slow and fast lanes for the purpose of improving traffic management and expanding the lanes. It is possible to charge vehicles through charging points that are dispersed across the city. Green cities can be built to manage rubbish through the use of plants and intelligent irrigation, along with controlling air pollution, absorbing carbon dioxide, and emitting oxygen. In order to provide users with information regarding traffic congestion, parking places, and other civic amenities, Wi-Fi can be utilized.
- By incorporating reasoning capabilities into language models, they are able to perform exceptionally well in increasingly difficult activities, such as problem-solving, decision-making, and organizational planning. This not only improves their performance on a variety of tasks, but it also increases their robustness when they are not distributed. It is vital to take into consideration more practical and significant applications, like as decision-making, legal reasoning, or scientific reasoning, in order to accurately evaluate the reasoning abilities of LLMs. When conducting research, it is essential to determine whether the particular task being investigated is significant and whether the proposed approach can be generalized to apply to tasks and applications that are more practical.

CONCLUSIONS

LLMs are not merely instruments; rather, they are the catalysts for advancement. The acceleration of sustainable development, the addressing of global difficulties, and the creation of a more fair world are all attained through the utilization of their potential. As we continue to investigate the possibilities offered by LLMs, we must be certain that the implementation of these technologies is in accordance with ethical considerations and is beneficial to mankind as a whole.

Our ability to use technology in a responsible and useful manner will determine a better future and world for us, and this necessitates more cooperation.

REFERENCES

A. S. of Civil Engineers (ASCE). (2024). "Engineers often need a Civil lot of Engineering Water to Magazine, keep 2024. Data centers [Online]. cool," Available: https://www.asce.org/publications-and-news/civil-engineering-source/ civil-engineering-magazine/issues/magazine-issue/article/2024/03/ engineers-often-need-a-lot-of-water-to-keep-data-centers-cool

Ahmad, N., Hussain, S., Ahmad, K., & Conci, N. (2015). "Computer vision based room interior design," A. Verikas, P. Radeva, and D. Nikolaev, Eds., Dec. 2015, p. 98751G. DOI: 10.1117/12.2228438

Al-Othman, A., Tawalbeh, M., Martis, R., Dhou, S., Orhan, M., Qasim, M., & Ghani Olabi, A. (2022). Artificial intelligence and numerical models in hybrid renewable energy systems with fuel cells: Advances and prospects. *Energy Conversion and Management*, *253*, 115154. DOI: 10.1016/j.enconman.2021.115154

Andrae, A. S. (2020). Hypotheses for primary energy use, electricity use and co2 emissions of global computing and its shares of the total between 2020 and 2030. *WSEAS Transactions on Power Systems*, *15*, 50–59. DOI: 10.37394/232016.2020.15.6

Bahrini, A., Khamoshifar, M., Abbasimehr, H., ... (2023). ChatGPT: Applications, opportunities, and threats. Systems and Information Engineering Design Symposium (SIEDS). IEEE, 2023: 274-279. DOI: 10.1109/SIEDS58326.2023.10137850

Bai, M., Chen, Y., Zhao, X., Liu, J., & Yu, D. (2022). Deep attention ConvLSTM-based adaptive fusion of clear-sky physical prior knowledge and multivariable historical information for probabilistic prediction of photovoltaic power. *Expert Systems with Applications*, *202*, 117335. DOI: 10.1016/j.eswa.2022.117335

Bai, Y., Kadavath, S., Kundu, S., ... (2022). Constitutional AI: Harmlessness from AI Feedback. arXiv preprint arXiv:2212.08073.

Baidu, (2023). https://yiyan.baidu.com/

Beta (2024). Be.ta labs newsroom: Innovations in green ai. Be.Ta Labs. [Online]. Available: https://www.betalabsllm. com/new

Beta Labs. (2024) Be.ta labs: Pioneering sustainable ai. Be.Ta Labs. [Online]. Available: https://www.betalabsllm.com/

S. Bharati, M. R. H. Mondal, P. Podder, and V. B. S. Prasath, (2022). "Federated learning: Applications, challenges and future directions," .DOI: 10.3233/HIS-220006

Brown, T., Mann, B., & Ryder, N.. (2020). Language models are few-shot learners. *Advances in Neural Information Processing Systems*, *33*, 1877–1901.

Collins, C., Dennehy, D., Conboy, K., & Mikalef, P. (2021). Artificial intelligence in information systems research: A systematic literature review and research agenda. *International Journal of Information Management*, *60*, 102383. DOI: 10.1016/j.ijinfomgt.2021.102383

Deng, Z., Liu, J., Luo, B., Yuan, C., Yang, Q., Xiao, L., Zhou, W., & Liu, Z. (2023). "Autopcf: Efficient product carbon footprint accounting with large language models,". [Online]. Available: https: //arxiv.org/abs/2308.04241

Ding, S., Li, R., & Tao, Z. (2021). A novel adaptive discrete grey model with time-varying parameters for long-term photovoltaic power generation forecasting. *Energy Conversion and Management*, *227*, 113644. DOI: 10.1016/j.enconman.2020.113644

Er, N. I., Singh, K. D., Couturier, C., & Bonnin, J.-M. (2021). "Towards A Simple and Efficient VDTNRouting Protocol for Data Collection in Smart Cities," [Online]. Available: https://arxiv.org/abs/2108.09044v2

Faiz, A., Kaneda, S., Wang, R., Osi, R., Sharma, P., Chen, F., & Jiang, L. (2024). "LLMcarbon: Modeling the end-to-end carbon footprint of large language Models". [Online]. Available: https://arxiv.org/abs/2309.14393

Fu, Z., Chen, F., Zhou, S., Li, H., & Jiang, L. (2024). "Llmco2: Advancing accurate carbon footprint prediction for LLM inferences,". [Online]. Available: https://arxiv.org/abs/2410.02950

Guermoui, M., Bouchouicha, K., Bailek, N., & Boland, J. W. (2021). Forecasting intra-hour variance of photovoltaic power using a new integrated model. *Energy Conversion and Management*, *245*, 114569. DOI: 10.1016/j.enconman.2021.114569

Halbreich, U. (2023). Impact of urbanization on mental health and well being. *Current Opinion in Psychiatry*, *36*(3), 200–205. DOI: 10.1097/YCO.0000000000000864 PMID: 36939353

Hameed, A. A. (2019). "Smart city planning and sustainable development," IOP Conf. Ser. Mater. Sci. Eng., vol. 518, no. 2, p. 022042, DOI: 10.1088/1757-899X/518/2/022042

Heidarpanah, M., Hooshyaripor, F., & Fazeli, M. (2023). Daily electricity price forecasting using artificial intelligence models in the Iranian electricity market. *Energy*, *2023*(263), 126011. DOI: 10.1016/j.energy.2022.126011

Intelligent Cities. (2023). "Intelligent Cities and Globalisation of Innovation Networks- Nicos Komninos- Google Books." https://books.google.com.pk/books?hl=en&lr=&id=GjZ8AgAAQBAJ&oi=fnd&pg=PP1& dq=13.%09Komninos,+N.+Intelligent+Cities+and+Globalisation+of+Innovation+Networks.+London:+Routledge.+2008+&ots=RgUe1ZaQDQ&sig=rxPT0ICvjE4Ix5gGzRnOrmjuca8&redir_esc=y#v=onepage&q=13

Jha, S. K., Bilalovic, J., Jha, A., Patel, N., & Zhang, H. (2017). Renewable energy: Present research and future scope of Artificial Intelligence. *Renewable & Sustainable Energy Reviews*, *77*, 297–317. DOI: 10.1016/j.rser.2017.04.018

Joshi, S., Saxena, S., Godbole, T., & Shreya, . (2016). Developing Smart Cities: An Integrated Framework. *Procedia Computer Science*, *93*, 902–909. DOI: 10.1016/j.procs.2016.07.258

Kellil, N., Aissat, A., & Mellit, A. (2023). Fault diagnosis of photovoltaic modules using deep neural networks and infrared images under Algerian climatic conditions. *Energy*, *263*, 125902. DOI: 10.1016/j.energy.2022.125902

Kirmani, A. R. (2022). Artificial Intelligence-Enabled Science Poetry. *ACS Energy Letters*, *8*(1), 574–576. DOI: 10.1021/acsenergylett.2c02758

Li, Y., Tan, X., & Zhu, J. (2023). "Making ai less 'thirsty': Uncovering and addressing the secret water footprint of ai models," arXiv preprint arXiv:2304.03271. [Online]. Available: https://arxiv.org/abs/2304. 03271

Luccioni, A. S., Viguier, S., & Ligozat, A.-L. (2022). "Estimating the carbon footprint of bloom, a 176b parameter language model,". [Online]. Available: https://arxiv.org/abs/2211.02001

Manaris, B. (2020). *Advances in Computer Science*. AkiNik Publications., DOI: 10.22271/ed.book.784

Mathew, A. (2023). Is Artificial Intelligence a World Changer? A Case Study of OpenAI's Chat GPT. *Recent Progress in Science and Technology*, *5*, 35–42. DOI: 10.9734/bpi/rpst/v5/18240D

Nastjuk, I., Trang, S., & Papageorgiou, E. I. (2022). Smart cities and smart governance models for future cities: Current research and future directions. *Electronic Markets*, *32*(4), 1917–1924. DOI: 10.1007/s12525-022-00609-0

Olawade, D. B., Wada, O. J., David-Olawade, A. C., Kunonga, E., Abaire, O., & Ling, J. (2023). Using artificial intelligence to improve public health: A narrative review. *Frontiers in Public Health*, *11*, 1196397. Advance online publication. DOI: 10.3389/fpubh.2023.1196397 PMID: 37954052

T. A. Oliveira, M. Oliver, and H. Ramalhinho, (2020). "Challenges for Connecting Citizens and Smart Cities: ICT, E-Governance and Blockchain," Sustain. 2020, Vol. 12, Page 2926, vol. 12, no. 7, p. 2926, .DOI: 10.3390/su12072926

Openai. (2023) https://chat.openai.com/

Pandiyan, P., Saravanan, S., Usha, K., Kannadasan, R., Alsharif, M. H., & Kim, M.-K. (2023). Technological advancements toward smart energy management in smart cities. *Energy Reports*, *10*, 648–677. DOI: 10.1016/j.egyr.2023.07.021

Perkins M. (2023). Academic Integrity considerations of AI Large Language Models in the post-pandemic era: ChatGPT and beyond. Journal of University Teaching & Learning Practice, 20(2): 07.

Rillig, M. C., Agerstrand, M. °., Bi, M., Gould, K. A., & Sauerland, U. (2023). Risks and benefits of large language models for the environment. *Environmental Science & Technology*, *57*(9), 3464–3466. DOI: 10.1021/acs.est.3c01106 PMID: 36821477

Ruan, Y., Liang, Z., Qian, F., Meng, H., & Gao, Y. (2023). Operation strategy optimization of combined cooling, heating, and power systems with energy storage and renewable energy based on deep reinforcement learning. *Journal of Building Engineering*, *65*, 105682. DOI: 10.1016/j.jobe.2022.105682

Samsi, S., Zhao, D., McDonald, J., Li, B., Michaleas, A., Jones, M., Bergeron, W., Kepner, J., Tiwari, D., & Gadepally, V. (2023). *"From words to watts: Benchmarking the energy costs of large language model inference," in 2023 IEEE High Performance Extreme Computing Conference*. HPEC.

Shao, Z., Han, J., Zhao, W., Zhou, K., & Yang, S. (2022). Hybrid model for short-term wind power forecasting based on singular spectrum analysis and a temporal convolutional attention network with an adaptive receptive field. *Energy Conversion and Management*, *269*, 116138. DOI: 10.1016/j.enconman.2022.116138

Shilpi, S., & Ahad, M. (2020, June). Blockchain Technology and Smart Cities. A Review. *EAI Endorsed Trans. Smart Cities*, *4*(10), 163846. DOI: 10.4108/eai.13-7-2018.163846

Silva, B. N., Khan, M., & Han, K. (2018). Towards sustainable smart cities: A review of trends, architectures, components, and open challenges in smart cities. *Sustainable Cities and Society*, *38*, 697–713. DOI: 10.1016/j.scs.2018.01.053

Solatorio, A. V., Vicente, G. S., Krambeck, H., & Dupriez, O. (2024). "Double jeopardy and climate impact in the use of large language models: Socio-economic disparities and reduced utility for non-english speakers," [Online]. Available: https://arxiv.org/abs/2410.10665

Sun, Y., Wang, S., Feng, S., ... Ernie. (2021). 3.0: Large-scale knowledge enhanced pre-training for language understanding and generation. arXiv preprint arXiv:2107.02137.

Sun, Y., Wang, S., Li, Y., Feng, S., Tian, H., Wu, H., & Wang, H. (2020). Ernie 2.0: A continual pre-training framework for language understanding. *Proceedings of the AAAI Conference on Artificial Intelligence*, *34*(05), 8968–8975. DOI: 10.1609/aaai.v34i05.6428

T. center. (2024). Editorial, water [Online]. "Demand consumption Available: for Ai sky is high," driving data TechCrunch, https://techcrunch.com/2024/08/19/demand-for-ai-is-driving-data-center-water-consumption-sky-high

Ullah, A.. (2023). Smart cities: The role of Internet of Things and machine learning in realizing a data-centric smart environment. *Complex & Intelligent Systems*. Advance online publication. DOI: 10.1007/s40747-023-01175-4

Z. Ullah, F. Al-Turjman, L. Mostarda, and R. Gagliardi, (2020). "Applications of Artificial Intelligence and Machine learning in smart cities," Comput. Commun., vol. 154, pp. 313 323, .DOI: 10.1016/j.comcom.2020.02.069

Verma, B., Snodgrass, R., Henry, B., Smith, B., & Daim, T. (2020). "Smart cities- an analysis of smart transportation management," in Managing Innovation in a Global and Digital World, Wiesbaden. *Springer Fachmedien Wiesbaden*, *2020*, 367–388. DOI: 10.1007/978-3-658-27241-8_23

Wala, T., Chand, N., & Sharma, A. K. (2020). "Energy Efficient Data Collection in Smart Cities Using IoT," in Convergence in the information industries. Telecommunications, broadcasting and data processing 1981-1996, pp. 632–654. DOI: 10.1007/978-3-030-40305-8_30

Wang, D., Zhou, Q., & Du, Y.. (2022). Research on Distributed PV Monitoring System Based on Ubiquitous Power IOT Architecture. Journal of Physics: Conference Series. *IOP Publishing*, *2166*(1), 012025.

Xinghuo. (2023). https://xinghuo.xfyun.cn/

Yu, Y., Niu, T., Wang, J., & Jiang, H. (2023). Intermittent solar power hybrid forecasting system based on pattern recognition and feature extraction. *Energy Conversion and Management*, *2023*(277), 116579. DOI: 10.1016/j.enconman.2022.116579

Zahoora, U., Khan, A., Rajarajan, M., Khan, S. H., Asam, M., & Jamal, T. (2022). "Ransomware detection using deep learning based unsupervised feature extraction and a cost sensitive Pareto Ensemble classifier," Sci. Reports, 121, vol. 12, no. 1, pp. 1–15, Sep. 2022, DOI: 10.1038/s41598-022-19443-7

Zhou, G., Bai, M., Zhao, X., Li, J., Li, Q., Liu, J., & Yu, D. (2022). Study on the distribution characteristics and uncertainty of multiple energy load patterns for building group to enhance demand side management. *Energy and Building*, *263*, 112038. DOI: 10.1016/j.enbuild.2022.112038

Zichichi, M., Ferretti, S., & D'Angelo, G. (2022). Blockchain-Based Data Management for Smart Transportation. *Blockchain-Based Data Management for Smart Transportation*, *2022*, 631–659. DOI: 10.1007/978-3-031-07535-3_20

Chapter 15
Edge Artificial Intelligence–Enabled 6G Communication Security System for Connected Vehicles in Revolutionizing Urban Development and Governance

Priya Kohli
Department of Computer Science and Engineering, Graphic Era University (Deemed), Dehradun, India

Sachin Sharma
https://orcid.org/0000-0002-7821-3685
Amity School of Engineering and Technology, Amity University, Mohali, India

ABSTRACT

6G in a rising innovation which can handle the robotized vehicular communication environment well in revolutionizing urban development and governance. It may be a promising innovation which can result in encouraging moo idleness, less communication overheads, etc. Security and protection is the major challenge confronted in 6G environment due to its energetic environment. Conventional ML procedures were sent prior but due to expanding vehicles on street and with various associated

DOI: 10.4018/979-8-3373-1375-7.ch015

IoT gadgets, it has ended up exceptionally troublesome to recognize a genuine and solid source of information which is drifted wirelessly over the arrange. We offer an outline of different confirmation plans proposed over time which are utilized in 6G IoE-based vehicular communication environment. Within the setting of 6G vehicular communication, we examined potential security employments of the Internet-of-Everything (IoE) and open inquire about issues on security conservation in revolutionizing urban development and governance.

I. INTRODUCTION

Automobiles tend to be basic component within the upcoming automated environment. It may be a promising innovation that encourages the conclusion client with coterminous association, security and less delay whereas exchanging information over the remote organize. Mechanized vehicle environment appears to be incredible but various researcher and businesses are endeavoring this objective by sending fifth era (5G) wirelessly associated system. 5G technique is a modern and potential technology which facilitates customer-oriented schemes that visions to fulfil the needs of almost all the gadgets deployed over the network. Due to the deployment of diverse techniques and gadgets under connected environment, it becomes impossible to fuse all the diversified technologies and address individual's need. Thus, 5G technology isn't visioned to transpose its framework, i.e., LTE, rather it facilitates in providing a single bridge for all technologies to gather all the services into a single unit to facilitate it to the end user. From industrial viewpoint, such approach will facilitate with huge profits on the investments made. 5G technique sights to facilitate its services in air with numerous modern technologies. Additionally, this plan will be executed over the prevailing wireless-connected technique which includes LTE, inflated speed data-packet acquisition, central data transfer system, Wi-Fi, etc. However, it is essential to identify characteristics of 5G technology so that diversified gadgets can be facilitated with a unified platform. The primary challenge while deploying connected vehicles comprises of shortage of range, high response time, etc. Under enormous wireless connected environment, 5G standards, results in abject ductile and unguaranteed facilitating of services. Some research has already been taken place under LTE-based connected vehicles and 5G which inspires the researchers and industrialists to enhance the communication-based network. The upcoming era which is based on beyond 5G (B5G) and sixth generation (6G) will support much higher and efficient gadgets with higher demand-resolving techniques for the automated automobiles. Under such scenarios, BS5 and 6G are expected to handle secured data transmission of enormous data. Data transmission rate is one of the most essential characteristics of B5G and 6G technology as it facilitates up to 1TBPS to support the ever-growing congestion on road. Wireless communication systems facilitate two steps to enhance the data-transfer rate. Those two approaches are: enhancing the capabilities of spectrum and uplifting the data transfer bandwidth. There are numerous techniques prevailing which can enhance the capabilities of spectrum range when B5S and 6G is deployed over wireless network. Among such technologies, ultra-massive multiple input multiple out (MIMO) is the popular one which is mostly deployed as it comprises of more than 100 RSUs. Under B5S and 6G communication environment, enhanced spectrum range of mm/THz frequency with GHz/THz is facilitated to the connected vehicles. B5G and 6G connected vehicles supports unusual internet-of-things i.e., internet of vehicles (IoV). This will allow a wide range of connected intelligent automobiles on road with massive data transfer over dynamic environment. Vehicular communication environment aims to facilitate intelligence and automated environment to the drivers, thus every automobile under B5G and 6G environment will have numerous sensors, camera, radars, etc, over it to support diversified services. Thus, connected vehicles for B5G and 6G environment should be deployed over MIMO and mm/THz techniques. The day break of 6G communication messengers a transformative time for urban scenes, promising a worldview move in how cities work and are represented. At the heart of this transformation lies the consistent integration of edge AI with associated vehicle innovations, making a vigorous communication security framework able of tending to the burgeoning requests of present day urban portability. As cities hook with expanding populations, activity congestion, and the basic for economical advancement, the require for brilliantly, secure, and productive transportation frameworks has never been more basic. The ordinary centralized cloud-based models, whereas capable, battle to convey the real-time responsiveness and information protection requested by the complicated environment of associated vehicles. This is often where edge AI rises as a urgent enabler, pushing computational control closer to the information source, subsequently relieving inactivity and improving security. By handling and analyzing information at the network's edge, inside the prompt region of vehicles, edge AI encourages quick decision-making, empowering basic applications such as independent driving, real-time activity administration, and proactive security measures. The integration of 6G communication with edge AI-enabled associated vehicle frameworks is balanced to revolutionize urban advancement and administration by cultivating a more cleverly, responsive, and secure transportation framework. The sheer volume of information produced by associated vehicles, enveloping sensor readings, area data, and communication logs, presents both an opportunity and a challenge. On one hand, this information holds gigantic potential for optimizing activity stream, foreseeing clog designs, and improving street security. On the other hand, it raises noteworthy concerns with respect to information security and security, as delicate data might be helpless to unauthorized access or malicious assaults. Traditional security components, depending on centralized servers and cloud foundation, regularly demonstrate insufficient in tending to these challenges. Edge AI-enabled security frameworks, be that as it may, offer a decentralized and proactive approach to defending information and guaranteeing the keenness of communication networks. By embedding AI calculations inside edge gadgets, such as roadside units and base stations, these frameworks can identify and react to security dangers in real-time, without the require for steady communication with centralized servers. Additionally, the low-latency capabilities of 6G communication, coupled with the computational proficiency of edge AI, empower the improvement of progressed applications that were already unattainable. For occurrence, real-time activity administration frameworks can use edge AI to analyze sensor information from associated vehicles and alter activity signals powerfully, in this manner lessening congestion and moving forward travel times. Independent driving frameworks can advantage from edge AI's capacity to prepare sensor information locally, empowering fast decision-making in complex and erratic driving scenarios. Besides, edge AI can encourage the advancement of personalized versatility administrations, such as ride-sharing and on-demand transportation, by analyzing client inclinations and optimizing steering calculations. The affect of edge AI-enabled 6G communication security frameworks amplifies past transportation, impacting broader angles of urban administration. By giving real-time information and experiences, these frameworks can engage city organizers and policymakers to create educated choices with respect to foundation advancement, asset assignment, and open security. For illustration, information from associated vehicles can be utilized to distinguish zones with tall activity clog or mischance rates, empowering focused on mediations to progress street security and decrease natural affect. Moreover, edge AI can encourage the improvement of shrewd city applications, such as cleverly lighting and squander administration, by analyzing sensor information and optimizing asset utilization. Be that as it may, the execution of edge AI-enabled 6G communication security frameworks moreover presents a few challenges. These incorporate the require for vigorous and dependable edge foundation, the advancement of proficient AI calculations that can work inside resource-constrained situations, and the foundation of standardized conventions for information sharing and communication. Besides, guaranteeing the security and security of information handled at the edge requires cautious thought of encryption procedures, get to control components, and information anonymization methodologies. Tending to these challenges requires a collaborative exertion including analysts, industry partners, and policymakers. By working together, able to open the complete potential of edge AI-enabled 6G communication security frameworks and clear the way for a more cleverly, feasible, and secure urban future.

II. LITERATURE REVIEW

There has as of now been a parcel of consider drained the past around the challenges of security, security, and message astuteness in 5G-based vehicular communication systems. Here, a brief rundown of already distributed work has been secured. Gyawali et al. (2021) proposed a framework where VEC keeps all gathered responses from automobiles by deploying dempster shafer and the outcome is utilized to forecast the standard numeric value of accurate data received. After this, author deployed reinforcement DL algorithms to optimize the updated rules to automobiles so that they can transmit verified and accurate response. Thus, author presented that the proposed framework is best in-terms of total number of verified and accurate responses gathered from an individual automobile over the dynamic environment. Rasheed et al. (2020) proposed a network protocol based on edge computing. The author also presented a modern security and reliability protection framework to enhance the reliability of the automobile over the dynamic environment by deploying edge-computing. The prime challenge under edge-computing is it has major loopholes while processing data over an individual node. Thus, security vulnerability increases with it. To protect the processing at edge from an adversaries, iCLASC is introduced, where signature-based encryption is done with without certificate. It too incorporates information exchange convention to compute the activity detecting data. The convention sent to ensure the security and unwavering quality has various key-features such as: mystery, data-integrity, association confirmation, unwavering quality, etc. Moreover, comparisons of the proposed conspire with the existing plans in terms of computational fetched, communication overhead and security highlight investigation. The proposed conspire outflanks all the past strategies and appears palatable security and communication execution requires for 5G-V2X Communication. Boualouache and Engel (2021) proposed a novel combined learning-based conspire for identifying inactive portable assailants in 5G vehicular edge computing. The creator to begin with recognizes a set of procedures that can be utilized by aggressors to productively track vehicles without being outwardly recognized. At that point they create an effective machine learning (ML) show to distinguish following assaults based as it were on the getting signals. The plot empowers combined learning (FL) at the edge to guarantee collaborative learning whereas protecting the protection of vehicles. Additionally, FL clients employments a semi-supervised learning approach to guarantee exact self-labeling. The tests illustrate the viability of the plot to identify detached versatile assailants rapidly and with tall precision. In fact, as it were 20 gotten guides are required to realize 95curacy. This exactness can be accomplished inside 60 FL rounds utilizing 5 FL clients in each FL circular. The gotten comes about are too approved through reenactments. Reebadiya et al. (2021) proposed a BC-based secure and brilliantly detecting and following engineering for AV framework utilizing past 5G communication organize. The proposed design guarantees secure detecting and following of question through BC by conveying AI calculations at the edge servers. Moreover, the past 5G organize empowers communications with moo idleness and tall unwavering quality to meet the wants of the time-sensitive applications. The proposed framework is assessed by considering the parameters as versatility and information exchange time against the conventional LTE-A and 5G communication systems. Letaief et al. (2021) provides a comprehensive outline of federated learning (FL), a disseminated machine learning approach. FL addresses the challenges of information protection and security by empowering demonstrate preparing on decentralized gadgets whereas keeping information locally. The study investigates the advancement of FL, beginning from its roots in centralized learning and advancing to disseminated on-site learning. It covers different angles, counting FL's engineering, communication conventions, and security contemplations. Moreover, it dives into progressed points such as personalized FL, heterogeneous FL, and the integration of FL with other advances like blockchain. The creators analyze the current state of FL investigate, highlighting key challenges and potential future headings, emphasizing its potential to revolutionize machine learning in data-sensitive applications. Sharma, Tyagi, et al. (2024a) investigates the integration of Artificial Intelligence (AI) into Green 6G systems, centering on models, scenarios, and applications, especially for Autonomous Connected Vehicles (ACVs). The creators highlight the require for energy-efficient 6G systems to back the developing requests of AI-driven applications. AI is situated as a key enabler for optimizing arrange execution, asset allotment, and vitality utilization in 6G. The chapter examines different AI-enabled structures, counting edge AI and unified learning, which are pivotal for low-latency and privacy-preserving applications. It dives into scenarios where AI improves ACV functionalities, such as brilliantly activity administration, prescient upkeep, and upgraded security. The creators emphasize the potential of AI to make a maintainable and proficient 6G biological system, tending to the challenges of expanding information activity and vitality utilization in future communication systems. Haider et al. (2024) focuses on the application of combined learning (FL) inside the Internet of Things (IoT) environment. It addresses the unique challenges postured by IoT gadgets, such as constrained assets, heterogeneous information, and protection concerns. The overview comprehensively audits existing FL arrangements custom fitted for IoT, categorizing them based on components like communication proficiency, security conservation, and personalization. It looks at different strategies utilized to relieve communication overhead, handle information heterogeneity, and guarantee secure demonstrate conglomeration. The creators highlight the significance of FL in empowering dispersed insights and privacy-preserving analytics in IoT applications. Moreover, the paper distinguishes key inquire about holes and diagrams future headings, counting the improvement of more strong and productive FL calculations for resource-constrained IoT situations, and the integration of FL with rising advances like edge computing and blockchain. Nawaz et al. (2024) investigates the application of Federated Learning (FL) inside the Mechanical Web of Things (IIoT). It highlights how FL addresses the challenges of information security, security, and computational impediments characteristic in IIoT situations. The study gives a comprehensive diagram of FL structures and calculations custom fitted for IIoT, centering on angles like communication effectiveness, information heterogeneity, and security conventions. It talks about different FL techniques, counting flat and vertical combined learning, and their appropriateness for diverse IIoT scenarios. The paper emphasizes the significance of FL in empowering dispersed insights and collaborative demonstrate preparing without compromising touchy mechanical information. Moreover, it recognizes key challenges, such as managing with non-IID information conveyances and resource-constrained gadgets, and traces potential future investigate bearings, counting the integration of FL with edge computing and blockchain for upgraded security and proficiency in IIoT applications. Teimoori et al. (2024) examines the integration of federated learning (FL) with 6G systems. It investigates how FL addresses the developing requests for information security and conveyed insights in next-generation communication frameworks. The paper studies different 6G applications profiting from FL, counting independent driving, shrewd healthcare, and mechanical computerization. It traces the interesting challenges of actualizing FL in 6G, such as dealing with gigantic information volumes, different gadget capabilities, and exacting idleness prerequisites. The authors talk about potential arrangements, counting optimized FL calculations, edge computing integration, and novel communication conventions. Besides, the study highlights the openings for FL to upgrade 6G execution, empowering personalized administrations, effective asset administration, and vigorous security. It concludes by distinguishing future inquire about bearings, emphasizing the require for collaborative endeavors to realize the complete potential of FL in 6G systems. Ibn-Khedher et al. (2023) analyzes how 6G innovations, especially edge computing, can improve the Internet of Autonomous Vehicles (IoAV). It explores the integration of advances like versatile edge computing, unmanned airborne vehicles, arrange work virtualization, software-defined organizing, and artificial intelligence to improve IoAV arrange execution past 5G capabilities. The paper highlights the merging of 6G and IoAV, centering on assembly the exacting necessities of next-generation associated and independent vehicle applications. It addresses the challenges inside the 6G-IoAV investigate field and proposes potential future bearings. The consider emphasizes the basic part of 6G in giving the low-latency, high-reliability communication vital for secure and effective independent vehicle operation Sheraz et al. (2024) studied on AI-enabled Digital Twin Networks (DTNs) in 6G would investigate how these innovations revolutionize network. It would look at the integration of AI to make and oversee DTNs, which are virtual reproductions of physical systems. The study would cover how these DTNs improve organize optimization, expectation, and administration in 6G. It would likely address the benefits of utilizing AI to robotize and progress the precision of DTN reenactments. The paper would consider the challenges in actualizing such frameworks, counting information synchronization, computational complexity, and security. It would too investigate potential applications and future bearings, emphasizing the part of DTNs in empowering brilliantly and versatile 6G systems.

III. OVERVIEW OF EDGE ARTIFICIAL INTELLIGENCE

AI is an approach to construct brilliantly machines competent of carrying out errands as people do. AI frameworks regularly illustrate at slightest a few of the taking after practices related with human insights: arranging, learning, thinking, problem-solving, information representation, recognition, movement, and control and, to a lesser degree, social insights, and imagination. The combination of AI and edge computing is normal since there's a clear crossing point between them. Particularly, edge computing points at planning a huge number of collaborative edge gadgets and servers to handle the produced information in vicinity, and AI endeavors for reenacting brilliantly human conduct in devices/machines by learning from information. The expansion and rising demand of IoT gadgets, multi-modal information such as audios, images, videos etc, of the environment are constantly sniffed at the automobile's end. With this, intelligent algorithms are a must to handle such enormous information collected through sniffing of dynamic environment. Such AI-based techniques helps in extracting valuable information so that quick and accurate decisions can be taken on time. Additionally, DL can be deployed to recognise the adversaries, malicious data etc, over the edge-nodes, by considering congestion on road, direction of heavy traffic, dampness, warmth, force of air, ariel conditions. The valuable information processed from the dump of information can be given as an input to the real time forecasting technique which plans for mass transit, control over traffic-flow, movable automobile warnings in corresponding to the dynamic surrounding. Deep Learning (DL) algorithms were widely accepted because of its fourfold: information, gadgets, algorithms, and hardware-devices. Deployment of DL algorithms and hardware is essential, but information and application's role is neglected throughout. DNN with numerous layers of neurons can be deployed with DL algorithms over the network to enhance the results. This will be leading in training of huge parameters under DNN, and thus huge data is required for training purpose. This showcases the essentialness of the datasets while building

AI. After identifying the need of data-sets next major challenge is where the data is sourced from. Earlier, information were gathered and stored under repositories. Though, with the huge deployment of IoT devices, storage is reversed. As per Cisco, enormous datasets will be gathered at the edge. A huge amount of bandwidth resources will be consumed, if such enormous data is being processed with AI-based techniques over the cloud. Edge-based computing is trending with its obvious advantages over cloud-based computing. It's nature of providing a unified platform to all the diversified technologies makes it different from all other computing techniques. After conducting some experiments by Microsoft team, it is being found that applications based on voice-recognition, AR/VR and real-time gaming gets best results when edge computing is deployed. It renders real-time, HD-based videos/images from surveillance for processing, and results in low computation cost, high privacy and reliability, low-latency. With such automation framework, numerous RSUs tends to behave like an edge-server which are pre-installed at some specific gap so that passing-by vehicle can establish connection with it and thus processing time and response time is reduced. Additionally, if any automobile tends to acquire some information, it can be filtered and provided. Thus, security and privacy can be maintained in such a way, thereby maintaining the efficiency of the network. Edge Artificial Intelligence (Edge AI) calculations are vital for empowering real-time, localized handling and decision-making in a tremendous cluster of applications, especially inside resource-constrained situations just like the Internet of Things (IoT), independent vehicles, and smart cities. Unlike traditional cloud-based AI, which depends on centralized servers for information preparing, Edge AI calculations work specifically on edge gadgets, closer to the information source. This nearness altogether diminishes idleness, preserves transmission capacity, and improves information security, making it an crucial apparatus for applications requesting quick reactions and secure information dealing with. The landscape of Edge AI calculations is different, enveloping a extend of procedures custom fitted to the particular imperatives and necessities of edge gadgets. One noticeable category includes demonstrate compression and optimization. These algorithms center on diminishing the estimate and complexity of AI models, making them reasonable for sending on gadgets with constrained computational assets and memory. Procedures such as show pruning, quantization, and information refining play a crucial part in this region. Demonstrate pruning includes evacuating excess or less noteworthy associations inside a neural organize, subsequently diminishing its estimate without essentially affecting its exactness. Quantization, on the other hand, decreases the accuracy of show parameters, ordinarily from 32-bit floating-point numbers to 8-bit integrability, driving to considerable diminishments in demonstrate estimate and computational requests. Information refining includes preparing a littler, more effective demonstrate to imitate the behavior of a bigger, more precise demonstrate, viably exchanging information whereas diminishing complexity. Another vital angle of Edge AI calculations is their capacity to handle real-time information streams. Streaming analytics and online learning calculations are basic for processing and analyzing information because it arrives, empowering prompt reactions to changing conditions. These calculations regularly utilize methods like sliding window examination, incremental learning, and versatile sifting to extricate significant bits of knowledge from nonstop information streams. For occurrence, in independent vehicles, gushing analytics can be utilized to prepare sensor information from cameras and LiDAR in real-time, empowering fast discovery of deterrents and people on foot. So also, in industrial IoT applications, online learning calculations can be utilized to screen machine execution and identify irregularities in real-time, empowering prescient upkeep and avoiding gear disappointments. Besides, Edge AI calculations must be outlined to handle the heterogeneity and inconstancy of edge gadgets. These gadgets regularly differ in terms of computational control, memory capacity, and vitality assets, requiring calculations that can adjust to these limitations. Federated learning, a disseminated machine learning approach, addresses this challenge by empowering show preparing on decentralized gadgets without requiring the exchange of raw information to a central server. This approach not as it were upgrades information security but too diminishes communication overhead, making it especially reasonable for IoT applications with various resource-constrained gadgets. Furthermore, methods like exchange learning and meta-learning can be utilized to adjust pre-trained models to modern assignments or situations with constrained information, empowering quick arrangement of AI applications on differing edge gadgets. Security and protection are fundamental concerns in Edge AI, requiring the advancement of strong calculations that can secure touchy information and anticipate malicious assaults. Strategies such as homomorphic encryption, secure multi-party computation, and differential protection are utilized to protect information during handling and communication. Homomorphic encryption permits computations to be performed on scrambled information without unscrambling it, guaranteeing information security indeed when handled on untrusted edge gadgets. Secure multi-party computation empowers different parties to mutually compute a work without uncovering their person inputs. Differential security includes noise to information to ensure person protection whereas still empowering exact factual examination. These security measures are especially imperative in applications such as healthcare and back, where information protection is basic. Edge AI calculations are revolutionizing the way we handle and analyze information, empowering real-time, localized insights in a wide extend of applications. By tending to the challenges of asset imperatives, heterogeneity, and security, these calculations are clearing the way for a more intelligent, effective, and secure future. As edge computing proceeds to advance, the advancement of imaginative Edge AI calculations will stay a basic area of inquire about and advancement, driving headways in different spaces and changing the way we connected with innovation.

IV. IMPORTANCE OF 5G COMMUNICATION SECURITY SYSTEM

Upcoming era will be all about autonomous automobiles which facilitates with uninterrupted connection amongst dynamic nodes, high reliability, less delay rate while transmitting data. Though, it seems unrealistic but numerous industrialist and scientists have joined their hands together in evolving new generation intelligent automobile with the help of fifth-generation (5G) telecommunication framework. 5G-based technology focuses on consumer-based connectivity that visions to satisfy the gadget's necessity while establishing a dynamic connection throughout the journey. In real-world, it is not easy to provide a single platform for all diversified connected applications/gadgets which facilitates the end user with some services. Thus, 5G technique doesn't limit its vision to only provide exchanging of messages with existing framework i.e., LTE, rather it facilitates the vehicles, gadgets with a single platform so that each modern technology-based gadgets can blend with the environment to render their services. From industrial viewpoint, such approach will facilitate with huge profits on the investments made. 5G technique sights to facilitate its services in air with numerous modern technologies. Additionally, this plan will be executed over the prevailing wireless-connected technique which includes LTE, inflated speed data-packet acquisition, central data transfer system, Wi-Fi, etc. However, it is essential to identify characteristics of 5G technology so that diversified gadgets can be facilitated with a unified platform. The primary challenge while deploying connected vehicles comprises of shortage of range, high response time, etc. Under enormous wireless connected environment, 5G standards, results in abject ductile and unguaranteed facilitating of services. Some research has already been taken place under LTE-based connected vehicles and 5G which inspires the researchers and industrialists to enhance the communication-based network. Numerous connected vehicles requires particular reliable and non-reliable gadgets. An essential component of 5G telecommunication system is ProSe services. At present, it focuses on facilitating the automobile with the information of nearby available application or service by deploying locale information. Under 5G-based IoT environment, Prose is specific to numerous unsolicited communications or tends to exchange messages over a limited locale. The major data source for ProSe are locale-based data and data transferring trends over social platforms. This technique is based on ad-hoc locale gathering and generates an opportunity for data transferring under dynamic environment. It can also be deployed and used as a framework under safety-concerns. Thus, by deploying ad-hoc networking with connected vehicles, inflated information transfer rate and reduction of congestion over the network along with enormously huge network efficiency can be attained. To use the utilities provided by ProSe, all the automobiles are required to get themselves registered over eNB, thus user can apply filtration over the services in order to attain their preferences only. After attaining relevant services, automobiles can access advertisements over 5G-based environments. For example, an alert generated by any collision-avoidance gadget delivers the driver after the incident has occurred is of no use. Under such real-time situations, beacons has proved its worth by transmitting data before time under huge wirelessly connected vehicular environment. But their message fault while transferring cannot be guaranteed because of low-bandwidth ranges between different nodes. The importance of 5G communication security system for connected vehicles is highlighted in Fig. 1.

Figure 1. Importance of 5G communication security system for connected vehicles

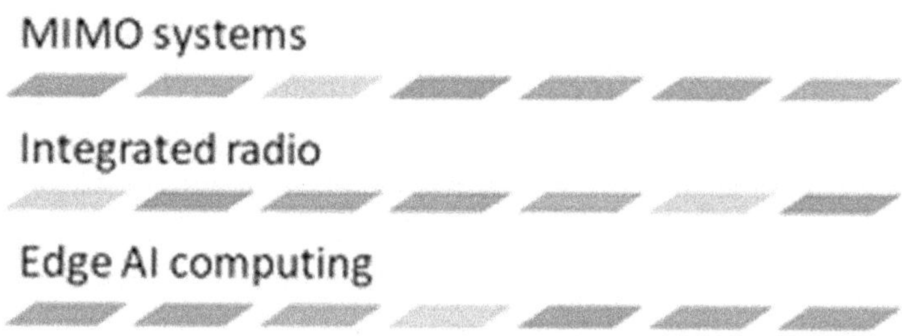

- Security of the 5G enabled massive multiple-input multiple-output (MIMO) systems for connected vehicles: Massive MIMO is one of the keys empowering innovation for next-generation systems, which bunches together receiving wires at both transmitter and the recipient to supply tall ghastly and vitality productivity utilizing moderately basic handling. Beneath vehicular communication engineering, effectiveness of RSUs can be expanded by sending MIMO over the organize. The MIMO arrangement of the radio wire shows expanded shared coupling due to its dispersing between radio wire components, which diminishes segregation.
- Security of the 5G enabled integrated radio for connected vehicles: The wireless communication systems deploys spectrums to enable transmission of data wirelessly. 5G communication network deploys high-range radio frequencies that have less clustering for efficient and secured communication amongst numerous automobiles. Additionally, if any automobile tends to acquire some information, it can be filtered and provided. Thus, security and

privacy can be maintained in such a way, thereby maintaining the efficiency of the network.

5G communication security frameworks for associated vehicles utilize a run of calculations to guarantee information keenness, privacy, and accessibility.

- Public Key Infrastructure (PKI) Algorithms
- RSA (Rivest–Shamir–Adleman): For advanced signatures and key trade.
- Elliptic Curve Cryptography (ECC): For efficient key era and trade, reasonable for resource-constrained vehicles.
- X.509 Certificates: For confirming the personality of vehicles and foundation.
- Diffie-Hellman (DH) and Elliptic Curve Diffie-Hellman (ECDH): For secure key establishment.
- IKEv2 (Internet Key Exchange version 2): For secure VPN setup.
- AKA (Authentication and Key Agreement): For secure access to 5G networks.
- AES (Advanced Encryption Standard): For encrypting data transmitted between vehicles and framework.
- ChaCha20: A stream cipher known for its speed and security.
- RSA and ECC: For encrypting and decrypting data utilizing open and private keys.
- Anomaly Detection Algorithms: Machine learning algorithms (e.g., Support Vector Machines, Neural Networks): For identifying abnormal arrange activity designs.
- Statistical analysis: For distinguishing deviations from normal behavior.
- Intrusion Prevention System (IPS) Algorithms
- Signature-based detection: For coordinating known assault designs.
- Behavioral analysis: For distinguishing malevolent behavior based on organize movement.
- TLS/SSL (Transport Layer Security/Secure Sockets Layer): For secure communication over the internet.
- IPsec (Internet Protocol Security): For secure communication at the organize layer.
- IEEE 1609.2: For secure message trade in V2X communication.
- 5G-AKA: 5G version of AKA, which gives better security than prior forms.
- SUCI (Subscription Concealed Identifier): Ensures the subscriber's character.
- SHA-256 (Secure Hash Algorithm 256): For confirming the astuteness of information.
- HMAC (Hash-based Message Authentication Code): For message confirmation.

- RSA and ECDSA (Elliptic Curve Digital Signature Algorithm): For confirming the genuineness of messages.
- Lightweight cryptographic calculations: planned to run productively on edge devices.
- Organize Slicing Security Algorithms

V. CHARACTERISTICS OF 5G COMMUNICATION SECURITY SYSTEM

After 4G, 5G tends to uplift the connected vehicle environment with speed, efficiency, less delay rate, huge battery backup, enormous capabilities and an efficient network. Apart from rendering speedy data transmission, 5G facilitates a unify platform for diversified tools and services like IoT-based tools/gadgets, etc. All such characteristics of 5G facilitates the automobiles with uninterrupted connectivity, health-care monitoring system by deploying numerous sensors, package tracking tools, etc throughout the dynamic environment. Though, 5G facilitates with numerous advantages, still it is less sufficient to handle the ever-growing congestion of automobiles, privacy warnings, and numerous cyberattacks on road. Thus, to built a fully secured and trustworthy platform for the automobiles to communicate in the dynamic environment, a flexible and scalable security protocol should be maintained for 5G networks. After the advent of 5G communication architecture, scientists have divided them in two equal thought process. According to some, it will bring numerous and diverse privacy related issues along with numerous cyberattacks on the automobiles, RSU, etc. 5G is a powerful technology which will enable the automobiles to establish the connection in a large-scale. It will facilitate the environment with high-bandwidth, low latency. Some popular characteristics of 5G communication security systems are:

- Confidentiality: With the deployment of various cryptographic algorithms and AI techniques, communication system makes sure to keep sensitive data confidential to an individual like, driver's real-time locale, private keys of a registered user, etc.
- Integrity: Data integrity is the key aspect while transferring messages over dynamic environment. Integrity of data should be preserved in terms of complete data, correctness, received duly on time, etc.
- Availability: As compared with 4G, 5G communication network is more dynamic, powerful, and reliable. The bandwidth speed facilitated by 5G is much higher than 4G. Thus, wireless network should be available throughout the

journey. Adversaries should be prevented to interfere or to alter the network which may lead to unavailability of network to the end-user.

- Encryption: Vehicular communication establishes a wireless connection and allows the nodes to transmit the data wirelessly. Encrypting algorithms plays a vital role while transmitting data from V2V, V2R, R2R and V2E communication technique.
- Authentication: Registered nodes should be verified before allowing them to enter inside the network. RSUs and various IoE gadgets should be verified too after every time slice (TS) expires. This may help in establishing a trustful connected network
- Connected vehicle user privacy: Preserving user's privacy is an essential aspect while establishing connection between any nearby vehicle or RSU. Numerous crimes like theft, murder, etc can take place if real-time data or automobile's real identity is revealed with other users over the network. Though, this data is crucial for the crime branch to track any criminal. Thus, such information is kept securely with the trusted authority (TA) of the network.
- Enhanced end user experience (UX): With the advancement of network technology from 4G to 5G, automobiles tend to establish real-quick connection with nearby RSUs and enjoy music, movies, online games, shopping, advertisement of which food outlet is on the way, etc uninterruptedly throughout the dynamic geographical environment.
- Simplified network operations: With the high power and high transmission rate of 5G, vehicles establish connection with each other in bi-directional mode where they can send and received crucial messages about the environment in which they are moving.
- Increased connected vehicles service creation agility: Service agility or service velocity time should be minimum while developing a superior connected network. Whenever a service is requested by any dynamic node, the time taken by the deployed IoE technology to fetch the service should be minimum so that driving experience can be enhanced. For example, playing online songs should be in continuous motion rather than multiple pauses in-between.
- Improved 5G network capabilities of connected vehicles: No doubt, 5G is much more powerful and capable as compared to 4G networks. It is being designed to handle 100X increase in traffic and network. The area coverage 5G provides ranges between 30-300GHz, approximately 500 meters. But with the increasing popularity of connected vehicles and traffic flow, 5G is not enough to handle the network. There is a need to incorporate much more powerful and more area coverage than 5G.
- Mutual connected vehicles authentication capabilities: Connected vehicles should be capable enough to authenticate the nearby vehicle or RSU

before establishing any connection. Numerous sensors and IoE gadgets are pre-installed over the automobile to handle such events over the dynamic environment.

- Enhanced connected vehicles subscriber identity protection: Numerous certificate-based solutions are facilitated under connected network which verifies an authenticated and unregistered user over the network. The certificate-based verification facilitates on-demand solutions while authenticating another connected user over the dynamic environment.
- Critical infrastructure security: The surrounding is dynamic under vehicular communication network. Thus, there is a need to authenticate the sensor-enabled devices deployed over the network which tends to establish connection and transmit data. Authentication is very crucial as any adversary may tend to mislead an authenticated user over the network.
- Critical 5G network security: 5G has empowered the network with high bandwidth which makes it available throughout the dynamic geographical changes. This hinders the adversaries to modify the data over the network as network is powerful and available throughout the journey.
- Critical connected vehicles cloud security: Cloud measure utilizes different contraptions and district sway, adaptability of contraptions, virtualization of programs and gear system, advanced QoS, combining of saves that can be shared by various conclusion clients. The foremost challenging danger in vehicular cloud computing is security and security of the vehicle. In this way, the VCC structure ought to guarantee confidence and must give a secured environment for communication.
- Critical 5G Internet of Things (IoT) security: Vehicular communication network enables a vast deployment of IoT technologies for facilitating diverse services to the automobiles. Authentication of such IoE gadgets who tends to connect wirelessly should be done after every specific interval of time.
- Critical 5G access control measures: Verified users/authenticated automobiles should be allowed to access services over the network. A trusted authority (TA) allocates a PKI to individual dynamic node and a certificate-based verification. This may restrict outsiders to access the sensitive data transmitted over the network designated for registered users.
- Critical protection and backup data of connected vehicles: Due to vast connected network, it is essential to deploy huge repositories to store the data of the automobiles. The data stored over a centralized server or on local machine should be protected by adversaries. If such data is accessed by an unauthorized user, whole network may be crashed, as user's privacy and security is compromised.

- Critical monitoring and testing of connected vehicles system: A time slice (TS) is attached to every verification certificate. After the expiration of the time slice, connected vehicles are required to authenticate themselves again over the dynamic network to prove their identity. Thus, numerous AI/ML based techniques may be deployed to test the authenticity of the automobile.
- Critical firewalls: To improve immediate commercial vehicle (ICV), traditional methods such as, vehicle gateway firewall encryption and authentication of individual movable nodes is an essential part while verifying registered user over the network. It acts as a barrier that acts in between private and public network.

VI. ADVANTAGES

With the coming of edge computing, existing advances may create due to edge computing, and unused advances based on edge computing have been created. Security has continuously been a key issue for both wired and remote systems, and numerous analysts have went through decades attempting to handle this issue. Unveiling drivers' secret profiles may lead to ponder radiation. For occasion, in the event that any automobile locale is followed, it'll be simple to anticipate their previous and winning district. As before long as the locale's relic is collected, aggressors might at that point conjecture the driver's day-to-day plans by connecting these measurements with unused prove [Fig. 2]. This collected result can be mutilated for a few illegal acts like taking one's vehicle, kill, seizing, etc.

- Avoidance hazardous events: Declining of real-time road accidents. Firewall/ Network Security Device (NSD) are deployed over the wireless network to prevent the data accessibility and to decline the automobile's security vulnerability. Illegal invasion over the network can be prevented by deploying numerous techniques to overcome reliability and privacy challenge over 5G and B5G network.
- Terminating of malware: Deploying techniques based on signature-verification aids to focus on the intrusion to invade the network and disrupts it. Additionally, by deploying sandboxing, attack pattern or actions can be judged at each end. As soon as any attack is identified, it should be blocked over the network.
- Detecting anomalies: If attacks are not traced by deploying primary filters, numerous ML techniques, big-data tools can be deployed to upgrade the network's efficiency and overall throughput. Security-based sensors are attached

over the dynamic network under 5G environment by installing numerous switches, routers, etc.

- Domain Name System intelligence: Such systems are deployed over the network to sniff and sense any intrusion attack, or any spiteful data inserted over the network.
- Threat intelligence paramount: To prevent adversaries interference over the dynamic environment, attackers attempt to attack over the data/automobile should be examined. Thus, a proficient team should be hired who can examine the attack pattern, and ratio of attack over a particular section of the wireless network under 5G environment.
- Higher transmission speed: 5G communication network facilitates with high data transfer speed up to 20GBPS. It is more powerful than 4G communication network. 5G has provided a platform to other IoT gadgets to establish connection wirelessly.
- Lower latency: Latency is lower in 5G networks when compared with 4G communication networks. It works best when operated on millimetre waves.
- Remote execution: Data processing can take place on local nodes over the network. With high speed 5G network, data computation can take place over the nodes itself rather than compiling it over a huge, centralized server making the network slower.
- Flexible networking: Dynamic vehicular communication requires, nodes to be connected dynamically. Numerous RSUs should be installed so that OBUs can establish connection under dynamic environment.
- Higher throughput: As compared to 4G networks, 5G provides high throughput and low latency and computational cost over the network. It provides up to 20GBPS and more than 100 MBPS data transfer rate.
- Multiple services deployment: 5G network communication facilitates the network as well as the end user with multiple services. It provides services in network resource facing services where it provides a reliable connection in between numerous edge clouds, core clouds and application cloud, network facing services where 5G provides connection in between various vertical components and vertical edge components, Customer facing services where 5G provides end to end connection with numerous automobiles and RSUs on road.
- Higher mobility: With increase throughput and lower latency, 5G facilitates with intact connection while automobiles are moving. The interconnection between RSUs and OBUs is changing under dynamic environment.
- Higher energy efficiency: Data collection and computation is done remotely over individual's node over the network. This enhances the performance of all the connected devices under dynamic environment.

- Higher data volume: 5G provides higher data transfer rate as compared to 4G networks. Dynamic exchange of data on real-time basis is achieved with the high speed and reliability of 5G networks. The ever-growing demand of vehicular communication urges the need to empower 5G so that more reliability and speed can be provided to the automobiles.
- Higher reliability: As 5G is powerful, it facilitates the automobiles to establish connection with other RSUs and OBUs with security and privacy. Numerous authentication and privacy-preserving techniques are proposed using 5G networks so that reliability can be preserved over dynamic environment.

Figure 2. Advantages.

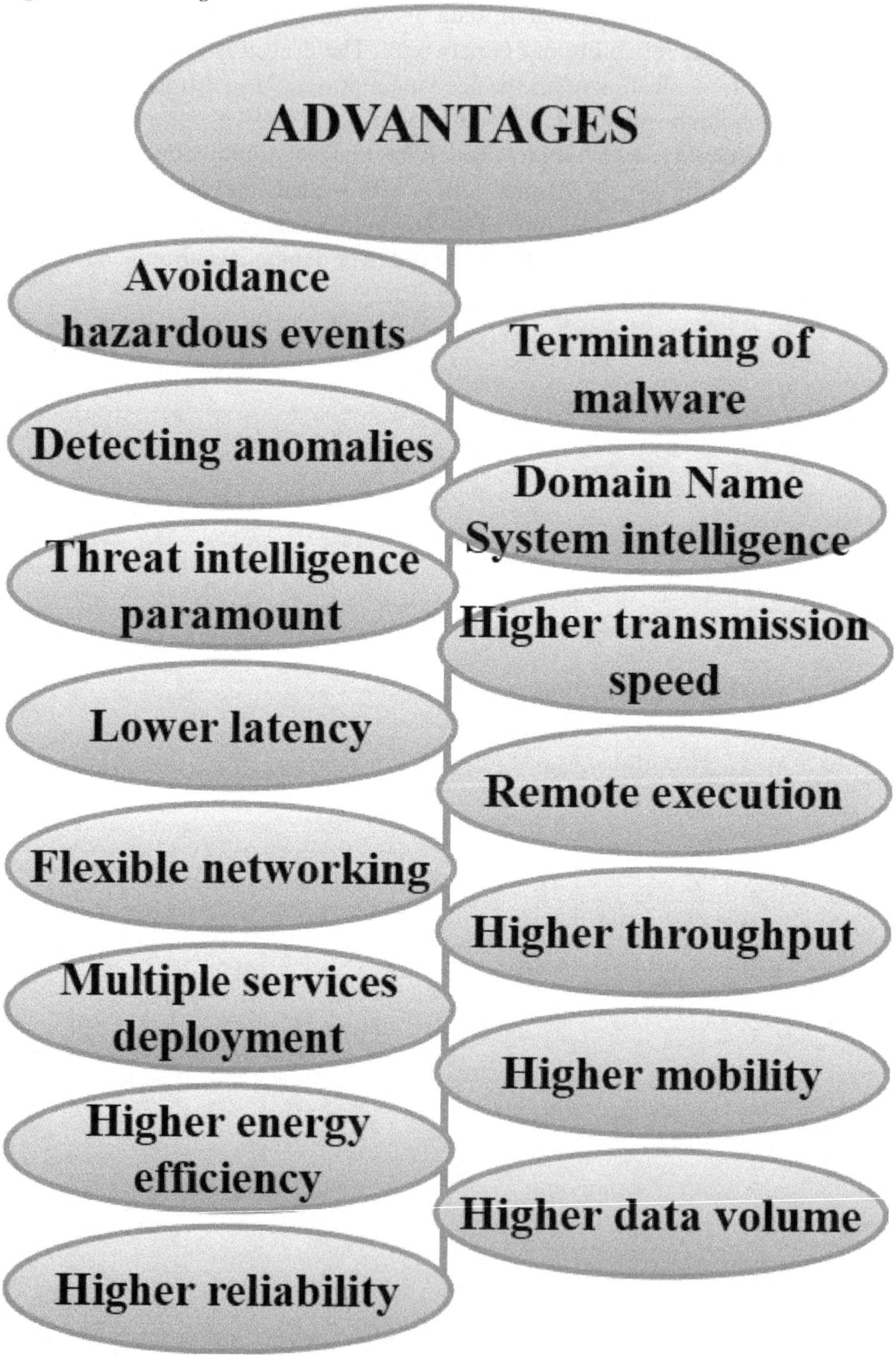

VII. CHALLENGES

The advancement of 5G and past 5G communication strategy encourages with the arrangement of various winning challenges such as store, preparing, security of client, and control confinements that makes a difference in building a able and an brilliantly transportation framework to proficiently oversee blockage on streets and to overhaul the driver's driving encounter beneath computerized vehicular environment. 5G may quicken the speed at which cyber dangers are recognized and inevitably permit quicker information examination, information downloads and communication over organizations universally. A few other challenges confronted beneath 5G communication security frameworks are:

- Maximize misconfiguration: Misconfiguration is a common problem. This enables the attacker to get hold of the core building blocks of the network.
- Less control of privileged access: If privacy and security is not managed strictly over the dynamic environment, it becomes easy for the adversaries to access the services prevailed by registered users of the network. This can lead to message alteration, misleading data, false identity over the network.
- Less visibility: 5G network communication has a shorter length wave which means it can transfer data much faster than 4G network but within a shorter distance. The wavelength provided by 4G was approx. 10miles and wavelength provided by 5G is near about 1000 feet.
- Less technical staff: With the development of 5G network from 4G, it has facilitated the network to incorporate multiple advanced IoE gadgets and data processing at individual's node storage. There is a need to manage all such gadgets efficiently else the network may drag down.

VIII. OPEN SOURCE TOOLS

Assessing the security of an Edge AI-enabled 6G communication framework for associated vehicles requires a multifaceted approach. Here's a breakdown of open-source devices categorized by their work, which can help in this evaluation:

- Nmap: A capable arrange scanner utilized for finding has and administrations on a organize, distinguishing open ports, and identifying vulnerabilities. It's basic for mapping the arrange topology of the 6G foundation.
- Wireshark: A arrange convention analyzer that captures and analyzes organize activity in real-time. It's significant for assessing communication conventions, recognizing peculiarities, and recognizing potential security breaches.

- Metasploit Framework: An infiltration testing system that gives a collection of misuses, payloads, and assistant modules. It permits security experts to mimic real-world assaults and evaluate the system's strength.
- OWASP Zap (Zed Attack Proxy): A web application security scanner that distinguishes vulnerabilities in web-based interfacing of the communication framework. This can be significant for any web-based administration or control interfacing.
- Scapy: An effective Python-based intuitively packet control program and library. It can be utilized to produce or interpret bundles of a wide number of conventions, send them on the wire, capture them, coordinate demands and answers and much more.
- OpenSSL: A toolkit for actualizing SSL/TLS conventions and cryptographic calculations. It can be utilized to test the quality of cryptographic executions, analyze certificate chains, and assess the security of key exchange mechanisms.
- GnuTLS: Another open source usage of the TLS and SSL conventions.
- Cryptanalysis Tools (e.g., John the Ripper, Hashcat): These instruments are utilized for password cracking and hash investigation, which can be important for surveying the quality of verification instruments.
- TensorFlow Security Tools: Whereas not a single apparatus, TensorFlow gives assets and rules for secure show arrangement. You'll be able too discover apparatuses that offer assistance with demonstrate solidifying.
- ONNX Runtime Security: In the event that utilizing ONNX models, looking into the ONNX runtime security documentation is vital.
- Federated Learning Frameworks (e.g., Flower, FedML): These systems can be utilized to reenact and analyze the security of unified learning arrangements, counting secure accumulation methods and differential protection components.
- Tools for Differential Privacy Analysis: Libraries in python, and R that offer assistance to evaluate the sum of security that differential security calculations give.
- OpenVAS: A defenselessness scanner that identifies security shortcomings in frameworks and applications. It can be used to distinguish known vulnerabilities within the 6G framework and edge gadgets.
- OWASP Dependency-Check: A computer program composition examination instrument that identifies freely known vulnerabilities contained inside a project's conditions. This is often supportive to guarantee all the open source libraries utilized are up to date and secure.
- NS-3 (Network Simulator 3): A organize test system that permits analysts to show and reenact complex arrange scenarios, counting 6G communication

and connected vehicle environments. It can be utilized to survey the execution and security of the framework beneath different conditions.

- SUMO (Simulation of Urban Mobility): A highly convenient, open source, microscopic and continuous road traffic simulation package outlined to handle expansive street systems. It is supportive to test the interaction of the associated vehicles inside the urban environment.

IX. ASSESSMENT PARAMETERS

Assessing the security of an Edge AI-enabled 6G communication framework for associated vehicles within the setting of urban advancement and administration requires assessing a run of parameters. These parameters can be broadly categorized into security, execution, unwavering quality, and societal affect. Here's a breakdown:

- Authentication and Authorization: It is utilized to degree the quality of authentication protocols (e.g., 5G-AKA, PKI), adequacy of access control components, and resistance to pantomime and replay assaults.
- Data Secrecy and Integrity: It is utilized to degree the adequacy of encryption calculations (e.g., AES, ECC), keenness of information transmission and capacity (e.g., hash capacities, advanced marks), and assurance against information breaches and unauthorized get to.
- Intrusion Detection and Anticipation: It is utilized to degree the exactness of irregularity location calculations, viability of intrusion prevention systems (IPS) and reaction time to security episodes.
- Edge AI Security: It is utilized to degree the vigor of AI models against ill-disposed assaults, security of unified learning forms (e.g., secure accumulation, differential protection), and assurance of AI models and information at the edge.
- Vulnerability Assessment: It is utilized to degree the recurrence and viability of powerlessness checking, opportuneness of fix administration, and resistance to known and zero-day misuses.
- Network Security: It is utilized to degree the security against Refusal of Benefit assaults, secure arrange cutting, and secure steering conventions.
- Latency: It is utilized to degree the end-to-end inactivity of communication, and handling idleness at the edge, and idleness affect on real-time applications (e.g., autonomous driving).
- Throughput: It is utilized to degree the information transmission rate, transfer speed utilization, and capacity to handle tall information volumes from associated vehicles.

- Reliability and Accessibility: It is utilized to degree the arrange uptime and stability, excess and fault resistance, and capacity to preserve network in challenging situations.
- Scalability: It is utilized to degree the capacity to handle expanding numbers of associated vehicles, adaptability of edge computing assets, and asset utilization of the Edge AI calculations.
- Fault Resilience: It is utilized to degree the how well the framework handles component disappointments, and excess inside the framework.
- Flexibility: It is utilized to degree the how well the framework recuperates from attacks, and capacity to preserve usefulness amid disturbances.
- Accessibility: It is utilized to degree the rate of time the framework is operational, and Mean time between failures (MTBF).
- Protection: It is utilized to degree the assurance of individual information from associated vehicles, Compliance with data privacy regulations (e.g., GDPR), and transparency of information collection and utilization.
- Security: It is utilized to degree the affect on street security and mischance decrease, unwavering quality of independent driving highlights, and adequacy of crisis reaction frameworks.
- Urban Efficiency: It is utilized to degree the affect on activity stream and blockage lessening, optimization of asset allotment (e.g., stopping, open transport), and contribution to savvy city activities.
- Administration: It is utilized to degree the capacity to implement activity directions and arrangements, straightforwardness and responsibility of urban administration, and moral contemplations of AI utilization.
- Environmental Impact: It is utilized to degree the control utilization of the edge gadgets, and affect on the lessening of emanations due to activity optimization.
- Entrance Testing: It will be reenacting real-world assaults to distinguish vulnerabilities.
- Vulnerability Scanning: It will be utilizing computerized instruments to identify known vulnerabilities.
- Organize Checking: It will be analyzing organize activity to distinguish anomalies and security episodes.
- Execution Testing: It will be measuring idleness, throughput, and unwavering quality beneath different conditions.
- Recreation and Modeling: It will be utilizing simulation tools to assess the system's behavior in complex scenarios.
- Real-World Testing: It will be conveying the framework in controlled situations to survey its execution and security.

- Privacy Impact Assessments (PIA): It will be assessing the potential affect of the framework on person protection.
- Ethical Impact Assessments: It will be assessing the moral suggestions of the framework.

X. CASE STUDY

A case study centering on a pilot program inside a major US city, such as Austin, Texas, pointing to revolutionize its activity administration and open security utilizing an Edge AI-enabled 6G communication security framework for associated vehicles. Austin, hooking with quick populace development and expanding activity clog, looked for to use cutting-edge innovation to form a more proficient and secure urban versatility environment. The city collaborated with a consortium of telecom suppliers, car producers, and AI engineers to send a pilot arrange over a assigned zone, centering on a high-traffic passage and a private zone. The conveyed framework utilized 6G framework with deliberately put edge computing servers, empowering close real-time preparing of information from associated vehicles. These vehicles, prepared with progressed sensors and communication modules, transmitted information with respect to their area, speed, and encompassing environment. Edge AI calculations analyzed this information to distinguish activity irregularities, anticipate blockage hotspots, and distinguish potential security dangers. For occasion, the framework might distinguish a sudden lull in activity stream, analyze the contributing components, and powerfully alter activity light timings to relieve clog. Moreover, it might distinguish vehicles showing sporadic behavior, possibly showing impeded driving, and alarm law authorization in real-time. Security was foremost in this pilot program. The 6G organize utilized vigorous encryption conventions and verification instruments to guarantee information secrecy and judgment. Edge AI models were solidified against ill-disposed assaults, and combined learning methods were actualized to ensure client protection by preparing models locally on vehicle information. The framework too joined interruption discovery frameworks that ceaselessly checked network traffic for suspicious action, giving an extra layer of security. The pilot program yielded noteworthy advancements in activity stream and security. Real-time activity administration decreased blockage by 20%, driving to shorter commute times and diminished fuel utilization. The system's capacity to identify and react to security dangers brought about in a 15% diminishment in activity mischances inside the pilot zone. Besides, the city utilized the information collected by the framework to optimize foundation arranging, recognizing ranges requiring street changes or open transportation improvements. The administration angle of the framework was carefully considered. An information administration system was built up to guarantee straightforwardness and responsibility in information collection and utilization. The city engaged with community partners to address security concerns and guarantee open believe. The framework was planned to comply with significant information protection directions, such as the California Consumer Privacy Act (CCPA), and utilized anonymization strategies to ensure person protection. This case ponder represents how Edge AI-enabled 6G communication security frameworks can change urban advancement and administration. By leveraging real-time information and progressed AI calculations, cities can make more productive, secure, and maintainable transportation biological systems. The pilot program in Austin illustrates the potential of this innovation to address urban challenges and make strides the quality of life for inhabitants, whereas keeping security and security at the bleeding edge.

A case study based in a European smart city, such as Barcelona, Spain, centering on the arrangement of an Edge AI-enabled 6G communication security framework for associated vehicles to improve urban versatility and maintainability. Barcelona, known for its imaginative keen city activities, pointed to address challenges related to activity clog, contamination, and person on foot security by leveraging progressed 6G innovation. The city propelled a pilot program in a assigned range, including a active commercial area and a private neighborhood, to test the system's adequacy. The sent 6G organize utilized a thick arrange of little cells and edge computing servers, empowering ultra-low idleness communication between associated vehicles and the city's framework. Vehicles prepared with progressed sensors and 6G communication modules transmitted real-time information on their area, speed, emanations, and encompassing environment. Edge AI calculations handled this information at the edge, empowering quick decision-making and localized control. For occurrence, the framework seem analyze activity stream designs, identify clog hotspots, and powerfully alter activity light timings to optimize activity stream and decrease outflows. It may too recognize vehicles surpassing speed limits or emanating over the top toxins, activating cautions for activity administration specialists. Security and security were basic contemplations in this pilot program. The 6G arrange utilized vigorous encryption conventions and confirmation instruments, following to exacting European information security controls, such as GDPR. Edge AI models were secured against ill-disposed assaults, and federated learning was utilized to prepare models on vehicle information without compromising client security. Additionally, the framework joined interruption discovery and avoidance components to protect against cyber dangers. The pilot program yielded noteworthy enhancements in urban versatility and maintainability. Real-time activity administration decreased blockage by 25%, driving to shorter commute times and decreased fuel utilization. The system's capacity to screen and control vehicle emanations contributed to a 15% decrease in discuss contamination inside the pilot zone. Besides, the framework improved person on foot security by identifying vehicles drawing closer crosswalks and cautioning people on foot by means of versatile apps. The administration viewpoint of the framework was carefully overseen. A information administration system was set up, guaranteeing straightforwardness and responsibility in information collection and utilization. The city locked in with nearby inhabitants and partners to address protection concerns and construct believe within the framework. The framework was outlined to comply with GDPR controls, guaranteeing that individual information was prepared legally and safely. This case think about in Barcelona illustrates the potential of Edge AI-enabled 6G communication security frameworks to convert urban improvement and administration in Europe. By leveraging progressed innovation and a solid accentuation on security, protection, and supportability, European cities can make more proficient, secure, and ecologically inviting urban situations. The Barcelona pilot program highlights the significance of collaborative organizations between innovation suppliers, city specialists, and nearby communities in realizing the benefits of smart city activities.

XI. FUTURE PERSPECTIVES

The integration of edge AI with 5G communication systems has the potential to revolutionize the security of connected vehicles. This combination can bring new levels of intelligence and automation to the security of these systems, enabling real-time threat detection, prevention, and response. Here are some of the key future perspectives of edge AI-enabled 5G communication security systems for connected vehicles:

- Real-time threat detection: Edge AI algorithms can be trained to analyze vast amounts of data generated by connected vehicles, including network traffic and sensor data, in real-time. This can enable the detection of cyber threats and attacks in near real-time, allowing for rapid response and mitigation.
- Improved security for autonomous vehicles: As autonomous vehicles become more prevalent, the need for robust security systems becomes increasingly important. Edge AI can play a crucial role in securing autonomous vehicles by providing real-time threat detection and prevention, as well as autonomous response in the event of an attack.
- Intelligent network traffic analysis: Edge AI algorithms can be used to analyze network traffic generated by connected vehicles to identify patterns of behavior that may indicate a security threat. This can help to detect potential security risks before they cause harm.

- Advanced encryption and secure data transfer: Edge AI can be used to enhance encryption and secure data transfer methods, ensuring that sensitive data transmitted between connected vehicles and the cloud remains protected.
- Predictive maintenance and security: Edge AI algorithms can be trained to analyze data from connected vehicles, including sensor data, network traffic, and other relevant information, to predict potential security risks and maintenance issues before they occur.
- Quantum-Resistant Cryptography: As quantum computing progresses, the require for quantum-resistant cryptographic calculations will gotten to be vital for securing 6G communications.
- AI-Driven Security: AI will be progressively utilized to identify and react to modern cyber dangers in real-time, leveraging progressed peculiarity location and prescient analytics.
- Homomorphic Encryption and Secure Multi-Party Computation: These advances will improve information security by empowering computations on scrambled information and secure collaborative examination, individually.
- Blockchain Integration: Blockchain innovation can improve information astuteness and security by giving decentralized and tamper-proof information administration.
- Federated Learning Advancements: Federated learning will advance to handle more complex information dispersions, heterogeneous gadgets, and energetic situations, empowering more personalized and proficient AI models.
- Neuromorphic Computing: Neuromorphic computing, mirroring the human brain, will empower more proficient and energy-saving AI handling at the edge, significant for resource-constrained vehicles.
- Explainable AI (XAI): XAI will ended up progressively imperative for guaranteeing straightforwardness and responsibility in AI-driven decision-making, especially in safety-critical applications like independent driving.
- AI-powered digital twins: These will empower prescient upkeep, and genuine time reenactment of activity streams, and optimization of asset assignment.
- Terahertz (THz) Communication: 6G will use THz frequencies to realize ultra-high information rates and moo inactivity, empowering more progressed applications like holographic communications and immersive encounters.
- Satellite-Terrestrial Integration: Consistent integration of satellite and earthly systems will guarantee omnipresent network, especially in inaccessible and underserved regions.
- Standardization and Interoperability: Stronger standardization endeavors will guarantee interoperability between distinctive 6G systems and associated vehicle frameworks, cultivating a more cohesive environment.

- Dynamic Network Slicing: More advanced network slicing capabilities will empower the creation of customized organize administrations for particular applications, such as crisis reaction and independent driving.
- Data-Driven Decision-Making: Real-time information from associated vehicles and edge AI will empower city organizers and policymakers to form more educated choices with respect to foundation improvement, activity administration, and open security.
- Smart Infrastructure: Integration of 6G and AI into smart foundation, such as smart activity lights and smart stopping frameworks, will optimize asset utilization and make strides urban effectiveness.
- Enhanced Public Safety: Real-time checking and examination of activity information will empower quicker crisis reaction times and proactive mischance avoidance.
- Personalized Mobility Services: AI-powered mobility-as-a-service (MaaS) stages will give personalized and efficient transportation choices, lessening congestion and making strides openness.
- Digital Governance: The utilize of computerized twins and AI will lead to more effective, transparent, and responsive urban administration.

XII. CONCLUSION

A quick expansion of IoT-based devices and gadgets are seen in final few a long time. Such gadgets covers personal-care IoT, health-care IoT, trade IoT building up a work organize within the environment. It is expected that 6G will be a game-changer in handling massive cyber exercises along side IoT-based tools. Since of various associated gadgets, DDOS assault may well be effectively done over the network. Such an assault beneath 6G IoT environment, decreases the unwavering quality, security and security of the car as well as the driver. This could be considered as an open challenge for analysts and vehicle businesses. The integration of edge counterfeit insights (AI) and 5G communication frameworks holds incredible guarantee for improving the security of associated vehicles. By leveraging the real-time handling capabilities of edge AI and the high-speed and low-latency capabilities of 5G, these frameworks can give progressed risk location, anticipation, and reaction, whereas too empowering secure information exchange and prescient support. Besides, the combination of edge AI and 5G has the potential to revolutionize the way associated vehicles work, giving a more cleverly and secure environment for independent driving, which is getting to be progressively vital as the number of independent vehicles develops.

REFERENCES

Boualouache, A., & Engel, T. (2021). Federated learning-based scheme for detecting passive mobile attackers in 5G vehicular edge computing. *Annales des Télécommunications*, *77*(3–4), 201–220. DOI: 10.1007/s12243-021-00871-x

Gyawali, S., Qian, Y., & Hu, R. (2021). Deep reinforcement learning based dynamic reputation policy in 5G based vehicular communication networks. *IEEE Transactions on Vehicular Technology*, *70*(6), 6136–6146. DOI: 10.1109/TVT.2021.3079379

Haider, S. A., Ramesh, J. V. N., Raina, V., Maaliw, R. R., Soni, M., Nasurova, K., Patni, J. C., & Singh, P. P. (2024). Secure artificial intelligence for precise vehicle behavior prediction in 6G consumer electronics. *IEEE Transactions on Consumer Electronics*, *70*(1), 3898–3905. DOI: 10.1109/TCE.2024.3369399

Ibn-Khedher, H., Laroui, M., Alfaqawi, M., Magnouche, A., Moungla, H., & Afifi, H. (2023). 6G-edge support of Internet of Autonomous Vehicles: A survey. *Transactions on Emerging Telecommunications Technologies*, *35*(1), e4918. Advance online publication. DOI: 10.1002/ett.4918

Letaief, K. B., Shi, Y., Lu, J., & Lu, J. (2021). Edge Artificial Intelligence for 6G: Vision, enabling technologies, and applications. *IEEE Journal on Selected Areas in Communications*, *40*(1), 5–36. DOI: 10.1109/JSAC.2021.3126076

Nawaz, M. W., Zhang, W., Flynn, D., Zhang, L., Swash, R., Abbasi, Q. H., Imran, M. A., & Popoola, O. (2024). 6G edge-networks and multi-UAV knowledge fusion for urban autonomous vehicles. *Physical Communication*, *67*, 102479. DOI: 10.1016/j.phycom.2024.102479

Rasheed, I., Zhang, L., & Hu, F. (2020). A privacy preserving scheme for vehicle-to-everything communications using 5G mobile edge computing. *Computer Networks*, *176*, 107283. DOI: 10.1016/j.comnet.2020.107283

Reebadiya, D., Rathod, T., Gupta, R., Tanwar, S., & Kumar, N. (2021). Blockchain-based secure and intelligent sensing scheme for autonomous vehicles activity tracking beyond 5G networks. *Peer-to-Peer Networking and Applications*, *14*(5), 2757–2774. DOI: 10.1007/s12083-021-01073-x

Sharma, S., Tyagi, R., & Mohan, S. (2024a). Artificial intelligence and green 6G network-enabled architectures, scenarios, and applications for autonomous connected vehicles. In River Publishers eBooks (pp. 187–212). https://doi.org/DOI: 10.1201/9781003515920-9

Sheraz, M., Chuah, T. C., Lee, Y. L., Alam, M. M., Al-Habashna, A., & Han, Z. (2024). A comprehensive survey on revolutionizing connectivity through Artificial Intelligence-Enabled Digital twin Network in 6G. *IEEE Access : Practical Innovations, Open Solutions*, *1*, 1. Advance online publication. DOI: 10.1109/ACCESS.2024.3384272

Teimoori, Z., Yassine, A., & Hossain, M. S. (2024). Smart Vehicles Recommendation System for Artificial Intelligence-Enabled Communication. *IEEE Transactions on Consumer Electronics*, *70*(1), 3914–3925. DOI: 10.1109/TCE.2024.3360320

Chapter 16
Human-Centered Design for Smart Cities:
Integrating Social Aspects in Planning and Policy

Ali Maqousi
https://orcid.org/0000-0002-3242-804X
Department of Information Security, University of Petra, Amman, Jordan

Kashinath Basu
https://orcid.org/0000-0002-0831-3752
Oxford Brookes University, UK

Ammar Almomani
https://orcid.org/0000-0002-8808-6114
Department of Computer Information Science, Higher Colleges of Technology, Sharjah, UAE

Mouhammd Alkasassbeh
https://orcid.org/0000-0001-8396-7441
Princess Sumaya University for Technology, Jordan

ABSTRACT

Cities worldwide seek new approaches to urban development that prioritize people, governance, and sustainable progress. Human-centered design focuses on social inclusion, participatory planning, and context-based methods to guide technology adoption in city environments. This chapter examines how integrating social factors into policy frameworks leads to smarter cities that strengthen equity and civic trust. It explores planning strategies that incorporate community voices, institutional shifts that facilitate inclusive governance, and the importance of shaping technology to serve

DOI: 10.4018/979-8-3373-1375-7.ch016

public needs. The research gathered qualitative and quantitative data from global initiatives and identified best practices for participatory design in urban projects. The findings suggest that citizen empowerment and transparent processes promote balanced and ethical smart city ecosystems. This work highlights a transformative pathway toward people-first urban innovation.

1. INTRODUCTION

Smart city agendas continue to influence major decisions in urban regions. Planners and policymakers often evaluate innovative technologies while seeking solutions for pressing challenges. These challenges include resource allocation, socioeconomic inequality, and participation in local governance. The current global discourse recognizes that a city cannot be deemed smart if it fails to empower its inhabitants. Over a decade of research has underscored how urban development strategies that emphasize digital infrastructures alone tend to neglect human dimensions (Hollands, 2008; Meijer & Rodríguez Bolívar, 2016). Scholars warn about a growing gulf between techno-centric city visions and inclusive models that engage the broader community (Sadowski & Bendor, 2019). City stakeholders and citizens frequently share aspirations for improved quality of life, transparency in management, and resilient public services. Yet attempts to embed these aspirations into coherent policy often remain fragmented (Datta, 2018).

Formal policy statements sometimes define the smart city as a place where data, analytics, and connected devices converge to optimize services. Substantial energy is spent on urban informatics, data platforms, sensor networks, and artificial intelligence. These instruments can facilitate efficient mobility, real-time monitoring of infrastructure, and responsive resource use. However, scholars such as Hollands (2015) note that technological sophistication does not guarantee equitable outcomes or broad participation. Indeed, studies show that governance systems designed around corporate priorities may position residents as passive consumers rather than active co-creators (Sadowski & Bendor, 2019; Cardullo & Kitchin, 2019). Social dimensions such as inclusiveness, shared decision-making, and local identity can be overshadowed by the pursuit of efficiency.

There is mounting evidence that human-centered design for smart cities offers a viable path toward bridging this gap. Human-centered design fosters collaborative innovation that addresses local needs and contexts (Concilio & Rizzo, 2016). Approaches guided by co-creation, open engagement, and transparent governance structures can empower communities to shape the future of their cities (Paskaleva, 2011). Planners who acknowledge the range of community experiences discover new perspectives and sometimes intangible benefits, such as trust and social cohesion

(Gil-García, Pardo, & Nam, 2015). Scholars propose that inclusive governance systems generate more resilient and legitimate pathways for urban innovation (Sweeting, de Alba-Ulloa, Pansera, & Marsh, 2022). When citizens are invited to engage with data platforms and community planning, they become partners in shaping more equitable urban spaces (Kummitha, 2024).

This chapter explores how a people-first perspective can be integrated into smart city planning and policy. It draws upon a body of academic research, policy documents, and empirical findings that illuminate the synergy between social inclusion and technical progress (Datta, 2018; Tekin & Dikmen, 2024; OECD, 2020). It considers inclusive governance mechanisms, digital equity, and community-based knowledge as key elements in shaping a robust urban future. Its central assumption holds that participatory engagement in policy formation and planning fosters trust, fosters accountability, and harnesses the capabilities of technology for public benefit (UN-Habitat, 2022).

To situate the argument, this introduction reviews the evolving narratives about smart city governance. Early conceptions favored market-led technology solutions (Townsend, 2013). Critics pointed out that these solutions sometimes neglected important social questions, including who controls data, whose interests are served, and how local values inform urban projects (Greenfield, 2013). Recent scholarship reframes these questions through a human lens. Instead of asking whether technology can automate or optimize urban processes, researchers examine whether communities can shape and steer these transformations toward common goals (Joss, Sengers, Schraven, Caprotti, & Dayot, 2019).

The chapter proposes that comprehensive smart city strategies must expand beyond hardware and software. Human-centered urban design merges social equity with technical innovation to create an integrated planning approach. In many policy realms, technology is presented as a neutral force, but design choices reflect values and priorities (Martin, Evans, & Karvonen, 2018). A deeper engagement with local contexts ensures that decisions account for historical inequalities, urban demographics, and community aspirations. Engaged governance fosters transparency and collaboration, thereby mitigating the risk of top-down initiatives that do not resonate with community needs (World Economic Forum, 2021).

Following this introduction, the chapter outlines theoretical underpinnings for human-centered smart cities. This theoretical framing demonstrates how the interplay between policy design, institutional structures, and civic engagement shapes the smart city agenda. It then moves to examine practical frameworks that enable inclusive governance. These frameworks emerge from municipal case studies and guiding policy reports from international agencies (OECD, 2020; European Commission, 2016). Later sections discuss methodological approaches for integrating social dimensions, including participatory planning and collaborative technology design.

The discussion then addresses the tensions between top-down modernization and bottom-up innovation. It reviews case examples where inclusive planning translated into tangible improvements for diverse populations. The chapter then offers policy recommendations and outlines how cross-sector collaboration can yield effective strategies. Finally, it proposes future directions for research and practice.

2. THEORETICAL PERSPECTIVES ON HUMAN-CENTERED DESIGN FOR SMART CITIES

2.1 Conceptual Foundations of Smart Cities

Smart city thinking has evolved from its initial emphasis on advanced technologies to an expanded understanding that includes governance, infrastructure, and social well-being (Albino, Berardi, & Dangelico, 2015). Authors like Hollands (2008) showed the potential pitfalls of technology-driven visions that marginalize communities. Early definitions of smart cities highlighted energy efficiency, communications networks, and data analytics. Over time, analysis revealed that such definitions lacked a robust sociopolitical dimension. The scholarly conversation turned toward frameworks that recognized governance and citizen participation as vital elements (Gil-García et al., 2015).

Academic literature often conceptualizes the smart city as a dynamic system where technology is employed to achieve improved service delivery, environmental stewardship, and economic growth (Townsend, 2013). This perspective focuses on the city's ability to leverage digital platforms to optimize processes, build interoperability among sectors, and respond to changing urban demands. Technology remains integral to this vision, yet the concept of "smartness" has become more nuanced. Studies increasingly suggest that urban intelligence depends on the relationships between technology, governance, and social inclusion (Meijer & Rodríguez Bolívar, 2016). Inclusive policies that encourage citizen co-creation and accountability help ensure technology initiatives serve public interests (Sweeting et al., 2022).

Human-centered design stands as a response to concerns about narrow, technocratic programs. Concilio and Rizzo (2016) argued that design thinking principles—such as empathy, iterative prototyping, and multi-stakeholder collaboration—can help shape future urban transformations. When applied to city planning, these principles foster deeper participation at each stage of project development. Participatory strategies shift the focus from technology's capabilities to the question of how local communities envision progress (Cardullo & Kitchin, 2019). This shift aligns with the broader notion of "smart enough" cities, which emphasize proportional solutions that align with public aspirations (Green, 2019).

2.2 Social Inclusion in the Smart City Discourse

Analysts examine how social inclusion emerges within smart city conversations. Vanolo (2016) observes that some programs portray residents as data producers or customers, limiting their active role in governance. Bastos, Fernández-Caballero, Pereira, and Pacheco Rocha (2022) found that many e-participation applications still do not guarantee robust forms of engagement. Instead, these platforms sometimes reflect institutional interests or technology vendor objectives. Human-centered design counters this dynamic by emphasizing shared ownership and collective goal-setting. Scholars advocate for governance that enables a broad range of participants to voice concerns, influence outcomes, and monitor implementation (Cowley, Joss, & Dayot, 2018).

The literature also addresses inclusive growth strategies that reduce digital divides. Unchecked digitization can create inequalities, where certain groups lack access to digital resources (OECD, 2020). World Bank (2016) has warned that technology alone does not yield equitable benefits without supportive policies. Inclusive governance structures can offer pathways to mitigate such risks. These structures recognize social disparities and employ targeted measures, such as community training in digital literacy, open data initiatives that use accessible interfaces, and consultation sessions that accommodate different languages and cultural contexts (Tekin & Dikmen, 2024). In this way, technology becomes a tool that supports collective well-being rather than a driver of marginalization.

2.3 Governance Theories and Civic Engagement

Governance theories contribute important insights to human-centered design for smart cities. Traditional governance models often revolve around hierarchical planning by municipal authorities (Meijer & Rodríguez Bolívar, 2016). Collaborative governance seeks a broader distribution of decision-making authority among agencies, private sector entities, and community organizations. Smart city frameworks that adopt collaborative governance approaches can facilitate open access to information, co-production of services, and deliberation over policy priorities (Datta, 2018).

Innovations in digital democracy, such as participatory budgeting platforms, underscore the possibility of more direct forms of civic engagement (Bastos et al., 2022). Citizen feedback can inform infrastructure decisions, social service allocations, and environmental initiatives. However, these platforms must be structured to avoid tokenistic participation. Mechanisms for informed deliberation and meaningful feedback loops can build trust in local government. Kummitha (2024) argues that robust engagement strategies include multiple channels—online tools, in-person gatherings, and community alliances—to broaden representation. Such participatory methods reinforce the conviction that cities thrive when governance processes integrate the knowledge and experience of residents (de Waal & Dignum, 2017).

2.4 Human-Centered Design Principles

The essence of human-centered design in urban contexts revolves around empathy, iteration, and co-creation. Planners conduct in-depth discussions with various stakeholders to identify local issues before selecting technological solutions. Pilot projects or prototypes are tested in small-scale environments, then refined through continuous feedback. This participatory process attempts to ensure that technology aligns with community priorities. Cardullo (2020) stresses the significance of co-production arrangements, where municipal agencies and citizens share responsibilities and design tasks. Such arrangements demand institutional readiness to handle diverse viewpoints and navigate social complexities.

Human-centered design also emphasizes the intangible outcomes of collaboration, such as strengthened social networks and heightened trust. Instead of imposing solutions, designers act as facilitators who leverage local knowledge to generate solutions that fit local constraints (Srivastava & Mostafavi, 2018). This shift disrupts top-down planning while offering a more dynamic form of citymaking. Inclusive governance further promotes civic identity, since people feel recognized and valued within urban processes (Aurigi & Odendaal, 2021).

Figure 1, outlines the key stages: understanding user needs, collaborative design, prototyping, feedback integration, and implementation.

Figure 1. Human-Centered Design Process for Smart Cities

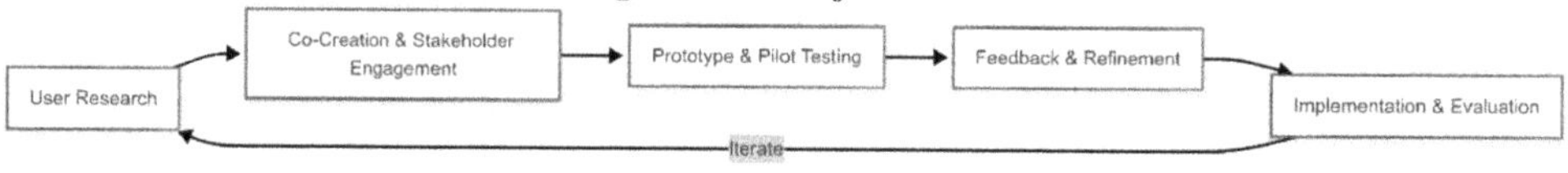

2.5 Relevance to Contemporary Policy Debates

Recent policy debates reflect growing recognition that the path to sustainable urban futures must be grounded in participatory processes. The New Urban Agenda (United Nations, 2017) calls for people-centered development strategies that foster equity and collective decision-making. Various national guidelines for smart city programs, such as India's Smart Cities Mission (Ministry of Housing and Urban Affairs, 2015), outline citizen involvement as a requirement for receiving project funding. Similar priorities appear in the G20 Smart Cities Alliance, which emphasizes transparent data governance and inclusive stakeholder engagement (World Economic Forum, 2021). These initiatives illustrate how the push for people-centered design is increasingly encoded in policy documents.

Yet challenges remain. Institutional inertia, resource constraints, and conflicting stakeholder interests can undermine participatory goals (Sadowski & Bendor, 2019). Researchers suggest that bridging rhetorical commitments and on-the-ground practices requires consistent political will, robust frameworks, and accountability tools (Manville et al., 2014). This chapter aims to explore how these frameworks and tools can be integrated into planning and policy processes so that human-centered design becomes a living practice, not an empty slogan.

3. INSTITUTIONAL AND POLICY CONTEXTS FOR SOCIAL INTEGRATION

3.1 Global Policy Drivers

Global organizations like the United Nations, the OECD, and the World Bank have circulated guidelines on smart city development that highlight social inclusion and governance. The UN-Habitat (2022) guide focuses on mainstreaming human rights in digital transformations. It addresses data ethics, privacy considerations, and participatory governance measures as mechanisms for aligning technology with the public interest. The OECD (2020) underscores inclusive growth as a shared objective of smart city interventions, suggesting that data-driven services must be paired with equitable access to digital infrastructure. The World Economic Forum (2021) contributes benchmarks for ethical smart city development, referencing issues like transparency, cybersecurity, and citizen involvement.

Such documents mark a shift away from technology-dominated narratives and toward frameworks that require stakeholder engagement. The prominence of these guidelines within policy circles has pressured local governments to demonstrate social impact in their smart city proposals (European Commission, 2016). Planners increasingly adopt language about co-creation, citizen-centered solutions, and equity goals. These commitments manifest in projects that provide free Wi-Fi in underserved neighborhoods, digital literacy training, and community-run data platforms. However, the extent to which local contexts can realize these ambitions varies. Implementation often hinges on political will, resource availability, and the strength of civic institutions (Calzada, 2021).

3.2 National and Municipal Initiatives

Many nations have launched programs that encourage municipal actors to integrate technology with community engagement. India's Smart Cities Mission stands out for making citizen participation an official criterion in project selection (Ministry of Housing and Urban Affairs, 2015). Municipalities that propose initiatives must show community consultations and feasible governance arrangements. Similarly, the European Union's Urban Agenda encourages local experimentation with living labs and co-design techniques (Manville et al., 2014). In Latin America, city governments have explored open-data portals and e-government tools to engage populations in public planning (Sweeting et al., 2022).

Case studies demonstrate how these policy frameworks play out in practice. Mexico City's approach to citizen participation includes hackathons, open innovation challenges, and digital forums for consultation (Sweeting et al., 2022). London's strategy involves inclusive design for transport, housing, and health, as part of its drive toward a socially cohesive smart city (Tekin & Dikmen, 2024). Dublin's smart city programs employ a "scaffold" approach that progresses from informing residents to enabling co-creation (Cardullo & Kitchin, 2019). These instances reflect varied governance traditions and highlight differences in how local cultures shape participatory methods.

3.3 Institutional Readiness and Collaboration

Institutional readiness is crucial for embedding human-centered design principles. Administrations may lack expertise in participatory processes, data governance, or cross-departmental coordination. Overcoming these gaps sometimes requires capacity-building programs that train officials in facilitation, design thinking, and technology ethics (Rodríguez-Bolívar, 2019). Partnerships with universities, civic organizations, and private firms can bring diverse skill sets into government. Some cities form advisory councils or steering committees that include representatives from nonprofits, academia, and neighborhood associations (Cowley et al., 2018).

Collaboration extends to horizontal and vertical alignment within government layers. Municipal agencies overseeing transportation, environment, housing, and social services might converge around shared policy goals. Meanwhile, broader levels of government—regional or national—can support local initiatives through funding and legislative mandates (Townsend, 2013). Harmonizing these collaborations is often a policy challenge, since bureaucratic structures may resist integrated approaches. Transparent frameworks that clarify roles, responsibilities, and accountability help anchor human-centered design in the institutional setting (OECD, 2020).

3.4 Policy Gaps and Ongoing Debates

Though policy documents advocate inclusiveness, critics argue that real-world smart city programs continue to prioritize technology procurement over civic empowerment (Sadowski & Bendor, 2019). The alignment between high-level rhetoric and practical outcomes remains inconsistent. Some municipal strategies pay lip service to engagement while sustaining top-down practices (Cardullo, 2020). Others implement token surveys rather than deeper deliberations (Bastos et al., 2022). These critiques highlight the possibility that human-centered design rhetoric might be co-opted to legitimize existing power structures without transforming them.

Additionally, the interplay of corporate interests and public welfare remains contested. Private-sector partners often supply the technological backbone of smart city solutions. Their involvement can expedite innovation, yet scholars warn about potential conflicts between profitability motives and long-term community well-being (Hollands, 2015). Strategies to mitigate these concerns include transparent procurement, open data standards, data-privacy guidelines, and robust oversight mechanisms (World Economic Forum, 2021). The involvement of civil society groups in shaping contract terms can further safeguard public interests.

In summary, policy contexts provide a framework for embedding social aspects into smart city plans. Global, national, and municipal guidelines emphasize inclusive governance and human rights-based approaches. Actual implementation hinges on institutional readiness, resource allocation, and sustained collaboration. Persistent policy gaps and debates reveal that the path toward human-centered design is neither linear nor guaranteed. These contextual insights set the stage for examining methodological approaches that can translate policy intentions into tangible outcomes.

4. METHODOLOGICAL APPROACHES FOR INTEGRATING SOCIAL ASPECTS

4.1 Participatory Planning Frameworks

Participatory planning frameworks create opportunities for integrating social dimensions throughout the smart city lifecycle. This section explains how inclusive methods support project definition, design, implementation, and evaluation. The principle is that stakeholders actively collaborate in shaping strategies, rather than merely responding to proposals (Schuurman, Baccarne, Mechant, & De Marez, 2012). Various methodological tools exist, such as community workshops, design sprints, living labs, and co-creation platforms. Each tool facilitates interaction between experts, policymakers, and the public, allowing local knowledge to emerge.

Table 1. Common Participatory Planning Methods for Smart City Projects

Method	Focus	Potential Outcome	Reference
Community Workshops	Face-to-face dialogue with residents	Identifies local needs and shared values	Schuurman et al., 2012
Design Sprints	Rapid prototyping with cross-functional teams	Tests feasibility of new solutions	Concilio & Rizzo, 2016
Living Labs	Real-world experimentation and iterative feedback	Generates user-driven innovations	Paskaleva, 2011
Co-creation Platforms	Digital interfaces for joint idea generation	Encourages ongoing collaboration	Datta, 2018

In practice, these methods should be tailored to local conditions. Workshops can help gather input on challenges and goals from citizens, especially when planners dedicate time to building trust before launching technical proposals. Design sprints condense project cycles into brief, intensive sessions that deliver quick prototypes for review. Living labs further embed prototypes within communities for real-time feedback, exposing design flaws and generating context-relevant improvements. Digital co-creation platforms can expand engagement beyond physical events, yet they also raise questions about digital access and literacy (Bastos et al., 2022).

4.2 Data-Driven Insights for Community Needs

Data-informed decision-making is a hallmark of many smart city initiatives. Yet conventional approaches sometimes emphasize big data from sensors and administrative systems at the expense of qualitative insights (Joss, Sengers, Schraven, Caprotti, & Dayot, 2019). A human-centered methodology pairs quantitative data with narratives from citizens, who bring depth and nuance to the problem context. Crowdsourcing tools, social media analyses, and open data portals can capture local experiences if carefully structured (Schuurman et al., 2012). Rather than viewing residents as mere data producers, the process can treat them as co-researchers who interpret and contextualize metrics.

For instance, a city may employ real-time traffic data to optimize transportation routes. Adding input from neighborhood associations might reveal hidden access barriers for pedestrians or cyclists. The resulting plan could adjust traffic priorities to accommodate diverse modes of transport, reflecting a more inclusive mobility approach. When data analysis aligns with local perceptions, solutions become responsive to actual challenges (Allam & Newman, 2018). This synergy of data and human insight strengthens the likelihood that outcomes will be acceptable and beneficial.

4.3 Cross-Sector Collaboration

Human-centered smart city methods thrive in cross-sector contexts where government, private sector, academia, and communities share resources and knowledge (Paskaleva, 2011). Multidisciplinary teams bring varied expertise that enriches problem definitions and solution paths. Partnerships with research institutions, for instance, can enhance evaluation metrics that gauge social impacts of digital innovations (Meijer & Rodríguez Bolívar, 2016). Companies can contribute operational knowledge, while civic groups can ensure accountability.

Table 2. Key Actors in Cross-Sector Collaboration and Their Contributions

Actor	Contribution	Potential Pitfalls	Reference
Government	Policy mandates, regulations, funding	Bureaucratic inertia, siloed management	OECD, 2020
Private Sector	Technical expertise, infrastructure investments	Profit motives, proprietary systems	Hollands, 2015
Academia	Research skills, data analysis, training	Limited real-world applicability	Calzada, 2021
Civic Groups	Grassroots advocacy, accountability	Unequal resources, internal fragmentation	Cardullo, 2020

Close collaboration demands recognition of divergent interests and power imbalances. Mechanisms such as Memoranda of Understanding, clear project charters, and shared governance boards can maintain transparency and define responsibilities (European Commission, 2016). Further, iterative check-ins ensure that partnership goals remain aligned over time. Inclusive methods involve consistent engagement with community members, including historically marginalized groups. This approach contrasts with superficial consultations that fail to incorporate community feedback into policy or project outcomes (Manville et al., 2014).

Figure 2, maps out the contributions and interactions of these key actors, emphasizing their roles in fostering participatory and inclusive urban innovation.

Figure 2. Cross-Sector Collaboration in Smart City Governance

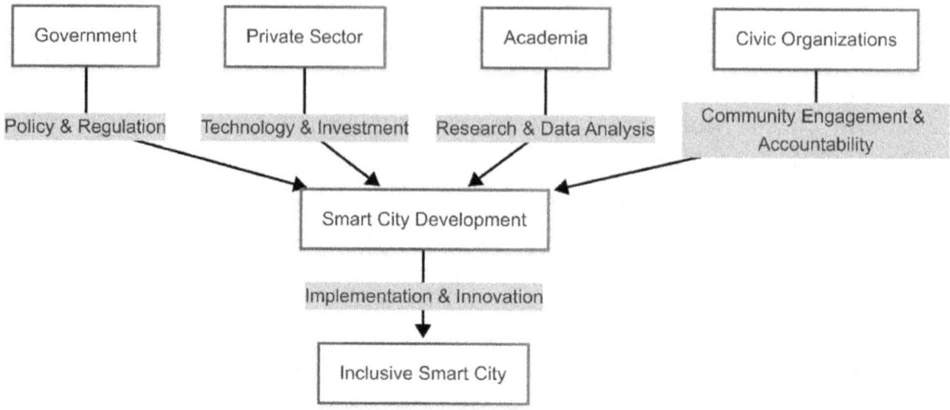

4.4 Design Thinking in Policy Formulation

Design thinking methodologies, typically applied to product development, can inform policy creation for smarter cities (Concilio & Rizzo, 2016). Policymakers can adopt iterative cycles: define the policy challenge, gather input from those affected, prototype policy instruments, pilot them in targeted locations, and refine them based on feedback. By integrating community perspectives early, policy design avoids a top-down approach that might generate resistance.

Studies suggest that iterative policy formation strengthens legitimacy. Active involvement in early stages encourages shared ownership among residents, organizations, and political leaders (Rodríguez-Bolívar, 2015). This inclusive process also tests assumptions, thereby reducing the risk of unintended outcomes. For example, a policy for e-participation might start as a small pilot in certain neighborhoods. Over time, policy refinements address accessibility concerns, privacy questions, and local preferences for communication tools. Once the pilot demonstrates viability, it can expand citywide. This approach encourages continuous learning rather than one-time, rigid policies.

4.5 Measuring Social Outcomes

Empirical studies show that measuring social outcomes is often overlooked in technology-driven initiatives (Martin et al., 2018). Human-centered methods incorporate metrics that go beyond cost-efficiency or user adoption rates. They might examine how well a project fosters social trust, reduces exclusion, or enhances public knowledge. Mixed-methods evaluations can combine quantitative surveys, focus group insights, and administrative data to provide a holistic view.

Frameworks for outcome measurement can integrate references to the Sustainable Development Goals, which stress reducing inequalities and promoting resilient communities (United Nations, 2017). Although many city dashboards show real-time environmental indicators or transit data, human-centered dashboards might include metrics related to citizen satisfaction, inclusive access to digital services, or diversity of engagement in decision processes (Srivastava & Mostafavi, 2018). Institutional commitment to these metrics signals a genuine interest in social impact.

Methodological clarity on participatory planning, data integration, cross-sector collaboration, design thinking, and social impact measurement helps ground the chapter's subsequent exploration of real-world implementations. Effective use of these methods can anchor human-centered ideals in the routines of city governance.

5. IMPLEMENTING HUMAN-CENTERED DESIGN IN PRACTICE

5.1 Case Insights from Global Cities

Cities that embrace human-centered smart city strategies often follow a multistage process: stakeholder engagement, planning with community input, iterative solution development, and open evaluation. This section offers examples to illustrate how these approaches function. It references case materials from academic studies and official policy reports.

Case studies in Dublin, Ireland, highlight the role of incremental engagement in building trust. Researchers found that Dublin's government progressed from gathering feedback to empowering citizens to propose new technological applications (Cardullo & Kitchin, 2019). These initiatives included accessible data dashboards for local communities, fostering transparent dialogues. Although early efforts were limited, sustained municipal support enabled deeper involvement over time.

In London, the city's smart strategy integrates social inclusion targets by addressing housing equity, transport accessibility, and health outcomes (Tekin & Dikmen, 2024). Participation platforms encourage residents to report local issues and suggest improvements. Policy evaluations found that many suggestions were adopted, leading to better alignment between city services and community demands. Yet challenges arose regarding digital literacy gaps among older adults and non-English speakers. The city responded by partnering with grassroots organizations to offer training and translation support.

Port Louis in Mauritius pursued a localized smart city approach that resonates with cultural identities and ecological needs (Allam & Newman, 2018). Methods included engaging faith-based groups and community elders in dialogues about sustainable resource use. The city integrated data collection on energy use with local traditions of communal gatherings, creating a hybrid approach that resonated with cultural norms. This example underscores how local culture shapes technology adoption.

5.2 Tensions between Top-Down and Bottom-Up Approaches

Despite promising initiatives, many cities encounter tensions that slow the integration of social considerations. Corporate-led programs can deliver infrastructure and capital investments rapidly, but some fail to incorporate public interests. Conversely, bottom-up experiments may struggle to secure funding, scale solutions, or gain political traction (Cowley et al., 2018). Balancing these forces requires municipal leadership with a clear mandate to protect public welfare.

For instance, corporate sponsors might propose advanced monitoring systems for water management. Local communities might have alternative priorities, such as workforce development or public health services. Inclusive policy frameworks mandate that both perspectives are heard. Decision-makers who adopt human-centered design weigh the benefits of data-driven optimization against the potential loss of community agency (Hollands, 2015).

Figure illustrates how policy acts as a bridge between technological innovation and civic engagement.

Figure 3. Conceptual Framework for Balancing Top-Down and Bottom-Up Approaches

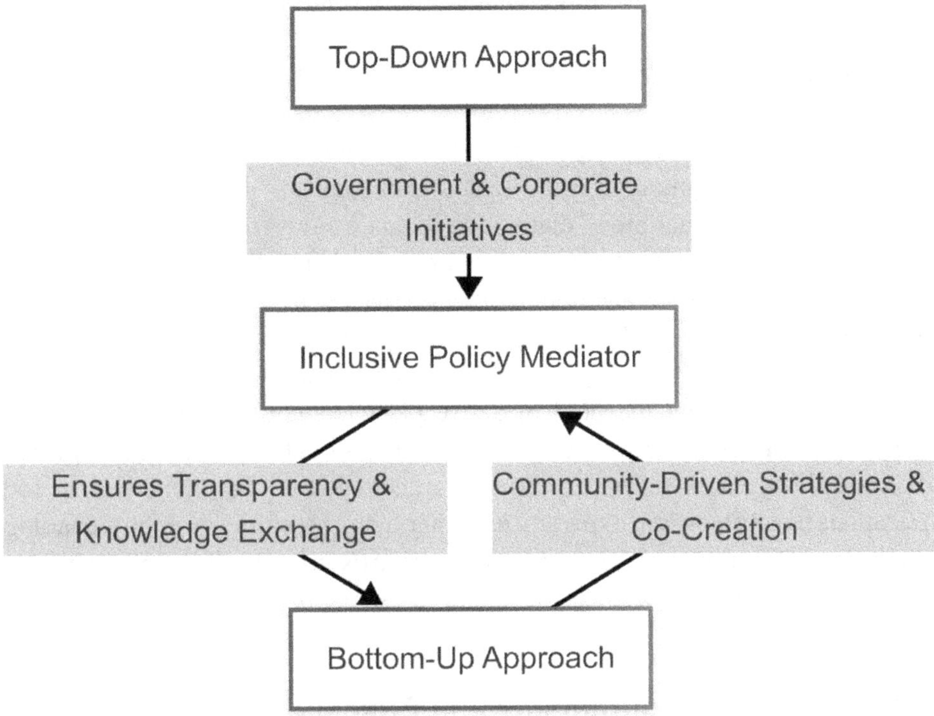

This diagram displays a mediator role for inclusive policy that ensures transparency in partnerships and encourages knowledge exchange. Human-centered design thrives when these roles and responsibilities are explicit. Participants negotiate solutions that reflect multiple interests rather than adopting a binary approach.

5.3 Collaborative Technology Development

Collaborative technology development involves codevelopment of digital solutions with user groups, local innovators, and city officials. Hackathons, open data initiatives, and civic tech partnerships exemplify this process (Townsend, 2013). Residents bring first-hand perspectives on public services, while developers refine technical specifications. City agencies provide policy directives and funding support.

Such initiatives have proliferated in cities like Barcelona, where an open-data portal facilitates community-driven apps for public transport updates or cultural event listings (Manville et al., 2014). The co-created apps reflect local interests, from accessible park guides to real-time air quality indexes. The synergy of municipal support and creative citizen input fosters a sense of collective ownership. Cities that adopt these methods often institutionalize them by dedicating resources to training, open challenges, and iterative prototyping cycles (Schuurman et al., 2012).

5.4 Community Training and Empowerment

Social inclusion in planning requires that residents can meaningfully participate. Training programs in digital literacy, data analysis, and civic engagement help address barriers that block many individuals from formal processes (OECD, 2020). When local governments partner with universities, libraries, or nonprofits, they can deliver workshops and online modules that enhance community skills. For instance, a municipality might conduct sessions showing how to interpret open data dashboards and how to submit proposals on e-participation platforms.

These efforts expand the pool of active participants. They also enhance the sophistication of community input, since trained residents can articulate informed critiques and suggestions. Some programs target youth, encouraging them to code applications that reflect their experiences. Others engage seniors through technology ambassadors who organize peer-to-peer instruction (Rodríguez-Bolívar, 2019). Over time, these initiatives strengthen the social infrastructure necessary for inclusive governance.

5.5 Maintaining Accountability and Ethical Standards

Smart city projects that gather data, automate processes, or employ predictive analytics carry ethical responsibilities. Residents often express concerns about surveillance, data privacy, and algorithmic biases (Greenfield, 2013). Human-centered design demands proactive safeguards and clear communication about data usage. Some cities implement data charters or codes of conduct that outline consent procedures and transparency standards (World Economic Forum, 2021).

Advisory boards, ethics committees, or public consultations can ensure that technology applications align with social values (Allam & Newman, 2018). For example, facial recognition systems introduced for public safety might be subject to oversight committees that evaluate their impact on civil liberties. By setting explicit standards for accountability, city leaders signal a commitment to the public good.

Taken together, these practices reveal how human-centered approaches can function in real-world contexts. They do not guarantee success, but they expand opportunities for communities to shape the technological transformations that define modern cities. Through steady institutional support, careful planning, and a respect for local voices, policymakers can embed social considerations into each stage of smart city development.

6. NAVIGATING CHALLENGES IN INTEGRATING SOCIAL ASPECTS

6.1 Political and Economic Pressures

Smart city agendas sometimes operate within political cycles that prioritize visible infrastructure or high-profile technology projects (Townsend, 2013). Elected officials might champion rapid solutions to display immediate results, marginalizing the slower, more consultative methods of human-centered planning. Economic considerations, including real estate development or corporate partnerships, can overshadow the broader social mission (Green, 2019).

When these pressures drive decision-making, inclusivity can become secondary. Large infrastructure vendors may emphasize hardware rollouts or sensor networks over intangible social outcomes. Public officials seeking quick wins might adopt solutions that lack robust stakeholder input (Hollands, 2015). The result can be an uneven power dynamic where corporations shape urban priorities in ways that do not reflect community needs.

6.2 Digital Inequalities

Despite the spread of internet access and mobile technologies, digital divides persist across demographics and regions (OECD, 2020). Smart city applications risk reinforcing these gaps if they assume universal connectivity. Lower-income neighborhoods often have weaker infrastructure, limiting participation in online platforms. Older adults, migrants, and people with disabilities may face additional barriers.

Cities mitigate digital inequalities through targeted programs that expand broadband coverage, distribute subsidized devices, and promote digital literacy (World Bank, 2016). Some adopt universal design principles that accommodate diverse users, ensuring that e-participation tools support text readers, translations, and offline interactions. Planners who acknowledge these divides can better balance high-tech solutions with inclusive approaches (Tekin & Dikmen, 2024).

6.3 Data Governance and Privacy

Data-intensive systems collect vast amounts of personal and behavioral information, raising questions about privacy, consent, and control (Greenfield, 2013). Without robust governance, data can be commodified or misused, especially when private sector entities dominate the technology ecosystem (Sadowski & Bendor,

2019). This scenario can undermine trust and deter people from engaging with smart city initiatives.

City authorities can adopt data governance frameworks grounded in transparency, security, and accountability (World Economic Forum, 2021). Strategies include anonymizing data, using consent-based data sharing, and storing sensitive information under public oversight. Residents should be informed about how their data is gathered, who has access, and how it is protected. Clear legal and regulatory guidelines enforce these protections.

6.4 Organizational Silos

Implementing human-centered design often challenges established bureaucratic practices. Government departments may function in isolation, with little coordination on cross-cutting projects (Rodríguez-Bolívar, 2015). Without interdepartmental alignment, integrated solutions—such as a mobility initiative that spans transport, environment, and social services—can stall.

Breaking silos requires leadership commitment to transversal teamwork. Official mandates can require departments to collaborate on planning processes, share data, and coordinate budgets (Anthopoulos, 2017). Joint task forces or steering committees also encourage knowledge exchange. In some cities, dedicated offices of innovation streamline collaboration by organizing cross-sector workshops and channeling resources to interdepartmental initiatives (Manville et al., 2014).

6.5 Socio-Cultural Barriers

Efforts to promote collaboration and co-creation can encounter cultural resistance. Some residents might distrust government motives, especially in contexts with historical marginalization (Datta, 2018). Others might show limited interest in technology-based solutions due to skepticism or practical constraints. Linguistic diversity, cultural norms around authority, or disparate community priorities can hinder unified engagement.

Context-sensitive outreach and community-building efforts address these complexities. Municipalities that cultivate relationships with neighborhood associations, cultural groups, and trusted local figures often achieve more fruitful dialogue. Providing interpretation services and recognizing different communication styles can further reduce cultural barriers (Allam & Newman, 2018).

Through these challenges, human-centered design still offers strategies to incorporate social considerations into smart city systems. The next sections examine strategies for policy alignment, cross-departmental integration, and community empowerment that address these barriers.

7. Strategies to Strengthen Human-Centered Integration

7.1 Policy Alignment and Legislative Support

Strong policies supported by legislation create an enabling environment for human-centered city projects. Municipal statutes can institutionalize participatory planning, requiring public consultations or co-creation approaches in major initiatives. City charters may include clauses that recognize digital equity as a public good. At higher levels, national laws might regulate data privacy and platform accountability, reinforcing local standards (UN-Habitat, 2022).

These provisions protect against policy reversals when leadership changes. They also offer legal grounds for citizens or advocacy groups to challenge noncompliant projects. Policy alignment happens when these mandates cascade from national to local levels, with each tier reinforcing inclusive guidelines (Calzada, 2021). Dedicated budget allocations for participation and digital inclusivity further ensure that commitments move beyond rhetoric.

7.2 Coordinated Funding Mechanisms

Financing human-centered smart city projects can be complex, particularly when returns on investment are not immediately quantifiable (Greenfield, 2013). In response, some authorities set up dedicated funds or incentives for participatory innovation. Alternatively, public-private-people partnerships distribute costs and risks across sectors (Rodríguez-Bolívar, 2019). In these arrangements, private partners might finance technology infrastructure, while communities contribute local expertise and oversight. Governments provide policy guarantees, such as open data requirements, ensuring that private solutions serve the public interest.

Philanthropic organizations or impact investors may also support pilot programs that prioritize social outcomes, particularly in contexts where government resources are limited (Saunders & Baeck, 2015). Multi-tiered funding strategies, drawing from municipal budgets, national grants, and international programs, can sustain inclusive initiatives over the long term (European Commission, 2016).

7.3 Capacity Building within Public Institutions

Formal training in participatory methods, data ethics, and design thinking can empower public servants to champion human-centered practices (Rodríguez-Bolívar, 2015). Workshops and mentorship programs, possibly in partnership with universities, expose policymakers to emerging tools and methodologies. Officials learn to manage consultation processes, interpret citizen feedback, and coordinate multi-stakeholder projects.

Table 3. Capacity Building Focus Areas for Municipal Officials

Focus Area	Skills Gained	Long-Term Impact	Reference
Participatory Methods	Facilitation, conflict resolution	More inclusive policy formulation	Concilio & Rizzo, 2016
Data Ethics	Privacy standards, responsible AI design	Trust in data-driven services	World Economic Forum, 2021
Design Thinking	Prototype-based policy development	Agile, citizen-focused programs	Townsend, 2013
Cross-Sector Collaboration	Partnership strategies, contract negotiation	Shared governance of smart city initiatives	OECD, 2020

Integrating these skills into job requirements and performance metrics encourages ongoing application. Some cities create innovation units or labs within government that facilitate iterative experimentation. Over time, a culture shift may occur, normalizing human-centered design in daily tasks.

7.4 Fostering Grassroots Innovation

Community-led innovation often emerges when residents organize around localized issues, from neighborhood safety to environmental quality (Srivastava & Mostafavi, 2018). By recognizing this energy, municipalities can provide micro-grants or technical assistance that enable small-scale pilot projects. These grassroots solutions may later scale up through government support.

Open data portals and hackathon events can channel grassroots creativity, allowing civic-minded individuals to propose tech-based solutions (Schuurman et al., 2012). Initiatives in some Latin American cities have delivered low-cost open-source tools for water management, connecting remote communities to real-time information (Manville et al., 2014). Municipal governments that build flexible interfaces—technical and administrative—often benefit from grassroots problem-solving capacity.

7.5 Robust Oversight and Monitoring

Accountability mechanisms ensure that human-centered mandates translate into real progress. Independent bodies or citizen review boards can monitor compliance, publish findings, and recommend improvements (UN-Habitat, 2022). Routine public reporting on performance indicators, including social impact metrics, strengthens transparency. Public hearings and digital dashboards may display how funds are allocated and whether projects meet inclusive objectives (Kummitha, 2024).

When oversight reveals shortcomings, well-defined procedures can trigger corrective actions. For instance, if a data system lacks adequate privacy safeguards, the responsible agency must implement improvements under a stipulated timeline. Persistent noncompliance might invite sanctions or funding cuts. This systematic monitoring and enforcement process closes the gap between promises and outcomes (Manville et al., 2014).

These strategies direct attention to the policy, institutional, and cultural dimensions that sustain inclusive smart city design. The interplay of legislative support, stable funding, training programs, grassroots empowerment, and oversight can produce a fertile environment for embedding social aspects in planning and policy.

8. FUTURE TRAJECTORIES AND INNOVATIONS

8.1 Technological Shifts and Opportunities

Emerging technologies, including machine learning, distributed ledgers, and immersive interfaces, may transform how cities operate. For example, artificial intelligence can optimize traffic flows, but it can also reinforce biases if not developed ethically (Greenfield, 2013). Citizen co-design methods for AI solutions ensure transparency and accountability in algorithmic decision-making. Blockchain tools might decentralize data management, giving communities more control over personal information (Anthopoulos, 2017).

Extended reality platforms could create virtual forums for city planning, where residents visualize proposed infrastructure in simulated environments (Heitlinger, Foth, & Clarke, 2023). These possibilities expand the spectrum of engagement, but they must remain grounded in real community needs.

8.2 More-Than-Human Perspectives

Recent scholarship calls for designing beyond anthropocentric assumptions, integrating ecological systems and nonhuman life in urban agendas (Heitlinger et al., 2023). Urban infrastructure can incorporate wildlife corridors, green roofs, and water systems that respect biodiversity. Sensing technologies might monitor habitats to understand environmental changes. By involving environmental experts and community stewards, human-centered design can evolve into multi-species design.

8.3 Policy Coherence with Global Goals

The Sustainable Development Goals and the New Urban Agenda press cities to address climate adaptation, resource equity, and inclusive livelihoods (United Nations, 2017). Smart city plans that align with these frameworks must treat technology as an enabler rather than an end. International collaboration, peer-to-peer learning between cities, and open-access knowledge platforms can accelerate adoption of inclusive practices. Over time, standardized metrics may emerge that help cities benchmark their progress on social inclusion within digital transformations (OECD, 2020).

8.4 Ethical and Regulatory Innovation

As digital tools permeate governance, ethical regulations will likely expand. Concepts such as "data trusts" and public interest algorithms may become central to sustaining democracy in technology-rich environments (Allam & Newman, 2018). Social impact assessments can become prerequisites for large-scale smart city deployments, similar to environmental impact statements. Legal frameworks that treat data as a collective asset might redistribute benefits from corporate data monetization back to communities (Sadowski & Bendor, 2019).

9. DISCUSSION

Human-centered design for smart cities responds to critiques of technology-led urban approaches. Scholars have questioned the mismatch between grand technological claims and actual community needs (Hollands, 2015). This chapter's discussion highlights an emergent consensus that social inclusion, participatory governance, and contextual design are prerequisites for meaningful smart city development (Vanolo, 2016). Authors like Cardullo and Kitchin (2019) emphasize the layers of engagement that shift residents from passive recipients to active co-creators. Evidence suggests that inclusive planning yields multiple benefits, including trust, innovation, and resilience. Yet it demands institutional reforms that foster collaboration among government, private firms, academics, and civic groups (Manville et al., 2014). Public officials need to internalize participatory values and acquire corresponding competencies (Concilio & Rizzo, 2016). Cross-sector funding and policy alignment bolster these efforts.Challenges persist around political pressures, digital divides, privacy, and organizational silos. Even among cities with a proclaimed commitment to inclusive design, real implementation can be piecemeal (Sadowski & Bendor, 2019). Translating guidelines into practice requires robust oversight, iterative learning, and flexible governance structures (World Economic

Forum, 2021). These considerations underscore the complexity of embedding social aspects in planning and policy.As technology evolves, new risks and opportunities will appear. Novel tools can deepen participation or erode freedoms, depending on how they are governed (Green, 2019). A human-centered city must remain vigilant, adopting an ethical stance toward data, environment, and community well-being. This vigilance includes multi-scalar policy coherence and global knowledge exchange (United Nations, 2017).

Recommendations and Implications for Practice

Municipal leaders, planners, and researchers can draw on the following implications to guide future projects. First, city administrations benefit from establishing concrete participatory guidelines, accompanied by dedicated resources and training. Second, data governance structures must enforce privacy and transparency. Third, cross-sector partnerships and grassroots inclusion can spark local innovation. Fourth, ongoing evaluation of social impacts is crucial to confirm that initiatives achieve equitable outcomes.

From a governance perspective, these strategies can recalibrate power relations and embed accountability mechanisms. In practice, they involve harmonizing technical solutions with community perspectives in everyday procedures. City leaders who invest in human-centered design see it as an iterative commitment rather than a single intervention. Aligning these efforts with broader global directives—such as the New Urban Agenda—heightens the potential for inclusive and sustainable outcomes.

10. CONCLUSION

Human-centered design offers a transformative path for cities seeking to harness emerging technologies while preserving social equity and civic engagement. By foregrounding inclusive governance, transparent data practices, and community empowerment, smart city agendas can transcend narrow efficiency goals. This chapter has traced the theoretical underpinnings, policy contexts, methodological approaches, and practical insights that support integrated social dimensions in urban innovation.

Such approaches shift the status quo, urging planners and officials to relinquish top-down control in favor of participatory co-creation. They align with global calls for sustainable, rights-based urban development. Although challenges remain, many cities worldwide demonstrate that a people-first orientation is feasible. Ongoing research can refine metrics for social outcomes, strengthen institutional frameworks, and clarify best practices for bridging digital divides. The journey toward truly human-centered smart cities is continuous, requiring consistent advocacy, adaptable policy, and a collective commitment to equity. This focus on integrating social aspects is not an optional feature but a pivotal requirement for cities that wish to be both modern and just.

REFERENCES

Albino, V., Berardi, U., & Dangelico, R. M. (2015). Smart cities: Definitions, dimensions, performance, and initiatives. *Journal of Urban Technology*, *22*(1), 3–21. DOI: 10.1080/10630732.2014.942092

Allam, Z., & Newman, P. (2018). Redefining the smart city: Culture, metabolism and governance—Case of Port Louis, Mauritius. *Smart Cities*, *1*(1), 4–25. DOI: 10.3390/smartcities1010002

Anthopoulos, L. G. (2017). *Understanding smart cities: A tool for smart government or an industrial trick?* Springer. DOI: 10.1007/978-3-319-57015-0

Aurigi, A., & Odendaal, N. (Eds.). (2021). Shaping smart for better cities: Rethinking and shaping relationships between urban space and digital technologies. Academic Press (Elsevier). DOI: 10.1016/B978-0-12-818636-7.00019-6

Bastos, D., Fernández-Caballero, A., Pereira, A., & Pacheco Rocha, N. (2022). Smart city applications to promote citizen participation in city management and governance: A systematic review. *Informatics (MDPI)*, *9*(4), 89. DOI: 10.3390/informatics9040089

Calzada, I. (2021). Smart city citizenship. Elsevier (Academic Press).

Cardullo, P. (2020). *Citizens in the "smart city": Participation, co-production, governance*. Routledge. DOI: 10.4324/9780429438806

Cardullo, P., & Kitchin, R. (2019). Being a "citizen" in the smart city: Up and down the scaffold of smart citizen participation in Dublin, Ireland. *GeoJournal*, *84*(1), 1–13. DOI: 10.1007/s10708-018-9845-8

Concilio, G., & Rizzo, F. (Eds.). (2016). *Human smart cities: Rethinking the interplay between design and planning*. Springer. DOI: 10.1007/978-3-319-33024-2

Cowley, R., Joss, S., & Dayot, Y. (2018). The smart city and its publics: Insights from across six UK cities. *Urban Research & Practice*, *11*(1), 53–77. DOI: 10.1080/17535069.2017.1293150

Datta, A. (2018). The digital turn in postcolonial urbanism: Smart citizenship in the making of India's 100 smart cities. *Transactions of the Institute of British Geographers*, *43*(3), 405–419. DOI: 10.1111/tran.12225

de Waal, M., & Dignum, M. (2017). The citizen in the smart city: How the smart city could transform citizenship. *Information Polity*, *22*(2–3), 143–152.

European Commission (EIP-SCC). (2016). *Inclusive smart cities: A European manifesto on citizen engagement*. European Innovation Partnership on Smart Cities and Communities.

Gil-García, J. R., Pardo, T. A., & Nam, T. (2015). What makes a city smart? Identifying core components and proposing an integrative framework. *Information Polity, 20*(1), 61–87. DOI: 10.3233/IP-150354

Green, B. (2019). *The smart enough city: Putting technology in its place to reclaim our urban future*. MIT Press. DOI: 10.7551/mitpress/11555.001.0001

Greenfield, A. (2013). *Against the smart city (The city is here for you to use, Vol. 1)*. Do Projects.

Heitlinger, S., Foth, M., & Clarke, R. (Eds.). (2023). *Designing more-than-human smart cities: Beyond sustainability, towards cohabitation*. Oxford University Press.

Hollands, R. G. (2008). Will the real smart city please stand up? *City (London, England), 12*(3), 303–320. DOI: 10.1080/13604810802479126

Hollands, R. G. (2015). Critical interventions into the corporate smart city. *Cambridge Journal of Regions, Economy and Society, 8*(1), 61–77. DOI: 10.1093/cjres/rsu011

Joss, S., Sengers, F., Schraven, D., Caprotti, F., & Dayot, Y. (2019). The smart city as global discourse: Storylines and critical junctures. *Journal of Urban Technology, 26*(1–3), 3–18. DOI: 10.1080/10630732.2018.1558387

Kummitha, R. K. R. (2024). Smart city governance: Assessing modes of active citizen engagement. *Regional Studies*. Advance online publication.

Manville, C., Cochrane, G., Cave, J., Millard, J., Pederson, J., & Thaarup, R.. (2014). *Mapping smart cities in the EU*. European Parliament.

Martin, C. J., Evans, J., & Karvonen, A. (2018). Smart and sustainable? Five tensions in the visions and practices of the smart-sustainable city. *Technological Forecasting and Social Change, 133*, 269–278. DOI: 10.1016/j.techfore.2018.01.005

Meijer, A., & Rodríguez Bolívar, M. P. (2016). Governing the smart city: A review of the literature on smart urban governance. *International Review of Administrative Sciences, 82*(2), 392–408. DOI: 10.1177/0020852314564308

Ministry of Housing and Urban Affairs, Government of India. (2015). *Smart Cities Mission: Statement and guidelines*. New Delhi: MoHUA, Govt. of India.

Organisation for Economic Co-operation and Development (OECD). (2020). *Smart cities and inclusive growth: Building on the outcomes of the 1st OECD Roundtable.* Paris: OECD Publishing.

Paskaleva, K. (2011). The smart city: A nexus for open innovation? *Intelligent Buildings International, 3*(3), 153–171. DOI: 10.1080/17508975.2011.586672

Rodríguez-Bolívar, M. P. (Ed.). (2015). *Transforming city governments for successful smart cities.* Springer. DOI: 10.1007/978-3-319-03167-5

Rodríguez-Bolívar, M. P. (Ed.). (2019). *Setting foundations for the creation of public value in smart cities.* Springer. DOI: 10.1007/978-3-319-98953-2

Sadowski, J., & Bendor, R. (2019). Selling smartness: Corporate narratives and the smart city as a sociotechnical imaginary. *Science, Technology & Human Values, 44*(3), 540–563. DOI: 10.1177/0162243918806061

Saunders, T., & Baeck, P. (2015). *Rethinking smart cities from the ground up.* Nesta.

Schuurman, D., Baccarne, B., Mechant, P., & De Marez, L. (2012). Smart ideas for smart cities: Investigating crowdsourcing for urban innovation. *Journal of Theoretical and Applied Electronic Commerce Research, 7*(3), 49–62. DOI: 10.4067/S0718-18762012000300006

Srivastava, P., & Mostafavi, A. (2018). Challenges and opportunities of crowdsourcing and participatory planning in developing infrastructure systems of smart cities. *Infrastructures, 3*(4), 51. DOI: 10.3390/infrastructures3040051

Sweeting, D., de Alba-Ulloa, J., Pansera, M., & Marsh, A. (2022). Easier said than done? Involving citizens in the smart city. *Environment and Planning C. Politics and Space, 40*(6), 1365–1381.

Tekin, H., & Dikmen, İ. (2024). Inclusive smart cities: An exploratory study on the London smart city strategy. *Buildings (Basel, Switzerland), 14*(2), 485. DOI: 10.3390/buildings14020485

Townsend, A. (2013). *Smart cities: Big data, civic hackers, and the quest for a new utopia.* W. W. Norton.

UN-Habitat. (2022). *Mainstreaming human rights in the digital transformation of cities: A guide for local governments.* United Nations Human Settlements Programme.

United Nations. (2017). *New Urban Agenda.* UN-Habitat.

Vanolo, A. (2016). Is there anybody out there? The place and role of citizens in tomorrow's smart city. *Futures, 82*, 26–36. DOI: 10.1016/j.futures.2016.05.010

World Bank. (2016). *World Development Report 2016: Digital dividends*. World Bank.

World Economic Forum. (2021). *Governing smart cities: Policy benchmarks for ethical and responsible smart city development.* Geneva: World Economic Forum.

Chapter 17
Digital Twins and Social Intelligence for Urban Early Warning Systems

Ali Al Maqousi
https://orcid.org/0000-0002-3242-804X
Department of Information Security, University of Petra, Amman, Jordan

Ahmad Al-Qerem
https://orcid.org/0000-0003-2187-6194
Computer Science Department, Faculty of Information Technology, Zarqa University, Jordan

Kashinath Basu
https://orcid.org/0000-0002-0831-3752
Oxford Brookes University, UK

Amjad Aldweesh
https://orcid.org/0000-0001-9358-1323
College of Computing and Information Technology, Shaqra University, Saudi Arabia

Mouhammd Alkasassbeh
https://orcid.org/0000-0001-8396-7441
Princess Sumaya University for Technology, Jordan

ABSTRACT

Early warning and public warning systems exist to reduce harm in urban regions through timely alerts and coordinated actions. Officials often face challenges in converting high-volume data into clear messages for residents, which shows a gap

DOI: 10.4018/979-8-3373-1375-7.ch017

in existing systems. This chapter examined how digital twin platforms and social intelligence approaches boost alert dissemination in dense metropolitan areas. The analysis included peer-reviewed research, policy documents, and selected case studies. Findings showed that merged sensor data and social input enhanced detection and coverage of warnings. This suggests that better integration of new tools strengthens preparedness for disruptive events. The chapter adds an overview of methods to align technology, institutions, and communities for consistent, real-time responses.

1. INTRODUCTION

Cities handle multiple threats, from extreme weather to public health hazards, in crowded settings. Administrations must convey timely alerts that encourage protective actions among residents, businesses, and agencies (Nam & Pardo, 2011). Traditional broadcast methods and isolated sensors sometimes perform well in stable situations, but they can stumble when confronted with data floods or abrupt hazards (Rinaldi, Peerenboom, & Kelly, 2001). The urban sphere now features greater technology adoption, including devices that gather location data, real-time analytics, and online networks. These developments open new avenues for immediate warnings. Yet, effective use of such tools requires coordinated approaches and acceptance by the public (Mitchell, 2007).

Digital twins and social intelligence help fill gaps in current methods (Ford & Wolf, 2020). Digital twins simulate built and natural environments, maintaining live streams of data that mirror the physical world. They can run predictive models to spot dangers and share forecasts with officials. Social intelligence collects information from the public through social media or crowdsourcing, enabling feedback about unseen or sudden events. Combining these elements may produce strong warning capabilities in major cities (Xie & Liu, 2023). However, many deployments remain narrow or pilot-level, and the overall scope is not entirely clear. This chapter aims to provide a broad discussion of these technologies, methods, and governance issues, illustrating their effect on early warning outcomes.

This introduction frames the need for multi-level solutions that draw upon digital models and collective input. Emergency management relies on data accuracy, interdepartmental coordination, and clarity in communicating action steps (Oh, Lee, & Lee, 2013). A deeper understanding of how digital twins and social intelligence can shape these tasks is essential. The chapter proceeds by surveying the literature, elaborating on the convergence of sensor infrastructure, real-time analytics, and engaged citizens. It then outlines a methodology, reviews leading examples, and proposes a framework for better integration. Ethical and governance questions also emerge, tied to privacy, fairness, and accountability (Brauneis & Goodman, 2018).

By merging technology and policy insights, this work reveals paths toward dynamic, inclusive early warning systems in modern urban settings.

1.1. Background and Context of Urban Early Warning Systems

Urban communities often exist in settings where infrastructure, population density, and social factors create interdependencies that increase the potential for harm. Flood events in coastal cities can disrupt transportation networks and hinder medical services. Earthquakes or industrial accidents in built-up areas may cause large-scale damages that require swift alerts (Rinaldi et al., 2001). Traditional early warning approaches built on official notices and sirens can reach many people but may not reflect real-time conditions or localized events. Over-reliance on top-down channels may cause delays, miscommunication, or limited targeting (Zhang & Huang, 2019). With more data sources emerging, new digital options arise.

Digital twin technology captures sensor data in real time, maintaining a city-scale model that updates when conditions shift. Simulations can run with parameters for traffic, energy, or weather, identifying vulnerabilities and possible disruptions (Hoskere, Narazaki, & Spencer, 2023). Meanwhile, social intelligence taps into social media posts, location-based apps, and volunteer group reports. These signals can help locate unexpected events or confirm official data (Vanolo, 2016). Merging official measurements with local insights expands the situational understanding needed for immediate alerts and resource deployment (Singh, Sharma, Yoon, Shojafar, & Cho, 2020).

Researchers and practitioners see advantages in this integration, but actual usage faces obstacles. Fragmented agency structures, cost factors, and questions on data sharing limit adoption (Johns, 2021). Concerns also arise regarding misinformation, privacy, and the need for robust governance. The next parts of this text explore where digital twins and social intelligence fit into warning systems, highlighting how synergy can address persistent shortfalls (Nam & Pardo, 2011). This discussion builds the basis for analyzing how to link technology, institutions, and the public to strengthen city resilience.

1.2. Problem Statement and Objectives

Many cities acknowledge that modern data sources can enrich early warning, yet practical integration of digital twins and social feedback remains spotty or incomplete (Chen & Zhang, 2022). Instances of floods, seismic shocks, pandemics, or fires show that large volumes of data often do not translate into timely, clear warnings. Municipal agencies may run advanced sensor networks but lack the organizational capacity to coordinate or validate results with community-level intelligence (Mazzetto, 2024). Decision-makers also face competing demands, including data privacy, budget constraints, and multiple stakeholder interests. This chapter aims to clarify how digital twins and social intelligence can work together in urban early warning. It has four main goals: (1) review the literature to identify current trends in digital modeling and real-time data usage, (2) examine select case studies that illustrate success or difficulty in merging these tools, (3) propose strategies to streamline integration, and (4) highlight ethical and policy concerns that come with data-driven alerts. Addressing these objectives provides a roadmap for municipalities considering next-generation alert systems. Insights gathered here may help guide decisions about investments, cross-agency partnerships, and operational protocols.

2. LITERATURE REVIEW

The study of early warning spans many fields, including disaster management, urban planning, and digital governance (Rinaldi et al., 2001). Each perspective sheds light on how warnings function, from sensor-level detection to community-based communication. Digital twins emerged from engineering circles, where they offered ways to track complex machinery, but they have expanded to city-scale simulations (Ingram, 2020). Social intelligence, meanwhile, draws on communication and data science theories related to online networks and collective information sharing (Malone & Bernstein, 2015). This review covers relevant themes in each domain, then synthesizes them to reveal convergent possibilities.

2.1. Evolution of Early Warning Systems

Early warning once depended on analog devices and broadcast alerts via radio or television (Ramaswami, Weisz, & Pataki, 2016). Government offices compiled data from weather stations or seismic sensors, then delivered bulletins that residents were expected to heed. Over time, digital networks allowed automated triggers and more precise targeting. Research shows that robust early warning demands four interconnected elements: hazard knowledge, monitoring, communication, and readiness to act (UNDRR, 2022). Missing any element can reduce system success. Studies track how new technology strengthens each stage. Remote sensing and satellites feed accurate hazard estimates (Oh et al., 2013). Big data tools organize sensor inputs from across a city in near real time (Zeng & Wu, 2020). Mobile devices bring location-based warnings to personal devices, improving outreach during crises (DHS, 2023). Although these advances help, fragmentation remains. Agencies and private actors do not always share data or adopt shared formats, and some groups distrust government technology. The global literature thus highlights that technology alone does not deliver optimal results unless institutions collaborate (World Bank, 2022).

2.2. Digital Twin Concepts and Applications

Digital twins mirror physical systems, updating continuously based on sensor data (Ford & Wolf, 2020). They exist in manufacturing, aviation, and urban design. In a city context, digital twins hold infrastructure details roads, utilities, buildings—merged with real-time signals from sensors that track traffic flow, energy usage, air quality, and more (European Space Agency, 2023). This structure enables simulations that show potential outcomes of events. If a flood is predicted, the twin can estimate where water might accumulate, how evacuation routes might be blocked, or which power lines risk malfunction. Academic work points out that city-scale digital twins require large data volumes, stable computing, and strong governance for data management (Mazzetto, 2024). Scholars examine how digital twins can enhance planning and daily operations (Komninos, 2014). Fewer publications detail their role in early warning, though some indicate that real-time modeling can identify anomalies that lead to faster alerts (Hoskere et al., 2023). Tensions emerge around data ownership, privacy, and accountability, especially if these platforms belong to private entities (Brauneis & Goodman, 2018). Cities that adopt digital twins often rely on collaborations among public, private, and academic sectors, but these alliances can produce complex governance structures (Johns, 2021).

2.3. Real-Time Social Intelligence in Urban Governance

Real-time social intelligence refers to data and insights from social media, crowdsourcing, and other communication channels that update quickly. Researchers note that residents often post incident details faster than official channels can verify them (Xie & Liu, 2023). Flood images, tweets about tremors, or messages about resource shortages appear as events unfold (Vanolo, 2016). Authorities who monitor such content can fill information gaps. This helps refine the official picture of a crisis, boosting the speed and local relevance of warnings (Gardner, 2021). However, social intelligence data can contain errors, rumors, or malicious content (Singh et al., 2020). Studies on crisis informatics show that verifying user posts, filtering spam, and detecting misinformation present real problems (Schecter, Pilny, Leung, Poole, & Contractor, 2018). Machine learning approaches classify messages by location, topic, or credibility, but no method is perfect (Weber, 2010). Ethical questions about privacy also arise if authorities scrape large amounts of user data. People may feel wary about constant monitoring by government or third parties (Brauneis &

Goodman, 2018). Still, the potential for immediate input from community members has led many cities to explore ways to incorporate social data into their operations.

2.4. Synthesis of Key Literature Insights

The literature suggests that effective early warning emerges when sensor networks, modeling tools, and communication structures align (Rinaldi et al., 2001). Digital twins can deliver detailed simulations, while social intelligence captures direct observations and opinions. By combining both, agencies gain a multi-layered view of conditions (Zeng & Wu, 2020). This approach may reduce delays caused by dependence on official sensor data alone, while also filtering some noise from unverified social content. Yet many researchers note that integrated systems remain in early stages, and thorough explorations of scaling methods, data ethics, and long-term maintenance are needed (Nam & Pardo, 2011). Governance is a recurring theme. The technology behind digital twins and social intelligence is advancing, but successful usage depends on trust, institutional support, and transparent policies (Johns, 2021). Some authors call for new frameworks that include risk assessments for data handling, oversight panels, and cross-agency task forces (Deakin, 2014). Others argue for continuous improvement in social media analytics to handle misinformation and reflect local language practices (Vanolo, 2016). The next sections delve into research methods, case examples, and recommended strategies for bridging theoretical advances and real-world deployments.

3. METHODOLOGY

The study supporting this chapter used a mixed approach that included a systematic literature review, case analysis, and the synthesis of official reports. This methodology captured both theoretical viewpoints and on-the-ground realities of digital twin and social intelligence adoption in major cities (Siemens, 2005). The multi-step process is outlined below.

3.1. Literature Review Procedures

The project began with a targeted review of peer-reviewed journals, conference papers, and policy publications on early warning, digital twins, and social intelligence. Relevant articles were located through subject-specific databases, including IEEE Xplore and academic platforms linked to urban studies (Zeng & Wu, 2020). Search terms included "early warning," "digital twin," "social intelligence," "urban risk," and "crowdsourced alerts." Each publication was screened for relevance to integrated alert systems. The final set encompassed research from multiple fields engineering, policy, data science, and urban management. After collecting the texts, a coding scheme extracted details on definitions, methods, challenges, and proposed solutions. Codes also flagged references to governance, ethics, or cross-agency partnerships (Schecter et al., 2018). The coding process served as a map for organizing themes in subsequent sections of the chapter. Gaps were identified, including limited empirical data on how digital twins have improved or struggled in actual city alerts.

3.2. Comparative Case Study Selection

The second methodological component involved case selection and analysis. Cases were chosen to illustrate diverse risks, geographic settings, and technology maturity (Smart Cities Council, 2019). Government reports, academic articles, and interviews (when available) informed the assessment of each case's timeline, data flows, success factors, and outcomes (Xie & Liu, 2023). The studied sites included Rotterdam (flood), Tokyo (earthquake), Singapore (pandemic), and parts of California (wildfire). Each place applied digital modeling or social data in some capacity, though the depth of implementation varied (Morrow, 2022). Data were collected from official statements, local media, and scholarly papers. Key performance indicators included alert latency, coverage, data quality, and user feedback. The analysis compared these indicators and identified patterns of adoption challenges. The goal was not to produce a comprehensive survey of all cities but to depict varied approaches that highlight success and pitfalls.

3.3. Synthesis of Secondary Data and Policy Documents

The third method involved reviewing secondary data from intergovernmental bodies such as the United Nations, the World Bank, and the International Telecommunication Union, as well as national agencies like the United States Department of Homeland Security (DHS, 2023). These reports offered statistical data, policy guidelines, and performance metrics for early warning and digital governance. They also provided insight into official stances on data ethics, interoperability, and capacity building (Brauneis & Goodman, 2018). By cross-referencing policy insights with case details, the study inferred how local programs might align or conflict with recognized best practices. This step helped frame the final recommendations, ensuring they addressed multi-scalar governance rather than city-specific conditions alone.

3.4. Analytical Framework

All findings were integrated through a framework that places digital twins and social intelligence at the core of early warning. The framework considers variables like technology readiness, inter-agency collaboration, funding, and public trust. It looks at how these factors interact to shape outcomes in warning dissemination (Ford & Wolf, 2020). Each case and literature source was examined to see where the interplay of modeling, social input, and governance either facilitated or hindered performance. The framework also acknowledges that successful warning systems rely on cyclical processes. Data collection feeds analysis, which informs alerts, which then prompt responses, generating new data for improvement (Zhang & Huang, 2019). In this cycle, digital twins offer predictions, and social intelligence refines them, but governance structures must mediate how these results become official alerts. The chapters that follow implement this framework to highlight strengths, limitations, and emerging strategies for next-generation warning solutions.

4. DIGITAL TWINS IN MODERN URBAN EARLY WARNING SYSTEMS

Cities that adopt digital twins for risk mitigation seek real-time models that capture environmental shifts, infrastructure usage, and resource demands (European Space Agency, 2023). This section explains how digital twins contribute to early warning processes, covering conceptual groundings, typical architectures, and recent developments.

4.1. Conceptual Foundations of Digital Twins in Risk Management

Digital twins link physical assets to virtual counterparts through continuous data exchange (Ingram, 2020). In risk management, the twin processes sensor inputs water levels, structural loads, seismic vibrations—to produce near-live representations of city systems. Planners and emergency teams run simulations for "what if" scenarios, anticipating chain reactions that might arise from infrastructure breakage or severe natural events (Rinaldi et al., 2001). This predictive capacity can shrink the time between a recognized hazard and a response. A digital twin's advantage lies in revealing interconnected vulnerabilities. Modern cities have interwoven power grids, transit systems, and communications networks (Komninos, 2014). A simple malfunction in one area may cascade. The twin's integrated data architecture highlights these linkages, offering advanced notice about potential compounding disruptions (Ford & Wolf, 2020). Still, building such a twin demands standardized data formats, stable computing resources, and multi-stakeholder collaboration. Planners need to confirm data authenticity and keep the model updated as urban conditions evolve (Mazzetto, 2024).

4.2. Architectural Components and System Integration

Digital twin frameworks have layers for data ingestion, cleaning, modeling, and visualization (Hoskere et al., 2023). The ingestion layer taps into sensor networks, geographic databases, or even historical logs. The cleaning stage removes duplicates or errors, ensuring a consistent data feed (Guinard, Trifa, & Wilde, 2010). Modeling then converts inputs into simulations of physical systems, often supported by machine learning to detect patterns (Wang, Zhang, & Li, 2021). Visualization layers generate dashboards or 3D maps that officials can interpret quickly.

Table 1. Key Components of Digital Twin Architectures in Urban Warning

Component	Purpose	Implementation Notes
Sensor Ingestion	Captures real-time data from infrastructure, environment	Often uses IoT feeds or legacy systems
Data Processing	Cleans, aggregates, and analyzes inputs	Cloud-based or on-premise solutions
Modeling Layer	Simulates physical systems and hazard scenarios	Involves machine learning, dynamic updates
Visualization	Displays outputs to planners, responders	Dashboards, 3D maps, integrated UIs
Feedback Loops	Routes insights to decision-makers, triggers alerts	Links with command centers, apps

Note. Adapted from Ford and Wolf (2020).

Integration with existing command systems is not trivial. Many cities already use traffic management platforms or utility monitoring tools (Deakin, 2014). Linking these with a digital twin involves bridging data silos or adopting shared data standards. Agencies also face challenges in adjusting protocols, staff training, and software licensing (Rinaldi et al., 2001). Despite these hurdles, some local governments push forward because they see a chance to unify data streams and produce earlier alerts.

4.3. Current Developments and Limitations

Major metropolitan areas experiment with city-scale digital twins. Singapore builds a national-level twin to improve planning, resource distribution, and disaster readiness (Johnson, 2022). European projects study how twin platforms can model flooding or pollution (European Space Agency, 2023). These efforts show promise, yet results remain uneven. Some report improved forecasting for floods or traffic disruptions, but few analyses provide long-term evaluations of how digital twins reduce casualties or economic harm (Smart City Institute Japan [SCIJ], 2022).

Cost and complexity affect rollout. High-end hardware, specialized modeling software, and skilled experts are not always available (World Bank, 2022). Governance also matters. Where data is regulated or siloed, building a unified twin is slow (Brauneis & Goodman, 2018). Critics worry that digital twins might encourage surveillance if they track personal movement. Advocates say anonymization strategies can reduce risk, but controversies persist (Johns, 2021). Overall, digital twins hold clear potential for early warning, but success depends on aligned policy, budget, and social acceptance.

5. REAL-TIME SOCIAL INTELLIGENCE FOR PUBLIC WARNING

Early warning once relied on official bulletins and top-down communication (Vanolo, 2016). Now, widespread internet use turns the public into active contributors of hazard information. This section examines the nature of social intelligence, the data it processes, and ways it can connect with official alert mechanisms.

5.1. Foundations of Social Intelligence in Crisis Management

Social intelligence centers on real-time updates from the public during disruptive events (Malone & Bernstein, 2015). Through tweets, posts, or group chats, individuals share locations of floods, landslides, or damaged infrastructure (Xie & Liu, 2023). These decentralized signals often appear before formal announcements. Officials who monitor them can detect anomalies and refine the official view of conditions. However, inaccuracies or hoaxes can appear as well, so the data requires filtering and verification (Gardner, 2021).

Studies note that social intelligence brings speed and granularity to risk management (Singh et al., 2020). Residents on the ground can capture hyper-local details that sensors cannot. In times of crisis, volunteer groups often assist agencies in tagging or classifying user reports (Zwitter & Boisse-Despiaux, 2018). Trusted digital communities can thus expand capacity for detection and coverage. Still, building trust involves open communication about how data is used and what steps authorities will take (Vanolo, 2016).

5.2. Types of Data and Analytical Techniques

Social intelligence includes text, images, and even video streams (Schecter et al., 2018). Posts might be geotagged, making it easier to place incidents on a map. Analytical techniques vary. Keyword monitoring picks out terms related to floods or power outages (Gardner, 2021). Sentiment analysis classifies the tone of posts, detecting panic or concern. Image recognition tools scan photos for signs of damage or environmental hazards (Zeng & Wu, 2020). These algorithms run at scale, though they produce false positives and sometimes miss relevant context.

Below, **Table 2** summarizes major categories of social intelligence techniques, along with their benefits and challenges:

Table 2. Comparative Analysis of Social Intelligence Techniques

Technique	Data Type	Key Benefit	Challenge
Keyword Monitoring	Text (posts, tweets)	Quick scan for relevant signals	High noise, false positives
Sentiment Analysis	User comments	Gauges mood and urgency	Context misunderstanding
Image Recognition	Photos, videos	Locates visual evidence of damage	Computing resource demands
Geotagged Feeds	Location metadata	Pinpoints hotspots	Variable accuracy, privacy concern

Agencies rely on data pipelines that ingest social media feeds and apply classification or clustering. A machine learning model might rank data points by credibility, using factors like user history or cross-verification (Xie & Liu, 2023). Data managers must follow regulations that protect user privacy, including methods that anonymize or aggregate personal details (Brauneis & Goodman, 2018). Ethical guidelines often recommend that authorities only store relevant data and discard extraneous records. This ensures compliance with data protection laws and respects civil liberties.

5.3. Integrating Social Intelligence into Official Alert Channels

Official warning protocols are often formal, cautious, and hierarchical. Social data can be noisy, scattered, and unverified (Gardner, 2021). Merging them demands structured processes. Some cities set up central dashboards that highlight unusual social media volume in a specific area (Singh et al., 2020). A flagged anomaly leads a duty officer to confirm the source or request on-site checks. If validated, the system triggers an alert flow—text messages, app notifications, or sirens—directing residents to take precautions (Nam & Pardo, 2011).

Figure 1 below (a sequence diagram) illustrates how real-time reports feed a city's digital twin, leading to official alerts through integrated channels.

Figure 1. Sequence Diagram for Alert Integration

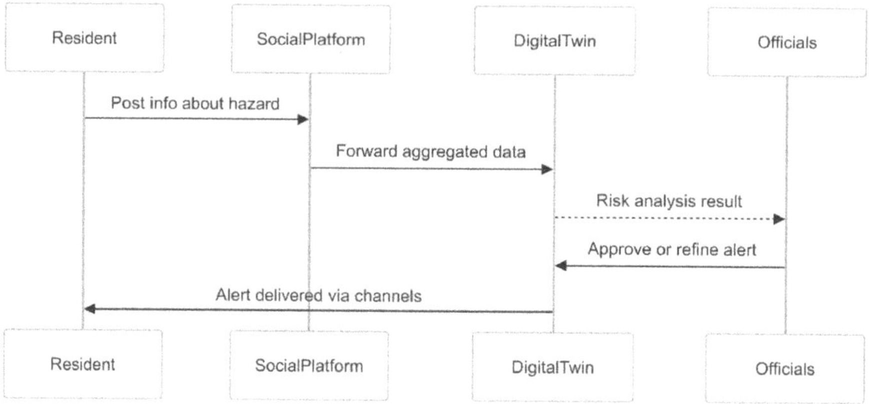

Coordinating official channels with social data boosts reach and clarity. Different platforms can reinforce a single message or adapt it to a location. Misinformation remains a worry, so some municipalities engage public figures or local community leaders to confirm official instructions (Vanolo, 2016). The synergy of real-time social input and established warning systems can shrink reaction times. However, the approach only works if agencies prepare staff to handle unpredictable spikes in data and have guidelines for releasing information. Overloading people with false alarms can erode trust in official channels (Xie & Liu, 2023).

6. SYNERGIES BETWEEN DIGITAL TWINS AND REAL-TIME SOCIAL INTELLIGENCE

Digital twins and social intelligence each offer distinct contributions. Twins give structured, sensor-driven views of infrastructure and environment. Social data brings human observations and local insights (Ford & Wolf, 2020). When combined, they can fill each other's gaps. The model identifies potential risk zones, while user reports confirm or update local severity. This synergy can help shape well-informed alerts in real time.

6.1. Convergent System Architecture

A convergent architecture fuses data pipelines for sensor feeds and social streams. The digital twin's simulation engine updates with official inputs—like meteorological readings—and crowd inputs on actual flooding or quake damage (Singh et al., 2020). The system flags mismatches between sensor data and user accounts, prompting staff to investigate. That feedback loop refines the twin's risk estimates (Ford & Wolf, 2020). The final result is a dynamic model that merges large-scale sensor coverage with granular, real-time observations.

Building this system demands robust data ingestion, machine learning, and stable cloud infrastructure (Wang et al., 2021). Interoperability is key, since digital twins often rely on specific data formats. Social media feeds may be unstructured, requiring advanced parsing (Guinard et al., 2010). Collaboration among agencies, tech firms, and community groups helps sort out roles. Despite the complexity, a well-designed system can speed up hazard detection and focus official interventions. This approach also fosters adaptiveness, since each crisis event updates the twin with ground truth information.

6.2. Enhanced Situational Awareness

Merging digital twin outputs with social data boosts situational awareness. Sensors track water rising near a river, while local residents post pictures of road washouts in real time. Officials gain a multi-layered view that helps them see not only the probable flood path but also how it affects daily life (Xie & Liu, 2023). This reduces reliance on limited vantage points. If a sensor fails, social feedback can signal problems. If social media rumors spread, data from sensors can debunk them (Vanolo, 2016).

This multi-layer approach moves beyond raw data collection. It frames the city as a web of interactions, with local voices feeding the digital model. Managers can pinpoint hotspots, plan evacuations, or direct rescue teams with more confidence (Nam & Pardo, 2011). Over time, these processes can refine official strategies, shaping better protocols for future events. The synergy lowers false alarms and fills knowledge gaps, making warnings more accurate (Ford & Wolf, 2020).

6.3. Operational Efficiency and Collaborative Governance

A combined system can streamline alert tasks. Machine learning filters large data volumes, highlighting areas of possible concern (Wang et al., 2021). Officials focus on verifying those signals instead of scanning raw feeds. This speeds up the warning cycle. Collaborative governance also emerges. Multiple agencies—transportation, utilities, public health—view the same twin and the same social data feed (Rinaldi et al., 2001). They coordinate responses without duplicating efforts.

Joint decision-making requires shared communication and agreement on data standards. Partnerships with private tech firms might expedite system design but also introduce commercial interests (Johns, 2021). The city must ensure that the platform serves public goals. If implemented carefully, integrated digital-socio intelligence can reduce the time from first detection to official alert, while ensuring that each department sees relevant information. This synergy can then create a better environment for risk management (Oh et al., 2013).

7. EMPIRICAL CASE ANALYSES

To illustrate practical applications of digital twins and social intelligence, this section examines four case studies: Rotterdam (flood risk), Tokyo (earthquake), Singapore (pandemic), and California (wildfire). Each example highlights methods, benefits, and barriers in real-world settings.

Table 3 provides a comparative overview of these case study outcomes in system effectiveness.

Table 3. Case Study Outcomes in System Effectiveness

Location	Hazard	Integration	Reported Outcome
Rotterdam	Flood	Digital twin + social media checks	Faster pump deployment, less flood damage
Tokyo	Earthquake	Building twin + social data for damage cues	Quicker focus on problem areas
Singapore	Pandemic	National twin + crowd updates on hotspots	Targeted health interventions, privacy debates
California	Wildfire	Fire spread models + local posts	Improved small-scale response, challenges in big fires

7.1. Case Study: Flood Early Warning in Rotterdam

Rotterdam faces chronic flood threats due to low-lying terrain. The city uses a digital twin that tracks real-time data on tides, rainfall, and water pumps (European Space Agency, 2023). The system includes a sensor network that relays water levels to a central platform. Planners also monitor social media for citizen reports of localized flooding. When a sensor reading differs from user posts, officials conduct checks. This cross-verification has prevented some false alarms.

Below, **Figure 2** outlines the typical process flow for urban flood early warning, showing how sensor data and social input form a feedback cycle:

Figure 2. Process Flow for Urban Flood Early Warning

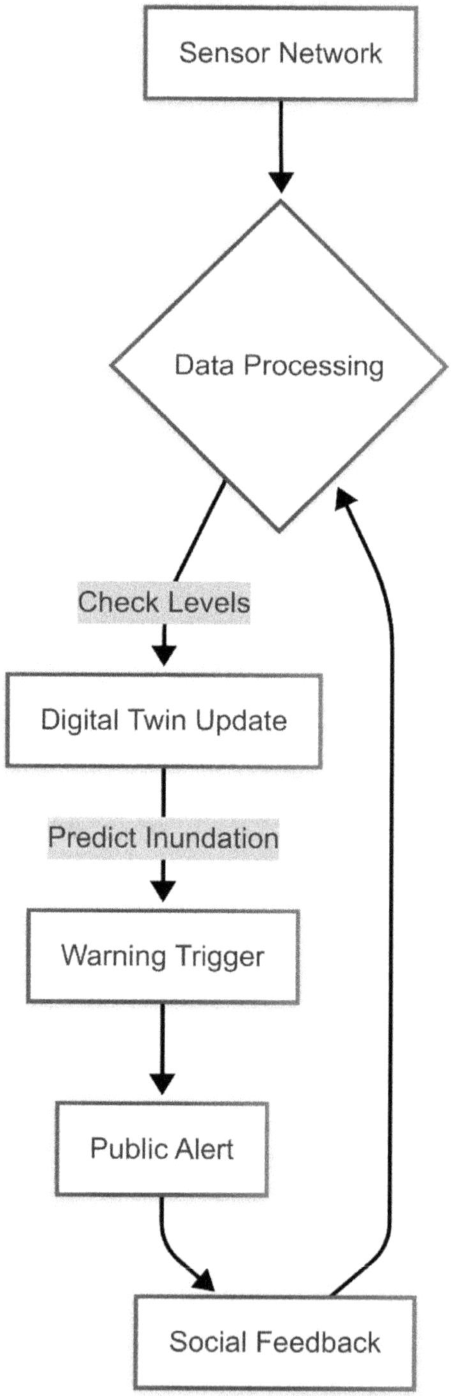

During a recent flood scare, community members posted images of a flooded street on local platforms, which city staff confirmed. Workers were dispatched to deploy pumps before water spread more widely. The digital twin updated its model to reflect changed drainage capacity. Observers in local government reported that this quick reaction minimized property damage (European Space Agency, 2023). Officials still note that the system can be difficult to maintain. Weather patterns shift, and sensor calibration is ongoing. Plus, not all posted images are authentic. Rotterdam's experience shows the value of combining structured sensor data with immediate citizen input, though it requires staff training and trust in the system's processes.

7.2. Case Study: Earthquake Preparedness in Tokyo

Tokyo's seismic risk prompted the development of a digital twin that hosts data on buildings, bridges, and underground structures (Smart City Institute Japan [SCIJ], 2022). The twin updates when ground motion sensors record tremors. Analysis then predicts possible building damage or transit shutdowns. At the same time, local authorities mine social media for reports of structural cracks or power outages. If those posts converge in a zone that the twin flags as high-risk, local response units focus on that area (Oh et al., 2013).

This layered approach helps city officials refine warnings. In one instance, mild tremors were registered, and the twin estimated no serious damage, but social data indicated multiple collapsed walls in a zone of older buildings. The city updated its model, recognized an overlooked factor, and redirected emergency services (SCIJ, 2022). Tokyo invests heavily in sensor infrastructure, but the quake risks remain high. Officials plan more integration, possibly linking the twin with predictive analytics that incorporate crowd-sourced updates. This process demands consistent budgets and strong partnerships with telecom providers.

7.3. Case Study: Pandemic Monitoring in Singapore

Singapore's digital twin, built initially for urban planning, saw use during a pandemic (Johnson, 2022). Authorities tracked hospital occupancy, mobility patterns, and confirmed infection clusters. Social media monitoring revealed crowd behavior and panic buying or localized supply issues (Pereira, 2023). The twin integrated these signals, enabling officials to see high-risk zones. This helped direct medical teams and guidance to areas with rising infections.

Although the approach improved situational awareness, questions arose about privacy. Some residents were concerned that the digital twin, along with social tracking, might reveal personal data (Brauneis & Goodman, 2018). The government responded with statements explaining data usage, emphasizing anonymized analytics. Singapore's strong top-down governance and technical capacity aided adoption, though civil rights groups called for transparency checks (Johns, 2021). In the end, the city contained pandemic surges, and officials credited real-time data. Critics pointed out potential overreach in data collection, fueling ongoing debates about balancing health security and individual freedom.

7.4. Case Study: Wildfire Threat in California

Wildfires in California cause property loss and evacuations each year. State and local agencies use sensor arrays and satellite imaging to track heat spots and humidity, feeding data into risk models (Morrow, 2022). In some counties, these models function as digital twins for forested regions. At the same time, social media provides local signs of smoke or fast-moving fire lines. Fire departments combine official model outputs with tweets and images from residents in the field (World Bank, 2022).

Rapid integration helps in small fires but can be overwhelmed in large incidents. In major wildfires, social media spikes, and agencies struggle to filter the mass of messages (Rinaldi et al., 2001). Some localities have introduced volunteer groups that classify posts, which lessens the burden on official staff. Still, wildfire spread can outpace modeling updates, leading to partial or lagging data (Morrow, 2022). The case underscores the need for scalable platforms and streamlined communication across state, federal, and private groups.

7.5. Lessons Learned from Comparative Cases

These four examples show how digital twins and social intelligence can strengthen alerts. Faster detection, targeted intervention, and potential reductions in damage were reported (Ford & Wolf, 2020). However, each city also faced technical or governance obstacles, such as data overload, misinformation, cost, or privacy concerns (Vanolo, 2016). Rotterdam and Tokyo illustrate how pairing sensor readings with local reports speeds up validation. Singapore shows the role of a national twin but also spotlights potential overreach. California highlights scaling issues in large disasters.

One recurring insight is that integrated systems work best when there is agency coordination and clear processes for verifying data (Nam & Pardo, 2011). Public trust is another factor: if users doubt official motives or suspect intrusion, they might withhold crucial details or disregard alerts (Brauneis & Goodman, 2018). The next section proposes ways to address these challenges, building on the synergy described earlier. These insights inform strategies for designing systems that serve diverse hazards in different governance settings.

8. STRATEGIC FRAMEWORK AND BEST PRACTICES

This section offers a strategic framework and recommended practices for fusing digital twins and social intelligence into urban early warning. The framework draws from the research base and the case findings, emphasizing governance, interoperability, community involvement, capacity building, and iterative evaluation (Mazzetto, 2024).

8.1. Data Governance and Security

Clear policies must guide data collection, storage, and usage (Brauneis & Goodman, 2018). City agencies often handle sensitive sensor data and personal posts. A multi-layer governance plan clarifies roles, sets data-sharing protocols, and secures systems from hacks (Johns, 2021). Encryption and strict access controls protect networks, while guidelines for anonymizing user data reduce privacy risks. Oversight panels or third-party audits can review compliance and address community concerns.

Security extends to risk management of the digital twin itself. If the twin is compromised, an attacker could feed false data, leading to misdirected alerts. Agencies must institute practices like network segmentation, real-time intrusion detection, and incident response drills (Ford & Wolf, 2020). In some cities, public-private partnerships fund the needed hardware, but these arrangements call for clarity on data rights to prevent exploitation.

8.2. Interoperability and Standardization

Interoperability ensures that multiple agencies and systems exchange data easily (Rinaldi et al., 2001). Early warning merges streams from meteorological services, police, public works, and volunteer networks. Without shared formats or communication protocols, integration stalls (Deakin, 2014). Bodies like the International Telecommunication Union (ITU) issue guidelines on sensor data formats. Adopting or adapting them helps unify digital twin inputs.

Standard application programming interfaces (APIs) and reference models simplify connections. This step requires top-level coordination. Municipal regulations can push for open data standards, compelling private utilities to share crucial readings. Though standardization takes time, it saves effort in future expansions. Interoperability also lowers vendor lock-in, letting agencies switch software without losing data continuity (Komninos, 2014).

8.3. User-Centric Design and Community Engagement

Public warning systems function when people receive and trust alerts (Nam & Pardo, 2011). Designing user-centric channels means using plain language, direct instructions, and multiple formats—SMS, apps, television—for broad coverage (Gardner, 2021). Engaging communities in system co-creation also builds trust. Surveys, focus groups, and pilot tests reveal local needs and preferences. This can improve the system's credibility.

Social intelligence thrives when residents see a benefit and believe that their input is valued (Vanolo, 2016). Municipalities can foster communities of digital volunteers, training them to tag or verify posts. Clear disclaimers about data handling reduce fear of surveillance. In areas with limited connectivity, in-person networks supplement digital alerts. This multi-channel approach mitigates inequities in technology access and fosters resilience (Oh et al., 2013).

8.4. Continuous Training and Capacity Building

Sophisticated data tools need skilled personnel (World Bank, 2022). Operators must interpret digital twin outputs and manage social streams. Training spans technical topics, crisis communication, and data ethics (Morrow, 2022). City staff can learn to calibrate sensors, refine machine learning models, and handle public inquiries. Partnerships with universities or research centers can strengthen skill pipelines (Zeng & Wu, 2020).

Capacity building goes beyond one-time workshops. As technologies evolve, staff need refresher sessions. Exercises and simulations test cross-agency teamwork. Encouraging staff to share lessons from each event creates institutional memory (Malone & Bernstein, 2015). Over time, agencies become more agile in adjusting warning protocols, adopting new analysis methods, or refining privacy measures.

8.5. Periodic Audits and Adaptive Management

Complex systems benefit from continuous audits. Key metrics include alert latency, false alarm rates, community feedback, and coverage. Authorities can measure these metrics at intervals, using the results to fine-tune data pipelines or operational steps (Johns, 2021). Discrepancies between model forecasts and actual outcomes reveal gaps in the twin's algorithms or sensor accuracy (Hoskere et al., 2023). Similarly, user complaints about unclear instructions show a need for message improvements.

Adaptive management treats warning systems as living programs. Feedback loops drive changes in real time. If the city invests in new sensors, the twin's parameters update. If certain neighborhoods do not engage online, outreach strategies shift

(Vanolo, 2016). Officials can publish results of these audits, enhancing transparency. This helps maintain public trust, as people see that the city recognizes imperfections and seeks solutions. Adapting to shifting hazards or technologies keeps the system relevant.

9. ETHICAL AND GOVERNANCE CONSIDERATIONS

Warnings that rely on digital twins and social intelligence raise ethical dilemmas about privacy, data rights, and algorithmic decision-making (Brauneis & Goodman, 2018). This section surveys key concerns and potential governance responses.

9.1. Privacy and Data Ethics

Digital twins gather detailed data on infrastructure, traffic, and sometimes personal devices. Social media analysis may capture user identities or location details if not processed carefully (Johns, 2021). These flows can reveal personal patterns when aggregated. Without safeguards, authorities or commercial partners might misuse them. Privacy frameworks thus play a vital role, enforcing data minimization and anonymization (Vanolo, 2016). Oversight bodies can audit compliance and investigate complaints.

Ethical concerns also arise in how data is collected. Are people informed that their posts might be used for official risk analyses? Is there an opt-out option? In some jurisdictions, existing laws regulate data collection. In others, new rules are needed. Transparent explanations of data usage and storage can reduce suspicion (Gardner, 2021). If residents suspect hidden motives, trust diminishes, and they may avoid contributing information.

9.2. Algorithmic Accountability

Models in digital twins and social media filters decide which alerts to send, to whom, and when (Zhang & Huang, 2019). Algorithmic systems can contain biases if they train on partial datasets. They might issue more warnings in areas with heavier sensor coverage or stronger digital presence, leaving some neighborhoods behind (Mazzetto, 2024). If an alert fails or is incorrect, who is responsible? Clear guidelines on model validation can help. External audits and transparent design notes can reveal how inputs shape results (Brauneis & Goodman, 2018).

False alarms harm credibility, while missed warnings can harm public safety (Vanolo, 2016). Officials must set thresholds for triggering official notices and have backup checks in place. The system should log decision paths, letting reviewers see how data turned into a message. This oversight is crucial when budgets push agencies toward automated solutions (Xie & Liu, 2023). Accountability measures also encourage continuous improvement, since flawed models risk public backlash.

9.3. Governance Models for Inclusive Resilience

Governance strategies vary. Traditional top-down models assign roles to public agencies, but digital twins and social intelligence require broader collaboration. Civil society groups, private tech firms, or academic labs may all hold key data or expertise (Morrow, 2022). A multi-stakeholder model can distribute tasks like data analytics, community outreach, or policy oversight (Malone & Bernstein, 2015). Each participant has input on system goals.

Inclusive governance also ensures that disadvantaged communities receive equitable protection. If social media analysis misses individuals who lack internet, those areas might get slower alerts (Oh et al., 2013). City councils can mandate bridging strategies. Transparent budgeting and open policy debates reduce corruption. Over time, an inclusive model that merges official authority with public engagement may improve readiness (Nam & Pardo, 2011). The next section explores open research areas that can refine these governance practices.

10. FUTURE DIRECTIONS AND RESEARCH GAPS

Digital twins and social intelligence continue to evolve. Broader trials in different contexts are needed to confirm how these tools improve or fail in actual crises (World Bank, 2022). Researchers can investigate how well integrated systems handle compound disasters, like hurricanes triggering industrial accidents. Cultural differences also shape how communities respond to data collection or warnings (Zhang & Huang, 2019). More cross-national studies can clarify best practices under varied governance styles.

Another gap lies in algorithmic transparency. As city simulations adopt advanced machine learning, interpretability decreases (Brauneis & Goodman, 2018). Methods to explain model outputs to decision-makers or the public are crucial. Studies could explore new explainable AI approaches for real-time risk decisions (Heidegger & Schmitt, 2023). Also, effective solutions for misinformation remain elusive. Tools that spot false social posts can fail under large volumes or changing user behaviors (Xie & Liu, 2023). Future work can refine detection algorithms or outline new collaboration approaches with social media platforms.

Long-term sustainability is also an open question. Funding, staff turnover, and shifting political priorities threaten system continuity. Research on stable governance frameworks can ensure that digital twins and crowdsourced data remain relevant. That means refining public-private partnerships, clarifying data ownership, and building institutional capacity to adapt as hazards or technologies shift (Morrow, 2022). Addressing these research gaps may increase the reliability and acceptance of digital-socio integrated systems in global cities.

11. CONCLUSION

Early warning and public warning systems aim to reduce harm during crises. This chapter explored how digital twins and real-time social intelligence can reshape these systems in dense urban landscapes. It drew on published research, official documents, and case examples spanning floods, earthquakes, pandemics, and wildfires. Results point to the merits of merging sensor-driven models with crowdsourced observations. The synergy can accelerate alerts, refine risk estimates, and prompt timely interventions.

Yet significant barriers remain. Building city-scale twins demands budgets, technical talent, and governance structures that embrace data sharing. Social data helps, but misinformation risks and privacy concerns persist. Each case showed that partial solutions can bring gains, but stable, integrated systems need broad policy support, inclusive engagement, and constant learning. Ethical considerations around privacy, algorithmic biases, and accountability also require attention. Cities should strive for user-centric approaches that explain how data is gathered and used, preserving trust in official alerts.

Moving forward, research must examine how integrated alerts adapt to diverse cities and multiple hazards. The environment of data-driven governance is shifting, and authorities must remain flexible. If approached with care, digital twins and social intelligence can help modern cities act faster and communicate clearer warnings that save lives and reduce disruption. Successful deployments will strike a balance between technological progress, legal norms, and public interests, forming a shared path toward safer urban futures.

REFERENCES

Brauneis, R., & Goodman, E. P. (2018). Algorithmic transparency for the smart city. *Yale Journal of Law & Technology.* Retrieved from en.wikipedia.org

Chen, Y., & Zhang, B. (2022). Digital transformation in disaster management: The convergence of digital twins and artificial intelligence for early warning systems. *Computers, Environment and Urban Systems*, *94*, 101789.

Deakin, M. (2014). From city of bits to e-topia: Taking the thesis on digitally-inclusive regeneration full circle. *Journal of Urban Technology, 21*(1), 79-95. Retrieved from en.wikipedia.org

DHS. (2023). Public alert and warning systems: Leveraging technology for emergency management. DHS Report.

European Space Agency. (2023). Digital Twin Earth: A digital replica of our planet.

Ford, D. N., & Wolf, C. M. (2020). Smart cities with digital twin systems for disaster management. [Retrieved from ascelibrary.org]. *Journal of Management Engineering*, *36*(4), 04020027. DOI: 10.1061/(ASCE)ME.1943-5479.0000779

Gardner, A. (2021, March 18). Don't write off government algorithms—Responsible AI can produce real benefits. *The Conversation.* Retrieved from en.wikipedia.org

Guinard, D., Trifa, V., & Wilde, E. (2010). A resource-oriented architecture for the web of things. In *Internet of Things (IOT)* (pp. 1-8). IEEE. Retrieved from en.wikipedia.org

Heidegger, M., & Schmitt, C. (2023). The philosophical foundations of smart city governance: Ethics and AI-driven decision-making. *AI & Society*, *38*(1), 45–67.

Hoskere, V., Narazaki, Y., & Spencer, B. F. (2023). Digital twins as testbeds for vision-based post-earthquake inspections of buildings. In *European Workshop on Structural Health Monitoring* (pp. 1–10). Springer., Retrieved from en.wikipedia.org DOI: 10.1007/978-3-031-07258-1_50

Ingram, J. (2020). *Understanding BIM: The past, present, and future*. Routledge.

Johns, F. (2021). Governance by data. *Annual Review of Law and Social Science*, *17*(1), 53–72. en.wikipedia.org. DOI: 10.1146/annurev-lawsocsci-120920-085138

Johnson, L. (2022, September 12). Singapore's digital twin of entire country. *Geospatial World.* Retrieved from en.wikipedia.org

Komninos, N. (2014). *Intelligent cities and globalization of innovation networks*. Routledge.

Malone, T. W., & Bernstein, M. S. (Eds.). (2015). *Handbook of collective intelligence*. MIT Press.

Mazzetto, S. (2024). A review of urban digital twins integration, challenges, and future directions in smart city development. [Retrieved from mdpi.com]. *Sustainability (Basel)*, *16*(19), 8337. DOI: 10.3390/su16198337

Mitchell, W. (2007). Intelligent cities. *e-Journal on the Knowledge Society, 5*, 1-8. Retrieved from en.wikipedia.org

Morrow, G. (2022). The robot in city hall: The limitations, structure, and governance of smart city technology regimes. Retrieved from en.wikipedia.org

Nam, T., & Pardo, T. A. (2011). Conceptualizing smart city with dimensions of technology, people, and institutions. In *Proceedings of the 12th Annual International Conference on Digital Government Research* (pp. 282-291). Retrieved from en.wikipedia.org

Oh, E., Lee, S., & Lee, H. (2013). Understanding the adoption of smart city policies: The Korea and Japan cases. *Journal of Comparative Policy Analysis*, *15*(5), 477–492.

Pereira, D. (2023, May 23). Speculative design: "Virtual Singapore" is a massive, fully functional digital twin of the Asian city-state. *ArchDaily*. Retrieved from en.wikipedia.org

Rinaldi, S. M., Peerenboom, J. P., & Kelly, T. K. (2001). Identifying, understanding, and analyzing critical infrastructure interdependencies. *IEEE Control Systems*, *21*(6), 11–25. DOI: 10.1109/37.969131

Schecter, A., Pilny, A., Leung, A., Poole, M. S., & Contractor, N. (2018). Step by step: Capturing the dynamics of work team process through relational event sequences. *Journal of Organizational Behavior*, *39*(9), 1163–1181. en.wikipedia.org. DOI: 10.1002/job.2247

Siemens, G. (2005). Connectivism: A learning theory for the digital age. *International Journal of Instructional Technology & Distance Learning*, *2*(1), 3–10.

Singh, S., Sharma, P. K., Yoon, B., Shojafar, M., Cho, G. H., & Ra, I.-H. (2020). Convergence of blockchain and artificial intelligence in IoT network for the sustainable smart city. *Sustainable Cities and Society*, *63*, 102364. en.wikipedia.org. DOI: 10.1016/j.scs.2020.102364

Smart Cities Council. (2019). *Smart cities readiness guide: The planning manual for building tomorrow's cities today.*

Smart City Institute Japan (SCIJ). (2022). Digital twins and disaster risk reduction: Emerging trends and future directions. SCIJ Report.

Vanolo, A. (2016). Is there anybody out there? The place and role of citizens in smart city policies. *Futures*, *82*, 26–36. DOI: 10.1016/j.futures.2016.05.010

Wang, F., Zhang, X., & Li, D. (2021). Digital twins in smart cities: Technologies, applications, and governance implications. *Sustainable Cities and Society*, *69*, 102820.

Weber, R. H. (2010). Internet of Things – New security and privacy challenges. *Computer Law & Security Review*, *26*(1), 23–30. DOI: 10.1016/j.clsr.2009.11.008

World Bank. (2022). *Digital transformation for urban resilience: The role of smart cities in climate adaptation and disaster management.* World Bank Group.

Xie, Y., & Liu, X. (2023). Real-time public warning systems and social media analytics: Integrating AI-driven intelligence into disaster response mechanisms. *Journal of Urban Technology*, *30*(2), 114–137.

Zeng, M., & Wu, H. (2020). Machine learning-based predictive analytics for real-time flood early warning in urban settings. *Natural Hazards*, *102*(3), 2673–2695.

Zhang, C., & Huang, W. (2019). The role of big data and artificial intelligence in early warning systems for urban risk management. *Urban Studies (Edinburgh, Scotland)*, *56*(15), 3215–3232.

Zwitter, A., & Boisse-Despiaux, M. (2018). Blockchain for humanitarian action and disaster resilience: Challenges and opportunities. *Journal of International Humanitarian Action*, *3*(1), 1–14.

Chapter 18
Challenges and Opportunities in Implementing Smart City Technologies in Developing Countries

Syed Mohd Faisal
https://orcid.org/0000-0003-2422-3535
Koneru Lakshmaiah Education Foundation, India

Wasim Khan
https://orcid.org/0000-0003-2311-1451
Symbiosis Institute of Technology, Symbiosis International University (Deemed), Pune, India

Mohammad Ishrat
https://orcid.org/0000-0002-9699-4454
Koneru Lakshmaiah Education Foundation, India

ABSTRACT

Smart city technologies offer transformative opportunities for developing countries but face challenges such as infrastructural deficits, financial constraints, outdated policies, and digital divides. Despite these obstacles, technologies like IoT, AI, and big data enable resource optimization and efficient urban management. Successful initiatives in India, Kenya, and Brazil demonstrate the potential for enhanced governance and urban resilience. To fully realize these benefits, developing countries must strengthen digital infrastructure, foster Public-Private Partnerships, and implement

DOI: 10.4018/979-8-3373-1375-7.ch018

policy standardization and cybersecurity measures. Investing in digital literacy is crucial to bridging the technological gap. Strategic planning and collaboration can help these nations leverage smart city solutions for sustainable urban growth and improved living conditions.

1. INTRODUCTION

The concept of smart cities is revolutionizing urban development by integrating digital technologies, data-driven solutions, and sustainable practices to enhance the quality of life for citizens. As urban populations continue to grow, cities around the world face mounting challenges related to infrastructure, resource management, pollution, transportation, and governance. Smart cities aim to address these issues by utilizing advanced technologies such as the Internet of Things (IoT) (Zikria et al., 2021), Artificial Intelligence (AI)(Jan et al., 2023), big data analytics, and cloud computing (Sadeeq et al., 2021). These innovations enable real-time monitoring, efficient resource distribution, and improved public services, making cities more responsive and sustainable. In developing countries, the need for smart city initiatives is even more critical. Rapid urbanization has led to overburdened transportation systems, inadequate sanitation, power shortages, and inefficient governance. Traditional urban planning methods struggle to keep up with the escalating demands of growing populations, resulting in deteriorating infrastructure and declining public service quality. Smart city technologies (Hassan et al., 2021) provide a viable solution by enhancing automation, promoting sustainable resource usage, and improving urban governance. A key driver of smart city implementation is the increasing adoption of IoT and AI, which facilitate efficient management of public utilities and services. IoT devices, such as smart meters, sensors, and automated traffic management systems, enable cities to optimize energy consumption, reduce water wastage, and mitigate congestion. AI-driven data analytics further enhance decision-making processes by analyzing patterns, predicting trends, and identifying areas that require intervention. Through these technological advancements, cities can improve efficiency while reducing costs.

Despite the benefits, implementing smart cities in developing nations comes with several challenges. Financial constraints, outdated infrastructure, lack of skilled workforce, and policy barriers often slow down the adoption of new technologies. Governments must work collaboratively with private sector players through Public-Private Partnerships (PPPs) to mobilize investments and drive digital transformation (Almarri & Boussabaine, 2023). Establishing clear regulatory frameworks and policies is crucial to ensuring data privacy, cybersecurity, and interoperability of smart city systems. Developing countries can harness the potential of smart cities by focusing on key areas such as digital connectivity, intelligent transport systems, and e-governance. Digital inclusion plays a vital role in ensuring that smart cities benefits reach all segments of society, reducing the digital divide and promoting social equity. By prioritizing investments in smart education, telemedicine, and smart grid technologies, developing nations can accelerate their journey toward modernization.

Figure 1. Components of smart city

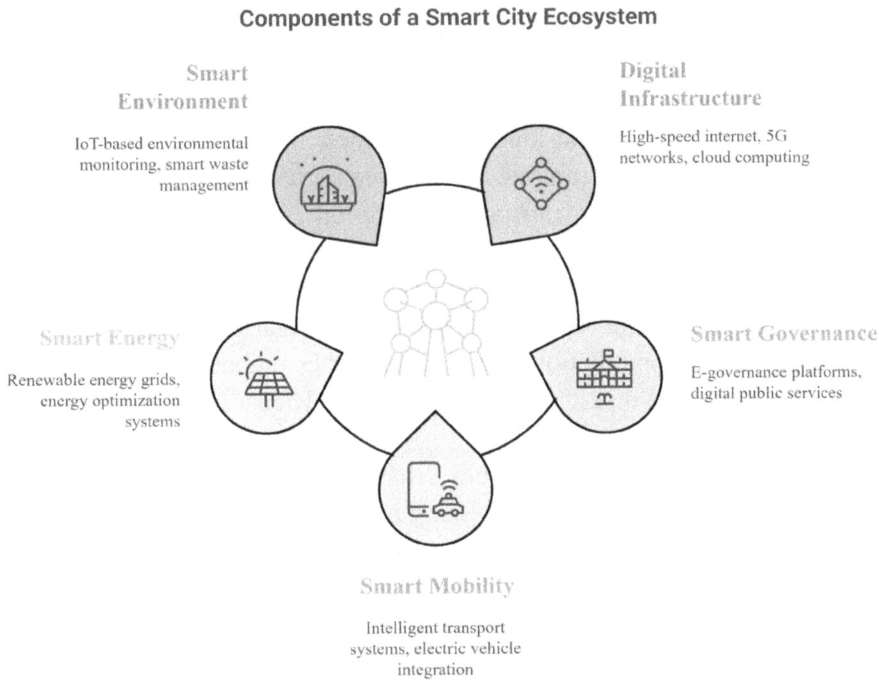

Figure 1 shows the components of smart cities and the key reasons for Smart City Implementation in Developing Countries is listed below:

- Rapid Urbanization: Cities are expanding at an unprecedented rate, leading to increased demand for infrastructure, housing, and essential services. Smart city technologies help manage this growth effectively.

- Traffic Congestion and Transportation Issues: Intelligent traffic management systems, automated toll collection, and smart public transport solutions can reduce congestion and improve urban mobility (Karimi et al., 2021).
- Energy and Resource Optimization: Smart grids, renewable energy integration, and real-time monitoring of utilities help optimize energy and resource consumption, ensuring sustainability.
- Enhanced Public Safety: AI-driven surveillance systems, smart street lighting, and predictive policing improve safety and security for urban populations (Gautam et al., 2025).
- Sustainability and Environmental Benefits: Smart waste management, water conservation technologies, and pollution control mechanisms contribute to a greener and more sustainable urban environment.
- Economic Growth and Job Creation: The implementation of smart city initiatives fosters technological innovation, attracts foreign investments, and creates employment opportunities in emerging sectors.
- Better Governance and Transparency: Digital governance platforms enable seamless interaction between citizens and government agencies, ensuring transparency, efficiency, and reduced corruption.
- Disaster Management and Urban Resilience: Real-time data analytics and AI-based disaster prediction systems help cities prepare for and respond effectively to natural disasters and emergencies (Richardson, 2021).

With this we can say that smart cities have the potential to transform urban living in developing countries by addressing infrastructural challenges, optimizing resource management, and improving governance. While financial and policy-related obstacles exist, strategic planning, technological adoption, and collaborative efforts between governments and private enterprises can pave the way for sustainable and inclusive urban development. By embracing digital transformation, developing nations can ensure that their cities remain future-ready, resilient, and capable of supporting their growing populations.

While the vision of smart cities offers promising solutions to the challenges of rapid urbanization, resource management, and governance inefficiencies, their implementation is not without obstacles. In developing countries, the adoption of smart city technologies is particularly complex due to infrastructural limitations, financial constraints, policy barriers, and digital divides. These challenges must be critically examined to understand the feasibility of smart city development and identify strategies for overcoming these hurdles. The following section delves into the key challenges associated with implementing smart city initiatives in developing countries, outlining the economic, technological, and policy-related barriers that must be addressed to enable successful urban transformation.

2. CHALLENGES IN IMPLEMENTING SMART CITY TECHNOLOGIES IN DEVELOPING COUNTRIES

The development of smart cities is a promising initiative that enhances urban infrastructure, improves public services, and fosters sustainable living. However, implementing smart city technologies in developing countries presents numerous challenges due to economic, infrastructure, policy, and technological constraints. This section explores these challenges in depth, categorized under various key domains, with supporting tables and proposed figures to illustrate the complexities involved.

2.1. Infrastructure Deficiencies

A well-functioning infrastructure is the backbone of any smart city initiative. However, many developing nations face critical infrastructural deficiencies that hinder the successful deployment of smart city technologies. These limitations affect the implementation of smart grids, IoT-based transportation systems, and digital governance platforms (Abbas et al., 2021).

2.1.1. Unreliable Power Supply

A stable power supply is essential for running smart technologies such as IoT devices, AI-driven city monitoring systems, and cloud-based data centers. Unfortunately, many developing countries suffer from frequent power outages due to outdated electricity grids, limited renewable energy sources, and inconsistent power distribution networks. As a result, smart street lighting, automated traffic control systems, and real-time surveillance networks often face operational disruptions. The dependence on fossil fuels further exacerbates the issue, making energy management a major obstacle in implementing smart city technologies (Gandhi et al., 2020).

2.1.2. Limited Internet Connectivity

Smart cities rely on seamless connectivity to function efficiently. High-speed internet and widespread broadband penetration are essential for real-time data sharing between urban systems. However, developing nations face severe limitations in internet infrastructure, particularly in rural and semi-urban areas. The high cost of broadband services further restricts accessibility, making it difficult for local governments to implement data-driven governance solutions. Without proper connectivity, IoT-based sensors, AI-powered analytics, and cloud computing cannot be effectively utilized in smart city applications (Ullah et al., 2024).

2.1.3. Inefficient Transportation Systems

Congested roads, outdated public transport networks, and poor traffic management systems are common in many developing cities. Implementing intelligent transport solutions, such as AI-driven traffic signals, smart parking systems, and real-time public transport tracking, requires extensive modernization of road infrastructure. However, inadequate funding and lack of urban planning strategies often delay the integration of smart mobility solutions.

2.2. Financial Constraints

The development of smart cities requires substantial financial investment. From deploying IoT-enabled infrastructure to training a technologically skilled workforce, the costs associated with smart city projects are often prohibitive for developing nations. Many governments struggle to allocate sufficient budgets for digital transformation due to competing priorities such as healthcare, education, and social welfare(Farooqui et al., 2023).

2.2.1. High Initial Costs

The upfront cost of setting up smart city technologies, such as smart grids, AI-driven governance platforms, and IoT-based monitoring systems, is immense. The procurement of advanced technology, installation of network infrastructure, and deployment of cloud-based services require billions of dollars in investment. For many developing countries, securing such funds remains a major hurdle.

2.2.2. Dependency on International Aid and Private Investment

Due to financial constraints, many developing nations rely on international aid, foreign loans, and external investments to fund smart city projects. However, these funding sources often come with conditions that may not align with national priorities. Additionally, private investors are sometimes reluctant to invest in large-scale urban projects due to perceived financial risks, lack of guaranteed returns, and bureaucratic inefficiencies.

2.2.3. Limited Government Budget Allocation

Governments in developing nations face numerous budgetary challenges, with limited resources allocated to urban innovation. Many national budgets prioritize essential services such as healthcare, education, and poverty alleviation, leaving minimal funds for technological advancements in urban planning. As a result, smart city projects often get delayed or are only partially implemented (Al-Worafi, 2023).

2.3. Policy and Regulatory Barriers

The successful implementation of smart cities requires well-defined policies and regulations that govern technology use, data privacy, and cybersecurity. However, many developing countries lack the necessary legal and administrative frameworks to regulate and support smart city initiatives.

2.3.1. Absence of Standardized Policies

One of the key challenges in developing smart cities is the absence of clear policies and regulatory frameworks. Many governments do not have standardized guidelines for smart infrastructure development, which leads to inconsistencies in project execution. Without well-defined policies, it becomes difficult to establish interoperable systems across different sectors such as transportation, healthcare, and security(Razmjoo et al., 2021).

2.3.2. Cybersecurity and Data Privacy Concerns

With the increasing adoption of digital governance and IoT-based monitoring systems, cybersecurity and data privacy have become major concerns. Many developing nations do not have robust cybersecurity laws to protect citizens' personal data, making them vulnerable to cyber threats, hacking, and data breaches. The lack of clear legal frameworks for data protection discourages citizens from adopting digital services, further slowing down smart city implementation.

2.3.3. Bureaucratic Delays and Administrative Inefficiencies

Bureaucracy and administrative inefficiencies often slow down smart city initiatives. Many smart projects require approval from multiple government agencies, leading to lengthy delays. Additionally, corruption, lack of transparency, and inefficiencies in governance contribute to the slow implementation of smart technologies (Gupta et al., 2022).

2.4. Common Cybersecurity Threats to Smart Cities

As smart cities rely on interconnected digital technologies such as the Internet of Things (IoT), Artificial Intelligence (AI), cloud computing, and big data analytics, they become attractive targets for cyber threats. The increasing dependence on these technologies creates vulnerabilities that, if exploited, can disrupt critical city functions, compromise citizen data, and hinder public services. This section explores the most common cybersecurity threats faced by smart cities, highlighting the risks associated with data security, infrastructure protection, and regulatory gaps.

2.4.1. Data Breaches and Privacy Violations

Smart cities collect and store vast amounts of personal and operational data through sensors, cameras, and digital services. Weak encryption, misconfigured databases, and poor access control mechanisms can result in unauthorized access, leading to data breaches. These breaches can expose sensitive citizen information, including personal identities, financial records, and healthcare data, increasing the risk of identity theft and fraud.

2.4.2. Ransomware and Cyber Attacks on Critical Infrastructure

Ransomware attacks target essential smart city services, such as power grids, water treatment plants, and transportation systems, by encrypting data and demanding ransom for its release. Such attacks can disrupt daily city operations, causing significant economic and societal damage. For instance, a cyberattack on a city's energy grid can lead to prolonged blackouts, affecting businesses, hospitals, and emergency response services.

2.4.3. IoT Device Vulnerabilities and Botnet Attacks

Smart cities integrate numerous IoT devices, including smart meters, traffic sensors, surveillance cameras, and environmental monitoring systems. Many of these devices lack robust security features, making them vulnerable to hijacking. Cybercriminals can exploit these weaknesses to launch botnet attacks, using compromised devices to conduct Distributed Denial-of-Service (DDoS) attacks, which can cripple city-wide digital infrastructure.

2.4.4. Man-in-the-Middle (MitM) Attacks on Communication Networks

Smart cities rely on real-time data transmission between IoT devices, cloud servers, and central control systems. Hackers can intercept and manipulate this communication through Man-in-the-Middle (MitM) attacks, altering data flows, falsifying sensor readings, or disrupting automated control mechanisms. This can lead to severe consequences, such as manipulated traffic signals causing accidents or false emergency alerts creating panic.

2.4.5. Supply Chain Attacks on Smart City Technologies

Many smart city technologies are sourced from multiple vendors, creating vulnerabilities in the supply chain. Malicious actors can introduce backdoors or security flaws during the manufacturing process, compromising software and hardware components. A compromised supplier can unknowingly distribute insecure devices or software updates, leading to long-term security risks for the city's infrastructure.

2.4.6. Lack of Standardized Cybersecurity Policies

The rapid deployment of smart city technologies often outpaces the development of security policies and regulations. Many developing countries lack standardized cybersecurity frameworks, resulting in inconsistent security practices, weak incident response mechanisms, and unpatched vulnerabilities. Without clear governance, cities face challenges in enforcing cybersecurity best practices and ensuring compliance across all digital infrastructure components.

Cybersecurity threats pose significant risks to the functionality and safety of smart cities. Without proper security measures, these threats can compromise sensitive data, disrupt essential services, and undermine public trust in digital governance. Addressing these vulnerabilities requires a proactive approach, including regulatory improvements, advanced threat detection, and collaborative security strategies. The next section explores best practices for securing smart city infrastructure, ensuring resilience against cyber threats while maintaining operational efficiency.

2.5. Technological and Digital Divide

The implementation of smart city technologies in developing countries faces numerous obstacles, including infrastructural deficiencies, financial constraints, policy and regulatory barriers, technological gaps, and environmental concerns. Many developing nations lack the essential infrastructure, such as reliable power grids, high-speed internet, and efficient transportation systems, which are critical for the smooth operation of smart city solutions. Financial constraints further exacerbate the situation, as the high initial costs of smart technologies, coupled with limited government budgets and dependency on foreign investments, slow down large-scale implementation. Additionally, the absence of standardized policies, weak cybersecurity regulations, and bureaucratic inefficiencies hinder the seamless integration of digital solutions in urban governance. The technological and digital divide remains another significant challenge, as low digital literacy among citizens and a shortage of skilled professionals limits the adoption and maintenance of smart technologies. Environmental concerns, such as inefficient waste management, high carbon emissions, and poor sanitation infrastructure, further complicate the transition to smart cities. Despite these challenges, with strategic investments, public-private partnerships, and strong policy frameworks, developing nations can overcome these barriers and successfully implement smart city initiatives, driving sustainable urban growth and improving the quality of life for their citizens.

2.6. Environmental and Sustainability Challenges

Implementing smart city technologies in developing countries presents a complex array of challenges, including infrastructural deficiencies, financial limitations, regulatory barriers, technological gaps, and environmental sustainability concerns. The lack of essential infrastructure, such as reliable electricity, high-speed internet, and efficient transportation systems, significantly hampers the integration of smart solutions. Frequent power outages disrupt IoT networks, cloud computing, and smart grids, leading to inefficient city operations. Similarly, inadequate broadband penetration and expensive internet services restrict digital connectivity, limiting access to e-governance platforms, real-time traffic management, and smart utility services. Another significant barrier is financial constraints, as smart city development requires substantial investments in hardware, software, and skilled personnel. Most developing countries struggle with budget allocations, prioritizing essential sectors like healthcare and education over technological advancements. Consequently, governments often rely on foreign aid, private investments, and public-private partnerships to fund these projects (Razmjoo et al., 2021). However, financial dependence on international agencies and foreign investors can create long-term economic burdens and policy dependencies. Regulatory and policy-related challenges also impede smart city implementation, as many developing nations lack standardized legal frameworks for data governance, cybersecurity, and technology regulations. The absence of strict cybersecurity measures increases risks related to data breaches, cyber-attacks, and misuse of personal information, discouraging citizen participation in digital governance initiatives. Additionally, bureaucratic inefficiencies, corruption, and lack of interdepartmental coordination further delay the execution of smart projects. The digital divide remains another pressing issue, as low digital literacy prevents many citizens from accessing and benefiting from smart city services. The shortage of skilled professionals, such as data scientists, AI engineers, and IoT specialists, limits the development and maintenance of smart infrastructure, making it difficult for cities to sustain technological progress. Environmental and sustainability challenges further complicate the scenario, as many developing nations struggle with ineffective waste management, high carbon emissions, and poor sanitation infrastructure. While smart cities aim to promote sustainability through IoT-enabled waste collection, automated recycling, and green energy solutions, these technologies require significant initial investment, which is often out of reach for developing economies. The continued reliance on non-renewable energy sources, such as coal and oil, increases air pollution and carbon emissions, counteracting the environmental benefits of smart urbanization. Additionally, poor urban planning and rapid population growth result in excessive strain on water resources, inadequate sewage treatment, and increased pollution, reducing the overall effectiveness of smart city solutions. Addressing these challenges requires a multi-faceted approach, including strategic investments in infrastructure, policy reforms, financial incentives for private sector involvement, and large-scale digital literacy programs. Governments must collaborate with international organizations, technology firms, and academic institutions to establish frameworks that promote cybersecurity, innovation, and smart urban planning. Expanding access to affordable internet, modernizing energy grids, and promoting green technology adoption are critical steps toward ensuring the successful deployment of smart cities in developing nations (A. Ansari et al., 2024). Moreover, fostering digital inclusion through training programs and educational initiatives will help bridge the technological divide, allowing citizens to actively participate in smart governance and benefit from urban digital transformation. Despite these challenges, the potential of smart city technologies to improve living standards, enhance governance, and drive sustainable economic growth makes it imperative for developing nations to prioritize digital urban development, ensuring a future where technology-driven cities are both inclusive and resilient.

While the implementation of smart city technologies in developing nations is fraught with challenges, these obstacles also present unique opportunities for innovation and growth. The rapid pace of urbanization, coupled with advancements in digital infrastructure, offers developing countries a chance to leapfrog traditional urban development models and adopt smart solutions that enhance efficiency, sustainability, and quality of life. By strategically addressing financial, technological, and policy-related barriers, governments and private sector stakeholders can unlock new pathways for smart city transformation. The following section explores the key opportunities that developing nations can leverage to accelerate smart city adoption, improve governance, foster economic growth, and promote sustainable urban living.

3. OPPORTUNITIES FOR SMART CITY IMPLEMENTATION IN DEVELOPING COUNTRIES

Despite the numerous challenges, developing countries have significant opportunities to leverage smart city technologies to improve urban living standards, drive economic growth, and promote sustainability. These opportunities arise due to rapid urbanization, technological advancements, international collaborations, and the growing demand for efficient public services. Figure 2 shows the basic architecture of smart cities and table 1 shows the Strategic Opportunities for Smart City Growth. Here are some of the key opportunities:

Figure 2. Smart City Architecture Overview

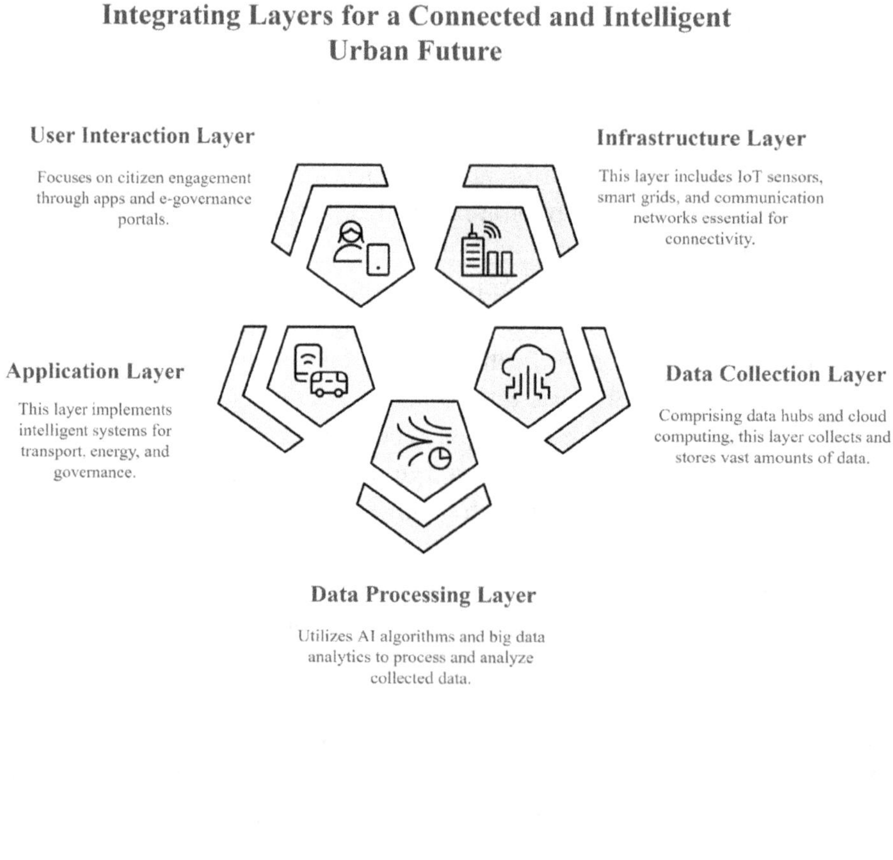

3.1. Leapfrogging Traditional Infrastructure

Developing countries have the advantage of bypassing outdated infrastructure systems by adopting modern, cost-effective smart technologies directly. Unlike developed nations, which often have legacy systems that are expensive to upgrade, emerging economies can implement state-of-the-art solutions without extensive overhauls. This approach allows them to avoid the high costs associated with upgrading existing systems and instead invest in more efficient and scalable technologies(Zaidi & Faisal, 2018). For example, in countries with limited broadband infrastructure, mobile technology has emerged as a powerful tool to provide digital services such as mobile banking, e-governance, and telemedicine. In Kenya, the mobile payment system M-Pesa revolutionized financial transactions by allowing users to send and receive money through their mobile phones, bypassing the need for traditional banking infrastructure. This not only enhanced financial inclusion but also spurred economic growth by empowering small businesses and rural communities. Similarly, developing nations can leapfrog traditional power grids by investing in smart grids integrated with renewable energy sources like solar and wind power. This allows them to overcome the challenges of unreliable electricity supply and high carbon emissions, leading to more sustainable urban development. By adopting these advanced technologies, developing countries can accelerate their digital transformation and improve the quality of life for their citizens.

3.2. Economic Growth and Job Creation

Smart city initiatives drive economic growth by attracting foreign investments, promoting local startups, and creating employment opportunities in technology-driven sectors. These initiatives foster a vibrant startup ecosystem by encouraging innovations in emerging technologies such as the Internet of Things (IoT), Artificial Intelligence (AI), and data analytics. This digital economy enables local entrepreneurs to develop innovative solutions for urban challenges, ranging from intelligent transportation systems to smart energy management. Additionally, the increasing demand for skilled professionals in smart infrastructure management, cybersecurity, and data analytics leads to significant job creation in these emerging sectors. For example, in India, the Smart Cities Mission has facilitated the growth of startups specializing in smart mobility solutions, such as ride-sharing platforms and intelligent traffic management systems. These innovations have improved urban mobility and created numerous job opportunities in technology development, customer support, and data analysis. By nurturing a culture of innovation and providing employment opportunities, smart city initiatives contribute to sustainable economic growth and help bridge the digital divide in developing countries.

3.3. Improved Governance and Public Services

Smart city technologies enable efficient governance and better public service delivery through digitization and data-driven decision-making. By leveraging digital platforms and advanced analytics, governments can enhance transparency, accountability, and citizen participation. This technological integration streamlines administrative processes, reduces bureaucratic delays, and promotes responsive governance. E-governance platforms play a crucial role by providing online portals and mobile applications that facilitate seamless interactions between citizens and government agencies (Malodia et al., 2021). These platforms simplify public services such as tax payments, license renewals, and grievance redressal, reducing paperwork and increasing transparency. Smart healthcare systems are another significant application of smart city technologies. Digital health records, telemedicine services, and AI-driven diagnostics improve healthcare accessibility and operational efficiency, especially in underserved areas. For example, in Estonia, an advanced e-governance system allows citizens to access a wide range of public services online, including healthcare, education, and taxation, with just a digital ID. This system has enhanced citizen participation, increased government transparency, and significantly reduced administrative costs. By adopting similar smart governance solutions, developing countries can improve public service delivery and build trust between citizens and government institutions (Farooqui et al., 2024).

3.4. Environmental Sustainability and Resilience

Smart city solutions contribute to environmental sustainability by optimizing resource usage and reducing carbon footprints. These technologies enable cities to manage resources more efficiently and minimize environmental impact. One of the key opportunities lies in smart waste management, where IoT-enabled waste bins are equipped with sensors monitor fill levels and optimize collection routes using AI-driven analytics. This approach reduces fuel consumption, minimizes operational costs, and decreases carbon emissions by preventing unnecessary trips. Additionally, sustainable urban mobility solutions, such as intelligent transportation systems and electric vehicle integration, help reduce traffic congestion and air pollution. By leveraging real-time data on traffic patterns, smart traffic management systems can dynamically adjust signal timings, improving traffic flow and reducing vehicle emissions. Smart cities also enhance disaster resilience by utilizing AI-based predictive analytics and real-time monitoring systems to anticipate natural disasters and respond proactively (Dwivedi et al., 2024). For example, in Japan, advanced earthquake early warning systems combine IoT sensors and AI analytics to provide real-time alerts, allowing citizens and emergency services to prepare for and mitigate the impact of earthquakes. By implementing these smart city solutions, developing countries can promote environmental sustainability, enhance urban resilience, and improve the overall quality of life for their citizens(Farooqui et al., 2023)(M. S. H. Ansari & Mehrotra, 2020).

3.5. Social Inclusion and Quality of Life

Smart city initiatives promote social inclusion by bridging the digital divide and enhancing the quality of life for citizens. These initiatives empower communities by ensuring equitable access to digital services and resources. By investing in digital literacy programs, smart cities enable citizens to acquire the necessary skills to participate in the digital economy, thus promoting economic empowerment and social mobility. This approach not only enhances individual opportunities but also contributes to the overall economic development of the community. Additionally, smart city platforms provide accessible public services, ensuring that essential services such as healthcare, education, and social welfare reach marginalized communities. By making these services available through digital platforms, smart cities eliminate geographical barriers and reduce disparities in service delivery(Padrón Nápoles et al., 2021). For example, in India, the Digital India initiative has successfully promoted digital literacy among rural populations, enabling them to access government services, banking, and healthcare through mobile applications. This has significantly improved the quality of life for underserved communities and fostered social equity. By bridging the digital divide and ensuring inclusive access to public services, smart city initiatives create more equitable urban environments and contribute to sustainable social development (Sindakis & Showkat, 2024).

3.6. Public-Private Partnerships and International Collaboration

Collaboration between governments, private companies, and international organizations drives innovation and investment in smart city initiatives. These collaborations enable resource sharing, knowledge transfer, and funding, which accelerate digital transformation and urban development. Public-Private Partnerships (PPPs) play a crucial role in facilitating investments and driving the adoption of smart technologies by leveraging the expertise and resources of private enterprises. These partnerships help bridge the financial gap and reduce the burden on public funds while promoting innovation and efficiency. Additionally, international collaborations with organizations such as the World Bank and UN-Habitat provide technical expertise, policy guidance, and financial aid, which are essential for overcoming the financial and infrastructural challenges faced by developing countries. For example, in Nigeria, a partnership between the government and international tech companies led to the implementation of smart energy solutions, improving electricity distribution and reducing power outages in urban areas. By fostering collaborative ecosystems, smart city initiatives benefit from diverse expertise, enhanced investment opportunities, and sustainable urban growth(Umeh et al., 2024).

3.7. Strategic Urban Planning and Policy Development

Developing countries can strategically plan smart cities by adopting forward-thinking policies and regulations that create an enabling environment for digital transformation and sustainable urban development. Clear and standardized regulations for data governance, cybersecurity, and technology interoperability are essential to ensure the secure and efficient implementation of smart city solutions. By establishing robust cybersecurity frameworks, governments can protect sensitive data, build public trust, and encourage citizen participation in digital governance systems. Moreover, policy standardization enhances interoperability between different smart city platforms, enabling seamless integration and efficient data sharing across various sectors, such as transportation, healthcare, and public safety. In addition to regulatory frameworks, sustainable urban development plays a critical role in the strategic planning of smart cities. By integrating smart solutions into urban planning, zoning, and infrastructure development, governments can promote long-term sustainability and resource optimization(M. S. H. Ansari & Mehrotra, 2019). This includes incorporating intelligent transportation systems, renewable energy solutions, and efficient waste management practices in city planning (Masik et al., 2021). For example, Singapore's Smart Nation initiative demonstrates the effectiveness of strategic policy planning in creating a technologically advanced urban environment. The government established clear regulations on data privacy and cybersecurity while promoting sustainable urban development through green building standards and intelligent transport systems. This holistic approach has positioned Singapore as a global leader in smart city implementation. By adopting similar forward-thinking policies and integrating smart solutions into urban planning, developing countries can enhance urban efficiency, promote sustainability, and improve the quality of life for their citizens (Sha & Taeihagh, 2024).

Table 1. Strategic Opportunities for Smart City Growth

Opportunity	Description	Example
Leapfrogging Traditional Infrastructure	Direct adoption of advanced technologies, bypassing legacy systems.	Kenya's mobile payment system M-Pesa revolutionized financial inclusion.
Economic Growth and Job Creation	Development of startups and job opportunities in emerging tech sectors.	Smart Cities Mission in India boosted the startup ecosystem in urban mobility.
Improved Governance and Public Services	Digital governance platforms enhance transparency and efficiency.	Estonia's e-governance system provides citizens with access to public services online.
Environmental Sustainability and Resilience	Smart waste management, intelligent transportation, and renewable energy integration.	Smart Rio's AI-driven flood monitoring system in Brazil.
Public-Private Partnerships	Collaborative investments and international cooperation drive innovation.	Nigeria's collaboration with tech companies for smart energy solutions.

As developing countries explore the vast potential of smart city technologies, numerous opportunities emerge to enhance urban living, drive economic growth, and promote sustainability. From leapfrogging traditional infrastructure to leveraging public-private partnerships, these nations are uniquely positioned to implement innovative solutions that address urban challenges. However, while theoretical opportunities highlight the feasibility of smart city initiatives, real-world implementations offer deeper insights into their impact and effectiveness. The following section presents case studies of smart city initiatives across various developing nations, showcasing how strategic planning, technological adoption, and collaborative efforts are transforming urban environments and improving the quality of life for citizens.

4. CASE STUDIES OF SMART CITY INITIATIVES IN DEVELOPING COUNTRIES

Smart city initiatives in developing countries are transforming urban landscapes by leveraging technology to address unique challenges. These projects focus on enhancing infrastructure, improving public services, and promoting sustainable development. Table 2 shows the comparative analysis of smart city initiatives. Few famous case studies on the smart city are explained below:

4.1. Rio de Janeiro, Brazil: Integrated Operations Center

Rio de Janeiro has implemented the Rio Operations Center (Centro de Operações Rio - COR) to enhance urban management and emergency response. Established in 2010, COR integrates data from various city departments, utilities, and public services into a centralized command center. This integration enables real-time monitoring of city operations, facilitating efficient responses to emergencies such as floods and landslides. The system has improved coordination among agencies, leading to more effective management of urban challenges (Martins et al., 2025).

4.2. Prayagraj, India: Smart City Transformation

Prayagraj, formerly known as Allahabad, is undergoing a transformation under India's Smart Cities Mission. The city has implemented projects focusing on waste management, disaster management, water management, and citizen services. Collaborations with international agencies, such as the United States Trade and Development Agency (USTDA), have facilitated the development of smart infrastructure. Initiatives include the introduction of smart transport systems, riverfront development, and the digitization of public services to enhance efficiency and transparency(Rana, 2023).

4.3. Addis Ababa, Ethiopia: City Corridor Project

The Addis Ababa City Corridor Project aims to upgrade key routes and improve connectivity within the city. Launched in December 2022, the project focuses on constructing bicycle routes, pedestrian walkways, parks, libraries, and additional housing. The initiative seeks to transform Addis Ababa into a hospitable and livable metropolis by enhancing urban infrastructure and public spaces. However, the project has faced controversies related to housing demolitions and concerns about its economic and societal benefits (Al-Sudaimi, 2024).

4.4. Vijayawada, India: Golden Mile Project

Vijayawada's Golden Mile Project is India's first smart street initiative, implemented along a 2.9 km stretch of M.G. Road. The project includes free Wi-Fi, intelligent street lighting, smart parking facilities, and connected transport systems. Managed through a City Digital Platform, these features enhance urban mobility and public safety. The project exemplifies how targeted smart infrastructure can improve the quality of urban life (Sridharan et al., 2017).

4.5. Chiang Mai, Thailand: Smart City Development

Chiang Mai is advancing towards becoming a smart city by integrating Information and Communications Technology (ICT) with the Internet of Things (IoT). Initiatives include smart transportation solutions, such as the introduction of bike-sharing programs, and smart agriculture projects that utilize wireless sensor systems for efficient irrigation. These efforts aim to promote sustainable urban development and improve the quality of life for residents (Kitika & Suwatcharapinun, 2024).

Table 2. Comparative Analysis of Smart City Initiatives

Country	Initiative	Key Features	Impact
India	Smart Cities Mission	Digital governance, intelligent traffic management, renewable energy integration.	Improved urban mobility, energy efficiency, and transparency.
Kenya	Smart Nairobi Initiative	IoT-based environmental monitoring, digital governance.	Enhanced public health and responsive public services.
Brazil	Smart Rio Project	AI-driven flood monitoring, smart waste management.	Increased urban resilience and sustainability.
Indonesia	Jakarta Smart City	Intelligent transportation, digital governance.	Reduced traffic congestion and enhanced public service delivery.
Rwanda	Kigali Digital Transformation	High-speed internet, e-governance, IoT-based monitoring.	Improved digital connectivity and sustainable resource management.

These case studies demonstrate that, despite challenges, developing countries are making significant strides in implementing smart city technologies. Through strategic planning, international collaboration, and community engagement, these cities are leveraging technology to create more sustainable, efficient, and livable urban environments.

The case studies of smart city initiatives in developing countries highlight the significant progress made in integrating digital technologies to address urban challenges. These examples showcase the potential of smart solutions in improving public services, enhancing urban resilience, and fostering economic growth. However, while these projects demonstrate success, they also reveal the complexities involved in smart city implementation, particularly in developing regions with infrastructural, financial, and policy constraints. To build on these successes and overcome existing challenges, strategic policy interventions, robust governance frameworks, and innovative partnerships are necessary. The following section outlines key future directions and policy recommendations that can help developing countries maximize the benefits of smart city initiatives, ensuring sustainable, inclusive, and technology-driven urban growth.

5. COMPARATIVE ANALYSIS OF SMART CITY IMPLEMENTATION ACROSS REGIONS

The adoption of smart city technologies varies significantly across regions due to differences in infrastructure, governance, investment levels, and technological readiness. While developed nations have well-established digital frameworks and strong cybersecurity measures, many developing regions face challenges related to funding, policy gaps, and digital literacy. This section provides a comparative analysis of smart city implementation across major global regions, highlighting their success rates, challenges, and key initiatives.

5.1. Global Smart City Implementation Trends

Smart city success depends on several factors, including digital infrastructure, investment in emerging technologies, and policy effectiveness. Table 3 presents a comparative analysis of smart city implementation across different regions, considering key indicators such as digital infrastructure development, cybersecurity readiness, policy effectiveness, and financial investment.

Table 3. A comparative analysis of smart city implementation across different regions

Region	Smart City Readiness Index (Out of 100)	Digital Infrastructure Development (%)	Cybersecurity Readiness Score (Out of 10)	Policy & Governance Effectiveness (Out of 10)	Investment in Smart City Initiatives (USD Billion)	Notable Smart City Projects
North America	85	90%	8.5	9.0	120	New York, Toronto, San Francisco
Europe	82	88%	8.8	9.2	100	Amsterdam, Barcelona, London
Asia-Pacific	78	85%	7.5	8.0	140	Singapore, Seoul, Tokyo
Middle East	75	80%	7.2	7.8	90	Dubai, Riyadh, Doha
Latin America	65	70%	6.5	6.8	50	Bogotá, Mexico City, São Paulo

continued on following page

Table 3. Continued

Region	Smart City Readiness Index (Out of 100)	Digital Infrastructure Development (%)	Cybersecurity Readiness Score (Out of 10)	Policy & Governance Effectiveness (Out of 10)	Investment in Smart City Initiatives (USD Billion)	Notable Smart City Projects
Africa	50	55%	5.0	5.5	30	Nairobi, Cape Town, Kigali
South Asia	60	65%	5.8	6.2	40	New Delhi, Mumbai, Colombo

5.2. Regional Insights on Smart City Development

5.2.1. North America – Leading in Technological Innovation

North America is a global leader in smart city adoption due to its advanced digital infrastructure, high cybersecurity readiness, and strong policy frameworks. Cities like New York, Toronto, and San Francisco have integrated AI, IoT, and big data analytics to improve urban mobility, public safety, and energy efficiency. Government funding and private-sector investments have played a crucial role in scaling smart city projects across the region (Dwivedi et al., 2024).

5.2.2. Europe – Strong Governance and Policy-Driven Smart Cities

European cities such as Amsterdam, Barcelona, and London emphasize sustainability and data privacy in their smart city strategies. The European Union's Smart Cities Marketplace initiative has driven regional collaboration, ensuring cities follow standardized governance models and cybersecurity frameworks. Europe's strong focus on environmental sustainability and citizen engagement sets it apart from other regions (Ulfik, 2024).

5.2.3. Asia-Pacific – Rapid Smart City Growth and Digital Transformation

Countries like Singapore, South Korea, and Japan are at the forefront of smart city development in the Asia-Pacific region. Singapore, in particular, has implemented nationwide IoT networks, AI-driven governance, and digital identity systems to improve urban living. However, countries such as India and Indonesia still face infrastructure challenges, requiring increased investments and policy improvements (Sanada & Zappa, 2025).

5.2.4. Middle East – Smart Cities Driven by Mega Investments

The Middle East has witnessed rapid progress in smart city initiatives, driven by large-scale government investments. Cities like Dubai, Riyadh, and Doha have focused on AI-powered infrastructure, smart transportation, and digital governance. However, the region still faces cybersecurity concerns, requiring stronger regulatory measures to ensure data security and privacy (Taleb, 2024).

5.2.5. Latin America – Emerging Smart Cities with Investment Challenges

Smart city adoption in Latin America is growing, with cities like Bogotá, Mexico City, and São Paulo implementing digital governance and smart mobility solutions. However, limited financial resources, weak cybersecurity measures, and fragmented policies slow down the widespread implementation of smart city technologies. Public-private partnerships (PPPs) are increasingly being used to overcome these challenges (Mutambik, 2024).

5.2.6. Africa – Early-Stage Smart City Development

Africa lags behind in smart city development due to infrastructure limitations, lack of digital literacy, and low investment levels. However, cities like Nairobi, Cape Town, and Kigali are pioneering digital transformation projects, focusing on mobile-based solutions, IoT-powered energy grids, and smart urban planning. Greater international collaboration and investment will be critical for Africa's smart city growth (Agyemang et al., 2024).

5.2.7. South Asia – Growth Potential with Infrastructure Challenges

South Asian cities such as New Delhi, Mumbai, and Colombo are gradually adopting smart city technologies. India's Smart Cities Mission has driven digital urban transformation, but poor connectivity, financial constraints, and weak cybersecurity regulations remain obstacles. Strengthening infrastructure and digital governance policies will be key to advancing smart city adoption in the region (Chakraborty et al., 2024).

The implementation of smart city technologies varies widely across regions, influenced by infrastructure development, policy frameworks, investment levels, and cybersecurity preparedness. North America and Europe lead in successful smart city adoption, while Asia-Pacific and the Middle East are rapidly advancing. In contrast, Latin America, South Asia, and Africa require further investments, regulatory improvements, and stronger digital infrastructure to fully realize their smart city potential. Understanding these regional differences helps identify key challenges and opportunities, shaping strategic recommendations for future smart city initiatives. The following section will discuss policy directions and best practices for strengthening smart city implementation across the globe.

6. FUTURE DIRECTIONS AND POLICY RECOMMENDATIONS

To successfully implement smart city technologies in developing countries, it is essential to adopt strategic policies, innovative approaches, and collaborative frameworks. These directions not only address existing challenges but also unlock new opportunities for sustainable urban development. The following recommendations provide a roadmap for governments, private enterprises, and international organizations to maximize the benefits of smart city initiatives. Figure 3 shows the Stakeholder roles in smart city development.

6.1. Strengthening Digital Infrastructure

Developing countries must prioritize the development of robust digital infrastructure, including high-speed internet, cloud computing, and smart grids. Investing in 5G networks and expanding broadband access are critical to ensuring seamless connectivity for smart city applications such as IoT devices, real-time data analytics, and digital governance platforms. Governments should encourage public-private partnerships (PPPs) to mobilize resources and leverage private sector expertise for infrastructure development. For example, Rwanda's collaboration with international telecommunications companies to expand 4G coverage nationwide has significantly improved digital connectivity, enabling the deployment of smart city solutions such as intelligent traffic management and digital public services (M. S. H. Ansari & Mehrotra, 2022).

6.2. Promoting Public-Private Partnerships (PPPs)

Public-Private Partnerships play a crucial role in accelerating smart city development by leveraging the financial resources, technological expertise, and innovation capabilities of the private sector. Governments should create conducive regulatory frameworks and financial incentives to attract private investments in smart infrastructure projects. Transparent and flexible PPP models are essential to ensure mutual benefits and sustainable collaborations. For example, India's Smart Cities Mission actively involves private technology firms and international organizations, leading to successful implementations of smart mobility solutions and digital governance platforms.

6.3. Establishing Clear Policy and Regulatory Frameworks

To ensure the secure and efficient deployment of smart city technologies, developing countries need to establish standardized policies and regulatory frameworks. These should cover data governance, cybersecurity, data privacy, and interoperability standards. Robust cybersecurity laws are essential to protect citizens' personal data and prevent cyber threats, while data governance policies ensure transparent and ethical data usage. Policy standardization also promotes system interoperability, facilitating seamless integration across various smart city platforms. Singapore's Smart Nation initiative serves as a model, demonstrating the importance of clear regulatory frameworks in enabling secure and efficient digital ecosystems.

6.4. Enhancing Digital Literacy and Capacity Building

Bridging the digital divide and promoting digital inclusion requires significant investments in digital literacy programs and capacity building. Governments should collaborate with educational institutions, international organizations, and technology firms to provide digital skills training and technical education, empowering citizens to participate in the digital economy. This approach also addresses the shortage of skilled professionals required for the maintenance and management of smart city infrastructure (Kumar Sahu et al., n.d.). For example, South Africa's Digital Skills Development Initiative offers coding and digital literacy programs to students and job seekers, fostering a digitally skilled workforce.

6.5. Emphasizing Environmental Sustainability and Resilience

Smart city initiatives must prioritize environmental sustainability by integrating renewable energy solutions, smart waste management systems, and sustainable urban mobility options. Governments should promote the adoption of green technologies, such as solar and wind energy, through financial incentives, tax benefits, and supportive policies. Additionally, smart cities should incorporate disaster resilience strategies, including predictive analytics, real-time monitoring systems, and AI-driven disaster management platforms. Japan's AI-based earthquake early warning system is an excellent example of enhancing urban resilience through predictive analytics and real-time data monitoring.

6.6. Fostering International Collaboration and Knowledge Exchange

International collaboration and knowledge exchange are essential for developing countries to learn from global best practices and adopt innovative smart city solutions. Governments should actively engage with international organizations, smart city networks, and global technology firms to gain technical expertise, funding, and policy guidance. Collaborative research and development initiatives enable local startups to innovate and develop context-specific solutions. For example, the ASEAN Smart Cities Network facilitates cross-border collaboration among Southeast Asian countries, promoting knowledge sharing and joint smart city projects.

6.7. Encouraging Community Participation and Stakeholder Engagement

Smart city development should be citizen-centric, ensuring that urban solutions address the real needs of communities. Governments should encourage community participation and stakeholder engagement through public consultations, digital feedback platforms, and participatory urban planning. Involving citizens in decision-making processes enhances public trust, ensures inclusivity, and promotes the adoption of digital governance systems. For instance, Barcelona's Decidim platform enables citizens to participate in policymaking, ensuring transparent and participatory governance.

6.8. Investing in Research and Innovation

To drive continuous improvement and innovation in smart city solutions, governments should invest in research and development (R&D) initiatives. Collaborations with academic institutions, technology firms, and startups foster innovation and facilitate the development of cutting-edge urban technologies. Additionally, governments should establish smart city testbeds and innovation hubs, allowing startups and researchers to experiment with emerging technologies. For example, Singapore's Smart Nation Sandbox provides a platform for startups to test and pilot new urban solutions, accelerating the commercialization of innovative technologies.

Figure 3. Stakeholder roles in smart city development

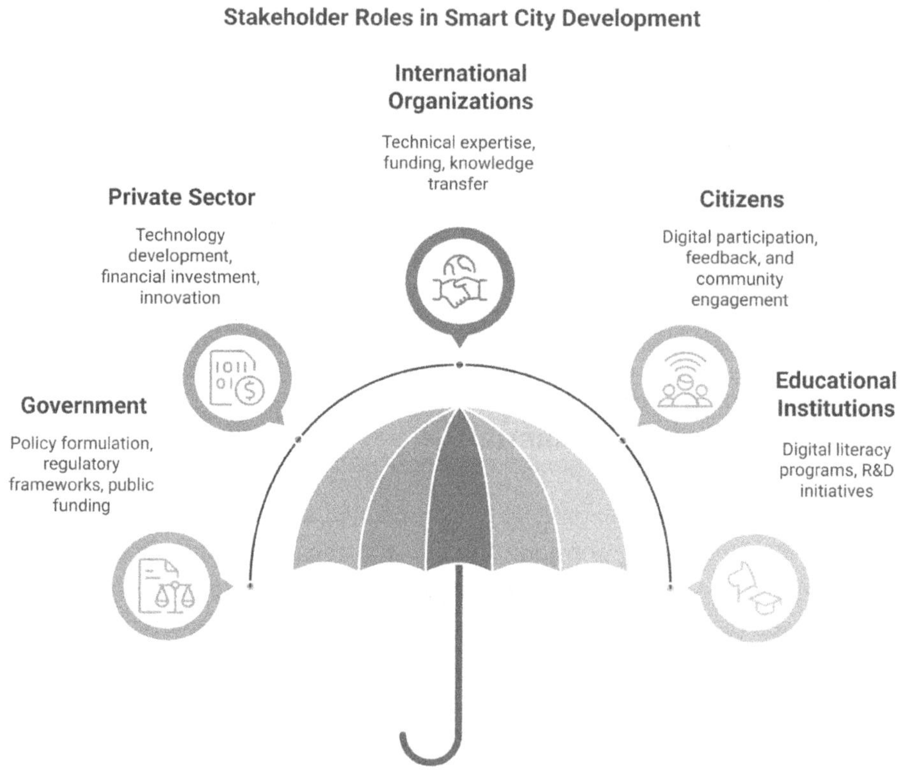

The successful implementation of smart city technologies in developing countries requires a holistic approach, encompassing strategic infrastructure investments, public-private partnerships, clear regulatory frameworks, and citizen-centric urban planning. By strengthening digital infrastructure, enhancing digital literacy, fostering international collaboration, and prioritizing environmental sustainability, developing countries can overcome existing challenges and unlock the transformative potential of smart city solutions. Governments, private enterprises, international organizations, and local communities must work collaboratively to create inclusive, sustainable, resilient urban ecosystems. By adopting these strategic policy recommendations and future directions, developing countries can pave the way for the next generation of smart cities, driving sustainable urban growth and improving the quality of life for their citizens.

7. CONCLUSION

The successful implementation of smart city technologies in developing countries requires a comprehensive and strategic approach. This involves strengthening digital infrastructure, fostering public-private partnerships, establishing clear regulatory frameworks, enhancing digital literacy, and prioritizing environmental sustainability. By adopting these strategies, developing nations can effectively overcome the challenges associated with infrastructural deficiencies, financial constraints, policy barriers, and technological gaps. Developing countries have the advantage of leapfrogging traditional infrastructure systems by directly adopting modern, cost-effective smart technologies. This enables them to bypass outdated systems and invest in state-of-the-art solutions such as mobile-based services, smart grids integrated with renewable energy, and digital governance platforms. For instance, countries like Kenya and India have demonstrated the transformative potential of smart technologies in financial inclusion and urban mobility, respectively. Public-Private Partnerships (PPPs) play a crucial role in mobilizing investments and leveraging technological expertise from the private sector. These partnerships facilitate resource sharing, innovation, and efficient implementation of smart city projects. Additionally, international collaborations with organizations such as the World Bank and UN-Habitat provide technical expertise, funding, and policy guidance, helping developing countries navigate financial and infrastructural challenges. Clear regulatory frameworks are essential for ensuring secure and efficient deployment of smart city technologies. Policies related to data governance, cybersecurity, and technology interoperability promote transparency, data security, and system integration. Countries like Singapore have set examples by implementing robust cybersecurity frameworks and standardized data governance policies, ensuring public trust and effective digital ecosystems. Digital literacy and capacity building are critical for bridging the digital divide and promoting social inclusion. By investing in digital education and skills development, developing countries can empower citizens to participate in the digital economy and benefit from smart city services. This also addresses the shortage of skilled professionals required for maintaining smart city infrastructure.

Environmental sustainability and urban resilience are key pillars of smart city development. Integrating renewable energy solutions, smart waste management systems, and intelligent transportation systems ensures sustainable resource management and reduces carbon footprints. Additionally, predictive analytics and real-time monitoring systems enhance disaster resilience and urban safety. By strategically implementing these policy recommendations and future directions, developing countries can transform urban landscapes, enhance governance, and improve the quality of life for their citizens. The collaborative efforts of governments, private enterprises, international organizations, and local communities are crucial for creating inclusive, efficient, and sustainable smart cities. This strategic approach paves the way for the next generation of urban ecosystems, ensuring a future that is resilient, innovative, and sustainable.

REFERENCES

Abbas, K., Tawalbeh, L. A., Rafiq, A., Muthanna, A., Elgendy, I. A., & Abd El-Latif, A. A. (2021). Convergence of blockchain and IoT for secure transportation systems in smart cities. *Security and Communication Networks*, *2021*(1), 5597679. DOI: 10.1155/2021/5597679

Agyemang, E., Anderson, B., Patiño, J., & Tremolieres, M. (2024). Toward achieving smart cities in Africa: Challenges to data use and the way forward. *Data & Policy*, *6*, e13.

Al-Sudaimi, M. Z. (2024). Developing, Enhancing, and Solving Problems of Transportation System in Addis Ababa. *Labyrinth: Fayoum Journal of Science and Interdisciplinary Studies*, 2(2), 69–78.

Al-Worafi, Y. M. (2023). Healthcare facilities in developing countries: infrastructure. In *Handbook of medical and health sciences in developing countries: Education, practice, and research* (pp. 1–21). Springer.

Almarri, K., & Boussabaine, H. (2023). Critical success factors for public–private partnerships in smart city infrastructure projects. *Construction Innovation*. Advance online publication. DOI: 10.1108/CI-01-2022-0020

Ansari, A., Dutt, D., & Kumar, V. (2024). Revolutionizing urban Waste: Eco-Innovation for Saharanpur's sustainability (Class-II urban Centers). *Waste Management Bulletin*, *2*(1), 184–190. https://doi.org/https://doi.org/10.1016/j.wmb.2024.01.006

Ansari, M. S. H., & Mehrotra, M. (2019). Development of smart cities and its sustainability: A smart city framework. *International Journal of Innovative Technology and Exploring Engineering*, *8*(11), 646–655.

Ansari, M. S. H., & Mehrotra, M. (2020). Securing M2M communication in Smart Cities. *2020 International Conference for Emerging Technology (INCET)*, 1–4.

Ansari, M. S. H., & Mehrotra, M. (2022). IoT Technologies, Security Attacks and their Security Measures under Smart City Framework. *Grenze International Journal of Engineering & Technology (GIJET)*, *8*(2).

Chakraborty, B., & Parkhi, A. Nishant, & Saha, R. K. (2024). India's smart City mission through the lens of sustainable development goals. In *SDGs in the Asia and Pacific Region* (pp. 1519–1548). Springer.

Dwivedi, U., Rajawat, A. S., Goyal, S. B., Faisal, S., Sulakhe, V. N., & Sudhir, M. (2024). AI-Enabled UAVs for Advanced Network Management in the Era of 6G Communications. In Vasant, P., Panchenko, V., Munapo, E., Weber, G.-W., Thomas, J. J., Intan, R., & Shamsul Arefin, M. (Eds.), *Intelligent Computing and Optimization* (pp. 349–358). Springer Nature Switzerland.

Farooqui, N. A., Ashraf, I., & Jaiswal, R. (2024). Modernizing healthcare through IoT-based e-health systems. In *Intelligent Networks* (pp. 318–330). CRC Press.

Farooqui, N. A., Mehra, R., & Faridi, S. B. (2023). An intellectual analysis of structural healthcare systems in India using intelligence-based techniques. In *Security Implementation in Internet of Medical Things* (pp. 37–58). CRC Press.

Gandhi, P., Bhatia, S., Kumar, A., Alojail, M. A., & Rathore, P. S. (2020). *Internet of Things in Business Transformation: Developing an Engineering and Business Strategy for Industry 5.0*. John Wiley & Sons.

Gautam, V., Sunidhi, S., & Prasad, S. (2025). AI-Powered Surveillance for Smart Cities. In *Internet of Vehicles and Computer Vision Solutions for Smart City Transformations* (pp. 245–265). Springer. DOI: 10.1007/978-3-031-72959-1_11

Gupta, D. N., Kumar, R., & Ansari, S. H. (2022). Federated learning for an iot application. In *Federated Learning for IoT Applications* (pp. 53–66). Springer. DOI: 10.1007/978-3-030-85559-8_4

Hassan, R. J., Zeebaree, S. R., Ameen, S. Y., Kak, S. F., Sadeeq, M. A., Ageed, Z. S., AL-Zebari, A., & Salih, A. A. (2021). State of art survey for iot effects on smart city technology: Challenges, opportunities, and solutions. *Asian Journal of Research in Computer Science*, *22*, 32–48. DOI: 10.9734/ajrcos/2021/v8i330202

Jan, Z., Ahamed, F., Mayer, W., Patel, N., Grossmann, G., Stumptner, M., & Kuusk, A. (2023). Artificial intelligence for industry 4.0: Systematic review of applications, challenges, and opportunities. *Expert Systems with Applications*, *216*, 119456. DOI: 10.1016/j.eswa.2022.119456

Karimi, H., Ghadirifaraz, B., Shetab Boushehri, S. N., Hosseininasab, S.-M., & Rafiei, N. (2021). Reducing traffic congestion and increasing sustainability in special urban areas through one-way traffic reconfiguration. *Transportation*, 1–24.

Kitika, C., & Suwatcharapinun, S. (2024). Smart district with the comparison on urban studies of internet infrastructure and new digital activities A case study of Chiang Mai Old City, Thailand. *International Review for Spatial Planning and Sustainable Development*, *12*(3), 200–217. DOI: 10.14246/irspsd.12.3_200

Kumar Sahu, V., Pandey, D., Singh, P., Haque Ansari, M. S., Khan, A., Varish, N., & Khan, M. W. (n.d.). An empirical analysis of evolutionary computing approaches for IoT security assessment. *Journal of Intelligent & Fuzzy Systems, Preprint*, 1–13.

Malodia, S., Dhir, A., Mishra, M., & Bhatti, Z. A. (2021). Future of e-Government: An integrated conceptual framework. *Technological Forecasting and Social Change, 173*, 121102. https://doi.org/https://doi.org/10.1016/j.techfore.2021.121102. DOI: 10.1016/j.techfore.2021.121102

Martins, P., Hojda, A., & de Moraes Batista Simão, M. (2025). City Command and Control Centers as Think Tanks for Organization of Big Events. In Autero, A., de Moraes Batista Simao, M., & Karppi, I. (Eds.), *Smart Urban Safety and Security: Interdisciplinary Perspectives* (pp. 225–262). Springer Nature Singapore., DOI: 10.1007/978-981-97-2196-2_11

Masik, G., Sagan, I., & Scott, J. W. (2021). Smart City strategies and new urban development policies in the Polish context. *Cities (London, England), 108*, 102970. DOI: 10.1016/j.cities.2020.102970

Mutambik, I. (2024). Unlocking the Potential of Sustainable Smart Cities: Barriers and Strategies. *Sustainability (Basel), 16*(12), 5061. DOI: 10.3390/su16125061

Padrón Nápoles, V. M., Gachet Páez, D., Esteban Penelas, J. L., García Pérez, O., Martín de Pablos, F., & Muñoz Gil, R. (2021). Social inclusion in smart cities. In *Handbook of smart cities* (pp. 469–514). Springer. DOI: 10.1007/978-3-030-69698-6_42

Rana, A. (2023). *Strategies For Redevelopment In Context Of Smart City.*

Razmjoo, A., Østergaard, P. A., Denai, M., Nezhad, M. M., & Mirjalili, S. (2021). Effective policies to overcome barriers in the development of smart cities. *Energy Research & Social Science, 79*, 102175. DOI: 10.1016/j.erss.2021.102175

Richardson, N. (2021). Emergency Response Planning: Leveraging Machine Learning for Real-Time Decision-Making. *Emergency (Tehran, Iran), 4*, 14.

Sadeeq, M. M., Abdulkareem, N. M., Zeebaree, S. R. M., Ahmed, D. M., Sami, A. S., & Zebari, R. R. (2021). IoT and Cloud computing issues, challenges and opportunities: A review. *Qubahan Academic Journal, 1*(2), 1–7. DOI: 10.48161/qaj.v1n2a36

Sanada, K., & Zappa, M. (2025). Japan's international cooperation on smart city development in Asia: International effort beneath the smart rhetoric in India and in Thailand. *Research in Globalization*, 100270.

Sha, K., & Taeihagh, A. (2024). Designing adaptive policy packages for inclusive smart cities: Lessons from Singapore's smart nation program. *Sustainable Cities and Society, 115*, 105868. https://doi.org/https://doi.org/10.1016/j.scs.2024.105868. DOI: 10.1016/j.scs.2024.105868

Sindakis, S., & Showkat, G. (2024). The digital revolution in India: Bridging the gap in rural technology adoption. *Journal of Innovation and Entrepreneurship, 13*(1), 29. DOI: 10.1186/s13731-024-00380-w

Sridharan, N., Ray, R., & Soni, A. (2017). *From Smart Agriculture to Smart Economy: Case of Vijayawada City Region. Smart Economy in Smart Cities: International Collaborative Research: Ottawa, St. Louis, Stuttgart, Bologna, Cape Town, Nairobi, Dakar, Lagos, New Delhi, Varanasi, Vijayawada*. Kozhikode.

Taleb, L. (2024). Challenges of Smart Sustainable Cities in the Middle East. *Available atSSRN* 4985808. DOI: 10.2139/ssrn.4985808

Ulfik, A. (2024). Innovative and Smart Cities of the Future. In *The Use of Information and Communication Technologies (ICT) in the Management of the Innovative and Smart City* (pp. 19–40). CRC Press. DOI: 10.1201/9781003465157-2

Ullah, A., Anwar, S. M., Li, J., Nadeem, L., Mahmood, T., Rehman, A., & Saba, T. (2024). Smart cities: The role of Internet of Things and machine learning in realizing a data-centric smart environment. *Complex & Intelligent Systems, 10*(1), 1607–1637. DOI: 10.1007/s40747-023-01175-4

Umeh, C. A., Nwankwo, A. U., Oluka, P. O., Umeh, C. L., & Ogbonnaya, A. L. (2024). The role of renewable energies for sustainable energy governance and environmental policies for the mitigation of climate change in Nigeria. *European Journal of Applied Science. Engineering and Technology, 2*(2), 71–98.

Zaidi, T., & Faisal, S. (2018). An overview: Various attacks in VANET. *2018 4th International Conference on Computing Communication and Automation (ICCCA)*, 1–6.

Zikria, Y., Ali, R., Afzal, M. K., & Kim, S. W. (2021). Next-generation internet of things (iot): Opportunities, challenges, and solutions. *Sensors (Basel), 21*(4), 1174. DOI: 10.3390/s21041174 PMID: 33562343

Chapter 19
Comprehensive Framework for Smart City Assessment Indicators, Methods, and Practical Applications

Ali Maqousi
https://orcid.org/0000-0002-3242-804X
Department of Information Security, University of Petra, Amman, Jordan

Ahmad Al-Qerem
https://orcid.org/0000-0003-2187-6194
Computer Science Department, Faculty of Information Technology, Zarqa University, Jordan

Kashinath Basu
https://orcid.org/0000-0002-0831-3752
Department of Computing and Communication Technologies, Oxford Brookes University, UK

Saad Alateef
https://orcid.org/0009-0002-3219-0833
School of Computing Science, Newcastle University, UK

ABSTRACT

This chapter examines smart city assessment practices in relation to urban development strategies. It addresses the ongoing challenge of selecting robust indicators and deploying methodological tools that capture complex urban processes. The

DOI: 10.4018/979-8-3373-1375-7.ch019

objective is to propose a comprehensive assessment framework that integrates context-specific requirements with systematically derived evaluation criteria. A mixed-methods approach was adopted, drawing on empirical case reviews and existing standards. The findings revealed critical dimensions influencing project design, implementation, and stakeholder engagement. They also highlighted convergences in global guidance on performance tracking. The results suggest that cities can refine their evaluation processes by aligning them with clearly articulated priorities. This chapter contributes an adaptable framework that can guide practitioners in various urban contexts.

1. INTRODUCTION

Cities have grown in size and complexity, prompting analyses on how to manage resources and services under mounting social, economic, and environmental pressures (Albino, Berardi, & Dangelico, 2015). Decision-makers turn to digital innovations and integrated policy strategies to address these pressing concerns. Although "smart city" initiatives embrace the inclusion of technology-driven systems for transportation, energy, governance, and other domains, the concept remains multifaceted (Angelidou, 2017). Diverse interpretations and aims have generated varying approaches to implementation and evaluation (Nam, 2019). As these initiatives evolve, researchers recognize the urgency for more unified and systematic frameworks that facilitate accurate assessments of both existing and planned interventions (Patrão, Moura, & de Almeida, 2020). Many cities that aim to enhance quality of life, environmental stewardship, and economic viability have endeavored to adopt data and technology in daily operations, yet their progress is rarely comparable in uniform ways (Joss, Cook, & Dayot, 2017). Although several indicator sets and rating systems exist, clear consensus on how to ensure robust evaluations remains elusive (Sharifi, 2019). Each city appears unique, shaped by governance patterns, resource availability, and societal priorities (Meijer & Bolívar, 2016). This diversity underscores the need for an assessment framework that identifies relevant dimensions while preserving adaptability.

The phenomenon of urban digitization has led many local governments to adopt solutions involving real-time data analytics, Internet of Things platforms, and other emergent tools (Hashem et al., 2016). Such transformations prompt queries regarding the appropriate design of monitoring systems that capture progress in inclusive and comprehensive ways (Trindade et al., 2017). Existing literature emphasizes the challenges encountered in aligning technical, policy, and social objectives within singular assessment designs (Bibri & Krogstie, 2017). Standardization bodies, including the International Telecommunication Union (ITU) and the International Organization for Standardization (ISO), have devised recommendations for performance metrics (International Telecommunication Union, 2016; International Organization for Standardization, 2019). Local administrations, however, often face difficulties adopting these guidelines without adjustments. In that sense, clarity emerges about the need for frameworks that can incorporate established global benchmarks while enabling flexibility (British Standards Institution, 2014; European Commission, Joint Research Centre, 2019).

Understanding the background of this evolution is essential. Policymakers and scholars have moved from seeing technology as an external factor to be appended to urban planning, toward a more integrated vision of built environments and digital ecosystems (Gil-García, Pardo, & Nam, 2015). New governance models seek to transform collaborative practices, public engagement, and trust-building in local affairs (Meijer & Bolívar, 2016). Meanwhile, the impetus to achieve sustainability targets shapes broad objectives, reinforcing attention on resource efficiency, carbon mitigation, and equitable service access (Ahvenniemi, Huovila, Pinto-Seppä, & Airaksinen, 2017). Multiple vantage points must be reconciled to generate meaningful evaluation criteria. By addressing these overlapping layers, it becomes possible to devise a systematic framework that illuminates performance and identifies pathways for refinement (Sharifi, 2019).

Section 1 sets out the fundamental context for understanding why cities seek consistent approaches for evaluating smart city strategies. Section 2 tracks the emergence and evolution of relevant assessment perspectives. Section 3 explores core indicators that appear in varied standardization efforts. Section 4 reviews prevalent methods for data collection and analysis. Section 5 outlines a conceptual framework that unites these elements in a structured approach. Section 6 examines case illustrations to validate the proposed method in practice, while Section 7 discusses broader applications. Section 8 highlights key obstacles in real-world adoption and governance processes. Section 9 offers conclusive insights, suggesting future directions for refining assessment protocols. Through this comprehensive investigation, the chapter aims to propose a scalable model that can aid decision-makers, researchers, and stakeholders in systematically appraising smart city interventions.

Current urban challenges are characterized by three major problems which include environmental modifications and population pressures and structural inequalities (Bibri & Krogstie, 2017). City administrations have created smart initiatives for condition management that span from digital service delivery to data-based policy generation (Allam & Dhunny, 2019). Success at implementing solutions depends on technology but requires more than the adoption of new devices or platforms for an accurate assessment. Generating full benefits assessments incorporates multiple substantial elements like social inclusion together with economic viability and sustainability alongside governance. Several initiatives keep depending on basic performance metrics that give limited understanding of city-wide effects (Sharifi, 2019). Several conflicting sets of standards and strong methodologies continue to remain fragmented while multiple frameworks exist independently of uniform standards (Patrão et al., 2020). A better understanding of this deficit serves as the foundation for adopting a unified solution.

Several studies note that conceptual ambiguity has led to an overemphasis on technology rather than broader transformative goals (Kummitha & Crutzen, 2017). Some interpret smart city developments as primarily hardware-oriented expansions, emphasizing sensors and networks. Others prioritize citizen engagement and novel policy processes that hinge on open data and collaborative approaches (Joss et al., 2017). Discrepancies persist in which indicators and dimensions deserve prominence. Moreover, city-specific contexts—geography, size, demographic patterns, resource constraints—further complicate attempts at standardized evaluation (Mora, Deakin, & Reid, 2019). A harmonized but adaptive framework could mitigate inconsistencies while respecting local differences.

The chapter thus asserts that although partial solutions exist, there remains a need for a comprehensive framework that clarifies a) which indicators matter most for diverse urban goals, b) how to gather relevant evidence and interpret results systematically, and c) how to integrate findings into governance structures (Meijer & Bolívar, 2016). By undertaking a broad examination of the literature, international standards, and real-world cases, this text aims to present a structured methodology for urban stakeholders worldwide.

The primary aim is to formulate a holistic smart city assessment model grounded in scholarly research, best-practice examples, and recognized standards (Nam, 2019; Sharifi, 2019). Specifically, the objectives include reviewing existing definitions of smart city success, identifying core elements that appear in recognized indicator sets, synthesizing methodologies for measuring and analyzing relevant data, and contextualizing these elements in an adaptable evaluation framework. The chapter also aims to provide practical illustrations of how these ideas manifest in actual city contexts. It addresses methodological tools that facilitate comprehensive data gathering, bridging policy considerations and measurable outcomes. By focusing on both theoretical underpinnings and practical realities, the proposed model aspires to offer guidance with global applicability.

2. HISTORICAL EVOLUTION OF SMART CITY ASSESSMENT

Smart city assessments have evolved alongside the development of digital and urban policies. Initially, the 1990s and early 2000s saw city managers experimenting with information and communication technologies to optimize services. At the time, measurement tended to revolve around internet penetration, basic connectivity, or e-government readiness (Calzada, 2020). Over time, broader sustainability agendas, spurred by global climate agreements and local activism, expanded the scope of assessments (UN-Habitat, 2022). Cities began measuring energy efficiency, water consumption, and transportation patterns under the banner of "sustainable urban development" (Angelidou, 2017). The term "smart city" gained traction around the mid-2000s, reflecting a convergence of digital infrastructure, environmental stewardship, and citizen-centric governance (Albino et al., 2015). At that stage, many analyses focused on technology adoption rates or project-based achievements.

Subsequent years witnessed attempts to formalize the concept. Scholars sought to unify "smart" and "sustainable" city principles, acknowledging that technology alone does not guarantee long-term prosperity if underlying governance remains siloed (Bibri & Krogstie, 2017; Ahvenniemi et al., 2017). National programs emerged to guide cities through structured approaches, such as India's Smart Cities Mission (Ministry of Urban Development, Government of India, 2015). International organizations developed standards to promote consistent data collection and reporting. The British Standards Institution introduced PAS 181 for strategic guidance in 2014, and ISO built on existing sustainable city indicators with a specific focus on smart elements (British Standards Institution, 2014; International Organization for Standardization, 2019). Although these standards provided frameworks, city administrations often customized them to fit local priorities.

Evaluation grew increasingly sophisticated with the integration of big data analytics, real-time sensors, and machine-learning algorithms (Allam & Dhunny, 2019). Researchers recognized that classical performance indicators lacked the granularity and dynamism to capture the pace of urban digitalization. Emphasis shifted toward resilience, adaptability, and inclusive growth (Organisation for Economic Co-operation and Development, 2020). During this period, many programs sought to incorporate equity measures, bridging digital divides and ensuring that marginalized communities benefitted from new services (Deloitte Center for Government Insights, 2019). By blending social, economic, environmental, and technological indicators, stakeholders realized that a singular emphasis on infrastructure is insufficient (Joss et al., 2017). This historical evolution underscores the layered nature of assessment practices and foreshadows ongoing debates about what constitutes a balanced evaluation system.

2.1. Contemporary Approaches to Standards and Guidelines

The evaluation of modern cities depends on guideline systems developed by several institutions. ISO 37122:2019 presents standardized indicators for smart urban environments as a continuation of the indicators available in ISO 37120 which covers city service delivery and quality of life evaluation (International Organization for Standardization, 2019). IT prescribes KPIs for intelligent sustainable urban centers that measure performance within three domains consisting of connectivity and sustainability alongside quality of life (International Telecommunication Union, 2016). The European Commission through its Smart City Guidance Package seeks to unify energy management with mobility operations and ICT improvements by promoting combined strategy planning and execution (European Innovation Partnership on Smart Cities and Communities, 2018). The Smart Cities Council developed the Smart Cities Readiness Guide which demonstrates the requirement for ready leadership and management capabilities under the concept of "governance readiness" (Smart Cities Council, 2017).

Such guidelines do not serve as strict regulations but rather as reference points that help cities assemble relevant metrics. National-level policies, including the United States National Institute of Standards and Technology (NIST) Key Performance Indicators framework, further illustrate how local contexts shape recommended indicators (National Institute of Standards and Technology, 2022). The result is a multifaceted mosaic in which local governments face the challenge of selecting from multiple overlapping sets of indicators. Many city leaders voice confusion over which framework to prioritize, or how to reconcile divergences among them (Myeong, Jung, & Lee, 2018). This complexity explains why many municipalities still adopt selective approaches, favoring indicators that align best with immediate goals. The present chapter advocates a comprehensive approach that harmonizes these global standards without sacrificing contextual nuances (Sharifi, 2019).

2.2. Role of Stakeholders in Shaping Assessment Practices

Assessment criteria do not emerge in a vacuum. Stakeholders such as municipal officials, private-sector firms, civic groups, and international organizations shape the focus of measurement (Angelidou, 2017). Large technology vendors might stress connectivity indicators that reflect the robustness of digital infrastructure, while community advocates highlight equity and inclusiveness. Environmental organizations underscore resource efficiency, and local governments seek direct links to financial feasibility (Van Zoonen, 2016). Scholars thus point out that indicator selection is often a negotiation among varied priorities. Although standardization bodies and global indexes, such as the IESE Cities in Motion Index (Berrone & Ricart, 2020) or the IMD Smart City Index (IMD Smart City Observatory, 2023), attempt to offer neutral perspectives, they inevitably embed assumptions about which dimensions matter most.

Public engagement in assessment design can guide more equitable outcomes. Cities with robust participatory processes sometimes co-create indicators alongside local communities, leading to metrics that resonate more closely with local realities (Nam, 2019). This participatory element becomes particularly significant for underrepresented groups. Without inclusive processes, data might obscure or exclude certain experiences (Deloitte Center for Government Insights, 2019). Indeed, the direction of future measurement systems may hinge on balancing top-down benchmarks and bottom-up knowledge (Meijer & Bolívar, 2016). A thorough framework must thus consider stakeholder diversity, not merely in the final selection of indicators but also in governance mechanisms that shape how data is collected and interpreted.

3. CORE INDICATORS IN SMART CITY EVALUATION

Indicators serve as visible signals of performance, offering tangible benchmarks for monitoring progress (Sharifi, 2019). They transform abstract goals, such as "improved quality of life," into measurable factors tied to real-world conditions. Although standard frameworks vary, many share core thematic areas that include economy, society, environment, governance, technology infrastructure, and mobility (Myeong et al., 2018). By uniting these domains, evaluations can capture cross-cutting issues and avoid narrow conceptions of "smartness." This section reviews widely referenced categories, gleaned from international standards and scholarly research, that constitute a foundation for any comprehensive assessment strategy.

3.1. Economy and Innovation

The measurement of economic growth alongside entrepreneurship and technology-based job development represents typical urban indicator selection (Rodríguez-Bolívar, 2015). The density of startups and research collaborations with innovation hubs allow the monitoring of digital infrastructure's effects on market competitiveness and productivity (Kummitha & Crutzen, 2017). The wider evaluative structures may consist of assessments for economic diversity and resilience. The focus of city rankings differs between global competitiveness and foreign direct investment attraction since smaller cities value local business vitality and digital literacy according to Komninos (2015). The different systems of assessment frequently produce uncertainties about what really makes an economy thrive. Solid measurement approaches will establish how technological projects affect sustainable growth alongside inclusivity development. The measurement model includes data on patent applications along with online business growth and startup development programs (Mora et al., 2019). These quantitative measurements show direct progress indicators for an innovative economic development.

3.2. Social Inclusion and Citizen Engagement

The smart city discourse now focuses more on inclusivity together with civic participation as Joss et al (2017) argue. The degree to which citizens participate in digital consultations alongside participatory budgeting initiatives serves as usual performance indicators. Knowledge programs which teach digital literacy serve as a fundamental dimension to reduce digital inequalities (Deloitte Center for Government Insights, 2019). Various assessment approaches incorporate service accessibility metrics that provide data about broadband distribution across low-income residential areas according to Van Zoonen (2016). A high number of unique community-led hackathons alongside different collaborative events demonstrate community engagement. Local citizen satisfaction toward e-government platform functions serves as one evaluation criterion (Gil-García et al., 2015). Sophisticated social outcome assessment now includes pooled information from citizen surveys since metrics alone do not fully reveal social system changes (Meijer & Bolívar, 2016).

3.3. Environmental Sustainability

Indicators related to environmental sustainability vary significantly. Classic examples include tracking carbon emissions, waste management efficiency, and air quality (Trindade et al., 2017). Some protocols focus on renewable energy adoption, such as solar panel installations or microgrid deployments (UN-Habitat, 2022). Water resource management and green space expansion also appear among frequently cited categories. In a smart city context, technology-based solutions such as intelligent lighting systems or sensor-based waste collection can reduce consumption and optimize resource allocation (Mohanty, Choppali, & Kougianos, 2016). Yet measuring environmental outcomes calls for consistent methodologies over extended periods. Comparisons among cities require standardized baselines (International Organization for Standardization, 2018). As environmental conditions shift under climate change, more frameworks incorporate resilience measures that capture a city's capacity to cope with or adapt to severe weather events (Bibri & Krogstie, 2017).

3.4. Governance and Policy

Governance-oriented indicators scrutinize institutional readiness, policy integration, and regulatory environments (Meijer & Bolívar, 2016). Many efforts focus on transparency measures, open data availability, or public trust in digital services (Hashem et al., 2016). Others track interdepartmental collaboration, reflecting how well municipal agencies align efforts toward overarching goals (European Commission, Joint Research Centre, 2019). Some standards propose specific governance KPIs, covering strategic vision, leadership structures, and citizen engagement in decision-making (British Standards Institution, 2014). A thorough assessment will connect these governance aspects with cross-sector performance, examining how agile policy processes adapt to emerging conditions. As data privacy and cybersecurity gain prominence, relevant indicators must address legal frameworks, data protection policies, and the handling of personal information (Van Zoonen, 2016).

3.5. Technology Infrastructure

Infrastructure metrics have remained central to smart city evaluations, reflecting connectivity, interoperability, and the presence of advanced communication networks (Albino et al., 2015). Indicators might quantify broadband speeds, coverage, or sensor density in public spaces (Hashem et al., 2016). Cloud adoption, data center capacity, and network reliability factor into technology readiness measures (Mora et al., 2019). The rise of the Internet of Things has expanded interest in real-time data analytics for traffic management, air quality monitoring, or public safety (Mohanty et al., 2016). A balanced assessment should not limit itself to describing hardware or software availability. The real question concerns how well these technological elements integrate with broader policy and societal aspirations (Kummitha & Crutzen, 2017). That alignment often separates cities that install solutions for show from those that embed them in a coherent vision of transformation.

3.6. Mobility and Transport

Mobility assessment focuses on how effectively cities integrate intelligent transportation systems, shared mobility services, and sustainable modes of travel (Berrone & Ricart, 2020). Indicators might assess public transport coverage, congestion levels, commute times, and adoption of electric or hybrid fleets (McKinsey Global Institute, 2018). Some frameworks track how digital apps enable route optimization or how integrated e-ticketing systems improve user convenience (European Innovation Partnership on Smart Cities and Communities, 2018). Safety outcomes, pedestrian friendliness, and cycling infrastructure can further illuminate the connectivity of urban spaces (IMD Smart City Observatory, 2023). As with other dimensions, collecting real-time data can strengthen evidence-based decisions, provided governance structures can handle, interpret, and secure that data (Nam, 2019). Mobility remains a core aspect because it influences economic productivity, environmental footprint, and overall quality of life.

Table 1 presents a concise sample of indicators gleaned from major frameworks. This set is not exhaustive but underscores recurring themes across global standards (International Telecommunication Union, 2016; International Organization for Standardization, 2019; Smart Cities Council, 2017).

Table 1. Illustrative Categories of Core Indicators

Category	Representative Indicators
Economy & Innovation	Startup density, R&D investment, digital entrepreneurship rates
Social Inclusion	Broadband access in underserved areas, civic participation, e-service uptake
Environmental	Carbon emissions, green space ratio, renewable energy penetration
Governance	Transparency scores, policy alignment, open data initiatives
Technology Infrastructure	Broadband speed, network coverage, sensor deployment, IoT data flows
Mobility & Transport	Public transport coverage, average commute times, adoption of electric mobility solutions

Each domain aligns with recognized dimensions in widely adopted smart city evaluations (Nam, 2019). Still, effective use of these indicators necessitates robust methods for data gathering and analysis.

4. METHODOLOGICAL APPROACHES FOR SMART CITY ASSESSMENT

Analysis methods must capture both the breadth and depth of urban dynamics. Researchers have used quantitative metrics, qualitative assessments, and mixed methods to evaluate performance. Quantitative approaches rely on numerical indicators aggregated into composite scores or indices, a format popular with policymakers seeking concise overviews (Yigitcanlar et al., 2018). Qualitative methods draw on interviews, focus groups, and ethnographies to uncover nuanced experiences, especially among marginalized communities (Meijer & Bolívar, 2016). Cities that combine these approaches can identify patterns and causal explanations more effectively (Gil-García et al., 2015). This section explores a selection of commonly employed methodological tools and addresses considerations for ensuring consistency and rigor.

4.1. Quantitative Metrics and Composite Indices

Quantitative measures typically form the backbone of city rankings and benchmarking exercises (Berrone & Ricart, 2020; IMD Smart City Observatory, 2023). By aggregating data on infrastructure, environment, or governance, analysts produce single scores for easier comparison. While straightforward to present, such composites can obscure internal variance (Kummitha & Crutzen, 2017). For instance, a city might excel in broadband penetration but lag in social inclusion. Weighted scoring systems attempt to account for varying importance among indicators. The weighting process, however, can prove subjective. Analysts must remain transparent about assumptions, data sources, and normalization procedures (Myeong et al., 2018). Rigor also depends on data availability and consistency across municipalities. Gaps in official statistics, differences in national accounting systems, and informal economies can reduce the reliability of purely quantitative approaches (Nam, 2019).

4.2. Qualitative Evaluations

Qualitative methods enrich understanding by capturing experiences that numbers alone cannot express (Joss et al., 2017). Researchers may conduct interviews with key stakeholders, including municipal officials, technology vendors, and community representatives. Focus groups can yield insights on how residents perceive changes in service delivery or public space enhancements (Deloitte Center for Government Insights, 2019). Ethnographic or observational methods further uncover the lived realities of interacting with digital applications or public Wi-Fi networks. Qualitative assessments can reveal hidden barriers to adoption or areas where technology fails to meet local needs. By highlighting perspectives that might not emerge in large datasets, these techniques promote more holistic evaluations. That said, qualitative data can be time-consuming to collect and interpret, making it less appealing for large-scale comparisons (Gil-García et al., 2015).

4.3. Mixed-Methods Frameworks

Combining quantitative and qualitative approaches addresses the shortcomings of relying on any single technique (Trindade et al., 2017). Mixed-methods frameworks typically involve collecting numerical data on key indicators while also gathering stakeholder feedback (Sharifi, 2019). The integration stage can use triangulation to cross-check findings, reinforcing validity. A city might show strong performance in broadband coverage but only moderate satisfaction levels among specific user groups. Investigating the discrepancy may clarify underlying issues. Mixed methods also allow layering of data over time, charting how new digital infrastructure affects community well-being or local economic development. Implementation involves planning for iterative cycles, in which each round of data collection informs subsequent interventions. This adaptability reflects an understanding that smart city programs evolve continuously (Bibri & Krogstie, 2017).

4.4. Key Data Sources and Collection Practices

Data come from numerous sources, including municipal records, national statistics bureaus, satellite imaging, sensors, crowdsourced platforms, and surveys (Allam & Dhunny, 2019). Integration requires consistent definitions and interoperable formats. Cities often struggle with legacy systems and fragmented data ownership, impeding seamless aggregation (Hashem et al., 2016). Governance arrangements may stipulate data-sharing agreements between agencies, as well as rules protecting sensitive information (Van Zoonen, 2016). Ensuring data quality and reliability demands clear guidelines on frequency of updates, sampling methods, and error margins (NIST, 2022). In resource-limited contexts, patchy data can hamper comprehensive assessments. Partnerships with academia or private firms sometimes fill these gaps by providing technical expertise or complementary data streams (Nam, 2019). Regardless of the source, clarity in how data is curated and validated is critical for producing accurate insights.

4.5. Challenges of Consistency and Comparability

Comparing cities necessitates consistent methodologies (European Innovation Partnership on Smart Cities and Communities, 2018). Local differences in governance structures, legal definitions, and baseline conditions can influence data availability. Some indicators, such as greenhouse gas inventories, require standardized calculation protocols to ensure fair comparisons (ISO, 2019). When data is lacking, proxies may be introduced, but that approach risks skewing results (Sharifi, 2019). Additionally, time-lags in data release can undermine the real-time ethos of many smart city programs (Myeong et al., 2018). Even within a single city, multiple agencies might track overlapping metrics differently, complicating cross-departmental analyses. The recognized solution involves adopting common standards, cross-verifying data, and maintaining open dialogues about how to reconcile nuances. Methodological rigor, supported by transparency and stakeholder collaboration, mitigates these challenges (Joss et al., 2017).

5. PROPOSED COMPREHENSIVE SMART CITY ASSESSMENT FRAMEWORK

Drawing on the indicators reviewed in Section 3 and the methodologies in Section 4, this section proposes a versatile framework that can be adapted to various contexts. It integrates broad thematic areas with flexible data collection strategies, supported by stakeholder participation at each stage. The framework aims to unify the technical aspects of measurement with the policy dimension of governance, thus providing a coherent roadmap for city leaders and researchers. In essence, it aspires to address the limitations of one-size-fits-all solutions by allowing for local adjustments while preserving methodological rigor.

5.1. Conceptual Foundations

City assessments should start by defining the main vision that guides the city's future direction. Strategic goals including economic vitality combined with social equity and environmental sustainability have their reflections through indicator sets according to Nam (2019). Administrators can make collected data actionable for policy guidance through the proper alignment of targets with both established global standards and local requirements according to Patrão et al. (2020). The second principle demands integration allowing various departments to link their data through a single governance structure. Each measurement framework for technology and environment and mobility and governance exists as a part of the overall collective analytical outlook (Gil-García et al., 2015). The final pillar addresses adaptability. This framework contains continuous feedback systems allowing local indicators to modify according to changing area conditions (Sharifi, 2019). Local urban areas stay adaptive to changing priorities and emerging technological breakthroughs.

5.2. Framework Structure and Stages

The proposed framework follows a sequence of key phases: goal definition, indicator selection, data gathering, analysis, policy alignment, implementation, and continuous revision. In practice, these steps may overlap, but they create a structured approach for designing and executing city assessments (Meijer & Bolívar, 2016). Figure 1, presented as a Mermaid flowchart, offers a high-level representation of these phases and their interconnections.

Figure 1. Process Flow of the Proposed Smart City Assessment Framework

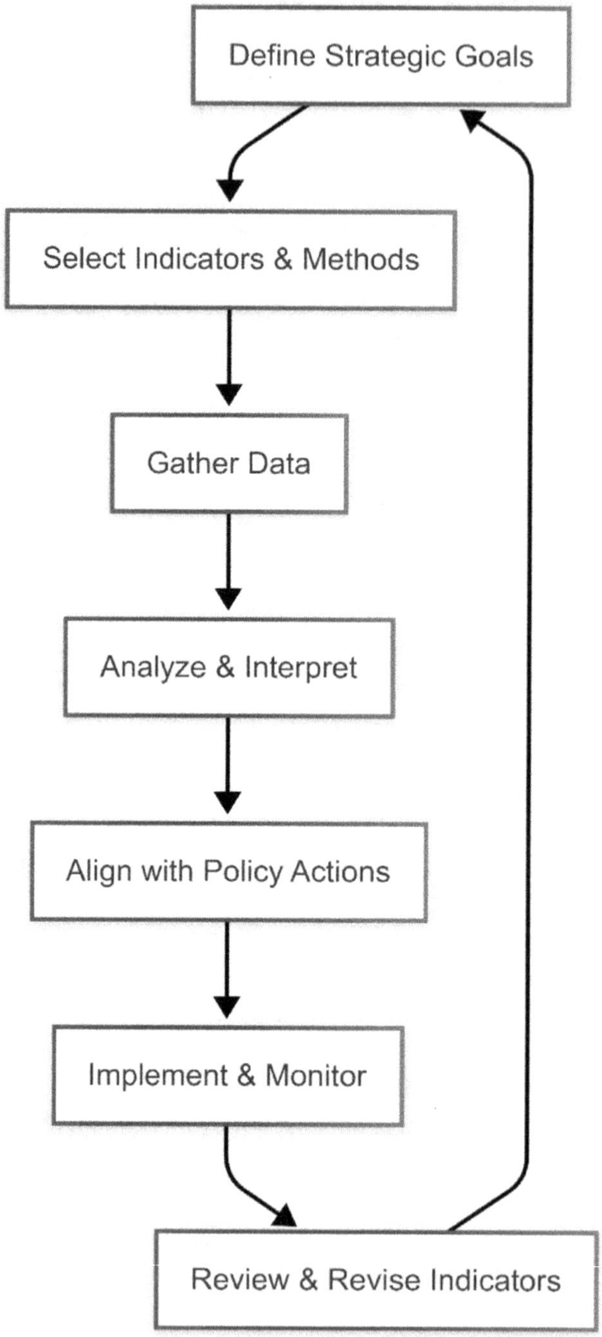

In this conceptual flow, the cycle repeats, illustrating how continuous learning refines subsequent iterations. After local authorities decide on a set of objectives, they choose indicators reflecting these aims. Data collection follows, informed by robust methodologies that combine quantitative and qualitative sources (Trindade et al., 2017). Analysis and interpretation lead to conclusions about performance. Policy recommendations then emerge, guiding interventions or program expansions (Mora et al., 2019). Monitoring the changes prompts further assessments, generating an iterative loop. Although the general progression may seem linear, feedback mechanisms ensure flexibility and responsiveness.

5.2.1. Phase 1: Strategic Goal Definition

Each city starts by articulating its priorities, possibly drawn from local development plans or stakeholder consultations. Some cities may emphasize sustainable mobility, while others concentrate on digital inclusion or economic diversification (Kummitha & Crutzen, 2017). Establishing clarity ensures that subsequent indicators remain relevant to tangible policy objectives (Angelidou, 2017). Engaging citizens and other stakeholders at this early stage helps foster shared ownership of the process (Nam, 2019).

5.2.2. Phase 2: Indicator Selection and Methodology

Drawing on established frameworks such as ISO 37122 or ITU's KPIs, city leaders compile a customized set of measures that address local context (International Telecommunication Union, 2016; ISO, 2019). The selection process involves balancing comprehensiveness with feasibility. Experts in policy, technology, and social development collaborate to refine choices, ensuring coverage of economy, inclusion, environment, governance, technology, and mobility (Trindade et al., 2017). Methodological decisions also arise, determining whether the city will rely on composite indices, in-depth surveys, or data analytics platforms (Sharifi, 2019).

5.2.3. Phase 3: Data Gathering

Implementation of data collection strategies begins. The city identifies sources of existing data, such as administrative records or sensor feeds, and addresses gaps through tailored surveys or new deployments (Hashem et al., 2016). Coordinating across agencies prevents duplication. A standard data governance policy clarifies roles, responsibilities, and privacy safeguards (Van Zoonen, 2016). Regular data audits help maintain accuracy and timeliness.

5.2.4. Phase 4: Analysis and Interpretation

Once data are compiled, analysts examine trends, compare them against benchmarks, and identify correlations. Mixed methods can reveal deeper insights by combining numeric patterns with qualitative feedback (Trindade et al., 2017). Policymakers then interpret findings to see whether existing targets are being met (Myeong et al., 2018). Visualization tools, dashboards, and data storytelling techniques can help communicate results to diverse audiences (IMD Smart City Observatory, 2023).

5.2.5. Phase 5: Policy Alignment and Action

Conclusions from the analysis guide policy adjustments or resource allocation. If mobility indicators highlight underuse of public transport, authorities might invest in route optimizations or public awareness campaigns (European Innovation Partnership on Smart Cities and Communities, 2018). If social inclusion metrics reveal digital disparity, the city could introduce subsidized broadband programs. Tying assessment outcomes to budgetary and strategic decisions deepens the relevance of evaluation processes (Mora et al., 2019).

5.2.6. Phase 6: Implementation and Monitoring

Policy changes and new programs must be enacted, with clear lines of accountability (Meijer & Bolívar, 2016). Monitoring involves continual tracking of indicators to measure progress over time. Monthly or quarterly reviews can detect emerging issues, while annual reports consolidate performance data for public disclosure (National League of Cities, 2016). Integrated dashboards may provide real-time insights, boosting transparency and responsiveness (Hashem et al., 2016).

5.2.7. Phase 7: Review and Revision

Urban priorities or technologies evolve. Periodic reviews enable the updating of indicators or data collection protocols (Sharifi, 2019). The city might refine weightings if certain indicators become less relevant or if stakeholders demand a deeper focus on emerging issues (Gil-García et al., 2015). This cyclical process ensures that the assessment framework remains dynamic, rather than a static checklist.

Stakeholder involvement bolsters the quality of the assessment process at each phase. Figure 2 visualizes the interaction among citizen groups, local government, and private sector entities. This simplified sequence diagram highlights collaborative decision points and data-sharing loops (Bibri & Krogstie, 2017).

Figure 2. Stakeholder Engagement Sequence Diagram

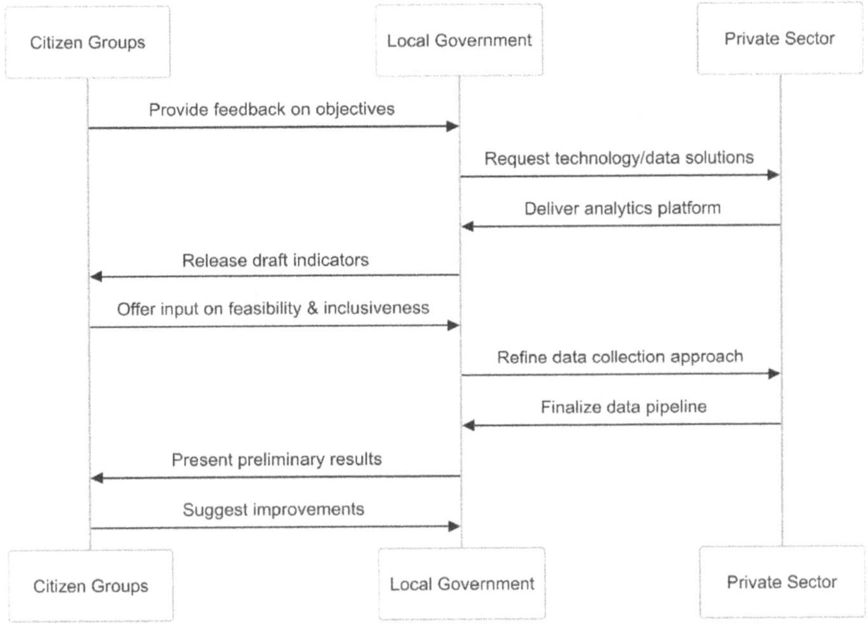

This diagram underscores the iterative nature of stakeholder engagement, affirming that thorough communication can align indicators with genuine community needs (Nam, 2019).

5.4. Data Architecture for Integrated Analysis

Many cities rely on distributed technology systems, making it critical to establish a coherent data architecture. Key elements include a central data platform, secure interfaces for external access, and interoperability standards. The final figure in this section, presented as a Mermaid class diagram, showcases a high-level view of data entities relevant to smart city assessment. It conveys relationships among municipal departments, private providers, and civic users (Hashem et al., 2016).

Figure 3. Class Diagram for Smart City Assessment Data Architecture

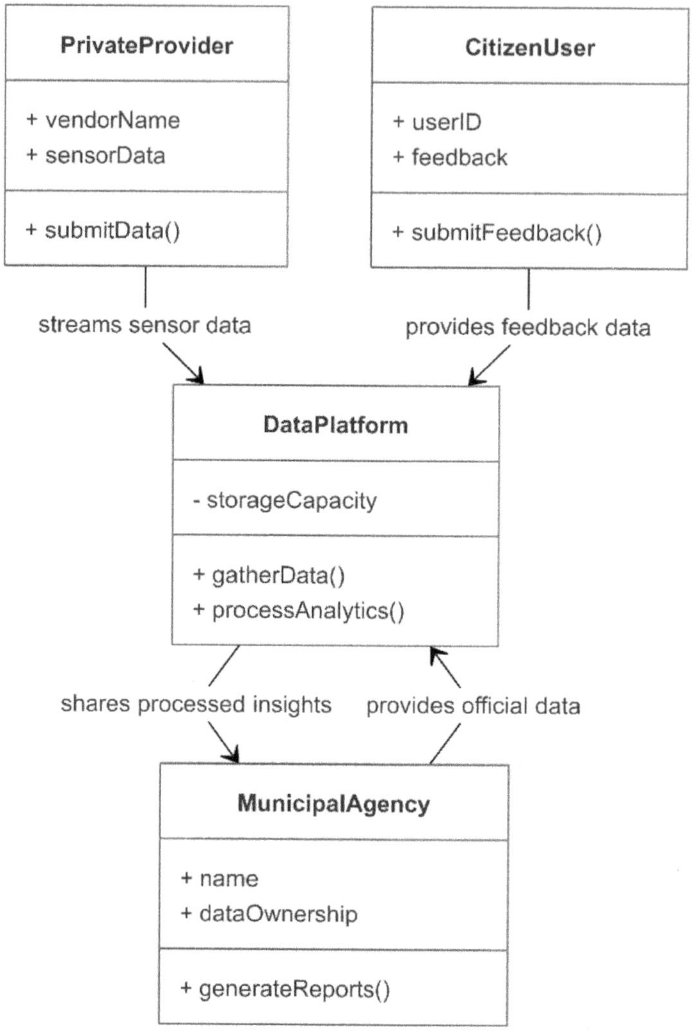

This simple depiction lays out the objects that interact within a city's digital ecosystem (Mora et al., 2019). The DataPlatform class manages ingestion and processing, receiving data from municipal agencies and private providers. Citizens contribute feedback, which can be integrated into analytics for governance improvements. By establishing clear relationships and data flows, the architecture supports consistent measurement and continuous evaluation (Nam, 2019).

Table 2. Essential Elements for a Comprehensive Smart City Assessment Framework

Component	Description
Strategic Alignment	Linking indicators to articulated city priorities
Stakeholder Engagement	Involving citizens, businesses, and public entities in selecting indicators and collecting data
Data Integration	Creating interoperable architectures for seamless sharing of real-time and historical data
Mixed-Methods Evaluation	Combining quantitative metrics with interviews, focus groups, and observational data
Policy Responsiveness	Translating findings into actionable strategies with defined timelines
Continuous Improvement	Adapting indicators and methods based on emerging technologies and evolving city needs

Each component signifies a strategic pillar needed for robust evaluations that are flexible, inclusive, and outcome-oriented (Bibri & Krogstie, 2017).

6. PRACTICAL ILLUSTRATIONS AND CASE CONTEXTS

To ground the proposed framework in real-world scenarios, this section presents select city experiences. Although these examples are generalized for illustrative purposes, they draw on documented practices in Europe, Asia, and North America. They underscore how diverse governance systems and socio-economic conditions can shape assessment outcomes (Albino et al., 2015).

6.1. Illustrative Example: A Mid-Sized European City

A mid-sized city introduced a unified platform to monitor energy consumption across municipal buildings. Drawing on ISO 37122 energy-related indicators, local officials aggregated real-time meter data to track daily usage patterns (International Organization for Standardization, 2019). The city also surveyed building occupants to understand behaviors influencing energy demand. When analyzing results, they discovered that schools had spiking consumption in early mornings. Qualitative discussions with staff revealed lighting and heating systems automatically switched on hours before actual classroom use. The city adjusted building control schedules, leading to documented energy savings of 15%. This example illustrates how a mixed-method approach—combining sensor data with interviews—can uncover practical areas for improvement (Myeong et al., 2018).

6.2. Illustrative Example: A Large Asian Metropolis

A heavily populated city's government sought to address traffic congestion by installing intelligent traffic signals linked to a central control room (Mohanty et al., 2016). Evaluation metrics included average commute time, congestion indexes, and public transport ridership. The city also used public opinion polls to gauge perceptions of commuting quality (Deloitte Center for Government Insights, 2019). Analysis suggested improvements in major corridors but revealed limited benefits in outer districts, where the infrastructure upgrade lagged. Residents there faced longer commutes and inconsistent transit schedules. Policy-makers reallocated budget to expand the system's coverage, incorporating more bus rapid transit lines. By using an iterative cycle, the local administration revised indicators to measure not just city-wide congestion but also district-level variations (Nam, 2019). This refined lens illuminated disparities that a broad average might mask.

6.3. Illustrative Example: North American Regional Hub

A regional hub in North America prioritized open data for fostering innovation (Gil-García et al., 2015). The city launched a portal featuring real-time data feeds on public health services, housing, and economic development. Data usage metrics and civic hackathon participation became core indicators of digital engagement (Deloitte Center for Government Insights, 2019). Analysis revealed a spike in community-led app creation addressing local issues, including a platform that matched social services to homeless individuals. Local non-profits reported enhanced communication channels with city officials, eventually influencing policy changes related to resource allocation. Through regular stakeholder forums, the city updated its indicator set to capture the social impact of digital solutions, rather than merely measuring portal usage statistics (Meijer & Bolívar, 2016). This case highlights how flexible assessment fosters new social linkages and policy innovation.

6.4. Reflections on Case Insights

The application of indicators requires context-awareness to produce practical knowledge as demonstrated by these scenarios (Mora et al., 2019). Supplying a combination of quantitative and qualitative data methods revealed fundamental causes that produced numerical statistics. Organizations adapted their solutions to address different regional priorities that included matters such as energy system improvements and congestion reduction and social problem-solving initiatives. Stakeholder involvement served as a critical aspect in determining appropriate metrics alongside discovering unexposed disparities between areas or population groups (Trindade et al., 2017). The framework enables cities to enhance their strategies through its cyclical operational method which accommodates new data findings (Nam, 2019). The set of illustrations demonstrates how strong adaptive frameworks enable cities to achieve more equitable sustainable outcomes through urban development.

7. POTENTIAL APPLICATIONS BEYOND THE CORE SECTORS

Though the discussion thus far has centered on standard domains like energy, mobility, and governance, the framework can be extended into other areas. Smart city approaches increasingly touch fields such as healthcare, education, public safety, and cultural heritage. Expanding the framework into these domains raises questions about specialized indicators, unique stakeholders, and distinct data flows. Nonetheless, the core principles—strategic alignment, stakeholder engagement, robust data integration, mixed methods, policy responsiveness, and continuous improvement—apply equally well.

7.1. Healthcare and Public Well-being

Some cities deploy telemedicine platforms and monitor public health data to optimize hospital resources (Meijer & Bolívar, 2016). Indicators might track the effectiveness of emergency response systems, vaccination coverage, or mental health service accessibility. Digital health initiatives often require sensitive handling of personal data, mandating robust privacy protections (Van Zoonen, 2016). Additionally, evaluating outcomes can blend clinical data with patient feedback. By situating these metrics within a broader assessment framework, city leaders can see how public well-being intersects with socio-economic and environmental factors, such as housing conditions or air quality (Sharifi, 2019).

7.2. Education and Workforce Development

Cities aiming to cultivate a technologically savvy population may integrate coding classes in public schools or foster collaborations with local universities (Angelidou, 2017). Assessment indicators might include enrollment in STEM programs, digital literacy rates among adults, and the number of institutional partnerships with businesses (Kummitha & Crutzen, 2017). Qualitative evaluations could examine teacher perspectives, student experiences, or barriers to accessing digital tools. Linking educational initiatives to broader city objectives—such as stimulating entrepreneurship—underscores how cross-sector synergy can strengthen outcomes (Mora et al., 2019).

7.3. Public Safety and Emergency Management

Smart city technologies support real-time crime monitoring, predictive policing, or natural disaster response (McKinsey Global Institute, 2018). Common indicators assess response times, incident clearance rates, and community trust in policing. Yet these strategies raise ethical dilemmas around surveillance and data privacy (Van Zoonen, 2016). The proposed framework advises a balanced approach that combines quantitative data with dialogues about accountability and civil liberties. Engaging community advocates in designing security-related indicators can foster trust (European Commission, Joint Research Centre, 2019). In addition, ensuring the reliability of technologies used in emergencies is critical, requiring rigorous testing and secure infrastructure.

7.4. Cultural Heritage and Tourism

Tourism in cities that preserve heritage sites benefits from digital signposting, interactive maps, and augmented reality guides (Townsend, 2013). Assessments might track visitor satisfaction, foot traffic patterns, and local economic gains. More advanced evaluations monitor how digital transformations affect resident life, especially regarding overcrowding or displacement concerns (Komninos, 2015). When integrated into a city's broader strategy, heritage-related indicators can balance economic goals with cultural preservation. Traditional methods of tourism measurement, such as visitor counts or hotel occupancy rates, become more nuanced if combined with feedback from local communities and real-time analytics on tourist behavior (Nam, 2019).

Table 3. Selected Extensions of Smart City Assessment Framework

Domain	Possible Indicators
Healthcare	Response times, telemedicine usage, patient satisfaction
Education	STEM enrollment, digital literacy, teacher training
Public Safety	Emergency response efficiency, perceived safety scores
Cultural Heritage & Tourism	Visitor flows, local economic impact, preservation efforts

This table illustrates the adaptability of the proposed framework. Indicators must always fit local conditions, preserving stakeholder relevance (Sharifi, 2019).

8. IMPLEMENTATION CHALLENGES AND STRATEGIES FOR MITIGATION

Multiple obstacles hinder the successful use of structured evaluation frameworks because they demand technical sophistication and institutional cooperation while also requiring funding resources together with public dedication and compliance with privacy requirements (Deloitte Center for Government Insights, 2019). The analysis section defines the obstacles in addition to recommending ways to overcome them.

8.1. Technical and Data Management

Many cities encounter problems from old infrastructure systems and limited digital capabilities of their workforce (Hashem et al., 2016). Cities which hold data in sheets or paper documents need substantial financial resources to implement complex analytic approaches. Advanced integration becomes difficult because different departments use inconsistent data formats which create fragmentations in data views (Myeong et al., 2018). Cities can address these problems by creating different stages of infrastructure upgrades as well as staff training in data management and implementing shared interoperability standards (International Telecommunication Union, 2016). Public entities should collaborate with educational institutions and private sector providers yet need to manage data ownership through appropriate contractual arrangements (Nam, 2019).

8.2. Institutional Siloes

Siloed structures persist in many municipal administrations, with each department setting its own priorities and using different metrics (Meijer & Bolívar, 2016). Cross-department coordination requires political will and clear incentives. Appointing an overarching smart city coordinator or committee can foster interdepartmental collaboration (Rodríguez-Bolívar, 2015). Shared digital platforms and data governance policies make collaboration more feasible by standardizing definitions and encouraging transparent information exchange (British Standards Institution, 2014). Regular joint sessions among departments to align on indicator sets create a culture of shared responsibility (Mora et al., 2019).

8.3. Privacy and Ethical Concerns

Smart city data collection can intrude into personal information, raising fears about surveillance or commercial exploitation (Van Zoonen, 2016). Public trust hinges on transparent data usage policies, robust encryption, and clear governance frameworks. Legal guidelines must spell out how data is stored, who accesses it, and under what conditions it can be shared (Organisation for Economic Co-operation and Development, 2020). Ethical review boards or advisory committees can examine proposed technologies or analytics, ensuring alignment with public interest (European Innovation Partnership on Smart Cities and Communities, 2018). In an iterative framework, privacy indicators must be continuously monitored and updated as new technologies emerge (Nam, 2019).

8.4. Financial Constraints

Developing robust assessment systems can require substantial resources, including hardware, software, training, and staff (Deloitte Center for Government Insights, 2019). Smaller or financially constrained municipalities may find comprehensive approaches prohibitively costly. Strategies to mitigate this involve leveraging open-source tools, seeking grants, forming public-private partnerships, and phasing implementation over time (Sharifi, 2019). Transparent cost-benefit analyses can demonstrate how improved measurement leads to more efficient resource allocation in the long run (European Commission, Joint Research Centre, 2019). Some global organizations also offer technical assistance for cities, especially in emerging economies, to reduce initial barriers.

8.5. Stakeholder Buy-In and Resistance

A recurring obstacle emerges when projects lack public support. Residents may not see tangible benefits or may fear data misuse (Van Zoonen, 2016). Business entities can also resist changes if they perceive costs or disruptions. Clear communication strategies that outline project objectives, expected outcomes, and privacy safeguards can address anxieties (Nam, 2019). Local community meetings, digital forums, and participatory design processes invite feedback and build trust. Governments can highlight successful implementations from peer cities to illustrate potential gains. Ultimately, generating a sense of shared ownership alleviates skepticism (Joss et al., 2017).

9. DISCUSSION: ALIGNING FRAMEWORK ADOPTION WITH GOVERNANCE MODELS

Assessment systems achieve success by maintaining alignment with particular conditions found in local governance. Each city has unique administrative traditions whereas political culture along with legislative mandates differ from one city to another (Meijer & Bolívar, 2016). Cities operate within two opposing governance frameworks whereby strong mayors control centralized systems versus decentralized governance structures run by various agencies. Open data policies receive support from specific geographical areas although particular regions implement security-based restrictions that limit data sharing activities (Van Zoonen, 2016). Dissimilarities in public-private partnerships impact how expertise together with resources move between partners. The proposed framework can function in different governance settings but it needs powerful leadership and multisector partnerships to achieve its full benefits (Rodríguez-Bolívar, 2015).

The continuous learning environment grows under the guidance of city leaders through multiple successive cycles. Each review process enhances the strategy by improving departmental relationships and displays new societal requirements (Nam, 2019). The adaptable cyclical process strengthens the resilience of municipalities so they can quickly respond to economic and environmental disturbances. The implementation of the framework fails to resolve all municipal challenges. Careful consideration of institutional change should focus on removing organizational barriers because it could enhance transparency according to Myeong et al. (2018). Data sharing formalization and performance audit requirements might need legislative approval to become official requirements. Public leaders who support this framework need to explain how strong evaluations produce concrete improvements that benefit their citizenry (Gil-García et al., 2015). The whole effort faces transformation from being a procedural exercise to an actual driver of change because it lacks demonstrable results.

10. CONCLUSION

Smart city strategies provide potential solutions for urban areas to develop environmentally sustainable inclusive efficiency (Albino et al., 2015). Systematic evaluation methods extending past isolated pilot projects or superficial indices are necessary to fulfill this promise. The analysis presented a complete assessment model which combines universal industry standards alongside numerical measurements with qualitative feedback processes derived from stakeholder perspectives (Sharifi, 2019). The assessment framework guides leaders to view evaluation as a continuous learning process through which they should aim for direct governance alignment with local needs (Meijer & Bolívar, 2016). Municipalities follow a framework which includes strategic clarity and effective stakeholder engagement and reliable data practices to manage development of smart solutions (Nam, 2019). The numerous examples demonstrate how evaluation principles adapt to different projects and locations to create significant change in urban environments. Future investigations need to establish and perfect quantitative measures for assessing advanced domains including artificial intelligence ethic challenges and social equity and climate sustainability objectives. The assessment of urban interventions for sustainable and inclusive growth becomes more significant when global challenges continue to multiply..

REFERENCES

Ahvenniemi, H., Huovila, A., Pinto-Seppä, I., & Airaksinen, M. (2017). What are the differences between sustainable and smart cities? *Cities (London, England)*, *60*, 234–245. DOI: 10.1016/j.cities.2016.09.009

Albino, V., Berardi, U., & Dangelico, R. M. (2015). Smart cities: Definitions, dimensions, performance, and initiatives. *Journal of Urban Technology*, *22*(1), 3–21. DOI: 10.1080/10630732.2014.942092

Allam, Z., & Dhunny, Z. A. (2019). On big data, artificial intelligence and smart cities. *Cities (London, England)*, *89*, 80–91. DOI: 10.1016/j.cities.2019.01.032

Angelidou, M. (2017). The role of smart city characteristics in the planning of urban environments. *Journal of Urban Technology*, *24*(4), 3–18. DOI: 10.1080/10630732.2017.1348880

Anthopoulos, L. G. (2017). *Understanding Smart Cities: A Tool for Smart Government or an Industrial Trick?* Springer International Publishing. DOI: 10.1007/978-3-319-57015-0

Association, G. S. M. (2019). *Creating Smart Cities: The Role of Mobile in the Digital Transformation of Urban Spaces*. GSMA.

Berrone, P., & Ricart, J. E. (2020). *IESE Cities in Motion Index 2020: World's Smartest Cities*. University of Navarra – IESE Business School.

Bibri, S. E., & Krogstie, J. (2017). Smart sustainable cities of the future: An extensive interdisciplinary literature review. *Sustainable Cities and Society*, *31*, 183–212. DOI: 10.1016/j.scs.2017.02.016

British Standards Institution. (2014). [– *Smart City Framework. Guide to Establishing Strategies for Smart Cities and Communities*. London: BSI.]. *PAS*, *181*, 2014.

Calzada, I. (2020). *Smart City Citizenship*. Elsevier.

Deloitte Center for Government Insights. (2019). *Inclusive Smart Cities: Delivering Digital Solutions for All*. Deloitte Development LLC.

European Commission, Joint Research Centre. (2019). *The Future of Cities: Opportunities, Challenges and the Way Forward*. Publications Office of the European Union.

European Innovation Partnership on Smart Cities and Communities. (2018). *Smart City Guidance Package: A Roadmap for Integrated Planning and Implementation of Smart City Projects*. European Commission.

Gil-García, J. R., Pardo, T. A., & Nam, T. (2015). What makes a city smart? Identifying core components and proposing an integrative and comprehensive conceptualization. *Information Polity*, *20*(1), 61–87. DOI: 10.3233/IP-150354

Hashem, I. A. T., Chang, V., Anuar, N. B., Adewole, K., Yaqoob, I., Gani, A., Ahmed, E., & Chiroma, H. (2016). The role of big data in smart city. *International Journal of Information Management*, *36*(5), 748–758. DOI: 10.1016/j.ijinfomgt.2016.05.002

IMD Smart City Observatory. (2023). *IMD Smart City Index 2023*. International Institute for Management Development.

International Organization for Standardization. (2018). *ISO 37106:2018 – Sustainable cities and communities – Guidance on establishing smart city operating models for sustainable communities*. ISO.

International Organization for Standardization. (2019). *ISO 37122:2019 – Sustainable cities and communities – Indicators for smart cities*. ISO.

International Telecommunication Union. (2016). *Key Performance Indicators for Smart Sustainable Cities*. ITU.

Joss, S., Cook, M., & Dayot, Y. (2017). Smart cities: Towards a new citizenship regime? A discourse analysis of the UK smart city standard. *Urban Studies (Edinburgh, Scotland)*, *54*(8), 1824–1840. DOI: 10.1177/0042098016633257

Komninos, N. (2015). *The Age of Intelligent Cities: Smart Environments and Innovation-for-All Strategies*. Routledge.

Kummitha, R. K. R., & Crutzen, N. (2017). How do we understand smart cities? An evolutionary perspective. *Cities (London, England)*, *67*, 43–52. DOI: 10.1016/j.cities.2017.04.010

McKinsey Global Institute. (2018). *Smart Cities: Digital Solutions for a More Livable Future*. McKinsey & Company.

Meijer, A., & Bolívar, M. P. R. (2016). Governing the smart city: A review of the literature on smart city governance. *International Review of Administrative Sciences*, *82*(2), 392–408. DOI: 10.1177/0020852314564308

Ministry of Urban Development, Government of India. (2015). *Smart Cities Mission: Statement and Guidelines*. Government of India.

Mohanty, S. P., Choppali, U., & Kougianos, E. (2016). Everything you wanted to know about smart cities: The Internet of Things is the backbone. *IEEE Consumer Electronics Magazine*, *5*(3), 60–70. DOI: 10.1109/MCE.2016.2556879

Mora, L., Deakin, M., & Reid, A. (2019). Strategic principles for smart city development: A multiple case study analysis of European best practices. *Technological Forecasting and Social Change*, *142*, 70–90. DOI: 10.1016/j.techfore.2018.07.035

Myeong, S., Jung, Y., & Lee, E. (2018). A study on determinant factors in smart city development: An analytic hierarchy process analysis. *Sustainability (Basel)*, *10*(8), 2606. DOI: 10.3390/su10082606

Nam, T. (2019). Determining the type of smart city: A conceptual model for assessment. *Smart Cities*, *2*(2), 179–197. DOI: 10.3390/smartcities2020012

National Institute of Standards and Technology. (2022). *Smart Cities and Communities: A Key Performance Indicators Framework (NIST Special Publication 1900-206)*. Gaithersburg, MD: U.S. Department of Commerce, NIST. DOI: 10.6028/NIST.SP.1900-206

National League of Cities. (2016). *Trends in Smart City Development*. NLC.

Organisation for Economic Co-operation and Development. (2020). Smart Cities and Inclusive Growth: Building on the Outcomes of the OECD Roundtable. Paris: OECD Publishing.

Patrão, C., Moura, P., & de Almeida, A. T. (2020). Review of smart city assessment tools. *Smart Cities*, *3*(4), 1117–1132. DOI: 10.3390/smartcities3040055

Rodríguez-Bolívar, M. P. (Ed.). (2015). *Transforming City Governments for Successful Smart Cities*. Springer. DOI: 10.1007/978-3-319-03167-5

Senyo, P. K., Liu, K., & Effah, J. (2019). Digital business ecosystem: Literature review and a framework for future research. *Government Information Quarterly*, *36*(3), 400–413. DOI: 10.1016/j.giq.2019.02.001

Sharifi, A. (2019). A critical review of selected smart city assessment tools and indicator sets. *Journal of Cleaner Production*, *233*, 1269–1283. DOI: 10.1016/j.jclepro.2019.06.172

Shi, F., & Shi, W. (2023). A critical review of smart city frameworks: New criteria to consider when building smart city framework. *ISPRS International Journal of Geo-Information*, *12*(9), 364. DOI: 10.3390/ijgi12090364

Silva, B. N., Khan, M., & Han, K. (2018). Towards sustainable smart cities: A review of trends, architectures, components and challenges. *Sustainable Cities and Society*, *38*, 697–713. DOI: 10.1016/j.scs.2018.01.053

Smart Cities Council. (2017). *Smart Cities Readiness Guide (Expanded Edition)*. Smart Cities Council.

Townsend, A. M. (2013). *Smart Cities: Big Data, Civic Hackers, and the Quest for a New Utopia*. W. W. Norton & Company.

Trindade, E. P., Hinnig, M. P., da Costa, E. M., Marques, J. S., Bastos, R. C., & Yigitcanlar, T. (2017). Sustainable development of smart cities: A systematic review of the literature. *Journal of Open Innovation*, *3*(1), 11. DOI: 10.1186/s40852-017-0063-2

UN-Habitat. (2022). *World Cities Report 2022: Envisaging the Future of Cities*. United Nations Human Settlements Programme.

Van Zoonen, L. (2016). Privacy concerns in smart cities. *Government Information Quarterly*, *33*(3), 472–480. DOI: 10.1016/j.giq.2016.06.004

World Economic Forum. (2021). *Governing Smart Cities: Policy Benchmarks for Ethical and Responsible Smart City Development*. Geneva: World Economic Forum.

Yigitcanlar, T., Kamruzzaman, M., Buys, L., Ioppolo, G., Sabatini-Marques, J., da Costa, E. M., & Yun, J. H. J. (2018). Understanding "smart cities": Intertwining development drivers with desired outcomes in a multidimensional framework. *Cities (London, England)*, *81*, 145–160. DOI: 10.1016/j.cities.2018.04.003

Chapter 20
Digital Solutions for Urban Household Waste Management:
Challenges and Opportunities for Sustainable Cities

Utkarsh Nawal Kishor Singh
https://orcid.org/0009-0008-6073-7668
Amity School of Economics, Amity University, Noida, India

Kavita Indapurkar
https://orcid.org/0000-0003-4388-2915
Amity School of Economics, Amity University, Noida, India

ABSTRACT

This research explores the structure of urban household waste management, focusing on challenges, practices, and perceptions of digital solutions. Key issues include inadequate infrastructure and electronic waste handling, as identified through literature reviews and empirical analysis. Household attitudes toward waste management highlight practices like waste reduction, segregation, and individual accountability. The study evaluates the willingness of families to adopt emerging technology interfaces such as apps and web-based services, revealing favorable attitudes toward digital waste management systems. Suggestions include enhancing waste collection infrastructure, promoting environment friendly behaviours, and fostering collaboration among government bodies, tech-based businesses, and local authorities. The findings underscore the importance of coordinated efforts to address waste management challenges and advance sustainable practices for a cleaner and healthier urban future.

DOI: 10.4018/979-8-3373-1375-7.ch020

INTRODUCTION

In today's world, waste management is an essential component of sustainable development, closely related to socioeconomic advancement, environmental conservation, and public health. As nations move from lower-income to the middle and higher-income status, their waste management demands vary. Furthermore, due to the greater population centres that have been created by rapid urban growth and population expansion, it is becoming increasingly difficult to collect all of the waste and procure land for its treatment, (Kaza, 2018). This challenge is further amplified by our reliance on the traditional waste management systems that rely on landfill-based disposal and manual waste collection, which have been criticized for their long-term ecological impact and inefficiency in handling growing urban wastes volumes. (Patrizia Ghisellini, 2022)

As a result, waste is often seen as an afterthought in production cycles and is handled only when the urgency to address the issue cannot be merely resolved by disposal (Seadon, 2010). In fact, Municipalities, which are primarily responsible for waste management, frequently face additional hurdles due to institutional, financial, and human resource limitation which results in significant service backlogs and inefficiencies in the existing waste management system (Karani, 2007).

The management, collection, and disposal of household waste has always been a global concern. This is because proper and efficient solid waste disposal and collection has been recognized as vital for the general well-being and hygienic conditions of metropolitan societies since the nineteenth century (Purity, 2016). Due to reasons such as the density of cities, cultural diversity, shifts in lifestyles, growing populations, and expanding metropolitan landscapes, waste generation has expanded tremendously. Due to which municipalities and households are constantly facing challenges in waste segregation, collection, disposal and management (Kumar, 2020).

Furthermore, the behaviour of households while practising waste management approaches reveals a complex interaction between social customs, financial incentives, and environmental conscience. (Rodrigues, 2020) assert that social factors have a major influence on altering waste management behaviours and emphasise the interconnectedness of social and ecological elements in determining how households' approach sustainable waste management. Household engagement is essential for a waste management initiative to be successful, and household participation is heavily impacted by social attitudes and behaviours (Hilles, 2011).

The rise in popularity of smartphone applications influencing human behaviour is a sign of a broader movement towards technological integration into daily life. While health-related applications have received greater attention, there has also been a rise in interest in using persuasive technology to assist sustainable activities (Varsolo Sunio, 2017), such as waste management. Similarly, studies on health and education apps indicate that using an app can successfully encourage behavioural change, even though research on the persuasive power of so-called "green apps" is still in its early phases (Wildt, 2023), (Brauer, 2016). Traditional waste management techniques have undergone a significant transformation as a result of emerging digital waste management technology, that offers operational efficiency, provides innovative tools such as IoT-enabled monitoring, blockchain-based waste tracking and online platforms that boost productivity, transparency, increases public involvement and facilitates data-driven decision making. Hence, it becomes crucial to address the willingness of individuals to invest in such efficient waste services (Peng Jiang, 2023), (Kayamo, 2022).

The primary purpose of this study, "Digital Solutions for Urban Household Waste Management: Challenges and Opportunities for Sustainable Cities", is to examine the interconnection between the opportunities and challenges associated with managing household waste. Making sound decisions as we transition to a more sustainable approach requires an understanding of present methods and the public's perceptions of household waste management (Fadhullah, 2022). This research examines the behavioural dynamics, regulatory implications, and technology potential surrounding household waste management in an attempt to stimulate productive debates and practical recommendations for the development of sustainable urban futures.

LITERATURE REVIEW

Challenges faced in the process of Waste Disposal and Management

(Sapuay, 2018) identified that urbanisation has led to major resource and environmental challenges for cities and necessitated a thorough review of their waste management and disposal approaches. In many areas, deficiencies in infrastructure, budget constraints, and outdated technology have given rise to illegal dumping and presented substantial risks to the public's health and quality of life, as discussed by (Singh, 2022). Beyond logistical inefficiencies, researchers have stressed the global concern of solid waste disposal, calling for sustainable and socially responsible solutions, such as the recycling initiatives and circular economy practices (Abdel Shafy, 2018), (Geetha, 2020). Furthermore, behavioural interventions play a crucial role in tackling waste segregation inefficiencies. For example, (Loan, 2023) elucidates the role of Nudge theory in prompting waste separation at source and highlights the need for well-planned behavioural strategies (Nudges) in significantly improving waste management effectiveness.

Behavioural influences towards practising Sustainable Waste Management

Various researchers have reported that the perception, attitude and behaviour of an individual towards waste management helps to better understand the underlying determinants affecting their waste management practices. (Omran, 2009) state that greater accessibility and understanding of recycling resources have a favourable impact on recycling engagement. Additionally, (Seng, 2018) underlines that education, income levels and dissatisfaction with municipal waste services significantly shape household behaviours regarding waste disposal. According to (Rawshan Ara Begum, 2009), in the construction sector, waste disposal strategies are influenced by a contractor awareness, company size and education background, underscoring the importance of industry-specific behavioural assessments. Furthermore, the necessity of thorough habit assessment in waste management research is emphasised by (Knussen, 2008), who highlights the impact of habitual behaviour, specifically past recycling behaviour and perceived absence of habit, in shaping recycling intentions. Lastly, (Pandit, 2021) propose that including the perspectives of future generations may affect the preference for sustainable waste management laws, further encouraging family behaviours in favour of efficient waste management practices. Given these findings, it is evident that behavioural factors extend beyond traditional waste disposal habits and influence the adoption of emerging waste management solutions, including digital technologies.

Willingness of Households to adopt emerging technology interface for Waste Management

A subject receiving more attention in the literature is households' willingness to use technological interfaces for waste management. In their investigation of China's rural waste management, (Han, 2019) highlights the importance of effective policy measures, the impact of socioeconomic factors, and the willingness of the public to pay and participate. Likewise, (Véliz, 2022) offer perspectives from Chile, emphasising the readiness of construction firms to allocate resources towards better demolition and construction, hence facilitating the development of more advanced waste management strategies. By examining the willingness of Jakartan residents to pay for services related to adaptive management of municipal solid waste, (Suryawan, 2023) expand on this conversation and emphasise the importance of educating people about adaptive strategies for sustainable waste solutions. In addition, (Crawford, 2017) investigate how well mobile apps support kids' connections to nature, indicating the possible use of tech interfaces to influence and promote waste management participation. And lastly, (Cellina, 2021) explore biases concerning app-based persuasive technologies, providing insightful information that may be applied to the evaluation of users' willingness to pay for technological interfaces in waste management.

Together, these studies demonstrate that while digital waste solutions hold promise, their adoption depends on policy frameworks, economic incentives and behavioural motivations. Thus, bridging the gap between waste management challenges, behavioural tendencies, and digital innovation is crucial for ensuring a systematic and effective transition towards tech-driven waste management solutions.

RESEARCH QUESTIONS

1. What are the primary challenges in effectively disposing of waste that urban households face?
2. How do urban households manage waste within their homes, and what are the influencing factors behind their behaviours?
3. To what extent are urban households willing to adopt technological interfaces for managing and disposing of waste?

RESEARCH OBJECTIVES

- Objective 1 - To evaluate the challenges that urban households encounter in waste disposal.
- Objective 2 - To examine the behaviour of urban households in practicing waste management techniques in their homes.
- Objective 3 - To assess the willingness among urban households to adopt emerging technology interface in waste disposal and management.

HYPOTHESIS

Hypothesis 1

(H0): The challenges faced by urban households in waste disposal does not significantly affect their willingness to adapt technological interfaces for waste management.

(H1): The challenges faced by urban households in waste disposal significantly affect their willingness to adopt technological interfaces for waste management.

Hypothesis 2

(H0): Household behaviours towards waste management do not significantly affect their willingness to adapt technological interfaces for waste management.

(H1): Household behaviours towards waste management significantly affect their willingness to adopt technological interfaces for waste management.

RESEARCH METHODOLOGY

This study employs a questionnaire survey as its research methodology in order to gather primary data. The questionnaire included statements about the different objectives based on dependent and independent variables. Each statement was rated using a 5-point Likert scale, wherein a score of 5 indicates strong agreement with the statement. The questionnaire was sent to the people via different social media platforms like LinkedIn, WhatsApp, Instagram, Facebook ensuring a wider reach and allows for the gathering of diverse perspectives from urban households. SPSS software (v.27) was employed to handle and analyse the collected data.

To determine the connection among the variables, Exploratory Factor Analysis (E.F.A.) was done EFA was chosen to identify the underlying structure of variables (latent constructs) influencing household willingness to adopt digital waste solutions (Ali Akbar Jowkar, 2013). This method helps uncover underlying dimensions that are not directly measurable but significantly impact the study (Hair J. H., 2014). After E.F.A., SMART PLS (v.4) was employed to carry out PLS-SEM in order to test the proposed hypothesis. Unlike traditional regression models, PLS-SEM is better suited for handling complex models with multiple latent variables, allowing for simultaneous assessment of direct and indirect relationships, ensuring higher reliability in structural path analysis. (Sarstedt, 2017).

Figure 1. Hypothesized Research Model

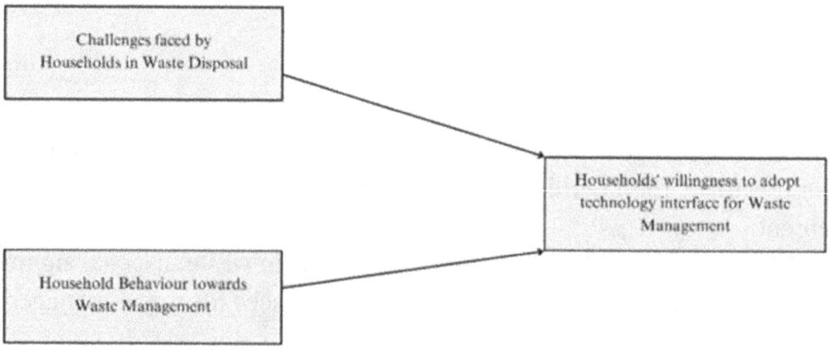

The Kaiser Meyer-Olkin value, that talks about the adequacy of the data, came out to be 0.789, 0.789, 0.922 for the three objectives respectively, which is good as suggested by Kaiser (Shrestha, 2021).

Using Cochran Formula (Cochran, 1977), the ideal Sample Size came out to be approximately 385. Accordingly, the researchers had circulated the questionnaire to 518 participants of which 413 were found to be appropriate for further analysis.

Cochran Formula: **n = (Z^2).(p).(1 - p) / (e^2)**

Here:

Z = Z-score for the desired level of confidence.

p = estimated proportion of population that has a specific trait.

e = error margin (expressed as a proportion).

DATA INTERPRETATION

Data Adequacy: KMO & Bartlett's Test

Figure 2. KMO and Bartlett's Test

OBJECTIVE 1		
Kaiser-Meyer-Olkin Measure of Sampling Adequacy.		0.789
Bartlett's Test of Sphericity	Approx. Chi-Square	921.939
	df	21
	Sig.	0.000
OBJECTIVE 2		
Kaiser-Meyer-Olkin Measure of Sampling Adequacy.		0.789
Bartlett's Test of Sphericity	Approx. Chi-Square	943.463
	df	28
	Sig.	0.000
OBJECTIVE 3		
Kaiser-Meyer-Olkin Measure of Sampling Adequacy.		0.922
Bartlett's Test of Sphericity	Approx. Chi-Square	3249.908
	df	36
	Sig.	0.000

Source: Author's Calculation

Objective 1: The KMO value of 0.789 is moderately good. The degree of connectivity between the observed variables in the data set is assessed by the Barlett's test. The computed chi-square value of 921.939 and the significant result (Sig. <.000) suggest a good correlation between the variables. These results of the two tests measure and provide strong evidence for the interrelatedness of researcher's chosen factors and the sufficiency of researcher's data (Mohsen Tavakol, 2020).

Objective 2: Figure 2, the KMO value of 0.789 is moderately good. The Bartlett's Test assesses the degree of connectivity between the observed variables in the data set. The computed chi-square value of 943.463 and the significant result (Sig. <.000) suggest a good correlation between the variables. These results of the two tests measure and provide strong evidence for the interrelatedness of researcher's chosen factors and the sufficiency of researcher's data (E.F.A.-Exploratory Factor Analysis).

Objective 3: The KMO value of 0.922 is moderately good in Figure 2. The Bartlett's Test assesses the degree of connectivity between the observed variables in the data set. The computed chi-square value of 3249.908 and the significant result (Sig. =.000) suggest a good correlation between the variables. These results of the two tests measure and provide strong evidence for the interrelatedness of the researcher's chosen factors and the sufficiency of the researcher's data.

EXPLORATORY FACTOR ANALYSIS

Figure 3. Total Variance Explained (using Principal Component Analysis)

OBJECTIVE 1									
	Initial Eigenvalues			Extraction Sums of Squared Loadings			Rotation Sums of Squared Loadings		
Component	Total	% of Variance	Cumulative %	Total	% of Variance	Cumulative %	Total	% of Variance	Cumulative %
1	3.187	45.522	45.522	3.187	45.522	45.522	2.078	29.681	29.681
2	1.139	16.278	61.799	1.139	16.278	61.799	2.002	28.605	58.286
3	0.928	13.257	75.056	0.928	13.257	75.056	1.174	16.770	75.056
4	0.655	9.356	84.412						
5	0.402	5.750	90.162						
6	0.366	5.233	95.395						
7	0.322	4.605	100.000						
Extraction Method: Principal Component Analysis.									

OBJECTIVE 2									
	Initial Eigenvalues			Extraction Sums of Squared Loadings			Rotation Sums of Squared Loadings		
Component	Total	% of Variance	Cumulative %	Total	% of Variance	Cumulative %	Total	% of Variance	Cumulative %
1	3.351	41.883	41.883	3.351	41.883	41.883	2.475	30.941	30.941
2	1.221	15.265	57.149	1.221	15.265	57.149	1.815	22.683	53.624
3	0.807	10.089	67.238	0.807	10.089	67.238	1.089	13.614	67.238
4	0.714	8.929	76.167						
5	0.610	7.622	83.789						
6	0.575	7.184	90.973						
7	0.462	5.781	96.753						
8	0.260	3.247	100.000						
Extraction Method: Principal Component Analysis.									

OBJECTIVE 3									
	Initial Eigenvalues			Extraction Sums of Squared Loadings			Rotation Sums of Squared Loadings		
Component	Total	% of Variance	Cumulative %	Total	% of Variance	Cumulative %	Total	% of Variance	Cumulative %
1	6.096	67.736	67.736	6.096	67.736	67.736	3.924	43.598	43.598
2	1.126	12.512	80.248	1.126	12.512	80.248	2.653	29.473	73.071
3	0.372	4.137	84.385	0.372	4.137	84.385	1.018	11.314	84.385
4	0.329	3.660	88.045						
5	0.266	2.950	90.995						
6	0.255	2.831	93.826						
7	0.213	2.372	96.198						
8	0.196	2.178	98.376						
9	0.146	1.624	100.000						
Extraction Method: Principal Component Analysis.									

Source: Author's Calculation

Objective 1:Figure 3 displays the overall variance explained and the eigenvalues. Principal Component Analysis is the extraction technique used here. Before extraction, the dataset contains 7 linear components and post-extraction, the dataset is divided into three distinct linear components based on the eigenvalues and correlation. These three factors together explain 75.056% of the variance. Consequently, these three factors can explain 75.056% of the common variance shared amongst the 7 variables. (Indapurkar, 2017)

Objective 2: Variance explained and eigenvalues are presented in **Figure 3** as a result of applying Principal Component Analysis for extraction. The dataset initially contained 8 linear components before the extraction process. Upon extraction and rotation based on the eigenvalues and correlation, the dataset is now segmented into three distinct linear components. These three factors collectively represent

67.238% of the total variance, indicating that these factors can explain 67.238% of the common variance shared by the 8 variables.

Objective 3: Variance explained and eigenvalues are presented in **Figure 3** as a result of applying Principal Component Analysis for extraction. The dataset initially contained 9 linear components before the extraction process. Upon extraction and rotation based on the eigenvalues and correlation, the dataset is now segmented into three distinct linear components. These three factors collectively represent 84.385% of the total variance, indicating that these factors can explain 84.385% of the common variance shared by the 9 variables.

Figure 4. Factor Loadings, Reliability & Validity

OBJ 1: Issues faced in HH Waste Disposal	Factor Loadings (λ)	λ^2	1 - λ^2	Composite Reliability	Average Variance Explained	Reliability Statistics (Cronbach's Alpha)	No. of Items
F1: Infrastructure and Accessibility of Waste Collection & Disposal	0.65	0.42	0.58	0.79	0.56	0.741	7
	0.86	0.75	0.25				
	0.72	0.52	0.48				
TOTAL	2.23	1.69	1.31				
F2: Collection and Disposal Efficiency	0.65	0.42	0.58	0.81	0.60		
	0.75	0.56	0.44				
	0.90	0.81	0.19				
TOTAL	2.30	1.79	1.21				
F3: Electronic Waste Management	0.89	0.80	0.20	0.80	0.80		
OBJ 2: HH Behaviour towards Waste Management	**Factor Loadings (λ)**	**λ^2**	**1 - λ^2**	**Composite Reliability**	**Average Variance Explained**	**Reliability Statistics (Cronbach's Alpha)**	**No. of Items**
F1: Waste Reduction Behaviour	0.67	0.45	0.55	0.84	0.57	0.793	8
	0.87	0.75	0.25				
	0.76	0.58	0.42				
	0.70	0.49	0.51				
TOTAL	3.00	2.28	1.72				
F2: Waste Segregation and Disposal Practices	0.63	0.40	0.60	0.77	0.53		
	0.84	0.70	0.30				
	0.70	0.49	0.51				
TOTAL	2.17	1.59	1.41				
F3: Personal Responsibility and Behaviour	0.96	0.93	0.07	0.93	0.93		
OBJ 3: HH Willingness to adopt technology interface for WM	**Factor Loadings (λ)**	**λ^2**	**1 - λ^2**	**Composite Reliability**	**Average Variance Explained**	**Reliability Statistics (Cronbach's Alpha)**	**No. of Items**
F1: Willingness to Engage & Learn about Digital Solutions	0.77	0.60	0.40	0.91	0.67	0.940	9
	0.83	0.69	0.31				
	0.84	0.71	0.29				
	0.83	0.68	0.32				
	0.82	0.67	0.33				
TOTAL	4.09	3.35	1.65				
F2: Belief in Effectiveness of Technology Interfaces	0.89	0.80	0.20	0.88	0.71		
	0.84	0.71	0.29				
	0.79	0.63	0.37				
TOTAL	2.53	2.14	0.86				
F3: Willingness to Invest in Technology	0.76	0.57	0.43	0.57	0.57		

Source: Author's Calculation

The values of the Cronbach's Alpha, which was used to calculate the Factor's Reliability, are displayed in **Figure 4**. A value greater than or equal to 0.7 signifies that the factors are accurate and reliable. (Hair J. J., 2006). As seen in Figure 4, the variables for each of the study's objectives (Objective 1- 0.741, Objective 2- 0.793, and Objective 3- 0.94) had sufficient magnitude of Cronbach's alpha.

Convergent validity is a tool that can be used to determine the level of correlation between several indicators of a same construct. The computation of the average variance extracted, the composite reliability, and the factor loading of the items must be performed to verify convergent validity. The Principal Component

Analysis method was applied to extract the factors. The relationship between each variable and the underlying components is communicated via factor loading values (Shrestha, 2021). Moreover, only variables with loadings of > 0.5 were included in the analysis indicating that they are representative of the factor. Each Objective in the study consists of 3 Factor (F1, F2, F3).

Objective 1 (OBJ 1) - To evaluate the challenges that households encounter in waste disposal.

Factor 1 (F1), reflecting the adequacy of waste collection infrastructure and accessibility of disposal facilities, exhibits moderate to strong positive correlations with its constituent variables (3 questions). Question 2 "There are separate bins for biodegradable, non-biodegradable, specific biodegradable waste in the colony" notably contributes significantly to this factor, indicating robust waste segregation practices. Factor 2 (F2), representing collection and disposal efficiency, shows moderate to very strong positive correlations with its variables (3 questions), with Question 3 "The disposal vehicle efficiently collects the waste with very little or no waste being spilled" being the most influential. This suggests effective waste management practices and efficient collection services. Factor 3 (F3) underscores the specific focus on electronic waste management, with Question 1 "There is provision for the collection of Electronic Waste" displaying a very strong positive correlation, indicating a significant emphasis on managing electronic waste separately within the locality.

Objective 2 (OBJ 2)- To examine the behaviour of urban households in practising waste management techniques in their homes.

Factor 1, Waste Reduction Behaviour, encompasses household practices focused on minimising waste generation. This factor takes into account behaviours like keeping separate bins for segregated waste (.672), reusing poly bags on a regular basis (.868), shopping using reusable bags to reduce waste (.764), and using biodegradable garbage bags for disposing (.700). Segregation of Waste and Disposal Practices, under Factor 2, embodies responsible waste management practices linked to waste segregation and proper disposal. Composting waste that is organic (.632), disposal of electronic waste separately (.837), and reusing materials creatively (.701) are all included. Factor 3, Personal Responsibility and Behaviour, emphasises individual accountability and active participation in managing waste, as indicated by a strong preference for carrying one's own bag while shopping (.963). Together, these factors shed light on how households manage their waste and emphasise the significance of encouraging sustainable practices to reduce environmental impact.

Objective 3 (OBJ 3)- To assess the willingness among urban households to adopt emerging technology interface in waste disposal and management

Factor 1, "Willingness to Engage & Learn about Digital Solutions," highlights respondents' eagerness to participate in educational activities and community initiatives related to waste management through digital platforms, with strong positive correlations observed for questions related to online workshops, learning about electronic waste disposal, and collaborating with other households. Factor 2, "Belief in Effectiveness of Technology Interfaces," underscores respondents' robust belief in the efficacy of technology interfaces for waste management, as indicated by very strong positive correlations with questions assessing beliefs about apps-based services, online platforms for awareness spreading, and website/app-based services for recycling. Factor 3, "Willingness to Invest in Technology," reflects a moderate inclination among respondents towards investing in waste management technology, evidenced by a moderate positive correlation with the question pertaining to investing in apps promoting waste reduction tools or equipment. These findings collectively suggest a positive attitude and readiness among urban households to embrace emerging technology interfaces for effective waste management practices.

Composite Reliability is an indicator of scale item internal consistency (Netemeyer, 2003). Composite reliability values between 0.6 and 0.7 are considered appropriate; however, in a more advanced stage, the value needs to be above 0.7. The values of composite reliability in Figure 4 indicate the scale items' internal consistency, which are all more than 0.7. The convergent validity is confirmed by Average Variance Extracted (AVE) ≥ 0.5, as stated by (Fornell, 1981) and it can be seen that all of the AVE values in Figure 4 are greater than 0.5.

PARTIAL LEAST SQUARE STRUCTURAL EQUATION MODELLING (PLS-SEM)

After conducting the E.F.A., all the factors with relevant factor loadings were taken into account to run the Partial Least Square Structural Equation Modelling (PLS-SEM) model. As hypothesised in **Figure 1**, the PLS-SEM model with Latent Variables were connected accordingly i.e., CHALLENGES_WM (signifying the Challenges faced by Households in Waste Disposal) was connected to TECH_WM (indicating Households' willingness to adopt technology interface for Waste Management) and BEHAVIOUR_WM (defining Household Behaviour towards Waste Management) was connected to TECH_WM as shown in **Figure 2** below. In order to test the model (path relationship), R-square values, standard beta, t-values using a bootstrapping process with a resample of 5000, and the effect size (using f-square) was taken into consideration. (Hair J. H., 2014).

Figure 5. PLS-SEM Model

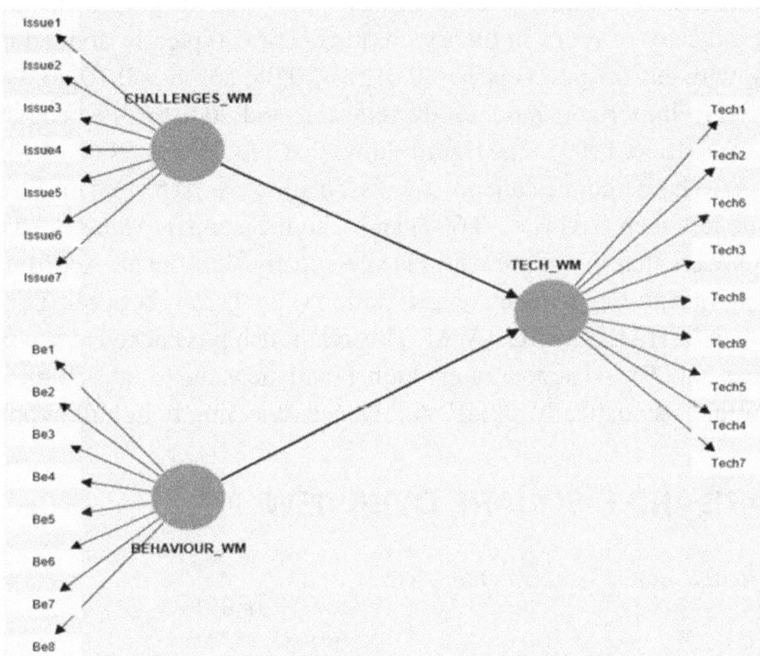

PATH COEFFICIENTS, P-VALUES AND T-VALUES

Figure 6. Path Coefficients – Mean, STDEV, T values, P values

Path	Original sample (O)	Sample mean (M)	Standard deviation (STDEV)	T statistics (|O/STDEV|)	P values
BEHAVIOUR_WM -> TECH_WM	0.531	0.53	0.039	13.559	0.000
ISSUES_WM -> TECH_WM	-0.254	-0.255	0.045	5.692	0.000

Source: Author's Calculation

PLS-SEM uses Path coefficients, which are also sometimes referred to as standardised beta coefficients, to determine the significance and strength of the proposed connections between the latent components (Götz, 2010). The bootstrapping technique is commonly employed here to evaluate the significance of hypothesised connections by analysing the t-value for the path coefficients (Hair J. R., 2011), (Efron, 1992) and (Yung, 1994). The path coefficient values range between -1 to +1, wherein values that near +1 indicate strong positive linear relationship, and vice versa for negative values (Hair J. J., 2016). Though the p-value is regarded as a constant indicator of proof in theory, in practice it is typically divided into three categories, with cut-off points at $p \leq 0.01$, $p \leq 0.05$, and $p > 0.10$, to distinguish between highly important, moderately relevant, and statistically insignificant at standard levels (Rice, 1989). The figure shows that TECHNOLOGY_WM and BEHAVIOR_WM have a significant positive association (i.e., 0.531). This is supported by a p value less than 0.05 (i.e., 0.000) and a high T statistic value (13.559), both of which indicate that the relationship is statistically significant. Additionally, the data indicates a significant negative association (i.e., -0.254) between TECHNOLOGY_WM and CHALLENGES_WM. This relationship is backed by a p value less than 0.05 (i.e.,0.000) and a moderately high T statistic value (5.692), indicating that the association is statistically significant. Hence, rejecting both null hypotheses.

R-SQUARE AND F-SQUARE OVERVIEW

Figure 7. R-square & F-square Overview

	R-square	R-square adjusted
TECH_WM	0.363	0.36
Path	**f-square**	
BEHAVIOUR_WM -> TECH_WM	0.441	
ISSUES_WM -> TECH_WM	0.101	

Source: Author's Calculation

The R-square value represents the extent to which exogenous variables explain the variance (expressed as a percentage) in the predictive power of the research model, with its value ranging from 0 to 1. This means that the model's explanatory power improves with increasing r-square values (Huang, 2013). According to Cohen (Cohen, 1988), as a rule of thumb, R-square values could be classified as weak if they fall between 0.02 and 0.12, moderate if they fall between 0.13 and 0.25, and considerable if they are equal to or above 0.26. And as shown in Figure 7, the R-square value of the current study came out to be 0.363, suggesting that 36.3% of the variation in

Willingness of households to adopt Technological interface for Waste Management is caused by Challenges faced by households in Waste Management and Behaviour of households towards Waste Management. When evaluating the magnitude of a local effect, Cohen's f-square is utilised, wherein the effect size assesses the degree, magnitude, or strength of the association among the latent variables (Wong, 2013). The findings show that the path from BEHAVIOR_WM to TECH_WM has an f-square value of 0.441, suggesting that, besides what is explained by other factors in the model, the BEHAVIOR_WM variable accounts for about 44.1% of the variance in TECH_WM. It represents the effect size of BEHAVIOUR_WM on TECH_WM after considering the effects of other variables, whereas the f-square value for the path from ISSUES_WM to TECH_WM is 0.101, indicating that in addition to the other variables in the model, the ISSUES_WM variable accounts for around 10.1% of the variance in TECH_WM. The effect size of ISSUES_WM on TECH_WM is displayed after considering the effect of other factors.

DISCUSSION

The analysis of PLS-SEM proves helpful in determining the association among the variables of urban households' waste management practices and their willingness to adopt technology interfaces for waste management.

The research finding shows a significant positive association between the behaviour of Urban households towards waste management (BEHAVIOUR_WM) and their willingness to adopt technology interface (TECH_WM) for waste management (path coefficient = 0.531, $p < 0.001$), suggesting households that efficiently manage waste by practising careful disposal and waste separation methods are more likely to adopt technological waste management solutions. Furthermore, the crucial role that household behaviour plays in determining the adoption of technology interfaces is further highlighted by the considerable effect size (f-square = 0.441). Since the relationship is significant, the null hypothesis (H0) is rejected, and the alternative hypothesis (H1) is accepted, meaning household behaviour significantly influences the willingness to adopt technological interfaces.

The study also reveals a negative association between the Challenges that households face in urban areas (CHALLENGES_WM) and their willingness to adopt technology interface (TECH_WM) for waste management (path coefficient = -0.254, $p < 0.001$), implying that urban households are less likely to use technological interface for managing waste since they face fewer challenges with the same, such as effective waste collection and disposal services. The effect size (f square = 0.101) is relatively smaller, suggesting that the challenges have a relatively lesser influence on household's willingness to adopt technological solutions than their behaviour towards waste management. Since the relationship is significant, the null hypothesis (H0) is rejected, and the alternative hypothesis (H1) is accepted, meaning challenges in waste disposal do impact the willingness to adopt technology interfaces, but in the negative direction.

However, it is essential to place these findings in the context of households, which is the main focus of the study. In situations where households do not face waste management issues due to established services and infrastructure there seems to be a negative relation between challenges and the willingness to adopt technological interfaces. This suggests that when challenges are fewer pressing households may not feel as compelled to seek digital solutions resulting in a decreased inclination towards adopting such interfaces. Therefore, these findings underscore the significance of taking factors into account when examining what motivates households to embrace technological interfaces, for waste management purposes.

LIMITATIONS

While this study provides valuable insights, certain limitations must be acknowledged. First, response bias may be present, as participants might have provided socially desirable responses regarding their waste management behaviour. Second, since the survey was disseminated through social media platforms (LinkedIn, WhatsApp, Instagram, Facebook), there is a self-selection bias, as individuals already inclined toward sustainability and digital solutions were more likely to participate than those who have partial to no knowledge about the topic. Third, while PLS-SEM is robust, it cannot fully account for unobserved heterogeneity. Lastly, the sample is primarily composed of urban residents, limiting the generalizability of findings to rural settings where waste management infrastructure and digital literacy levels may differ significantly.

Thus, future researchers should consider a broader demographic representation, including rural populations, to ensure more comprehensive insights to validate findings.

CONCLUSION AND SUGGESTION

The findings of this study highlight the need for targeted policy interventions that encourage digital adoption while addressing behavioural and structural barriers. To translate these insights into action, a set of strategic recommendations alongside each finding is proposed to enhance urban household waste management and promote sustainable practices.

The study reveals that urban households' behaviour towards sustainable waste management significantly impacts their willingness to adopt technological interfaces. Households that actively practice waste segregation and disposal are more inclined to integrate digital solutions, reinforcing the idea that behavioural awareness is a key driver of technology adoption. In this regard, public-private partnerships (PPPs) can play a pivotal role in the successful deployment and scalability of these digital solutions. Collaboration between governments and municipalities can collaborate with private technology firms or startups and waste management service providers can ensure financial feasibility, technology innovation and efficient service delivery. Government can work with startups to introduce app-based (or web-based) waste collection and monitoring, sensor equipped smart bins, blockchain-based waste tracking systems, facilitating real-time waste monitoring and automation. And to further streamline the waste management process, these platforms must integrate separate alternatives for the disposal and collection of organic, inorganic, and electronic waste simultaneously. In order to ensure widespread acceptance, adoption and usage, these apps should be user-friendly, multilingual (to cater to a variety of demographics), and compatible with various devices, making them accessible across diverse demographics.

Conversely, the study finds that urban households who face fewer challenges in managing their wastes are less likely to adopt digital tools, as they perceive existing systems as sufficient. This indicates that adoption of technological interface is driven by necessity rather than awareness of long-term benefits. To address this, municipalities must launch awareness campaigns and engage in dialogues with residents to highlight the long-term benefits of digital waste management. These efforts should demonstrate how technology can further optimize waste tracking, improving efficiency, and contribute to environmental sustainability beyond basic waste collection services.

The study also reveals that even if some households recognize the long-term benefits, they lack the financial motivation to invest in digital waste management interfaces. Households with lower disposable income may perceive these technologies as an added expense rather than an investment, leading to reluctance in adoption (Income effect). Additionally, the concept of Present Bias explains how households prioritize immediate savings over future efficiency benefits, further limiting their willingness. To tackle this, government can offer them subsidies, cash-back incentives for app-based waste tracking, tax rebates, gradual payment models (such as pay-as-you-use) and annual benefits as incentives to encourage long-term usage and reduce the cost barriers associated with accessing and using these digital tools.

The study also indicates that while some urban households already have efficient waste collection systems, a significant proportion still face infrastructural gaps, such as inconsistent waste collection services, lack of proper disposal facilities, insufficient public dustbins and lack of separate provisions for collection and disposal of electronic waste. These gaps contribute to irregular waste disposal behaviours and hinder efforts to promote sustainable waste management practices. To enable appropriate waste disposal, municipalities must give top priority to improving the infrastructure for waste collection, including door-to-door waste collection services, availability of public dustbins, provisions for e-waste disposal and regularizing disposal vehicles in the localities. To tackle the increasing concern over e-waste pollution, government authorities must also invest in dedicated infrastructure for the collection, recycling and proper disposal of electronic waste.

The findings also point out that household behaviour towards practising sustainable waste management techniques is largely influenced by access to convenient and affordable waste reduction options. Hence, a comprehensive approach is necessary to encourage sustainable practices among urban households for managing and reducing waste. To strengthen household participation, government and local bodies should introduce behavioural incentives, such as composting programs, promote upcycling practices, and mandate the use of reusable shopping bags. Additionally, online education programs should be developed to foster community engagement, improve waste management knowledge, and cultivate a sense of shared responsibility among the households.

The study also highlights that, practice of segregated waste disposal remains inconsistent among urban households, posing a challenge to effective waste management. In order to enforce compliance and promote responsible behaviour, the government should seek to establish regulations mandating waste segregation at source. This should be accompanied by a structured penalty system for non-compliance, including fines for illegal dumping at household as well as institutional level, covering sectors such as hotels, hospitals, schools, railroads, etc., and provide financial support for the development of innovative waste management initiatives such as, Smart Waste Bins, AI-powered Waste Sorting and Recycling Facilities, Waste to Energy (WTE) Projects, Blockchain-based Waste Tracking System, etc. These measures will ensure a systematic transition toward sustainable urban waste practices.

This study states that while digital waste management solutions are well-suited for urban areas, their adaptability in rural areas remains uncertain. Differences in infrastructure, digital literacy, and waste disposal habits mean that a direct transition may not be effective. Hence, pilot programs should be conducted in select rural areas to assess the adaptability of these digital waste solutions, allowing policymakers to make necessary adjustments before implementing them nationwide.

The findings highlight that the effectiveness of waste management policies and interventions is often unclear due to lack of systematic monitoring and evaluation. In order to address this, municipalities should establish a comprehensive monitoring and evaluation framework to measure the success of their interventions. This framework should track key performance indicators, measure the effectiveness of adopted strategies and identify the loopholes that need to be rectified. Following this technique, policymakers must continue to improve their policies and programs to meet the wants of urban households, allowing users to practise waste management that is viable.

Lastly, given the increasing readiness of urban residents to use digital platforms for waste disposal, this study supports the introduction of smart, technology-driven waste management systems in at least 100 smart cities by 2027. This initiative not only aligns with India's Swachh Bharat Abhiyaan (which emphasizes sanitation and urban cleanliness), but also with Smart Cities Mission, which advocates for IoT-enabled waste collection, real-time tracking and AI driven waste sorting as essential components of sustainable urban development. Additionally, this approach supports United Nations Sustainable Development Goals (SDGs), particularly SDG 11 (Sustainable Cities and Communities) and SDG 12 (Responsible Consumption and Production) by promoting efficient waste disposal, circular economy principles, and data-driven policy interventions. The integration of such initiatives can serve as a scalable model for other developing nations, demonstrating how digital waste solutions contribute to global environmental sustainability efforts.

REFERENCES

Abdel Shafy, H. I., & Mansour, M. S. M. (2018). Solid waste issue: Sources, composition, disposal, recycling, and valorization. *Egyptian Journal of Petroleum*, *27*(4), 1275–1290. DOI: 10.1016/j.ejpe.2018.07.003

Ali Akbar Jowkar, H. D. (2013). A factor analysis of identifying the customer behaviour patterns: A case study in Tehran. *European Online Journal of Natural and Social Sciences*, •••, 7.

Brauer, B. E. (2016). Green by app: the contribution of mobile applications to environmental sustainability. *Pacific Asia Conference on Information Systems*, (p. 220).

Cellina, F. V. (2021). Self-selection and attrition biases in app-based persuasive technologies for mobility behaviour change: Evidence from a Swiss case study. *Computers in Human Behaviour, 125*.

Cochran, W. (1977). *Sampling Techniques* (3rd ed.). John Wiley & Sons.

Cohen, J. (1988). *Statistical Power Analysis for the Behavioral Sciences* (2nd ed.). Erlbaum Associates.

Crawford, M. R., Holder, M. D., & O'Connor, B. P. (2017). Using Mobile Technology to Engage Children with Nature. *Environment and Behavior*, *49*(9), 959–984. DOI: 10.1177/0013916516673870

Efron, B. (1992). Bootstrap Methods: Another Look at the Jackknife. In *Breakthroughs in statistics: Methodology and Distribution* (Vol. 2, pp. 569–593). Springer Series in Statistics, Springer. DOI: 10.1007/978-1-4612-4380-9_41

Fadhullah, W. I., Imran, N. I. N., Ismail, S. N. S., Jaafar, M. H., & Abdullah, H. (2022). Household solid waste management practices and perceptions among residents in the East Coast of Malaysia. *BMC Public Health*, *22*(1), 1. DOI: 10.1186/s12889-021-12274-7 PMID: 34983455

Fornell, C. L., & Larcker, D. F. (1981). Evaluating structural equation models with unobservable variables and measurement error. *JMR, Journal of Marketing Research*, *18*(1), 39–50. DOI: 10.1177/002224378101800104

Geetha, R., & Rajalakshmi, S. (2020). Problem faced by the Public due to the Improper Waste Disposal and Behaviour of Waste Disposal. *International Journal of Social Sciences and Management*, *7*(2), 70–77. DOI: 10.3126/ijssm.v7i2.28593

Götz, O. L.-G. (2010). Evaluation of structural equation models using the partial least squares (PLS) approach. In *Handbook of Partial Least Squares* (pp. 691–711). Springer. DOI: 10.1007/978-3-540-32827-8_30

Hair, J. H. (2014). *A Primer on Partial Least Squares Structural Equation Modeling (PLS-SEM)*. Sage Publications.

Hair, J. J. (2006). *Multivariate Data Analysis* (6th ed.). Pearson.

Hair, J. J. (2016). *A Primer on Partial Least Squares Structural Equation Modeling (PLS-SEM)*. Sage Publications.

Hair, J. R., Ringle, C. M., & Sarstedt, M. (2011). PLS-SEM: Indeed a Silver Bullet. *Journal of Marketing Theory and Practice, 19*(2), 139–152. DOI: 10.2753/MTP1069-6679190202

Han, Z. Z., Zeng, D., Li, Q., Cheng, C., Shi, G., & Mou, Z. (2019). Public willingness to pay and participate in domestic waste management in rural areas of China. *Resources, Conservation and Recycling, 140*, 166–174. DOI: 10.1016/j.resconrec.2018.09.018

Hilles, D.-A. (2011). *Society and Household Behaviour*. Culture and Attitudes & Their Role in Solid Waste Management.

Huang, C. C., Wang, Y.-M., Wu, T.-W., & Wang, P.-A. (2013). An empirical analysis of the antecedents and performance consequences of using the moodle platform. *International Journal of Information and Education Technology (IJIET), 3*(2), 217–221. DOI: 10.7763/IJIET.2013.V3.267

Indapurkar, K. (2017). Financial Literacy Among Educated Urban Youth: Issues and Challenges. *International Journal of Economic Research*, •••, 14.

Karani, P., & Jewasikiewitz, S. M. (2007). Waste management and sustainable development in South Africa. *Environment, Development and Sustainability, 9*(2), 163–185. DOI: 10.1007/s10668-005-9010-7

Kayamo, S. E. (2022). Willingness to pay for solid waste management improvement in Hawassa city, Ethiopia. *Journal of Environmental Management, 302 (Part A)*, 113973.

Kaza, S. Y.-T. (2018). *What a Waste 2.0: A Global Snapshot of Solid Waste Management to 2050.* Retrieved from World Bank Group: https://documents.worldbank.org/en/publication/documents-reports/documentdetail/697271544470229584/what-a-waste-2-0-a-global-snapshot-of-solid-waste-management-to-2050

Knussen, C., & Yule, F. (2008). I'm Not in the Habit of Recycling: The Role of Habitual Behavior in the Disposal of Household Waste. *Environment and Behavior, 40*(5), 683–702. DOI: 10.1177/0013916507307527

Kumar, A., & Agrawal, A. (2020). Recent trends in solid waste management status, challenges, and potential for the future Indian cities – A review. *Current Research in Environmental Sustainability, 2*, 100011. Advance online publication. DOI: 10.1016/j.crsust.2020.100011

Loan, L. T., & Balanay, R. M. (2023). Towards reinforcing the waste separation at source for Vietnam's waste management: Insights from the Nudge Theory. *Environmental Challenges, 10*, 100660. Advance online publication. DOI: 10.1016/j.envc.2022.100660

Mohsen Tavakol, A. W. (2020). Factor Analysis: A means for theory and instrument development in support of construct validity. *International Journal of Medical Education, 11*, 245–247. DOI: 10.5116/ijme.5f96.0f4a PMID: 33170146

Netemeyer, R. G. (2003). *Scaling procedures: Issues and applications*. Sage Publications. DOI: 10.4135/9781412985772

Omran, A. M. (2009). Investigating Households Attitude Toward Recycling of Solid Waste in Malaysia: A Case Study. *International Journal of Environmental Research, 3*, 275–288.

Pandit, A. N., Nakagawa, Y., Timilsina, R. R., Kotani, K., & Saijo, T. (2021). Taking the perspectives of future generations as an effective method for achieving sustainable waste management. *Sustainable Production and Consumption, 27*, 1526–1536. DOI: 10.1016/j.spc.2021.03.019

Patrizia Ghisellini, A. N. (2022). Toward circular and socially just urban mining in global societies and cities: Present state and future perspectives. *Frontiers in Sustainable Cities*.

Peng Jiang, L. Z. (2023). Blockchain technology applications in waste management: Overview, challenges and opportunities. *Journal of Cleaner Production, 421*, 138466. DOI: 10.1016/j.jclepro.2023.138466

Purity, U. I. (2016). Waste Management and Sustainable Development in Nigeria: A Study of Anambra State Waste Management Agency. *European Journal of Business and Management, 8*, 132–144.

Rawshan Ara Begum, C. S. (2009). Attitude and behavioural factors in waste management in the construction industry of Malaysia. *Resources, Conservation and Recycling, 53*(6), 321–328. DOI: 10.1016/j.resconrec.2009.01.005

Rice, W. R. (1989). Analyzing Tables of Statistical Tests. *Evolution; International Journal of Organic Evolution, 43*(1), 223–225. DOI: 10.2307/2409177 PMID: 28568501

Rodrigues, S. J. (2020). Behavioural aspects of solid waste management: A systematic review. *Journal of the Air & Waste Management Association, 70*(12), 1268–1302. DOI: 10.1080/10962247.2020.1823524 PMID: 32970533

Sapuay, G. P. (2018). Sustainable Solid Waste Management and Sustainable Development in the Philippines. *International Conference in Urban and Regional Planning.*

Sarstedt, M. R. (2017). Partial Least Squares Structural Equation Modeling. In Homburg, C. K. (Ed.), *Handbook of Market Research* (pp. 1–40). Springer. DOI: 10.1007/978-3-319-05542-8_15-1

Seadon, J. K. (2010). Sustainable waste management systems. *Journal of Cleaner Production, 18*(16–17), 1639–1651. DOI: 10.1016/j.jclepro.2010.07.009

Seng, B. F. (2018). Households' knowledge, attitudes, and practices toward solid waste management in suburbs of Phnom Penh, Cambodia. *Waste management & research: The journal of the International Solid Wastes and Public Cleansing Association. ISWA, 36*(10), 993–1000.

Shrestha, N. (2021). Factor Analysis as a Tool for Survey Analysis. *American Journal of Applied Mathematics and Statistics, 9*(1), 11. DOI: 10.12691/ajams-9-1-2

Singh, D. A. (2022). Impact of Solid Waste on Water at Chapra (Bihar). *International Journal For Multidisciplinary Research, 4*(5).

Suryawan, I. W.-H., & Lee, C.-H. (2023). Citizens' willingness to pay for adaptive municipal solid waste management services in Jakarta, Indonesia. *Sustainable Cities and Society, 97*, 97. DOI: 10.1016/j.scs.2023.104765

Varsolo Sunio, J.-D. S. (2017). Can we promote sustainable travel behaviour through mobile apps? Evaluation and review of evidence. *International Journal of Sustainable Transportation, 11*(8), 553–566. DOI: 10.1080/15568318.2017.1300716

Véliz, K. D.-R., Ramírez-Rodríguez, G., & Ossio, F. (2022). Willingness to pay for construction and demolition waste from buildings in Chile. *Waste Management (New York, N.Y.), 137*, 222–230. DOI: 10.1016/j.wasman.2021.11.008 PMID: 34800746

Wildt, K. K. (2023). Time spent on separating waste is never wasted: Fostering people's recycling behaviour through the use of a mobile application. *Computers in Human Behaviour, 139.*

Wong, K. K.-K. (2013). Partial least squares structural equation modeling (PLS-SEM) techniques using SmartPLS. *Marketing Bulletin*, *24*(1), 1–32.

Yung, Y. F., & Bentler, P. M. (1994). Bootstrap-corrected ADF test statistics in covariance structure analysis. *British Journal of Mathematical & Statistical Psychology*, *47*(1), 63–84. DOI: 10.1111/j.2044-8317.1994.tb01025.x PMID: 8031706

APPENDIX

Table 1. Definition of Variable Used

Challenges faced by Households in Waste Disposal	**CHALLENGES_WM**
There is a door-to-door waste collection service in my society/ colony on a daily basis.	Issue1
There are separate bins for biodegradable, non-biodegradable, specific biodegradable waste in my society/ colony.	Issue2
There are an adequate number of public dustbins in my locality.	Issue3
There are facilities for proper management of collected waste at the common point in my area.	Issue4
The disposal vehicle regularly collects waste from the common point in my locality.	Issue5
The disposal vehicle efficiently collects the waste with very little or no waste being spilled.	Issue6
There is provision for the collection of Electronic Waste in my locality/society.	Issue7
Household Behaviour towards Waste Management	**BEHAVIOUR_WM**
I have separate bins for segregated waste in my house.	Be1
I always reuse the poly bags.	Be2
I use reusable bags for shopping to reduce waste.	Be3
I compost organic waste in my household.	Be4
I dispose of electronic waste separately from my other household waste.	Be5
I use a biodegradable trash bag for disposing of my household waste.	Be6
I upcycle (creative reuse) good quality waste material instead of disposing it off. (Eg- Glass Jar)	Be7
I prefer carrying my own bag when I go shopping.	Be8
Households' willingness to adopt emerging technology interface for Waste Management	**TECH_WM**
I am willing to participate in online workshops or training sessions to learn more about solid waste management practices.	Tech1
I am willing to learn how to safely dispose of electronic waste.	Tech2
I am willing to collaborate with other households in my community to implement sustainable waste management practices using digital platforms	Tech3
I believe that technology support can help promote the adoption of solid waste management practices	Tech4
I am willing to monitor and track my household waste management practices to assess their effectiveness using app-based service	Tech5
Belief in effectiveness of app-based service for household waste collection, tracking, and monitoring	Tech6

continued on following page

Table 1. Continued

Challenges faced by Households in Waste Disposal	CHALLENGES_WM
Belief in effectiveness of online platforms for spreading awareness and community engagement	Tech7
Belief in effectiveness of website/app-based service for recycling, reusing, and upcycling waste products (IoT)	Tech8
I am willing to moderately invest in applications that help in promoting tools or equipment to reduce waste	Tech9

Table 1 defines all the variables considered in this model.

About the Contributors

Ali Al Maqousi is an Associate Professor of Information Security at the University of Petra in Jordan and serves as the Director of the Office of External Funding and Technology Transfer. He holds a Ph.D. in Computer Science (Computer Networks) from Oxford Brookes University, UK, and specializes in cybersecurity, computer networks, blockchain, and smart systems. With over 30 peer-reviewed publications, Dr. Al Maqousi has led and contributed to numerous research initiatives, including high-impact Erasmus+ projects. These include BITTCOIN-JO, which focuses on establishing Technology Transfer Offices in Jordan; RL4Eng, which develops remote and virtual labs for engineering education; Pro-GREEN LABs, promoting sustainable development skills in architecture; and COMMO, a mobility program enhancing international academic exchange across the Mediterranean and Western Balkans. Dr. Al Maqousi contributed to the organization of four international conferences as Organization Chair (AEECT 2011, IT-DREPS 2013, AEECT 2013, and AEECT 2015) and two international conferences as General Co-Chair (JIEEEC 2017 & IT-DREPS 2017) and one international conference as a publication chair (ICCIAA 2025). His work has supported innovation, capacity building, and educational modernization through collaboration with institutions across Europe, the Middle East, and Africa. He is active in academic quality assurance, supervises graduate research, and serves as a reviewer for international journals. Dr. Al Maqousi is also a senior member of IEEE and the Jordanian Engineers Association, reflecting his strong commitment to advancing research, education, and cross-border collaboration in higher education.

Ammar Almomani earned his Ph.D. in Advanced Internet Security and Monitoring from Universiti Sains Malaysia (2013). He is a Professor at the Higher Colleges of Technology, UAE, and a consultant in AI and cybersecurity. Dr. Almomani has over 20 years of experience in academia and industry, specializing in areas such as network security, cryptography, and IoT-based cybersecurity.

Recognized among the top 2% of researchers worldwide, he has authored over 150 publications and holds several patents. He has also played key roles in curriculum development and accreditation processes for academic programs.

Amjad Aldweesh received his Ph.D. in Blockchain Technology and Smart Contracts from Newcastle University, UK (2019). He is an Associate Professor at Shaqra University, Saudi Arabia, with expertise in blockchain systems, network security, and algorithm design. Dr. Aldweesh's work focuses on leveraging blockchain technologies to enhance data security and contribute to Saudi Arabia's Vision 2030 goals. He has published extensively and has developed and taught courses in cybersecurity and blockchain technology.

Mohammad Alauthman is an Associate Professor in the Information Security Department at the Faculty of Information Technology, University of Petra, Amman, Jordan. His research interests include network security, intrusion detection systems, and applying AI techniques—such as machine learning and deep learning—for botnet and DDoS detection, spam filtering, IoT security, and network traffic classification. He earned his Ph.D. in Computer Science from Northumbria University, UK, in 2016. Dr. Alauthman has received multiple research grants supporting advanced AI-driven intrusion detection systems and international collaboration. He is also actively involved in Erasmus+ projects, including BITTCOIN-JO (technology transfer), RL4Eng (remote engineering labs), Pro-GREEN LABs (green competences in education), and COMMO (mobility and cooperation across Mediterranean and Balkan institutions), contributing to innovation, sustainability, and cross-border academic development.

***

Adaikkammai A is a faculty member in the Department of Computer Science and Business Systems at RMD Engineering College, Tamil Nadu. She is dedicated to teaching, research, and mentoring students in emerging technologies. With a strong academic background, she actively contributes to scholarly work and technical advancements. Her commitment to education and innovation enhances the academic excellence of the institution.

Uzma Abbas holds a PhD from the University of Jammu. Her pioneering research on "Rights of Forest Dwellers: A Critical Study of the Forest Rights Act 2006" has paved the way for significant discourse on indigenous rights. Her academic excellence is underscored by a gold medal in her LLM (Criminal & Security Law) from Noida International University and an impressive 82.7% score in the University

Grant Commission's National Eligibility Test (NET). Committed to interdisciplinary exploration, Dr. Abbas is currently pursuing a Master's in Political Science from IGNOU. She has shared her expertise at national and international seminars, focusing on critical issues surrounding human rights and environmental law. Her publications appear in esteemed peer-reviewed journals, including "Phalonk" and the "Indian Journal of Socio-Legal Studies." Dr. Abbas also serves as a Faculty at Dogra Law College, inspiring the next generation of legal minds. A polyglot proficient in English, Hindi, Urdu, Kashmiri, and beginner's Arabic, she embodies a holistic approach to education, with interests spanning literature, gender studies, environmental preservation, and the arts. Dr. Uzma Abbas's work continues to bridge the gap between scholarship and social impact, fostering a deeper understanding of the intricate relationships between law, society, and the environment.

Mahapara Abbass, a distinguished academician and researcher in the Department of Civil Engineering at Maharishi Markandeshwar (Deemed to be University), Mullana-Ambala, has made significant contributions to the field of structural engineering and sustainable construction materials. Her academic and research endeavors are reflected in an impressive portfolio of publications. Dr. Abbas has authored several research papers in prestigious SCI and Scopus-indexed journals, such as Multiscale Multidisciplinary Modeling, Experimentation and Design, Journal of Building Pathology and Rehabilitation, and Lecture Notes in Civil Engineering. In addition to her journal articles, she has presented her work at renowned conferences. Dr. Abbas's expertise also extends to scholarly book contributions, where she has authored/co-authored several book chapters in critically acclaimed volumes, including Advances in Geotechnics and Structural Engineering and Lecture Notes in Civil Engineering. Further demonstrating her influence in the field, she has published research papers and reviews, which have appeared in platforms such as Elsevier and SCI and SCOPUS indexed journals. Her research portfolio exemplifies a deep engagement with cutting-edge topics like geopolymer concrete, sustainable construction practices, and innovative materials in civil engineering, underscoring her prominent role in advancing the frontiers of civil engineering.

Faisal Aburub is a professor of Information Systems within the Faculty of Administrative and Financial Sciences at University of Petra, Jordan. Faisal completed his PhD in the University of the West of England - Bristol-UK. He joined University of Petra in September 2001. Professor Aburub currently is Dean of Scientific Research and Graduate Studies at University of Petra. His primary areas of research are business process modelling, business process reengineering, organizational agility and ERP systems. His research has been published extensively in academic journals and conferences. Professor Aburub's research has focused significantly on bridging the gap between system models and business process models. His research has focused on using practical methods for modelling complex organizational settings and the potential role of IT systems within them.

Shalom Akhai is a distinguished figure in engineering, boasting 17+ years of experience in academia, research, and technical applications. With a robust portfolio of 100+ publications in esteemed journals, conferences, and book chapters, he demonstrates a commitment to advancing knowledge. As a prolific author, Dr. Akhai has co-authored several technical textbooks and holds over 50 patents, underscoring his innovative approach and influence in shaping the engineering landscape. Founder of IGNIS Technical Solutions, a consultancy firm translating his expertise into real-world applications, Dr. Akhai's expertise and dedication to education have solidified his position as a leading expert in his field.

Shaikha Al-Sanad is the program manager & research scientists for the Sustainability & Reliability of Infrastructure Program at the Kuwait Institute for Scientific Research (KISR). The team is involved in risk and reliability assessment of infrastructures, structural health monitoring of various infrastructures in Kuwait (Tall buildings, bridges, and wind turbine towers), computational modelling and reliability analysis of concrete structures, and geotechnical modelling. Dr.Shaikha serves several level government boards. Dr Shaikha's currently leading a couple of ongoing projects on structural optimization of wind turbines in Kuwait, a white paper on infrastructure, and risk assessment of mega projects. Her research interest extends to the areas of includes, structural reliability of wind turbine structures, SHM of infrastructures, risk assessment of megaprojects, Research interests extend to the areas of asset management, risk and reliability engineering, construction project risk management, the identification and mitigation of the risks of construction, building procurement, sustainable built environment and sustainable assessment of building performance, project complexity, and the design of change support tools and project management techniques to reduce carbon footprints, supply chain management, and statistical analysis. She has authored and published several peer reviewed international journal and international conferences papers, chapters, technical reports on these areas. She professionally trained several professionals in engineering and management fields. Dr. AlSanad earned her PhD degree in Civil Engineering from the esteemed University of Manchester, UK, and holds MSc and BSc degrees in Civil Engineering from the University of Kuwait. She has earned several professional certifications, including an Associate Value Specialist (AVS) certification, a Project Management Professional (PMP) certification, and an ISO 3100 Risk Manager certification. In addition, Dr. AlSanad is a member of several international and local professional organizations, as well as various technical and policy committees. Dr. AlSanad has had the privilege of engaging in research collaborations with esteemed international universities and institutions. These collaborations have allowed her to broaden her knowledge, establish fruitful connections, and contribute to the global research community. Her expertise and contributions in these collaborations have been instrumental in advancing the field and addressing complex challenges. With a strong reputation for her meticulous approach and thorough research, Dr. AlSanad is highly respected and valued by her peers and colleagues. Her wealth of experience, combined with her passion for continuous learning and improvement, positions her as a leading professional in her industry. Dr. AlSanad possesses a wealth of experience in organizing and leading conferences, workshops, and seminars within her field of research expertise. Her proficiency in event coordination and leadership is demonstrated through her successful track record in conceptualizing, planning, and executing impactful academic gatherings. She has successfully chaired sessions and collaborated with experts in her research areas. Driven by her commitment to knowledge dissemination and professional networking, she has consistently delivered high-quality events that foster intellectual exchange, facilitate collaboration, and advance the understanding of her research domain. Dr. AlSanad brings extensive teaching and mentoring experience to her role, having guided students at various academic levels in Kuwait and the United Kingdom. She has delivered professional training in engineering and management, while also supervising numerous master's degree students as their thesis advisor. Furthermore, Dr. AlSanad has served as an examiner for students at esteemed universities in the United Kingdom. Her commitment to education and dedication to fostering student growth make her a valued contributor to the academic community. Overall, Dr. AlSanad's exceptional professional achievements, extensive research collaborations, and unwavering commitment to excellence make her a distinguished and influential figure in her field. she had the privilege of engaging in research collaborations with esteemed international universities and institutions. Her dedication to the field of expertise and her commitment to excellence make her a highly respected and valued professional in her industry.

Mohammad Nazmi Al Sheikh Hasan is a PhD researcher in Artificial Intelligence and Data Science at Brunel University London, specializing in student performance prediction using machine learning. He holds an MSc in Computer Information Systems from the Arab Academy for Banking and Financial Sciences and a BSc in Computer Science from the University of Petra, Jordan. With over 17 years of experience as a university lecturer, Mohammad has taught various courses in programming, databases, artificial intelligence, and system analysis. He has also made significant contributions to e-learning development, particularly in

Moodle-based learning management systems. His research focuses on integrating Intended Learning Outcomes (ILOs) data to enhance predictive models in education. An Oracle Certified Professional, Mohammad has extensive expertise in software development, database administration, and academic research. His work has been published in international conferences and journals, covering topics such as learning analytics, cybersecurity, and e-learning quality assurance. Beyond academia, he has played a key role in the development and management of e-learning platforms and has served on accreditation and quality assurance committees.

Md Shamsul Haque Ansari had completed his Ph.D. from Jamia Millia Islamia (Central University), New Delhi-110025, INDIA, and MCA from UP Technical University, Lucknow – 201306, INDIA. He has qualified UGC-NET in 2015. He has more than 19 years of rich experience including academics, research and administration. He is currently working as "Assistant Professor in the Department of Computer Science and Engineering at the Koneru Lakshmaiah Education Foundation, Guntur, Andhra Pradesh, India". His research interests include Lightweight cryptography, Random number generation, Internet of Things, Artificial Intelligence and Datamining. Apart from that he has good hands-on experience in Database Management System with various tools like Oracle/DB2/MySQL. He has published various papers in International Journals and Conference proceedings including Web of Science and Scopus indexed Journals. He has also published various book chapters in Scopus indexed Journals. He is an active member of various societies such as International Association of Engineers (IAENG), Computer Science Teachers Association (CSTA), and Institute of Research Engineers and Doctors (IRED). He has also worked as reviewer for various international conferences.

B. Yamini is a faculty member at SRM Institute of Science and Technology (SRMIST), Kattankulathur, Tamil Nadu. She is actively involved in research, teaching, and scholarly publications in her field. With a strong academic background, she contributes to advancing knowledge and student development. Her dedication to research enriches the academic environment of SRMIST.

Kashinath Basu is a Senior Lecturer in Computer Science at Oxford Brookes University. He has over over 20 years of research and teaching experience in the field of computer science, especially focussing around networking and web technologies. His recent research includes application of AI/ML and big data technologies in the softwarisation of network infrastructure, cloud computing and cyber security and application of AI/Ml and big data in the domain of networks and cloud. Dr Basu regularly publishes in prestigeous journals, conferences and books and has been in editorial board, organising committees and chairs of several international scholastic events. He also serves in a number of IEEE and Internet Engineering Task Force committees on internation standards and has active research collaboration with a number of global technology companies.

Arti Chouksey, Assistant Professor, Department of Civil Engineering, Deenbandhu Chhotu Ram University of Science and Technology, Murthal, Sonipat, Haryana, India.

Nafees Akhter Farooqui had completed a BSc (Hons.) in Statistics from AMU, Aligarh, MCA from Integral University, Lucknow, and Ph.D. (Computer Science & Engineering), from DIT University, Dehradun, Uttarakhand, India. He has 14 years of teaching experience and presently working as "Assistant Professor in the Department of Computer Science and Engineering at the Koneru Lakshmaiah Education Foundation-Deemed to be University, Guntur, Andhra Pradesh, India". His research interests include Artificial Intelligence, Machine Learning, Deep Learning, Computer Vision, Pattern Recognition, Natural Language Processing and Data Mining. He has published approx. 35 papers in International Journals and Conference proceedings including Web of Science and Scopus indexed Journals. He also published various book chapters in Scopus indexed Journals. He has published two books for National Publishers etc. He has been a member of Association of Information Science and Technology (ASIS&T) since 2024, Computer Science Teachers Association (CSTA) since 2023, International Association of Engineers (IAENG) since 2017, ACM since 2011. He guided various projects of UG and PG level Students. He received awards from various professional bodies.

Manshu Goyal is a dedicated law graduate and a practicing advocate at the District Court of Modinagar, Ghaziabad. With a strong academic foundation in legal studies, he graduated with a degree in law from Swami Vivekanand Subharti University, Meerut, where he excelled in subjects such as criminal law, civil litigation, and legal drafting. Since entering the legal profession, Manshu has gained valuable experience representing clients in a wide range of cases, including family disputes, property matters, and criminal defenses.

Wael M. Hadi is a distinguished computer scientist and academic leader who currently serves as Dean of the Faculty of Information Technology at the University of Petra in Jordan. He also holds the rank of Professor of Data Science. Over the course of his career, he has advanced through various roles, including Head of the Computer Information Systems Department, Chair of the Information Security program, and Director of the E-Learning Center. He earned his Ph.D. in Computer Information Systems, which laid a strong foundation for his extensive research in Artificial Intelligence, Machine Learning, Data Mining, and Big Data analytics.

His work covers a wide spectrum of areas, from renewable energy and groundwater resource management to medical diagnostics and Arabic text mining. Notably, Professor Hadi has made significant contributions in associative classification, introducing novel algorithms that enhance both the speed and accuracy of data-driven solutions. In addition to his research and leadership duties, he has contributed to numerous Erasmus projects, fostering international academic collaborations and expanding IT education opportunities. With an extensive publication record and high citation metrics, Professor Hadi continues to champion innovation, mentorship, and excellence at both institutional and global levels.

Ala Hamarsheh is an associate professor at the Faculty of Engineering and Information Technology of the Arab American University of Jenin. Dr. Hamarsheh has obtained a PhD in engineering sciences from Vrije Universiteit Brussel (VUB)/ Brussels-Belgium in 2012. He graduated in computer science at the Faculty of Science, Birzeit University, Palestine, in 2000. He obtained an MSc degree in computer science at the Kind Abdullah II School for IT, The University of Jordan, Jordan, in 2003. Dr. Hamarsheh has published numerous papers in international refereed journals and conferences.

S. Ida Evangeline, presently working as an Assistant Professor in the Department of Electrical and Electronics Engineering at the Government College of Engineering, Tirunelveli, Tamilnadu, India. She obtained her Bachelor's in Electrical and Electronics Engineering from Manonmaniam Sundaranar University in 2003, and Master's in Power Systems Engineering from Anna University, Chennai, Tamilnadu, India in 2005. She completed her PhD degree in 2023 at Anna University, Chennai, Tamilnadu, India. She has published six research papers in international journals. Her current research interests include optimal power flow, renewable energy, soft computing, machine learning, and deep learning.

Kavita Indapurkar, with an experience of teaching in higher education institutions in India for over 25 years, has held several academic leadership positions and is presently Professor and is heading the School of Economics at Amity University, Uttar Pradesh, Noida Campus. A PhD in Economics and an MBA in finance, qualified at National level test for teaching in higher education in India, Prof. Dr. Kavita Indapurkar finds her research interests at the crossroads of behavioural aspects of people as consumers of various goods and or services or how do they make decisions.

Mohammad Ishrat with a 20+ International and National academic career in Computer Science and Engineering, holds a Doctorate and master's degree, showcasing his expertise. He is currently an Associate Professor at KL University

(NAAC A++), India. Previously, he has authored many research articles Patents, Book chapters in the fields of Machine Learning, Data Mining, Deep Learning, and Future Networks etc. He has extensive teaching and research experience at various universities, including King Abdul Aziz University, Jeddah, KSA, University of Technology & Applied Science, Oman, and Integral University, Lucknow, India.

Wasim Khan with over 17 years in academia, is a seasoned expert in Computer Science Engineering. His educational journey, which includes a B.Tech., MTech., and a Ph.D., underscores a deep commitment to his field. He has made significant academic contributions, evidenced by numerous patents and a vast array of publications, including conference papers and book chapters. He is currently an Senior Assistant Professor at Symbiosis University Pune (NAAC A++ University), India. His research interests include machine learning, deep learning, social network analysis, anomaly detection, and network intrusion detection.

Hitesh Mohapatra received the B.E. degree in Information Technology from Biju Patnaik University of Technology (BPUT), Odisha in 2006, and the MTech. Degree in CSE from Odisha University of Technology and Research (OUTR) University, Odisha in 2009. He received his Ph.D. in Computer Science & Engineering in 2021 from Veer Surendra Sai University of Technology (VSSUT), Burla, India. He has contributed 30 SCI and Scopus indexed research papers, 21 international/national conferences and books on Software Engineering and C Programming respectively. He has 15 years of teaching experience both in industry and academia. He has served the research community with various capacities like session chair, technical chair, keynote speaker etc. His research interests include wireless sensor network, smart city, smart grid and smart water. Currently he is working as Associate professor at School of Computer Engineering, KIIT DU, Bhubaneswar, and Odisha.

Girija P is associated with Vel Tech Rangarajan Dr. Sagunthala R&D Institute of Science and Technology, Chennai. She is committed to teaching, research, and innovation in her area of expertise. Her contributions to academics and research help in shaping future professionals. She actively engages in scholarly publications and technical advancements.

Ananya Pandey is a Research Scholar in School of Law at Christ University, Bangalore. She has her research interests in the field of Constitutional Law, Environment Law, Human Rights, Food Security, Intellectual Property Law and Jurisprudence.

Swati Pathak, Assistant Professor, Chandigarh Group of Colleges Jhanjeri, Mohali, Punjab, India - 140307, Chandigarh Engineering College, Department of Civil Engineering.

Siva Subramanian R is associated with the Department of Computer Science and Engineering at R.M.K. College of Engineering and Technology. He actively contributes to research and scholarly publications. He is committed to mentoring students and driving technical innovation in his field. His work strengthens the academic and research environment of the institution.

Nagarajan S is a faculty member in the Department of Information Technology at R.M.K. Engineering College, Tamil Nadu. He is dedicated to teaching, research, and guiding students in technological advancements. With a strong academic background, he actively contributes to scholarly publications and innovative projects. His commitment to education and research plays a vital role in enhancing the institution's academic excellence.

Sachin Sharma has worked as a Professor at Amity School of Engineering and Technology, Amity University, Punjab, Mohali, India since January 2025. He also worked as Associate Dean of International Affairs and Professor, Department of Computer Science and Engineering at Graphic Era Deemed to be University, Dehradun, Uttarakhand, India from February, 2018 to January 2025. He has experience of 15+ years in industry and academia. He is also Co-founder and Chief Technology officer (CTO) of IntelliNexus LLC, Arkansas, USA based company. He also worked as a Senior Systems Engineer at Belkin International, Inc., Irvine, California, USA. He received his Philosophy of Doctorate (Ph.D.) degree in Engineering Science and Systems specialization in Systems Engineering from University of Arkansas at Little Rock, USA with 4.0 out 4.0 GPA and M.S. degree in Systems engineering from University of Arkansas at Little Rock with 4.0 out 4.0 GPA. Dr. Sharma has authored/coauthored over 270+ publications in the form of books, patents, and papers in refereed journals and conference proceedings. He holds 70+ US, Indian and international patents in the area of IoT, wireless communication.

Utkarsh Singh is a dedicated researcher with a background in Economics. He holds a Master's degree in Economics from Amity University, Noida, and a Bachelor's degree from the University of Mumbai. Utkarsh has honed his research skills through active participation in various research conventions and conferences, where he has presented compelling proposals on topics such as "Socio-Economic Impact Evaluation of Products Based on the Concept of Biomimicry" and "Enhancing Operational Excellence in Private Sector Banking." His research interests lie at the intersection of economics, technology, and sustainable development, with a focus on driving sustainable economic growth and operational efficiency. Utkarsh has also published research papers on topics such as "An Analysis of the Trade Dynamics of the Textile Sector Between India and BRICS Nations" and "Experiential Tourism in India and Its Journey Towards Sustainable Development" in IGI Global.

Venkata Ramana Kaneti is a faculty member in the Department of Computer Science and Engineering at VNR Vignana Jyothi Institute of Engineering and Technology, Hyderabad, Telangana. He is dedicated to teaching, research, and technological advancements in his field. With a strong academic and research background, he actively contributes to scholarly publications and student mentorship. His commitment to education and innovation enhances the academic excellence of the institution.

Sana Abbass, Assistant Professor, Department of Civil Engineering, Mahant Bachittar Singh College of Engineering and Technology, Babliana, Jammu, India.

Index

Symbols

A

B

C

D

E

F

G

H

I

L

M

P

R

S

T

U

W

www.ingramcontent.com/pod-product-compliance
Lightning Source LLC
LaVergne TN
LVHW080355011026
849161LV00009B/2316